The World Atlas of

Birds

The World Atlas of
Birds

Galley Press

The World Atlas of Birds
was edited and designed by
Mitchell Beazley Publishers Limited,
14-15 Manette Street, London W1V 5LB

First published in Great Britain 1974

© Mitchell Beazley Publishers Limited 1974

This edition published 1985 by Galley Press,
an imprint of W.H. Smith and Son Limited,
Registered No 237811 England. Trading as WHS
Distributors, St. John's House, East Street,
Leicester LE1 6NE.

ISBN 0-86136 704 9

Printed and bound in
Portugal by Printer Portuguesa

CONSULTANT EDITOR
Sir Peter Scott CBE DSC
*Hon. Director, The Wildfowl Trust, Slimbridge
International Vice-President, World Wildlife Fund*

FOREWORD BY
Roger Tory Peterson DSc
Special Consultant to the National Audubon Society

CHIEF CONTRIBUTING EDITORS
C. Hilary Fry PhD MA
*Senior Lecturer in Zoology, University of
Aberdeen*
J. J. M. Flegg PhD BSc ARCS
Director, The British Trust for Ornithology

ADVISORY EDITORS
Gwynne Vevers MBE DPhil FLS FIBiol
Assistant Director of Science, The London Zoo

Olin Sewall Pettingill Jr.
*Formerly Director, The Cornell Laboratory of
Ornithology*

CONTRIBUTORS
INTRODUCTION: THE WORLD OF BIRDS
Cyril Walker FLS
British Museum of Natural History

Peter Evans PhD DPhil MA
*Senior Lecturer in Zoology, University
of Durham*

Bryan Nelson DPhil BSc
*Senior Lecturer in Zoology, University
of Aberdeen*

Bernard Stonehouse DPhil MA BSc MInstBiol
*Chairman, Postgraduate School of
Environmental Science, University of
Bradford*

NORTH AMERICA: THE NEARCTIC REALM
John Farrand Jr. PhD MS
American Museum of Natural History

SOUTH AMERICA: THE NEOTROPICAL REALM
Alexander F. Skutch PhD
*Honorary President, The Audubon
Society of Costa Rica*

EURASIA: THE PALAEARCTIC REALM
J. J. M. Flegg PhD BSc ARCS
*Director, The British Trust for
Ornithology*

Prof. Jean Dorst
*Museum National D'Histoire Naturelle,
Paris*

AFRICA: THE ETHIOPIAN REALM
C. Hilary Fry PhD MA
Senior Lecturer in Zoology, University of Aberdeen

SOUTHERN ASIA: THE ORIENTAL REALM
Salim Ali DSc FNA
President, The Bombay Natural History Society

Guy R. Mountfort OBE
President, The British Ornithologists' Union

AUSTRALIA AND NEW ZEALAND:
THE AUSTRALASIAN REALM
Peter Slater

THE OCEANIC REALM AND WORLD-WIDE BIRDS
Mike Harris PhD BSc
Institute of Terrestrial Ecology

THE POLAR REALM
Bernard Stonehouse DPhil MA BSc MInstBiol
Chairman, Postgraduate School of Environmental Science, University of Bradford

CLASSIFICATION
Peter J. S. Olney BSc DipEd FLS
Curator of Birds, The Zoological Society of London

Foreword

Of all the higher forms of life the birds are the most beautiful, most musical, most admired, most watched and most defended. Indeed, there is scarcely a square mile of the earth's surface that some birds do not occupy, or travel across, except the interior of the Antarctic continent. Without them much of our world would seem ominously lifeless and silent.

Birds have always touched the lives of men in many ways, but they have long been taken for granted and the present plight of many species has brought them into sharper focus. Birds are far more than finches, doves and thrushes to enliven the garden, ducks and quail to fill the sportsman's bag, or rare waders to be ticked off on the bird-watcher's list. They are an "ecological litmus paper". They reflect changes in the environment quickly; they warn us of things out of balance, sending out signals whenever there is a deterioration in the ecosystem. It is inevitable that the intelligent person who watches birds must become a committed environmentalist. He is disturbed when a species becomes endangered and deplores the passing of a species because it means the abrupt termination of a long line of evolution.

This book offers the reader a fresh look at what birds are, what makes them tick, and what lies behind their extraordinary success in coming to terms with virtually every habitat available on our planet – from the polar regions to the equatorial rain-forests and from the mountain-tops to the sky and the open sea. Visiting the natural habitats of many of the world's most fascinating birds requires more time and wherewithal than most of us can command. Not everyone can travel to New Zealand to see a Kiwi or to Australia to observe an Emu. We may aspire to know at least our own native species, and, through the displays of captive birds in zoos and wildlife parks, a few species from other lands.

Recent years have seen the emergence of a new type of opportunity – guided tours to the uttermost ends of the earth for the primary purpose of observing the native bird-life. Antarctica, the northernmost reaches of Greenland, the headwaters of the Amazon and the highlands of Ethiopia – all are available. More than 25 years ago there were bird tours by ship around the islands of Scotland and Audubon-sponsored tours through Florida, but in recent years the coverage has extended to the whole world.

In lieu of such travel, the armchair voyager can be knowledgeable about every bird family, every zoo-geographical realm and every major habitat, through the pages of this lavishly illustrated book. The living bird is the key, rather than geography or taxonomy. Birds are the very affirmation of life and beauty. I commend this book – this avian gallery – to you for your pleasure.

Roger Tory Peterson

The Evolution of Flight

Fulmar
Fulmarus glaciali

The only mammals to have achieved powered flight, the bats differ from birds in having the whole hand adapted to support the wing. No fossils are known prior to the Eocene. Today there are more than 750 species

Fruit-eating bat
Family, Pteropodidae

During the six-hundred-million-year history of advanced life, four life-forms have forsaken their earthbound ancestors and evolved the power of flight. First to fly were the insects, about 220 million years ago, followed by flying reptiles, birds, who first appear in the fossil record about 150 million years ago, and finally mammals (the bats) recorded in rocks of Eocene age. All other "flying" creatures – fish, lizards, tropical frogs, squirrels and snakes – are capable only of partly controlled glides.

The speed with which a bird body decomposes and the fragile structure of the avian skeleton are not conducive to the preservation of bird remains as fossils and knowledge of early avian evolution is therefore scant. Little detail is available of the transitional stages through which the feather passed in its evolution from the reptilian scale, or of the stages by which the forelimb was modified into the avian wing.

The first recognizable fossil bird, the crow-sized *Archaeopteryx*, was discovered in 1861 in the fine Jurassic sediments of southern Germany. The bird exhibited many reptilian features and from the weak structure of the breast bone probably had very limited powers of flight. The next known birds occur some 30 million years later and show much more advanced avian features. The flightless, six-foot long *Hesperornis* of the Cretaceous period retained its primitive teeth but resembled modern divers, while its diminutive contemporary, *Ichthyornis*, was probably capable of strong flight.

By the beginning of the Tertiary period, about 70 million years ago, birds had shed virtually all their reptilian features and the first of the groups extant today had appeared – including the ducks, cranes, gulls and penguins. The Tertiary was a concentrated period of development of bird orders; a period that saw the emergence of about three-quarters of the present-day avian families and also some spectacular birds like the seven-foot flightless *Diatryma* of North America. Later periods saw the evolution of the huge "elephant birds" of Madagascar and the giant moas of New Zealand – both of which are now extinct, perhaps due in part to man.

MILLION
YEARS
AGO
100
110
120
130
140
150
160
170
180
190

Zalambdalestes

One of the earliest-known placental mammals, *Zalambdalestes* was probably a tree-dwelling creature and a primitive forerunner of the tree shrews

Archaeopteryx lithographica

The discovery, in 1861, of the fossil remains of *Archaeopteryx* gave rise to one of the most exciting – and controversial – debates ever to shake the world of palaeontology. The first discovery, the imprint of a single feather, was quickly followed by an even more important find, an almost complete skeleton which, but for the earlier discovery and the undoubted marks of feathers on the forearm, would have immediately been designated the remains of a reptile.

Certainly this first true bird retains many of the characteristic features of its reptilian ancestry. Its jaws were armed with strong teeth; the bones of the head and jaw are reptilian in character, and the bird retained a long reptilian tail. But this creature was feathered, and this feature alone was enough to designate *Archaeopteryx* the first known bird – the furthest back man has yet been able to reach into the ancestry of the 8,600 bird species we know today.

Thrinaxodon
Thrinaxodon, an advanced mammal-like reptile of the Triassic period, was probably close to the main line of evolution that led to the mammals

10

Great Skua
Catharacta skua

Sooty Falcon
Falco concolor

Magpie
Pica pica

The Tertiary period, 60 to 10 million years ago, saw the rapid emergence of "modern" bird families, but the major evolutionary explosion occurred over the past few million years, giving rise to more than 8,600 species

Modern insects are the most successful life-forms ever evolved on earth. Today there are more than 700,000 recorded species; the total may be much higher

Locust
Locusta sp

Pteranodon

The pterosaurs died out in the Cretaceous period, leaving no surviving relatives. Pteranodon (illustrated) was the largest-ever flying creature with a wingspan in excess of 27 feet

Ornithosuchus

The thecodont reptiles were one of the dominant groups during the Triassic period. Related to the dinosaurs and pterosaurs, they probably gave rise to the first birds

Primitive wingless insect, 300 million years ago

Insects reached their zenith in the Carboniferous 350 to 270 million years ago. The largest species was the giant dragonfly, *Meganeura*, 29 inches from wing-tip to wing-tip

Birds in prehistory

Known only from North America, from the Eocene of New Mexico and Wyoming. Similar contemporaries in Europe

Diatryma steini
6-7 feet tall; ground-dwelling raptor

Flightless aquatic predator known from the Cretaceous chalk deposits of Kansas

Hesperornis regalis
6 feet long; tooth-billed fish-eater

Tern-like piscivore dated Upper Cretaceous. Not known whether or not the bill was toothed

Ichthyornis victor
8 inches long; tern-like fish hunter

The earliest true bird, discovered in the Jurassic deposits of southern Germany in 1861. Had the first specimens not shown feather imprints, the skeletons would almost certainly have been classified as reptiles

Archaeopteryx lithographica
18 inches long; the first true bird

Feathers: The Unique Adaptation

Grey Sea Eagle
Haliaeetus albicilla

The main structural features of the bird's wing as viewed from below. 1 Primary flight feathers, 2 Secondary flight feathers, 3 First digit (alula), 4 Second digit, 5 Third digit, 6 Fused metacarpals, 7 Carpals (wrist), 8 Radius, 9 Ulna, 10 Humerus

Compared with the human arm, the forelimb of a bird exhibits both loss, and modification, of bones. Major differences are seen in the wrist and hand region, where several bones are fused, and in the structure of the shoulder

A unique outer covering

The most distinctive characteristic of a bird is its covering of feathers – a unique feature that sets it apart from all other members of the animal kingdom. The major functions of feathers are to assist in flight and to provide the insulation vital to the conservation of the bird's body heat. For both these functions the feather is intricately and admirably adapted. Although the evidence is not recorded in fossil form, it is likely that, just as the birds evolved from reptilian ancestors, feathers have evolved from the reptilian scale. Both are formed of the same horny substance – the protein keratin.

There are four basic types of feathers. The most important are the vaned feathers in which a strong central shaft supports two converging webs of parallel, diagonal rows of filaments, to each of which are attached a multitude of tiny interlocking barbules that give the structure its remarkable lightness and strength. All the flight feathers are vaned; the primaries, that provide forward propulsion in flight, and the secondaries, that form the main

aerofoil of the inner wing and create the uplift necessary for flight. The bird's outer covering of body feathers also consists of vaned feathers.

A second major group, the down feathers, form a warm insulating layer close to the body beneath the vaned feathers. They are most abundant in those species, such as sea-birds and Arctic residents, that must withstand severe cold. Less important are the filoplume feathers that appear as a fine, hair-like fuzz, visible for example when a game-bird is plucked. Some species also have bristle feathers having a sensory function. They are found around the mouths of aerial feeders, such as Swifts, and around the base of the Kiwi's bill, where they assist this ground feeder in foraging for worms and grubs among leaf debris.

The number of feathers depends on the bird's size, species and sex. A Whistling Swan may have as many as 25,000; a Hummingbird as few as 900. Feathers are regularly replaced during the bird's life, usually during an annual moult. New feathers grow at the base of the old, forcing

out their predecessors and taking their place. If flight feathers are broken the bird's ability to fly may be drastically reduced until the next moult, but a feather pulled out intact may be replaced within two months. The main flight feathers rest in sockets in the wing bones and are held by an elastic tendon and by the skin.

Aerofoil and propeller

The wing is a remarkably versatile appendage far removed from the reptilian forelimb from which it evolved. The skeleton is similar in form to that of a human arm though the bird's upper arm is proportionally smaller. Also, the bird's "wrist" and "palm" bones, which support the main flight feathers, are fused to provide greater strength. The bird has three digits; two support the flight feathers while the third, at the front of the wing, carries the "alula" or "bastard wing", a small group of feathers that are manipulated to control the airflow over the wing and give stability at low (near stall) speeds, encountered, for example, when the bird is about to land.

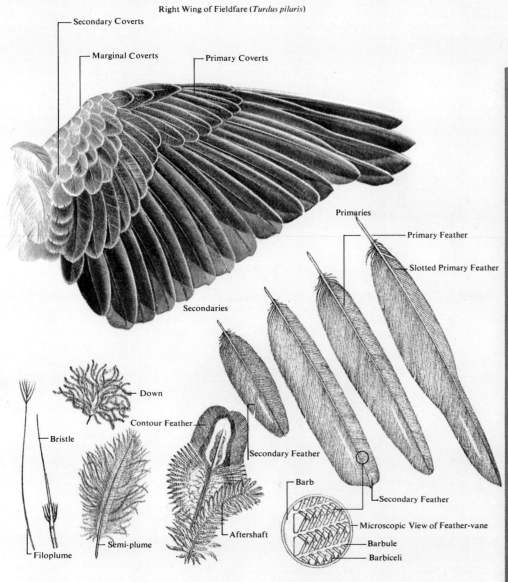

Right Wing of Fieldfare (*Turdus pilaris*)

Secondary Coverts

Marginal Coverts

Primary Coverts

Primaries

Primary Feather

Slotted Primary Feather

Secondaries

Down

Contour Feather

Bristle

Secondary Feather

Barb

Secondary Feather

Aftershaft

Microscopic View of Feather-vane

Semi-plume

Barbule

Filoplume

Barbiceli

The bird's superb insulation is provided by the down feathers underlying the outer contour feathers. Down feathers are not vaned. Some contour feathers (see above) have a downy aftershaft. Filoplumes and bristles are specialized forms

All the main flight feathers, and the body contour feathers, are vaned. A strong, light central shaft, the rachis, supports the branching barbs that form the vane. The barbs are in turn locked together by the barbules and barbiceli, giving strength and lightness

The wing itself is a sophisticated aerofoil, having a thickened leading edge and a finely tapered trailing edge. It is cambered downward so that air flowing over the wing must travel farther and faster than air passing beneath, so reducing the air pressure above and creating lift. Subtle adjustments of the wing's "angle of attack" allow the bird total control of its speed and attitude. Large birds of prey are able to spread their primary feathers in flight so that each feather acts as a separate miniature aerofoil, providing extra lift. In soaring birds the tips are deeply slotted to reduce turbulence at the wing tip.

The control of temperature
Although one of the main functions of feathers is to insulate, the bird must control the degree of insulation and be able to dissipate the enormous amount of heat that is generated by the massive flight muscles. Surface muscles attached to the skin are employed to raise and separate the body feathers to permit this excess heat to escape as though through a multi-slotted

ventilator system. Outwardly, the bird appears to be completely covered in feathers, but this is not strictly so. The feathers actually grow in well-defined regions of the body known as feather tracts or pterylae, and overlay the bare areas or apteria. There are, however, a few exceptions; the feathers of the ostriches, penguins and South American screamers are distributed over the whole body and several of the temperate-zone penguins must stand and pant, holding their wings (flippers) away from the body, in order to lose the heat generated whilst swimming.

Form and function
Wings vary enormously in shape and size depending on the life-style of the bird. High-speed hunters, like the Hobby, have back-swept scimitar wings that create little drag in flight; large soaring species, like eagles and vultures, have long broad wings with deeply slotted primaries to enable the birds to utilize every available up-draught, while many forest-dwelling birds, like the tanagers and owls, have short, broad wings ideally suited to fast manoeuvring.

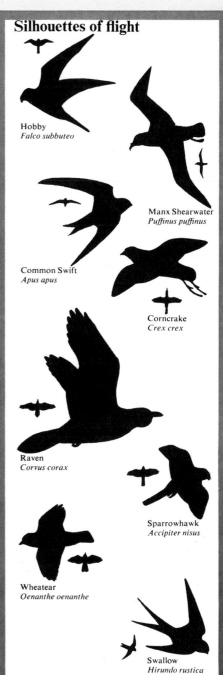

Silhouettes of flight

Hobby
Falco subbuteo

Manx Shearwater
Puffinus puffinus

Common Swift
Apus apus

Corncrake
Crex crex

Raven
Corvus corax

Sparrowhawk
Accipiter nisus

Wheatear
Oenanthe oenanthe

Swallow
Hirundo rustica

The mechanical demands of flight, and the additional demands imposed by each species' life-style, have led to the evolution of a wide variety of wing shapes.

Purely aerial birds like the falcons, swifts and swallows, have slender back-swept wings which give the bird great speed and manoeuvrability. The long, narrow wings of the shearwaters, petrels and albatrosses, however, are designed for gliding and soaring and will carry the bird for hours with scarcely a wingbeat.

The short, broad wings of the corncrake and sparrowhawk have contrasting functions; the corncrake flies rarely, and then for only short distances, while the sparrowhawk is an active aerial hunter whose wing- and tail-form enable it to follow every twist and turn of its intended prey.

Broad, deeply slotted wings enable the ravens, eagles and vultures to utilize the thermals and updraughts of high ground and cliffs as they soar in search of food.

Masters of the Air

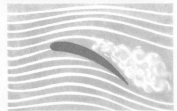

In stable flight, the air pressure difference at a and b creates lift

Too high an angle of attack causes the airflow to break up as turbulence

The alula creates a slot – streamlining the airflow and preventing a stall

Hovering flight

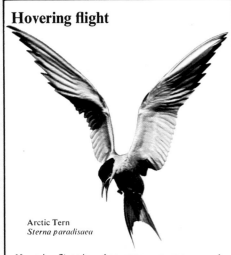

Arctic Tern
Sterna paradisaea

Hovering flight is a phenomenon more commonly associated with insects than with birds and, indeed, the complex wing action of the hummingbird has been compared to that of an insect. While hovering, these tiny birds are able to flap their wings at the astonishing rate of up to 80 beats a second; by comparison, a pigeon can manage a maximum of only ten beats a second. Hovering almost motionless before a flower to feed, the hummingbird drives its wings powerfully downwards then rotates them so that, on the up beat, the wings are "wrong-side" up. The forward thrust of the down beat is immediately counterbalanced by the backward thrust of this second power stroke and the bird remains fixed in one spot. Terns and some hawks are able to hover for only a few seconds, and then only when facing into a wind which, flowing across the aerofoil of the wing, provides the required lift.

The techniques of flight

The manner in which any bird flies may be classified in one of four ways; gliding, soaring, flapping or hovering, each one of which involves a sophisticated and quite instinctive use of aerodynamics. Each bird species specializes in those types of flight best suited to its physical environment and to its manner of feeding.

Gliding is the simplest form of flight and requires virtually no expenditure of energy. The bird is kept aloft simply by the airflow above and beneath the aerofoils of its stiffly held wings. Enough lift is gained to counteract the pull of gravity. However, friction between the wings and the airflow gradually slows the bird down and without any remedial action the bird would fall to earth. To increase the amount of lifting force the bird may flap its wings, expending some energy, or glide into a thermal updraught, which requires no energy output.

For soaring flight the bird inclines its head downwards at a shallow angle and, with a slight increase in speed, glides into upward-moving air currents. The soaring bird can, by subtle movements of body and wings, fly on a horizontal plane or gain height, and with very little effort may remain in the air for hours at a time. Soaring flight often takes the form of a rising spiral as the bird must remain within the roughly cylindrical column of rising air. From the top of the spiral the bird breaks away into a long and effortless glide. Flapping flight over great distances requires an enormous output of energy quite beyond most large soaring birds such as storks and eagles, and migrant storks must ride the air currents throughout their annual journeys from the Baltic to South Africa.

Flapping flight may take either of two forms; one for take-off and rapid climbing flight, another for forward horizontal flight. For simple forward motion the bird uses its wing like an oar, strong down strokes generating enough thrust and lift to keep the bird airborne. The upward stroke in this flight is passive. Take-off and rapid climbing require a far greater degree of lift, and power is utilized on both up and down strokes.

Hovering flight is probably the most highly specialized of all flight forms and is virtually restricted to the hummingbirds. The degree of lift generated is just sufficient to counterbalance the force of the wind and the pull of gravity. With the exception of the Kestrel, few birds are able to hover for more than a few seconds – often as a precursor to a hunting dive.

Soaring flight

Gannet
Morus bassanus

Long, narrow wings are characteristic of pelagic birds like shearwaters, petrels and albatrosses – all birds that habitually soar and glide. Flapping flight is exhausting and inefficient with this type of wing and these birds, though supreme in the air, are generally clumsy when taking off and landing

A powerful upward current is produced whenever the wind hits an obstacle such as a cliff or hill. The rising airflow is used by many cliff-nesting gulls while, in inland situations, the updraughts are utilized by eagles and other soaring birds

An offshore wind, flowing over the edge of a cliff (or hill) creates eddy currents. Soaring birds like the gulls, fulmars and choughs make full use of these eddies, while the heavyweight auks could barely reach their nests without the aid of the updraughts

SOARING ON THERMALS

As the land surface heats up unevenly, the air tends to rise over the "hot spots". This rising column of air is contained by cold air streaming down the sides – eventually to undercut the hot air mass so that it rises as an unstable bubble

SOARING ON THE WIND

Flight track

Picking up speed in the faster airflow 50 to 100 feet above the waves, soaring sea-birds swoop down to skim the surface. Here the wind velocity is reduced by friction and the bird turns to soar into the headwind

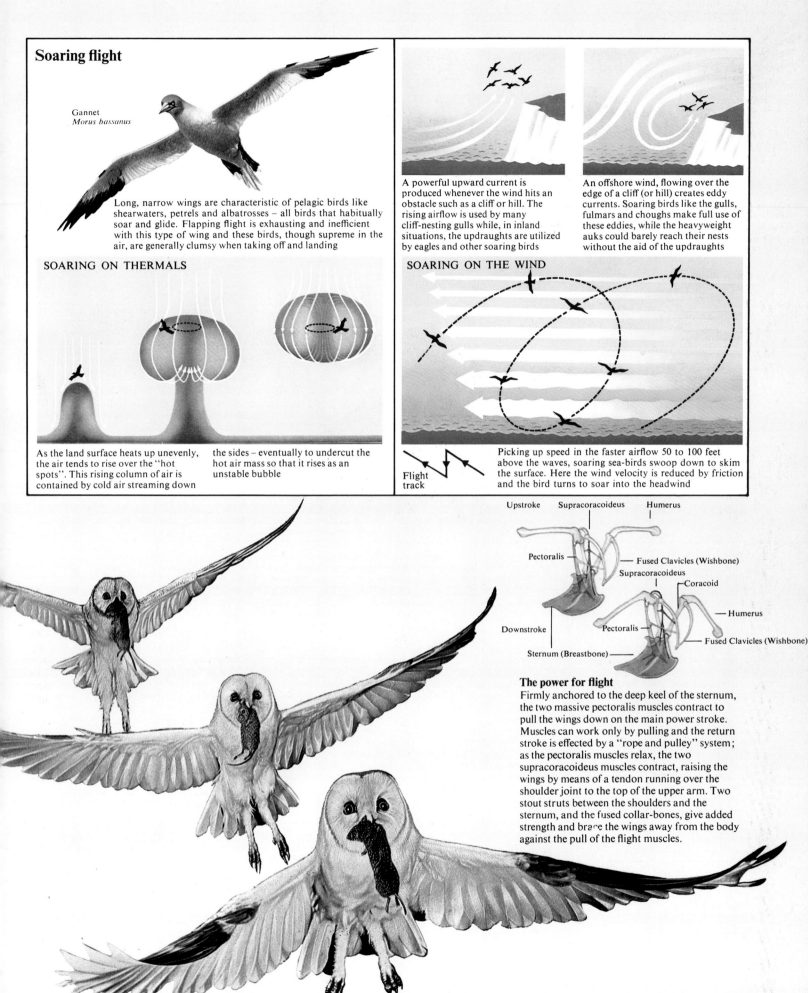

Upstroke Supracoracoideus Humerus

Pectoralis — — Fused Clavicles (Wishbone)

Supracoracoideus

—Coracoid

Downstroke

Pectoralis —

— Humerus

Sternum (Breastbone) —

— Fused Clavicles (Wishbone)

The power for flight

Firmly anchored to the deep keel of the sternum, the two massive pectoralis muscles contract to pull the wings down on the main power stroke. Muscles can work only by pulling and the return stroke is effected by a "rope and pulley" system; as the pectoralis muscles relax, the two supracoracoideus muscles contract, raising the wings by means of a tendon running over the shoulder joint to the top of the upper arm. Two stout struts between the shoulders and the sternum, and the fused collar-bones, give added strength and brace the wings away from the body against the pull of the flight muscles.

15

Landing . . .

As the bird comes in to land, the eyes are fixed on the "target" area; the wings and tail are spread to reduce speed and the body begins to rotate into a more upright position.

A bird coming in to land is an animal undergoing a major transformation – an airborne creature in the process of changing into a land animal. Through millions of years of evolution the bird's body structure has become equipped for this sudden change; the landing process involves the utilization of appendages, bones and muscles that have evolved specifically to facilitate the transformation and to support the bird's weight and movements when it is not aloft. The wings play a vital role in landing, partly as brakes, to reduce speed before making contact with the ground, partly as stabilizers to maintain balance and control, but the bird's undercarriage, consisting of its feet, legs and tail, and the muscles and bones which permit their manipulation, has an even more complex landing function. The undercarriage is braced and extended to withstand the shift of the bird's weight from its wings to its legs, and to establish immediate balance on the ground, counteracting forward momentum and gravitational pull. To meet these formidable requirements, the undercarriage has evolved from

Just before contact is made, the body is rotated still further; the wings beat against the direction of movement to reduce speed, and the legs are stretched forward to grip the perch.

the long heavy tail, hindlimbs and underpart of the lower body of the bird's reptilian ancestor into a sturdy, compact, reinforced structure.

An important element of the reinforcement lies in the pelvic bones, which support the hip joints. The pelvic bones are fused together to provide greater strength, to carry the substantial, though seemingly minute, impact of landing, in addition to the bird's terrestrial weight. The fused pelvis bones are, in turn, attached to a rigid horizontal backbone to spread the load of the bird's body, a necessary distribution, particularly in landing, because much of the weight is concentrated beneath the backbone. As for the tail, in addition to assisting flight manoeuvring, it contributes significantly to braking during landing, its feathers spreading to reduce velocity. On land, the tail is often used as a prop by Woodpeckers and other tree-climbers, and by birds pulling worms from the ground. In the last stage of the bird's descent during landing, the legs, which are usually drawn up under the feathers in flight to aid streamlining, are stretched forward to meet the ground. The toes, particularly the long, pointed front toes, are held rigid to provide a firm support. Some species have claws on the tips of their toes for gripping perches – particularly important for birds which sleep on perches and for birds of prey whose livelihood depends on their ability to seize, and hold, their prey. The web-footed legs of aquatic birds have a different primary purpose. They are the bird's swimming appendages and are set farther back than the legs of land-birds in order to act as water propellers. This positioning results in reduced balance on land and a clumsy waddling walk characteristic of swimming birds.

The undercarriage

The bones of the bird's leg are, like those of the wing, reduced in comparison with the human limb, and in places either absent or highly modified. The whole structure is designed as an efficient shock absorber – light yet strong and equipped with powerful muscles situated high up near the bird's centre of gravity. There are no muscles in the lower part of the leg; the toes are operated by tendons stretched over the "false knee" or ankle joint.

Sternum

Pygostyle

Tibiotarsus

Ambiens muscle

Sternum

Pygostyle

Flexor muscle

Flexor tendons

Pubis

Semitendinosus muscle

Phalanges (Toes)

Tendons operate the toes and control grip

Femur (Thigh)

Patella (Knee)

Tibiotarsus

Fibula

Tarsals (Ankle)

Fibia (Lower Leg)

Phalanges

Tarsometatarsus

Phalanges

By spreading the alula, or "bastard wing", the bird controls any tendency to stall as it makes its final approach. The airflow over the wing aerofoil is smoothed and turbulence is reduced. The wings beat forward to arrest the bird's motion and the outstretched legs take the shock of impact. In perching birds (passerines) the foot is structured so that, on coming to rest with the leg bent at the ankle, tendons in the leg are pulled taut and the foot closes.

Perching, Walking and Swimming

Over countless generations, birds have evolved to fill almost every available ecological niche, their wing shapes, bills, body forms and feet all perfectly adapted to their chosen way of life.

Feet have become adapted to swimming, wading, running, climbing, perching and every intermediate combination of activity. Swimmers' feet may be webbed between all four toes to give maximum propulsion, as in the case of the cormorants, or between three toes, as with the ducks, auks and gulls. The aquatic grebes, phalaropes and coots have horny lobes fringing the toes instead of web membranes. The lily-trotter illustrates one of the more extreme forms of wader specialization; the toes are greatly extended and spread the bird's weight over a wide area – allowing it to walk with ease on floating vegetation.

Runners and walkers, too, have their extreme forms. The ostrich is the only bird with just two toes, and these have cushion-soles to prevent the bird sinking in loose sand. Many ground-dwelling seed-eaters, notably the fowl, have strong feet ideally suited to scratching food from the ground. Some of the tree-climbing species like woodpeckers and tree-creepers have two toes pointed forward and two back, while "clinging" birds like the swifts, have all four toes directed forward.

Powerful talons are characteristic of hunters and scavengers whose livelihood depends on their ability to strike surely.

Species illustrated

1 Little Owl	9 Lapwing
2 Osprey	10 Avocet
3 Peregrine Falcon	11 Coot
4 Yellow-headed	12 Red-throated Diver
Amazon Parrot	13 Mallard
5 Swift	14 Northern Jacana
6 Ostrich	15 Skylark
7 Ptarmigan	16 Kingfisher
8 Green Woodpecker	17 Cardinal

17

Techniques of Feeding

Beaks are feeding tools, their enormous variety of form enabling birds to utilize almost every conceivable feeding niche. The major feeding modes of flesh-tearing, seed-crushing, fishing, grazing and insect-catching, to each of which several distinct groups of birds are adapted, are complemented by subtle gradations. Even among the seed-eating finches there is a complete range of bill-form from the tiny bill of the Siskin to the massive crushing equipment of the Hawfinch.

The beak, however, is just one part of the bird's total equipment and should not be viewed in isolation. The powerful, hooked bill of the eagle would be of little use without the flight technique for soaring, and hence spotting likely prey, nor would the bill be of great use without the massive talons with which the eagle seizes and carries its prey. Similarly the algae-filtering bill of the Flamingo and the serrated bill of the Merganser would be of little use without the other physical and behavioural adaptations of these species.

Physical appearance, behaviour, habitat, nesting site and breeding habits must all be considered if a bird is to be understood.

The insect-eaters
Generally slender, pincer-like bills of varying length. Some species have bristles around the mouth to assist in catching airborne insects. 1 Swift, 2 Swallow, 3 Great Tit, 4 Icterine Warbler, 5 Collared Flycatcher, 6 Akiapolaau

Hunter *above*
The Osprey, *Pandion haliaetus*, is one of the world's most widespread piscivorous predators. This handsome hunter inhabits mountain-lake regions, coastal marshes, rivers and estuaries in the temperate and tropical regions of every major continent except South America. Diving feet first on to a surface-swimming fish, the Osprey clamps two toes on each side of its prey.

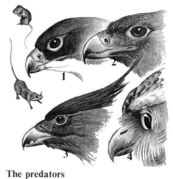

The fish-eaters
Long, sharp bills, often hook-tipped and with serrated margins. 1 Brown Noddy Tern, 2 Red-breasted Merganser, 3 Cormorant

The predators
Powerful, hooked bills for tearing and cutting flesh and skin. 1 Peregrine Falcon, 2 Golden Eagle, 3 Cuckoo Falcon, 4 Eagle Owl

The seed- and nut-eaters
Usually short, stout bills, some strongly curved. In some species, e.g. the Crossbill, the bill tips overlap. 1 Parrot, 2 Common Partridge, 3 Siskin

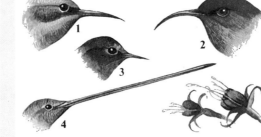

The nectar-feeders
Characterized by very long slender bills; many species also have brush-tipped tongues. 1 Scarlet-breasted Sunbird, 2 Honeyeater, 3 and 4 Hummingbirds

The fruit-eaters
The bills are very varied and often do not immediately indicate the bird's food preference.
1 Black-casqued Hornbill, 2 Common Wood Pigeon, 3 Mistletoe Bird

Scavenger
The tube-nosed Fulmar

Filter-feeder
The Avocet

Vegetarian/omnivore
The Ostrich

Omnivore
The Common Crow

The Senses

The bird's senses are, like the rest of its physiology, perfectly adapted to the demands of its way of life. Vision and hearing are acutely developed, while the senses of smell, taste and touch are relatively weak.

To most species, sight is the key to survival and consequently the eyes are large; the bigger the eye, the more light-sensitive cells it can contain. To the hunter, sight is necessary for spotting prey – often small creatures at great distance from the eye. Conversely, the prey species depend on keen, all-round vision to warn of approaching danger. Lacking any sophisticated verbal language, birds communicate largely by signal, and keen vision is necessary to catch, and correctly interpret, a fleeting danger signal. Hearing, too, is an important factor in the bird's life, both for communication and in food gathering. Though similar in hearing range to the human ear, the bird's hearing is far more acute and only by slowing down a recorded bird song can the human ear detect many of the faster notes and subtle variations in tone that make up the call. Smell may be an important sense to some scavenging species.

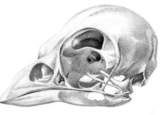

The bones of the bird's skull are extremely thin, though fused together and braced internally to give great strength. The heavy jaws and teeth of mammals are replaced by the bird's gizzard – situated nearer the bird's centre of gravity

Cortex
Unlike the thick, convoluted cortex of a mammal, that of the bird brain is thin and poorly developed. The cortex controls learning and intelligence in mammals

Optic lobe
Very large and well developed, this area of the brain receives impulses from the eyes and co-ordinates vision, the bird's most important sense

Cerebellum
The flight-control area of the bird brain – the control centre for balance and co-ordination. Notably less well developed in flightless species

Olfactory bulb
A small projection of the forebrain receives impulses associated with the sense of smell. It is small in comparison with that of a mammal

Hindbrain
The main "junction box" for the bird's nervous system. The nerves associated with hearing, taste and the motor functions originate in the hindbrain

Striatum
The striatum is the seat of learning and intelligence in birds

Touch and smell

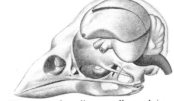

The sense of smell, generally weak in birds, is seated in the olfactory bulb. Nerves passing to the hindbrain carry impulses from touch- and heat-sensitive receptors in the bill and from sensitive bristles in some species, e.g. the Kiwi

Kiwi

Woodcock

Very few birds make use of the tactile sense, though it is almost certainly present in a poorly developed form. Two species that depart from the norm and utilize this sense in searching for food are the Kiwi of New Zealand and the Woodcock, represented by a number of species throughout the world.

The Woodcock (p109) probes deep into the loose earth and leaf-litter of the forest floor, detecting worms and grubs with the sensitive nerves concentrated in the bulbous tip of its bill. The Kiwi (p211) also has a concentration of nerve endings in the region of the bill tip, but in this species the tactile sense is reinforced by sensitive bristles around the base of the bill, which detect any movements within the leaf-litter, and further by a well-developed sense of smell. The remarkable mound-building Mallee Fowl of Australia (p194) has a further refinement of the tactile sense; probing into the incubating mound, the bird is apparently able to judge accurately the temperature of the decomposing vegetation.

Sight

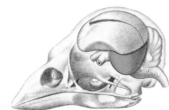

Visual impulses from the bird's eyes are transmitted via the optic nerves and are interpreted by the well-developed optic lobes of the brain. Control of focusing and eye movements derives from the major nerves situated in the hindbrain

Wood Pigeon
A great many seed-eating and ground-dwelling species are preyed upon by hawks, falcons, cats and even foxes. In order to survive, they need a very wide range of vision, and in the case of the Wood Pigeon this field of vision covers 340 degrees of the horizon. The bird's binocular vision, however, covers only 24 degrees, immediately in front of the bird's head.

Tawny Owl
While the pigeon's eyes are sited at the sides of the head, to increase the field of vision for defence, the hunter's eyes are generally placed near the front of the head so as to increase the field of binocular vision. The forward gaze is more effective in keeping an intended victim in view, and the binocular vision is vital to the predator's ability to judge distance when making a strike.

Woodcock
Probing the leaf-litter with its long bill, the feeding Woodcock would be a vulnerable target for predators but for the extreme specialization of its eyes. These are placed high on the sides of the head, and well back, giving the bird a field of vision of 360 degrees. The Woodcock has a narrow field of binocular vision both forward and to the rear, for feeding and defence.

Hearing

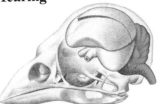

Nerves in the hindbrain are closely associated with hearing and with equilibrium. The acoustic nerve runs from the ear to the brain, carrying information relating to sounds received, and with information on orientation.

Oilbird

Although all birds have a well-developed sense of hearing, very few have adapted to make use of this sense for navigational purposes. Two birds that have adapted in this way are the Oilbird (p82) of South America and the Cave Swiftlet (p171) of the forest caves of southern Asia. The Oilbird is a large cave-dwelling bird that leaves the darkness of its nesting site at dusk to forage for food. Flying through the forest, the bird emits a rapid series of clicking calls, "reading" the presence of obstacles from the returning echoes – in exactly the same manner as a bat. So accurate is the bird's navigation that it is able to pluck nuts and small fruits from the forest trees, even in darkness, without pausing to land. The Cave Swiftlet is an insect-eater, leaving the darkness of its cave to hunt in the evening light, or occasionally during the day. These birds use exactly the same echo-location technique on flying back into the darkness of the cave after one of their feeding trips and their uncanny flying skills remove the risk of in-flight collisions.

The Retreat from Winter

The migration of birds is the world's most extraordinary mass movement of living creatures. Many thousands of millions of birds leave their breeding areas each year, fly enormous distances – often thousands of miles – and then fly back again some months later. Birds migrate to find adequate sustenance and optimal conditions for survival. The approach of winter signals an imminent curtailment of their food supply; days grow shorter, reducing available foraging time; insects, and later seeds and berries, become less plentiful. Most birds would be unable to find enough to eat during protracted northern rainy seasons or after snowfalls.

Migration is instinctive. Well before cold or famine sets in birds depart for more agreeable environments. They remain in those environments until the days again begin to grow long, the food once more begins to become abundant and the climate again begins to turn agreeable in the breeding areas they forsook for the winter; until conditions in those breeding habitats are again more favourable.

Although migration is geared to external conditions birds have internal mechanisms which are triggered several months before migration time. Most migration flights are long and exhausting and extensive preparations have to be made. The migrant must boost its store of body fat as a future energy reserve; many insect-eaters turn from their normal diet to sugar-rich berries in order to boost their reserves of energy. Some birds which normally roost at night, but which fly at night during migration, also change the rhythm of their daily activity to prepare for their journey. Willow Warblers kept in captivity under conditions resembling the wintering quarters to which they migrate, nevertheless begin hopping restlessly up and down through most of the night as the migration period draws near. Birds undergo similar behaviour changes in the spring as the time for their return migration approaches. The internal timing mechanisms for preparation and migration are vitally important, particularly for the return voyage. If a

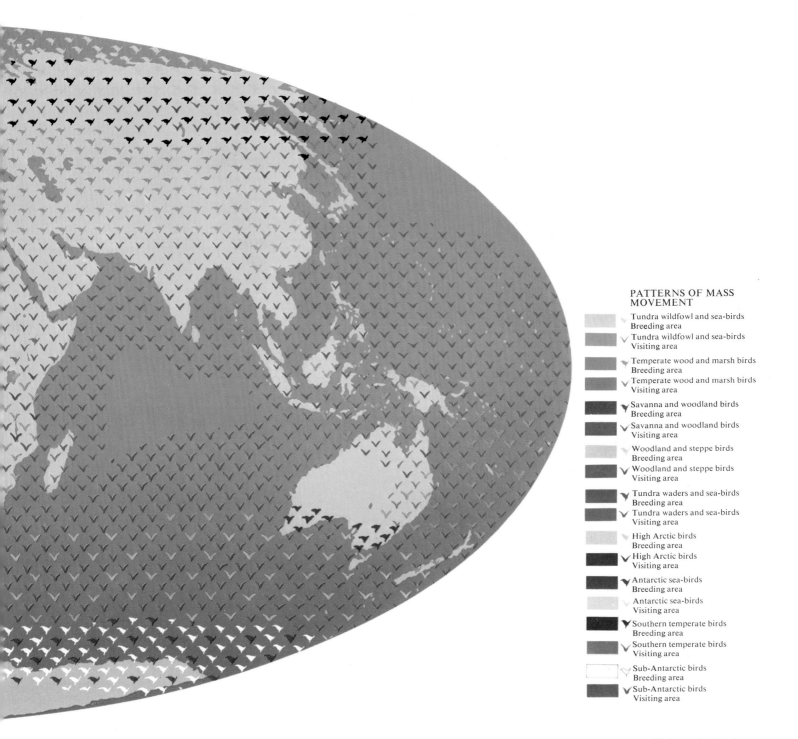

bird returns to its breeding area too early, there may not yet be enough available food. If it returns too late, it may be limited in its choice of preferred nesting territory.

Migration probably originated with major climatic upheavals in the earth's past, the most recent of which, and therefore the most influential today, were the Ice Ages. As the glaciers retreated, some species followed northwards in the wake of the ice – often to recolonize their former territories, sometimes expanding their range into new areas; but winters remained severe in northern latitudes and the birds would have had to fly south again on annual food-searching pilgrimages, gradually establishing regular breeding quarters

and wintering quarters as well as a regular migratory flight pattern. However, continued and continuing changes in basic climatic conditions have altered, and continue to alter, the migratory habits of some species. For example, northern birds like the Blackbird, which winter in temperate northern regions, are pushing farther north on their return migratory flights as northern summer temperatures gradually edge up to higher levels.

While most birds migrate every year, some, like the Cedar Waxwing, are "eruptive" migrants. Whether they migrate usually depends on year-to-year changes in the availability of food in their breeding habitats. If the autumn berry crop is good,

they may not migrate; if food is in short supply, they must migrate to survive.

There are also "internal" migrants whose breeding areas and migratory destinations are geographically relatively close. The Quelea bird of Africa moves with the insect- and seed-producing rains, but does not travel very far. The Pochard ducks which breed in southern Germany migrate to a man-made Bavarian lake, their migratory path extending only a comparatively few miles.

There are many specific, and general, differences in migratory habits, patterns and paths. But all have a common and instinctive motive – self-preservation and, thereby, the perpetuation of the species.

Patterns of Migration

THE THREE MAJOR MIGRATION SYSTEMS OF THE WORLD

The migratory journeys that many birds make each year are potentially extremely hazardous. Many fly vast distances and must rely on the availability of food *en route*. Weather is unpredictable and migrants may be blown dangerously off course. Throughout the journey they face the peril of predators; small migrant birds are an important component of the diet of Eleanora's Falcon, a predator that nests at both ends of the Mediterranean route, astride the flight paths of many migrants. Migration is, however, essentially a voyage for survival and would be self-defeating if the dangers and physical demands of the trip proved too great. Consequently, birds generally seek reasonably direct, and the least obstructed, flight paths. For this purpose they have divided the world into three major migratory systems, separated by imposing geographic barriers.

The Nearctic-Neotropical (North America-South America) system has as its boundaries the Atlantic and Pacific Oceans, seas which are far too vast for most land-birds to negotiate, though some sea-birds, like the Arctic Tern, overfly broad oceans with little difficulty. The other two migratory systems, the Eurasian-African and the East Asian-South Asian-Australasian, are separated on the Eurasian landmass by forbidding mountain ranges and immense expanses of inhospitable desert. There is some overlapping of migratory paths on the boundary of these last two systems; generally, however, birds travelling to and from winter quarters remain within their migratory systems, traversing roughly north-south routes. But some species migrate on an approximately east-west axis. These include Siberian shore-birds and geese which congregate at the beginning of winter on the western shores of Britain and in Ireland, attracted by ice-free estuaries warmed by the gulf stream and rich in food. Redheaded ducks of America's prairie states migrate to the Atlantic coast of the United States, but such lateral migrations also usually remain within the boundaries of one of the main migratory systems.

Birds migrate along broad or narrow fronts or a combination of both. Perhaps millions of water-fowl, *en route* to their South American wintering quarters, use the narrow-fronted Mississippi flyway,

which is at times only a few miles wide. Large birds, like the Great Shearwater, that nest in restricted areas and migrate to areas that are only a little less restricted, follow narrow migratory corridors; to do otherwise would be dangerously wasteful of energy. But the breeding habitats of most land-birds cover wide areas; for some, like the Swallow and the Willow Warbler, they can be several thousand miles across. Their wintering areas are equally broad, and as a consequence these species tend to migrate along broad fronts. The migratory path of the Ruff, for example, can be as much as 3,000 miles wide. However, some broad front migrants often converge on narrow flight corridors to avoid longer sea crossings than are otherwise necessary. For example, White Storks, which breed in northern and central Europe, cross into Africa over the narrow Strait of Gibraltar or through the Middle East; they require regular access to air currents rising from the land to power their soaring, gliding migratory flight. Honey Buzzards from central Europe converge on the same two corridors into Africa, but they are more capable of prolonged flapping flight and some fly directly across the central Mediterranean. Direction in migration can also be influenced by heredity.

Migration is a crucial part of a bird's existence; its life and the life of its species depend on it. The method of migration and behaviour during migration are, therefore, extremely significant. The Sedge Warbler flies from northern Europe to its African wintering centres with one phenomenal expenditure of effort – about four days and nights of non-stop flying. However, most other species must rest *en route*. Most fly at night and stop during the day, primarily because feeding – essentially refuelling – is easier during the day, and also because the stars provide additional navigational aids and predators are easier to avoid at night. Some small day migrants, like Swallows and Swifts,

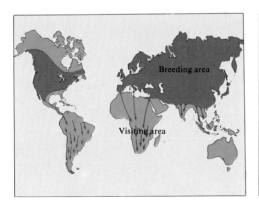

Swallow
Often leaving their breeding grounds later than most migrants, the Swallows travel by day – moving south along a broad front to winter in Africa and southern Asia

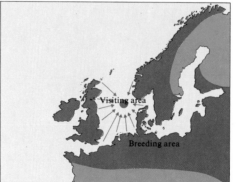

Shelduck
Shelducks migrate to Heligoland for their annual moult. During the moult the birds are flightless. Unlike the outward mass migration, the birds return in small groups

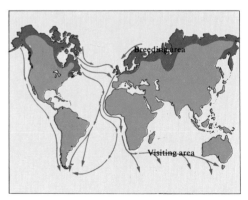

Arctic Tern
This long-range migrant breeds in the high Arctic regions and migrates each year to wintering grounds on the northern fringes of the Antarctic pack-ice. The round trip utilizes Atlantic winds

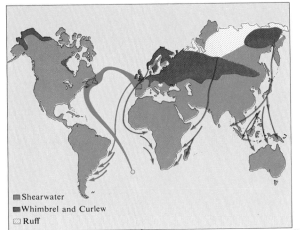

Great Shearwater
The birds breed almost exclusively on the southern Atlantic islands of the Tristan da Cunha group. Leaving the breeding grounds in late April they sweep north and east across the North Atlantic in a migration journey lasting for almost nine months, feeding on fish and squid as they move. Though the birds remain at sea their movements are hampered in July by the moult

Ruff
One of the many species to breed in the high Arctic regions, the Ruffs move south in late August and early September. The main northern populations travel to Africa to winter in coastal habitats south of the Sahara desert, but a few smaller populations based in the northern Palaearctic migrate east-west and spend the winter months in the temperate lands of the Mediterranean region

Whimbrel and Curlew
The Curlew populations breed in the temperate marshland and moorland regions of the Palaearctic, generally moving only slightly farther south in the winter months. The Whimbrels breed to the north of the Curlews, in Arctic and sub-Arctic heath and marshland, and "leap-frog" over their neighbours to migrate to coastal habitats of Africa, Asia, South America and Australia

The Shearwater, Ruff, Whimbrel and Curlew are among the world's long-range migrants, travelling many thousands of miles each year.

can feed as they fly, simply opening their mouths to devour insects carried up on air currents. Species that migrate relatively short distances and that, therefore, are less burdened by feeding problems, generally travel by day. Shore-birds, whose behaviour is geared to the tides rather than to the time of day or night, perform their migratory hops at virtually any time of the day or night.

Some species, like the Wood Sandpiper, break off their migratory flights for the essential annual moult, moving on after they have replaced their feathers; but for others, migration is primarily aimed at allowing the birds to moult in a suitable area. For example, Shelducks from all over western Europe gather each July on the Heligoland sandbanks and stay there until the autumn, after which they return, with their plumage completely renewed, to their breeding areas. Like many other wildfowl, Shelducks are flightless during the moulting period and require a refuge where they will be safe from predators and where there is an abundance of food. Other species have conflicting migratory habits; part of a population may migrate to

distant wintering areas while part, occupying the same breeding habitat, may remain in the "home" range the year round. This generally occurs where a certain amount of food can be relied upon in the breeding area during the winter, but where there might not be enough to feed the entire resident population. In the case of these "partial migrants", the hazards of migrating are sometimes matched by the danger that severe winter conditions will reduce the available food supply for the sedentary individuals. In the greater scheme of things "partial migration" appears to be a testing of possibilities – a preparation for the possible migration of the entire species if changing climatic conditions make this a necessity.

Similarly, closely related species living near each other may have very different migratory habits, with one species overflying the other to head for wintering quarters, while the other remains where it is throughout the year. Whimbrels of northern Scandinavia "leapfrog" over their sedentary Curlew cousins as they migrate to tropical Africa for the winter. They then overfly the Curlews again in the spring

when they return to their breeding grounds in the north.

There has been much scientific research into the migratory habits of birds, but though much has been discovered about the techniques and mechanics of migration, less is known about the biological apparatus that tells each bird when it is time to migrate, or about the remarkable internal compass that gets some birds to roughly the same wintering grounds each year and back to the breeding habitat. A close examination of the bird's "body-clock" operation has confirmed that it works efficiently, but has not disclosed how it keeps accurate time. As for the bird's internal compass, various theories have been advanced. It may be based on external navigational aids like the sun and the stars; it may be influenced by variations in the earth's magnetic field; the bird's interpretation of low frequency sound waves and polarized light may be a factor; winds may play an important role. All these factors are currently the focus of detailed research programmes, but a comprehensive explanation of how birds navigate is still to be found.

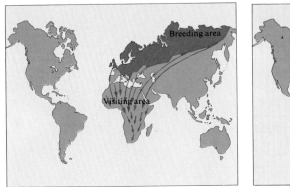

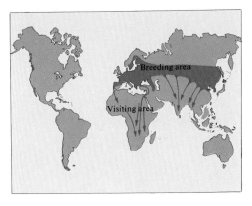

Willow Warbler
The tiny Willow Warblers of the northern forests migrate in September each year. Usually flying at night, the birds make their way south through the Mediterranean region to central Africa

White Stork
Like many of the larger migrant species, the White Stork chooses its route so as to avoid long sea crossings. Gibraltar, Italy and the Middle East region provide the easiest routes to Africa

Honey Buzzard
The Honey Buzzard often covers more than 6,000 miles in a single journey. Eurasian birds migrate to Africa; eastern Asian populations to Burma and Southeast Asia

The Language of Birds

It is almost impossible for a human, fully accustomed to intelligent communication by speech, to comprehend the difficulties facing a bird that must behave in precisely the right way in a wide range of complex social situations without benefit of verbal communication. Most male birds must win and defend a territory, attract and form a pair bond with a mate, and co-operate in reproduction. All this must be accomplished by postures and movements plus a limited range of vocal signals. The display may be dramatic and conspicuous or quiet and subtle, a complex sequence of movements or a single discrete motion. Whatever the sequence of signals used, the individual at whom the display is directed must interpret the meaning correctly and react accordingly.

This complex language of posture and movement may achieve many ends; in territorial display, the distancing of a rival; in courtship, the establishment of the rapport necessary before copulation can take place; in many long-lived birds, the maintenance of a strong pair bond.

The variety of display

The range of courtship display is immense. If, in rapid succession, an observer was to witness wing-drooping finches, dancing cranes, weed-presenting grebes, fish-offering terns, waltzing junglefowl, bill-fencing gannets and a host of other posturing birds, mainly male, it would seem as though every possible expressive act had been pressed into service. But it is all far from haphazard. Apart from the often obvious relationship between the bird's morphology and its way of life (aerial, aquatic, cursorial) and its display, there are deep underlying ecological motivations. Lek, and other communal displays, can only occur in species in which the male has been freed from nesting duties. A lek super-cock may fertilize many hens and could never assist in caring for several broods at one time.

The origins of display

Just as feathers have evolved from scales, and wings from the quadruped forelimb, so displays have evolved from a "pool" of common, everyday activities. Courtship displays are commonly derived from the movements associated with simultaneous aggression and fear mixed with sexual approaches. The combination of actions, enhanced by ritualization and subsequent association with conspicuous structures or colours, eventually becomes a formalized signal. A female entering a male bird's territory will normally elicit the automatic aggressive response directed at any intruder – the more so if her plumage is very like that of the male. An appeasement display, generally derived from juvenile behaviour or from gestures indicating submission, is necessary to block the male's aggression and allow courtship and mating to proceed.

Some courtship displays, however, incorporate apparently quite irrelevant actions such as preening, bill-wiping or even sleeping. These are usually the result of conflict arising from the simultaneous arousal of incompatible emotions. The emotions "block" each other and leave the way open for a third type of response known as "displacement behaviour".

Hawfinch
Coccothraustes coccothraustes

Great Frigatebird
Fregata minor

Robin
Erithacus rubecula

Life before birth

The number of eggs laid in a single clutch; the size, shape and weight of the egg; shell pigmentation, and frequency of laying, may all vary enormously between birds of different families. Some variation may also be seen between members of the same species, sometimes explained by disturbance or diet deficiencies – sometimes for no apparent reason save natural variation.

The egg-forming process, though not the speed at which it proceeds, is identical in all birds and is here illustrated by the domestic hen, *Gallus gallus*.

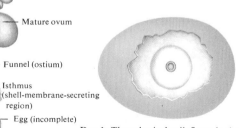

Small ova (eggs)

Mature ovum

Magnum (albumen-secreting region)

Funnel (ostium)

Isthmus (shell-membrane-secreting region)

Egg (incomplete)

Uterus (shell-secreting region)

Cloaca

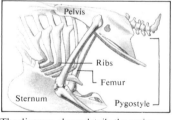

Pelvis

Ribs

Femur

Sternum

Pygostyle

The diagram above details the major anatomical features appearing in the radiographs. Six hours after release from the oviduct, the newly forming egg lies just beneath the pelvis

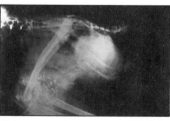

Eight and a half hours after release the albumen, or "egg white", has already been secreted in the magnum and is enclosed in a fine transparent membrane, secreted by the isthmus

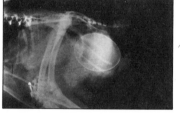

Eleven and a half hours after release, the new egg shows clearly as shell material is deposited on the shell-membrane, stretched tight by the absorption of water

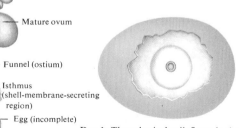

Day 1: The spherical yolk floats in the fluid albumen with the blastodisc, an early stage of the embryo, at the top; nearest the source of heat from the incubating adult

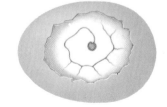

Day 3: The minute embryonic heart, with the main blood vessels already formed, is actively beating only three days after the egg is laid and before the chick is recognizable

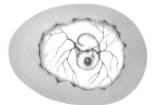

Day 9: Oxygen which has permeated the pores of the shell, and nutrients from the yolk, are fed to the developing chick by a fine, hair-like mass of delicate blood vessels

Blackcock
Lyrurus tetrix

Ruffed Grouse
Bonasa umbellus

Yellow-thighed Manakin
Pipra mentalis

Greater Bird of Paradise
Paradisaea apoda

Ruff
Philomachus pugnax

Kingfisher
Alcedo atthis

Adelie Penguin
Pygoscelis adeliae

Gannet
Morus bassanus

Black-headed Gull
Larus ridibundus

Shag
Phalacrocorax aristotelis

Pintail
Anas acuta

Jackdaw
Corvus monedula

Pochard
Aythya ferina

Features of courtship display

The sign language used by birds must be extremely versatile in order to communicate information as diverse as a warning to an approaching stranger, and an invitation to an unmated female to form a pair.

The birds illustrated are shown in a variety of display activities associated with courtship. The first, and often most obvious, form of display is that of a male "advertising" for a mate. This may take the form of a ground display like the drumming display of the Ruffed Grouse, or a flight display, perhaps made even more dramatic by a sexual adornment – like the brilliant red gular pouch of the Frigatebird.

Food-presenting is an important display element in many species, e.g. the Robin and Kingfisher, and may even become ritualized, "food-presenting without food",as a means of cementing an existing pair bond. This behaviour is a feature of the Hawfinch pair bond.

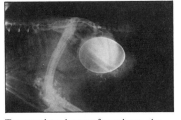

Twenty-three hours after release, the shell advances along the uterus pointed end first. Almost the full thickness of shell material has, by this time, been secreted

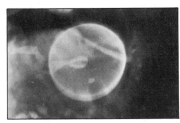

Twenty-five hours after release, a rather curious development occurs. From passing along the uterus pointed end first, the egg is completely rotated for the remainder of the journey

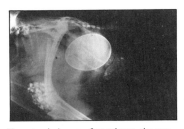

Twenty-six hours after release, the egg is laid, blunt end first. The egg is not forced out by mass muscle movement, as in defaecation, but is passed from the body in the prolapsed uterus

Day 15: The yolk mass is reduced as the chick takes on a recognizable bird form. The eye is the dominant feature, but other details, notably the bill and feet, are visible

Day 20: The dominant feature of the fully developed chick is the foot. At 21 days, the chick cracks the egg with a tiny "egg-tooth" on the bill and emerges into the outside world

Nidifugous (precocial) chicks are down-covered at birth

Nidicolous chicks are born naked and unable to walk

Clutch and egg size

The variation in the size of egg laid by individual birds of different species is quite remarkable. Smallest of all eggs is that of the Bee Hummingbird, *Mellisuga helenae*, weighing only 0.18 ounces and less than half an inch in length. At the other extreme, the African Ostrich, *Struthio camelus*, lays the world's heaviest egg, averaging well in excess of three and a half pounds. Compared with the bird's own body weight, the egg of the Kiwi, *Apteryx* spp, is one of the heaviest. At about 18 ounces, the egg accounts for almost 25 per cent of the adult bird's own weight.

The largest average clutch is generally accredited to the American Bobwhite, *Colinus virginianus*, with an average of between 12 and 24 eggs though, with 12 to 20 eggs in a clutch, the Common Partridge, *Perdix perdix*, comes second.

Incubation periods vary just as widely as egg-weight and size. The passerines generally have short incubation periods; the Hawfinch, *Coccothraustes coccothraustes*, takes nine to ten days, the Skylark, *Alauda arvensis*, usually 11. The longest incubators are to be found among the sea-birds. The Great Wandering Albatross, *Diomedea exulans*, incubates its single egg for 75 to 82 days.

The Nearctic and Neotropical Realms

The avifaunas of the neighbouring Nearctic (North American) and Neotropical (Central and South American) realms have less in common than might be expected. For more than 50 million years, North America has drifted westwards from Greenland and Europe, but during the last three million years has shared with Eurasia a history of repeated and widespread glaciations that have given rise to corresponding patterns of vegetational zones – tundra, coniferous and deciduous forests, grassland and desert. By contrast, South America was part of the ancient super-continent of Gondwanaland, which included Africa, India, Australia and Antarctica – an enormous landmass separated from the lands to the north by wide oceans. Breaking free, South America drifted westwards more than 100 million years ago, becoming isolated long before the evolution of modern bird families. For millions of years, birds of the Palaearctic and Nearctic realms have experienced similar climatic conditions, and the avifauna of North America includes several species common to Europe and the rest of the circumpolar belt of tundra and boreal forest.

Connexions between North and South America were tenuous throughout the Tertiary period, when broad equatorial seas filled the Amazon basin and isolated the lands to the south. South America was thus able to evolve an avifauna of its own, showing affinities with Africa and North America but far richer than either and with a high proportion of endemic species.

Tundra

Boreal forest

Temperate woodland

Mediterranean vegetation

Sub-desert and steppe

Desert

Wooded savanna

Sea and marsh

Montane vegetation

Tropical rain-forest

Plateau steppe

Birds illustrated in the American section of the atlas are shown below in silhouette. The colour of each silhouette corresponds with the key colour of the bird's habitat

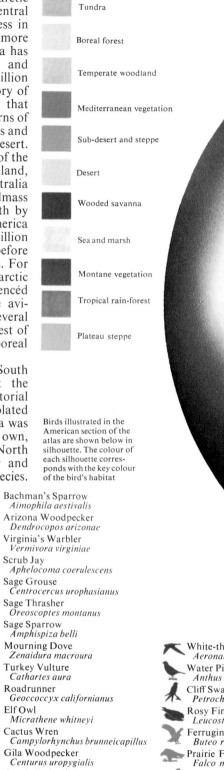

Parasitic Jaeger
Stercorarius parasiticus

Arctic Loon
Gavia arctica

American Golden Plover
Pluvialis dominica

Snowy Owl
Nyctea scandiaca

Raven
Corvus corax

Spruce Grouse
Canachites canadensis

Hawk Owl
Surnia ulula

White-winged Crossbill
Loxia leucoptera

Goshawk
Accipiter gentilis

Kirtland's Warbler
Dendroica kirtlandii

Steller's Jay
Cyanocitta stelleri

Chestnut-backed Chickadee
Parus rufescens

Townsend's Solitaire
Myadestes townsendi

Williamson's Sapsucker
Sphyrapicus thyroideus

Cassin's Finch
Carpodacus cassinii

Scarlet Tanager
Piranga olivacea

Yellow-throated Vireo
Vireo flavifrons

Turkey
Meleagris gallopavo

Red-headed Woodpecker
Melanerpes erythrocephalus

Red-shouldered Hawk
Buteo lineatus

Ivory-billed Woodpecker
Campephilus principalis

Bachman's Sparrow
Aimophila aestivalis

Arizona Woodpecker
Dendrocopos arizonae

Virginia's Warbler
Vermivora virginiae

Scrub Jay
Aphelocoma coerulescens

Sage Grouse
Centrocercus urophasianus

Sage Thrasher
Oreoscoptes montanus

Sage Sparrow
Amphispiza belli

Mourning Dove
Zenaidura macroura

Turkey Vulture
Cathartes aura

Roadrunner
Geoccoccyx californianus

Elf Owl
Micrathene whitneyi

Cactus Wren
Campylorhynchus brunneicapillus

Gila Woodpecker
Centurus uropygialis

Gambel's Quail
Lophortyx gambelii

Wrentit
Chamaea fasciata

Black-chinned Sparrow
Spizella atrogularis

Poorwill
Phalaenoptilus nuttallii

Pinyon Jay
Gymnorhinus cyanocephalus

Black-crested Titmouse
Parus atricristatus

Blue-grey Gnatcatcher
Polioptila caerulea

California Condor
Gymnogyps californianus

White-throated Swift
Aeronautes saxatalis

Water Pipit
Anthus spinoletta

Cliff Swallow
Petrochelidon pyrrhonota

Rosy Finch
Leucosticte tephrocotis

Ferruginous Hawk
Buteo regalis

Prairie Falcon
Falco mexicanus

Greater Prairie Chicken
Tympanuchus cupido

Burrowing Owl
Speotyto cunicularia

Western Meadowlark
Sturnella neglecta

Brown-headed Cowbird
Molothrus ater

Chestnut-collared Longspur
Calcarius ornatus

Lark Bunting
Calamospiza melanocorys

Killdeer
Charadrius vociferus

Bobolink
Dolichonyx oryzivorus

Eastern Bluebird
Sialia sialis

Painted Bunting
Passerina ciris

Scissor-tailed Flycatcher
Muscivora forficata

Pied-billed Grebe
Podilymbus podiceps

Marsh Hawk
Circus cyaneus

Canvasback
Aythya valisineria

Whooping Crane
Grus americana

Yellow-headed Blackbird
Xanthocephalus xanthocephalus

Red-winged Blackbird
Agelaius phoeniceus

Franklin's Gull
Larus pipixcan

Sora Rail
Porzana carolina

Great Blue Heron
Ardea herodias

Canada Goose
Branta canadensis

Brown Pelican
Pelecanus occidentalis

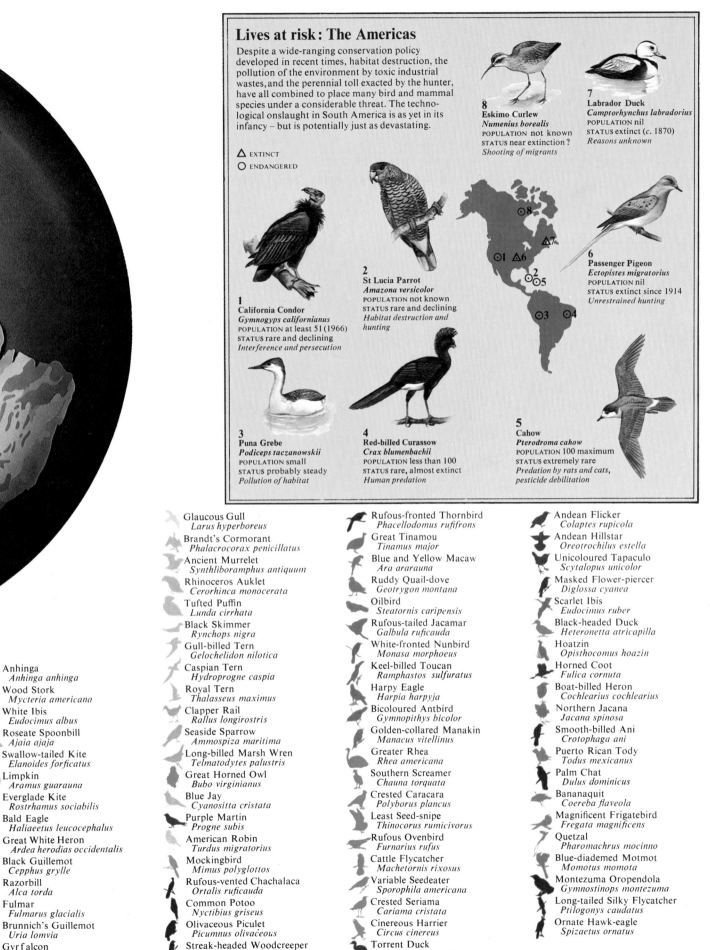

Lives at risk: The Americas

Despite a wide-ranging conservation policy developed in recent times, habitat destruction, the pollution of the environment by toxic industrial wastes, and the perennial toll exacted by the hunter, have all combined to place many bird and mammal species under a considerable threat. The technological onslaught in South America is as yet in its infancy – but is potentially just as devastating.

△ EXTINCT
○ ENDANGERED

8 Eskimo Curlew
Numenius borealis
POPULATION not known
STATUS near extinction?
Shooting of migrants

7 Labrador Duck
Camptorhynchus labradorius
POPULATION nil
STATUS extinct (c. 1870)
Reasons unknown

1 California Condor
Gymnogyps californianus
POPULATION at least 51 (1966)
STATUS rare and declining
Interference and persecution

2 St Lucia Parrot
Amazona versicolor
POPULATION not known
STATUS rare and declining
Habitat destruction and hunting

6 Passenger Pigeon
Ectopistes migratorius
POPULATION nil
STATUS extinct since 1914
Unrestrained hunting

3 Puna Grebe
Podiceps taczanowskii
POPULATION small
STATUS probably steady
Pollution of habitat

4 Red-billed Curassow
Crax blumenbachii
POPULATION less than 100
STATUS rare, almost extinct
Human predation

5 Cahow
Pterodroma cahow
POPULATION 100 maximum
STATUS extremely rare
Predation by rats and cats, pesticide debilitation

Anhinga
Anhinga anhinga

Wood Stork
Mycteria americana

White Ibis
Eudocimus albus

Roseate Spoonbill
Ajaia ajaja

Swallow-tailed Kite
Elanoides forficatus

Limpkin
Aramus guarauna

Everglade Kite
Rostrhamus sociabilis

Bald Eagle
Haliaeetus leucocephalus

Great White Heron
Ardea herodias occidentalis

Black Guillemot
Cepphus grylle

Razorbill
Alca torda

Fulmar
Fulmarus glacialis

Brunnich's Guillemot
Uria lomvia

Gyrfalcon
Falco rusticolus

Glaucous Gull
Larus hyperboreus

Brandt's Cormorant
Phalacrocorax penicillatus

Ancient Murrelet
Synthliboramphus antiquum

Rhinoceros Auklet
Cerorhinca monocerata

Tufted Puffin
Lunda cirrhata

Black Skimmer
Rynchops nigra

Gull-billed Tern
Gelochelidon nilotica

Caspian Tern
Hydroprogne caspia

Royal Tern
Thalasseus maximus

Clapper Rail
Rallus longirostris

Seaside Sparrow
Ammospiza maritima

Long-billed Marsh Wren
Telmatodytes palustris

Great Horned Owl
Bubo virginianus

Blue Jay
Cyanositta cristata

Purple Martin
Progne subis

American Robin
Turdus migratorius

Mockingbird
Mimus polyglottos

Rufous-vented Chachalaca
Ortalis ruficauda

Common Potoo
Nyctibius griseus

Olivaceous Piculet
Picumnus olivaceous

Streak-headed Woodcreeper
Lepidocolaptes souleyetii

Rufous-fronted Thornbird
Phacellodomus rufifrons

Great Tinamou
Tinamus major

Blue and Yellow Macaw
Ara ararauna

Ruddy Quail-dove
Geotrygon montana

Oilbird
Steatornis caripensis

Rufous-tailed Jacamar
Galbula ruficauda

White-fronted Nunbird
Monasa morphoeus

Keel-billed Toucan
Ramphastos sulfuratus

Harpy Eagle
Harpia harpyja

Bicoloured Antbird
Gymnopithys bicolor

Golden-collared Manakin
Manacus vitellinus

Greater Rhea
Rhea americana

Southern Screamer
Chauna torquata

Crested Caracara
Polyborus plancus

Least Seed-snipe
Thinocorus rumicivorus

Rufous Ovenbird
Furnarius rufus

Cattle Flycatcher
Machetornis rixosus

Variable Seedeater
Sporophila americana

Crested Seriama
Cariama cristata

Cinereous Harrier
Circus cinereus

Torrent Duck
Merganetta armata

Andean Flicker
Colaptes rupicola

Andean Hillstar
Oreotrochilus estella

Unicoloured Tapaculo
Scytalopus unicolor

Masked Flower-piercer
Diglossa cyanea

Scarlet Ibis
Eudocimus ruber

Black-headed Duck
Heteronetta atricapilla

Hoatzin
Opisthocomus hoazin

Horned Coot
Fulica cornuta

Boat-billed Heron
Cochlearius cochlearius

Northern Jacana
Jacana spinosa

Smooth-billed Ani
Crotophaga ani

Puerto Rican Tody
Todus mexicanus

Palm Chat
Dulus dominicus

Bananaquit
Coereba flaveola

Magnificent Frigatebird
Fregata magnificens

Quetzal
Pharomachrus mocinno

Blue-diademed Motmot
Momotus momota

Montezuma Oropendola
Gymnostinops montezuma

Long-tailed Silky Flycatcher
Ptilogonys caudatus

Ornate Hawk-eagle
Spizaetus ornatus

The Palaearctic Realm

Tundra

Boreal forest

Temperate woodland

Mediterranean vegetation

Sub-desert and steppe

Desert

Wooded savanna

Sea and marsh

Tropical rain-forest

Birds illustrated in the Palaearctic section of the atlas are shown below in silhouette. The colour of each silhouette corresponds with the key colour of the bird's habitat

Rough-legged Buzzard
Buteo lagopus

Ptarmigan
Lagopus mutus

Snow Bunting
Plectrophenax nivalis

Dunlin
Calidris alpina

Great Grey Owl
Strix nebulosa

Siberian Jay
Perisoreus infaustus

Capercaillie
Tetrao urogallus

Brambling
Fringilla montifringilla

Sparrowhawk
Accipiter nisus

Greater Spotted Woodpecker
Dendrocopos major

Tree-creeper
Certhia familiaris

Jay
Garrulus glandarius

Woodcock
Scolopax rusticola

Willow Warbler
Phylloscopus trochilus

Hawfinch
Coccothraustes coccothraustes

Blackcap
Sylvia atricapilla

Steppe Eagle
Aquila rapax

Sociable Plover
Vanellus gregarius

Rosy Pastor
Sturnus roseus

Demoiselle Crane
Anthropoides virgo

Partridge
Perdix perdix

Little Owl
Athene noctua

Skylark
Alauda arvensis

Rook
Corvus frugilegus

European Roller
Coracias garrulus

Dartford Warbler
Sylvia undata

Imperial Eagle
Aquila heliaca

Rock Thrush
Monticola saxatilis

Hobby
Falco subbuteo

Nightjar
Caprimulgus europaeus

Stonechat
Saxicola torquata

Hoopoe
Upupa epops

Houbara Bustard
Chlamydotis undulata

Pallas's Sandgrouse
Syrrhaptes paradoxus

Desert Wheatear
Oenanthe deserti

Ground Jay
Podoces pandari

Golden Eagle
Aquila chrysaetos

Dipper
Cinclus cinclus

Merlin
Falco columbarius

Ring Ouzel
Turdus torquatus

Snowfinch
Montifringilla nivalis

Bittern
Botaurus stellaris

Marsh Harrier
Circus aeruginosus

Ruff
Philomachus pugnax

Bearded Reedling
Panurus biarmicus

Great Crested Grebe
Podiceps cristatus

Common Sandpiper
Tringa hypoleucos

Mute Swan
Cygnus olor

Grey Wagtail
Motacilla cinerea

Eider
Somateria mollissima

Redshank
Tringa totanus

Black-headed Gull
Larus ridibundus

Shelduck
Tadorna tadorna

Red-breasted Merganser
Mergus serrator

Slavonian Grebe
Podiceps auritus

Shore Lark
Eremophila alpestris

Knot
Calidris canutus

Oystercatcher
Haematopus ostralegus

Ringed Plover
Charadrius hiaticula

Herring Gull
Larus argentatus

Little Tern
Sterna albifrons

Shag
Phalacrocorax aristotelis

Kittiwake
Rissa tridactyla

Chough
Pyrrhocorax pyrrhocorax

Puffin
Fratercula arctica

Swift
Apus apus

Tawny Owl
Strix aluco

Blackbird
Turdus merula

Blue Tit
Parus caeruleus

Collared Dove
Streptopelia decaocto

Extending from Iceland in the west to Japan in the east, and from the Arctic coast to the Himalayas and the Yangtze River, the huge Palaearctic realm covers a wide range of climates from polar to sub-tropical, and numerous clearly defined zones of vegetation each harbouring a characteristic group of plants and animals. The avifauna, however, is surprisingly poor in comparison with that of neighbouring areas; the Palaearctic realm supports less than two-fifths of the number of species found in South America and only half as many as Africa. Two possible reasons for this paucity are the lack of a truly tropical zone and the drastic changes in climate during the last three million years, caused by the advance and retreat of the ice-fields.

The first true bird

Throughout the Mesozoic and most of the Tertiary period, warm temperate conditions extended north across the Palaearctic almost to the shores of the Arctic Ocean. Much of what is now Europe and Asia was at that time low-lying and marshy, flooded periodically by warm shallow seas. In this mild habitat dwelt the earliest Palaearctic birds, including *Archaeopteryx*, a primitive, toothed creature about the size of a crow. Superb fossil remains of this bird were discovered 150 million years later in the limestone rocks of a Bavarian slate quarry.

The coming of the ice

Great sheets of ice began to spread down across the Palaearctic between two and three million years ago, descending in broad glacial streams from the highlands and spreading out over the plains of grassland and forest. Ice-fields also formed in the highlands of Europe, in the Alps, the Pyrenees and the highlands of Britain and Scandinavia, advancing and retreating four times during the last 800,000 years. At each advance the forests and grasslands were destroyed and their animal- and bird-life forced to retreat southwards. As the ice retreated, barren ground was left to be invaded by tundra vegetation and a few hardy animals and birds. Later, this vegetation was replaced by heathland and scrub; later still by woodland and grassy plains. Since the end of the last glaciation, some 20,000 years ago, the vegetation zones have been largely stable, though minor shifts still occur in response to local changes.

The birds of the Palaearctic

Relatively few species are peculiar to the Palaearctic region. One-eighth of all its species also occur in North America; rather more are shared with Africa, and nearly one-fifth extend into the Oriental realm. The wide tundra regions, inhospitable in winter, are invaded in summer by immense numbers of migrants from the south who feed on the rich wetland vegetation and teeming insects throughout the long summer days and retreat again to warmer climes at the beginning of winter.

Lives at risk: Europe and Asia

Although large areas of Eurasia have been populated for thousands of years, and the demands of hunting communities have always placed pressures on the continent's wildlife, it is only since the great age of expansion – the Industrial Revolution – that these pressures have begun to take a heavy toll of mammal, fish and bird life. Land clearance for large-scale farming and for urbanization and industrial use have destroyed large areas of natural habitat and, at an ever-increasing rate, the toxic waste of industrial processing pollutes much of what remains.

Although no European species, with the exception of the Great Auk, has become extinct in modern times, the effects of man's expansion is placing many in considerable danger. Predators, which find their food sources contaminated by pesticides, and woodpeckers and marsh birds who rely on specialized habitats, are particularly at risk. Legislation to preserve areas of unspoiled habitat and to effectively restrict the use and disposal of harmful chemicals is improving the plight of many animals and birds, but only responsible action by all nations will avert the inevitable extinction of at least some of Europe's birds.

1
Great Auk
Pinguinus impennis
POPULATION nil
STATUS extinct (c. 1844)
Unrestrained hunting

2
Cyprus Dipper
Cinclus cinclus
POPULATION nil
STATUS extinct
Habitat destruction

3
Iwo Jima Rail
Poliolimnas cinereus
POPULATION nil
STATUS extinct
*Introduced predators/
interference*

4
Spectacled Cormorant
*Phalacrocorax
perspicillatus*
POPULATION nil
STATUS extinct (c. 1852)
Unrestrained hunting

5
Siberian White Crane
Grus leucogeranus
POPULATION about 2,000
STATUS rare and declining
*Habitat destruction/
persecution*

6
Brown Eared Pheasant
Crossoptilon mantchuricum
POPULATION not known
STATUS rare and declining
*Deforestation and
persecution*

7
Japanese Crested Ibis
Nipponia nippon
POPULATION 12 in Japan
STATUS very rare
*19th C. hunting/20th C.
deforestation*

⊙ ENDANGERED

△ EXTINT

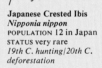

8
Chinese Monal
Lophophorus lhuysii
POPULATION not known
STATUS very rare
Human predation

9
Spanish Imperial Eagle
Aquila heliaca
POPULATION 100
STATUS very rare
Persecution by man

10
Audouin's Gull
Larus audouinii
POPULATION about 1,000
STATUS rare and localized
*Egg predation by man and
gulls*

11
Bald Ibis
Geronticus eremita
POPULATION less than 500
STATUS rare and declining
*Natural causes/
pesticides (?)*

12
Tristram's Woodpecker
Dryocopus javensis
POPULATION not known
STATUS rare but recovering
Destruction of forest

The Ethiopian Realm

The Ethiopian realm, which includes virtually all of Africa, is a largely stable tropical region encompassing a wide range of varied and generally rich habitats for birds. Most Ethiopian species have evolved in isolation. Though long separated from South America, Africa was in contact with India during most of the early Tertiary, when avian evolution was at its most intense. Nevertheless, the two regions have few species in common, indicating very little east-west movement of birds during the last few million years. South of the Sahara, Africa is immensely rich in birds, both in species and in numbers. The lowland evergreen rain-forests extending across the middle of the continent have a wealth of specialized forms living high above the ground in the dense canopy vegetation. Much of this is relatively new habitat, recovered from desert conditions within the last two million years. The swamps of the Upper Nile drainage area are inhabited by many species and great numbers of fish-eating birds. The mountain evergreen forests of the Cameroons, Kenya and Abyssinia, isolated remnants of a once-continuous forest which extended from Abyssinia almost to the Cape, have their own peculiar avifauna, and the grassy savannas and dry scrub zones carry immense populations of small seed-eating and insectivorous birds. In addition to its own massive populations, the Ethiopian realm supports huge flocks of migrant birds during the northern winter months.

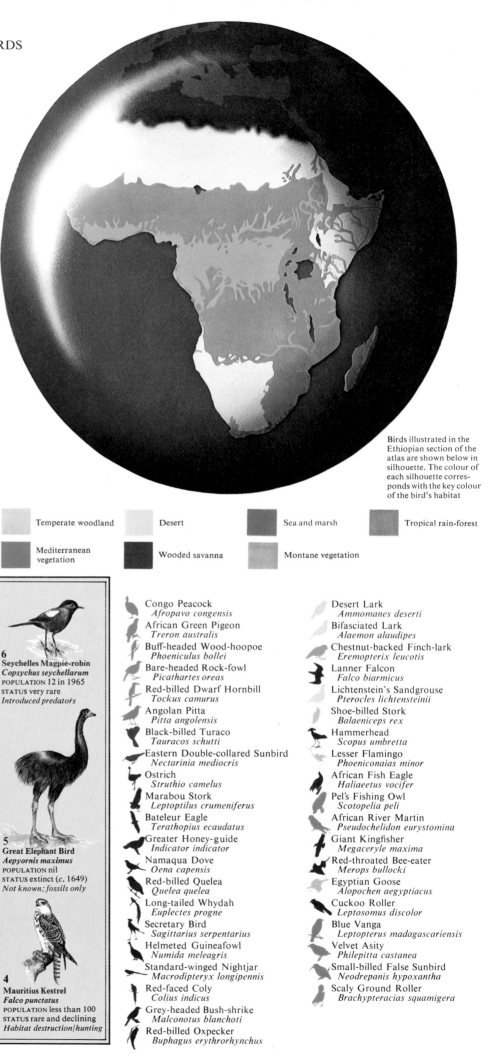

Birds illustrated in the Ethiopian section of the atlas are shown below in silhouette. The colour of each silhouette corresponds with the key colour of the bird's habitat

Temperate woodland

Desert

Sea and marsh

Tropical rain-forest

Mediterranean vegetation

Wooded savanna

Montane vegetation

Lives at risk: Africa

Africa's bird-life has suffered less at the hand of man than much of its mammal life. No continental bird has become extinct in recent times though 21 species are listed as endangered. The future of most can be secured – but only if the activities of hunter, farmer and engineer are controlled so that habitats are not too drastically altered. For island species the future is bleak; many birds have already succumbed to predation or land clearance and five are today listed as endangered.

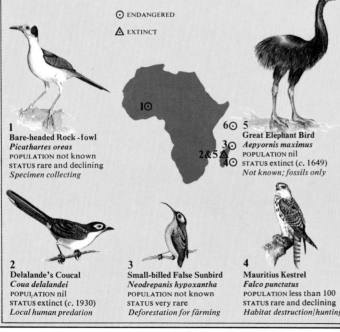

6
Seychelles Magpie-robin
Copsychus seychellarum
POPULATION 12 in 1965
STATUS very rare
Introduced predators

⊙ ENDANGERED

△ EXTINCT

1
Bare-headed Rock-fowl
Picathartes oreas
POPULATION not known
STATUS rare and declining
Specimen collecting

5
Great Elephant Bird
Aepyornis maximus
POPULATION nil
STATUS extinct (c. 1649)
Not known; fossils only

2
Delalande's Coucal
Coua delalandei
POPULATION nil
STATUS extinct (c. 1930)
Local human predation

3
Small-billed False Sunbird
Neodrepanis hypoxantha
POPULATION not known
STATUS very rare
Deforestation for farming

4
Mauritius Kestrel
Falco punctatus
POPULATION less than 100
STATUS rare and declining
Habitat destruction/hunting

Congo Peacock
Afropavo congensis

African Green Pigeon
Treron australis

Buff-headed Wood-hoopoe
Phoeniculus bollei

Bare-headed Rock-fowl
Picathartes oreas

Red-billed Dwarf Hornbill
Tockus camurus

Angolan Pitta
Pitta angolensis

Black-billed Turaco
Tauracos schutti

Eastern Double-collared Sunbird
Nectarinia mediocris

Ostrich
Struthio camelus

Marabou Stork
Leptoptilus crumeniferus

Bateleur Eagle
Terathopius ecaudatus

Greater Honey-guide
Indicator indicator

Namaqua Dove
Oena capensis

Red-billed Quelea
Quelea quelea

Long-tailed Whydah
Euplectes progne

Secretary Bird
Sagittarius serpentarius

Helmeted Guineafowl
Numida meleagris

Standard-winged Nightjar
Macrodipteryx longipennis

Red-faced Coly
Colius indicus

Grey-headed Bush-shrike
Malconotus blanchoti

Red-billed Oxpecker
Buphagus erythrorhynchus

Desert Lark
Ammomanes deserti

Bifasciated Lark
Alaemon alaudipes

Chestnut-backed Finch-lark
Eremopterix leucotis

Lanner Falcon
Falco biarmicus

Lichtenstein's Sandgrouse
Pterocles lichtensteinii

Shoe-billed Stork
Balaeniceps rex

Hammerhead
Scopus umbretta

Lesser Flamingo
Phoeniconaias minor

African Fish Eagle
Haliaeetus vocifer

Pel's Fishing Owl
Scotopelia peli

African River Martin
Pseudochelidon eurystomina

Giant Kingfisher
Megaceryle maxima

Red-throated Bee-eater
Merops bullocki

Egyptian Goose
Alopochen aegyptiacus

Cuckoo Roller
Leptosomus discolor

Blue Vanga
Leptopterus madagascariensis

Velvet Asity
Philepitta castanea

Small-billed False Sunbird
Neodrepanis hypoxantha

Scaly Ground Roller
Brachypteracias squamigera

The Oriental Realm

The Oriental realm includes the mountain deserts and wooded foothills of the Himalayas and Hindu Kush, the monsoon forests and mangrove swamps of Southeast Asia and Indonesia, the deciduous and mixed forests of India, Burma and Thailand, and the hot deserts of northern India and Pakistan. Between the Oriental and Australasian realms lies a broad transitional zone of islands, including the Celebes, Timor and Lombok. Birds from both realms intermingle within this zone, observing seemingly arbitrary boundaries which probably reflect the geological newness of many of the islands. Borneo, Java, Sumatra and possibly the Philippines, were originally part of mainland Southeast Asia, isolated by rising sea levels during the late Pleistocene. India, formerly an isolated landmass far to the south, with its own flora and fauna, joined the Eurasian landmass about 40 million years ago – the impact of its arrival buckling the continental plates and thrusting up the Himalayan rampart. The mingling and redistribution of species that followed continues even today, with many of the region's rich array of species spreading into neighbouring areas.

Like the Ethiopian realm, the Oriental realm has suffered little from the drastic climatic fluctuations that have recently had so profound an effect on the more northerly land areas. Much of its vegetation has remained relatively unchanged for millions of years and this stability has encouraged the evolution of many endemic species.

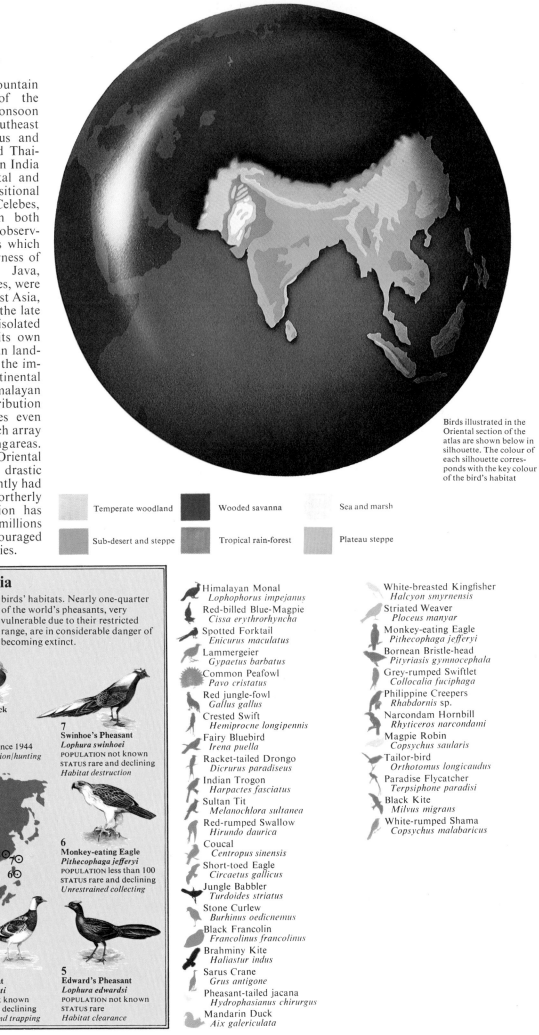

Birds illustrated in the Oriental section of the atlas are shown below in silhouette. The colour of each silhouette corresponds with the key colour of the bird's habitat

Temperate woodland   Wooded savanna   Sea and marsh

Sub-desert and steppe   Tropical rain-forest   Plateau steppe

Lives at risk: Southern Asia

Of the 31 Oriental species listed as endangered, three are members of the crane family; 11 are island species; the rest are all victims of excessive human interference in the birds' habitats. Nearly one-quarter of the world's pheasants, very vulnerable due to their restricted range, are in considerable danger of becoming extinct.

⊙ ENDANGERED

△ EXTINCT

8
Pink-headed Duck
Rhodonessa caryophyllacea
POPULATION nil
STATUS extinct since 1944
Habitat destruction/hunting

7
Swinhoe's Pheasant
Lophura swinhoei
POPULATION not known
STATUS rare and declining
Habitat destruction

1
Great Indian Bustard
Choriotis nigriceps
POPULATION not known
STATUS rare and declining
Habitat destruction/hunting

2
Jerdon's Courser
Cursorius bitorquatus
POPULATION nil
STATUS extinct since 1900?
Limited habitat available

6
Monkey-eating Eagle
Pithecophaga jefferyi
POPULATION less than 100
STATUS rare and declining
Unrestrained collecting

8△ 4⊙ 7⊙
2△
3⊙ 5⊙ 6⊙

3
Red-faced Malkoha
Phaenicophaeus pyrrhocephalus
POPULATION not known
STATUS rare and declining
Habitat clearance

4
Elliot's Pheasant
Syrmaticus ellioti
POPULATION not known
STATUS rare and declining
Deforestation and trapping

5
Edward's Pheasant
Lophura edwardsi
POPULATION not known
STATUS rare
Habitat clearance

Himalayan Monal
Lophophorus impejanus

Red-billed Blue-Magpie
Cissa erythrorhyncha

Spotted Forktail
Enicurus maculatus

Lammergeier
Gypaetus barbatus

Common Peafowl
Pavo cristatus

Red jungle-fowl
Gallus gallus

Crested Swift
Hemiprocne longipennis

Fairy Bluebird
Irena puella

Racket-tailed Drongo
Dicrurus paradiseus

Indian Trogon
Harpactes fasciatus

Sultan Tit
Melanochlora sultanea

Red-rumped Swallow
Hirundo daurica

Coucal
Centropus sinensis

Short-toed Eagle
Circaetus gallicus

Jungle Babbler
Turdoides striatus

Stone Curlew
Burhinus oedicnemus

Black Francolin
Francolinus francolinus

Brahminy Kite
Haliastur indus

Sarus Crane
Grus antigone

Pheasant-tailed jacana
Hydrophasianus chirurgus

Mandarin Duck
Aix galericulata

White-breasted Kingfisher
Halcyon smyrnensis

Striated Weaver
Ploceus manyar

Monkey-eating Eagle
Pithecophaga jefferyi

Bornean Bristle-head
Pityriasis gymnocephala

Grey-rumped Swiftlet
Collocalia fuciphaga

Philippine Creepers
Rhabdornis sp.

Narcondam Hornbill
Rhyticeros narcondami

Magpie Robin
Copsychus saularis

Tailor-bird
Orthotomus longicaudus

Paradise Flycatcher
Terpsiphone paradisi

Black Kite
Milvus migrans

White-rumped Shama
Copsychus malabaricus

The Australasian Realm and Antarctica

Australasia includes the continent of Australia, the large neighbouring islands of New Guinea, Tasmania and New Zealand, as well as a host of smaller oceanic islands. Australia itself, which has long been isolated geographically from the rest of the world, is a vast, mainly low-lying landmass with extensive dry desert plains, eucalyptus forests and savannas, and a tropical northern fringe with rain-forests and mangrove swamps. Its broad range of habitats allows for a wide variety of birds, including many species of parrots, flightless emus and cassowaries, and mound-building megapodes. New Guinea, Australia's northern neighbour, is a heavily forested island with a backbone of high, scrub-capped mountains, while Tasmania, to the south, has damper forests of beech, eucalyptus and conifers. Both islands share many species of birds with Australia. New Zealand's green islands of forest-clad alps and grassy plains, isolated from Australia for 100 million years or more, have developed a higher proportion of their own species. Almost all the birds of the Australasian realm show kinship with Oriental forms, but have had time to evolve and diversify to meet local conditions. Despite their difference in size, New Guinea and Australia each support about 650 species, while New Zealand, much smaller in area, supports about 250 species.

Antarctica and Australia were joined throughout the Mesozoic and early Tertiary, separating and drifting towards their present geographical positions during the last 30 million years. Antarctica must have shared much of Australia's flora and fauna, and carried a large menagerie of plants and animals southwards through the late Tertiary. The growth and spread of the ice-cap first modified and then destroyed practically all of Antarctica's living creatures. Its present bird fauna is exclusively marine, including enormous numbers of petrels and penguins, and smaller numbers or terns, gulls, skuas, sheathbills and cormorants.

Temperate woodland

Mediterranean vegetation

Sub-desert and steppe

Desert

Wooded savanna

Sea and marsh

Tropical rain-forest

Birds illustrated in the Australasian section of the atlas are shown below in silhouette. The colour of each silhouette corresponds with the key colour of the bird's habitat

Superb Lyrebird
  Menura novaehollandiae
Pink Robin
  Petroica rodinogaster
Golden Whistler
  Pachycephala pectoralis
Sulphur-crested Cockatoo
  Cacatua galerita
Tawny Frogmouth
  Podargus strigoides
Black-headed Pardalote
  Pardalotus melanocephalus
Orange-winged Sitella
  Neositta chrysoptera
Golden-backed Honeyeater
  Melithreptus laetior
Kookaburra
  Dacelo gigas

Barking Owl
  Ninox connivens
Bronze Cuckoo
  Chalchites lucidus
White-winged Triller
  Lalage suerri
Red-backed Kingfisher
  Halcyon pyrrhopygia
Owlet-nightjar
  Aegotheles cristatus
Emu
  Dromaius novaehollandiae
Crested Pigeon
  Ocyphaps lophotes
Cockatiel
  Nymphicus hollandicus
Singing Bushlark
  Mirafra javanica

Wedge-tailed Eagle
  Aquila audax
Budgerigar
  Melopsittacus undulatus
Purple-crowned Lorikeet
  Glossopsitta porphyrocephala
Bourke's Parrot
  Neophema bourkii
Princess Parrot
  Polytelis alexandrae
Cinnamon Quail-thrush
  Cinclosoma cinnamomeum
Rufous-crowned Emu-wren
  Stipiturus ruficeps
Striated Grass-wren
  Amytornis striatus
Night Parrot
  Geopsittacus occidentalis

Gibber Chat
  Ashbyia lovensis
Australian Dotterel
  Peltohyas australis
Black Swan
  Cygnus atratus
Spotted Crake
  Porzana fluminea
Short-tailed Shearwater
  Puffinus tenuirostris
Brolga
  Grus rubicunda
Magpie Goose
  Anseranas semipalmata
Cassowary
  Casuarius casuarius
Topknot Pigeon
  Lopholaimus antarcticus

Lives at risk: Australia and New Zealand

Neither Australia nor New Zealand felt the effects of human settlement until comparatively recently and even today it is not man who is having the greatest effect on the wildlife of these island continents but the animals he has introduced. Rabbits, casually introduced into Australia in 1859, spread like a plague and are one of the most destructive elements in the Australian landscape – rapidly reducing once-rich grasslands to sterile scrub of little use to grassland birds. Less dramatically, the widespread rearing of cattle and sheep has had a similar effect wherever the natural vegetation cover has been eroded.

In New Zealand, no fewer than ten introduced species of deer now inhabit the forests and, despite vast numbers being shot every year, their effect on the natural vegetation has been as destructive as that of Australia's rabbits. So delicately balanced was the flora and fauna of Australia and New Zealand that virtually every species introduced by man has had a profound and lasting effect on the native plant and animal life.

The effects of hunting on the bird life of Australasia has been less drastic than on other continents, but man is nevertheless directly responsible for the extinction of some of the world's most curious species, and for the reduction in numbers of many more. The last surviving moas are thought to have died out about 1350, after years of predation by peoples of the moa-cultures, and even today many of New Guinea's magnificent birds of paradise are a prime target for native hunters and illicit traders alike.

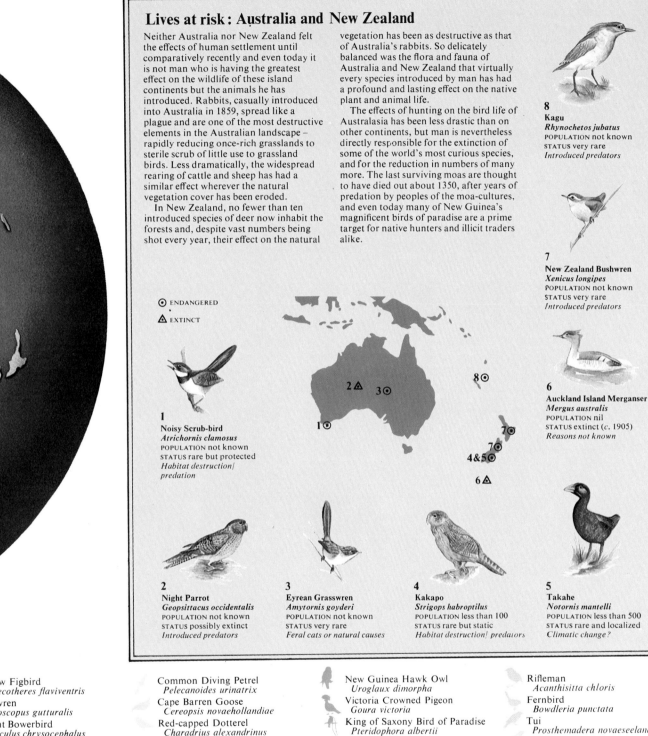

⊙ ENDANGERED

△ EXTINCT

8
Kagu
Rhynochetos jubatus
POPULATION not known
STATUS very rare
Introduced predators

7
New Zealand Bushwren
Xenicus longipes
POPULATION not known
STATUS very rare
Introduced predators

6
Auckland Island Merganser
Mergus australis
POPULATION nil
STATUS extinct (c. 1905)
Reasons not known

1
Noisy Scrub-bird
Atrichornis clamosus
POPULATION not known
STATUS rare but protected
Habitat destruction/predation

2
Night Parrot
Geopsittacus occidentalis
POPULATION not known
STATUS possibly extinct
Introduced predators

3
Eyrean Grasswren
Amytornis goyderi
POPULATION not known
STATUS very rare
Feral cats or natural causes

4
Kakapo
Strigops habroptilus
POPULATION less than 100
STATUS rare but static
Habitat destruction/predators

5
Takahe
Notornis mantelli
POPULATION less than 500
STATUS rare and localized
Climatic change?

Yellow Figbird
Sphecotheres flaviventris

Fernwren
Oreoscopus gutturalis

Regent Bowerbird
Sericulus chrysocephalus

Noisy Scrub-bird
Atrichornis clamosus

Brush Bronzewing
Phaps elegans

Ground Parrot
Pezoporus wallicus

Rufous Bristlebird
Dasyornis broadbenti

Mallee Fowl
Leipoa ocellata

White-browed Wood-swallow
Artamus superciliosus

Common Diving Petrel
Pelecanoides urinatrix

Cape Barren Goose
Cereopsis novaehollandiae

Red-capped Dotterel
Charadrius alexandrinus

Little Penguin
Eudyptula minor

Red-headed Honeyeater
Myzomela erythrocephala

New Holland Honeyeater
Meliornis novaehollandiae

Magnificent Riflebird
Ptiloris magnificus

Princess Stephania's Bird of Paradise *Astrapia stephaniae*

Greater Bird of Paradise
Paradisaea apoda

New Guinea Hawk Owl
Uroglaux dimorpha

Victoria Crowned Pigeon
Goura victoria

King of Saxony Bird of Paradise
Pteridophora albertii

Kagu
Rhynochetos jubatus

Brown Kiwi
Apteryx australis

Takahe
Notornis mantelli

New Zealand Pigeon
Hemiphaga novaeseelandiae

Kakapo
Strigops habroptilus

Kea
Nestor notabilis

Rifleman
Acanthisitta chloris

Fernbird
Bowdleria punctata

Tui
Prosthemadera novaeseelandiae

Kokako
Callaeas cinerea

Magpie Lark
Grallina cyanoleuca

Crimson Rosella
Platycercus elegans

Superb Blue-wren
Malurus cyaneus

Willie Wagtail
Rhipidura leucophrys

Pied Currawong
Strepera graculina

Yellow-tailed Thornbill
Acanthiza chrysorrhoa

North America

The Nearctic Realm

Separated from Europe and Asia for at least 70 million years by the widening gulf of the Atlantic Ocean, and from South America by the periodic inundation of the fragile Panamanian land-bridge, the huge continent of North America has evolved a complex and fascinating avifauna. Most North American birds have evolved in isolation from their Palaearctic relatives, but the narrow gap of the Bering Strait has allowed a limited degree of interchange between North America and Asia right up to the present day. Island-hopping immigrants from tropical South America form another important element – particularly in the southern states where, only a few million years ago, tropical conditions prevailed.

Ranged in broad longitudinal bands, the natural vegetation zones of North America include examples of almost every possible habitat. From the bleak ramparts of the western Rockies, through deserts and plains to the undulating wooded hills of the east, and from the frigid wastes of Arctic Canada to the humid swamps of the Florida Everglades, this vast continent provides a rich and varied range of living conditions for more than 750 bird species.

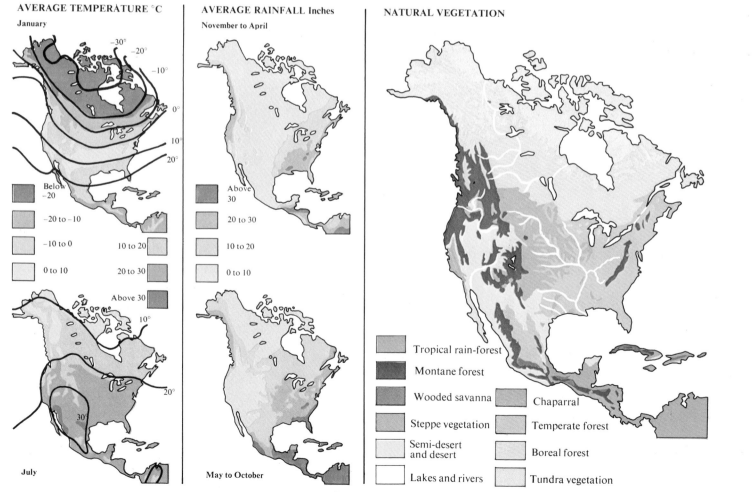

AVERAGE TEMPERATURE °C

January

-30° -20° -10° 0° 10° 20°

Below -20
-20 to -10
-10 to 0
0 to 10
10 to 20
20 to 30
Above 30

July

10° 20° 30°

AVERAGE RAINFALL Inches

November to April

Above 30
20 to 30
10 to 20
0 to 10

May to October

NATURAL VEGETATION

Tropical rain-forest
Montane forest
Wooded savanna
Steppe vegetation
Semi-desert and desert
Lakes and rivers
Chaparral
Temperate forest
Boreal forest
Tundra vegetation

Tundra: The Arctic Wilderness

A vast and lonely tundra stretches across the northern part of the North American continent. It extends from the Arctic Ocean to northeastern Manitoba and northern Ontario, though outcroppings of Alpine tundra, supporting forms of life otherwise found only in the Arctic, may be found in mountains as far south as New Mexico. The North American tundra is similar in climate and vegetation to that of Eurasia. The birds that inhabit these generally inhospitable, treeless plains on both continents are, therefore, also similar and in many cases are the same species.

Despite its bleak appearance, the tundra is capable of supporting an enormous variety of plant and animal life, though their annual reproductive cycles must be compressed into a few short weeks each summer. Great populations of shore-birds, gulls and water-fowl hurry north each year, to quickly rear a single brood and just as quickly withdraw, often departing before they have completed the post-nuptial moult. Sandpipers, for example, may appear in later summer on their southward migration still clad in their breeding plumage. Most of the time, the climate of the tundra is so hostile that only the hardiest of birds, like the Raven, can remain in the north all the year round. Nevertheless, ecologically, the tundra is subject to increasingly widespread human disturbance.

Right: Tundra vegetation on the shores of Hudson Bay

Arctic Loon
Gavia arctica

At sunrise in the bleak tundra west of Hudson Bay, and in Alaska, the mournful wailing of the Arctic Loons may be heard for miles. The birds begin arriving on the northern breeding grounds in May and soon lay their eggs (usually two), either directly on the ground or in a crudely built nest of earth and aquatic vegetation.

The young cannot fly for two months after hatching, and the family remains together until the birds leave the tundra in late August.

Most of the population of this species winters along the Pacific coast, as far south as Baja California. Diet consists of a wide variety of aquatic animals and occasionally plants, enabling the birds to take advantage of whatever food may be available in their harsh environment.

Golden Plover
Pluvialis dominica 10in
A remarkable annual migration of more than 15,000 miles

Tundra
- Extent of tundra
- **Distribution of species**
  American Golden Plover
  Pluvialis dominica
- Summer range
- Winter range
- Migration route

Arctic Loon
Gavia arctica 26in
The family group remains intact until the autumn dispersal

Golden Plover
Pluvialis dominica

The Golden Plover performs one of the most spectacular migrations of any North American bird – a round-trip of about 15,000 miles. At the end of the breeding season, these birds fly from their home in Arctic Canada to the coasts of Nova Scotia and Labrador. After fattening themselves there on crowberries, they fly non-stop to the northern coast of South America, from where, after a brief respite, they move south again over the Amazon Basin, to arrive at their wintering grounds on the *pampas* of Argentina in September. By January, flocks of plovers are on the move again, travelling northwards across the Amazon Basin and the Caribbean to reach the northern tundra by way

of the Great Plains of America.

Numbers were severely depleted in the days when plovers were shot as they migrated across the plains in spring. But, unlike the Eskimo Curlew, *Numenius borealis* (which may now be extinct), the Golden Plover responded well to protection, and large flocks once again make this remarkable annual journey.

The Golden Plover's nest, a slight depression in the tundra vegetation, is hard to find. Four eggs are laid and the incubating bird departs long before the observer is near, rising conspicuously from the ground some distance away in a decoy movement so as not to betray the nest location. The adult birds depart on migration before the fledglings are able to fly, leaving their offspring to find their way to Argentina unaided.

Vulnerable hunter

This splendid owl of the Far North is largely dependent for food on the population of lemmings (small rodents that generally abound in the tundra) and its breeding success is closely linked to that of its prey. The lemming population follows a four-year cycle in which a steady increase in numbers accelerates into a population explosion followed by a drastic crash in the total numbers. When the crash occurs, the Snowy Owl is faced with a serious food shortage and in winter it may be forced far south of its normal range. Some individuals move south into Canada and the northern parts of the United States where their presence, as infrequent visitors, is a welcome event for ornithologists.

Mortality is high during the irruption years and the Snowy Owl returns in much smaller numbers to the bleak breeding grounds in the spring. In such lean years, the lemming population has not yet recovered, there is still insufficient food for young birds, and the owls frequently fail to breed. Even if they do succeed in nesting, they lay

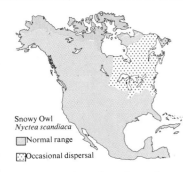

Snowy Owl
Nyctea scandiaca
☐ Normal range
☐ Occasional dispersal

smaller clutches. Just how the number of eggs is regulated to coincide with the food supply is not known, but generally by the time the lemming population has recovered, the population of owls is also at its usual level.

The nest of the Snowy Owl is usually placed on a rise in the tundra, and the number of eggs varies from three to as many as a dozen, depending on the state of the lemming cycle. The female incubates alone, while the male spends his time finding food for the pair and vigorously defending the nest against intruders.

Snowy Owl   23in
Nyctea scandiaca

Parasitic Jaeger
Stercorarius parasiticus   18in
Non-breeding birds remain away from the breeding grounds

Raven
Corvus corax   25in
One of the few birds capable of withstanding the Arctic winter

Parasitic Jaeger
Stercorarius parasiticus

The jaegers are closely related to the gulls, and indeed may be regarded as highly predatory gulls. They differ from gulls in their faster, more powerful flight and in having a more strongly hooked bill. Whether on their breeding grounds or spending the winter off southern coasts, jaegers obtain much of their food by robbing other sea-birds – chasing a gull or tern until it gives up the food it has captured. They also feed on carrion, small mammals, insects, the eggs and young of other birds and even on crowberries. Because jaegers (except the Long-tailed, *S.longicaudus*) do not depend on any one source of food, their numbers do not undergo the drastic fluctuations seen in the Snowy Owl population.

On the breeding grounds the jaeger lays two or three spotted eggs in a shallow depression in the tundra. The young are clad in a coat of uniformly grey-brown down. After breeding, the jaegers depart for the winter, which is spent at sea in more southerly latitudes. Recent evidence suggests that only the older birds return to the breeding grounds the following spring; first-year birds remain on the wintering grounds. This is probably a mechanism preventing the young birds, which would not breed, from competing for food with the potential parent birds.

There are three species of jaeger, differing only in size, and their relative sizes are probably associated with differences in food – another mechanism for avoiding competition. Larger still is the Skua, *Catharacta skua*, which, because of its great size, does not compete with the jaegers.

Raven
Corvus corax

A large relative of the crows, the Raven is a characteristic bird of the Far North no less than of the deserts and sea coasts in much of the Northern Hemisphere. Like other crows it is omnivorous, and, since it eats practically anything, is one of the few birds capable of spending the entire winter on the northernmost land in the Arctic. Mainly a scavenger, the Raven is numerous around settlements in the Arctic, where it raids garbage dumps for food. In other regions, however, it is sensitive to persecution and therefore less common.

The nest is a large mass of sticks placed on a ledge in a cave or in a pine tree. Three to five dull, spotted eggs require incubation for about three weeks. The young grow quickly and acquire plumage very like that of the parents, except that it lacks the glossy sheen of the adult, and the elongated feathers of the throat are not so well developed.

Very adaptable birds, Ravens are not migratory, although some individuals may wander southwards in winter, turning up in southern Canada and the northern United States.

The Common Raven has a number of close relatives in various parts of the world. One of these is the Rufous-necked Raven, *C.ruficollis*, a bird of the deserts of North Africa and south-western Asia. Another is the so-called Hawaiian Crow, *C.tropicus*. At some time in the remote past ravens managed to establish themselves on the Hawaiian islands, where they evolved into the species found there today.

Taiga and Boreal Forest

South of the tundra, the vast boreal, or northern, coniferous forest extends far into the northernmost parts of the United States. The dominant trees are spruce, fir and larch. Rising from land scoured by glaciers during the last Ice Age, the forest is dotted with lakes, ponds and marshes. Its bird-life is somewhat distinct from that of the similar forests that extend across Siberia and into northern Europe. Some species, such as the Hawk Owl and White-winged Crossbill, can be found in both hemispheres, but many others are only distantly related to Old World birds; some not at all. In the last category are the many warblers of the family Parulidae, small insectivorous birds that visit the conifers only for breeding before returning to their wintering grounds in the tropics. The birds that remain in the forest all year round – principally seed-eaters and birds of prey – usually belong to the same or closely related species as their Old World counterparts. Migrant species often have no close Eurasian relatives.

In Alaska, the American coniferous forest approaches that of Siberia most closely, and a few species from each continent have penetrated a short distance into the other, often by way of the Bering Strait. Typical North American birds, like the Myrtle Warbler and the Grey-cheeked Thrush, also breed in extreme northeastern Siberia, while the Siberian Tit and the Bluethroat have colonized parts of Alaska.
Right: The Great Grey Owl, a major forest predator

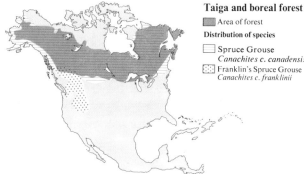

Taiga and boreal forest
- Area of forest

Distribution of species
- Spruce Grouse
  Canachites c. canadensis
- Franklin's Spruce Grouse
  Canachites c. franklinii

White-winged Crossbill
Loxia leucoptera 6½in
Exploits a food source denied to other finches

Spruce Grouse
Canachites canadensis 16in
Each male defends a separate forest territory

White-winged Crossbill
Loxia leucoptera

In the White-winged Crossbill (as in the related Red Crossbill, *L. curvirostra*) the tips of the mandibles are twisted across one another, giving the bird an odd, almost deformed appearance. This device enables the bird to remove seeds from the cones of pines and other conifers, exploiting a food source denied to other finches which share the northern coniferous forests. In years when the crop of conifer seeds fails, crossbills move south into the United States in large numbers, sometimes even reaching the Gulf of Mexico.

Crossbills belong to the group of finches that includes the canaries, siskins and goldfinches. Like these birds they have a musical, twittering song and build a loose, rather messy, cup-shaped nest. The young are fed largely on pulverized seeds regurgitated by the adults. In the winter, when the birds are feeding among the pines and larches, they resemble tiny parrots, climbing nimbly along the branches and hanging upside down to reach the cones.

Spruce Grouse
Canachites canadensis

The Spruce Grouse is the principal grouse of the vast coniferous forests of Canada and the northernmost part of the United States. Unlike the Sage Grouse, *Centrocercus urophasianus* (p51), and Greater Prairie Chicken, *Tympanuchus cupido* (p55), Spruce Grouse males do not share communal display grounds, but occupy separate territories, widely spaced in the forest, which are advertised by means of a display that involves strutting and raising the tail.

Females visit the males for mating and then build their nests. Since the birds occupy well-defined territories, the females are more aggressive towards intruders than female Greater Prairie Chickens. As with other grouse species, the male takes no part in incubating the eggs and raising the young.

In summer the Spruce Grouse feeds on berries and insects. In winter, when snow covers most other sources of food, the birds survive on an austere diet consisting almost entirely of conifer needles.

Goshawk
Accipiter gentilis 20in
*Fearless "bird hawk" of the
northern coniferous forests*

Kirtland's Warbler
Dendroica kirtlandii 5¾in

A precarious existence

Although a great many of the world's endangered species are island-dwellers, several mainland species are also restricted to very small and vulnerable populations. Two such species are members of the American Warbler family, the Parulidae. Bachman's Warbler, *Vermivora bachmanii*, is unaccountably rare, but the other, Kirtland's Warbler, *Dendroica kirtlandi*, is one of America's rarest birds because of its quite remarkable degree of specialization.

With a vast area of the North American continent covered with their jack-pine forest habitat, these birds, fewer than a thousand in number, remain in a very restricted area in north central Michigan. Curiously, their small range seems largely a matter of choice and not, as with so many endangered species, a product of enforced circumstance. Nor will any stand of jack-pine suffice; Kirtland's Warbler will

apparently adopt only young, secondary growth forest produced in the aftermath of a forest fire. At first, these trees grow in dense thickets, their lower branches trailing to the ground, and it is within the concealment of these lower branches, and the dense tangle of ground vegetation, that the warblers build their nests – often in loosely organized colonies. When the trees reach a height of between 16 and 20 feet the lower branches die, daylight is excluded from the ground and the dense herbage is lost, totally changing the habitat.

Kirtland's Warbler was first discovered outside its breeding range. In 1851 a migrating male was collected in Ohio and in 1879 the species was found to be wintering in the Bahamas, but not until 1903 was the species' breeding ground discovered. The birds show a remarkably accurate homing sense in their annual migrations to and from their restricted breeding area and this factor, taken with their unusual dependence on the forest fires common in that area, may partly explain the species' reluctance to extend its breeding range. Such a high degree of specialization is, however, dangerous. Fire is the key to its survival and improved fire control methods, plus the harvesting of jack-pine for the wood pulp industries, constantly threaten its precarious existence. Ironically, conservationists are now deliberately firing stands of pine in the breeding area in order to maintain the necessary breeding habitat and ensure the birds' survival.

Goshawk
Accipiter gentilis

One of the boldest of predators, the Goshawk frequently shows no fear even of man. This is the large, dashing "bird hawk" of the northern coniferous forests – well-suited, with its rather short, rounded wings and longish tail, to twisting and darting through the dense forest understorey in pursuit of mammals and birds up to the size of grouse. Also, the bird has a habit of perching quietly in a tall tree at the edge of a clearing, ready to make a long, swift stoop on prey moving on the ground below.

Although the Goshawk is relatively silent for most of the year, during the breeding season members of a mated pair are quite vocal in the early morning, screaming loudly to each other. The nest, a large, rough structure of sticks, is built mainly or entirely by the male. The female incubates the eggs and broods the young, fed on the nest by the male. Most of the food brought to the nest for the young consists of small birds carefully plucked by the parent.

While there is some southward movement every year, major invasions of Goshawks occur in years when food is in short supply in the north. When this happens, the birds may turn their attention to poultry farms, and are therefore shot in large numbers.

Besides inhabiting the northern forests, the species is also found in the mountains as far south as northern Mexico and as far east as Maryland. Outside of North America the Goshawk occurs in much of Eurasia and related species are found in Africa, Madagascar and the islands of the southwestern Pacific.

Hawk Owl
Surnia ulula

With a rather long tail and swift, swooping flight, the Hawk Owl is reminiscent more of a hawk than of an owl, and this accounts for its conglomerate name. This is a characteristic bird of the taiga, the vast forest of spruce and larch that extends across the northern parts of North America and Eurasia. Diurnal like the Snowy Owl, the Hawk Owl is usually easy to find – perched conspicuously in a tree-top at the edge of a clearing. Like many other birds of the far north, it is very tame, permitting the observer a close approach before it flies to another perch nearby to continue its normal activities.

The Hawk Owl preys on a wide variety of mammals and birds, including mice and other rodents, weasels, snowshoe hares, grouse and ptarmigan. Perhaps because it does not depend on any single food source, it seldom leaves its northern home in winter (as do the Snowy Owl and the Goshawk), and is rarely seen south of the taiga.

The Hawk Owl produces a generous clutch of eggs each year – usually seven, sometimes as many as nine – and, since incubation commences as soon as the first egg is laid, the nest contains young of different ages. In years when food is scarce, the older, more aggressive chicks are fed first, while the youngest weaken and starve. This process of natural selection is probably beneficial to the species. The alternative, raising a nestful of sickly, undernourished young in lean years, would produce individuals ill-equipped to survive the rigorous northern winter.

Hawk Owl
Surnia ulula 16in
*A wide-ranging and versatile
predator that seldom strays
south of the taiga*

Coastal and Montane Forest

In the Rocky Mountains and the ranges that extend along North America's Pacific coast, the forests consist mainly of pines and firs of various species, although the region also includes the famous Redwoods and Sequoias, the huge conifers of the California coastal ranges. The relationships of the bird-life of this region are complex. The coniferous forests are in broad contact with the spruce and fir zone which stretches across Canada, and many species have their closest affinities with birds of that habitat; indeed, many species occur in both. The Chestnut-backed Chickadee, shown here, is replaced in the Canadian forests by the Boreal Chickadee, while the Spruce Grouse and Goshawk of the northern coniferous forests also breed in the western mountains. Other species, like Steller's Jay, have their closest kin in the deciduous forests of eastern North America. Some, like Townsend's Solitaire, belong to groups that are distinctly montane; solitaires of one species or another occur in highlands throughout Central America and far into South America as well. Just as many of the birds of the northern coniferous forest migrate southwards in the autumn, so many of the species of these mountains move down into the lowlands at the onset of cold weather. In winter, birds like Cassin's Finch, which normally inhabit the highest part of the forest, flock down into the lowland valleys.
Right: Montane forest near Gibbon Falls, Wyoming

Coastal and montane forest

▨ Area of forest

Distribution of species

▭ Steller's Jay
Cyanocitta stelleri

▨ Chestnut-backed Chickadee
Parus rufescens

Townsend's Solitaire
Myadestes townsendi 8½in
*Builds a curious runway
in front of the nest*

Chestnut-backed Chickadee
Parus rufescens 4½in
*The New World equivalent of
the European tits*

Cassin's Finch
Carpodacus cassinii 6in
*Most characteristic bird of
the high montane forests*

Townsend's Solitaire
Myadestes townsendi

Visitors to the western mountains of North America know this member of the thrush family as a rather drab and very elusive bird, somewhat similar to the Mockingbird (p77). Like many forest species it makes up for its lack of colour with a rich and varied repertoire of songs.

During the summer months, the Solitaire stays high in the mountains, its breeding range extending from central Alaska as far south as the mountains of California and New Mexico. In winter, when food becomes scarce in the high regions, the birds flock down into the foothills and valleys where they feed on juniper berries – often competing for this favourite food with great flocks of American Robins (p77). Although the Solitaire feeds mainly on berries, and is able to run swiftly over rough ground, the bird is a skilled flier and will often supplement its diet with insects caught on the wing. This aspect of its feeding behaviour has earned Townsend's Solitaire the name of the "flycatching thrush".

Juniper forest is the bird's preferred habitat and individuals are reported to spend a great deal of their time perched as high as possible in an exposed juniper tree. The nest is a bulky cup of twigs and pine needles placed on the ground in the shelter of an overhanging rock or among the roots of a hillside tree. Often the bird will build a curious apron-like runway in front of the nest.

Chestnut-backed Chickadee
Parus rufescens

In North America the term chickadee refers to the dark-capped and dark-throated little birds known in Europe as the tits. The American species are more closely related to one another than are the Old World forms and so tend to have very similar ecological requirements. As a result, they are unable to co-exist side by side, as do many of the European tits, but instead replace each other geographically.

Almost no forested area in North America is without its local resident species. The Chestnut-backed Chickadee is the common representative of the family in the coast mountains and the dense coastal spruce forests. In general, the species shows a preference for the spruce, fir and lodgepole stands of higher ground and is commonly replaced in low-lying areas by the Black-capped Chickadee, *Parus atricapillus*.

The Chestnut-back is a confident, inquisitive creature, quite content to feed in close proximity to man and to visit feeding stations. When not breeding, they often join the company of nuthatches, creepers and kinglets, roaming the forests in search of insects and seeds.

Cassin's Finch
Carpodacus cassinii

Named after the distinguished nineteenth-century American ornithologist John Cassin, this finch is one of the most characteristic birds of the upper zones of the montane coniferous forests. They are widespread throughout the western mountains and occur from British Columbia south to the mountains of Arizona and New Mexico. Cassin's Finch is closely related to the more familiar Purple Finch, *C.purpureus*, and, more distantly, to the Scarlet Grosbeak, *C.erythrinus*, of Europe and Asia. So closely does it resemble the Purple Finch that the two species may only be separated by the most careful examination.

For much of the year, Cassin's Finch is almost exclusively vegetarian, consuming a wide variety of buds, seeds and small fruits. During the breeding season, which lasts from May to July, the birds tend to remain in one place but over the rest of the year they wander through the montane forests in mixed flocks with crossbills and grosbeaks. In cold winters the birds often descend from the mountains to lower elevations in order to feed.

Steller's Jay
Cyanocitta stelleri

This beautiful dark-blue, crested jay is represented by a number of very similar races, or sub-species, ranging throughout the coniferous forests and montane woodlands of North America. The eastern relative is the familiar Blue Jay, *C.cristata*, illustrated on page 77, while in the mountains of the west, the species sub-divides into three main races, the Coast Jay, *C.s.carbonacea*, resident in the humid coastal strip from Oregon to California, the Blue-fronted Jay, *C.s.frontalis*, occupying the timbered hills over much the same range, and the Black-headed Jay, *C.s.annectens*, more restricted to the northern montane forests.

These attractive forest jays are noisy and boisterous birds, ever alert and quick to break the forest calm with their harsh, penetrating warning cries at the first sign of danger. Though noisy by nature, the jay is remarkably discreet in the neighbourhood of its nest during the breeding season, flitting silently to its nest like a shadowy ghost. The nest is a neat construction of twigs and grass, cemented together with mud and placed in the branches of a conifer. Three to five pale blue-green eggs are laid on a soft lining of fine vegetation.

The main diet of the jays consists of seeds, nuts and fruit, but a varying amount of animal food, possibly up to 25 per cent of the total intake, consists of insects, spiders and occasionally young nestlings.

Steller's Jay
Cyanocitta stelleri 12in
Surprisingly discreet during the nesting season

Specialist woodpecker

Sapsuckers are an exclusively North American group of woodpeckers that take their name from their unusual method of feeding. While other woodpeckers are capable of extending the tongue far beyond the tip of the bill, sapsuckers lack this specialization and are therefore unable to probe deeply into crevices in search of their insect prey. Although they do, on occasion, dig insects out of wood, they are better known for their habit of boring small holes in the bark of living trees and feeding on the sap and on the insects that are attracted to it. Sapsuckers further differ from other woodpeckers in that the sexes are differently coloured, the female being a dull brown bird. The most familiar species is the Yellow-bellied Sapsucker, *Sphyrapicus varius* (illustrated), a bird of the eastern woodlands, while Williamson's Sapsucker, *S.thyroideus* is a bird of more purely coniferous forests. Like other woodpeckers, it excavates a nest cavity in the wood of a dead tree, and the eggs are laid on the natural deposit of wood dust in the bottom of the hole.

Yellow-bellied Sapsucker
Sphyrapicus varius 9½in

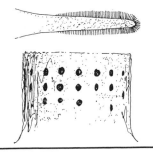

The brush-tipped tongue of the Sapsucker

Food begets more food

The sapsucker's curious adaptation affords it a rich diet of both plant and animal matter at one convenient feeding site. Boring a series of shallow holes around the trunk of a deciduous tree, the bird drinks the sweet sap as it oozes from the bark. A second food source is then provided by the insects, which, attracted by the sweet sap, also come to feed on the fluid and on the tender cambium layer that lies immediately beneath the protective outer bark.

Eastern Deciduous Woodland

When European settlers arrived on the eastern shores of North America, they found one of the richest habitats in the Northern Hemisphere. Deciduous trees of dozens of species extended, and still extend, from the Atlantic to well beyond the Mississippi River. There are more species of trees in the Great Smoky Mountains of Tennessee and North Carolina than in all of Europe. An equable climate and rich alluvial soils produce conditions in which literally thousands of species of plants may thrive. Many have their closest relatives in similar forests in China and Japan. But the link is an ancient one and relatively few species of birds show such a distribution pattern today. One that does so is the beautiful Wood Duck, or Carolina Duck, closely akin to the Mandarin Duck of eastern Asia and familiar as an introduced bird in Britain.

Most birds typical of this habitat are tropical in origin; the Scarlet Tanager, Yellow-throated Vireo and Turkey are all members of groups found in the New World tropics, although each of these species is confined to North America. The Red-headed Woodpecker and Red-shouldered Hawk are members of a group of species well represented in Central and South America. Comparatively few species in the eastern deciduous forest are also found in Eurasia; it is inhabited by an almost purely New World avifauna and only birds like the Barn Swallow and Sand Martin will remind European visitors of their own resident bird-life.

Red-headed Woodpecker
Melanerpes erythrocephalus 9½in
One of the few species to benefit from forest clearance and thinning

Eastern deciduous woodland

▦ Area of forest

Distribution of species

▢ Scarlet Tanager
Piranga olivacea

▨ Yellow-throated Vireo
Vireo flavifrons

Red-headed Woodpecker
Melanerpes erythrocephalus

This attractive, albeit rather pugnacious, woodpecker occurs over much of the United States and southern Canada east of the Rocky Mountains. The Red-headed Woodpecker's preference is for large, dead trees in open woodland, whether in clearings in the eastern deciduous forest or scattered along watercourses in the Great Plains. This may have been one of the species to benefit from forest clearance by the early settlers: in the unbroken virgin timber it would have been much less common than it is now.

Today there is competition with introduced starlings for nest sites, and a further restrictive factor is the birds' disastrous habit of darting on to roads in pursuit of insects. Where Red-headed Woodpeckers are common, however, they are often seen in the early morning, sitting in groups, calling shrilly. They are quarrelsome and noisy and often attack intruders.

In the mountains of the southwestern states and Central America, this species is replaced by the related Acorn Woodpecker, *M.formicivorus*.

Red-shouldered Hawk
Buteo lineatus

Decreasing in numbers in parts of its range – perhaps due to pesticides – the Red-shouldered Hawk is found in eastern North America. It inhabits low-lying, moist forest and the edges of swamps, while the Red-tailed Hawk, *B.jamaicensis*, allied to Europe's Common Buzzard, *B.buteo*, is a bird of the uplands. The Red-shoulder's closest relatives are in the American tropics. Generally a rather quiet, elusive bird, it is noisy and conspicuous in the mating season.

At all times of the year the Red-shouldered Hawk may be seen perched fairly low in the trees along the banks of streams and the margins of forest pools, carefully scanning the ground for prey. It is a rather sluggish bird, preferring to take frogs, snakes and mice, and seldom preys on birds as do the dashing bird hawks of the genus *Accipiter*.

Not as strongly migratory as the Broad-winged Hawk, *B.platypterus*, the Red-shoulder may be found on the northern breeding grounds in winter, feeding mainly on mice and other rodents.

Red-shouldered Hawk
Buteo lineatus 18in
Its decline may be partly due to pesticides in the food chain

Turkey
Meleagris gallopavo

As soon as European settlers arrived in the New World, the Turkey became a favourite bird of sport and the table, and before long this traditional bird of Thanksgiving Day had been exterminated over much of its original range. Nowadays, however, after careful protection and a programme of reintroductions, wild birds are once again widespread.

Like many species where the young find their own food, the Turkey lays a large number of eggs – up to 15 in a normal clutch. Frequently two or more hens lay their eggs in a single nest, and, after hatching, tend the chicks together. After three weeks the young are able to fly, and join the adults in roosting at night.

Centuries ago the species was taken to Europe, where it has become an important and familiar domestic bird. Occurring naturally, however, this is exclusively a New World group. The only other species, the Ocellated Turkey, *Agriocharis ocellata*, inhabits the forests of Yucatán and Guatemala.

Scarlet Tanager
Piranga olivacea

North of Mexico, tanagers are represented by only four species. The Scarlet Tanager is a well-known and characteristic resident of the northeastern woodlands. Despite its gay plumage, this is a difficult bird to see amid the dense foliage of the deciduous forest, but a cheerful and rather burry song reveals its presence. Although occurring in most deciduous and mixed woodlands in its range, the species reaches maximum numbers in mature oak forest, where the flimsy, shallow nest is placed on a horizontal branch up to 50 feet above ground.

Perhaps because of his bright colouring, the male does not assist the female in incubating, but he does participate in feeding the young. After the breeding season the male moults his bright plumage and is transformed to resemble the olive-green female. Shortly after the moult, the birds depart for their wintering grounds in northern South America, where so many other species of tanager are found.

Yellow-throated Vireo
Vireo flavifrons

Vireos resemble some wood warblers, but differ in their manner of feeding. While the warblers are active, nervous birds darting quickly among the leaves, vireos are more deliberate, carefully searching each leaf and twig for their insect prey. As they work the characteristic song is heard – a series of short musical phrases, endlessly repeated. In fact vireos are such persistent vocalists that they often capture, subdue and swallow a large insect while the singing goes on uninterrupted.

The Yellow-throated Vireo has the most pleasing song of all, a sound which evokes the rich, mature deciduous forests where the species is usually found. Here, sometimes as high as 60 feet, the Yellow-throat builds its nest, a small, neat cup suspended from the fork of a branch.

The Yellow-throated Vireo is a frequent victim of the parasitic Cowbird, and may respond to the unwanted egg by laying down a new nest lining over it and starting all over again.

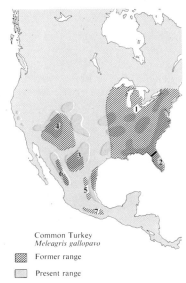

Common Turkey
Meleagris gallopavo

    Former range

    Present range

1   Common Turkey

2   Florida Turkey

3   Rio Grande Turkey

4   Merriam's Turkey

5   Gould's Turkey

6   Moore's Turkey

7   Mexican Turkey

Scarlet Tanager
Piranga olivacea 7in
The male loses his colourful courtship plumage at the end of the breeding season

Turkey
Meleagris gallopavo 49in
A native of the New World, introduced into Europe as a domestic food species

Yellow-throated Vireo
Vireo flavifrons 6in
Frequently chosen as an unwilling host to the eggs of the parasitic Cowbird

Cypress Swamps and Evergreen Woodlands

A great forest of tall pines spreads southwards from New Jersey across the coastal plains to Georgia and Florida, and then west across Louisiana to eastern Texas. This coniferous forest is isolated from the other forests of pines and firs in North America and, as might be expected, it is inhabited by a number of bird species found nowhere else. Both the Ivory-billed Woodpecker and Bachman's Sparrow are unique or "endemic" to the southeastern forest, although both have close relatives elsewhere. Other distinctive birds of this habitat include the Red-cockaded Woodpecker and the Brown-headed Nuthatch. Such affinities as the bird-life of this forest has are mainly western; the Ivory-bill has a near relative in the big Imperial Ivory-bill of western Mexico, and the Nuthatch is very closely allied to the Pygmy Nuthatch of the mountain forests of the far west. The great pines, as well as the other trees that grew in the river-bottom swamps where the Ivory-bill bred, provided an excellent source of timber, and much of this vast forest was cut down soon after the arrival of the settlers. This meant a drastic reduction in available habitat for many of the forest birds, and their numbers declined in consequence, but the clearing of the forest meant the opening up of millions of acres of new habitat to other birds that were originally confined either to brushy clearings and the edges of streams, or to the open grasslands beyond the limits of the forest.

Bachman's Sparrow
Aimophila aestivalis 6in
*Forest clearance has enabled
this bunting to extend its range*

Swamps and evergreen woodland

- Area of forest

Distribution of species

- Ivory-billed Woodpecker
  Campephilus principalis
- Bachman's Sparrow
  Aimophila aestivalis

Ivory-billed Woodpecker
Campephilus principalis 20in
*Over-specialization may already
have caused its extinction*

Bachman's Sparrow
Aimophila aestivalis

Despite their names, American sparrows are in fact buntings, related more closely to the familiar Yellow-hammer of Europe than to true sparrows. Bachman's Sparrow is the eastern North American representative of a large group found throughout much of the southwestern United States and Central America.

Unlike the ill-fated Ivory-billed Woodpecker (this page), Bachman's Sparrow has capitalized on forest clearance. Before the arrival of the European settlers in the southeastern states, this was a rather rare bird, confined to brushy places along the banks of streams in the southern pine forests. These virgin forests lacked a stratum of undergrowth. But, with the appearance of suitable under-storey, the species has colonized extensive areas and has now spread beyond the limits of the original pine forest, as far north as southern Ohio.

Bachman's Sparrow is a shy and retiring species, and during the breeding season is most easily located by its sweet, musical song.

Ivory-billed Woodpecker
Campephilus principalis

Apart from evidence that a few birds may still survive in southern Louisiana, there is a strong likelihood that the Ivory-billed Woodpecker is already extinct. Unlike other species, this highly specialized bird has dwindled with the logging of its habitat, the virgin river-bottom swamps of the southeastern states. When the primeval swamps were cleared, the supply of dead timber disappeared, and the woodpeckers, unable to exploit another food source, disappeared as well.

Incredibly each Ivory-bill pair requires no less than six square miles of timber. Only a tract of this size contains an adequate supply of large dead trees from which the birds obtain their food – chiefly the grubs of wood-boring beetles – by prying apart loose pieces of bark.

Even in the proper habitat, this species has always been difficult to find. The odd, tooting call, like the high, false note of a clarinet, is usually given only for a short time in the morning as the birds look for food.

Dry Oak Woodlands

In the lower reaches of the western mountains, below the level of the coniferous forest but above the deserts and grasslands, there exists a wide zone of broad-leaved trees, of which oaks of various species form a conspicuous part. Although this habitat is rather dry, it is watered for much of the year by mountain streams flowing down from cooler highlands, and local differences in topography and drainage create a complex variety of habitats. The populations of many species are accordingly somewhat localized. Close to the Mexican border, in the cool canyons of some of the desert mountain ranges of southern Arizona, a number of Mexican species are present in small numbers. One of these is the beautiful Copper-tailed Trogon, a member of a group of brilliantly coloured tropical species. Another is the Arizona Woodpecker, a more modestly coloured bird usually found in drier oak woodlands at higher elevations. Other species, such as Virginia's Warbler, are numerous farther north, in Utah, Colorado and the northern parts of Arizona and New Mexico. Insects are relatively scarce in this habitat and some species are adapted to feed on acorns. But the supply of acorns is unreliable as well and birds like the Scrub Jay are apt to be nomadic, constantly moving about in search of food. Insectivorous species, like Virginia's Warbler, are migratory and withdraw to the south when cold weather arrives.

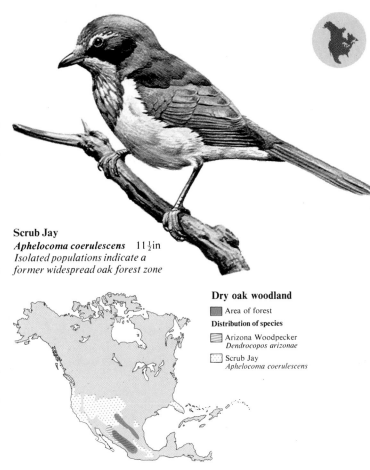

Scrub Jay
Aphelocoma coerulescens 11½in
Isolated populations indicate a former widespread oak forest zone

Dry oak woodland

■ Area of forest
Distribution of species
▤ Arizona Woodpecker
Dendrocopos arizonae
▦ Scrub Jay
Aphelocoma coerulescens

Arizona Woodpecker
Dendrocopos arizonae 7½in
Makes its nest hole in the soft wood of walnut and sycamore

Virginia's Warbler
Vermivora virginiae 4in
Breeding is timed to exploit the caterpillar "crop"

Scrub Jay
Aphelocoma coerulescens

Both the Scrub Jay and the related Mexican Jay, *A.ultramarina*, are found in the southwestern oak woods. But, while the Mexican Jay is a bird of the higher, richer oak zone (and is restricted to this habitat), the Scrub Jay is more numerous at lower elevations, and also occurs elsewhere in western North America as well as in Mexico. In addition there is an isolated population in the pine-oak woodlands of central Florida – evidence that in the recent past a belt of this habitat must have extended right across the southern United States.

Unlike the noisy, inquisitive Mexican Jay, the Scrub Jay is rather shy, and is usually seen darting into cover. The nest is a well-hidden, neatly built cup of twigs and weedstalks lined with fine grasses and horsehair.

For much of the year acorns and (where available) pinyon nuts form the bulk of the diet, but during the summer insects are added to the diet. Like many other jays, the Scrub Jay is a predator on the eggs and young of other birds. In winter the birds drift down from the mountains and may be found well out in the desert regions, foraging for food.

Virginia's Warbler
Vermivora virginiae

Virginia's Warbler is found at the lower edge of the oak zone, where the trees become scrubby and intermingled with cactus and yucca, and wherever the oak forest is interrupted by patches of dense brush. A retiring, inconspicuous bird in this dry habitat, Virginia's Warbler is the dull-coloured representative of the Nashville Warbler, *V.ruficapilla*, a brightly coloured species occupying wetter habitats to the north and east.

Virginia's Warbler builds its cup-shaped nest on the ground. The four eggs are laid in June, and hatching coincides with the period of maximum abundance of the small caterpillars on which the chicks are fed. After the young are fledged – and the caterpillars are again in short supply – family parties often move down into the lower foothills. Here they may be found along dry, bushy watercourses, in a habitat normally occupied by the closely related Lucy's Warbler, *V.luciae*.

Arizona Woodpecker
Dendrocopos arizonae

Although the Arizona Woodpecker is fairly common in the oak zone of desert mountains in the southwestern United States and northern Mexico, it is often overlooked because of its shyness. Frequently the first indication of the bird's presence is a quiet tapping, and only after a careful search is it located.

It is especially secretive during the breeding season, April, May and June, making investigation of nesting habits difficult. The nest cavity is usually placed up to 50 feet above ground, and the softer wood of the walnuts and sycamores is preferred to that of the oaks.

Farther south in Mexico, the Arizona Woodpecker is replaced by a similar species known as Strickland's Woodpecker, *D.stricklandi*, which differs in having the back barred with white.

Pinyon-Juniper and Mesquite

Between the sandy deserts of the southwest and the great expanse of grassland covering the central part of the North American continent is a broad belt of woodland. On the rocky slopes and tablelands of the Colorado Plateau, the dominant trees are pinyon pines and junipers. In the sandy and gravel soils of the flatter country, and along the rivers that flow southwestwards into the Gulf of Mexico, the most important constituent is mesquite, a member of the legume family. Although not nearly as rich in birds as the *Acacia* and *Commiphora* woodlands and savannas of Africa, these seemingly uninviting woodlands support a variety of species, some of which, like the Pinyon Jay, are largely restricted to the low coniferous growth on the plateaux.

The greatest diversity of species is found along the rivers, especially those far enough south to have a distinct Mexican element in their associated flora and fauna. On the plateaux, several species are dependent for food on the seeds of the pines. These species are somewhat nomadic, taking advantage of local differences in the abundance of cones. Although both these habitats support many species of birds which are numerous farther west, there is a definite eastern element too; birds like the Black-crested Titmouse have their closest kin in the forests of the southeastern part of the United States, while others, including the Blue-grey Gnatcatcher, occur from coast to coast in suitable habitats.

Blue-grey Gnatcatcher
Polioptila caerulea 4½in
A curious habit of tearing down a partly built nest to start afresh

Pinyon Jay
Gymnorhinus cyanocephalus 10in
Once fledged, the young join large wandering flocks

Pinyon-juniper and mesquite

- Range of Pinyon pine
  Pinus edulis

Distribution of species

- Pinyon Jay
  Gymnorhinus cyanocephala
- Black-crested Titmouse
  Parus atricristatus

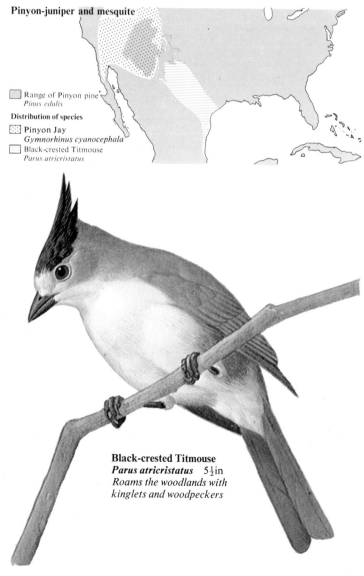

Black-crested Titmouse
Parus atricristatus 5½in
Roams the woodlands with kinglets and woodpeckers

Blue-grey Gnatcatcher
Polioptila caerulea

The Blue-grey Gnatcatcher is one of a group of species widespread throughout the tropics. Gnatcatchers are closely related to the kinglets or firecrests, and, with their soft grey plumage and rather long tails, they resemble tiny mockingbirds. The Blue-grey is the common species of the woodlands of the southern half of the United States and northern Mexico.

Although rather silent and inconspicuous during most of the year, the birds are noisy during the breeding season, when they are identified by characteristic lisping calls. The species is noted for its beautifully made nest – a delicate, cup-shaped structure of plant down and cobwebs, covered with lichen and saddled on a horizontal branch.

These birds have an odd habit of moving house, tearing down a partially completed nest and building a new one elsewhere. After the eggs have hatched the adults seem wholly preoccupied with feeding the young, oblivious of any human observers.

Pinyon Jay
Gymnorhinus cyanocephalus

Although the Pinyon Jay is practically omnivorous, its favourite food is the pinyon nut. Consequently the species is most numerous where pinyon pines occur. Movements are quite erratic – the birds appearing suddenly in an area where pinyon nuts are abundant.

More like small blue crows, these chunky, short-tailed jays are highly gregarious, moving through the pine- and juniper-covered hills in large, noisy flocks. Vocal for much of the year, the jays are silent in the breeding season, when they nest in colonies of a dozen or more pairs.

The nest, a bulky affair of twigs and strips of bark lined with softer material, is placed a few feet above ground in a pine or juniper. Although the Pinyon Jay has a nesting season lasting several months, all the nests in a colony are in the same stage of the cycle. The young leave the nest about three weeks after hatching and join large flocks moving through the countryside in search of food.

Black-crested Titmouse
Parus atricristatus

A common bird in the juniper country and riverine woodland of Texas and northeastern Mexico, the Black-crested Titmouse is the geographical replacement of the familiar Tufted Titmouse, *P.bicolor*, of the east. Like its relative, the Black-crested Titmouse is a sociable species, often moving about in loose association with wintering kinglets, creepers and woodpeckers.

The nest is built in a natural cavity or in a hole excavated in a dead stump. Five or six eggs are laid and the young, which leave the nest after about two weeks, resemble the adults. Two broods are usually raised, and the young remain with the adults until joining the mixed flocks ready for winter.

Like their relatives, the chickadees and Old World tits, these birds are confiding and inquisitive, and show little fear of man. They are frequent visitors to bird tables, and will accept man-made nest-boxes.

Black-chinned Sparrow
Spizella atrogularis 5in
*One of America's least-known
chaparral species*

Wrentit
Chamaea fasciata 6in
*The only American representative
of the babbler family*

Chaparral

From Oregon through California and into Baja California, there extends a distinctive habitat in which low evergreen oaks and resinous woody shrubs predominate. A fairly uniform environment, the chaparral supports relatively few species, but many of its plants produce edible berries and support vast insect populations, and what chaparral lacks in diversity of bird-life it makes up in numbers of individuals. Ground-dwelling and thicket-loving species are especially prominent. Chief among the latter is the resident secretive Wrentit, whose range coincides almost exactly with the limits of the chaparral community. A number of local sub-species are recognized. As a plant community, the chaparral is adapted to winter rains and is at least partly maintained by natural fires which stimulate germination of seeds and promote new growth. The habitat is, however, dependent on a delicate balance of forces; if fire sweeps the hillsides too often the woody growth dies and is replaced by grassland. Similar conditions exist in many parts of the world. In the Mediterranean Basin, South Africa, coastal Chile and southern Australia, plant communities like the Californian chaparral have developed, although each area has its own characteristic suite of constituent plants. Similarly, each of these widely separated chaparral communities has an avifauna which, while unrelated to the Californian birds, consists largely of similar ground-dwelling and thicket-haunting species.

Chaparral

☐ Area of chaparral

Distribution of species

☐ Poorwill
Phalaenoptilus nuttallii

☐ Wren Tit
Chamaea fasciata

Black-chinned Sparrow
Spizella atrogularis

A quiet, western cousin of the well-known Chipping Sparrow, *S. passerina*, the Black-chinned Sparrow covers a large area of rugged, brush-covered country in the southwestern United States and Mexico. The bird is very locally distributed: several pairs may be found nesting in one particular spot, but the species is absent from many square miles of apparently suitable habitat. As a result, the Black-chin is one of the least-known North American birds.

Judging from the few nests which have been found, the breeding habits of the species are typical of sparrows of this type. The nest is a loose, cup-shaped structure made of grass. The three or four eggs are pale blue, often with scattered spots. The birds are known to feed insects to their young, but the seeds from weeds and grasses probably form an important part of the diet. After the breeding season and during the winter the birds wander in small parties through the chaparral and, at this time of the year, are encountered purely by chance.

Wrentit
Chamaea fasciata

Although it is common, the Wrentit is a secretive little bird, and is more often heard than seen as it picks its way through dense brush. The species is restricted to the chaparral-covered slopes of Oregon, California and northern Baja California. In its movements and longish tail it is reminiscent of Marmora's Warbler, *Sylvia sarda*, a bird of similar habitat found on the coasts and islands of the western Mediterranean. The Wrentit is not a warbler, however, but is a member of the babbler family – the only one of this group in the New World.

Once mated, pairs remain together for life. Like many sedentary birds, Wrentits defend their territory all year round. The nest, a compact, well-made cup, is concealed in the vegetation a few feet above ground. Four pale blue eggs are laid in late March or April. Only one brood is produced each year, but if the first set of eggs is destroyed, the birds lay additional clutches and eggs may sometimes be found as late as June or early July.

Poorwill
Phalaenoptilus nuttallii

The Poorwill, a small, desert nightjar, is known for its mournful call echoing through the dry canyons and arroyos. More nocturnal than the larger nighthawks, the Poorwill feeds close to the ground, fluttering like a large moth among the bushes on rocky slopes. By day, asleep on the ground, it is only seen by chance, but at night its habit of sitting in the roadway makes it easy to find.

In 1946 the remarkable discovery was made of a hibernating Poorwill, hidden in a small niche in the wall of a canyon in the Chuckawalla Mountains of southern California. The bird had a very reduced heart-rate and respiration, and was thought to be dead at first. However, this or another bird returned to this same niche for four successive winters.

Recent work with captive Poorwills has shown that not only do the heart and respiratory rates decrease, but also that the body temperature drops well below normal. Prior to hibernation the bird accumulates a substantial amount of fat which it draws on gradually through the winter.

Poorwill
Phalaenoptilus nuttallii 8in
*Lays down reserves of fat
for its winter hibernation*

Colorado, Sonora and Mojave: The Hot Deserts

The prevailing winds in the southwestern United States are westerly, and as moisture-laden air moves inland from the Pacific, it is forced upwards by the long mountain ridges that flank the coast. Moisture is lost as rain as the temperature drops at these higher levels. The lowlands lying east of the mountains, in southeastern California, Arizona, New Mexico and western Texas consequently receive very little rainfall and form the closest approximation of a true desert to be found in North America. Even here, however, life is abundant. Particularly in southern Arizona, in the Sonoran Desert, the number of plant species is unexpectedly high. Great arborescent cacti cover the rocky slopes of the desert mountains and scores of flowering plants wait for the infrequent rains which bring them suddenly into bloom, producing great numbers of seeds before the fleeting moisture is gone. These seeds, and the insects that subsist on the plants that produce them, form the basis of a complex ecological community that includes a surprising number of bird species. Some, like Gambel's Quail, feed directly on the seeds; others, like the Roadrunner and Elf Owl, prey on smaller animals. At midday, there is little evidence of the abundant bird-life but a chorus of birdsong greets the dawn and despite its aridity, the desert supports one of North America's most interesting bird communities.

Right: Saguaro and Prickly Pear cacti; Southern Arizona

The hot deserts

☐ Area of desert

Distribution of species

▨ Gambel's Quail
Lophortyx gambelii

☐ Elf Owl
Micrathene whitneyi

Gambel's Quail
Lophortyx gambelii

The attractive Gambel's Quail occurs in a variety of habitats in the southwestern deserts, where it is generally found moving about in coveys of up to 40 individuals. These coveys consist of one or more family groups, and occupy a well-defined territory or home range. The birds remain within this home range throughout the year, living on the seeds and foliage of desert plants. While a whole covey may abandon an unfavourable area individuals seldom travel alone.

Late in the winter the birds split into pairs for breeding, each pair establishing a territory from which all other members are barred. Adults and young remain together until the autumn, when the winter coveys are re-established.

The familiar barking call of the Gambel's Quail is a location call used by members of a covey or pair to maintain contact when out of sight. Although the calls sound alike to human ears, the birds are known to distinguish the calls of their mates from those of strangers.

Elf Owl
Micrathene whitneyi 5½in
The world's smallest owl

Gambel's Quail
Lophortyx gambelii 11in
Barking calls enable the birds to maintain contact while feeding

Elf Owl
Micrathene whitneyi

No larger than a sparrow and smallest of all owl species, the Elf Owl nevertheless varies its insectivorous diet with occasional small birds. A rare sight by day, it becomes active at dusk, when it may be observed by flashlight, oblivious of the observer and tamely behaving quite normally. This tiny predator is a common inhabitant of the southwestern United States and neighbouring parts of Mexico, and its curious chirping call, beginning as the light fails, is a characteristic conclusion to the day in the saguaro country and oak canyons of the area.

Saguaro cacti provide favourite nest sites, although oaks and cottonwoods are often used. The Elf Owl, like other species, uses the abandoned nest-holes of the Gila Woodpecker for the three or four white eggs which it lays in May.

Cactus Wren
Campylorhynchus brunneicapillus 8in
*Its eggs and young are protected
by a formidable barrier of spines*

Roadrunner
Geococcyx californianus 22in
*A tireless and resourceful
desert predator*

Cactus Wren
Campylorhynchus brunneicapillus

The curious churring call of the Cactus Wren, largest of North American wrens, brings to mind the hottest days in the deserts of the southwestern states. Although this bird will build its nest in almost any cactus, yucca or thorn-bearing tree, the treacherous *cholla* cactus, bristling with dense clusters of extremely sharp spines, seems to be preferred. The birds move nimbly and apparently without harm over the spine-covered branches, and the domed nest is placed in the most inaccessible part of this arborescent cactus.

The nest is beautifully made of fine grasses and twigs and lined with feathers. It is used the year round for roosting as well as breeding. Because of the great difficulty of seeing into, or reaching, the nests little is known about the nesting habits of the species, although it is certain that both sexes incubate the eggs and carry insects to the nestlings.

For a while after fledging, the young birds are led back to the nest each evening but they quickly learn to build roosting nests of their own.

The Cactus Wren's adult diet consists mainly of insects, fruit pulp and seeds, with occasional small lizards. The species is well adjusted to the presence of man, and often nests in parks and gardens, where it has become quite tame. There are a number of closely allied species in the forests and dry habitats of tropical America.

Roadrunner
Geococcyx californianus

A swift-running, terrestrial cuckoo, the Roadrunner is a tireless and energetic predator, feeding on rodents, small birds and their eggs and young, insects, scorpions, snakes, lizards, seeds and fruit. Like many predatory birds, the Roadrunner responds to an imitation of the distress call of a bird – running eagerly up to a person making a squeaking sound. The bird is resourceful in its pursuit of prey and has even succeeded in capturing swifts by lying in wait for them near water and seizing them in the air as they swoop to drink.

While the majority of Old World cuckoos are brood parasites, all but a few of the New World species build their own nests. The nest of the Roadrunner is a bulky affair of sticks, leaves, snakeskins and the dried manure of cattle and horses, built a few feet above ground in a tree. Three to six eggs make up a normal clutch, but occasionally two females lay in the same nest, and clutches containing as many as 12 eggs have been found. Incubation begins as soon as the first egg is laid, so that the young in any nest are of varying ages.

Not surprisingly, this distinctive bird is the subject of much folklore, and it is widely believed that the bird will capture rattlesnakes by building a stockade of cactus spines around the snake and waiting for it to impale itself in an attempt to escape.

Fortified "trees" of the desert

The noisy and conspicuous Gila Woodpecker, *Centurus uropygialis*, is associated with giant cacti almost throughout its whole range. The forests of stately saguaro in southern Arizona and of equally imposing cardon cacti in Baja California form the heart of its breeding range, although the species nest periodically elsewhere in the southwestern deserts. The soft flesh of the cactus is ideal for the excavation of nest cavities, and only occasionally will the birds choose the wood of a willow or cottonwood. These nesting holes are important to other hole-nesting species that without the Gila Woodpecker would have very few nesting opportunities in the desert; Purple Martins (p76), House Finches, *Carpodacus mexicanus*, and Ash-throated Flycatchers, *Myiarchus cinerascens*, all benefit from abandoned nests. Curiously, the evidence of the woodpeckers' industry often outlasts the plant; the gourd-shaped relic of a nest among the desiccated ribs of a long dead saguaro is a common find in the desert and one that was exploited by the Indians who used them as drinking vessels. Far from damaging the cacti, the woodpeckers seem to act as tree surgeons, digging their holes where the flesh is damaged or diseased and thereby encouraging the formation of hard scar tissue.

The Gila Woodpecker is a perennial omnivore, feeding on birds' eggs and nestlings, seeds, fruits and nuts, in addition to insects. In the winter, they may also turn their unwelcome attention on orange or pecan crops. Insects are also the main food for the two or three broods reared each year. Once the breeding season is over, the birds tend to disperse somewhat.

Closely related to the Gila Woodpecker are the Red-bellied Woodpecker, *C.carolinus*, of the southeastern woodlands and the Golden-fronted Woodpecker, *C.aurifrons*, found in the juniper forests and riverine woodlands of Texas and northeastern Mexico.

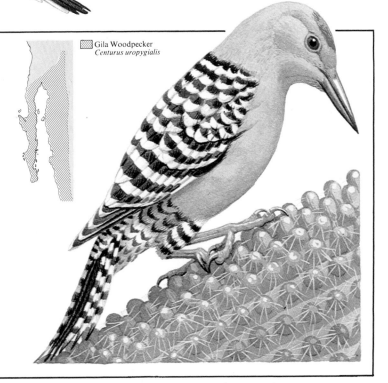

Gila Woodpecker
Centurus uropygialis

Shadscale and Sagebrush: The Cold Deserts

The dominant plant in much of the Great Basin and parts of southwestern Canada is sagebrush, a plant closely related to the wormwood of Eurasia. The silence of the grey-green expanse is broken only occasionally by the sound of a bird singing, and during the heat of midday the stillness is often complete. Because of the harshness of this environment and the fact that the resinous foliage of the sagebrush supports only a rather small insect population, only a few species of birds inhabit the sage country.

Each of the desert species has evolved its own way of coping with the relative sterility of the habitat. The Sage Grouse, for example, can eat the leaves and flowers of the sage itself; the Sage Thrasher manages to support itself on insects, and supplements its diet with berries when these are available; the Sage Sparrow lives principally on the seeds of low herbaceous vegetation while the Mourning Dove is a more generalized feeder that often moves long distances in search of food. Finally the Turkey Vulture subsists primarily on carrion, just as it does elsewhere in its range. Together, the bird species of the desert lands manage to co-exist, each specializing in one or another of the few available sources of food, and thereby avoiding competition. A few predators, like the Prairie Falcon and Ferruginous Hawk, hunt over the desert regions but breed in the more benign marginal lands.
Right: Sagebrush scrub in the desert of Arizona

Desert game-bird

The only dove in much of North America, the Mourning Dove, *Zenaidura macroura*, is found in abundance in a wide variety of habitats, including the sagebrush country of the Great Basin. The birds arrive in March or April and depart for their wintering grounds in the southern states in October. In the southern part of the range where the species is resident, breeding continues almost throughout the year.

As with most doves and pigeons, the Mourning Dove's nest is a flimsy affair, built of sticks, that scarcely seems able to support the eggs and young. The usual clutch is two eggs, but since several broods are raised each season, the annual production rate is high.

When not breeding, Mourning Doves travel in small flocks through the sagebrush, feeding largely on seeds and occasionally entering cultivated areas.

The Mourning Dove is a popular game-bird, but its adaptability and high rate of reproduction enable it to withstand the pressure of hunting.

Mourning Dove
Zenaidura macroura   12in

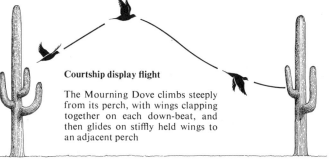

Courtship display flight

The Mourning Dove climbs steeply from its perch, with wings clapping together on each down-beat, and then glides on stiffly held wings to an adjacent perch

The cold deserts

☐ Area of desert

Distribution of species

▭ Sage Sparrow
  Amphispiza belli

Sage Thresher
Oreoscoptes montanus

▨ Winter range

▨ Summer range

Turkey Vulture
Cathartes aura

The Turkey Vulture is the most familiar of the New World vultures in North America. It is a widespread and common bird – no less numerous in cool sagebrush country than in the milder farmlands of the southeastern states. Although not very closely related to the Old World vultures, this species and the Black Vulture, *Coragyps atratus*, are similar in appearance and ecology to the Hooded Vulture, *Necrosyrtes monachus*, of Africa.

While the Black Vulture is a social bird, the Turkey Vulture is more solitary, nesting and hunting alone, and gathering only at roosts. Ungainly on the ground, it is a graceful bird in flight, soaring effortlessly as it scans the ground for food. Turkey Vultures come readily to human habitations to glean garbage and offal, and, although they gather at the carcases of large mammals, they are also adept at finding smaller items of carrion – even the bodies of mice and snakes hidden in the underbrush along roads and streams.

Sage Grouse
Centrocercus urophasianus

When spring arrives and the last of the snow melts in the sagebrush country, the Sage Grouse males gather at their traditional display grounds, or leks, and begin their elaborate posturing and strutting. These displays serve both to attract the females and to warn off other males. So, with the males in a highly aggressive state, the approaching females must first avoid being attacked. This is done by *not* displaying: while in some species of grouse the hen birds have elaborate displays of their own, the Sage Grouse female merely assumes a stationary, submissive posture which has the effect of blocking the attack drive of the male and allows mating to take place.

After mating, the females withdraw from the display area to nest. Seven or eight eggs are laid, but losses are heavy due to the depredations of coyotes, badgers, ground squirrels and magpies. Should a first nesting fail, a second attempt is unlikely since, as the season wears on, the male's fertility declines.

Sage Thrasher
Oreoscoptes montanus 8½in
The vulnerable eggs are shielded by a crude canopy of twigs

Sage Sparrow
Amphispiza belli 5½in
Its only defence is a nervous distraction display

Turkey Vulture
Cathartes aura 30in
Most widespread of the New World vultures

Sage Thrasher
Oreoscoptes montanus

As a breeding bird the Sage Thrasher is almost entirely restricted to the vast sagebrush plains of the interior of the western part of North America. Here it is a shy bird, darting quickly out of sight when discovered, and best seen in the early morning when it sings its melodious song from the top of a tall sage.

Like the other thrashers, these birds spend much time on the ground rummaging among dead leaves for the insects and spiders that are their chief prey. In late summer and autumn they feed heavily on berries.

The nest is placed on the ground or in the sagebrush, and is always very well concealed. Sometimes it is partially domed, or it may have a crude platform of twigs built above – apparently to shield the eggs and young from the sun. Both sexes incubate the eggs and care for the young.

After the post-breeding moult, the Sage Thrashers migrate south to wintering grounds in southern Arizona, New Mexico and Texas.

Sage Sparrow
Amphispiza belli

The modestly plumaged Sage Sparrow is one of the most furtive birds of the sagebrush. Foraging almost entirely on the ground, these birds run swiftly, tails held high over their backs. If approached, they are apt to dart quickly out of sight like mice.

This is a species best seen in the vicinity of the nest, for a brooding bird is reluctant to leave its eggs or young. It will remain on the nest until a visitor is very near, and then drop to the ground and run nervously about in full view. Eggs are found from March to June, but it is not clear whether clutches found late in the season are second nestings or attempts to breed after a first clutch has been destroyed.

Although the Sage Sparrow is confined (as a breeding bird) to sagebrush over most of its range, the populations of the coast ranges of California also inhabit the chaparral. During winter many birds remain on the breeding grounds, but some move south into the deserts of southern Arizonia and northern Mexico.

Sage Grouse
Centrocercus urophasianus 28in
The female's submissive posture blocks the fierce aggression of the breeding male

Mountain Peaks and Alpine Meadows

The great mountain ranges of western North America extend for more than 3,500 miles from the frozen tundra of Alaska, through the Rocky Mountains and Cascade ranges to the arid highlands of southern California and Mexico. At higher elevations the climate is like that of more northern latitudes; the succession of habitats one encounters in moving from the nothernmost parts of the continent southwards is, therefore, duplicated in descending the mountains. At the highest elevations, tundra similar to that of the Far North can be found, and characteristic birds, like the Water Pipit and the Ptarmigan, breed there, just as they do in northern Canada. Farther down the slopes, the forests support many species also found in the forests of Canada.

The complex topography of the mountains results in an irregular distribution of habitats. Small areas of tundra may be separated from one another by many miles, with the result that small populations of birds are locally isolated – often as sub-species, or races, characterized by differences in colour and pattern. For example, many strikingly different populations of the Rosy Finch exist in various parts of the mountains of western North America; some so distinct that they were long ago regarded as distinct species. However, no two of these populations occur together and they may, therefore, be considered members of a single species.

Right: Mountain crags in Glacier National Park, Montana

White-throated Swift
Aeronautes saxatalis 6½in
Possibly the fastest-flying species in North America

Water Pipit
Anthus spinoletta 6½in
Forsakes its mountain home to winter in the shelter of beach or river valley

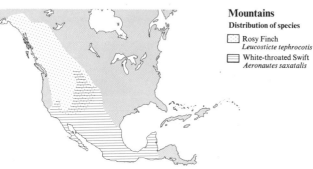

Mountains
Distribution of species

☐ Rosy Finch
Leucosticte tephrocotis

▤ White-throated Swift
Aeronautes saxatalis

White-throated Swift
Aeronautes saxatalis

The White-throated Swift builds its nest high up on the side of a cliff, quite inaccessible to most predators, including man. So insubstantial that it often cannot be seen at a distance, the nest is a shallow cup of feathers, twigs and grass glued together with saliva and attached to the wall of a crevice or cavity in the rock-face. The White-throated Swift is colonial, with about a dozen pairs making up each colony.

Four or five whitish eggs are usually laid, but, because of the difficulty of reaching the nests, the incubation and fledging periods are not known. However, it may be assumed that, as in other swifts (which are fed only occasionally during the day, and often not at all on cold days), the young develop very slowly.

The White-throated Swift is probably the fastest of North American species, plunging down the mountainsides at phenomenal speed. The birds range widely in search of insect food and, even in the breeding season, they are often seen over the desert lowlands, miles from the nesting site.

Water Pipit
Anthus spinoletta

Although many species of pipit occur in Eurasia, only two breed in North America. One of these, the Water Pipit, is widespread in the Old World. In North America the Water Pipit is a bird of the Arctic tundra and the highest, most windswept Alpine meadows. Here, far above the timber-line where there is so little other bird song, the rich flight song of the Water Pipit is especially beautiful.

The nest is placed in the shelter of a rock outcrop or in a clump of grass and contains five or six eggs, thickly spotted with brown. The young are fed almost entirely on insects. The Water Pipit is largely terrestrial, walking methodically over the ground, bobbing its tail, in search of the insects and small molluscs that form the bulk of its diet.

In the autumn the birds move down from the mountains, and, joined by migrant populations from the Arctic breeding grounds the species is a common winter bird, favouring beaches, sandy river-beds and open country throughout most of North America.

California Condor
Gymnogyps californianus

The huge California Condor is one of North America's rarest species, and recent estimates put the number of surviving birds as low as 50 to 60. Living entirely on carrion, the condor is restricted to a few areas in the mountains of southern California. The species has a very low reproductive rate; only a single egg is laid, and the young bird is dependent on the adults for more than a year. It is for this reason that the adults breed only once in two years. They are sensitive to interference and quickly abandon a nest that is disturbed.

Remains of California Condors have been found in Texas and New Mexico, where the species has not occurred for thousands of years – suggesting that the species has been declining since long before the coming of the white man to North America. While no doubt aggravated by human interference and the low reproductive rate, the decline is probably ultimately the result of the gradual disappearance, during the Pleistocene age, of the large mammals upon which the birds once depended for carrion.

Rosy Finch
Leucosticte tephrocotis

The Rosy Finch is another resident of the highest mountains, sharing the bleak Alpine meadows with the Water Pipit (p52). Like its neighbour, the Rosy Finch nests on the ground, but, whereas the nest of the pipit is a rather delicate affair, that of the Rosy Finch is a large bulky structure, often lined with Ptarmigan feathers.

Rosy Finches spend most of their time in large, active flocks, moving swiftly over the ground searching for seeds and insects. The birds roost together, often spending the night in nests long since abandoned by colonies of Cliff Swallows (this page). Although primarily a bird of the mountains, the Rosy Finch also

nests near sea level in Alaska. In winter, the mountain flocks move down into the lowlands, where they may wander some considerable distance; the species has been recorded as far from the mountains as Minnesota and Maine.

The Rosy Finch populations of different mountain ranges show considerable geographical variation in the amount of grey on the head, and until recently three distinct species were recognized.

Cliff Swallow
Petrochelidon pyrrhonota

The Cliff Swallow is very aptly named, for while today large numbers of these birds build their nests on the sides of barns and other buildings, the species' original nesting sites were the vertical faces of cliffs and the walls of canyons. Many still nest in the traditional situation today. The species is colonial and several hundred pairs may inhabit a single cliff, where they build their nests in densely packed groups. The nest, a flask-shaped structure made of mud, closely resembles that of the European House Martin, *Delichon urbica*, and the Red-rumped Swallow, *Hirundo daurica*.

This is the common swallow of the high mountains of the west, but it is also found in the eastern part of the continent where it has taken to nesting in smaller colonies, usually on buildings. In this newly acquired nesting site, however, it faces severe competition from House Sparrows, *Passer domesticus* (p 220), which often drive out entire swallow colonies and appropriate the nests for themselves. Even so, though not so numerous as many of the other North American swallows, the species has undoubtedly gained in numbers since adopting the urban habitat.

A compactly built, short-tailed bird, the Cliff Swallow bears little resemblance to many of its close relatives but, like other swallows, it is a long-distance migrant.

California Condor
Gymnogyps californianus

█ Present range

▨ Former range

California Condor
Gymnogyps californianus 50in
The magnificent "mountain vulture" – poised on the brink of extinction

Rosy Finch
Leucosticte tephrocotis 6in
Colour variations identify the different mountain races

Cliff Swallow
Petrochelidon pyrrhonota 5½in
A new lease of life in a new environment

Prairie Grasslands

The central part of North America, from west of the Mississippi to the base of the Rocky Mountains, and from the coast of Texas north into Canada, is covered by a vast sea of grass. These broad plains, which supported immense herds of bison as recently as a century ago, are the home of a distinctive community of birds. The absence of trees greatly reduces the number of ecological niches available to birds, and the habitat supports fewer species than the forests lying to the east. All species must nest on or near the ground and the nests must be cleverly concealed because they are within easy reach of predators. Finding the nests of grassland birds is consequently no easy task. Many of the birds of prey place their nests on rocky outcrops and are, therefore, more numerous on the western fringes of the plains, among the foothills of the Rockies. Most songbirds sing from an elevated perch of one sort or another, but such perches are seldom found in the open grasslands and birds like the Longspur and the Lark Bunting have solved this problem by resorting to aerial singing. They, and other birds, engage in striking aerial displays in which they conspicuously advertise their territories. In winter, heavy snows cover the ground, especially in northern parts of the Great Plains, and most of the birds withdraw – leaving the grassland fastness almost devoid of bird-life.

Right: Rolling prairie lands in northern Montana

Prairie grassland

Types of grassland

☐ Short grasses

▦ Mid-length grasses

▪ Long grasses

Distribution of species

▒ Chestnut-collared Longspur
Calcarius ornatus

Prairie grassland

Distribution of species

☐ Eastern Meadowlark
Sturnella magna

▨ Western Meadowlark
Sturnella neglecta

Chestnut-collared Longspur
Calcarius ornatus 6in
Much of its former range is now under the plough

Western Meadowlark
Sturnella neglecta 9in
Remained unrecognized for more than 80 years

Chestnut-collared Longspur
Calcarius ornatus

The longspurs are a group of four species, three of which, including the Chestnut-collared, are confined to the grasslands of North America. The fourth, the Lapland Longspur, *C.lapponicus*, is found in the Arctic tundra and occurs not only in North America, but also in Eurasia, where it is known as the Lapland Bunting.

The Chestnut-collared Longspur has suffered as the native grasslands of central North America have succumbed to cultivation. The species prefers rather dry, elevated prairie, much of which is today planted in wheat. In many areas the birds have ceased to breed, while in others they are found only on golf-courses, vacant lots and undisturbed land.

Fortunately there are still areas of suitable grassland left, and here populations are dense, the birds needing only an acre or two per territory. In this dry grassland, where vegetation is rather sparse, the longspurs build a nest rather like those of many larks – set in a depression in an open spot, yet hard to find.

Ferruginous Hawk
Buteo regalis 23in
A major predator on prairie dogs and ground squirrels

Ferruginous Hawk
Buteo regalis

The Ferruginous Hawk is a bird of the western grasslands and dry open country generally. Breeding in southern Canada and over much of the western United States, these birds winter in the southwestern states and northern Mexico. They are readily seen, perched on a tree, fence-post or rock outcrop, the blazing white underparts and rufous thighs making identification easy. The nest, often built on the ground, is used year after year. When built in a tree, it may be very big and is liable to be usurped by Horned Owls (p76).

The flight of this big raptor is rather laboured, and, like the Rough-legged Hawk (p102), the Ferruginous Hawk is frequently seen hovering. Prairie dogs and ground squirrels are the main prey.

Though the Ferruginous Hawk seldom molests livestock, it was for many years given no legal protection, and large numbers were shot. Though now protected, the species has failed to recover and is today a rare bird.

Western Meadowlark
Sturnella neglecta

The song of the Western Meadowlark has probably been heard in more countries than that of any other bird, as its melodious, flute-like notes are almost invariably found on the sound-tracks of Hollywood westerns. If the bird itself were to appear on the screen, it would be almost impossible to be sure it was not an Eastern Meadowlark, *S.magna*, the two species being almost identical in pattern and colour. Indeed, the fact that the western bird is a separate species was not discovered for more than 80 years after the eastern one was named. In 1844 the bird was given the name *neglecta* because the difference had been overlooked for so long.

As in many other birds that are close in coloration, the two meadow-larks may be distinguished by their songs, and it is by means of vocal differences that the two birds recognize each other. Although the ranges of the two species were originally separate, in recent years both have extended eastwards into the cleared lands in the Midwest. Now in some areas the ranges overlap, so that birds of the two species may be heard in adjoining fields.

That they are indeed separate species is now shown by the fact that they hybridize only rarely. These occasional mixed matings are thought to occur when a bird of one species strays into an area where normally only the other occurs.

The habits of the two meadowlarks are similar: both build domed nests of grasses and lay from three to seven eggs, and both are welcome residents in arable farmland since they eat insects damaging to crops.

A species in retreat

Since the arrival of European settlers the history of the Great Prairie Chicken, *Tympanuchus cupido*, has not been a happy one. Populations of the open pine barrens and grass-lands of the Atlantic coast, faced with uncontrolled hunting and the destruction of habitat by fire, were quickly exterminated. The last individual of this race, known as the Heath Hen, died in 1932 on the island of Martha's Vineyard in Massachusetts. Birds of the coastal prairies of Texas and western Louisiana have also declined, although a few isolated colonies still exist. Only in the centre of the continent, in South Dakota, Nebraska, Kansas and Oklahoma, are Prairie Chickens still present in numbers, and even here they face the encroachment of agriculture and the elimination of their native grasslands.

Although the birds feed to some extent on buds and foliage, seeds are a much more important part of the diet than in other grouse, and, after a heavy snowfall, prairie chickens may be dependent for a time on grain obtained from fields of cultivated maize and sorghum.

Each spring the males gather on communal display grounds, the booming call of the displaying birds being a characteristic early morning sound on the prairie. As with the Sage Grouse (p50), no pair bond is formed. The females visit the display grounds only for mating.

Prairie Chicken
Tympanuchus cupido
Former range
Present range

Greater Prairie Chicken
Tympanuchus cupido 17in

Prairie Grasslands

Safe – but for man

Once a familiar sight in the deserts and dry grasslands of western North America and the Kissammee Prairie of central Florida, the Burrowing Owl, *Speotyto cunicularia*, has been greatly reduced in numbers. Though safe from many of its natural enemies, the owl has suffered the depredations of the "sportsman" and the destruction of its habitat.

This tiny, long-legged owl is a terrestrial hole-nester, often taking possession of the abandoned burrows of prairie dogs, badgers, skunks and ground squirrels. Where necessary, the owl will enlarge the hole by scraping away the earth with its powerful feet and kicking it into a mound outside. In Florida, light sandy soils are widespread and the owls excavate their own burrows.

Six to 12 eggs are laid at the end of the burrow and, once fledged, the young emerge to await the hunting adults. When one of the parents returns with food, the young jostle one another for the prize, but are ever alert and scramble below at the first sign of danger.

Burrowing Owl
Speotyto cunicularia

Mirrored lifestyles of *pampas* and prairie

The lack of trees and dense ground cover, typical of desert and arid grassland, has encouraged the development of a thriving underground community. While the surface is patrolled by predators, a maze of tunnels provides a safe refuge in which the plains animals are able to raise their young. The Burrowing Owl inhabits both North and South America and in each continent shares its underground refuge with mammals, reptiles and rodents which, though of different species, fill exactly the same ecological niches.

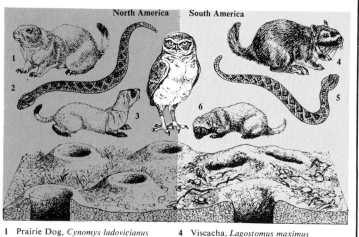

North America	South America

1 Prairie Dog, *Cynomys ludovicianus*
2 Rattlesnake, *Crotalus viridis*
3 Black-footed Ferret, *Mustela nigripes*
4 Viscacha, *Lagostomus maximus*
5 Rattlesnake, *Crotalus durissus*
6 Grison, *Galictis vittata*

female

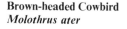

Brown-headed Cowbird
Molothrus ater 7in
Indiscriminate brood parasite of the American grasslands

male

Brown-headed Cowbird
Molothrus ater

Like many species of cuckoo, cowbirds are brood parasites, laying their eggs in the nests of other birds and leaving the foster parents to raise the young. Their parasitism is, however, not as highly specialized as that of some parasitic birds and there is not so great a tendency towards host specificity as in other parasitic groups. As a result, cowbirds have not developed the precise adaptations, such as egg mimicry, necessary to exploit particular host species.

Cowbird parasitism is successful because it has evolved in a different direction. Cowbirds lay their eggs in the nests of a great variety of species and the Brown-headed Cowbird, the only species in much of North America, is known to have parasitized no less than 205 different hosts. True, several of these are not in fact songbirds, and are therefore unsuitable as hosts (many songbirds react to the alien egg by abandoning the nest, ejecting the egg or covering it with a new nest lining) but, nevertheless, young cowbirds survive at a rate no lower than that of the songbird species they victimize.

Since they are not burdened with the task of building nests and rearing young, cowbirds are sociable all year round. They are particularly common in farmland, and are known for their habit of feeding around livestock. In primeval North America, cowbirds were associated with the great herds of bison that roamed the western plains. Since the settlement of this territory and the clearing of the forests, the cowbird has extended its range, but it is still most numerous in the grasslands.

Prairie Falcon
Falco mexicanus

Although in size and behaviour the Prairie Falcon resembles the Peregrine, *F.peregrinus*, it is actually a smaller ally of the Gyrfalcon, *F.rusticolus*, and is replaced in Eurasia by the Lanner and Saker falcons, *F.biarmicus and F.cherrug*. Like the Peregrine, which breeds in the same area, the Prairie Falcon is very sensitive to the pesticides that build up in the food chain, and at this time the bird is in danger of extinction.

In rough, hilly country both species nest on ledges and in shallow caves, the Prairie Falcon favouring the more arid regions, while the Peregrine usually builds close to water. Nesting, in the Prairie Falcon, is preceded by spectacular courtship flights, in which the male plummets from a great height, screaming loudly. The four or five eggs are incubated mainly by the female, attended and fed by the male, and both sexes bring food to the young.

The birds hunt for food by flying along a few hundred feet high ready to strike at small mammals and birds on the ground. So great is the speed of the attacking bird that, if the strike fails to hit the prey, the bird may tumble confusedly over the ground. Occasionally the Prairie Falcon takes prey in the air, in the manner of the Peregrine. In this, the bird is as adept as the Peregrine, and has even been seen to capture swifts on the wing.

After the nesting season, the birds move to lower elevations, generally in the same region. The young birds of any year may, however, wander widely and are often recovered several hundred miles from their place of birth.

Lark Bunting
Calamospiza melanocorys 7in
*Forced to retreat in the
face of arable farming*

male

female

Prairie Falcon
Falco mexicanus 17in
*Tumbles head over heels if
its hunting stoop fails to
find its target*

Lark Bunting
Calamospiza melanocorys

Lark Buntings are gregarious birds all year round, gathering in large flocks in winter, and also nesting in groups. Territories are often so small that singing males are just a few yards apart. In the breeding season, clad in bold black and white plumage, the males often indulge in a spectacular display flight, launching high into the air and then descending, singing ecstatically, with wings quivering. In parts of the prairie where the birds are numerous, dozens of displaying males may be seen in the air simultaneously.

The Lark Bunting builds its nest on the ground, concealed in the grass. The four or five pale blue eggs are incubated by the female alone, but the male joins in feeding the young. The birds usually raise a single brood and then depart quickly from the breeding zone.

After breeding, the buntings move south into the dry grasslands and deserts of the southwestern states and Mexico, where flocks roam the countryside searching for insects and seeds. They are commonly seen along roads in the desert, but, although the Lark Bunting is quite tame when breeding, it is shy in winter and takes to flight if approached.

Being a bird of the original grassland of the central part of the continent, the species has probably always been a victim of the Brown-headed Cowbird (p56). As the grasslands were taken over by agriculture, the Lark Bunting withdrew from much of its original range (and now rarely breeds in Minnesota and Iowa, where it was once common), but is still common in the higher, arid grasslands of the west, where the land is used to support cattle.

Farmland: The New Environment

It has been said that man is a grassland animal. Certainly man's principal sources of food are grasses, or animals that feed on grasses, and agricultural areas are often nothing more than man-made grasslands. Consequently, the birds most successful in adapting to agriculture have been grassland species. For many of these species, the clearing of eastern North America's forests created vast new areas of suitable habitat. As the forest species dwindled and disappeared, they were replaced by Sparrows, Killdeers, Bluebirds, Swallows and many other species that require open ground. but for a few species, the pendulum has begun to swing the other way. Much of the pastureland in the northeastern states is now becoming forest again. As this process continues, birds like the Bobolink, until recently an abundant migrant from the East Coast, will decline in numbers, and such species as the Redstart and the Ovenbird will probably take over the abandoned fields. For some grassland birds, the advent of agriculture has not been a blessing. The spread of agriculture resulted in the destruction of almost all of the suitable habitat of birds like the Prairie Chicken whose prime requirement is for unbroken and undisturbed prairie. Of all North American habitats, the grasslands have probably suffered most from human disturbance. For species which have not been able to adjust to cultivation, the future is bleak.
Right: Citrus groves in the Central Valley, California

Farmland

Distribution of species

- Painted Bunting
  Passerina ciris
- Bobolink
  Dolichonyx oryzivorus
- Scissor-tailed Flycatcher
  Muscivora forficata

Killdeer
Charadrius vociferus 10in
Its "distraction display" may be caused by a conflict of powerful instincts

Killdeer
Charadrius vociferus

The Killdeer is the noisy and conspicuous plover characteristic of ploughed fields, golf-courses and other open spaces, and seems to fill the niche occupied elsewhere by the various species of lapwing, which are absent from North America. Most of the Killdeer's relatives are smaller, rather inconspicuous birds of beaches and streams.

Like many other ground-nesting birds, the Killdeer performs a complex and extremely effective "injury-feigning" display whenever an intruder persists in an approach to its nest. This desperate response is preceded, at the intruder's first approach, by a simpler distractive measure. The bird runs from the nest (a shallow scrape, sometimes lined with a few pebbles or blades of grass) and takes to the air some distance away. If this has no effect, the bird will land and, one wing dragging uselessly behind, begin a laborious crawl. This persuasive display of injury diverts the predator's attention away from the four blotched eggs or the hatched young. If the distraction succeeds too well, and induces the predator to chase the struggling bird, the urge of self-preservation eventually overwhelms the protective instinct and the adult bird, making a miraculous "recovery" will fly off, calling loudly.

Eastern Bluebird
Sialia sialis

For the Eastern Bluebird the coming of European settlers was a mixed blessing: while forest clearance caused a big increase in the preferred habitat, introduced Starlings and House Sparrows offered fierce competition for the available nesting sites and the newcomers are in part responsible for the recent decline in bluebird numbers.

All but a few birds evacuate their breeding grounds in winter, and, while not the most consistent of spring migrants, this beautiful bird with its quiet, musical song is generally recognized as one of the heralds of spring. Sometimes the return is premature and large numbers of bluebirds perish in late winter storms.

On arrival, the birds set up territories centred around a nest-box or natural cavity fairly low in a tree. As in many hole-nesting species, the male selects the site and entices the female to accept it. Five or six pale blue eggs are laid, and the male participates both in incubation and in rearing the young. When the first brood has fledged, it is tended by the male while the female begins a second nesting.

Painted Bunting
Passerina ciris

An attractive bird, the Painted Bunting is a common summer resident in the southeastern states, favouring thickets at the edges of swamps and lowland forest, and breeding readily in well-planted parks and gardens in the towns and cities. The clearing of forest and its replacement by brushy secondary growth has created many square miles of new habitat, rich in the seeds and berries that are the birds' main food.

Two, three or even four broods are raised each season, the nest being a

Eastern Bluebird
Sialia sialis 7in
*Mixed blessings attended the arrival
of European settlers*

Scissor-tailed Flycatcher
Muscivora forficata 13in
*Streaming tail plumes enhance
the male's courtship displays*

Painted Bunting
Passerina ciris 5in
*Its fierce territorial battles
sometimes prove fatal*

well-made cup placed low-down in a dense thicket. The Painted Bunting male is a persistent singer and is very pugnacious, continually fighting with males in adjoining territories – sometimes to the death.

At the end of the breeding season the males lose their bright plumage and assume the greenish colour of the females. At this time of year the birds form flocks, often with the related Indigo Buntings, *P.cyanea*, in their brown winter plumage. Although a few birds winter along the Gulf Coast and in Florida, the majority migrate to the West Indies and Central America.

Scissor-tailed Flycatcher
Muscivora forficata

The Scissor-tailed Flycatcher is a striking inhabitant of the southern plains, very closely related to the kingbirds, *Tyrannus* spp. Like them it is noted for being very aggressive, readily attacking crows, hawks and even eagles. The species has an elaborate aerial display, much more spectacular than that of the kingbirds because of the lengthened outer tail feathers.

These birds are adept at capturing insects on the wing, but also take them from the ground. The cup-shaped nest is made of twigs, plant stalks and a great variety of other materials, including twine, horsehair and rags. The four to six spotted eggs are incubated by the female alone, while the male defends the nest with great vigour and aggression. Both adults feed the young. After breeding the birds gather in loose flocks and move south for the winter.

The Scissor-tail breeds in a com-paratively small area from Nebraska and Colorado south to southern Texas and Louisiana, and migrates along a rather direct route to the wintering grounds in Central America. Even so, a surprising number of birds have strayed to the Atlantic coast.

Bobolink
Dolichonyx oryzivorus

On crisp autumn days flocks of small, brownish birds pass overhead uttering their distinctive "pink-pink" call-note. They are Bobolinks, migrating from their summer homes in the lush northern farmlands and pastures to the wintering grounds on the *pampas* of Argentina. On the way south the birds pause along the Gulf Coast, where their former habit of raiding the rice fields earned them the name "rice birds".

The nest is placed on the ground and is extremely difficult to find, the bird darting away through the grass long before an intruder gets near. The five or six attractively spotted eggs are incubated by the female alone, while the male assists only in feeding the young.

Despite its finch-like bill, the Bobolink is a member of the American blackbird family, which includes the grackles, meadowlarks and American orioles. Bobolinks were formerly much more abundant: the return to secondary growth of much of the rich agricultural grasslands of the north-east, while assisting other species, has reduced the Bobolink's habitat, causing it to disappear from large areas. Nevertheless, the birds are probably more numerous now than they were in the days before the arrival of the European settlers.

Bobolink
Dolichonyx oryzivorus 7in
*Winters far to the south in
the Argentine pampas*

The Language of Colour

Among the birds of every continent will be found certain genera that contain a large number of species, with many of these species occurring together in the same area and even occupying parts of the same habitat. In Europe, for example, there are eight species of tits (genus *Parus*), while in the whole of temperate Eurasia there are no less than 26 species of leaf-warblers (genus *Phylloscopus*), a group which includes the familiar Willow Warbler and Chiff-chaff.

In North America the genus *Dendroica*, a group of colourful wood warblers, contains 20 species, while among the North American water-fowl there are 13 species of "puddle ducks" of the genus *Anas*. Each of these groups of closely related species is the result of a recent evolutionary radiation in which one or two ancestral forms have given rise, within the past million years or so, to the present array of species. In many such groups, the species are so closely related, and their lineages so recently diverged, that their ecological needs are still very similar, and therefore they cannot co-exist without competing for food and nesting sites. But in other groups, including all those mentioned above, the species have developed ecological differences, with the result that several different warblers may be found breeding in the same woodland and a number of allied species of ducks may occur together in a marsh. Although ecologically different, the birds are nevertheless quite closely related, and this co-existence of closely allied species creates a special problem. The birds are still genetically capable of interbreeding, but hybrids, either sterile or lacking in vigour, would contribute nothing to the welfare of the species. In both the ducks and the warblers, the striking and colourful plumage of the males is no accident; it is by means of these distinctive patterns that the birds recognize one another as belonging to the same species. The variety of colour serves the very serious purpose of preventing interbreeding between these closely allied species, and may be supported by other "isolating mechanisms". In the warblers, for example, the songs are also very different and contribute to species recognition. In some groups of birds the principal isolating mechanisms are vocal; the leaf-warblers of the genus *Phylloscopus* are almost identical in appearance and must rely entirely on differences in song to separate the species.

BIRDS ILLUSTRATED

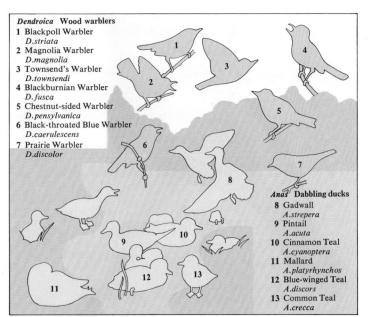

Dendroica Wood warblers
1 Blackpoll Warbler
    D. striata
2 Magnolia Warbler
    D. magnolia
3 Townsend's Warbler
    D. townsendi
4 Blackburnian Warbler
    D. fusca
5 Chestnut-sided Warbler
    D. pensylvanica
6 Black-throated Blue Warbler
    D. caerulescens
7 Prairie Warbler
    D. discolor

Anas Dabbling ducks
8 Gadwall
    A. strepera
9 Pintail
    A. acuta
10 Cinnamon Teal
    A. cyanoptera
11 Mallard
    A. platyrhynchos
12 Blue-winged Teal
    A. discors
13 Common Teal
    A. crecca

The Wood warblers (*Dendroica* spp)

Every spring, two dozen or more species of wood warbler pass through the eastern United States on their way to their northern breeding grounds. The dazzling variety of their plumage colour and pattern aids in species recognition and acts to prevent wasteful hybridization between closely related species. This diversity reaches its greatest degree of development in the genus *Dendroica*, several of whose members are illustrated. Although each of these species differs ecologically to some extent from the others, many of them may breed in the same woodland, where without these isolating mechanisms hybridization would probably occur. After the breeding season, when species recognition is no longer necessary, many of the birds assume a more drab plumage. Some, easily identifiable in spring, are very difficult to tell apart when they are in dull winter dress. One such bird is the Blackpoll Warbler, *D. striata*, which in the autumn is almost impossible to distinguish from the Bay-breasted Warbler, *D. castanea* – yet in the spring the two are easily separated. The Blackpoll is one of the northernmost of the warblers, and its spring migration is somewhat later than that of species that mainly breed farther south. Townsend's Warbler, *D. townsendi*, is a western species and a member of a group of warblers that includes the familiar Black-throated Green Warbler, *D. virens*. The members of this group are too closely related to be able to co-exist without competing ecologically, and consequently the members replace one another geographically. Since they nowhere breed in the same area, there is no danger of hybridization and the males of this group are all very similar. The Blackburnian Warbler, *D. fusca*, Magnolia Warbler, *D. magnolia*, and Black-throated Blue Warbler, *D. caerulescens*, are all birds of the cool coniferous forests of southern Canada and the northern United States. Each also occurs in the coniferous forests of the Appalachians. The Prairie Warbler, *D. discolor*, and Chestnut-sided Warbler, *D. pensylvanica*, are strikingly dissimilar, and both breed in brushy overgrown pastures and on scrubby hillsides. Both are much more abundant now than when unbroken forest covered much of eastern North America.

The dabbling ducks (*Anas* spp)

Several of the ducks shown here also occur in Europe, and any visitor to North America from Europe will immediately recognize the familiar Mallard, Pintail and Gadwall, while the Teal, called in America the Green-winged Teal, is but slightly different from the European bird and is presently considered to be only racially distinct. The Blue-winged Teal and Cinnamon Teal are confined to the New World, but are closely related to the Old World Garganey, *A.querquedula*. The females of all these birds look very similar – only the males show the great variety of patterns and colours that act as species markers. The aggressive male Mallards and Pintails will court and pursue any female duck; they are apparently unable to distinguish females of their own species from those of the others. It is up to the modestly coloured female, assisted by the bright patterns of the

males, to make the right choice and thus avoid hybridization.

The Mallard, *A.platyrhynchos*, is the largest of the *Anas* ducks and is widely distributed in the Northern Hemisphere. Strongly migratory, the Mallard has reached a number of oceanic islands, where on occasion small populations have remained. Here, remote from other members of the genus *Anas*, the bright male plumage is no longer necessary for species recognition and in many of these island populations the males are similar in colour to the females. The Gadwall, *A.strepera*, and Teal, *A.crecca*, breed in both North America and Eurasia. Both are strongly migratory, but except for a now extinct population of Gadwalls on Washington Island in the central Pacific, neither has been successful in colonizing remote oceanic islands. The Blue-winged Teal, *A.discors*, and Cinnamon Teal, *A.cyanoptera*, are two species confined to the New World. The Blue-winged Teal breeds only in North America.

Wetlands of the Interior

The inland fresh-water marshes of North America are among the richest and most interesting avian habitats on the continent. Those of the Prairie Provinces of Canada and adjacent parts of the United States are the largest and most productive. It is to these prairie marshes that the bulk of the North American water-fowl population migrates during the breeding season. Even the ducks, geese and swans that nest on the tundra use these marshes as important resting places during migration. No less important are the great areas of muskeg – the large, boggy tracts that are a characteristic feature of the coniferous forests. These are the breeding grounds for herons, rails and grebes, as well as for woodland ducks like Mergansers and Goldeneyes. Many of these marshes lie on the beds of what were once vast glacial lakes. Since the ice sheets receded following the last glacial period, these lakes have gradually diminished in size, leaving a rich alluvial soil which supports the complex plant and animal communities that exist today. This same soil is excellent for agriculture and the marshes have been extensively drained and planted with wheat. The enormous water-fowl population that once depended on these wetlands has dwindled to a fraction of its former size and the destruction of the habitat has reduced the population of ducks and geese in a way that hunting alone could never have done.

Right: Fresh-water lake in marshland; Algonquin Park

Red-winged Blackbird
Agelaius phoeniceus

The "Redwing" is one of the most successful and well-known North American birds. Highly adaptable, the species occurs throughout North America and south into Central America and the West Indies, nesting not only in marshes and swamps, but in moist habitat of any sort, even, on occasion, in upland meadows. In the marshes of California there is another species, the Tri-coloured Blackbird, *A. tricolor*, that resembles the Redwing closely in appearance but differs in nesting in immense colonies of as many as 200,000 pairs.

The Red-winged Blackbird is not colonial, although pairs often nest in loose association. In the north of its range, it is one of the first migrant species to return in spring, the males arriving first to establish territories. The familiar song is heard from every marsh and roadside pond, accompanied by a display in which the red wing coverts are prominent.

Two, occasionally three, broods are raised each season, the birds building a new nest for each set of eggs. The nest is a deep, skilfully made cup of grasses, placed in reeds, bushes or trees or, rarely, on the ground. In the breeding season the birds are almost entirely insectivorous, but in autumn and winter they gather in flocks – at times numbering hundreds of thousands – and may do considerable damage to crops, although even at this time of year they also consume large quantities of insects.

In the West Indies and South America there are a number of close allies of the Redwing, most having a bright patch of red, orange or yellow on the head or wing coverts.

Yellow-headed Blackbird
Xanthocephalus xanthocephalus

The guttural discords of the Yellow-headed Blackbird's song are one feature of the great prairie marshes sure to arrest the visitor's attention. Apart from its unmistakable croaking, the Yellow-head is distinguished by its feet – unusually large for a North American blackbird, but well suited to its nimble clambering among reeds.

In many respects, this bird recalls the smaller Redwing (this page), although there are no firm grounds for closely relating these two marsh-dwellers. The Yellow-head is less widespread than the Redwing and its breeding habits are less flexible, since it nests only in marshy areas. Wherever the two species coincide, the larger blackbird takes over the deeper water (its preferred breeding area) and the Redwing retires to the more exposed marsh fringes, where the dangers of predation are greater.

The Yellow-headed Blackbird's breeding cycle is synchronized with that of the large aquatic insects on which it feeds. Because hatching coincides with the greatest abundance of food, these birds rarely raise more than one brood in a season.

Since Yellow-heads nest colonially, the males are much occupied during the breeding season with singing and displaying in defence of their small territories. At this time, the males' bright plumage plays an important role in these aggressive displays. After the breeding season, when the birds gather in flocks, aggressive behaviour is reduced to a minimum, and the provocative breeding plumage of the males is replaced by a drab winter uniform.

Red-winged Blackbird
Agelaius phoeniceus 8in
Equally at home in lowland marsh and upland meadow

Yellow-headed Blackbird 9in
Xanthocephalus xanthocephalus
A passerine bird whose feet are adapted for marshland life

Interior wetlands
Distribution of species

Canvasback
Aythya vallisnaria

Red-winged Blackbird
Agelaius phoeniceus

Breeding range

Winter range

Yellow-headed Blackbird
Xanthocephalus xanthocephalus

Breeding range

Winter range

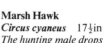

Marsh Hawk
Circus cyaneus 17½in
The hunting male drops food to his brooding mate

male

female

Marsh Hawk
Circus cyaneus

Though wrongly termed a hawk, this marshland predator is actually a harrier, and the sole representative of that group in North America. It is the same species as that known in Britain as the Hen Harrier.

Quartering its hunting area in a fast, silent, low-level flight, the Marsh Hawk is hidden from its prey until it is too late for the victim to take evasive action. It is a hunting technique perfectly adapted for the marshland habitat where frogs, mice, snakes and large insects abound amid dense, low vegetation.

Unlike the majority of birds of prey, the harriers commonly nest on the ground; the Marsh Hawk builds a large mound of reeds and rushes amid dense marsh vegetation. Although the female is responsible for building the nest, the male assists by foraging for materials, swooping low over the nest site and dropping the materials to his mate without alighting. This same technique is used in feeding the young; the male does most of the hunting and drops the food near the nest for the female to retrieve and feed to the nestlings.

Once fully fledged, the young birds disperse widely and marked juveniles have been recovered hundreds of miles from their place of birth.

Canvasback
Aythya valisineria

The Canvasback, and the similar Redhead, *A.americana*, are both close relatives of the European Pochard, *A.ferina*, and are probably the descendants of two separate colonizations of North America by the Pochard or its ancestors. A wary and fast-flying bird, the Canvasback is considered by hunters to be the aristocrat of North American ducks. Though many are taken every year, the numbers shot and the length of

the season are adjusted each year and any decline in the Canvasback population is more the result of the reclamation of its marshland habitat than a result of over-shooting.

Like other pochards, the Canvasback builds a well-made nest concealed in reeds and bulrushes along the edge of the marsh and usually over water. Nest material is added constantly during incubation in order to compensate for sinking of the sodden mass of vegetation. The hen alone builds the nest, incubates, and cares for the young; the male abandons his mate as soon as the eggs are laid.

Pied-billed Grebe
Podilymbus podiceps

The Pied-bill is the most familiar and widespread of the Western Hemisphere grebes and is a common resident of marshes and ponds from Canada to Patagonia. In the northernmost parts of its range, the Pied-billed Grebe is migratory – leaving its tundra home at the onset of winter and returning as soon as the ice breaks up in the spring. Soon after the birds return, the ponds and marshes resound with the sonorous, gulping territorial cries of the breeding males.

As in other members of the grebe family, the nest is a sodden mass of floating vegetation and, when alarmed, the brooding hen will pile masses of vegetation over her eggs before retiring to safety. The attractively striped young are often seen riding on the back of one of the adults.

The Pied-bill differs from its relatives in having an unusually large, stout bill – a feature that probably reflects the fact that hard-shelled crustaceans, such as crayfish, form a major part of the diet. On Lake Atitlan in Guatemala, there is a larger, flightless derivative of the Pied-bill, the Atitlan Grebe, *P.gigas*, often considered a separate species.

Canvasback
Aythya valisineria 22in
Descendant of an early Eurasian colonist

Pied-billed Grebe
Podilymbus podiceps 13in
Its powerful bill is adapted for a specialized diet

Muskeg and Marshland

Muskeg and marsh

Distribution of species

Franklin's Gull
Larus pipixcan

Canada Goose
Branta canadensis

Great Blue Heron
Ardea herodias

The Great Blue Heron is the North American representative of the familiar Grey Heron, *A.cinerea*, of Europe – the two are sometimes regarded as belonging to a single species. In the populations of southern Florida, Cuba and Yucatán, all-white individuals predominate, and it was long thought that these were a distinct species.

Despite its large size, the Great Blue Heron is a highly successful and adaptable bird, breeding throughout the United States and southern Canada. It avoids only the high mountains and the most parched stretches of desert. Although solitary breeding pairs are found, the species usually nests in colonies of from two or three pairs to several hundred, in such inaccessible places as islands or thick, swampy woods. Great Blue Herons often nest in association with other species of heron, returning year after year to the same group of trees. At the end of the breeding season the birds disperse, often moving far from the breeding site.

Sora Rail
Porzana carolina

The Sora, or Carolina Crake, is a small, short-billed rail closely related to the Spotted Crake, *P.porzana*, of Europe and western Asia. It is a widespread and abundant bird. During migration, individuals turn up in the smallest areas of marshy habitat. On the wintering grounds along the Gulf Coast, the Sora is often present in great numbers in the marshes and flooded fields of the rice country.

Like other rails, Soras are very secretive and adept at concealing themselves in the grass and reeds. Standing at the edge of a southern marsh, one might never suspect that there were any of these birds about at all, until a hand-clap or – better still – a tape-recording of the bird's whinnying call is immediately answered by a chorus of hidden Soras.

The nest of the Sora is a substantially made shallow cup, anchored to the reeds, often over fairly deep water. A typical clutch contains ten or 12 eggs, and occasionally as many as 18. The young, like those of all but the

Great Blue Heron
Ardea herodias 47in
The New World equivalent of the European Grey Heron

Sora Rail
Porzana carolina 9in
Trees and buildings are a dangerous hazard to this low-flying migrant

Franklin's Gull
Larus pipixcan 14in
The crowded conditions of the breeding colony provide a vital stimulus

most primitive rails, are covered with soft black down. Soon after hatching they leave the nest to wander about with the adults, in search of food.

The visitor to the marsh may all at once be approached by an adult Sora, calling plaintively and making no attempt to conceal itself. This is a good indication that a brood is nearby, and by carefully searching the vegetation one may find the tiny black young ones, crouched motionless among the catkins.

As cold weather approaches, Soras become increasingly restless until, on some particularly cold October night, virtually the entire population of an area departs on migration, to spend the winter in the southern United States, the West Indies and northern South America.

Franklin's Gull
Larus pipixcan

Each year Franklin's Gull migrates between its breeding grounds on the great marshes of the northern plains, and its winter home off the coast of South America. Spring flocks of these "prairie doves" are a beautiful sight as they migrate northwards across Texas and Oklahoma, their breasts showing the pinkish tinge of the breeding plumage.

At home on the prairie marshes, the birds nest in large, clamorous colonies numbering many thousands. Indeed, there is evidence that the species can only breed in groups of such size, since individuals require the stimulus provided by large numbers of other nesting birds. The nest is built of rushes and grass on a mass of floating vegetation. New material is added constantly to compensate for the fact that, as the season advances, the nest becomes saturated and slowly sinks.

The young are poor swimmers, and, unlike the young of gulls nesting on solid ground, do not leave the nest except in the face of extreme danger. When they do, they often struggle across the water to another nest, where they are readily adopted by the pair in residence.

On the marshes of the Atlantic and Gulf coasts, Franklin's Gull is replaced by the related Laughing Gull, *L.atricilla*.

Canada Goose
Branta canadensis

The most familiar of all American Geese, the Canada Goose is a widespread breeding bird found throughout much of the northern half of the continent, and, since its introduction into Europe, is well known and successful there as well. In North America the species is migratory, and a sure sign of the arrival of spring is the musical honking of a flock of Canada Geese – heard as the birds pass overhead in characteristic wedge-shaped

formation on their way to the northern breeding grounds.

Like other geese, Canadas pair for life, and they are closely attached to their breeding area. Here they are semi-colonial, with groups of birds nesting in close proximity for many generations and seldom inter-breeding with other such groups. The result is that many local differences in size and coloration have developed, and many such distinct populations are recognized as races. Some of the most distinctive of these have even been regarded as full species.

Even today, the question of whether the small bird known as Hutchins' Goose, *B.c.hutchinsii*, is best considered a race of the Canada Goose or a separate species has not been settled. Interbreeding between these birds and other small forms of the Canada Goose has not yet been discovered, so the possibility remains that Hutchins' Goose is reproductively isolated from the Canada Goose and is therefore a species in its own right.

Whooping Crane
Grus americana 50in (height)

Whooping Crane
Grus americana
▨ Present breeding range
▤ Present wintering range
▨ Former range

Perilous existence

If it were to be discovered today, the Whooping Crane, *Grus americana*, would probably be considered a bird of the muskeg – the low, swampy conifer country of the Canadian interior. The small surviving population of this most celebrated of endangered North American birds breeds in this habitat in southern Mackenzie, and winters at the Aransas National Wildlife Refuge on the Gulf Coast of Texas. In former times, however, the bird also bred in the aspen zone in the prairie provinces and in other wetland regions in the interior of the continent, as well as in a small area in the coastal marshes of Louisiana.

Once dangerously close to extinction, with a world population of less than two dozen individuals, these elegant white cranes have a current population that has stabilized at just under 50 birds. Indeed, because there is little suitable habitat remaining on the Texas coast (and the birds are highly territorial even on their wintering grounds), it is unlikely that there will ever be many more Whooping Cranes than there are now. Never as abundant as the related Sandhill Cranes, *G.canadensis*, these birds were shot in large numbers, and they suffered, too, the draining of many of the marshes in which they bred.

Each year the surviving population makes the long and perilous migration from the breeding grounds to the Texas coast, anxiously watched over by wildlife conservation officials both in Canada and the United States. While the birds are probably relatively safe on their remote breeding grounds, each year a few lives are lost, and they are quite vulnerable in Texas. If a severe hurricane were to strike Aransas while the birds were there, the entire population might well be wiped out.

Canada Goose
Branta canadensis 30in
Each racial group returns to its own traditional breeding ground

Gulf Coast and Everglades

Florida and the coast of the Gulf of Mexico provide a wide variety of wetland habitats. In southern Florida, particularly in the Everglades, there are vast saw-grass marshes, dotted with clumps of palms and interlaced with miles of meandering natural waterways. There are dark cypress swamps in the fresh-water interior and dense tangles of mangrove along the brackish coast. Farther west, along the coast of the Florida Panhandle and in the sprawling bayous of Louisiana, there are broad marshes where thousands of ducks and geese spend the winter months. Many of these habitats have a distinctly tropical look and, indeed, may be regarded as outposts of the American tropics. Many of the plants growing here belong to groups otherwise found in abundance in parts of Central and South America – an affinity that is also reflected in the bird-life. Although these plant and animal communities are separated from similar environments by the Gulf of Mexico and the arid coasts of Texas and Tamaulipas, it is certain that at some time in the past, tropical conditions extended all the way around the Gulf. When the climate cooled, the tropical wetlands of Florida and the northern Gulf Coast became isolated, as did that part of their bird-life which is correspondingly tropical in affinity, including the Wood Stork and the Everglade Kite. The small populations of tropical birds isolated in this way are consequently vulnerable.

Right: Open pools surrounded by reed-beds; Florida Everglades

Roseate Spoonbill
Ajaia ajaja 32in
The sole representative of its family in the Western Hemisphere

White Ibis
Eudocimus albus 25in
Elaborate appeasement displays forestall domestic violence

A curious development
Short, pink and fleshy, the bill of a newly hatched spoonbill is very much like that of any other chick and gives little indication of its future remarkable transformation. As the chick increases in size, the bill gradually lengthens and assumes a bulbous tip, finally attaining the proportions of the adult bill by the time the chick is fully fledged.

When the adult bird is feeding, the bill is held almost vertically in the water and is swept from side to side, the tip of the lower mandible raking through the bottom ooze. Any small animals that are disturbed by the scything bill are instantly trapped between the broad spatulate mandibles and, raising its head, the spoonbill tosses the morsel to the back of its throat.

Wood Stork
Mycteria americana 40in
Drought or frost may cause widespread nesting failures

White Ibis
Eudocimus albus

The White Ibis is a bird of lowland swamp and mangrove from Florida and Louisiana south through Central America and the West Indies to northern South America. This species is always gregarious, and evening flights to roost are a spectacular sight as thousands of birds stream into a large stand of mangroves.

The birds nest in March and April in colonies of thousands of pairs. The nests are shallow platforms of twigs and leaves, and contain three or four white eggs. The young leave the nest at about three weeks, but, unable to fly, remain perched nearby for another two weeks.

Members of a mated pair are unable to recognize one another as individuals, so a bird approaching a nest must perform an appeasement display if it is to avoid being attacked as an intruder.

Roseate Spoonbill
Ajaia ajaja

Spoonbills are very closely related to the ibises, and they share with them many details of behaviour and ecology. The chief difference between the two is that whereas ibises feed by probing their bills in the mud, spoonbills, with bills flattened at the tip, strain small fish and crustaceans from the water.

Flocks of Roseate Spoonbills, wading through shallow water and feeding by swinging their bills gracefully from side to side, are a familiar sight along the Gulf Coast of Florida and Texas. Like the White Ibis, the Roseate Spoonbill nests in colonies, but the young take longer to become independent of the adults.

In the past the species was persecuted for the millinery trade, but is now responding well to protection. The only spoonbill in the Western Hemisphere, the Roseate is somewhat different from those of the Old World, which form a close-knit group of white species.

Wood Stork
Mycteria americana

The Wood Stork, long known under the less appropriate name of Wood Ibis, is the only species of stork breeding in North America. Here the birds nest only in Florida, although formerly they may have nested more widely in the southeastern states. The species also nests in much of Central and South America.

In Florida, the birds are sensitive to drought and irregular frost. On occasion these factors cause widespread nesting failure, an event resulting in spectacular dispersals in which the birds are recorded as far away as Oklahoma and New England.

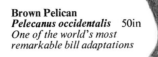

Brown Pelican
Pelecanus occidentalis 50in
One of the world's most remarkable bill adaptations

Aerial bombardment
In addition to scooping its prey while wading, the Brown Pelican often dives like a gannet to take fish at deeper levels

Specialist fishers of coast and swamp

The Brown Pelican, *Pelecanus occidentalis*, differs from the other six species of pelicans not only in the colour of its plumage – brown instead of white – but in being confined to salt-water habitats. In North America the species occurs on the low, sandy Gulf Coast and on the rocky coasts of southern California. Other populations are found along the coasts of Central and South America. On the cold Peruvian coast there is a distinctly larger form, considered by some to be a separate species.

Pelicans are known to use the distensible pouch to catch fish, but the manner in which this is accomplished is more complicated than it at first appears. As the bird darts forward, the elongated bones of the lower jaw spread outwards, then upwards, gathering in the fish and much sea-water as well. Then these two sides of the jaw draw together over the pouchful of fish and water, and the narrow upper mandible drops down. When the bird lifts its head from the water the huge bill points downwards, allowing water to drain out, and then, with a toss of the head, the bird swallows the fish that have been retained.

In this latter part of the process, the birds often attract the attention of the gulls that hover nearby and attempt to steal fish. Unlike the other pelicans, the Brown Pelican is an expert diver, plunging into the water from the air like a gannet.

Once familiar on the Gulf Coast, the Brown Pelican is now in danger of extinction because the water is saturated with pesticides, causing the birds to lay eggs with shells so frail that they collapse under the weight of the incubating bird.

Darters, or Anhingas, *Anhinga anhinga*, are birds of quiet, inland waters, where they capture fish and other aquatic animals. Because of their habit of swimming with only the head and long, slender neck above the surface, Darters are often called snakebirds.

These birds are closely allied to the cormorants, and more distantly to the pelicans and gannets. All these groups are alike in having all four toes united by a single web. Darters share many characteristics with the cormorants, including the habit of perching for long periods of time with the wings partially spread. But they have longer, broader tails than cormorants, and often soar high over the swamps, sometimes so high as to disappear from view.

Darters usually nest in colonies, often in association with herons, ibises and cormorants. The shallow, flimsy nests are placed in bushes or trees over the water, or occasionally the birds appropriate the nests of egrets. Four or five pale blue eggs are laid and the incubation period, shared by both parents, lasts for about four weeks.

Both parents bring food to the chicks, which are born naked but soon acquire a coat of buff-coloured down. When the young are two weeks old or more, they will leave the nest if disturbed, jumping into the water and diving for safety. When the danger is past, they are able to scramble back to the nest.

In addition to occurring in the swamps and marshes of the southeastern states, the Darter inhabits similar habitats in much of tropical America. Related species are found in Africa, Asia and Australia.

Darter
Anhinga anhinga 34in
The "snake-bird" of the Everglade swamp-forests

Drying out
Lacking the plumage oils typical of many water-birds, the Darter must dry out its wings after each dive

The Everglades: An Environment at Risk

The changing climatic conditions that isolated the tropical areas of the Gulf Coast and Florida Everglades from the similar areas of northern South America, also isolated a number of bird species that formerly ranged throughout the whole of the central American domain. Many of these birds are now, through a variety of causes, on the decline and their isolation makes it virtually impossible for their numbers to be replenished by new arrivals from the southern source region. Even without the interference of human activities such as the draining of marshland, many of these species are vulnerable; marginal populations have not the resilience to withstand the natural hazards of a particularly poor breeding season, an outbreak of disease or flooding of the nesting area, and it is almost certain that many tropical species, once resident in these regions, became extinct even before man made his presence felt.

Any action man may take to alter the natural form and balance of an environment has repercussions throughout that, and also neighbouring, habitats. Large areas of land in the Florida Everglades have been drained and reclaimed. The consequent alteration of the drainage pattern led immediately to a decline in the numbers of fresh-water snails in the pools and streams of the region, with near-disastrous effects on the Limpkin and the Everglade Kite – both species having adapted to feed almost exclusively on these aquatic invertebrates.

Great White Heron
Ardea herodias occidentalis 41in
Recently proved to be a distinctive race of the Great Blue Heron

A vital resource
The large and colourful snails, particularly those of the genus *Pomacea*, that abound in the Everglade swamps, are a major food source for the Limpkin and the Everglade Kite. Should swamp drainage schemes, or any other factor, reduce the snail population, the Limpkin will suffer a marked decline and the Kite may well disappear for ever.

Limpkin
Aramus guarauna 28in
A possible link with the primitive cranes

Limpkin
Aramus guarauna

The distinctive Limpkin is generally regarded as a close relative of the cranes, and it has been suggested that the Limpkin is a primitive bird, giving a clue as to what the remote ancestors of the cranes may have looked like. This bird is entirely American in distribution, and its strange, mournful cry, which has earned it the name of the "crying bird", may be heard in saw-grass marshes and swamps from Florida south to Argentina.

Like the Everglade Kite, which also inhabits may of these wetlands, the Limpkin is fond of large snails, but it also eats a wide variety of other aquatic animals such as crustaceans, frogs, fresh-water clams and insects. The birds open the molluscs by seizing them in their bills and striking them against a rock, or root, until the shells break. Suitable sites for breaking clam and snail shells are favourite resorts of the Limpkins, and are often marked by quantities of broken shell debris.

The Limpkin's nest is a bulky platform of reeds and marsh grasses, attached to standing vegetation, and usually placed in remote parts of the marsh. The clutch generally consists of four or five heavily spotted eggs, and the young birds are covered in attractive cinnamon-coloured down.

Although usually seen stalking about in marsh vegetation, the Limpkin is equally at home in the tree-tops, clambering among the branches with considerable agility. From such elevated perches the birds often utter their loud, rolling call – the sound reverberating far and wide over the saw-grass beds. Unlike the cranes, the Limpkin is non-migratory.

Great White Heron
Ardea herodias occidentalis

Long considered a separate species, the Great White Heron of southern Florida, Cuba and the coast of the Yucatán Peninsula in Mexico has recently been determined to be merely a form of the more widespread North American Great Blue Heron (p64). Many species of heron exhibit colour phases in which some individuals are grey, brown or patterned in one way or another, while others are completely white. Birds of these types interbreed freely. Their offspring are of one phase or the other; rarely intermediate.

In the case of the Great White Heron, the incidence of white individuals is so high that only recently has the true relationship of these birds been discovered. In most respects the white birds are very like their blue counterparts. They are large herons which feed in the brackish coastal waters consuming large quantities of crustaceans, insects and salt-water fishes.

While the typical Great Blue Heron is sometimes migratory, the white birds are mainly sedentary, although like other herons they disperse after the nesting season, the young birds especially turning up miles to the north in peninsular Florida.

Breeding may occur at any time of year, but is concentrated during the late autumn. The birds nest singly or in small groups, and vigorously defend their nesting territories not only against other Great Whites, but, as might be expected, against Great Blues as well. At other times of the year each bird defends an individual feeding territory, from which both white and typical birds are excluded.

Everglade Kite
Rostrhamus sociabilis 18in
*Its fate is tied to that of
the colourful Pomacea snail*

Endangered species: 1

Everglade Kite
Rostrhamus sociabilis

Everglade Kite
Rostrhamus sociabilis

A number of birds that are primarily species of the American tropics are present also in southern Florida, isolated by hundreds of miles from the nearest populations of their species. Such a bird is the Everglade Kite, whose North American population has been at a precariously low level for many years. Although Everglade Kites, also known as Snail Kites, are found from Mexico to Argentina and are abundant in some parts of their range, the North American population was once thought to be as low as four birds.

Like many endangered species, the kites are highly specialized, and, therefore, sensitive to every disturbance in their ecology. In the case of the Everglade Kite the problem is diet: it feeds almost entirely on large, colourful snails, and in some areas swamp-drainage has robbed the bird of its sole source of food.

Bald Eagle
Haliaeetus leucocephalus

The majestic Bald Eagle, national bird of the United States, was once an abundant species in the flat pinelands of Florida, feeding along the miles of estuaries and channels and building its great nests of sticks in the tall pines. Today this population is sadly diminished due to the contamination of the environment by pesticides. High levels of chlorinated hydrocarbons in the system have drastically reduced the birds' ability to reproduce. Only in remote parts of Alaska are Bald Eagles present in anything like their former numbers.

Although more closely related to the Grey Sea Eagle, *H.albicilla*, of the northern parts of the Old World, the Bald Eagle looks more like the African Fish Eagle (p156). This species, like the Bald Eagle, is a conspicuous and attractive inhabitant of estuaries and river edges, where it feeds principally on fish.

Swallow-tailed Kite
Elanoides forficatus

The Swallow-tailed Kite is perhaps the most aerial of all birds of prey, as it not only captures its food – mainly flying insects – on the wing, but also drinks while flying, skimming low over the water without pause. The birds even gather nesting material in flight, snapping dry twigs from the tops of trees as they pass. These graceful birds are highly sociable and are often seen in large flocks.

Swallow-tails nest in loosely associated groups, and when one nest is molested – as by a Fish Crow in search of eggs – neighbouring pairs join in the attack on the intruder.

Like the Everglade Kite (this page), this species is widespread in the American tropics, with a dwindling population in North America. Once breeding as far north as Minnesota, the Swallow-tailed Kite is now confined to southern river-bottom swampland.

In these relatively small areas there are rarely enough birds for a breeding colony, but the kites still build their small, neat nests high in the trees and raise two or three young. After the breeding season the North American birds migrate southwards to winter in the range of their South American relatives.

Endangered species: 2

Bald Eagle
Haliaeetus leucocephalus

Bald Eagle
Haliaeetus leucocephalus 30in
*Brought perilously close to
extinction by pesticides in
the Everglade food chain*

Swallow-tailed Kite
Elanoides forficatus 24in
*The most aerial of all
birds of prey*

Endangered species: 3

Swallow-tailed Kite
Elanoides forficatus

Salt Marshes and Estuaries

The action of the surf along the Atlantic coast has created a series of long, sandy islands which parallel the coastline. In quiet, sheltered waters behind these "barrier beaches", thick deposits of silt and decaying plant matter have accumulated, and from them sprout dense clusters of salt-marsh grasses. On the inland side of these marshes, incoming streams produce conditions not unlike those of fresh-water marshes. Farther out the water is more saline. Unlike nearby sandy beaches, the marshes, interlaced with warm, shallow estuaries and tidal channels, support a rich and varied community of organisms in which birds play an important part. Many are species, usually found in fresh-water marshes, which have adapted to the saline environment and tidal fluctuations. Red-winged Blackbirds, abundant in inland marshes, breed alongside Seaside Sparrows, which are restricted to these salt-marshes. Rails, ducks and sandpipers breed along the waterways. Clamorous colonies of Laughing Gulls build their shallow nests in remote and protected parts of the marsh. Herons, breeding in nearby groves of trees, search for fish and crabs in the shallow waters. There is a wealth of bird-life. But, as happens in wetland habitats throughout the world, many of the marshes have been drained and filled, and the day may not be far away when one will no longer be able to see the birds, nor indeed the wild plants and insects, of this intricate and interesting community.

Clapper Rail
Rallus longirostris 15in
*Secretive resident of the
salt Spartina marshes*

Seaside Sparrow
Ammospiza maritima 6in
*A slightly longer bill reflects
this sparrow's dietary preference*

Long-billed Marsh Wren
Telmatodytes palustris 5in
*The male's frantic nest building
is purely for effect*

Clapper Rail
Rallus longirostris

In the wide meadows of *Spartina* lining the estuaries of the east coast, the Clapper Rail is a familiar and common bird, though not so abundant as it was before the days of uncontrolled hunting. This species is confined to brackish and salt marshes, while the similar King Rail, *R.elegans*, is a bird of fresh-water marshes. The two may breed in the same coastal marsh, with the King Rail keeping to the inland edge where salinity is low. Occasionally, in zones of intermediate salinity, the two rails hybridize.

Secretive, like other rails, the Clapper conceals its nest in a clump of green marsh grass, often with a protective canopy of grass stems overhead. About a dozen spotted eggs are laid. Many different kinds of food are taken, including fiddler crabs and other crustaceans, small fish, snails, insects and seeds.

Seaside Sparrow
Ammospiza maritima

The modestly plumaged Seaside Sparrow is another common inhabitant of the salt meadows, usually favouring the ranker growth of *Spartina* along the edges of tidal channels and pools.

The bird itself is rather shy: if flushed from the marsh grass it flies quickly off and drops out of sight again. Seaside Sparrows are easiest to see early on warm spring mornings, when the newly arrived males advertise their territories by singing from clumps of grass or marsh elder.

The nest is concealed in a thick stand of *Spartina* or low in a marsh elder, and holds four or five spotted eggs. This species is more insectivorous than most sparrows, its less conical, more elongated bill perhaps reflecting this difference in diet.

The Seaside Sparrow is restricted to the narrow zone of salt-marsh extending from Cape Cod to southern Texas and, within this range, a number of races are recognized.

Long-billed Marsh Wren
Telmatodytes palustris

In winter, the spherical nests of the Long-billed Marsh Wren are found in great abundance in dense stands of *Phragmites* reeds. It is easy to overestimate the size of the summer population from these nests for the male Marsh Wren builds many dummy nests before the females arrive on the scene and build the actual breeding nests.

Male Marsh Wrens are highly territorial and in summer spend much time singing and displaying. They are frequently polygamous, each male having two or three mates on an enlarged territory. Four or five young are raised in each brood, and the birds usually nest twice. The male takes no part in incubation or feeding the young in the nest, but once the brood leaves the nest he feeds them while the female begins the second nesting.

Marsh Wrens are largely insectivorous, but are known for the habit – shared with other wrens – of piercing the eggs of other birds to drink the contents. Often this is detrimental to the nesting success of other species, causing heavy losses in Redwinged Blackbirds, rails and bitterns.

Sand and Shingle

Unlike the rocky coasts, the broad and inviting beaches stretching from Cape Cod along the Atlantic and Gulf of Mexico shorelines into Mexico provide suitable habitats for only a few kinds of birds. The smooth bottom of shifting sand supports a much smaller variety of marine organisms, many of which escape capture by burrowing. On land, the flat sandbars, and gravel banks, whose uniformity is broken only here and there by clumps of beach grass, offer an environment in which few birds can nest. Chief among them are terns and skimmers, which generally nest in large colonies on isolated spits and bars, protected by water from mammalian predators, and which subsist largely on small minnows, an important component of marine life in this environment. Suitable nesting sites are relatively scarce, particularly along the Atlantic coast, and it is not uncommon to find several species of terns, as well as skimmers, nesting in the same crowded colony. Scattered here and there along the beaches are nesting pairs of small plovers, including the Piping Plover and the Kent (or Snowy) Plover. These birds subsist on the insects and small crustaceans that may be found in the sand. Few other birds inhabit these sandy and pebbly stretches during the height of the breeding season, but during the migration the beaches are crowded with flocks of shorebirds, busily probing the sand along the line of breaking surf before continuing their journeys southwards.

Gull-billed Tern
Gelochelidon nilotica

The Gull-billed Tern has been made a refugee from its preferred salt-marsh habitat by the reclamation of coastal salt meadows, and now nests, along with other terns, on the shoreline. Gull-bill nests are usually found scattered among mixed colonies of terns, but the occasional colony composed exclusively of Gull-bills does occur. Different feeding habits prevent destructive competition with cohabitants like the Royal Tern, *Thalasseus maximus*, and the Caspian Tern, *Hydroprogne caspia*. These other tern species rely on a diet of small fish, caught by hovering over the water and then diving after minnows as they flit about near the surface. Gull-bills feed largely on insects, which they take from among marsh vegetation, or on the wing.

Another victim of the nineteenth-century passion for feathers, the Gull-billed Tern has not recovered from the severe depletion in numbers as well as the other tern species and it is still not common on the east coast.

Black Skimmer
Rynchops nigra

Along the beaches from Long Island south to Argentina, and on the great rivers of the Amazon Basin, flocks of skimmers are seen flying close to the surface, their elongated lower mandibles slicing through the water like knives. The instant the lower mandible of one of the birds strikes a small minnow, the upper mandible snaps down and a capture is made. Called the "cutta-water" by the people of Guyana, the Black Skimmer can, by this unusual method of feeding, compete successfully for food with the many species of tern with which it shares the shallow coastal waters.

In most respects skimmers resemble the closely related terns. Like them the Skimmer is a colonial nester, usually choosing a broad, level expanse of sand as a nest site. The newly hatched chicks have a lower mandible of normal length, enabling them to pick up food brought back by the adults and regurgitated on to the ground.

Gull-billed Tern
Gelochelidon nilotica   14½in
Forced on to the shore by marshland reclamation

Caspian Tern
Hydroprogne caspia   21in
One of the most aggressive of the tern species

Royal Tern
Thalasseus maximus   19in
Unlike many terns, the Royal cares for its young for several months after hatching

Black Skimmer
Rynchops nigra   18in
Its bill cleaves the water in a wave-skimming hunting flight

The Northern Cliffs

North America's northern cliffs stretch north from Cape Cod to Greenland on the Atlantic, and along the shores of the Arctic Ocean to its meeting with the Pacific. In summer, the fissures and ledges of the cliffs on the east coast overflow with enormous numbers of breeding birds. A multitude of gulls, the larger auks, kittiwakes, cormorants and gannets – species whose breeding grounds spread to the coastal cliffs of western Europe – fill every available breeding space on the rock face. Although enormous colonies are found on the Arctic cliffs, they contain fewer species. These extreme northern coasts are, during the breeding season, the almost exclusive preserve of Little Auk, Ivory and Glaucous gulls. Farther south these species are replaced by Razorbills, Kittiwakes and larger guillemots.

For their food the sea-birds plunder the northern seas and Newfoundland banks, whose cold waters harbour a wealth of marine life. In winter, the Arctic species move only as far as the edge of the pack ice, while the more southerly species feed farther out to sea.

Two species of falcon are also to be found breeding on the ocean cliffs, the Gyrfalcon of the high Arctic and the Peregrine farther south, and although these birds feed almost exclusively on their sea-bird neighbours, they make little impression on their vast numbers.

Right: Little Auks nesting among boulders; Greenland

Razorbill
Alca torda 16in
Slowly recovering from years of exploitation

Black Guillemot
Cepphus grylle 13in
Free from the nest-site pressures suffered by most of its relatives

Brünnich's Guillemot
Uria lomvia 16in
Often nests shoulder to shoulder with the related Common Guillemot

Fulmar
Fulmarus glacialis 18in
Wheeling hoards follow
the fishing fleets

Gyrfalcon
Falco rusticolus 20in
Prey species are taken from
behind after a spectacular chase

Juvenile plumage

Mature adult plumage

Glaucous Gull
Larus hyperboreus 28in
Voracious predator and scavenger
of the high Arctic colonies

Razorbill
Alca torda

The Razorbill is the largest living auk and a surviving relative of the flightless Great Auk, *Pinguinus impennis*, which became extinct during the last century. For many years the Razorbill was killed for its feathers, and by fishermen for use as bait, and the species was sadly depleted. Now protected, the bird is making a comeback and has recently re-established itself on the coast of Maine.

The birds nest on cliffs, often in guillemot colonies, or in small groups on boulder-strewn shores. An incubating bird does not adopt the upright penguin-like posture of the guillemots but crouches low over the egg, which, like the egg of many cliff nesters, is tapered to prevent it from rolling from the narrow, rocky ledge.

The young bird is fed by both parents and remains on the ledge until nearly full grown, though still unable to fly. It is then coaxed to the sea by the adult birds and, by following their example, soon learns to feed on shrimps and small fish by diving and swimming swiftly under water.

Black Guillemot
Cepphus grylle

The slender-billed Black Guillemot breeds on both coasts of the Atlantic and on the rocky shores of the Arctic Ocean. It is replaced, in the eastern Pacific, by the Pigeon Guillemot, *C.columba*, and in Japan by the Japanese Guillemot, *C.carbo*.

During the warmer months, the birds feed in the shallow coastal waters, taking Red Rock Eels from beneath the rocks of the sea-bed. In winter, the majority remain close to the breeding grounds or move out to sea.

The guillemots favour rocky talus slopes and clay banks, concealing their eggs in natural crevices or occasionally excavating their own nest-holes. Unlike the larger guillemots, or murres, they are not colonial in habit – possibly because, unlike the cliff-nesters, they have no difficulty in finding suitable nesting sites. The two attractively spotted eggs are laid either on the bare rock or on a flat bed of small pebbles and shells.

Brünnich's Guillemot
Uria lomvia

Brünnich's Guillemot, and the closely related Common Guillemot, *U.aalge*, are large auks that breed together in huge colonies, or "loomeries", on sea cliffs and stacks in the Arctic, North Atlantic and North Pacific Oceans. No attempt is made to build a nest and the single egg is laid on the bare rock ledge – the adult incubating in an upright posture. Although the two species often occur together, the Common Guillemot favours flatter surfaces and nesting colonies are partly segregated. In the high Arctic, where Brünnich's Guillemot occurs alone, the birds will utilize every available space, but elsewhere competition is fierce, though once established the birds in a colony are tolerant of their neighbours.

Competition for nest sites is probably the most important limiting factor on the population, for the sea provides an almost limitless supply of food and the species have no need to compete for their staple diet of molluscs, crustaceans and fish.

Gyrfalcon
Falco rusticolus

The largest and most magnificent of the falcons, the Gyrfalcon occurs throughout the Arctic, ranging widely over the tundra but nearly always resorting to coastal cliffs in the breeding season. It generally uses the abandoned nest of a Raven or Rough-legged Hawk, and the clutch of four large eggs is incubated almost without a break to protect the eggs from the severe cold. The male provides food for the brooding female, and for the young until they are fully fledged, but once the chicks are able to survive without the female's body heat, both parents hunt.

The Gyrfalcon's prey is invariably taken after a chase; very rarely will it strike at a bird from above. Since this predator depends on bird prey rather than on lemmings, it does not suffer from the periodic lemming "crashes" that so badly affect some of the Arctic raptors. However, should ptarmigan, a favourite and important prey species, be scarce, the Gyrfalcon may not breed.

Fulmar
Fulmarus glacialis

The Fulmar is a member of a large family, including the shearwaters, fulmars and petrels, all of which are characterized by their external nostrils, situated in a horny sheath lying along the top of the upper mandible. This same bill is a marked feature of the Giant, and Wilson's, Petrels, illustrated on page 222.

The majority of these birds are shy and timid, only visiting their nest burrows under cover of darkness, but the Fulmar is a bold and aggressive bird well able to defend itself, and its eggs, against predatory gulls and skuas. Fulmar colonies in the Arctic, nesting on cliffs and the flat tops of uninhabited islands, are estimated to number many hundreds of thousands of birds.

The Fulmar has increased in recent years around the shores of Britain; the birds, like their American counterparts, being attracted to the rich source of food provided by the North Atlantic fishing fleets.

Glaucous Gull
Larus hyperboreus

This large, powerful gull is known to most observers only as a rare winter visitor, for the birds nest far to the north on the cliffs and islands of the Arctic and North Atlantic Oceans.

Here the birds nest in huge colonies, building their shallow platform nests of seaweed, grass and moss on the most inaccessible ledges. Sometimes they will nest on small rocky islands in pools in the coastal tundra. Three eggs make up the usual clutch and, though the male does share the incubation, the female spends the greater part of her time on the nest while the male stands guard nearby. The young apparently winter farther south than the adult birds and, in coastal cities in North America, immature birds in their mottled brown and white plumage, far outnumber the mature gulls.

The Glaucous Gull is a voracious predator, taking a wide variety of prey including small mammals and the eggs and young of other cliff nesters, in addition to marine creatures and any available carrion.

The Pacific Coast

Along the entire Pacific coast, from sub-tropical Baja California in the south to Alaska and the Aleutian Island chain on the Arctic fringes, the shore is marked by abrupt cliffs or rugged boulder-strewn slopes. This imposing topography is a result of the ceaseless action of the surf wearing away at the land to form great seaward-facing escarpments. Watching the waves dashing against the rocks, it is easy to imagine that this environment is as hostile to birds as it is to man; this, however, is not the case. The warm Alaska and colder California currents running north and south along the coast create turbulent upwellings which draw a wealth of nutrients from the sea-bed. These nutrients are the first link in an aquatic food chain of which the fish-eating birds are the beneficiaries. These sea-bed minerals provide some of the basic food materials for plankton, the main food source for higher marine organisms.

The varied features of the shore-line itself, full of small recesses and coves, provides suitable habitat for an impressive selection of marine invertebrates and fishes which provide an abundant supply of food for birds. The nature of the coast also ensures that there is a great diversity of nesting sites among boulders, on cliff ledges and in caves, for a great number and variety of birds. Heading the list are the 16 species of auk which breed on the west coast of the Nearctic. Of these, 13 species are peculiar to the North Pacific and, where their breeding ranges overlap, the many members of this family neatly divide the nesting sites between them. Also present in large numbers are various species of cormorant, storm petrel and gull.

The rich marine life of these waters varies little with the seasons, and few of these birds are migratory; they merely move farther out to sea at the onset of colder weather. They are joined in winter by large numbers of migratory birds that have made the journey from their Arctic breeding grounds to take advantage of the abundance of food. Among these migrants are countless diving-ducks, mostly eiders and scoters, which stay at sea, while on shore oystercatchers, plovers and sandpipers forage among the rocks and seaweed.
Right: Guillemot colony, St. Paul's Rock, Bering Sea

Rhinoceros Auklet
Cerorhinca monocerata 15in
The characteristic plumes and "horn" are shed in winter

Tufted Puffin
Lunda cirrhata 15in
The golden plumes are important recognition features

Ancient Murrelet
Synthliborhamphus antiquum 10in
A quickening pace of life marks the climax of the breeding season

Rhinoceros Auklet
Cerorhinca monocerata

In winter the Rhinoceros Auklet loses not only the white head plumes, but also the odd, knob-like growth on the bill that gives it its name. This auklet is one of the most abundant and widespread of the family and nests along the North American coast from Alaska to Washington.

This species nests in burrows on wooded islands, and has been known to dig tunnels as long as 20 feet. Returning from the sea, the birds often land in the undergrowth some distance away and make their way to the nest on foot through the concealing vegetation. Both sexes incubate the single egg.

Unlike the Tufted Puffin (this page), the Rhinoceros Auklet is little in evidence at the colony during the day, most visits to the nest taking place under cover of darkness. The year's young desert the colony during a two-week exodus period.

Ancient Murrelet
Synthliborhamphus antiquum

The Ancient Murrelet breeds from Alaska south to Washington, generally nesting on rocky islands. But, while its neighbours dig deep burrows, the Ancient Murrelet either digs a very short one or merely conceals its two eggs under a log or in a crevice in the rocks.

Nesting is colonial and all of the nests in a single colony are at roughly the same stage in the cycle. The tempo of the colony changes, therefore, as the birds cease incubating and begin feeding the offspring – streaming back and forth from the sea with food for the young.

On several nights late in the season, adults gather on the water and utter a chorus of musical chirps, encouraging the young to come down to the sea. Soon there are stirrings in the brush, and hordes of young murrelets pour down the shore to plunge into the water and join their parents.

Tufted Puffin
Lunda cirrhata

The two curling tufts of golden feathers which give the Tufted Puffin its name, with the brightly coloured plates that cover the bill in the breeding season, are important in displays that serve not only in communication between members of this species, but also help the birds recognize others of their own species, thereby avoiding hybridization.

On the grass-covered islands where these delightful birds nest, they dig tunnels up to six feet long, ending in a small chamber where the single egg is laid. The young remain in the nest until feathered but not yet able to fly, when they leave to fend for themselves on the open water.

Brandt's Cormorant
Phalacrocorax penicillatus

Like the European Shag, *P. aristotelis*, Brandt's Cormorant is exclusively marine, breeding along the Pacific coast from British Columbia to Baja California. Its neighbour is the Pelagic Cormorant, *P. pelagicus*, and the two species divide the available habitat between them. The Pelagic Cormorant is confined to narrow ledges on steep cliffs, while the larger bird breeds on the flatter surfaces of islands and promontories.

On its guano-covered breeding site Brandt's Cormorant builds a shallow nest of seaweed and eelgrass and lays four white eggs. The young, born naked and helpless, soon acquire a coat of brownish down, and are fed by both parents, who arrive at the nest with their gullets crammed with small fish.

In these relatively inaccessible breeding places the cormorants are safe from most predators, but gulls may take a heavy toll of the eggs. Sometimes entire colonies are wiped out by these voracious predators, but the birds return.

Brandt's Cormorant
Phalacrocorax penicillatus 34in
Nest-site segregation helps to reduce competition

Auks of the Pacific seaboard

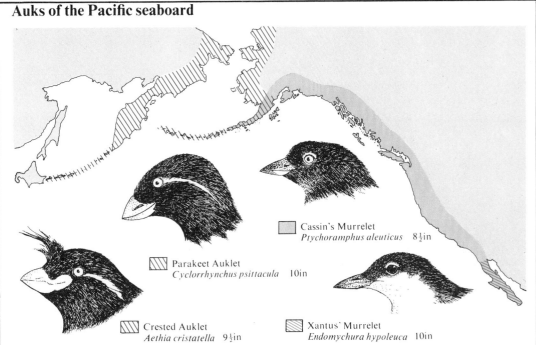

Parakeet Auklet
Cyclorrhynchus psittacula 10in

Crested Auklet
Aethia cristatella 9½in

Cassin's Murrelet
Ptychoramphus aleuticus 8½in

Xantus' Murrelet
Endomychura hypoleuca 10in

The North Pacific Ocean is the headquarters of the auk family, which includes the auks, guillemots, puffins and auklets. No less than 18 of the 22 auk species breed on its rocky shores, and of the six species which breed in the North Atlantic, two are also Pacific residents. Although the reasons for this situation are unclear, seizure of the whole Atlantic coast in the ice blanket during periods of glaciation may explain this concentration of species on Pacific shores, though some parts of the west coast, far to the south of the ice, would still have provided suitable breeding sites. This unevenness of distribution within a family creates a survival problem. All the alcids are stout, short-winged diving birds, that use their wings for propulsion under water, and are dependent on the sea for food. Despite basic similarities of form and habit, the Pacific auks have evolved several ways of avoiding competition with one another for food and nesting sites, the two vital resources of the environment. They come in all sizes from the diminutive Least Auklet which is only six inches long, to the three times larger guillemots, with a variety of bill shapes and sizes to match. These physical differences, and the fact that the birds hunt at various depths and in different parts of the shallow coastal seas, enable them to exploit a wide range of food sources. Their nesting habits are even more diverse. Some, like the larger guillemots, nest in crowded colonies on cliffs, while others are burrowing species, nesting, like the Tufted Puffin, on grassy islands or choosing sites high in the coastal mountain ranges, or in crevices among wave-lashed boulders. Only by this kind of diversity in their exploitation of habitat resources can the 18 auks species share the Pacific coast without crowding each other out of feeding grounds or nesting sites.

The City: Land of Opportunity

European cities developed gradually over many centuries, and the birds which inhabit them were able to adapt to the urban environment by degrees. By contrast, most North American cities sprang up comparatively rapidly, giving birds little chance to adjust to the new conditions. Nevertheless, American cities are not ornithological deserts. A surprising number of species now breed readily in city parks; others visit towns and cities during the non-breeding season. The three most important birds in American cities are the Rock Dove, the Starling and the House Sparrow, all introduced from Europe, already adapted to urban survival. They have been joined by many North American species able to make the necessary adjustment, and today the list of urban species is long. Some have even succeeded in establishing themselves in the centre of the largest cities. Aside from large numbers of people, to whom many species can readily adapt, the most serious obstacle to colonizing cities is probably the shortage of insects. Seed-eating birds like the House Finch have become common in the heart of New York City, but only the largest parks support such insectivorous birds as vireos and warblers. Perhaps the most dramatic urban adaptation has been that of several species of gulls which winter in cities and feed on garbage. As gulls adapted to this new winter food supply their numbers greatly increased.

Right: The urban habitat; New York City

Great Horned Owl
Bubo virginianus

Unlike the closely related Eagle Owl *B.bubo*, of Eurasia, the Great Horned Owl is tolerant of man, occasionally nesting in city parks, and, while the Eagle Owl has become rare in densely populated parts of Europe, the deep hooting of the Horned Owl is still heard within a few miles of New York.

The birds begin breeding early in the year, often using the abandoned nest of a crow or hawk, or else a hollow tree or rocky ledge. They are fierce in defence of the nest and more than one visitor to a nest has been knocked out of a tree or badly clawed. They feed on a variety of mammals and birds, even preying on skunks and the smaller owl species.

The Great Horned Owl occurs all the way from Alaska and northern Canada south to Tierra del Fuego.

Purple Martin
Progne subis

The Purple Martin is the North American representative of a group of species widespread in tropical America. These large swallows are popular because of their usefulness in feeding on mosquitoes and many other flying insects. In parts of the country people encourage them to breed by putting up nest-boxes. The species is colonial and the natural nest site is usually in a dead tree with ample woodpecker holes.

This fact was recognized long ago by the Indians of the southeastern states, who used to hang out hollow gourds – prototypes of today's elaborate martin houses. Martins must compete with other birds for these nest sites and the birds often find themselves ousted by introduced Starlings and House Sparrows.

Purple Martin
Progne subis 8in
A long history of amicable association with man

Great Horned Owl
Bubo virginianus 22in
Far more adaptable than its European relative

Blue Jay
Cyanocitta cristata

Blue Jay
Cyanocitta cristata 12in
*Its food-storing habits are
a boon to seed dispersal*

The Blue Jay is another of the most familiar birds of North America, although it is unpopular on account of its predatory habits. Blue Jays often rob the nests of other birds, and around feeding stations they are aggressive and domineering, driving away birds of other species. Also, these birds are well known for their habit of mobbing hawks and owls.

The Blue Jay is a member of a distinctive group of New World species occurring not only throughout North America, but also in the tropical and sub-tropical parts of the Western Hemisphere. It resembles the European Jays (p109) in being partial to acorns. On cool days in October the oak woods resound with the calls of Blue Jays busily gathering acorns and storing them in leaf litter or just beneath the surface of the soil. Often the birds fail to return to retrieve the acorns and eventually they take root; one of many cases where a food-storing habit actively helps seed dispersal.

Common in the less settled districts, the species is equally numerous in towns and cities and nests readily in city parks – living partly on table scraps and hand-outs. The bulky nest of twigs and sticks is placed up to 50 feet above ground. The young birds resemble the adults, but have shorter crests and less well-defined black breast bands.

Mockingbird
Mimus polyglottos

The characteristic and popular bird of the American South is the modestly coloured Mockingbird. An accomplished singer and excellent mimic, the Mockingbird has been compared favourably to the European Nightingale, *Luscinia megarhynchos*. Each of these birds evokes its own surroundings – in the case of the Mockingbird, the graceful gardens and plantations, and the lush countryside of the deep south.

In recent years the species has extended its range beyond the Mason-Dixon Line, and it is now numerous in the region around New York City, where its song seems strangely out of place. The bird often sings on warm spring nights, especially under a bright moon. At such times its song is remarkably beautiful, and includes accurate imitations of the songs of many other species. This talent for mimicry may have something to do with the fact that the Mockingbird is strongly territorial, driving out not only birds of its own species but those of other species, too.

Although the birds defend a territory all the year round they are especially aggressive in the breeding season, when the nest of leaves and twigs is concealed in dense shrubbery. Four or five eggs are normal. The young spend about two weeks in the nest, and when they leave the alarm call of the adults is heard for several days

American Robin
Turdus migratorius

This well-known species is not a true robin, in that it has no close kinship with the familiar Robin, *Erithacus rubecula*, of Europe. The North American bird is a large thrush, whose closest relatives are birds like the European Blackbird, *T.merula*, and Mistlethrush, *T.viscivorus*. The American Robin is so called because early colonists from the British Isles, noting the red breast, gave it the name of the familiar bird of their homeland.

Like its cousins in other parts of the world, the American Robin has adapted readily to the presence of man, nesting in yards and feeding tamely on lawns. In the wilder parts of its range, however, it retains the elusive habits characteristic of a forest bird.

The Robin builds itself a substantial cup-shaped nest of mud lined with grasses, in which four or five eggs are laid. These aggressive and successful birds produce up to three broods in a season. In late summer, when the population is at its peak, they feed heavily on fruit and insects,

Mockingbird
Mimus polyglottos 10½in
*One of America's most
accomplished mimics*

American Robin
Turdus migratorius 10in
*The misnomer dates back to
the colonization of America*

South America
The Neotropical Realm

Except for the intermittent formation and inundation of the fragile Panamanian land-bridge, South America has remained isolated throughout the greater part of its history and has developed an avifauna that reflects both the isolation and the periodic influxes of migrant species from the north. Its geography is a catalogue of superlatives. The rocky spine of the Andes reaches from north of the Equator almost to Antarctica; in the north, tropical forests of unequalled size and luxuriance clothe the heart of the continent, fed by the greatest of all river systems – the Amazon. Vast open grassland regions flank the forests, *llanos* in the north and *pampas* to the south of the Amazon Basin, and, farther south still, the continent tapers to a narrow ice-clad promontory surrounded by the cold waters of the southern oceans.

A wealth of benign lowland habitats supports the world's richest and most varied avifauna. Some 3,000 species are indigenous to the region, a total unequalled on any other continent, and every year the Neotropical realm is host to millions of visitors retreating from the cold winter of the Northern Hemisphere.

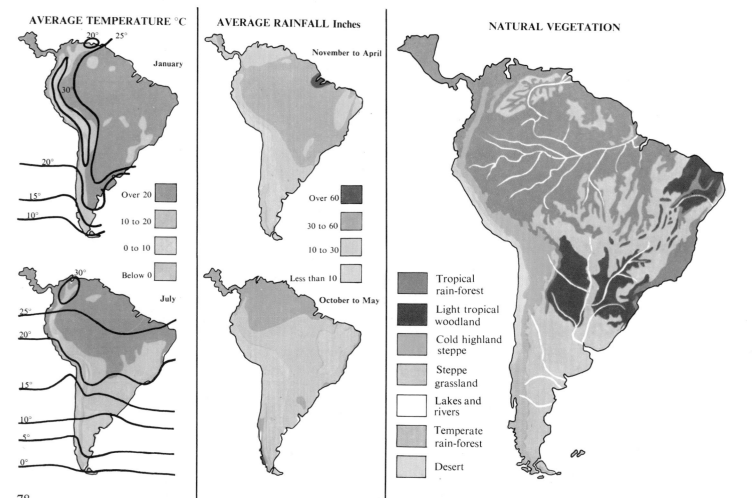

AVERAGE TEMPERATURE °C

January

July

Over 20

10 to 20

0 to 10

Below 0

AVERAGE RAINFALL Inches

November to April

October to May

Over 60

30 to 60

10 to 30

Less than 10

NATURAL VEGETATION

Tropical rain-forest

Light tropical woodland

Cold highland steppe

Steppe grassland

Lakes and rivers

Temperate rain-forest

Desert

BIRDS ILLUSTRATED

1 Scarlet Ibis
  Eudocimus ruber

2 Crimson Topaz Hummingbird
  Topaza pella

3 Long-tailed Manakin
  Chiroxiphia linearis

4 Toco Toucan
  Ramphastos toco

5 Blue-and-yellow Macaw
  Ara ararauna

6 Guanay Cormorant
  Phalacrocorax bougainvillii

7 Buffy-browed Guan
  Penelope superciliaris

8 Andean Condor
  Vultur gryphus

9 Frilled Coquette Hummingbird
  Lophornis delattrei

10 Greater Rhea
   Rhea americana

11 Magellanic Penguin
   Spheniscus magellanicus

Light Tropical Woodland

Forming an intermediate zone between the dense tropical rain-forest and the arid wastes of desert and scrub, the light tropical woodlands are characteristic of areas with poor soils and a prolonged dry season. The trees are generally much smaller than those of the rain-forest; the largest, with massive trunks, tending to spread their branches wide instead of soaring upward. Many trees and shrubs, including the abundant short, stout palms, are thorny and the vegetation is typically festooned with straggling shrubbery and slender vines making an impenetrable tangled mass.

Verdant in the rainy season – often a time of frequent deluges – these woods may become almost leafless in the dry season when many of the trees flower – bursting into a colourful profusion of white, yellow, pink and lavender blossom. As the season advances, seedpods burst under the blazing sun and drought-resistant epiphytes proliferate on leafless boughs, which become fantastically draped with long grey streamers of "Spanish moss", *Tillandsia usneoides*.

Although they are easier to observe, and therefore seem more abundant, far fewer birds are found here than in the food-rich rain-forest. Only hardy, catholic feeders can accommodate to a life in these regions of prolonged drought and sparse food supply, and large hunting and scavenging birds such as hawks, caracaras, chachalacas and parrots are the most common species.

Rufous-vented Chachalaca
Ortalis ruficauda 21in
An adaptable member of a seriously threatened family

Streaked-headed Woodcreeper
Lepidocolaptes souleyetii 8in
Stiffened tail-feathers give the bird extra support while climbing

Olivaceous Piculet
Picumnus olivaceus 3½in
One of the most agile of the pygmy woodpeckers

Rufous-vented Chachalaca
Ortalis ruficauda

The loud harsh cries of the Rufous-vented Chachalaca are heard throughout South America's woodlands. Stirring choruses surge back and forth as group after group joins in the cry "guacharaca – guacharaca" – the bird's Venezuelan name.

Chachalacas live in loose flocks, feeding on fruits, tender leaves and shoots which they gather as they walk gracefully among high, thin branches. The bulky, open nest of twigs, grass and sometimes green leaves is usually placed in a bush, and in it the female alone incubates her three white, unusually rough-shelled eggs.

Although many members of the guan family face extinction through hunting and the destruction of their rain-forest habitats, the chachalaca, who thrives in scrub and light woodland, may yet survive, even in agricultural regions, if prompt measures are taken to ensure its protection.

Streaked-headed Woodcreeper
Lepidocolaptes souleyetii

Insects, spiders and occasional small lizards and frogs form the main diet of the 60 species of woodcreeper inhabiting the mainland of tropical America.

Supporting themselves with the sharp, incurved tips of their stiff tail feathers, the woodcreepers run up the trunks of trees and along branches, prying into crevices and lifting up patches of moss or lichen in search of food. Unlike other species that inhabit the dense forests, the Streaked-headed Woodcreeper favours the forest edge, light woodland and scrub regions.

The male and female call to each other with clear musical trills while foraging, but at nightfall each retires alone into a sheltered tree-hole. During the mating season the birds seek out an obscure cranny into which they carry flakes of stiff bark. The female lays two eggs on this mat of bark fragments and incubates them with some, though rather inconsistent, help from her mate. Both parents feed the young, carrying insects one at a time to the ever-hungry nestlings.

Olivaceous Piculet
Picumnus olivaceus

Scampering about among slender dead branches high in the trees, this agile pygmy woodpecker has (unlike its larger relatives) no need to use its tail as additional support as it probes and digs under the bark for the ants that constitute the bulk of its diet.

In the mating season the male and female work in turn to carve out a neat cavity in the soft wood of a decaying tree or fence post, leaving a smoothly rounded doorway less than an inch in diameter. The female lays her two or three tiny, pure-white eggs on a bed of fine wood-chips at the bottom of the chamber and both sexes share the 14-day incubation.

The nestlings are naked and blind at birth and are fed on the larvae and pupae of ants. The young are able to fly after 24 days, but are led back to the nest each night – the whole family remaining together for several months and moving to a larger cavity if overcrowding becomes a problem.

Master-builders of the woodlands

In response to the mild summer climate and the relatively short breeding season available to them, most temperate-zone birds build simple open cup-nests. By contrast, their tropical relatives, who have a much longer breeding season, are able to build elaborate covered and hanging nests that protect their vulnerable eggs and young from the blazing sun and torrential rains.

Covered nests, supported from below, vary from the neatly woven pockets of the wrens to the massive structures of interlaced twigs built by some of the thornbirds. Pendent nests may be huge, intricately woven pouches suspended high above ground, like those of the New World orioles and their larger relatives the oropendolas. Less beautiful – but probably no less efficient – are the tangled structures built by the American flycatchers, whose short, thick bills are poor instruments for such delicate work as weaving.

The safety of the occupants depends more on inaccessibility than concealment. Tree-snakes have been seen to fall while trying to enter the downward-facing entrances of retort-shaped nests, and many birds build close to a wild wasps' nest for protection. The wasps will attack an intruder but seldom disturb the birds. Yet no bird has discovered an infallible method of protecting its offspring, and even the elaborate thornbirds nests are often plundered.

Rufous-fronted Thornbird
Phacellodomus rufifrons 6½in
Its multi-storey nest is constantly plagued by unwelcome lodgers

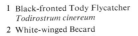

1 Black-fronted Tody Flycatcher
  Todirostrum cinereum

2 White-winged Becard
  Pachyramphus polychopterus

3 Sulphury Flat-bill
  Tolmomyias sulphurescens

4 Bananaquit
  Coereba flaveola

5 Yellow Oriole
  Icterus nigrogularis

6 Great Kiskadee
  Pitangus sulphuratus

7 Rufous-fronted Thornbird
  Phacellodomus rufifrons

Common Potoo
Nyctibius griseus 15in
Distorts its body as an aid to concealment

Rufous-fronted Thornbird
Phacellodomus rufifrons

Throughout the savannas and light woodlands the conspicuous, bulky nests of the Rufous-fronted Thornbird may be seen hanging from slender branches and vines up to 75 feet above the ground.

Varying from 15 inches to, occasionally, seven feet in height, the complex nest of interlaced twigs may contain up to eight individual chambers, each with its own entrance. Only one resident family breeds in the nest, but unrelated, homeless thornbirds may forcibly intrude as lodgers at nightfall. The commodious structures are coveted by a number of other species, some of which – like the Troupial – will forcibly evict the weaker thornbirds and take over the whole nest.

The female adopts one compartment as a brood-chamber and lays three eggs on a bed of vegetation and rubbish – sharing the 17-day incubation with the male. The young leave the nest after three weeks, but are escorted back each night to roost with the parents. Two broods are raised each season, and the family group usually consists of the parents, young chicks and older siblings.

Common Potoo
Nyctibius griseus

The plaintive cry of this strange relative of the nightjars can be heard on any moonlit night in the woodlands of tropical America.

By day the potoo drowses motionless on an elevated perch, but if an intruder approaches, this remarkable bird is able to elongate and flatten its normally short, stout body to such an extent that, with its great yellow eyes closed, it merges almost invisibly into the branch on which it rests.

The female lays her single large egg in a precariously shallow hollow in the top of a tree-stump or in a knot-hole in a branch. Male and female take turns incubating the egg; one sitting by day, the other by night. The egg is left unattended for only an hour or so each night, when both parents leave the nest to forage for flying insects.

The nestling potoo – hatched with a dense covering of white down – remains in the nest for 50 days and is fed each night on pellets of compressed insects. By the time it is half-grown the chick will adopt the cryptic concealment posture whenever it senses approaching danger.

Tropical Rain-forest

More than two and a half million square miles of South America are clothed by the world's largest, yet least-explored rain-forest, the *hylaea amazonica*.

The characteristic features of the rain-forest are constant; an evergreen canopy more than 100 feet high with scattered giants towering above it; a bewildering number of tree species growing in mixed stands; palms soaring aloft to spread their feathered fronds near the canopy; and everywhere, lianas draped in heavy loops and coiled round branches laden with epiphytic orchids, ferns, bromeliads and lichens. The heavier the forest, the more open is the undergrowth of shrubs, small spiny palms and ferns that thrive in the subdued light of the lower levels.

Brilliantly coloured birds like the tanagers, toucans, honeycreepers and macaws throng the well-lighted upper levels, while the dim, shadowy world at ground level is home to a variety of dull-coloured birds, including the ovenbirds, wrens, antbirds and manakins.

The Amazon forest alone supports more than 600 species of birds, many as yet not studied in detail, but sadly this last great wilderness of majestic trees and rich avian life is being broached as bulldozers carve out the track of the Trans-amazonica Highway – disturbing the ecology of the forest and threatening the extinction of hundreds of species.

Right: The light-dappled canopy of the Amazon rain-forest

Tropical rain-forest

▢ Area of tropical forest

Distribution of species

▢ Oilbird
  Steatornis caripensis

▢ Blue and Yellow Macaw
  Ara ararauna

Great Tinamou
Tinamus major

One of the most characteristic sounds of the South American rain-forest is the whirr of wingbeats as a large, stout bird, the Great Tinamou, erupts from the undergrowth and shoots out of sight between the tall well-spaced trunks.

As daylight fades this same bird may be heard to utter a deep cry that echoes through the forest like the notes of a great organ.

The Great Tinamou, a quail-like game-bird, is one of 40 members of the family Tinamidae that inhabit forests, thickets and grasslands from Mexico to Patagonia. Ground-dwelling and solitary, the members of this family lay some of the loveliest of all bird-eggs. Those of the Great Tinamou are a glossy bright blue and, like those of several related species, are laid on the ground to be incubated by the male alone.

Oilbird
Steatornis caripensis

In the total darkness of a forest cave, a persistent chattering chorus may be the only clue to the presence, high in the cave roof, of a wheeling multitude of large dusky-brown birds.

Like bats and some cave-swiftlets, Oilbirds navigate by echolocation, resting by day on ledges high in the cave, then streaming out into the gathering darkness to forage for food. They are superb fliers, "reading" the presence of obstacles from the echoes of their clicking calls. They feed on the single-seeded fruits of forest trees such as palms – plucking the fruit from the tree in mid flight and swallowing it whole.

The young, fed only on oily fruit, soon weigh 50 per cent more than the adults and must lose this excess weight during the three or four months spent in the nest before they learn to fly.

Oilbird
Steatornis caripensis 18in
A nocturnal feeder that navigates by echolocation

Great Tinamou
Tinamus major 18in
The rain-forest equivalent of the pheasant and partridge

Rufous-tailed Jacamar
Galbula ruficauda 9in
An acrobatic hunter with a marked preference for butterflies

Rufous-tailed Jacamar
Galbula ruficauda

The song of the Rufous-tailed Jacamar, long and melodious with ascending trills, is worthy of a true songbird. Reminiscent of a large hummingbird, it is the most widespread and adaptable of the 15 species of jacamar found on the mainland of tropical America.

Either singly or in pairs this species inhabits the more open parts of the rain-forest and the drier woodlands up to 3,000 feet above sea level. Perched on a low, exposed branch, the jacamar turns its head from side to side until it catches sight of a flying insect. Darting swiftly out, it seizes the victim with a snap of its long bill and returns to the perch, where, if the insect is large, the jacamar proceeds to beat it against the branch until the wings break off – a behaviour pattern very like that of some African bee-eaters (see Red-throated Bee-eater illustrated on p157).

Like other jacamars the Rufous-tailed catches many butterflies, including the spectacular tropical swallowtails, in addition to dragon-flies and glittering beetles that abound in the forest vegetation.

The Rufous-tailed Jacamar builds its nest in a burrow driven into an earth bank, a large termite mound or into the mound of clay around the roots of a fallen tree. With bills that seem too delicate for such heavy work, both male and female tunnel into the hard clay – the male often singing to, and feeding his mate as they work.

On the bare floor of the burrow the female lays her two plain white eggs and incubates them herself every night. During the day both parents share the task, alternating at intervals of a few hours, throughout the 19- to 23-day incubation period.

The freshly hatched nestlings are totally blind and, surprisingly, are covered with copious long white down. The parents bring them insects one at a time and, as the young mature, they become very loquacious – repeating calls and little songs as they await the next meal. Although the nest is never cleaned, the young birds' plumage is always fresh when they leave the nest after 25 days to begin their independent life.

Blue-and-yellow Macaw
Ara ararauna

Few families can match the dazzling array of colour displayed by the Psittacidae – the 315-strong family of mainly tropical birds that includes the parrots, macaws, parakeets, cockatoos and lories. The largest and most colourful of the 111 South American species are the 14 macaws found in the dense tropical rain-forests.

Like its relatives, the Blue-and-yellow Macaw flies over the forest canopy either in pairs or in large flocks made up of birds flying in pairs. Occasionally trios are observed, consisting of parents and a mature offspring or a pair accompanied by an interloper in search of a mate. Viewed from above, as from an aircraft, they make an impressive sight – their brilliant blue upper plumage contrasting with the dark green backdrop of the forest. Despite their conspicuous vivid colours the birds also advertise their presence with loud, raucous shrieks.

Macaws feed almost exclusively on the fruits of forest trees and show a preference for the nutritious, oil-rich kernels of many of the hard-shelled species. Thick shell-cases and even the toughest skins are no match for the macaw's powerful bill, which is quite capable of clipping through the strong wire mesh of most bird-cages.

Unfortunately, despite the wide range of the Blue-and-yellow Macaw, no detailed studies have been made of its habits or behaviour. Information is scant, but close observation of related species suggests that it probably nests in holes high in the trees, laying a small clutch of white, smooth-shelled eggs.

Ruddy Quail-dove
Geotrygon montana

Ranging from northern Argentina to Mexico and the West Indies, the Ruddy Quail-dove is one of the most widespread of South America's 45 pigeons.

With the curious head-bobbing gait characteristic of its family, the quail-dove forages over the leaf-littered forest floor in search of seeds and berries. A mated pair will often forage together – calling to each other intermittently with a low mournful cooing cry.

In contrast to the pure-white eggs of most pigeons, those laid by the Ruddy Quail-dove are a soft buff colour, ideally suited to the dim light of the forest, where egg-eating predators abound. The two inconspicuous eggs are laid in a flimsily built nest of coarse twigs and leaves, hidden low in a bush or on a tree stump amid dense foliage.

In common with all pigeons, the female quail-dove incubates the eggs throughout the night and is relieved by her mate at dawn – the male sitting through the day until late afternoon. The 11-day incubation is remarkably short for a pigeon and the young develop very quickly. The newly hatched nestlings are fed individually at first, but soon learn to feed simultaneously – one chick taking the regurgitated food from each side of the parent's bill. Feeds are quickly reduced from 22 per day to three or four sessions lasting about 25 minutes, and the young are able to walk at eight days old and fly well at ten. The camouflaged eggs, short incubation and rapid development of the young are all "survival" features developed over millions of years.

Blue-and-yellow Macaw
Ara ararauna 33in
Most brilliantly coloured of the South American parrots

Ruddy Quail-dove
Geotrygon montana 9in
Special breeding adaptations promote the survival of this ground-nesting dove

Tropical Rain-forest

Most nests in the tropical forests of America contain only two eggs. Clutches of three eggs are less common; clutches of four are rare; and clutches of five or six are quite exceptional, even in birds whose young leave the nest and feed independently within a few days of hatching. Yet many of these birds have close relatives beyond the tropics that lay much larger clutches. What causes this "latitude effect" as it is called?

As one moves away from the Equator, the days of spring and summer, when most birds breed, become longer, and with a longer working day parents can bring more food to their young. This explanation assumes that tropical birds can only adequately feed small broods. One would then expect unaided females to raise fewer young than their neighbours whose mates share the task of feeding the young, and yet they successfully raise just as many.

Evidently the size of the brood has been adjusted by complex evolutionary processes, not to the ability of parents to feed their young, but to the need to replace natural losses. Recent studies show that small birds living in the tropics live very much longer than their relatives in higher latitudes who must undertake long and dangerous migrations every year to avoid the rigours and deprivations of winter and who must therefore raise large broods in order to maintain their numbers.

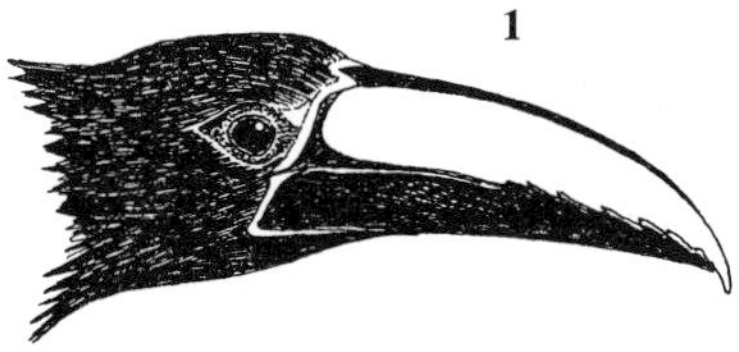

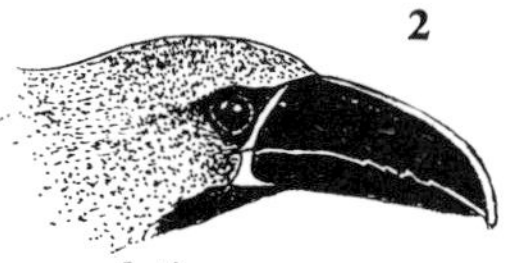

Toucan relatives
1 Black-necked Aracari
Pteroglossus aracari

2 Emerald Toucanet
Aulacorhynchus prasinus

3 Grey-breasted Mountain Toucan
Andigena hypoglauca

Keel-billed Toucan
Ramphastos sulfuratus 15in
Despite its size, the bill is light and capable of delicate manipulation

Bicoloured Antbird
Gymnopithys bicolor 5½in
Hunts in the wake of marching army ants

Golden-collared Manakin
Manacus vitellinus 4in
Gaudy bachelor with an impressive display

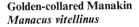

Golden-collared Manakin
Manacus vitellinus

The contrast between the rich and varied colours of the male manakin birds and their dull olive and green female counterparts plays a vitally important role in their breeding behaviour.

As far as is known, manakins never form pairs but in several species the males gather together in "leks", or courtship assemblies, in order to attract the females to mate.

The male Golden-collared Manakin chooses a spot among light undergrowth and, with meticulous care, removes all leaves and litter from a patch of ground between two or more slender upright stems. Above this display "court" he leaps back and forth between the uprights and with each jump makes a loud sharp *snap* with his modified wing-feathers. Several males may display in close proximity without interfering or intruding on each other's "courts".

An interested female will come and join one of the males in his dance – the two birds passing in mid-air as they leap back and forth. If copulation occurs, the female leaves to build a small, open nest, lay her two eggs, incubate them and raise the young all by herself.

The 60 or so species of manakins are all small, stout berry- and insect-eating birds and are found only in tropical America and the nearby offshore islands.

Keel-billed Toucan
Ramphastos sulfuratus

The 43 species of the toucan family (Ramphastidae) inhabit the woodlands of America from Mexico to northern Argentina. Most of them, including the larger toucans, *Ramphastos* sp, and the medium-sized aracaris, *Pteroglossus* sp, inhabit the warm lowland forests but the small green toucanets, *Aulacorhynchus* sp, and the montane *Andigena* species range into the cooler heights of the temperate hill zones.

Their huge, brightly-coloured bills are remarkably light in construction but little is understood of their significance. They may serve as recognition symbols between members of the various species and probably play some part in courtship display. The length of the bill does help the toucan when reaching out for the fruits that form a major part of its diet, but this alone would not account for its size and bright colour. Nor does the bill function as a weapon, although it is used to intimidate smaller birds whose nests the toucan sometimes plunders.

Both parents share the 16-day incubation of their two to four white eggs. The naked, pink-skinned nestlings develop very slowly and do not leave the nest until they are six or seven weeks old.

Bicoloured Antbird
Gymnopithys bicolor

Though they lack the brilliant colours of many tropical species, the 231 members of the antbird family are among the most attractive forest birds – their subtle plumage of black, white, brown, olive and rufous tones fitting them perfectly for a life spent foraging in the dim, twilight interior of the tropical rain-forest.

Antbirds are gregarious by nature and members of several species may gather together in mixed flocks – wandering through the lower levels of the forest in search of food. In any such gathering the Bicoloured Antbird is the most voluble and conspicuous member – its enthusiastic, if hardly musical, song often disclosing the presence of an otherwise quiet and unobtrusive flock. All antbirds live on a diet of insects and other small invertebrates and only very rarely is the diet supplemented with fruit.

The Bicoloured Antbird is one of a small group of species that have developed a highly refined hunting technique. Following in the track of a moving swarm of army ants, they prey on the insects, beetles and other small creatures driven out of the leaf-litter by the passage of the marching column. In common with many other antbirds, the male *G. bicolor* often presents his mate with a particularly choice insect – a behaviour pattern that probably serves to strengthen the pair-bond between the two birds.

The nest is usually built in the hollow, broken-off stump of a fallen palm, rarely more than a few feet above ground level and unobstructed by vegetation. Here, on a pad of leaf-fragments, the female lays the two heavily-marked eggs that are characteristic of all members of the family.

Harpy Eagle
Harpia harpyja

The handsomely barred and crested Harpy Eagle occupies the highest position in the forest food-chain, preying on all other birds and a wide variety of mammals including monkeys, sloths, agoutis, coatimundis and porcupines.

Weighing up to 16 pounds, the Harpy is one of the most powerful of all eagles and, like any large predator, it requires a large territory in which to hunt. Its population density is so low that nests are seldom seen and few have been studied in detail. The huge, untidy construction is usually placed high in the fork of a giant silk-cotton tree projecting above the level of the forest canopy.

A single chick is raised in alternate years and the young eagle is fed by the parents until it is at least nine months old and able to fly well.

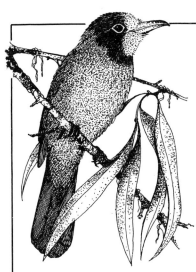

White-fronted Nunbird
Monasa morphoeus 11½in

Aerobatic hunters

The sombre plumage of the White-fronted Nunbird is relieved only by the white facial ruff at the base of its vivid orange-red bill. Like the 31 other species of the tropical American puffbird family, the Nunbird appears to take only animal food – chiefly insects and other small invertebrates with occasional frogs and lizards.

Confined to the warm and humid lowland forests, the White-fronted Nunbird hunts by perching in apparent lethargy until its acute sight detects a suitable target – perhaps a green insect amid green foliage more than 20 yards away. The prey is snatched from its perch in a darting flight that carries the Nunbird back to its own perch without pause.

The Nunbird nests in a long tunnel driven into level or gently sloping ground. The entrance is disguised by a collar of dead leaves and twigs and the nest chamber at the inner end is thickly lined with a carpet of dead leaves. The eggs have never been seen, but are probably white and unmarked as in other closely related species. Up to three nestlings are hatched – blind and completely naked and with prominent callous pads on the heels which are thought to protect the young bird's feet from chaffing against the lining of the nest-chamber.

Each nest is attended by three or four adult birds, the parents and the mature young of the previous brood, but food is seldom taken into the nest. Instead, the adult alights at the entrance to the nest and gives a characteristic call at which the young, even though blind and barely able to move, will grope their way along the five-foot burrow to seize the food from the donor's bill.

Sometimes the nest is found and totally destroyed by a powerfully-clawed mammal such as the tayra, but the attendant adults will continue to bring food for days – plaintively calling at the mouth of the shattered nest.

If all goes well the young fly from the nest when four weeks old, soaring instinctively upwards to perch high in the forest canopy. The young birds soon learn to take their food in a far more spectacular manner that prepares them for adult life. Instead of carrying food to the young, the adult perches up to 100 feet away, holding an insect or lizard in its bill and uttering the feeding call. The young bird swoops from its perch and snatches the food from the parent's bill, without alighting, in a perfect rehearsal of the adult hunting flight.

Harpy Eagle
Harpia harpyja 35in
At the pinnacle of the forest food-chain

Pampas and Llanos

Despite the ravages of modern farming and large-scale cattle ranching, the vast, seemingly endless, expanse of the Argentinian *pampas* remains one of the most impressive sights in this continent of extremes. Alternately parched by drought and flooded by torrential rains, swept by dust-storms in summer and cold gales in winter, the *pampas* is an inhospitable landscape – yet it supports a multitude of birds including the Greater Rhea, the Maguari Stork, the Southern Screamer and the Red-winged Tinamou.

Scarcely less famous are the *llanos* of Venezuela, which are also subject to extremes of climate as the stiflingly hot dry season alternates with the violent tropical thunderstorms of the wet. The *llanos* are less uniformly treeless than the older *pampas* regions and were the first vegetation zones to be called "savanna". The term is now used widely to describe any natural region of grassland diversified by scattered shrubs and deciduous trees growing singly or in open groves.

The savanna regions and the heavier gallery forest of the *caños* and water-courses are also home to many of South America's large and impressive birds. Buff-necked Ibises, Southern Lapwings, Caracaras and Great Black Hawks range the open grasslands while the wetter areas teem with flocks of Black-bellied Tree-ducks and stalking Jabiru.

Below: Scrub grassland of the Patagonian steppe

Least Seedsnipe
Thinocorus rumicivorus 7½in
The tidy hen removes every shell-fragment from the nest to avoid attracting predators

Least Seedsnipe
Thinocorus rumicivorus

The four seedsnipe species of the Neotropical Realm are relatives of the plovers and sandpipers and share with them an erratic, zigzag climbing flight and rasping cry. Confined to South America, but ranging throughout its length, the seedsnipes are partly migratory – flocking down from the bleak Andean heights in Ecuador and moving north from chilly Tierra del Fuego to Argentina as winter sets in.

The Least Seedsnipe is a bird of the open country, preferring dry barren ground which it covers swiftly despite its short legs. It is exclusively vegetarian. Sparsely covered *pampas*, the fleshy plants of semi-desert areas, and the pickings of stubble fields provide the buds and leaves, shoots and seeds on which the bird depends for both solid food and water.

The nest is a shallow ground-scrape amid stunted plants or on completely barren ground and in it the female lays her four eggs – their soft colours camouflaged against the nest lining of vegetation and dry dung. Despite this protection, every time the female leaves the nest during the 26-day incubation she swiftly covers the eggs with the lining materials. This obsession does not end when the eggs hatch. Removing all trace of the broken shells (a habit shared with the sandpipers and other relatives), the female continues to try to cover the active young with grass or dust whenever danger threatens. An adult bird will leave the nest, feigning weakness or an injury such as a damaged wing, in order to distract an approaching predator.

Southern Screamer
Chauna torquata

Well adapted to a life in open wet grasslands and marshes, the Screamer picks its way across floating vegetation on long, slightly webbed toes, feeding exclusively on aquatic plants, grasses and seeds.

This large goose-like bird has a laborious take-off that belies its aerial proficiency. Screamers will circle for hours, barely visible against the sky but easily identified by their strident calls, so well described by the "cha-ha" pronunciation of their American Indian name *cha-ja*. Though flocks combine in deafening chorus all year round, by day or night, grounded or airborne, pairs mate for life, and mated birds perform their own loud, ringing duets which carry for miles.

The three species of screamer are distinguished from all other birds by their pneumatic bones, long sharp spurs on the leading edge of each wing and the layer of tiny air cells underlying the whole skin surface. None of these peculiarities is fully understood, but the air-sacs and light bones may aid their soaring flight.

For all its community singing and gregarious behaviour the Screamer nests in isolation. The nest is a great pile of sticks and aquatic weeds standing a foot above the water of the marsh, or even afloat. A clutch of four to six white eggs is laid and the 42-day incubation is shared by both parents.

Easily tamed if taken from the nest when young, screamers become strongly attached to their "adopted" family and, because of their strident alarm calls, are frequently used as "watch-dogs" for domestic fowl.

Grassland and scrub

Types of grassland

- Grassland
- Savanna
- Deciduous forest and scrub

Llanos

Brazilian highlands

Gran Chaco

Pampas

Crested Caracara
Polyborus plancus 22in
Hunter-scavenger of the open plains

Southern Screamer
Chauna torquata 34in
A goose-like bird with surprising aerial skills

Crested Caracara
Polyborus plancus

Part predator and part scavenger this carrion-eating falcon pursues its distasteful life-style from southern Texas and Florida south to Tierra del Fuego.

Constantly on the lookout for sick or wounded birds and mammals, of any size, the Crested Caracara will operate either individually or as one of a group. Young sheep and goats are taken as soon as the adult's back is turned. Birds as large as the Great Egret, the White Ibis and the Southern Lapwing may be harassed over long distances by marauding caracaras, and flying pelicans are mobbed until they drop the food they are carrying. Lizards and snakes, young alligators and turtles, crabs, fishes, insects and palm-fruit – all form a part of the caracara's diet.

Avoiding rain-forest areas even when extensively cleared and cultivated, the Crested Caracara frequents more arid country, ranging across the savanna grasslands and treeless *pampas* with its characteristic head-bobbing walk. When foraging, the Caracara gives a dull, grunting call but, if the nest of a brooding pair is approached, the adults vibrate their bills to produce a loud rattle.

A favourite site for the large, untidy nest of coarse sticks and scavenged rubbish is the crown of a solitary palm, though any tall tree will suffice. On treeless *pampas* the Caracara builds its nest on the bare ground or chooses a mound rising above marshland.

The clutch of two or three variably-marked brown eggs is laid in the nest with little or no lining material and the 28-day incubation is shared by both the parents.

Greater Rhea
Rhea americana

Standing five feet tall and weighing more than 50 pounds, the flightless Greater Rhea ranges from the Brazilian *campo* south through *chaco* and steppe to the *pampas* of Argentina.

Although it may squat motionless when disturbed, the Greater Rhea can outrun a galloping horse. Sprinting on powerful, three-toed legs, the rhea flees with its neck outstretched and one wing raised high over its back like a small sail – twisting and turning abruptly to elude its pursuer.

Non-breeding rheas live in flocks of up to 30 birds, foraging over the open ground for roots, tender leaves, insects and occasionally small animals. The cock's loud, bellowing call heralds the start of the mating season. Rivals fight furiously with their necks entwined – circling round and round, biting and kicking until a trench is worn in the earth. After winning a harem of females, the cock selects a dry, sheltered spot and uproots the vegetation to create a depression. Lining the hollow with dry grass he repeatedly leads five or six chosen hens to the nest where they lay from 12 to 60 golden-yellow eggs measuring more than five inches long by three and a half in diameter.

The cock incubates the 20-ounce eggs alone for 35 to 40 days – repulsing even his own hens – and zealously guards the plaintively-whistling chicks throughout their growing period.

After five months' rapid growth the chicks attain adult size, but do not become sexually mature until they are two years old.

Greater Rhea
Rhea americana 52in
Flightless heavyweight that can outrun a galloping horse

Pampas and Llanos

Many plants openly display brightly coloured fruits and berries as an inducement to animals and birds to eat them and so disseminate the seeds. Insects and other animals, by contrast, have no wish to be eaten and try to escape predation by means of camouflage, poisonous secretions, defensive armament or flight. Accordingly, even when the food of an insectivorous bird is abundant, it may still be hard to catch – or even to find.

Some birds overcome this difficulty by employing other animals to drive their prey out into the open. In addition to the Cattle Tyrant, both the Smooth-billed and the Groove-billed Anis follow grazing animals in order to catch grass-hoppers and the thousands of small insects disturbed from the ground vegetation. The Cattle Egret, a bird of Old World origin which appeared in the Americas late in the last century, also forages in the company of herbivores. In woodland, where grazing animals are rare or absent, army ants perform the same service – their swarming legions attended by a motley crowd of birds, including manakins, wood-creepers, tinamous and occasionally hawks on the alert for small rodents and mammals.

Nor have birds been slow to benefit from man's labours. Swallows follow the tractor-drawn weed-cutters used to clear tropical pasture; gulls flock behind the plough, and urban birds reap the harvest exposed by lawn-mowers.

Cinereous Harrier
Circus cinereus 18in
Migrant hunter of the bleak upland plains

Open grasslands

Distribution of species

- Rufous Ovenbird
  Furnarius rufus
- Variable Seed-eater
  Sporophila americana
- Crested Seriema
  Cariama cristata

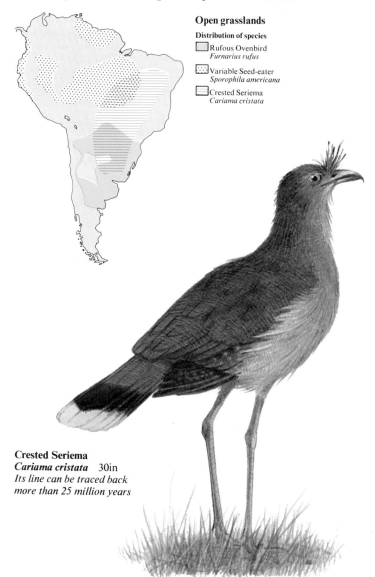

Crested Seriema
Cariama cristata 30in
Its line can be traced back more than 25 million years

Cinereous Harrier
Circus cinereus

The range of the Cinereous Harrier extends north from the bleak and windswept Falkland Islands to Paraguay and Brazil in the east and to the high, treeless regions of Ecuador and Colombia on the north-west coast. In the extreme south of its range this harrier is partly migratory – retreating northwards as the bitter cold of the sub-Antarctic winter grips the southern tip of the continent.

In Patagonia, the Cinereous Harrier is second only to the Chimango Caracara, *Milvago chimango*, in abundance and is a familiar resident of marshes and wet grassland regions. Soaring aloft with wings held in a characteristic deep "vee" configuration, *C. cinereus* sometimes takes small birds on the wing – a marked departure from the usual harrier hunting technique of an untidy attack on prey on the ground.

Crested Seriema
Cariama cristata

Seriemas are the sole survivors of a primitive group of giant ground-dwelling predatory birds that inhabited South America more than 25 million years ago. The two present-day species, related to the bustard family, are found only in the dry scrub grasslands between the Amazon rain-forest and the *pampas* of Argentina. Foraging in pairs or small groups, the Crested Seriema feeds on worms, snails, insects, fruit and small snakes, though, to its cost, it seems unable to distinguish between poisonous and harmless species.

When approached, the seriema

ceases its usual loud calling and, if danger threatens, takes to its heels in a precipitate head-down scamper, bounding over the ground on its long legs and only taking to the air if hard-pressed.

After an energetic, bustard-like courtship display accompanied by shrill yelping calls, the birds construct a compact nest of sticks anywhere from ground level to ten feet up in a tree. The two white eggs, irregularly streaked with brown, are incubated for 26 days and the downy chicks remain in the nest until well advanced.

When raised with domestic fowl, seriemas make efficient guardians – screaming at the approach of danger and even killing intruding snakes.

Rufous Ovenbird
Furnarius rufus

Few families can boast the remarkable variety of nest architecture displayed by the 215 members of the Furnariidae. The nests range from bank burrows and tree-holes to elaborate stick mansions (see Rufous-fronted Thornbird), and from mossy globes suspended in trees to clay fortresses shaped like the traditional earthen baking oven.

The six species of ovenbirds, or horneros, are widespread in South America – in habitats as varied as tropical rain-forest and *pampas*.

Nest building begins in autumn and continues into the mild, wet days of winter when mud is readily available. Perched on a firm, exposed foundation such as a fencepost or horizontal tree-limb, the nine-pound nest – a foot or more in diameter – is built up of mud strengthened with

Cattle Tyrant
Machetornis rixosus 8in

Opportunist "horsemen" of the plains

More than 370 species, differing widely in appearance and behaviour, make up the flycatcher family Tyrannidae – the largest of the avian families confined to the New World. Minute or thrush-sized; aerial or ground-dwelling; migratory or sedentary – the flycatchers have a representative in virtually every life-style available to an insectivorous bird.

It is almost impossible to choose a "typical" flycatcher, but one of the most interesting is the Cattle Tyrant *Machetornis rixosus*, known in Venezuela as the Jinete, or "Horseman", because of its curious habit of riding all day on the back of a large quadruped. Throughout its vast range from the Caribbean to Argentina the Cattle Tyrant patronizes pigs, horses, cattle and even dogs – ever alert for flying insects and hopping from its perch when hungry to forage in the grass for insects disturbed by the grazing animal.

The Cattle Tyrant is a born opportunist. It has learned to follow men mowing the lawns of Venezuelan oil camps; to glean dead and injured insects from the windscreens of cars and to gather those attracted by house-lights at night. Its nesting habits are no less versatile. In Venezuela the Cattle Tyrant will place its bulky nest of woven grass under the eaves of a house. In Argentina it builds a nest of slender twigs and leaves in a tree-hole, or builds its nest into that of a larger bird. The great woven twig edifices of some of the horneros are often found to contain flycatcher "lodgers". The nest of Rufous-fronted Thornbirds and Firewood Gatherers are also favoured, and the Cattle Tyrant will fight fiercely against other species with similar nesting habits in order to secure a prime site.

The Cattle Tyrant is sedentary throughout its range, even as far south as Buenos Aires where many birds are at least partially migratory. Once mated, pairs of tyrants remain together for the whole year – their union strengthened by their frequent duets of loud, shrill, rapidly repeated song.

Like many other flycatchers, the Cattle Tyrant has an erectile crest of brilliantly coloured crown feathers which, when raised in the excitement of courtship, or in a dispute over food, flash their message in a brilliant burst of orange-crimson colour.

fibrous vegetation and animal hairs. A side entrance gives access to a small antechamber from which a narrow passage curves round the inner wall to the grass-lined nest-chamber in which the female lays her five small white eggs.

Variable Seed-eater
Sporophila americana

The aptly named Variable Seed-eater is one of 30 distinctive finches inhabiting grasslands and fields from southern Texas to Argentina. The males of this varied genus are clad in black and white, grey, rufous and chestnut plumage, but the females, in tones of olive and buff, are difficult to identify.

Perched on a swaying grass-stem the Variable Seed-eater grasps the ear with one foot and strips the seeds with the strong, short bill characteristic of seed-eating birds. When ripe grass-seeds are scarce it will turn to mistletoes and small-fruited shrubs – supplementing its diet with insects.

Food supply governs the breeding season and in Costa Rica the Variable Seed-eater nests much later than most passerines in order to coincide with the rains.

Variable Seed-eaters are gregarious birds, nesting close together in dense stands of sugar-cane or grass – often in the company of other small birds. The female alone builds the slight, though strong, cup-nest of dark fibres and incubates her clutch of two or three pale- or blue-grey speckled eggs. The male, characterized by his enthusiastic and richly varied song, helps to feed the nestlings on regurgitated seeds until they leave the nest at 14 days old.

Rufous Ovenbird
Furnarius rufus 7½in
Builds a two-roomed house of mud and grass-fibres

Variable Seed-eater
Sporophila americana 4½in
Supplements its diet with fruit and insects when grass seeds are scarce

The Food-web of the Forest

No habitat on earth has greater complexity than the tropical rain-forest. Trees exist in a great profusion of species, soaring upwards in their struggle for life-giving sunlight. Festooned in lianas, mosses, fungi and epiphytic plants whose air-roots require no soil, they provide a rich and varied source of food unaffected by seasonal change.

The dense and continuous mass of the forest canopy acts as a great collector of energy, absorbing the sun's radiation and fixing it, by photosynthesis, in leaves, flowers and fruits. Green plants are thus the prime producers of energy – the basic resource on which the whole interlocking structure of the forest ecosystem depends.

Countless millions of insects feed on the juices, stems and leaves of the forest. With fruit-eating birds like the macaws, pigeons, tanagers and wood-quail, and the nectar-sipping hummingbirds, they form the primary level of consumers – those wholly dependent on plant food. These in turn provide food for a second rank of consumers, the insectivores and other small predators. While many are indiscriminate in their choice of food, others are highly specialized. The swifts take insects in flight, high above the canopy; woodpeckers and scythebills feed on bark-insects; cuckoos take caterpillars, while the jacamars feed on venomous wasps. Hawks and owls patrol the forest by day and night, preying on reptiles, small birds and mammals of the primary level.

Dominating the food-web are the elite hunters of the tertiary level. Few in number and requiring vast areas over which to hunt, the major predators, like the Ornate Hawk Eagle, prey on all below them in the forest hierarchy.

In a severe habitat such as desert or tundra, feeding relationships often take the form of a simple chain (say, hawk-lizard-spider-ant), a vulnerable situation in which a shortage of one link-member may drastically upset the whole structure. No such danger threatens the forest residents: food is so abundant that every bird and mammal is presented with a wide choice of foods, transforming the simple vulnerable chain into a complex and flexible food-web.

The energy pyramid

Tertiary consumers
Major predators occupy the highest level in the food-chain, taking their energy requirements from vegetarians and smaller carnivores alike

Secondary consumers
Insectivorous birds, omnivores and small predators like the Collared Falcon, form the middle links of the forest food-chain

Primary consumers
Energy is first converted from plant to animal matter by the fruit and seed eaters that form the broad base of the food pyramid

Producers
All energy is initially derived from sunlight – converted into usable food by photosynthesis. On the huge mass of the forest vegetation depends the structure of one of natures most complex biomes

Tertiary consumers

Secondary consumers

Primary consumers

Energy producers

Insects, bacteria and fungi break down organic remains and return minerals to the soil, completing the energy cycle and replenishing the nutrient supply

Birds illustrated

1 Crested Eagle
  Morphnus guianensis
2 White-collared Swift
  Streptoprocne zonaris
3 Hyacinth Macaw
  Anodorhynchus hyacinthinus
4 Short-billed Pigeon
  Columba nigrirostris
5 Blue-throated Piping Guan
  Pipile pipile
6 Silver-throated Tanager
  Tangara icterocephala
7 Squirrel Cuckoo
  Piaya cayana
8 Rufous-browed Pepper-shrike
  Cyclarhis gujanensis
9 Ornate Umbrella-bird
  Cephalopterus ornatus
10 Cayanne Jay
  Cyanocorax affinis
11 Black-eared Fairy
  Heliothryx aurita
12 Fork-tailed Woodnymph
  Thalurania furcata
13 Bronze-tailed Plumeleteer
  Chalybura urochrysia
14 Band-tailed Barb-throat
  Threnetes ruckeri
15 Long-tailed Hermit
  Phaethornis superciliosus
16 Semicollared Hawk
  Accipiter collaris
17 Collared Forest Falcon
  Micrastur semitorquatus
18 Spectacled Owl
  Pulsatrix perspicillata
19 Great Jacamar
  Jacamerops aurea
20 Chestnut Woodpecker
  Celeus elegans
21 Rufous-capped Spinetail
  Synallaxis ruficapilla
22 Red-billed Scythebill
  Campylorhamphus trochilirostris
23 Black-throated Trogon
  Trogon rufus
24 Cock-of-the-rock
  Rupicola rupicola
25 Red-capped Cardinal
  Paroaria gularis
26 Brazilian Tanager
  Ramphocelus bresilius
27 Grey-winged Trumpeter
  Psophia crepitans
28 Marbled Wood-quail
  Odontophorus gujanensis
29 Black-bellied Gnateater
  Conopophaga melanogaster
30 Grey-throated Leaf-scraper
  Sclerurus albigularis

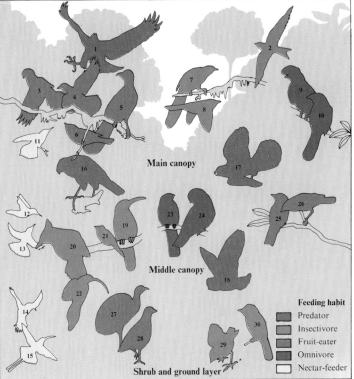

Main canopy

Middle canopy

Feeding habit
Predator
Insectivore
Fruit-eater
Omnivore
Nectar-feeder

Shrub and ground layer

Puna and Páramo

To mention the mountains of South America is to evoke visions of the Andes – that towering rampart of rock stretching from the Equator to the icy waters of Cape Horn. Apart from the short Santa Marta range in Colombia, only the Andes have large areas of life-supporting land above the tree-line, which, in the equatorial Andes, varies from 10,500 to 12,500 feet above sea-level. Above the tree-line vast open spaces slope upwards to meet the perennially snow-capped peaks – high moorlands that are deceptively mild in fair weather but bleak and desolate when shrouded in chilling cloud and mist.

From Ecuador north to Costa Rica these high treeless solitudes are known as *páramos*, characterized by the hardy Frailjón, *Espeletia*, standing amid grasses and the colourful blooms of cushion plants and shrubs. Farther south, in Peru, the *páramo* gives way to the drier *puna* – open tussock-grass moorland that provides grazing for llama and alpaca. The tallest of the *puna* plants, up to 30 feet high, is the bromeliad *Puya raimondii*, whose sword-like leaves are armed with cruel spines.

Many birds are well adapted to withstand the harsh climate and restricted food supply of the cold montane regions, and the Andean lakes and torrents provide an isolated and protected home to some of the world's most beautiful and fascinating water-birds.

Andean Hillstar
Oreotrochilus estella 4½in
*The high-altitude humming-bird
of páramo and puna*

Backbone of a continent

1 Cordillera Occidental
2 Cordillera Oriental
3 Sierra de Perija
4 Sierra de Merida
5 Pakaraima Mountains
6 Tumuc Mountains
7 Sierra Geral de Goias
8 Sierra do Espinhaco
9 Sierra do Mar

Unicoloured Tapaculo
Scytalopus unicolor

The Tapaculo is an exasperatingly elusive bird inhabiting the thorny scrub, cool mossy highlands and dank forests of southern Chile. A reluctant flier, it prefers to run or walk over the ground with its tail held high over its back – a habit that has earned some species the local name "gallito" or "little cock". Even the loud cry of this dull-coloured bird gives little clue to its whereabouts when it is foraging in dense cover.

The family name of the 29 species of tapaculo, Rhinocryptidae, refers to the peculiar flap of movable skin covering the bird's nostrils. Wren-sized to thrush-sized, they are found in montane habitats from Costa Rica to Cape Horn, some species occasionally venturing down into the warm lowland forest. Their food consists of larvae, mature insects and spiders gathered from the ground and from the scrub vegetation.

Tapaculos build a wide variety of nests. Some nest in burrows and others, more rarely, make use of hollow logs. Some species construct a domed nest of grass or twigs in the base of a thorn bush.

Two to four plain white eggs are laid, but little is known in detail of the Tapaculo's breeding behaviour. One authority was able to observe a nest of *S. unicolor* on the volcano Volcan Tungurahua in Ecuador. Both parents were seen carrying insects to the nest which consisted of a black ball of finely-woven moss-stems hidden in a narrow cleft in an earth bank and screened by a protective curtain of moss and *Selaginella* plants.

Andean Hillstar
Oreotrochilus estella

The hardy Andean Hillstar exhibits the perfect mastery of flight, the tiny body and the lavish ornamentation characteristic of the humming-bird family, Trochilidae.

Most of the 320 species of humming-birds are resident in the tropics – from lowland rainforest and desert to the high reaches of the snow-capped Andean peaks. The hillstar is well adapted to the harsh climate of *páramo* and *puna*, and is found up to 15,000 feet above sea level. Like other humming-birds the hillstar feeds largely on nectar sucked from flowers with its tubular tongue, but unlike many of its relatives it supplements this diet with insects and small spiders caught in or near the blooms of montane flowers.

To conserve energy on cold nights the hillstar allows its body temperature to fall to that of the surrounding air. To avoid excessive cooling it roosts in caves and mineshafts where the night temperature remains a few degrees above that outside.

With no help from the male the female hillstar builds a large, well insulated nest, sometimes fastening it with nectar to a cliff face where it can catch the first warming rays of the morning sun yet be protected from the harsh rays of midday, which could easily prove fatal to the naked nestlings.

Although nesting humming-birds are usually solitary, high on Volcán Cotopaxi another hillstar race has adopted a colonial habit with as many as five nests closely grouped in a sheltering cave.

Unicoloured Tapaculo
Scytalopus unicolor 6in
*Called "gallito" from its
strutting cock-like walk*

Masked Flower-piercer
Diglossa cyanea

The soberly clad flower-piercers of the mountains and *páramos* are the most highly specialized of the 39 honeycreepers inhabiting tropical America.

The Masked Flower-piercer alights near the head of a mountain flower and, holding the base of the bloom with the finely hooked tip of its upper bill, drives the sharp lower mandible through the petals. In a raid lasting only a second, the bird extracts the flower's store of nectar through the tiny hole with darting movements of its slender, brush-like tongue.

The flower receives nothing in return. No part of the bird ever comes near to the pollen-bearing stamens and so, unlike most nectar-feeding birds and insects, the flower-piercer cannot pay for its bounty by pollinating the flowers it visits in search of food.

The flower-piercers are similar in many ways to the unrelated hummingbirds. Both species obtain their protein requirements from insects caught on the wing and both nest

when flowers are most abundant – often at a time of year when few other small birds are nesting. Two eggs are laid in the small, compact open cup-nest and the young are fed on partly digested food regurgitated by the parents.

The flower-raiders

The luxuriant flowering plants of tropical America provide a rich food-source for nectar-feeders. *Salvia*, *Fuchsia*, *Centropogon* and *Cestrum* are all visited by hummingbirds, and flower-piercers will feed on any species having a tubular flower not too thick to be pierced. Tightly closed flowers like those of *Erythrina berteroana* and the huge pendent bells of daturas are available only to long-billed species like the Long-billed Starthroat, *Heliomaster longirostris*, and the Swordbill, *Ensifera ensifera*.

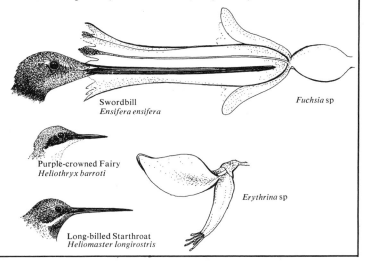

Swordbill
Ensifera ensifera

Fuchsia sp

Purple-crowned Fairy
Heliothryx barroti

Erythrina sp

Long-billed Starthroat
Heliomaster longirostris

Torrent Duck
Merganetta armata   15in
Undisputed master of the Andes' raging streams

Andean Flicker
Colaptes rupicola   14in
A woodpecker marooned in a treeless land

Torrent Duck
Merganetta armata

Fast-flowing, rock-strewn torrents in the high Andes provide a home for one of the world's most highly specialized water-birds. The Andean Torrent Duck has become adapted to feed on minute aquatic organisms, such as stonefly larvae, which are found only in the oxygen-rich conditions of turbulent water.

Swimming with apparent impunity only inches from the brink of a raging waterfall, the Torrent Duck dives in search of its food – probing among the rocks of the stream bed with its slender, flexible bill. The duck's streamlined body, unusually large feet and stiff, powerful tail enable it to swim submerged against strong currents, but it more often chooses to swim upstream on the surface, taking advantage of the relatively slack water near the bank or in the lee of boulders.

Each pair of birds will defend about half a mile of river as its territory. The female nests in an old kingfisher burrow or a cavity between the roots of a riverside tree and lays from three to five large eggs at intervals of up to a week. When the set is complete the female incubates the eggs for the unusually long period of 43 to 44 days.

The newly hatched young take to the water immediately, plunging unaided from a nest 60 feet above the water at the sound of the mother's call, protected only by their lightness and buoyant down. With remarkable stamina the young skitter over the turbulent water, scrambling over rocks with help from the drake, who, unlike most ducks, remains attentive to his mate and young throughout.

Andean Flicker
Colaptes rupicola

It is difficult to imagine woodpeckers in a land without trees, but the high montane areas of South America boast two species that have adapted to a life in open grassland. Both are flickers of the genus *Colaptes*. The Campo Woodpecker, *C. campestris*, inhabits the grasslands of the eastern lowlands, while the Andean Flicker is found throughout the bleak *puna* zone from 10,000 to 16,000 feet above sea level.

The Andean Flicker forages on stony slopes and level grassy areas, usually near a cliff or rocky outcrop which serves as a lookout post. Unlike most woodpeckers they are gregarious birds, sometimes gathering in parties of up to 30 as they move across the slopes digging out beetle larvae and plucking moth larvae from the tussock-grass.

Up to a dozen pairs may nest together as a colony in tunnels driven into a stream bank. To build each nest the birds loosen the earth with their bills, using their feet to kick the earth backwards and outwards. Male and female take turns digging the upward-sloping shaft three or four feet into the bank, widening the inner end into a simple, unlined nest-chamber. Andean Flickers are also known to burrow into the adobe walls of local buildings to roost but they have never been seen to breed in this situation.

In the harsh, cold environment of the *puna* many species, including ducks, hawks, parakeets, ovenbirds and flycatchers, find it to their advantage to raise their young in the shelter of burrows protected from extremes of wind and temperature.

Lakes, Rivers and Swamps

The varied aquatic habitats of South America range over the entire continent. High in the Andes, tumbling streams and still lakes are inhabited by Torrent Ducks, coots and gulls, while the shallow, saline lagoons, far above the tree line, are nesting refuges for the world's rarest flamingos.

Fed by the mountain torrents, broad rivers wind through the forested heart of the continent. Horned Screamers stalk in pairs through grassy tropical marshlands and, in the *pampas* regions of Argentina, dense stands of tule and sawgrass alternate with duckweed-covered pools to create an ideal habitat for multitudes of grebes, herons, ducks, storks and gallinules. Even the Venezuelan *llanos*, parched throughout the long dry season, is transformed into an aquatic environment by the torrential rains of the wet season.

Throughout tropical South America, low coastlines and river estuaries are blanketed by dense forests of red mangroves soaring to heights of a hundred feet or more above the impenetrable maze of their arched stilt-roots. Innumerable crabs scurry over the thick mud surrounding the roots, sharing with frogs, snakes and countless insects a dark world of brackish water inundated by each high tide. Pygmy Kingfishers and Yellow Mangrove Warblers hunt across the mud flats, and herons, ibises and spoonbills nest in the tangled mass of roots and branches.

Right: Adult Buff-necked Ibis feeding in fresh-water marsh

Rivers and swamps

- Hoatzin
  Opisthocomus hoazin
- Scarlet Ibis
  Eudocimus ruber
- Boat-billed Heron
  Cochlearius cochlearius

Scarlet Ibis
Eudocimus ruber 22in
*Plumage colour intensifies
as the bird grows older*

Eager feeder
*A young Boat-billed Heron
grasps its parent's bill to
receive regurgitated food*

Boat-billed Heron
Cochlearius cochlearius 24in
*A unique bill-form that
requires special classification*

Scarlet Ibis
Eudocimus ruber

The uniformly bright-red plumage of the Scarlet Ibis is one of the most striking sights in the world of birds, and a flock, flying across desolate coastal mudflats against a lowering sky, attracts the eye like a beacon.

Leaving their crowded roosts early in the morning, the birds spread out across the exposed mudflats at low tide or among the tangled vegetation of the mangroves at high tide, probing into the deep mud in their search for crabs and molluscs, small fishes and invertebrates.

The Scarlet Ibis is found far inland among the swamp regions of northern South America, but their known breeding colonies are nearly always among the great natural fortresses of the coastal mangrove swamps – remote and difficult to approach. In contrast to other colonial nesters they vary the site of the breeding colony year by year, but the reasons for this variation are not yet understood.

On a shallow nest of coarse sticks, from four to 40 feet above the high-water level, the female ibis lays two or three, rarely four, dull olive-green or buff eggs streaked with brown. The young hatch, nearly naked, after 23 days' incubation, but long before they are able to fly they leave the nest and scramble among the mangrove vegetation, using their bills and wings as well as feet in their ungainly but determined explorations. They fly at four weeks, but the dull grey juvenile plumage persists for several years. The scarlet adult plumage is acquired over a number of seasons and becomes progressively more intense as the bird gets older.

Boat-billed Heron
Cochlearius cochlearius

The grotesque, broad bill of the Boat-billed Heron is so different from the slender spear of typical herons that this odd bird has been placed in a family of its own – the Cochleariidae. The single species is found from southern Mexico to Peru and southern Brazil.

By day, the Boat-billed Heron rests quietly in coastal mangroves or in trees lining the banks of inland swamps. If a human should intrude among their perches, they flap about reluctantly – gazing apathetically down and emitting low, hoarse, croaking cries. By night, when they do most of their foraging, they are far more wary – flying off with deep "quok quok" calls the moment a beam of light disturbs them.

The birds have been observed standing or walking slowly through shallow water, scooping up their prey, which consists of swamp fishes and shrimps, rather than spearing it in the manner of true herons. In inland localities ants and other ground-swarming insects form a major part of the diet.

Boat-billed Herons nest in small colonies, sometimes in the company of ibises and other herons. Their crude, shallow nests of sticks are built in trees, and the female lays a clutch of two to four lightly spotted blue-white eggs. In large aviaries, where the birds have been successfully bred, both sexes have shared the incubation, turning the eggs frequently during the day. The young birds take their regurgitated meals by reaching up and grasping the parent's bill firmly between their own mandibles.

Hoatzin
Opisthocomus hoazin

Recently shown to be a highly aberrant cuckoo, this strange bird inhabits the shores of the great rivers of South America – the Amazon and the Orinoco.

Its food consists almost entirely of leaves, particularly those of the tall, cane-like water-arum *Montrichardia*, and, after a prolonged period of feeding, the Hoatzin's crop is so distended and heavy that the bird must rest with its breast supported against a branch, protected from abrasion by a callous pad.

Hoatzins live in sociable parties of between 10 and 30, which split into smaller groups at the approach of the breeding season. The female lays her eggs in an open stick nest placed in branches overhanging the river and the young are attended by up to four adult helpers as well as the parents.

If alarmed, the flightless young instinctively drop into the water to escape and then scramble back to the nest using their feet, bills and the sharp claws on the leading edges of their wings.

Black-headed Duck
Heteronetta atricapilla

Living amid dense marsh vegetation on both sides of the southern Andes, the Black-headed Duck dabbles and dives for seeds, duckweed and, occasionally, snails.

Although many ducks lay their eggs more or less frequently in the nests of other ducks, only the Black-headed species is totally parasitic in its breeding habits. After the spring mating the females lay their eggs in the nests of a variety of marsh-dwelling birds, particularly those of coots, pochards and ibises. Occasionally they will parasitize the nests of birds as different as Southern Screamers, Coscoroba Swans, Limpkins and even Chimango Caracaras.

The young hatch after about 25 days' incubation with the host's eggs, but remain with the foster-parents for only a few days before wandering from the nest to face the world alone. The young Black-headed Ducks make so few demands on their foster-parents that the species has been described as "the most perfect of all avian parasites".

Hoatzin
Opisthocomus hoazin 25in
Primitive wing-claws enable the young to regain the nest after a fall

---

The island-builders

Horned Coot
Fulica cornuta 24in

Eggs, nestlings and immature birds are a favourite prey of many predators, and the nesting habits of many species show a direct response to this ever-present threat.

To increase their chances of success, many inland water-birds build solitary nests on islets or hummocks surrounded by shallow water, but, despite the safety that an island home gives to a bird, only one species, the Horned Coot, *Fulica cornuta*, is known to build its own island.

A slaty black bird, and one of the largest members of its family, the Horned Coot is characterized by the forward-pointing horn on its forehead. In most coots the forehead is adorned by a frontal shield of flabby wattle, but in the Horned Coot this curious decoration is a muscular

organ of unknown significance.

In the bleak, arid upland wastes where Chile, Argentina and Bolivia meet, the Horned Coot makes its home in shallow lakes 12,000 to 14,000 feet above sea level. Because these lakes are so poor in water-plants, this coot has abandoned the floating nest typical of its relatives in favour of a huge platform of stones two or three feet high and up to 13 feet in diameter – a remarkable island of stones built up over a number of years and sometimes containing several tons of rock. The top of the platform is always just below water-level and on it the birds build a nest of aquatic plants gathered from the bed of the lake.

Farther north, where Andean lakes support a richer vegetation, the Horned Coot builds its island of plant materials instead of stones, but nowhere does it revert to the floating nest typical of its family.

Coots, grebes, inland terns and gulls all build floating nests and all face a common problem – that of keeping their eggs dry while incubating. As the nest-materials become waterlogged and sink, the birds must keep adding new material to keep the vulnerable eggs above the water. The Pheasant-tailed Jacana of Asia has a different solution. If the lily-pad supporting its nest rots, or if flood waters threaten the nest, this jacana simply rolls its egg across the lily-pads to a safe site and builds a new nest.

Artificial island of the Horned Coot

Black-headed Duck
Heteronetta atricapilla 14½in
The only totally parasitic member of the duck family

Central America: The Tenuous Link

As a biological province, Central America stretches for 1,400 miles from the Isthmus of Tehuantepec to eastern Panama. The varied topography, and its unique situation between two great landmasses, have given Central America a rich and diverse bird fauna containing species from both north and south.

Of its major natural habitats, the warm, moist Caribbean lowlands are the richest in species – particularly in puff-birds, manakins, woodcreepers, cotingas and tanagers. They are all families of South American origin which spread north-ward through a once-continuous belt of tropical rain-forest. The Pacific slopes north of the Gulf of Nicoya, and the dry inland valleys lying in the rain-shadow area facing the Caribbean Sea, are rich in dry-country species, many of which originated in the arid regions of southern North America.

Two vast highland regions guard the narrow land-bridge between the two Americas. The largest, centred on Guatemala, has extensive plateau-regions 10,000 feet above sea level with volcanic peaks rising to nearly 14,000 feet. Here, where the winter nights are cold, many northern species reach their southernmost limit. Beyond the lowlands of southern Nicaragua the land rises again to form the 12,500-foot Cordillera de Talamanca – a mountain barrier extending into western Panama and rich in Andean birds – notably many members of the ovenbird family.

Quetzal
Pharomachrus mocinno 14in
The magnificent 24-inch courtship train is battered by the rigours of parenthood

Blue-diademed Motmot
Momotus momota 15in
Long-term planning solves a nesting problem

Natural vegetation of Central America

■ Tropical rain forest

■ Montane zone

□ Deciduous forest and scrub

Blue-diademed Motmot
Momotus momota

Central America was probably the cradle of the motmot family, and eight of the nine known species are found in this region. The Blue-diademed Motmot is the most widespread and familiar species – a resident of clearings, secondary forest and even suburban gardens.

The long central tail-feathers are fully vaned when they first form, but the vanes are restricted near the tip and readily fall away to leave a length of naked shaft terminating in the "racquet" adornment common to six of the nine species.

Motmots feed on insects, small lizards and fruit, the Blue-diademed Motmot showing a marked preference for bananas. Male and female work together during the wet season to dig a long tunnel into a soft earth bank. The burrow is then abandoned until the following dry season when the female returns to lay her three white eggs. In physiology and behaviour the motmots closely resemble their near relatives, the kingfishers.

Quetzal
Pharomachrus mocinno

With its long tail-coverts streaming behind, the beautiful Quetzal darts through the forest plucking small fruits from the trees and occasionally pausing to pounce on an unwary frog or lizard. This national symbol of Guatemala ranges through cool highland forests 4,000 to 10,000 feet high, from Chiapas in Mexico to western Panama.

Contrary to a persistent myth, the Quetzal's nest-hole in a rotting tree-trunk has only a single entrance – like that of a woodpecker. Like other trogons, the elegantly-attired male incubates the two blue eggs through-out the day – his presence often being betrayed by the tail-feathers pro-jecting from the nest and waving in the breeze. If the female deserts the nest, the male will continue and successfully raise the nestlings alone, but usually a pair of adults will raise two broods in each season. By the time the second brood is fledged, the once-glorious train of the courting male is reduced to a frayed remnant.

Life-zones of the mountains

From luxuriantly forested foothills to barren rocky peaks, the vegetation zones of a mountain follow the same clear order as do the major zones encircling the earth between Equator and poles. Each zone supports its own characteristic suite of plants, birds, mammals and insects, the more adaptable perhaps spanning two or more zones while the most specialized species are quite rigidly confined to their own particular habitats. The diagram illustrates four species that have adapted to specific altitude bands.

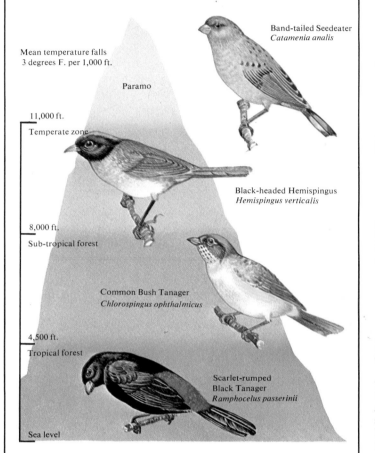

Mean temperature falls
3 degrees F. per 1,000 ft.

Paramo

Band-tailed Seedeater
Catamenia analis

11,000 ft.

Temperate zone

Black-headed Hemispingus
Hemispingus verticalis

8,000 ft.

Sub-tropical forest

Common Bush Tanager
Chlorospingus ophthalmicus

4,500 ft.

Tropical forest

**Scarlet-rumped
Black Tanager**
Ramphocelus passerinii

Sea level

Montezuma Oropendola
Gymnostinops montezuma 15in
*Isolated trees are festooned
with their woven nest-pouches*

Ornate Hawk Eagle
Spizaetus ornatus 24in
*One of the least-known
South American raptors*

Long-tailed Silky Flycatcher
Ptilogonys caudatus 9¾in
*Undaunted by the gales
of its mountain habitat*

Montezuma Oropendola
Gymnostinops montezuma

The 88 species making up the New World oriole family, Icteridae, occupy a wide range of habitats and life-styles. Some are terrestrial, others highly arboreal; some are social parasites that build no nests of their own, while others are among the most skilful of nest weavers. Among the latter are the dozen species of oropendolas, whose long, pear-shaped pouches may be seen hanging in clusters high in isolated trees.

A colony of Montezuma Oropendolas may contain more than 100 nests, each two to four feet long and up to nine inches wide at the base. The female alone weaves the pouch of fibrous plant materials, filling the bottom of the nest with a loose litter of leaf fragments which protect her eggs when the nest is buffeted by strong winds. The young oropendolas remain in the nest for a month after hatching – attended by the hen alone.

Ornate Hawk Eagle
Spizaetus ornatus

Despite its great range, this strikingly coloured raptor remains one of the least known of all South America's birds of prey. It inhabits the dense belts of tropical forest from Mexico to Argentina and has been observed to attack curassows and a number of other large, slow-moving ground-

birds. Other observations suggest that the Ornate Hawk Eagle may also hunt over small lakes and rivers – swooping to snatch water-snakes from the shallows.

The Ornate Hawk Eagle will occasionally take possession of a nest deserted by another member of the hawk family but, to date, the details of this handsome bird's breeding habits are a mystery.

Long-tailed Silky Flycatcher
Ptilogonys caudatus

Confined to the high mountains of Costa Rica and western Panama, the Long-tailed Silky Flycatcher weaves its way in straggling flocks across the top of the forest canopy, occasionally venturing forth into the more open wooded grasslands of the foothills.

Perching upright in the topmost branches of tall trees, quite undaunted by the fierce gales that sweep the exposed mountain ridges, the Silky Flycatcher launches itself into the air on long aerial sorties in search of the insects and berries that constitute the bulk of its diet.

Male and female work together to build a bulky, woven nest of finely branched mosses and lichens in which the two lightly marked grey eggs are laid. Although he takes no part in the 17-day incubation of the eggs, the male remains in close attendance and often brings food to the brooding female.

The Caribbean Islands

The great arc of the West Indian archipelago stretches for more than 2,000 miles from Florida and Yucatan to the northernmost fringe of the South American landmass.

This chain of islands, enclosing the Caribbean Sea, supports nearly every type of tropical vegetation with the exception of *páramo* and *puna*. Mangrove swamps line the island shores; marshes and tropical rain-forests clothe the wet windward slopes of forest-capped mountains and, in the dry rain-shadow of the higher ranges, the slopes are covered with drought-resistant xerophytic vegetation rich in cacti. Palms, including the stately Royal Palm, are common throughout the islands and true pines, absent from the continent south of Nicaragua, grow in abundance on Cuba and Hispaniola.

Despite their proximity to the American continents, the West Indies have been separated from them long enough to have developed a fauna of their own. Some of the most widespread and characteristic South American birds, such as the toucans, puffbirds, woodcreepers and manakins, are completely absent from the islands, but some of the families that have their origins in tropical North America – the thrashers and wood-warblers – are well represented. About 50 of the island genera are endemic, and two complete families, the palm-chats and the todies, are restricted to the four main islands – Cuba, Jamaica, Hispaniola and Puerto Rico.

Magnificent Frigatebird
Fregata magnificens 42in
Ruthless pirate of the tropical islands

Northern Jacana
Jacana spinosa 8in
The dominant female fiercely defends her weaker "husbands"

Northern Jacana
Jacana spinosa

Ruling the roost over as many as four "husbands" at once, the polyandrous female Northern Jacana helps each of her much lighter mates to defend his personal breeding territory within her own overall domain. For each she will lay four dull brown eggs, delicately marked with fine black lines, in a flimsy nest built on floating plants. The male incubates the eggs alone, and in order to keep the eggs dry as well as warm probably pushes his wing feathers beneath them – a behaviour pattern common to other members of the jacana family.

As soon as the downy chicks are able to use their long-toed feet well enough to pick their way across floating vegetation, they are led on foraging expeditions in search of food. Jacanas feed mainly on insects gleaned from the ponds, lagoons and marshes they inhabit and the birds are most often seen picking their way delicately over the floating plants – at times seeming to walk on the surface of the water. However, the jacana does occasionally leave its aquatic home to forage in grassland where insects are abundant.

Despite their rapid physical development, the young birds retain their dull juvenile plumage until well grown – perhaps as a partial defence against would-be predators. The adult bird is predominantly reddish-brown, but the briefly held statuesque pose adopted on landing, with the wings stretched almost vertically above the back, reveals the bright yellow-green flight feathers and the sharp yellow spur on each wing.

Smooth-billed Ani
Crotophaga ani 14in
Communal living

Smooth-billed Ani
Crotophaga ani

Belying the parasitic reputation of their family, these black cuckoos lead a closely knit, highly co-operative life. In groups of six or eight they build a bulky communal nest of coarse sticks in the middle of a jointly defended territory – roosting together in a compact huddle at night.

Each female contributes between four and seven eggs to a communal clutch of up to 30 eggs laid on a thick lining of green leaves that is constantly replenished throughout the nesting period. The eggs have an unusual chalky white covering over the blue inner shell and are incubated for 13 days by members of both sexes. A single male is left to stand guard over the clutch at night. The young are hatched black and naked but are able to leave the nest within five or six days if alarmed. Insects form the bulk of the ani's diet, and the whole group, including juveniles of an earlier brood, will forage together – often in the company of grazing animals. When insects are scarce the Ani will feed on berries and lizards.

Palm Chat
Dulus dominicus

The single species of Palm Chat lives only on the islands of Gonave and Hispaniola, where it is the most conspicuously abundant bird. Palm Chats are highly sociable birds that move through the forest in loose flocks in search of seeds, berries and flowers – sometimes plucking the fruit from the tree in full flight. They are often seen perching close together high in the trees, where they compensate for their lack of song with an enthusiastic repertoire of squeaks and buzzes, deepening to a mournful "cher – cher" at nightfall.

The huge communal nests of the Palm Chat are a prominent feature of the landscape. Up to ten feet high and four feet in diameter, the nest of interlaced twigs may completely enclose the main shaft of a Royal Palm. Each nest is an apartment block containing up to 30 individual chambers, each with its own entrance tunnel and each one the home of a mated pair. Between two and four spotted white eggs are laid in each nest, on a lining of shredded bark.

Palm Chat
Dulus dominicus 8in
Thirty families may share the huge tenement nest

Magnificent Frigatebird
Fregata magnificens

Easily recognized at any height by its deeply forked tail and narrow, angled wings, the frigatebird uses its superb manoeuvrability to harass boobies and other birds until they drop the food they are carrying. The pirate then swoops to catch its booty in mid-air – perhaps only to be forced to relinquish it to another of its kind. The frigatebird does forage for itself as well, deftly snatching flying fish from above the waves or taking squid and jellyfish from the surface-waters.

The birds breed in huge island colonies, building crude platforms of sticks and straws in low bushes or, occasionally, in mangrove trees or on the ground. Males display to cruising females by inflating their brilliant-scarlet throat-sacs while vibrating their outstretched wings and uttering guttural cries. Attracted by this bizarre display a female will respond by nibbling the male's feathers and rubbing her head across his pouch.

The single young must be guarded at all times, as unprotected nests are torn apart by other adults in search of nesting materials, and nestlings are ruthlessly savaged by cannibalistic neighbours.

The young remain in the nest for five months and even after learning to fly they return to the nest to be fed until nearly a year old. During the final months the chicks are fed by the female alone as the males withdraw from the colony. This prolonged burden of parental care restricts the females to breeding in alternate years while the less busy males are free to take a new mate each season and so breed annually.

Bananaquit
Coereba flaveola 4½in
Separate nests for male and female

Puerto Rican Tody
Todus mexicanus 4¼in
Each to its island

Bananaquit
Coereba flaveola

A bold and indiscriminate feeder and a tireless nest-builder, the self-sufficient Bananaquit is one of tropical America's most widespread songbirds.

Each adult builds a separate tightly woven globular nest in which it roosts alone throughout the year – excluding even its mate. The male does assist the female in building the slightly larger breeding nest and helps her to feed the young on regurgitated food, but the task of incubating the three spotted white eggs is left entirely to the female.

When the young fly, at about 19 days, they are rudely excluded from the nest and must immediately embark on their life-long career of nest-building.

Puerto Rican Tody
Todus mexicanus

The five species of tody (relatives of the motmots) are all confined to islands, though their habitats may be as diverse as rain-forest and desert scrub. Two are found on Hispaniola, one on Puerto Rico, one on Jamaica and one on Cuba and the neighbouring Isle of Pines.

Todies are identified by their harsh "cherek" cries, the rattling sound sometimes made by their primary feathers in flight, and by their habit of hunting on the wing – snatching small insects from the foliage without alighting.

They lay two to four pure-white eggs in a foot-long earth burrow, and, after hatching, the young are fed for 20 days in the nest-chamber.

Eurasia
The Palaearctic Realm

For more than a million years Europe and northern Asia were dominated by the ice ages. Vegetation zones were pushed southwards, and throughout the region, temperate and sub-tropical vegetation gave way to heath and coniferous forest. As the ice retreated, barely 10,000 years ago, scores of species began to spread north and west, recolonizing their former territories but leaving behind a number of Arctic species – isolated in the mountains of southern Europe by the rapid spread of temperate grass and woodland.

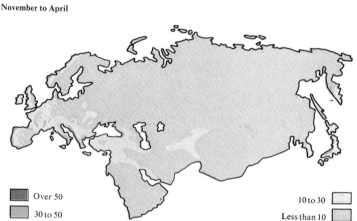

BIRDS ILLUSTRATED

1	Herring Gull *Larus argentatus*		
2	Arctic Skua *Stercorarius parasiticus*	**7**	Teal *Anas crecca*
3	Brent Goose *Branta bernicla*	**8**	Golden Pheasant *Chrysolophus pictus*
4	Grey Plover *Pluvialis squatarola*	**9**	Hoopoe *Upupa epops*
5	Red Footed Falcon *Falco vespertinus*	**10**	Scops Owl *Otus scops*
6	Night Heron *Nycticorax nycticorax*	**11**	Lammergeier *Gypaetus barbatus*

AVERAGE TEMPERATURE °C

January

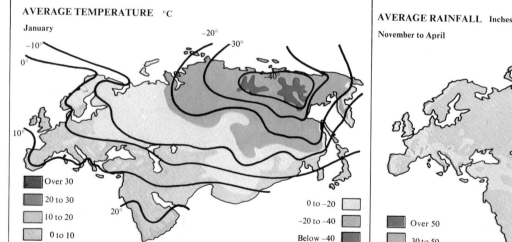

- Over 30
- 20 to 30
- 10 to 20
- 0 to 10
- 0 to −20
- −20 to −40
- Below −40

July

AVERAGE RAINFALL Inches

November to April

- Over 50
- 30 to 50
- 10 to 30
- Less than 10

May to October

NATURAL VEGETATION

Wooded savanna

Steppe

Desert

Lakes and rivers

Mediterranean vegetation

Temperate forest

Boreal forest

Tundra vegetation

The Arctic Breeding Grounds

Due to the severity of the Arctic climate, the bird-life of the north is more restricted than in temperate zones. Apart from a few mountain-dwelling species like the Meadow Pipit, most tundra birds are confined to the northern regions, where the climate is extremely harsh and long winters bring heavy snowfalls and temperatures permanently below freezing. The brief summer yields a rich growth of ground vegetation, but there are no trees in the tundra, and the few bushes, dwarf willows and birches grow only in sheltered places.

Birds survive by adapting their breeding habits to make full use of the short-lived summer. Flocks arrive as soon as the snow melts and nesting begins at once. With continuous summer daylight, plant growth is accelerated and the young are raised when food is most plentiful. As this favourable season is so short, almost all the species are long-range migrants that desert the tundra in winter.

Bird numbers fluctuate considerably from year to year. Marshes, peat-bogs and lakes offer the best food supply, notably insects, and these summer wetlands are filled with waders, ducks, scoters, geese, swans and divers. Fewer species feed on land, but prominent among them are wagtails, pipits, blue-throats and thrushes, Arctic Warblers and finches. The main predators ranging the Arctic wastes are Snowy Owls, Rough-legged Buzzards and skuas.

Right: Purple Sandpiper nesting in Arctic heathland

Rough-legged Buzzard
Buteo lagopus 23in
Breeding success is totally dependent on the availability of prey-species

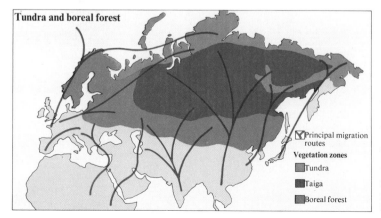

Tundra and boreal forest

Principal migration routes

Vegetation zones

Tundra

Taiga

Boreal forest

Rough-legged Buzzard
Buteo lagopus

The life-style of the Rough-legged Buzzard, a species widespread throughout the tundra, demonstrates perfectly the close relationship that often exists between predator and prey. The buzzard nests on the ground and is strictly adapted to a treeless environment – depending for food almost entirely on the local populations of lemmings and voles.

The rodent population varies considerably from one year to the next and the buzzard's breeding success follows every fluctuation. In a year of low rodent population, the number of breeding pairs of this Arctic hunter may be 15 times smaller than when lemmings and voles are abundant. Also, in lean years, the Rough-legged Buzzard leaves its breeding range much earlier, in much greater numbers and travels farther south than in seasons when food is plentiful.

Ptarmigan
Lagopus mutus

Ptarmigan constitute an important group of game-birds now almost entirely confined to the Arctic, apart from a few mountain species isolated in the Alps, the Pyrenees and the American Rockies at the close of the ice-ages.

One of the few full-time residents of the Arctic, the Ptarmigan is sheltered to some extent by a convenient seasonal camouflage. In winter it is protected from sub-zero temperatures by a dense, pure-white plumage, while its summer colouring of brown and black blends with the surrounding rock and lichen to shield the nesting bird from the eyes of predators. However, even in summer plumage the Ptarmigan retains the characteristic white feathers on its belly and wings and, in order not to attract the attention of predators, particularly the Golden Eagle, the bird spends most of its time on the ground – protected by the rich summer growth of heather, ling and low, shrubby vegetation.

The hen-bird alone incubates the clutch of five to nine mottled, red-brown eggs, but both parents will fiercely defend the nest against any intruder. Even if a chick is seized the parents will continue their efforts, thrashing the ground with out-stretched wings and feigning injury in an attempt to distract the attacker.

Ptarmigan feed mainly on the buds and twigs of dwarf willows. High in calories and available throughout the year, this diet allows the bird to remain in the tundra when most other species have departed for more hospitable regions.

Snow Bunting
Plectrophenax nivalis

The Snow Bunting's elaborate display is an object lesson in the effectiveness of visual signals in an open habitat. In courtship the male parades before the female with wings and tail spread to show the bold pattern of white patches on his otherwise black plumage. This striking pattern is also revealed in the song-flight as the male rises through the air with rapid fluttering wing-beats.

Feeding on a mixed diet of seeds, insects and larvae, the Snow Bunting occupies its breeding ground very early in the spring – building its nest in a rock crevice for protection.

Dunlin
Calidris alpina

Like most Arctic waders, Dunlin are wide-ranging migrants which spend the winter months along sea-coasts from Europe to tropical Africa and parts of Asia.

They arrive as soon as conditions are favourable and set about nesting immediately. The young are hatched when the food supply, mainly aquatic insects and larvae, is at its most abundant. The nestlings develop rapidly in the long, mild days of the brief Arctic summer and are able to fly south with the adult birds as soon as winter approaches and the food supply comes to an abrupt end.

Dunlin
Calidris alpina 7½ in
Nestlings develop quickly to beat the onset of winter

Snow Bunting
Plectrophenax nivalis 6½ in
Visual language in a barren habitat

Ptarmigan
Lagopus mutus 14½ in
Protective colouring varies with the seasons

Food for all seasons

Most waders are long-range migrants that show a marked change of habitat between breeding and wintering grounds. In summer, many establish themselves in moors, marshes and other fresh-water habitats, some even on barren ground at some distance from water. During migration they frequent sea-shores and are often found in immense concentrations on mudflats and sand beaches. Throughout the tundra summer the waders' main food consists of insects and larvae, with some seeds and berries, but in their marine habitats they feed mainly on molluscs, crustaceans and lugworms.

Curlew
Numenius arquata
The long, slender, down-curved bill can either pick morsels of food from the surface or probe deep into the mud for molluscs, worms or insects

Little Stint
Calidris minuta
One of the smallest waders, but one of the most active and lively. The short, straight bill is used to glean insects and crustacea from the surface

Bar-tailed Godwit
Limosa lapponica
The slender, delicately curved bill is driven deep into the mud with a side-to-side motion, probing for lugworms and other invertebrates

Spoon-billed Sandpiper
Eurynorhynchus pygmeus
Also called the Shoveller Sandpiper, the Spoonbill runs with rapid turning movements of the head. Small insects are sifted from the surface sand

Turnstone
Arenaria interpres
The short, stout, pointed bill is used to forage among stones and vegetation in search of small prey. Stone-turning is a characteristic hunting method

Boreal Coniferous Forest

Like an endless sea of firs, larches and pines, the vast expanse of the boreal forest and taiga stretches right across northern Europe and Asia. In the north the forest eventually gives way to the Arctic tundra, and on the southern margins the relentless acres of conifers are gradually relieved by scattered stands of birch, aspen and alder with an undergrowth of juniper, willow and fruiting bushes.

As a habitat, the forest lacks variety and can support far fewer species than the diverse woodlands of the temperate zone. Some birds adapt, but in general the pine forest is an austere habitat. Insect-eaters are uncommon and the few that do visit the pine forests move on quickly at the onset of winter, when food becomes scarce.

Best adapted are those birds that feed on conifer seeds – crossbills, grosbeaks, finches and nutcrackers. In all but the leanest years these species are the permanent residents of the northern forests. The productivity of the pine forests varies from year to year with abundant fruiting every two or three years. The bird population varies accordingly and, in lean years, many species migrate in search of new feeding grounds. The periodic invasions of western and central Europe by crossbills, nutcrackers and waxwings are often the result of a food shortage in the northern forests and may result in the temporary colonization of new areas.

Right: Stone pines – major food source for many species

The migrant specialists

While many seed-eating species must wait for conifer cones to open before they can feed on the tender seeds within, the crossbill's powerful beak, capable of exerting a pressure in excess of 100 lb/in² at the cutting edge, can shear through the hard outer case with ease and expose the seeds to the bird's long tongue. The Parrot Crossbill, specializing on tough pine-cones, has the heaviest bill, while the Common Crossbill (spruce) and the Two-barred Crossbill (larch) have lighter equipment.

The cone crop varies enormously from year to year and a prolific season is often followed by one of low productivity. In response to the ensuing food shortage, exacerbated by the population increase caused by a season of plenty, the birds irrupt in mass migrations. Occasionally the migrants successfully colonize a new area, but generally the birds breed only once before moving on or becoming extinct. While the adult birds successfully return to their normal breeding range, young born during the irruption tend to fly in the original migration direction, south or west, and the majority perish without ever returning to the home range.

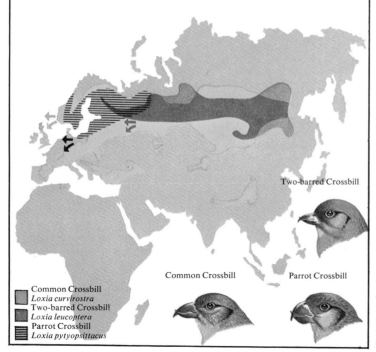

Common Crossbill

Two-barred Crossbill

Parrot Crossbill

Common Crossbill
Loxia curvirostra
Two-barred Crossbill
Loxia leucoptera
Parrot Crossbill
Loxia pytyopsittacus

Siberian Jay
Perisoreus infaustus 12in
Permanent resident of the cold northern forests

Siberian Jay
Perisoreus infaustus

The Siberian Jay is a more or less permanent resident of coniferous forests, with a marked preference for spruce and fir. Lodged in the fork of a tree, the jay's nest is built of twigs, lichens and herbaceous plants and is lined with mosses and feathers for warmth. Breeding starts in March or April and it may be two months before the young leave the nest.

Like many other Corvidae, this jay is a mixed feeder, preying on beetles, small birds and rodents as well as foraging for seeds and berries. In common with many birds of the taiga it probably also stores berries and seeds in a hollow tree for winter use. If the winter is exceptionally severe the Siberian Jay makes one of its rare excursions outside its chosen habitat in search of better conditions. In migration the birds form into small flocks within which the pair-bonds of mated birds remain permanent.

Capercaillie
Tetrao urogallus

Few, if any, forest species can match the elaborate and impressive courtship displays of the polygamous Capercaillie. In April and May the male takes up a display territory on a rock, in a tree or simply a patch of open ground and engages several females. Singing, leaping in the air and strutting about he cavorts before them noisily flapping his wings until, exhausted by the rigours of courtship and mating, he leaves the females in charge of the nest and young.

The species is restricted to mountains in Europe but is also found in the lowland forests of Siberia. The Capercaillie frequents larch, spruce and pine forests with a dense under-growth and, since it faces no competition for its winter food of conifer shoots and buds, is a year-round resident. In summer the diet is varied with grasses, leaves, fruits and, occasionally, insects.

Brambling
Fringilla montifringilla 5¾in
One of the long-range migrants,
travelling as far as
southern China

Great Grey Owl
Strix nebulosa 27in
Silent hunter of the
lemming and vole

Brambling
Fringilla montifringilla

Common throughout the forests of Europe, but particularly in the birch-woods and willow scrub of the northern taiga, the Brambling is a true insectivore. Vegetation plays a very minor role in the Brambling's food supply, which consists almost entirely of beetles, caterpillars, wasps and spiders. In fact this gregarious forest bird is so single-minded that sudden increases in the plant-lice population will attract the species in huge flocks – even at the height of the breeding season. This dietary preference explains why Brambling travel such vast distances in their annual migrations – flocks numbering many thousands of birds pouring south through Europe and Asia to spend the winter months in the south of France, Italy, the Near East and even India and southern China.

The Brambling resembles the Chaffinch, to which it is related, but its monotonous cheeping call is a far cry from the melodious song of its relative. From early June onwards it builds the compact nest typical of the finch family, but somewhat larger and, possibly as a response to the cold climate of its northern range, with thicker walls.

Great Grey Owl
Strix nebulosa

The Great Grey Owl is dependent for survival on the forest population of small rodents, and the numbers of rodents in any year profoundly affect the owl's breeding habits.

The predator's diet is based mainly on the lemming in the tundra regions and on forest lemmings, voles and mice, squirrels and even young sable in the forests. Very rare in western Europe, the Great Grey Owl may not breed at all in years when the prey-species population is unusually small, and even in moderate years the clutch-size may vary considerably (between one and five eggs), depending on the availability of food.

Though generally sedentary, the owl will adopt a nomadic life-style in lean years and may even make irregular migrations if conditions become serious.

The species is common in Siberia, where it frequents old, mature coniferous forest tracts, and in eastern Siberia its range extends into the deciduous woodlands farther south. Like all owls the Great Grey is a solitary creature, often utilizing nests abandoned by other large birds, and always choosing an exposed nest site high in the crown of a tree.

Capercaillie
Tetrao urogallus 34in
Noisy exhibitionist of the
mountain pine-forests

Temperate Deciduous Woodland

Rather less than 20,000 years ago, towards the end of the most recent ice-age, the polar ice-cap spread like a mantle over northern Europe and Asia. Deciduous forest was restricted to a narrow coastal strip along the Mediterranean Sea, extending east in a slender band to the southern shores of the Black Sea and the Caspian. Another belt of deciduous woodland lay along the foot of the northern slopes of the Himalayan range.

Gradually, as the ice retreated and the climate became more temperate, deciduous trees spread northwards and began to overtake the conifers. By about 5,000 years ago much of western Europe up to the shores of the Baltic had been successfully recolonized.

In the early phase of its development, this forest must have offered abundant and varied habitats for many species of birds. But, on reaching full maturity with a closed canopy restricting ground vegetation, this primarily oak forest could only have supported a much more restricted range of species.

Natural clearance and regeneration would have made only small areas of variety available, so bird-life would have remained restricted until man began to make an impact on the ecological picture with his agricultural clearances. Much of the avian richness of woodland Europe is a welcome by-product of forest clearance and timber management.
Below: Mixed deciduous woodland in southern Britain.

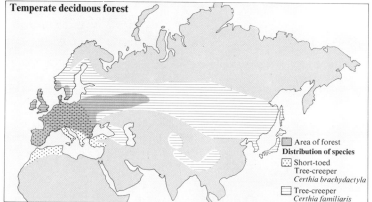

Temperate deciduous forest

Area of forest
Distribution of species
Short-toed
Tree-creeper
Certhia brachydactyla
Tree-creeper
Certhia familiaris

Willow Warbler
Phylloscopus trochilus

The Willow Warbler is one of the first migrant songbirds to return to the forests of Europe following a winter spent south of the Sahara. Its relative the Chiffchaff, *P. collybita*, arrives a few days earlier, having wintered no farther south than the Mediterranean.

Although these two birds look so similar, their songs offer a striking contrast. There are other distinctions, too. Both species feed largely on insects in the breeding season, but the Chiffchaff usually occupies a higher feeding station – preferring to hunt its food, and sing, from the canopy of a tall tree. The Willow Warbler tends to exploit areas with a better-developed shrub layer and is able to penetrate considerably farther north and west. It can colonize even stunted birchwoods at quite high altitudes.

A similar distinction occurs in nesting. The Willow Warbler builds a domed nest of grass on the ground amid the stems of other vegetation while the untidy, only partly hooded nest of the Chiffchaff may be up to three feet above the ground. With a longer migration journey into Africa, the Willow Warbler is usually single-brooded, while the Chiffchaff often raises two broods a year.

Willow Warbler
Phylloscopus trochilus 4¼in
*One of the first migrants
to return in spring*

Sparrowhawk
Accipiter nisus

In forest surroundings, predatory birds are at some disadvantage because of the physical obstacles littering their hunting grounds. The Tawny Owl, *Strix aluco*, overcomes these difficulties by waiting, perched over an open area, before dropping silently on to its ground-feeding prey as it moves, unsuspectingly, beneath.

The Sparrowhawk uses another technique to reap its harvest from the abundance of small forest birds. The long tail and short, rounded wings with deeply slotted primaries give the Sparrowhawk astonishing speed and the agility to manoeuvre through trees as it dashes after its prey – snatching the victim in mid-air.

The sexes are very different in size, the female often dwarfing the male. She can cope with prey as large as Woodpigeon, while the male rarely takes anything bigger than Fieldfare. The hen bird moults while incubating the eggs, renewing her feathers in time for her hunting ability to be of immense value in feeding the rapidly developing young.

Although each Sparrowhawk will take several small birds every day, the species occurs at surprisingly high densities without, apparently, adversely affecting the population of small-bird species.

Sparrowhawk
Accipiter nisus 13in
*Once endangered by
excessive use of pesticides*

Treecreepers
Certhia spp

Although they appear so very similar, the two species of treecreeper have adapted to quite different habitats – the Common Treecreeper, *C. familiaris*, to the coniferous forests of northern Europe and the Short-toed Treecreeper, *C. brachydactyla*, to the deciduous woodlands of central and southern Europe. It is generally thought that *familiaris* was isolated in the coniferous forests of Britain at the close of the ice-age and that it subsequently adapted to the fast-developing deciduous woodlands.

Treecreepers exploit the many dietary possibilities of bark, trunk and branches. Their needle-sharp, slightly curved beaks are perfectly adapted for seeking out insects and other small arthropods, concealed larvae and grubs. After the breeding season, mixed feeding flocks are a common sight in deciduous woodlands, and treecreepers regularly take their place along with tits, wrens, goldcrests and warblers. Between them the birds of the mixed forests

cover most feeding niches from the ground (province of the Great Tit) to the twigs and branches of the canopy (province of the Chiffchaff).

Apart from feeding expeditions, the treecreeper is one of the most sedentary of birds and is only rarely involved in movements beyond its home territory. In compensation, these birds have well-developed roosting behaviour. Individuals may roost in small hollows in the bark, and groups sometimes roost huddled together for warmth.

Treecreepers are best suited to forest areas, where there is a natural progression of vegetation – including fallen and decaying trees. Not only does this enhance food supplies, but their nests are most commonly situated behind flaps of peeling bark or in large splits in the timber. Much modern, controlled, forest, where decayed matter is cut out and removed, is therefore unsuitable for treecreepers.

The nest is usually boat-shaped to fit the cavity and normally has a bolt-hole at the rear to facilitate escape should the nest and young be threatened by predatory mammals.

Common Treecreeper
Certhia familiaris 5in
Forced to adapt by Britain's changing woodland flora

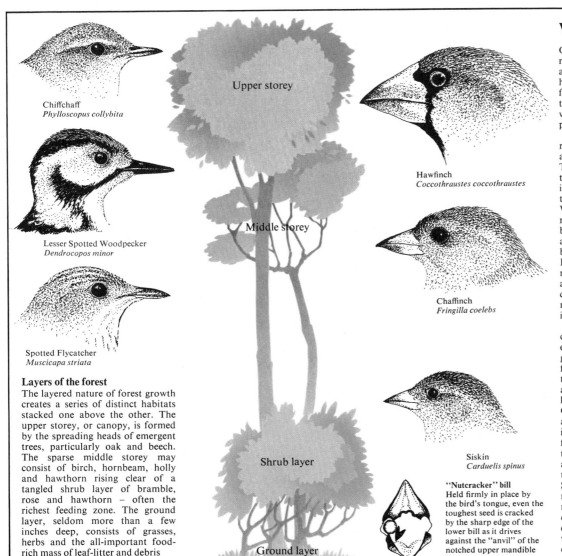

Chiffchaff
Phylloscopus collybita

Lesser Spotted Woodpecker
Dendrocopos minor

Spotted Flycatcher
Muscicapa striata

Upper storey

Middle storey

Shrub layer

Ground layer

Hawfinch
Coccothraustes coccothraustes

Chaffinch
Fringilla coelebs

Siskin
Carduelis spinus

"Nutcracker" bill
Held firmly in place by the bird's tongue, even the toughest seed is cracked by the sharp edge of the lower bill as it drives against the "anvil" of the notched upper mandible

Layers of the forest
The layered nature of forest growth creates a series of distinct habitats stacked one above the other. The upper storey, or canopy, is formed by the spreading heads of emergent trees, particularly oak and beech. The sparse middle storey may consist of birch, hornbeam, holly and hawthorn rising clear of a tangled shrub layer of bramble, rose and hawthorn – often the richest feeding zone. The ground layer, seldom more than a few inches deep, consists of grasses, herbs and the all-important food-rich mass of leaf-litter and debris

Woodland ecology

Open mixed woodland is one of the most varied and productive habitats available to birds. Wherever trees have fallen, or where man has formed coppices, the feeding opportunities of the enriched lower layers will attract a large and varied bird population.

Woodland birds display a wide range of adaptation in taking advantage of the niches available. The Chiffchaff spends most of its time high in the canopy gleaning insects, grubs and caterpillars from the foliage. The Lesser Spotted Woodpecker is more mobile – roaming up and down trunks and branches and probing among leaves and loose bark for insects and beetles. By contrast, the Spotted Flycatcher inhabits the more open middle storey, especially in glades and clearings. Perched on a convenient branch, this agile hunter makes darting forays after flying insects and beetles.

The finch family illustrates the diversity of feeding habit that may evolve within a single, closely related group. The Hawfinch, largest of the finches, spends its time in the tree-tops where, armed with a massive and powerful bill, it feeds on the largest and toughest seeds. The Chaffinch, equipped with a lighter and more versatile bill, feeds mainly in the shrub layer and on the ground, foraging amongst the close vegetation for seeds and insects, which are often caught on the wing. At the other extreme, the tiny, agile Siskin balances at the tips of the most slender twigs, feeding on minute seeds. Its bill is light and delicately pointed, enabling it to extract the seeds from alder cones when other sources of food are diminished in the winter months.

Woodland: The Dwindling Habitat

Great Spotted Woodpecker
Dendrocopos major 9 in
Wood-boring larvae are extracted with a barb-tipped tongue

Hawfinch
Coccothraustes coccothraustes 7in
The most powerful seed-crushing bill in the finch family

Blackcap
Sylvia atricapilla 5½in
Shares the rich habitat of secondary forest with the Garden Warbler

Great Spotted Woodpecker
Dendrocopos major

The mixed forests of Europe and Asia offer sufficient diversity of habitat to accommodate nine woodpecker species. Apart from a variation in size, they are all structurally similar, with their toes arranged two forward and two back (except in the Three-toed Woodpecker, *Picoides tridactylus*) to facilitate climbing. Stiff tail-feathers serve as an additional prop and the robust head and bill are designed to withstand the repeated hammer-blows of drilling. The bird's thick-necked appearance is due to the massive neck muscles, which provide the power to drill into the toughest wood.

The prime food source consists of wood-boring insects and larvae that are reached by chipping away the outer bark or by drilling into the living wood. Most woodpeckers have an immensely long tongue, which is coiled in a sheath within the skull and anchored at the base of the upper mandible. In the Great Spotted Woodpecker, the tongue has a horny barbed tip that is plunged into the larva in its burrow like an animated harpoon.

Tree fruits, especially nuts and pine cones, are regularly taken and are often removed to an "anvil" for opening. In some areas the Great Spotted Woodpecker has become a predator – preying on the young of other hole-nesting species. Woodpeckers themselves excavate deep flask-shaped nest-holes in a trunk or branch, a task that may take several weeks. In the breeding season, the strident calls of the adults and the screams of the hungry young are characteristic sounds of the forest.

Blackcap
Sylvia atricapilla

The Blackcap is an unobtrusive insect and fruit eater that, with the Garden Warbler, *S.borin*, has exploited the extensive secondary vegetation of artificially thinned deciduous forests.

Difficult to observe despite its distinctive plumage, the Blackcap tends to feed, nest and sing high in the undergrowth or even in the canopy, leaving the more dense lower cover to the Garden Warbler. The annual feeding cycles of the two species are much the same; insects are taken throughout the summer, but both switch to energy-rich fruits prior to migration.

Blackcaps winter in northern Africa and, unlike the Garden Warbler, seldom cross the Sahara. Their prolonged stay in the home range enables them to raise two broods to the Garden Warbler's one, and many Blackcaps now winter in western Europe without migrating.

Hawfinch
Coccothraustes coccothraustes

Capable of exerting a crushing pressure of nearly 200 lb/in² the massive bill of the Hawfinch represents the ultimate in finch feeding adaptation. The bill is used to crack open the seeds of wild cherry, damson and even hornbeam – a task quite beyond any other member of the finch family.

Like most seed-eating species, the Hawfinch is common in western Europe, where man's agricultural and forestry practices have led to an increase in secondary vegetation in clearings, glades and forest margins.

Woodcock
Scolopax rusticola

Only a handful of wading species has broken away from the coastal and wetland habitats associated with this group of birds. The Woodcock has done so successfully and is now widespread in any damp deciduous forest from the edge of the tundra south almost to the Mediterranean.

In some western areas the Woodcock is sedentary, but it migrates from northern regions where the soil freezes in winter and denies the bird's long bill access to the earthworms and other ground-invertebrates that make up the bulk of its diet.

Catholic in its choice of forest type, the Woodcock prefers open glades for its display flights in spring, but like many forest birds it is capable of fast, agile flight between closely spaced trunks. The eggs and chicks are as well camouflaged as the adults, which, even among ground-dwelling birds, are remarkable for their perfect cryptic colouring. The young, like those of most waders, leave the nest and disperse a few hours after hatching.

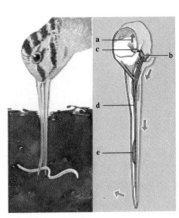

A sensitive probe
The Woodcock's bill is beautifully adapted for feeding in loose earth and leaf-litter. Probing deep into the soft humus, the Woodcock can feel the presence of worms and grasp them with the flexible upper mandible. As the muscle (a) contracts, a linkbone (b) rotates around a pivot (c) in the skull. Movement is transmitted through the slender bone (d) and the bill-tip flexes open, helped by a thinning (e) of the upper mandible.

Woodcock
Scolopax rusticola 14½in
Detects its prey with a remarkably sensitive bill-tip

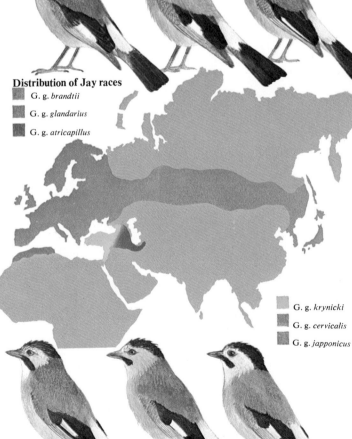

The Jay races of Eurasia

By far the most strikingly coloured of all European woodland birds, the Common Jay is widely distributed, in a number of different races, throughout Europe and Asia.

It is primarily a resident of oak and mixed deciduous woodland and feeds on acorns wherever these are available. However, the Common Jay is a versatile feeder, taking insects and larvae, seeds, eggs and young birds, fruit and buds. In some areas it has forsaken its usual preference for deciduous woodland and successfully adapted to a life in mixed coniferous forests, where it feeds mainly on the seeds of the Arolla pine, *Pinus cembra*. Like many members of the family Corvidae, the Common Jay hoards food during the late summer, burying each seed or acorn separately in the soft ground.

Between five and seven pale, speckled eggs are laid in late April, in a slightly built open nest, well concealed in a small tree or bush.

Many bird species that have a wide geographical range show local variations in plumage coloration from one part of the range to another. Although not recognized as full species in their own right, the members of these populations are different enough to be called subspecies, or races. Where races overlap, there is a gradual transition from one set of characteristics to the next, as interbreeding occurs wherever birds of the same species are in contact.

There are more than 20 recognized jay races in the Palaearctic realm, ranging from the familiar *G.g.glandarius* of western Europe to the much more localized *G.g.japonicus* of the Japanese islands.

1 *G.g.glandarius*
2 *G.g.brandtii*
3 *G.g.japonicus*
4 *G.g.cervicalis*
5 *G.g.krynicki*
6 *G.g.atricapillus*

Distribution of Jay races
G. g. *brandtii*
G. g. *glandarius*
G. g. *atricapillus*

G. g. *krynicki*
G. g. *cervicalis*
G. g. *japponicus*

Common Jay
Garrulus glandarius 15in
Its races are spread from Britain to the Japanese islands

The Windswept Grasslands

The broad belt of steppe country, stretching across Asia from eastern Europe to the Orient, forms an arid and windswept corridor offering little encouragement to plant-growth. The summer months are parched and dusty; those of winter, bitterly cold. Only in spring does plant-life burst forth to transform the steppe into a waving sea of feathergrass and wild flowers. Although the dominant plant species vary with latitude, the steppes have a superficial similarity, characterized by dry, open, uncultivated plains, or by rolling expanses of undulating country relieved by scattered areas of scrub vegetation.

Despite the apparent harshness of this domain, the steppes are surprisingly rich in bird-life. Those of Central Asia support nearly 250 of the species found in Europe – a total equal to that of the apparently more hospitable Mediterranean region where more species might be expected.

In the absence of trees, most steppe birds nest in the protection of grass tussocks and rocks or in cavities and burrows. The eggs are cryptically coloured and the adults themselves show a marked tendency toward drab, inconspicuous colours – though to a lesser extent than birds of the true deserts. As would be expected, woodland and aquatic species are poorly represented in the steppes, while raptors, wheatears, larks and shrikes are widespread.

Below: Rolling steppe country with scattered trees

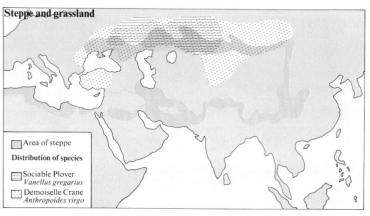

Steppe Eagle
Aquila rapax   28in
Versatility breeds success in the treeless steppes

Steppe and grassland

☐ Area of steppe

Distribution of species

☐ Sociable Plover
Vanellus gregarius
☐ Demoiselle Crane
Anthropoides virgo

Steppe Eagle
Aquila rapax

Found in a wide variety of habitats ranging from semi-desert to bushveld, and at altitudes from sea level to 7,000 feet, the Steppe Eagle is probably the most numerous eagle of its size in the world. Geographically, too, it is widespread, represented by races in Africa, Arabia and India. Most of the northern races migrate in winter, but those within the tropics tend to remain in their home range, supported by a more abundant food supply which they boost by scavenging more than their relatives.

In steppe conditions, shelter from chilling winds and the direct rays of the sun is vitally important – particularly to the brooding female and her vulnerable nestlings. The huge nest of sticks and branches is usually built in an isolated tree or on an exposed rock outcrop commanding a view across the plain, but, unlike most eagles, *A. rapax* will also nest on open ground – a useful adaptation to the steppe environment.

Demoiselle Crane
Anthropoides virgo

Although it may breed in the damp, marshy areas bordering rivers, the Demoiselle Crane is really a bird of arid lands and is found throughout savannas, semi-deserts and steppes, even at high altitudes. As in the Common Crane, *Grus grus*, elaborate and exciting communal displays serve to strengthen the bonds between mated pairs. The birds form a circle, the centre of which is occupied by a few individuals who take turns in leaping and dancing, calling and bowing, with wings outstretched.

Unlike the massive reed nest of the Common Crane, the Demoiselle makes little more than a shallow scrape in the ground, among stones, in which to lay her clutch of two or three brown-speckled olive-coloured eggs.

In common with most steppe birds, the Demoiselle feeds mainly on grasshoppers, locusts and beetles, but this diet is supplemented with lizards, which abound in the dry grasslands.

Sociable Plover
Vanellus gregarius

In the breeding season the Sociable Plover appears to favour relatively barren areas of open, rolling country where vegetation is sparse, even for the steppe. In winter, the birds retire to warmer areas of sandy soil with extensive grass cover, though summer and winter alike the bird seldom strays very far from water.

The Sociable Plover nests in a shallow depression near to, or even within, a tuft of grass or other low vegetation, and the eggs – usually a typical wader clutch of four – are effectively camouflaged, as are the nidifugous young. Both parents incubate and care for the young, feeding them on a wide variety of beetles, spiders and grasshoppers.

Sociable Plover
Vanellus gregarius 11½in
*Never far from water – even
in the most barren steppe*

Demoiselle Crane
Anthropoides virgo 38in
*Social bonds are strengthened
by elaborate dance displays*

Courtship contortionist

Few, if indeed any, of the world's ground-dwelling birds can compete with the bizarre and spectacular courtship display of the Great Bustard, *Otis tarda*. Starting well in advance of the nesting season and continuing long after the eggs have been laid, the male bustard displays either singly or in a group; at first to any female who happens to be present but later to a chosen individual hen. As females outnumber the males, each cock may in fact take more than one mate.

The most intense periods of activity are at dawn and dusk, and the display may continue through the night in fair weather with bright moonlight. Strutting and stamping before the female, the excited male shakes his plumage vigorously then raises his tail over his back to expose the snowy white underfeathers. The wings are drooped almost to ground level and then twisted over so that the white undersides of the flight feathers are uppermost. At the same time the head is sunk into the shoulders, and the gular pouch, visible only during the mating season, is inflated, almost completely hiding the bird's head. The result of these contortions is to transform the male from a handsome reddish-brown bird into a billowing, amorphous mass of brilliant white feathers.

Having held the display pose, sometimes for several minutes, the male reverts to his former self like the finale of a conjurer's performance.

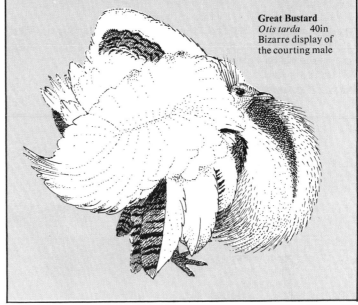

Great Bustard
Otis tarda 40in
Bizarre display of
the courting male

Rosy Pastor 8½in
Sturnus roseus
*Colourful relative
of the Starling*

Rosy Pastor
Sturnus roseus

Gregarious and noisy, generally omnivorous, the Rosy Pastor is very like its close relative, the Starling, *S. vulgaris*, with which it frequently forms mixed flocks. It is primarily a bird of barren open country, and in particular those areas of rocky outcrop that provide a profusion of convenient nesting cavities. Pastors are generally colonial in habit and breeding colonies may number several thousand birds.

In courtship, the male performs a frantic dance – running in circles round the hen with crest erect and wings quivering. Eventually the female joins in and the two rotate together until the hen stops and crouches to receive her mate.

The nest is a tangled mass of vegetation concealing a clutch of five or six eggs. In some years, productivity is unusually high and the population may irrupt far beyond the normal range. From the population centre in southeastern Europe, Rosy Pastors have travelled as far as Ireland.

Western Fields and Pastures

In changing the balance of nature, man has structured an environment vastly different from that which existed in primitive times, and, although the relatively slow pace of change has made adaptation possible for many species of wildlife, man's manipulation of the environment has led to a shift in the balance of avian communities. Species of the open habitats have found themselves in a more favourable position than those of the woodlands.

Bird populations are invariably much higher in man-made woodland than in natural forest. In fact, the structured woodland habitat is one of the most benign of all. Even in parkland, where the diversity of species is not quite so marked, a census taken in Switzerland revealed 170 pairs on only ten hectares, the predominant species being Blackbird, Greenfinch, Chaffinch, Canary, Great Tit, Goldfinch and Redstart. Less reassuring was a count taken in Britain. In a comparable area in the Midlands, only 11 to 50 pairs were seen – principally Blackbird, Hedgesparrow, Skylark, Robin and Chaffinch.

Vast arable fields are not conducive to a rich diversity of bird-life as relatively few species thrive alongside modern agriculture. Seed-eaters are more common than insectivores, but species that nest in branches or hollow trees have been driven from many agricultural regions.

Right: The varied patchwork of man-modified Europe

Partridge
Perdix perdix 12½in
Suffers heavy losses in areas of intensive modern farming

Partridge
Perdix perdix

Partridge are gregarious birds, normally living in coveys consisting of adults and young of several families. In early spring, considerable numbers gather in mating assemblies to display before dispersing in pairs to nest and breed.

Partridge are most numerous on agricultural land, especially where cereals are a main crop, as well as in pasture and other grassland offering suitable ground-cover. Intensive farming is, however, detrimental to the species: agricultural methods and equipment pose a constant threat to nests, eggs and young and in many European countries the decline of the species can be attributed to heavy losses incurred before the young are fledged.

The female scrapes out a shallow nesting hollow and in it lays a characteristically large clutch – anything from nine to 20 eggs with as many as 24 having been recorded. Predators take a heavy toll of the young, which are able to leave the nest soon after hatching. Partridge are mainly vegetarian but will also take worms and insects. Ants and their larvae are a favoured delicacy.

Little Owl
Athene noctua

The life-style of the Little Owl is so flexible that this tiny predator is one of the most widespread and successful members of its family. With a wide choice of diet, it needs only open habitat interspersed with convenient perches and potential nesting cavities to be able to live in quite high densities. Up to 20 pairs may breed in as little as one square kilometre.

The Little Owl nests in tree-holes, particularly in pollarded willows, in wall cavities, sometimes even in rabbit burrows. It has a wide range of food, up to 90 per cent of its diet consisting of invertebrates, especially earthworms and large beetles. The owl may also prey on a variety of small birds, mammals, reptiles and amphibians. Like most owls it hunts mainly at dawn or dusk, but it may also hunt by day.

Its catholic feeding and nesting habits allow the Little Owl to remain in its home range all year round, but numbers may suffer in very cold winters when heavy snowfalls drastically reduce the food available.

Little Owl
Athene noctua 9in
Tiny, but enormously successful

Skylark
Alauda arvensis 7¾in
Southern populations are joined, in winter, by their northern relatives

Rook
Corvus frugilegus 19in
Feeding groups post sentries to warn of approaching danger

Agricultural Europe

Distribution of species

Rook
Corvus frugilegus

Skylark
Alauda arvensis

Little Owl
Athene noctua

Common Partridge
Perdix perdix

Rook
Corvus frugilegus

Rookeries, for centuries a familiar feature of the landscape, normally consist of about 50 birds, but giant "conurbations" of up to 2,000 birds have been recorded. Rookeries are established in the tops of tall trees, with the nests, up to 50 in a single tree, placed close together.

Highly gregarious, rooks live in these colonies all year round and exhibit a number of group behaviour patterns. Flocks are very well organized, particularly on feeding grounds where scouts are deployed all round to pass visual and audible warnings of approaching danger. The Rook is skilful in flight and makes full use of wings that are longer and narrower than those of the Crow.

In western Europe populations are sedentary – augmented each winter by huge contingents of eastern Rooks that migrate across the plains of central Europe in flocks of thousands.

The Rook needs tall trees in which to roost and open grassland in which to feed – precisely those conditions found in agricultural land. But, though welcome during nesting when they destroy insects and larvae, the species incurs the farmer's wrath when it turns to young cereal shoots in the winter months.

Skylark
Alauda arvensis

The prolonged warbling song of the Skylark, lasting anything up to ten minutes, is one of the most familiar sounds of rural Europe. The male sings during his courtship flights, hovering or spiralling slowly up or down through several hundred feet, and in addition to proclaiming his readiness to mate, the far-carrying song serves to warn all other birds of his claim to a breeding territory.

Although the Skylark was originally found on grassy moors and marshland meadows, today it has spread widely through farmland, particularly in cereal-growing regions. An opportunist feeder switching from insects in summer to seeds in winter, the Skylark can remain in Europe throughout the year and is joined, in winter, by migrant populations from the colder eastern and northern regions of Europe.

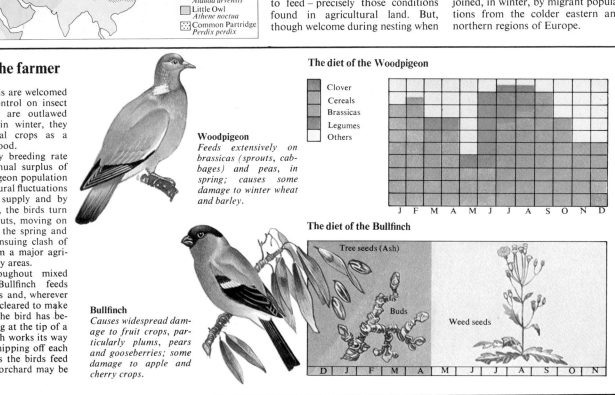

No friend to the farmer

Although some birds are welcomed by farmers as a control on insect pests, many more are outlawed when, particularly in winter, they turn to commercial crops as a major source of food.

Despite a healthy breeding rate that creates an annual surplus of young, the Woodpigeon population is kept stable by natural fluctuations in its winter food supply and by shooting. In winter, the birds turn increasingly to sprouts, moving on to ripening peas in the spring and summer, and the ensuing clash of interest brands them a major agricultural pest in many areas.

Widespread throughout mixed woodlands, the Bullfinch feeds mainly on tree buds and, wherever woodland has been cleared to make way for orchards, the bird has become a pest. Starting at the tip of a branch, the Bullfinch works its way towards the trunk nipping off each bud in turn and, as the birds feed in small flocks, an orchard may be stripped in hours.

Woodpigeon
Feeds extensively on brassicas (sprouts, cabbages) and peas, in spring; causes some damage to winter wheat and barley.

Bullfinch
Causes widespread damage to fruit crops, particularly plums, pears and gooseberries; some damage to apple and cherry crops.

The diet of the Woodpigeon

Clover
Cereals
Brassicas
Legumes
Others

J F M A M J J A S O N D

The diet of the Bullfinch

Tree seeds (Ash)

Buds

Weed seeds

D J F M A M J J A S O N

The impact of man

The natural environment, like its inhabitants, is in a constant state of evolutionary change. Lakes gradually fill in to become marshes, then carrs and finally forests, while open downland undergoes a similar series of transformations through scrub to mature woodland. This natural progression towards a stable "climax" vegetation is slow but inexorable, and can only be halted or changed by a massive input of energy from some external source. A climax situation that took, perhaps, several thousand years to develop, may be destroyed overnight by the ravages of hurricane, flood or forest fire, but once reduced to a barren waste, the land is slowly recolonized by wind-blown seeds and spores and the cycle begins anew.

Climax vegetation is seldom as rich in animal and bird life as the transitional phases that precede it. Maturing trees provide new niches for hole-nesting species and canopy feeders, but many other niches, particularly at ground level, are progressively lost. The resulting rise and fall in the resident bird population is best illustrated in the case of plantation forests where the intermediate stage of scrub vegetation is by far the richest in bird life.

During the past few centuries the land has been dominated by a rapidly expanding, and highly mechanized, human population. As living standards have risen, so too has man's demand for land – for agriculture, industry, housing and for the extraction of mineral resources lying beneath the surface. What was virgin forest a mere few hundred years ago is today largely covered by the vast urban sprawl of industrial society, and even the remaining forest areas are often as closely managed as any other commercial crop.

Progress, however, does not inevitably mean the destruction of wildlife: much of our modern environment is sterile, but intelligent management can turn gravel-pits into attractive havens for water-fowl, and the cropping of forested areas, with a 50-year turn-round, ensures a perpetual supply of richly diverse transitional habitats. The derelict scars left by the early industrialization of Europe can be erased and land reclaimed, but the continuing growth of monoculture is a dangerous trend – not only destroying valuable wildlife habitats but steadily weakening the structure of the soil and reducing its capacity to produce.

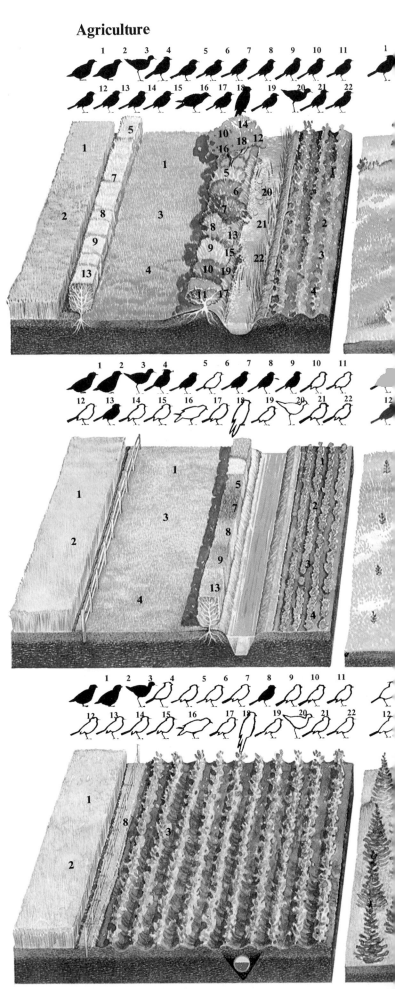

Agriculture

Key to bird symbols

Breeding resident	Breeding resident lost from habitat	Newly-acquired breeding resident	Non-breeding resident

---

Agricultural areas	Forested areas	Industrial areas
1 Partridge	1 Meadow Pipit	1 Willow Warbler
2 Pheasant	2 Hen Harrier	2 Reed Bunting
3 Lapwing	3 Merlin	3 Pied Wagtail
4 Skylark	4 Skylark	4 Lapwing
5 Dunnock	5 Redpoll	5 Moorhen
6 Wren	6 Linnet	6 Kingfisher
7 Blackbird	7 Nightjar	7 Water Rail
8 Corn Bunting	8 Stonechat	8 Sedge Warbler
9 Yellowhammer	9 Whinchat	9 Heron
10 Chaffinch	10 Long-tailed Tit	10 Sand Martin
11 Robin	11 Lesser Whitethroat	11 Little Ringed Plover
12 Blue Tit	12 Whitethroat	12 Mallard
13 Whitethroat	13 Greenfinch	13 Mute Swan
14 Great Tit	14 Goldfinch	14 Marsh Tit
15 Songthrush	15 Chiffchaff	15 Migrant waders
16 Carrion Crow	16 Jay	16 Coot
17 Long-tailed Tit	17 Chaffinch	17 Great Crested Grebe
18 Kestrel	18 Goldcrest	18 Tufted Duck
19 Greenfinch	19 Coal Tit	19 Black Redstart
20 Moorhen	20 Sparrowhawk	20 Starling
21 Reed Bunting	21 Wood Pigeon	21 House Sparrow
22 Sedge Warbler	22 Crossbill	22 Herring Gull

Industry

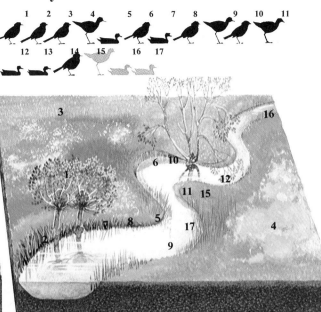

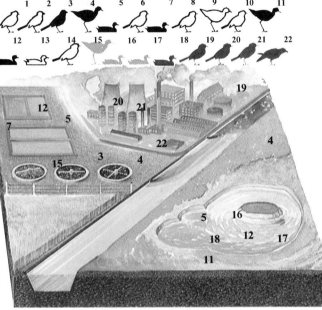

Creative reclamation

The vehicle dump is as sterile to wild-life as it is offensive to man; but simple landscaping can quickly turn a disused gravel-pit into an attractive lagoon – to the benefit of man and water-fowl alike

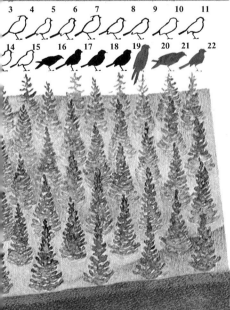

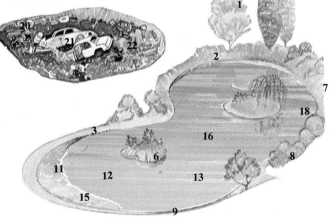

Farmland

The partial clearance of medieval forest, to provide arable land, greatly broadened the range of available habitats. Essential feeding and breeding cover was retained in the hedges and open ditches, while stands of woodland were preserved for fuel.

The pressures of a vastly increased population now demand that farmers utilize every inch of their land. Hedges are trimmed or replaced with wire fences, so destroying the nest-sites and song-posts of many species, and the food-rich ditch is canalized and often replaced by an underground drainage conduit.

The diversity of habitat that was possible, without conflict, a few centuries ago, has today been lost through the dictates of monoculture, and the consequent and inevitable loss of bird-life is clearly apparent in the sequence of diagrams far left.

Forestry

The pattern of change in forested areas, shown in the central series of illustrations, is very different from that in farmland – and far more beneficial to wildlife.

Areas of marginal land, often moorland and heath with a relatively impoverished bird fauna, are planted with conifers and, during the first 20 years of growth, provide a scrub-land habitat rich in ecological niches. Once the forest matures, light is excluded from the ground layer, the food supply is reduced, and many of the newly acquired species are lost. However, the natural life of a commercial plantation-forest is about 50 years for planting to felling and, as planting times are staggered, a constant supply of varied, scrub-type habitats is ensured.

Often several different tree species are planted, broadleaf as well as conifer, and "islands" of older timber are regularly left standing when the timber is harvested.

Industry

In terms of both visual impact and pollution, industry is capable of making the greatest scars on our landscapes. The canalization of rivers to provide transportation and cheap water, eventually to be used as great sewers for industrial waste, is just one of the many examples. When countryside vanishes beneath concrete, the loss of bird-life is bound to be considerable and yet there are a surprising number of hardy and adaptable species that have come to terms with man's activities.

Fortunately, concern for human (and environmental) health has led to many legislative controls, reducing atmospheric pollution and dumping and requiring the replacement of land disturbed by mineral extraction. Here man has the opportunity, and the responsibility, to repair the environment. There can be no excuse for derelict waste land when thought, and modest capital outlay, can create viable wildlife habitats.

The Mediterranean: Maquis and Scrub

In many ways the Mediterranean serves as much as a recuperative region for birds as it does for the people of Europe. Midway between the searing heat of the tropics and the frigid extremes of northern Europe, this is a benign régime characterized by mild, humid winters and warm, dry summers. Though lapsing to some extent in summer, the vegetation growth is adequate, and insects are to be found in varying densities throughout the year.

Bird-life is at its most sparse in the Mediterranean in summer, when conditions are least favourable. Species represented at this time are mainly tropical birds adapted to scrub habitat and dry conditions. They will have bred in spring and are ready to leave before the onset of winter. Predominant among winter visitors are passerines, such as warblers and thrushes, and ducks. Most are mixed feeders and can rely on a reasonable supply of insects, fruits and grasses.

In between, the Mediterranean also plays host to the transients – the long-range migrants. These are birds which, exhausted after their long flight across the Sahara and the open sea, break their northward migration in the spring. In autumn there are many more species that pause in the Mediterranean to build up their reserves of fat before travelling south to their southern-hemisphere winter quarters.
Right: Scrub terrain of the Mediterranean maquis

Dartford Warbler
Sylvia undata 5in
Nests in the protection of tangled thorn-thickets

Rock Thrush
Monticola saxatilis 7½in
Maintains an additional feeding territory up to a mile from the nest

Dartford Warbler
Sylvia undata

The Dartford Warbler is one of a group of warblers peculiar to the Mediterranean region, where several species exist side by side in the same area while occupying different ecological niches.

In the Mediterranean, the Dartford Warbler inhabits oak-woodlands and cistus-covered hills, but a sub-species, or race, is established in western France and southern England, where heather and gorse heathland provides a suitable habitat for year-round residence.

Common throughout the Mediterranean maquis, the Dartford Warbler preys on flies, beetles, butterflies and caterpillars, which it hunts with great agility among the tangled branches of thorn-bush vegetation. Its nest is cunningly concealed in this defensive entanglement and the bird is seldom seen except when perched on an exposed branch to sing. The male has an elaborate display flight – "dancing" through the air with wings and tail fanned out, singing loudly.

Due to the mild winter conditions, this warbler is never a true migrant, though it does desert the higher parts of its range in favour of lowland valleys during the winter. Some hardy individuals remain at quite high altitude even when the ground is covered in snow.

Rock Thrush
Monticola saxatilis

Moving over the ground in a succession of hops, or standing bolt upright like a Wheatear, the Rock Thrush spends the major part of its

European Roller
Coracias garrulus 12in
A non-stop traveller for nearly nine months of the year

life at ground level. It is a plump bird, the size of a Songthrush, but is characterized by its very short chestnut tail and rather long legs.

While the female is quiet and discreet, the male is more conspicuous in his behaviour, indulging in elaborate flight displays and bursts of clear ringing song. He vigorously defends the chosen nesting territory but, unusually, also defends a second territory up to a mile away where the pair forage for food for their brood.

The insect-feeding Rock Thrush favours a dry, warm habitat and is generally to be found at moderate elevations where the female builds a neat nest under stones or in a wall crevice among ruined buildings or on a stony hill-slope.

European Roller
Coracias garrulus

The European Roller is one of a number of species that spend so much of their time travelling that most of the year is taken up by migrations.

The itinerary is hectic: evacuating its territory at the end of the northern summer, the Roller flies an estimated 40 miles each day, and, after frequent stops, arrives in Kenya by late October/early November. It is seldom home and dry in South Africa before December, and by February it is time to depart on the long flight back to Europe, arriving late in April or at the beginning of May.

A jay-like bird with azure breast, bright chestnut back and blue wings, the Roller belongs to a group well established in the tropics, particularly in Africa, where a number of species are widespread. The European Roller is a true carnivore, preying on insects, beetles, lizards and even small rodents and young birds – often taken in a sudden shrike-like swoop from a lookout post. The nest is an insanitary affair built into a tree-hollow, mud-bank or wall crevice.

The Roller's call is harsh and discordant but very varied, and male and female often perch together, calling alternately in a crude duet.

Left holding the baby

The Common Cuckoo, *Cuculus canorus*, lays its eggs in the nests of a variety of birds, commonly Reed Warblers, Blackbirds, Meadow Pipits, Wagtails and Dunnocks. Hatching first, the nestling cuckoo ejects all the eggs of the foster-parent's clutch, pushing them out of the nest to smash on the ground below. The young Common Cuckoo grows so rapidly that a small foster-parent such as the Reed Warbler (illustrated) is barely able to keep pace with its exorbitant demands for food.

The Great Spotted Cuckoo, *Clamator glandarius*, is more selective in its choice of host and far less destructive. The foster-parent is usually a member of the crow family, often the Common Magpie. Hatching at the same time as the host's own chicks, the Great Spotted Cuckoo chick is fed as one of the brood and although it may, by strength and greater size, take more than a fair share of the food available, it makes no attempt to injure the other nestlings.

Great Spotted Cuckoo
Clamator glandarius

Common Cuckoo
Cuculus canorus

Imperial Eagle
Aquila heliaca

Largest and most impressive of Eurasia's birds of prey, the Imperial Eagle shuns mountainous regions and, unlike other eagles, makes its home in flat, open plains and steppes. Partly migratory, this handsome raptor is distributed from Spain (where strenuous efforts are now being made to snatch it from the brink of extinction) east to northwest India, the USSR and Mongolia.

After an acrobatic nuptial flight display, the mated pair select one of several nests in their territory, large untidy structures built high in isolated trees. As with most raptors, the female tends the nest while the male hunts for rabbits, reptiles, birds and occasionally carrion.

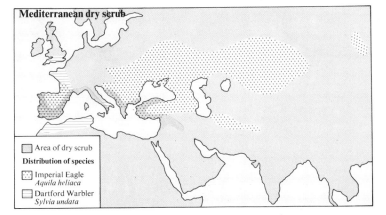

Mediterranean dry scrub

☐ Area of dry scrub
Distribution of species
☐ Imperial Eagle
   Aquila heliaca
☐ Dartford Warbler
   Sylvia undata

Imperial Eagle
Aquila heliaca 32in
A magnificent eagle, widespread in eastern Asia but on the brink of extinction in Spain

Heathland and Scrub

The terms scrub and heathland are used to describe, respectively, areas with low bushes, shrubs and regenerating woodland and areas supporting only herbaceous vegetation such as grasses and heathers. The two types frequently merge and some authorities consider heathland to be an early stage in the development of scrub vegetation, though the stability of some heathlands argues against this theory. Stable heathlands do occur in western Europe where poor drainage, salt spray, or too acid or too alkaline soils inhibit the growth of tall, woody scrub plants, but much of Europe's heathland is artificial – a consequence of the forest clearances in ages past, now maintained by modern agricultural practices, particularly livestock grazing.

Scrub forms an intermediate zone between woodland and grassland and thus supports birds characteristic of both in addition to its own typical fauna. Woodland birds found in scrub areas are usually those normally favouring glades and clearings, indeed exactly the same forest species that have successfully colonized and exploited farmland. Pure heathland, by contrast, tends to support a much smaller fauna.

As the flora, and consequently the associated insect-life, becomes more diverse in the progression from heathland to scrub, so the variety of bird-life increases in response to the increase in food supply, nesting sites and shelter.

Right: Gorse in full bloom in southern England.

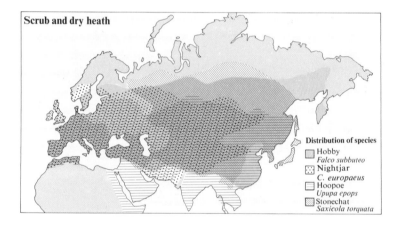

Scrub and dry heath

Distribution of species
Hobby
Falco subbuteo
Nightjar
C. europaeus
Hoopoe
Upupa epops
Stonechat
Saxicola torquata

Hoopoe
Upupa epops 11in
First impressions may deceive the hunter

Hoopoe
Upupa epops

The unimpressive undulating flight of the Hoopoe belies its true ability for, when pressed, this short-winged scrub-bird can evade and outdistance most falcons. It is a bird of dry, open heathland with scattered trees, and of woodland margins and farmland wherever suitable feeding and nesting situations are available.

A pedestrian feeder, the Hoopoe paces about the undergrowth, probing with its slender down-curved bill for terrestrial invertebrates. Flies, grasshoppers, beetles and snails form the bulk of its diet, but in the more southerly parts of the bird's range, lizards are regularly taken – particularly in the breeding season when hungry nestlings must be fed. Considering its dependence on large insects, the Hoopoe's successful penetration of Sweden, as a breeding species, is a sure sign of the bird's adaptability.

The nest-site is invariably a cavity of some sort. A hollow tree or pile of fallen rock will provide ideal shelter, but walls may also be utilized. No proper nest is built and the eggs are simply laid on the bare floor of the nest-hole. In southern Europe, the first eggs are laid late in April, but in the north the breeding season is delayed and the first eggs may not appear until June. Incubation begins before the clutch is complete and the resulting spread of ages within the brood is probably an important aid to survival in the colder parts of the range. Constantly supplied with food by her attentive mate, the female incubates the eggs alone and does not leave the nest until the young are sufficiently advanced for them to survive without the help of the mother's body-heat.

In flight, the black and white bars on the wings are conspicuous and, at dusk, the Hoopoe's broad-winged silhouette gives it the appearance of a huge moth. In courtship or dispute, the handsome crest is fanned open in a striking display.

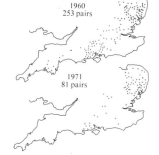

The butcher-birds

Closely resembling miniature hawks in their behaviour and hunting technique, the Great Grey Shrike and the Red-backed Shrike both hunt from conveniently placed lookout posts from which they swoop down on their unsuspecting prey.

Both are known as butcher-birds from their habit of storing food in a larder – impaling their prey on the spikes of a thorn-bush or, in the case of the adaptable and opportunist Great Grey Shrike, on the spines of a barbed wire fence. While the Red-backed Shrike feeds mainly on bumble-bees, grasshoppers and other large insects, the more powerful Great Grey takes larger prey, including mice, lizards and even fledgling birds

Great Grey Shrike
Lanius excubitor

Red-backed Shrike
Lanius collurio

1960
253 pairs

1971
81 pairs

Declining numbers
In recent years the population of the Red-backed Shrike has suffered a marked decline in southern England, possibly due to climatic changes in its African wintering habitat

Hobby
Falco subbuteo

The Hobby's elegantly back-swept wings enable this diminutive falcon to prey on such agile fliers as Swifts and Swallows as they traverse Europe on their annual migrations. Normally, however, small passerines up to the size of a thrush are the main prey-species, with large insects forming an important addition to the diet.

Wintering in Africa, the Hobby spends the summer in open heathland throughout Europe, always remaining within, or near, thinly wooded areas where it nests – sometimes building a nest of its own, but more often taking over that of a crow or other large tree-nesting species.

In courtship, male and female soar and wheel together in an exciting display flight from which the male periodically breaks away in order to stoop at the female. The clutch of two or three richly coloured red/brown eggs is incubated by the female alone, while the male supplies food for the brooding hen and later for the newly hatched young.

Stonechat
Saxicola torquata

Taking its name from a distinctive alarm-call reminiscent of two stones being clapped together, this characteristic bird of heath and moor has a marked preference for coastal areas of western Europe where the heath is diversified with scrub-vegetation and gorse. Elsewhere in Europe, and in Africa, it is associated with low-grade agricultural land.

Northern species are migratory, but even in the sedentary populations of southern Europe, some nomadic movement occurs outside the breeding season. This is in marked contrast to the classical migration pattern shown by the closely related Whinchat, *S.rubetra*. Favouring meadows and marshy areas during its summer

visits, the Whinchat seldom competes with its relative and may also be separated by altitude – always remaining on low-lying ground while the Stonechat is found as high as 12,000 feet.

At the start of the breeding season, the male Stonechat proclaims his territory in a series of song-flights, rising steeply from a perch and hovering briefly while uttering his scratchy, jangling song. The female builds her well-concealed nest low down, often in the base of a bush, and in it lays between three and seven eggs. She rarely leaves the nest, except for brief feeding forays, but, unlike most passerines, will defend territory in her own right – an activity usually reserved for the male.

Nightjar
Caprimulgus europaeus

The Nightjar is attracted to heathland by its wealth of insect-life and in particular by the dusk-flying species. The bird's huge eyes give it superb vision in the failing light of evening, and the enormous mouth, fringed with bristles, acts like a scoop as the Nightjar turns and darts after its prey. Despite the difference in diet, some observers consider the Nightjar a relative of the owls, but convergent evolution may have produced their similar adaptations to life as nocturnal hunters.

By day, the Nightjar's cryptic colouring makes it virtually impossible to detect when roosting on a rugged branch or sitting on its nest among dead leaves and bracken fronds.

After wintering in Africa, the Nightjar returns to its European breeding grounds very early in the season and invariably raises two broods. Each consists of two eggs which, like the helpless new-born chicks that follow, are superbly camouflaged as a defence against predators.

Hobby
Falco subbuteo 13in
Agile hunter of the Swallow and Swift

Stonechat
Saxicola torquata 5in
Takes its name from a strange alarm-call

Nightjar
Caprimulgus europaeus 10½in
Hidden by day – hunter by night

The Desert Corridor

A vast sinuous tract of desert and desolate steppe stretches across Eurasia from the Caspian Sea to Inner Mongolia. Conditions are severe with cruelly hot summers alternating with bitterly cold winters. Deserts of stone and clay support virtually no vegetation, but the great areas of sand desert bloom briefly with the intermittent rains, exerting a profound effect on the wildlife of the desert.

Nevertheless, some 300 bird species survive in this inhospitable land, including about 70 endemic species. Passerines, particularly warblers, shrikes, larks and finches, offer the greatest variety, but nightjars, waders, doves and raptors are all well represented. Most show colour adaptations, their grey and pale sandy tones fitting them for a life in a land with very little vegetation cover.

Seed-eaters are the most abundant desert species, especially in the stony regions, where fallen seeds remain exposed on the surface. Mixed feeders are mainly migrants or nomadic species, able to depart quickly to more favourable parts when food is scarce. Most notable, however, are the birds of prey, whose diet of moisture-rich living tissue enables them to live in the desert without recourse to drinking.

Right: Barren wilderness of the Oken desert, Tunisia.

Cold deserts

Types of desert	Distribution of species
Sand	Pallas's Sandgrouse *Syrrhaptes paradoxus*
Clay-pan	
Stone	

Desert Wheatear
Oenanthe deserti 6in
Creates its own climate in the safety of a nest-burrow

Ground Jay
Podoces pandari 10½in
Flight is of secondary importance to this fleet-footed ground bird

Pallas's Sandgrouse
Syrrhaptes paradoxus 16in
A seed-eating bird that cannot stray far from water

Ground Jay
Podoces pandari

Gaining some measure of protection from the unobtrusive grey tones of its plumage, the Ground Jay has adapted to an almost totally terrestrial way of life. It flies only rarely, and then reluctantly, preferring to run over the rough terrain. Using its wings to boost its stride to more than 12 inches, it has a turn of speed unequalled by any other bird of this size.

Restricted to two small areas, east of the Caspian Sea and south of Lake Balkhash, the Ground Jay avoids dense shrub growth. Although it is claimed to nest in abandoned burrows the thick-walled, cup-shaped nest is generally built in the base of a bush. The Ground Jay's diet consists mainly of insects and small lizards, but in winter when these are scarce seeds and buds are also taken. Like many desert species, the Ground Jay appears not to drink but to obtain its water requirements from its insect prey.

Desert Wheatear
Oenanthe deserti

Discreetly hidden beneath a mass of stones, in the base of a bush, or even four to five feet deep in a deserted rodent burrow, the nest of the Desert Wheatear is well protected against the unwelcome attention of foxes and predatory birds. In addition, the confined space of the nest-site creates its own microclimate – protecting the occupants from the violent daily temperature changes typical of arid regions.

Despite its misleading name, the Desert Wheatear is not a bird of the true deserts. It frequents the semi-arid steppes and barren scrublands bordering the true deserts but shuns sandy regions and areas of bare rock. The Desert Wheatear belongs to a genus confined to open habitats and one race has penetrated far into the Tibetan Plateau, where it is known to nest 12,000 feet above sea level.

Feeding mainly on insects and insect larvae, the species is partly migratory and is forced to evacuate the northern parts of its range in winter when food is scarce.

Pallas's Sandgrouse
Syrrhaptes paradoxus

Like several of its relatives, Pallas's Sandgrouse lives in semi-desert and arid steppe regions, generally where clay soils predominate, its plumage blending with the surroundings.

As a seed-eater, this Sandgrouse needs to drink frequently and so, like its Saharan relative Lichtenstein's Sandgrouse, *Pterocles lichtensteinii*, (p 145), it makes daily flights of several dozen miles from its barren nest-site to the nearest open water.

This routine limits the bird's distribution, particularly during the breeding season, and there is a tendency for the species to form large, loosely knit colonies.

Pallas's Sandgrouse migrates irregularly, depending on local weather conditions and the availability of food. Periodically the species irrupts far beyond the boundaries of its normal range and massive flocks have been recorded as far apart as eastern Manchuria and western Europe.

Pratincole
Glareola pratincola

Common throughout the arid grasslands and semi-deserts of Asia, the Pratincole inhabits a wide range of habitats from muddy lake shores and deltas to arid steppes and arable land. Its distribution is very erratic and seems to be governed only by the available food supply.

Pratincoles nest on bare ground, often on sandy or loamy soils, in low vegetation or in the dried hollows left by the feet of grazing cattle, and colonies may range from 20 or 30 birds to many thousands.

Grasshoppers, locusts, beetles, flies and mosquitoes form the bulk of the Pratincole's diet – the insects being caught both on the ground and in flight. The richest harvest of all is provided by the great swarms of locusts that periodically sweep across the grasslands and scrub regions during the breeding season. Like many northern species, the Pratincole winters in the dry steppe and savanna regions of Africa.

Houbara Bustard
Chlamydotis undulata

Effectively camouflaged against the desert landscape when at rest or feeding, the Houbara Bustard becomes strikingly conspicuous in flight when the bold black and white wing-patterning is fully exposed. This colour contrast is used to full effect during courtship displays, when the male struts before his chosen mate with wings and tail spread and the impressive ruff of long black and white feathers raised over the neck.

As with all birds of open habitats, visual signals play a vital role in many behaviour patterns; vocal signals, of paramount importance to birds of the woodlands where visibility is restricted, are of secondary importance.

The Houbara Bustard inhabits the wide belt of semi-desert and steppe stretching from Algeria to central Asia. A mixed feeder, collecting seeds and shoots and preying on beetles, grasshoppers, locusts and lizards, the Houbara Bustard gains enough water from insects and the fleshy parts of desert plants to fully maintain its water-balance.

Pratincole
Glareola pratincola 10in
Locust swarms ease the hunter's constant search for insect food

Houbara Bustard
Chlamydotis undulata 28in
Takes its water requirements from the flesh of desert plants

Mountains and Moorlands

Mountain and moorland regions are harsh and uncompromising environments, constantly exposed to extremes of wind and rain, to winter blizzards and summer droughts. The characteristic vegetation is sparse and lacking in variety; few trees can grow in such adverse conditions and the rolling expanses of heath and ling are broken only by scattered patches of gorse and stunted shrubs. Rocky crags and deeply incised stream gullies provide vital oases of shelter, often comparatively rich in seed and insect food, where ground-nesting birds may find some measure of protection.

These severe conditions naturally limit both the number and variety of birds found in upland regions. Some members of widespread lowland families, such as the Ring Ouzel from the thrush family, have adapted to moorland life, and tolerant species like the Meadow Pipit and the Wheatear are common though never in large numbers. Food is so sparsely distributed that even seed and insect eaters need large territories in which to feed, and the raptors, mainly buzzards and eagles, need many square miles.

Most species withdraw to the shelter of lowland or valley in winter but a few, notably the scavanging Raven and Golden Eagle, remain. Neither, however, is as well equipped as the Ptarmigan whose dense white winter plumage provides both camouflage and insulation against the cold.

Below: Typical moorland and mountains. Kerry Reeks, Ireland

Moorland and mountains

Distribution of species

Golden Eagle
Aquila chrysaetos

Ring Ouzel
Turdus torquatus

Merlin
Falco columbarius

Dipper
Cinclus cinclus

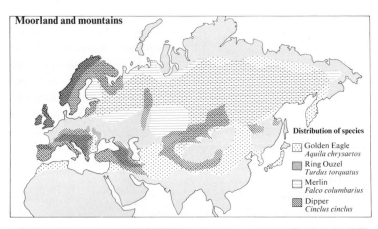

Merlin
Falco columbarius 11in
Upland birds are caught unawares by the Merlin's low-level hunting flight

Golden Eagle
Aquila chrysaetos 32 in
May hunt more than 25 miles from the nest

Snow Finch
Montifringilla nivalis 7 in
A familiar sight up to 15,000 feet above sea level

Ring Ouzel
Turdus torquatus 10in
Its powerful smell may distract the hill-farmer's working dogs

Dipper
Cinclus cinclus 7in

Merlin
Falco columbarius

Unlike the related Peregrine Falcon, which climbs high in the air to gather speed for its hunting stoop, the Merlin patrols the moor in a low-level flight, swooping over the vegetation so low that it is probably hidden from its prey until the last second before the strike.

Throughout its range the Merlin is a bird of open country, favouring bleak moorlands during the summer but ranging over marshes and estuaries in winter when the high ground is snow-covered. Except when the young are calling noisily for food, the Merlin's nest is difficult to locate. Normally it is hidden among bracken stems in a sheltered hollow high on the moor, or on an exposed bluff overlooking a valley. Nearby, a white-splashed rock marks the male's lookout post, an important site to which, after the kill, he often returns in order to pluck and dismember the prey before taking it to the nest.

The five or six young are fed by the parents for the first few weeks but soon begin their education, starting with large insects and quickly graduating to small birds. Although the main prey-species are Skylark and Meadow Pipit, the Merlin is a bold hunter and will tackle prey up to the size of a Golden Plover.

Golden Eagle
Aquila chrysaetos

Soaring effortlessly on upswept wings, the magnificent Golden Eagle patrols a hunting territory of many square miles. Making full use of every thermal upcurrent, it may remain on the wing for many hours without rest, constantly scanning the moor for hares, young deer, sick or injured sheep and ground-nesting birds. The prey is taken in a fierce stoop and only a nearby hole or rock-crevice will provide protection.

Occasionally the Golden Eagle will nest in a tall, exposed tree, but the preferred site for the huge nest of loosely interlaced sticks is high on a rocky crag or cliff face. Each territory may contain several sites which are used year after year by successive generations.

The male provides most of the food for the young, tearing the meat into delicate strips and passing it to the female who feeds the young. The nestlings quickly learn to dismember prey themselves and, as soon as they are fully fledged, they join the parents in hunting forays, remaining in the family group until the winter.

Snow Finch
Montifringilla nivalis

Spiralling down to its waiting mate, the displaying male Snow Finch is one of the most attractive mountain birds. Its dazzling white plumage is conspicuous in flight, but on the ground, in the narrow zone it frequents between the snow-line and timber-line, the soft grey tones of its back provide an effective camouflage.

The bird runs and hops over the rocky terrain, feeding on insects and the seeds of alpine plants. Its bulky nest, warmly lined with feathers and animal hairs, is built deep in a rock crevice or in an abandoned marmot burrow to give protection to the clutch of two delicate white eggs.

Ring Ouzel
Turdus torquatus

Colloquially known as the "Mountain Blackbird", the Ring Ouzel has a clear, piping song that is often the only bird-call to break the moorland silence. It is thought to be one of the few birds with a powerful smell and is therefore unpopular with game-keepers whose dogs may be distracted from their work.

Like all members of the thrush family, the Ring Ouzel has an alert, brisk manner, alternately running and pausing as it searches along the banks of streams and bogs for the earthworms that form the bulk of its diet. Later in the season the Ring Ouzel supplements its diet with the caterpillars that abound among the heather.

The male selects a song-post, usually in an isolated tree or on an exposed rock outcrop quite close to the nest, which is discreetly hidden against a low bank or background of vegetation. Occasionally the nest may be built several feet below ground, in a pothole or disused mineshaft. In the brief upland breeding season most pairs are able to raise only a single brood, compared with between three and five broods in the case of the lowland Blackbird. However, the single clutch of five Ring Ouzel eggs appears to suffer far fewer losses than the Blackbird.

Most Ring Ouzels migrate from the moorland tops during the winter. For alpine populations this may simply mean a move down to the foothills, but North European populations undertake the short-haul flight south to the warmer latitudes of the Mediterranean.

Fresh-water Marshlands

Of all modern ecosystems, that of fresh-water marsh is probably under the greatest threat. There is a constant clamour for land – for housing, industry and agriculture – and, although land may be reclaimed from the sea, the drainage or infilling of marshland is both easier and cheaper.

By its nature fresh-water marsh is level, though not necessarily low-lying, as any impediment to drainage will cause a marsh to develop. Such areas are characterized by a wide variety of rushes, sedges and rank grasses. Extensive stands of bullrushes and *Phragmites* reedbeds are common, but tree growth is restricted to willows and alders.

These severe limitations on the variety of plant life create a similar shortage in the supply of food on land and the marsh is usually considered to be a specialist habitat. Even the choice of nest-sites is very restricted. Where there are large areas of open water the distinction between marsh and lake becomes blurred, but there is always a lack of true terrestrial habitats.

Though water-birds are well represented, there are some striking gaps in the bird fauna. The marsh accommodates no breeding thrushes or crows, no finches or true tits, few warblers and only one bunting species. While the herons and their allies harvest the rich aquatic food source, the insect life of the marsh suffers relatively little predation.

Below: Rich vegetation of a lowland marsh, southern England

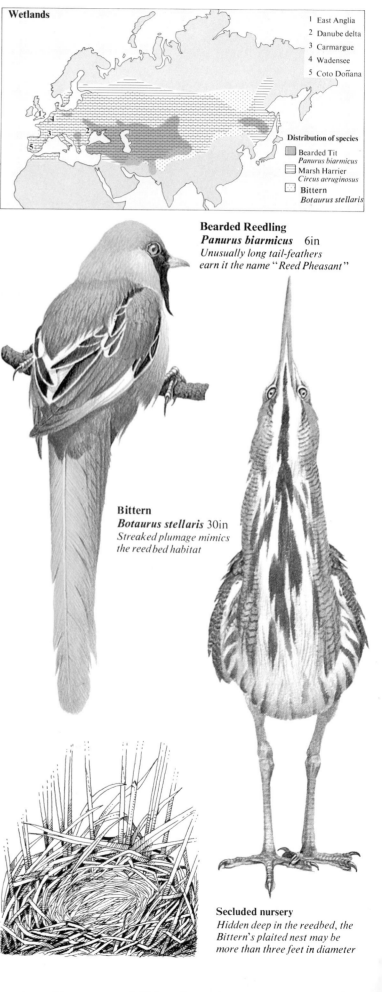

Wetlands

1 East Anglia
2 Danube delta
3 Carmargue
4 Wadensee
5 Coto Doñana

Distribution of species

Bearded Tit
Panurus biarmicus
Marsh Harrier
Circus aeruginosus
Bittern
Botaurus stellaris

Bearded Reedling
Panurus biarmicus 6in
Unusually long tail-feathers earn it the name "Reed Pheasant"

Bittern
Botaurus stellaris 30in
Streaked plumage mimics the reed bed habitat

Secluded nursery
Hidden deep in the reedbed, the Bittern's plaited nest may be more than three feet in diameter

Marsh Harrier 21in
Circus aeruginosus
The silent hunter

Bearded Reedling
Panurus biarmicus

Whirring across the waving reed-heads with its long tail-feathers streaming behind, the Bearded Reedling fully justifies its local name of Reed Pheasant. Closely related to the babblers, it was, until recently, erroneously called the Bearded Tit.

Reedlings usually move in family parties, foraging among the *Phragmites* reeds for their seeds, for which there is virtually no competition, and for larval and adult insects. Like many other small reed-dwelling birds, Bearded Reedlings are agile creatures and can perform the most unlikely contortions whilst feeding on the reed-heads.

In a good breeding season the Bearded Reedling will produce three, four or five broods in a neat nest built low down among the sedges. The population may therefore build up rapidly and the local population may disperse to new feeding grounds in order to relieve the pressure. Although not strong fliers, reedlings are able to cross the North Sea, but usually shun longer migrations.

Bittern
Botaurus stellaris

Like all members of the heron-egret family, the Bittern is superbly equipped to exploit the rich variety of vertebrate and invertebrate life of the fresh-water marsh. The powerful, dagger-like beak, set on a long neck, spears or seizes the prey in a lightning thrust after a long, patient stalk through the water. The eyes too are well adapted to this hunting technique as they can be swivelled to give the bird almost all-round vision without moving the head. Like other herons, the Bittern often augments its diet of fish and frogs with nestling birds and small lizards.

The Bittern rarely emerges from cover and, if disturbed, stretches its neck and body upwards so that the streaked plumage blends with the reed background. However, if pressed the bird erects its plumage in an impressive threat display.

Marsh Harrier
Circus aeruginosus

Many difficulties face a bird of prey operating in a marsh environment. Dense vegetation and a forest of slender reed stems form a very effective screen and prey-species are almost perpetually either in cover or within easy reach of the safety of water. To overcome these disadvantages the Marsh Harrier has a specialized hunting technique based on stealth and the element of surprise.

The Marsh Harrier flies a regular beat, quartering the marsh silently, gliding on stiffly held, upswept wings. Suddenly appearing, only inches above the reed-heads, the hunter can drop swiftly on to prey exposed by any small gap in the vegetation cover. The victim, be it a frog or vole, young coot or duck, has little chance of escape. Even if it should dive, the hunter's legs are so long, and so formidably taloned, that one lightning strike usually secures a meal.

Ruff
Philomachus pugnax

Although the female (called a Reeve) withdraws into the protection of the wetter, more densely vegetated areas of the marsh in the nesting season, Ruffs normally frequent the drier areas, particularly where grazing has shortened the ground vegetation.

The most remarkable feature of the Ruff's behaviour is the "lek", the spring gathering when males come together on a patch of open ground to compete for mates. Attired in widely varying hues, and with their ruffs fanned out, the males engage in ritual dances and mock-combat displays that will decide the order of dominance in the group without recourse to physical combat. The individual who triumphs will make his choice of one or more females and lead them away, but after mating the male retires to a solitary existence and takes no further part in raising the brood.

Ruff
Philomachus pugnax 12½in
*Social order established
at an annual gathering*

Reed-bed craftsmen

The tall, dense reedbeds of marshes provide a safe environment which is exploited by marsh-nesting birds.

The Penduline Tit, one of the most skilful of nest builders, weaves a retort-shaped nest of fine grasses and downy seed cases, suspended from the tip of a thin branch overhanging the water. The nest is safe from most nest-robbers, the only danger coming from members of the crow family, who may smash the nest to prey on eggs and young.

In contrast, the Bearded Reedling builds a rough, untidy nest of grass and reeds at the base of tall *Phragmites*, relying on the dense screen to protect the eggs and young.

The deep-woven cone of the Reed Warbler's nest is another masterpiece of design. Suspended part way up the tall reed-stems, it is almost immune from attack, unlike the more exposed ground-nest of the Moorhen which, anchored to the base of the reeds, may be left open to attack if the marsh dries out during a long period of drought.

Penduline Tit
Remiz pendulinus

Reed Warbler
Acrocephalus scirpaceus

Moorhen
Gallinula chloropus

Bearded Reedling
Panurus biarmicus

Lakes, Rivers and Streams

The apparently simple title "Lakes and Rivers" embraces an immense variety of habitats. The lakes of the far north, frozen for much of the year, or forming swiftly from meltwater in summer, differ greatly from the permanent lakes of the south where freezing is rare. Rocky or peaty lakes of upland Europe may have an acidic sterility that sets them apart from those on alkaline soils and these in turn differ enormously from the mild, placid waters of lowland regions.

Rivers too may vary greatly, each one unique in its rate of flow, the nature of its bed, the chemistry of its waters and the material it carries to the sea. Small rural streams may hold little more than a few Moorhens while the full sweep of a mature river will support a wide variety of waterfowl including grebes, herons, swans and ducks. Fast-flowing rivers, usually shallow and with rocky margins, are a feature of upland Europe and the northern tundra. Carrying relatively few species, they are yet the home of some of the most typical highland water-birds, notably the Dipper and the torrent-adapted Harlequin Duck. Few aquatic plants are able to flourish in the cold, turbulent waters of the mountain streams and the upland birds are dependent for food on aquatic invertebrates and the few fish that exist.

In contrast, the slow-moving, nutrient-rich lowland rivers contain a rich flora and their banks are thickly vegetated with grasses, shrubs, wild flowers and overhanging trees. Here the vegetarian Mute Swan and Coot may flourish, while the rich bankside vegetation and its associated insect life is available to an enormous variety of ducks, rails and members of the heron family. Smaller tributaries, especially those flowing between high banks, are the natural home of the Kingfisher and the insectivorous Sand Martin.

There is little difference between the slow-moving river and the lake it feeds, though to those species that build floating nests the static conditions are important, while steep banks may discourage many of the dabbling ducks. The surrounding vegetaion is of great importance to some waterfowl. Hole-nesters, like the Goldeneye, and tree-dwellers, like the Osprey, need stands of woodland, whereas many ducks, particularly the Teal, need flat expanses of grass in which to build their nests.

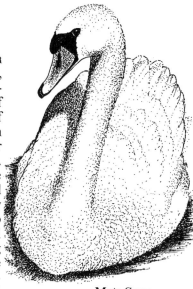

Mute Swan
Cygnus olor 60in

Mute Swan
Cygnus olor

While short-necked birds like the Coot must dive in search of their food, the swan is able to utilize vegetation as much as three feet below the surface simply by "upending" like a Mallard. The Mute Swan is primarily a grazing bird, cropping the short grasses in meadowland surrounding lakes and slow-moving rivers, and the aquatic vegetation of the lakes themselves.

The nest is an enormous mound of reeds, often more than six feet in diameter, usually built on the shore or on an island. The site is vigorously defended by the territorial male, even against human intruders, and an angry male may create havoc if disturbed by a brood of unwary ducklings. The Mute Swan normally nests in seclusion, but there are exceptional cases of colonial nesting (such as the Abbotsbury Swannery in southwest England) where the birds have been encouraged by man.

The Mute Swan's association with man stretches back to the twelfth century and today the species is common, partly domesticated, in parks throughout Europe. This elegant bird is a permanent resident in western Europe where it is joined in winter by large numbers of migrant Whooper and Bewick's Swans, *C.cygnus* and *C.bewickii*, from the arctic and sub-arctic regions of northern Asia and Iceland.

Great Crested Grebe
Podiceps cristatus 19in
The classic example of ritualized courtship behaviour

Great Crested Grebe
Podiceps cristatus

Breeding adults of the Great Crested Grebe are unmistakable in their mating plumage, their heads adorned with dark, double-horned "ear-tufts" and black-tipped, orange facial feathers. Their magnificent courtship displays are made up of several elaborate and stylized movements including the ritualized presentation of food and nest materials between male and female. At the climax of the nuptial dance, the two birds tread water furiously, raising their bodies vertically out of the water, and approaching each other slowly until they meet breast to breast. So complex and ritualized is the Grebe's courtship that it has become a classic study of mating behaviour.

All grebes show extensive adaptation to aquatic life. The powerful legs are set well back on the body, and the large feet, though not webbed with skin flaps, have horny lobes along the edge of each toe to provide a large surface area. The plumage is dense, with good insulating properties, and when alarmed, the bird is able to expel the air from its plumage and from its internal air-sac system and to gradually sink until only the head remains above water.

Anchored to rising strands of lake-bed vegetation, the floating nest is built of reeds and leaves, and even if the female is frightened from the nest by an intruder, she usually pauses long enough to cover the small, chalky white eggs with vegetation, both as concealment and to provide enough warmth for incubation to continue in her absence.

On hatching, the young are striped grey and white. Although they take to the water almost immediately, they remain dependent on the parents for several weeks, constantly being fed on fish and small aquatic molluscs. During this period, crows, harriers and marauding pike take a heavy toll and to avoid predation, the young often ride on the parent's back – remaining in position even when the adult dives beneath the surface.

Grey Wagtail
Motacilla cinerea

Usually regarded as one of the most attractive, and characteristic, passerine birds of fast-flowing, rocky mountain streams, the Grey Wagtail will also colonize slow-moving rivers wherever man has constructed weirs, mill-races and watercress beds. These artificial obstructions create the fast, turbulent water, well supplied with oxygen, in which aquatic invertebrates, the wagtail's main food, can proliferate. Old mill-races, buildings, bridges and sluices provide the bird with a wide variety of well-protected nesting sites in addition to stream-bank crevices and overhangs.

When brooding, the female is a "close-sitter", i.e. very reluctant to abandon her young, but if forced to flee in the face of an intruder, she will flutter from the nest with wings and tail widely spread in an efficient distraction display designed to confuse the would-be predator.

In summer, the Grey Wagtail usually remains near upland streams and waterfalls where it feeds in the splash-zone well clear of the full force of the water. In winter, however, this attractive bird frequents lowland rivers and sewage farms, often close to, or even within, urban areas.

The closely related Yellow Wagtail, *M. flava*, is one of the most widespread Palaearctic birds. Eight subspecies are recognized from moist open habitats ranging from northern Scandinavia to North Africa, and from arctic Russia to Egypt. *M. flava* is distinguished from the Grey, and all other wagtails, by its long tail, brilliant yellow undersides and green back, while the different subspecies, or races, are distinguished by the colour of their head-plumage.

Common Sandpiper
Tringa hypoleucos

An interesting similarity exists between the incessant tail-bobbing action of the Common Sandpiper and the tail-wagging movements characteristic of the wagtail family. Neither has been fully explained, but it is possible that the continuous movement helps to camouflage both these birds against the background of rippling water that is their feeding environment.

The Common Sandpiper is normally seen alone or in a small flock of a dozen or so birds, feeding on small aquatic animals either at the water's edge or in the shallows. In summer its preferred habitat is among the rocky lakes and streams of the uplands, but in winter it moves to the lowlands, feeding along both fresh-water and salt-water shores. The Common Sandpiper is less dependent on marshy ground than most waders and is often seen on the concrete and stone banks of culverts and reservoirs.

The nest is built in a grass tussock close to the water's edge and the young, well developed at birth as are most waders, are immediately active, scampering over the ground and diving beneath rocks at the first sign of danger. Although they are waders, the young birds are accomplished swimmers and both adults and young will take to the water, and even dive, in order to evade an attacking hawk.

The flight-pattern of the Common Sandpiper is very distinctive; several short, very shallow wing-beats followed by a glide in which the wings are held low and stiffly bowed. The birds are migrants and studies of ringed birds indicate that individuals use the same routes year after year on their flights to and from Africa.

Silhouettes of winter

Each winter, the reservoirs of Britain and Europe play host to many thousands of immigrant ducks from the Arctic. Virtually free from predators, these areas are rich in plant and animal foods. The sawbills, Goosander and Smew feed mainly on fish, while the Pochard, Tufted Duck and Goldeneye are mainly vegetarian. With the exception of an occasional heron feeding near the edge, and large flocks of immigrant Coot diving for food, the visitors face no serious competition. Even in the dull grey light of evening, many species are able to recognize each other, and be identified, by their shapes and the characteristic patterns of their plumage.

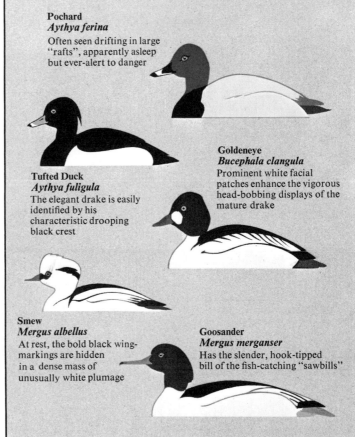

Pochard
Aythya ferina
Often seen drifting in large "rafts", apparently asleep but ever-alert to danger

Tufted Duck
Aythya fuligula
The elegant drake is easily identified by his characteristic drooping black crest

Smew
Mergus albellus
At rest, the bold black wing-markings are hidden in a dense mass of unusually white plumage

Goldeneye
Bucephala clangula
Prominent white facial patches enhance the vigorous head-bobbing displays of the mature drake

Goosander
Mergus merganser
Has the slender, hook-tipped bill of the fish-catching "sawbills"

Grey Wagtail
Motacilla cinerea 7in
Nests close to foaming streams and waterfalls

Common Sandpiper
Tringa hypoleucos 7¾in
Constant movement as an aid to concealment

Salt Marshes and Estuaries

Inundated by each high tide, the flat expanse of a coastal salt-marsh is one of natures richest biological habitats. Unfortunately it is also one of the most threatened. Vast areas of sea-washed mud are of little use to the farmer but offer rich returns to the developer – either as industrial sites or as recreational areas for yachting and water-skiing.

The character of each salt-marsh varies with the salinity of the water, the frequency with which it is inundated, and the duration of immersion. For bird-life, the richest feeding grounds are those that are exposed for long periods each day. Here, a full range of plant and animal life can develop – from the salt-loving species of the seaward margins to the fresh-water organisms of the landward side. Open marsh provides food for Brent Geese and Wigeon, while the soft grasses of drier areas are ideal for grazing ducks and geese. Pools and creeks, that disect the marsh in a maze of fine channels, yield ample food for a variety of opportunist feeders, including gulls and Shelducks. Perhaps the best-adapted of all marsh-birds are the waders, which, with their long legs and probing bills, are able to exploit the full range of niches.

As a nesting habitat, only those marshes exposed for long periods have any value. Isolated waders and ducks, and colonies of terns, are regular breeders, but passerines are limited to Pipits, Reed Buntings, Yellow Wagtails and finches.

Right: Shelduck feeding at low tide, East Anglia.

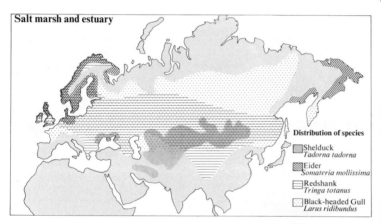

Salt marsh and estuary

Distribution of species

Shelduck
Tadorna tadorna

Eider
Somateria mollissima

Redshank
Tringa totanus

Black-headed Gull
Larus ridibundus

Shelduck
Tadorna tadorna 24in
*Leaves its mark
wherever it feeds*

Shelduck
Tadorna tadorna

The Shelduck is one of a small number of water-fowl that have features in common with both ducks and geese. In sand-dune areas the Shelduck nests in abandoned rabbit burrows, but on salt-marsh it builds a well-concealed nest of grasses tucked out of sight in long grass or against a sea-wall.

The large clutch (anything up to 16 eggs) is tended by the female, who leads her downy grey-and-white chicks to the water as soon as they have dried after hatching. Almost immediately the young are able to dive in search of food, but the adult feeds by sifting small invertebrates from the mud – sweeping the head from side to side and leaving a semi-circular pattern on the surface.

Eider
Somateria mollissima

Its heavy build, and the massive forehead containing well-developed salt-extracting glands, mark the Eider as one of the few predominantly marine ducks. A clumsy bird on land, the Eider breeds in large colonies on low-lying coastal flats within easy reach of its feeding grounds. Dabbling at low water, and able to dive as deep as 20 feet at high tide, the Eider is a major predator on mussels.

The nest of grasses and seaweed is built on rocks or among tussocks, and is warmly lined with dark down plucked from the breast. Such is the insulating quality of the down that it is harvested each year for the manufacture of quilts and high-altitude clothing.

Eider
Somateria mollissima 23in
*Its down is nature's
most efficient insulator*

Black-headed Gull
Larus ridibundus

Today the Black-headed Gull is perhaps the most familiar gull in the Palaearctic region, particularly in winter when it flocks inland to follow the plough in arable farmland. At the turn of the century records were rare, but now, despite its preference for salt-marsh, the species has established breeding colonies on many inland waterways. Colonies may number many thousands of birds and, in coastal situations, pairs at the seaward edge of a large colony are often in danger of being inundated by high tides.

Black-headed Gulls are prolific breeders and, in areas where predation losses are high, a pair may replace their clutch of two or three eggs several times in a season. Incubation begins with the first egg and young are usually hatched at daily intervals. The third chick of a brood, however, seldom survives and usually only a single chick reaches maturity.

Redshank
Tringa totanus

In the breeding season, the Redshank frequents the damp grasslands near coasts, lakes and reservoirs, and may even be found on marshy moors up to 1,000 feet above sea-level.

Its nest is built in a shallow hollow or in the base of a clump of vegetation and is thickly lined with dry grasses. The lining materials often meet above, and extend right round, the sitting bird – providing an excellent defence against predators. The eggs and chicks, however, are so perfectly camouflaged that even without this protection, they would be hidden.

The parent birds share the task of guarding and educating the young, which, like the young of most waders, are led to the water within a few hours of hatching.

Adult Black-headed Gull in pale winter plumage

Black-headed Gull
Larus ridibundus 14in
Prolific breeding keeps pace with the predators

Redshank
Tringa totanus 11in
Wrap-around nest-lining protects both eggs and young

The shore-line specialists

Birds of salt-marshes and estuaries, beaches and cliffs, have evolved a wide range of physical adaptations and feeding techniques in order to exploit the rich variety of food available. Long, slender bills enable the waders to probe into surface sand and mud for burrowing invertebrates; the broad, powerful bills of predatory ducks like the Eider and Scoter are adapted for crushing the hard shells of molluscs and shore-dwelling crabs, while one thrust of the Oystercatcher's bill cuts through internal muscles to leave the cockle's shell open and defenceless. Shelducks graze on the rich grasses of estuarine marshes while, beyond the surf-zone, sharp-eyed Terns hover before plunging on to small fish swimming near the surface.

Eider *below*
Uses its powerful bill to crush the tough shells of molluscs and shore-dwelling crabs

Redshank *above*
The slender bill is used to probe soft sand and mud for burrowing organisms

Oystercatcher *above*
The sharp, chisel-tipped bill makes short work of bivalved molluscs.

1 Redshank *Tringa totanus*
2 Oystercatcher *Haematopus ostralegus*
3 Shelduck *Tadorna tadorna*
4 Black-headed Gull *Larus ridibundus*
5 Eider *Somateria mollissima*
6 Little Tern *Sterna albifrons*

The Coast in Winter

Backed by extensive inland marshes, the calm expanse of sandbanks and mudflats of a major river estuary provide a vitally important haven for many bird species. This meeting point of river, sea and sky has more than aesthetic merit, for the physical nature of the estuary, with embracing headlands and sheltering bluffs, provides a wide range of feeding and nesting areas not to be found on exposed stretches of coastline.

In these quiet waters, mineral and organic riches washed from the land merge with the riches of the sea. Sediments of widely differing compositions are laid one over the other; equable sea temperatures, especially in northern temperate latitudes, encourage a great diversity of wildlife, and the great range of water salinity supports a specialized flora of salt-tolerant plants in addition to algae and other organisms.

These areas are of prime importance during winter and whenever birds are migrating. Breeding sites are restricted to islands and coastal margins, but for the non-breeding transients there is a vast range of feeding and roosting opportunities. Unfortunately, estuaries are also attractive to man. Sheltered anchorages and low-value marginal land are a magnet to industrial development, while the sluggish flow of a lowland river has little chance of scouring the estuary clean of spilt, and deliberately discharged, pollutants.
Right: Oystercatchers feeding on mudflats in East Anglia

Slavonian Grebe
Podiceps auritus 13in
*Forced to move south as
the Arctic lakes freeze*

Red-breasted Merganser
Mergus serrator 23in
*The "saw-toothed" bill ensures
a firm grip on slippery prey*

Shore Lark
Eremophila alpestris 7in
*Rich pickings at the
high-water mark*

Red-breasted Merganser
Mergus serrator

The three European "sawbill" ducks show striking structural adaptations to a diet composed mainly of fish. The bill is long and slender with a sharply hooked tip, and the margins of both the upper and lower mandibles are armed with a series of backward-pointing serrations that enable the duck to obtain a firm grip on its slippery prey.

These ducks generally breed in high latitudes, often beside lakes and rivers, and both the Goosander, *M.merganser*, and the Red-breasted Merganser have taken to nesting in hollow trees. The Merganser frequents sea lochs and fjords and, in winter, shows a far greater preference for marine and estuarine waters than any of its relatives.

Mergansers often hunt for food in small parties, but seldom, even when fish are plentiful, are they seen in large concentrations. Sculling along in close formation with their heads close to the surface, or even immersed, they dive in unison, driving powerfully down to fifteen feet or more below the surface.

Unlike the dabbling ducks, who feed at dusk, and many wader species, whose feeding is governed more by tide than time of day, mergansers feed almost entirely during the day.

Slavonian Grebe
Podiceps auritus

The shallow fresh-water lakes favoured by the Slavonian Grebe as breeding grounds lie in a narrow tract of Europe and Asia between 50° and 60° north. Here the lakes freeze in winter and throughout its range the Slavonian Grebe is a migrant, though a reluctant one – moving only as far south as proves necessary to escape the worst of the northern winter. In western Europe, the Slavonian Grebe is found around the Scottish coast, but is replaced by the closely related Black-necked Grebe, *P.nigricollis*, in many southern regions.

Only rarely do Slavonian Grebes form flocks. Usually they are seen in ones and twos, widely scattered over the estuarine waters that are their preferred winter habitat. The protective shelter of the estuary is of great importance as, unlike many species, grebes moult all their main flight feathers at once, instead of going through a gradual replacement process.

The Slavonian Grebe's diving action is neat and light. Jumping almost clear of the water, the bird plunges down to search for fresh-water invertebrates and, increasingly in the winter months, fish. As with many members of the duck family, plants and seaweeds form a regular and important addition to the diet.

Shore Lark
Eremophila alpestris

The placid conditions of a river estuary encourage the proliferation of salt-marsh plants like the Glasswort, *Salicornia*, and the Seablite, *Suaeda*, but little else. It is along the strand line, where there is no scouring action by river or sea, that small passerine birds like the Shore Lark may reap a rich harvest of seeds, arthropods, crustaceans and larvae among the rotting and often pungent tide-wrack of seaweeds and wind-blown plant debris. In a habitat offering little to passerine birds, either in the breeding season or in winter, this narrow feeding zone assumes a vital importance.

The Shore Lark breeds in the cold, rocky wastes of the high arctic regions but, like many northern species, moves south in the winter. In the company of Skylarks, Linnets, Buntings and several members of the pipit family, the Shore Lark winters along the shores of southern Britain and the low-lying coasts of the North and Baltic Seas, feeding along the tide-wrack zones until the warmth of spring allows their return to the arctic breeding grounds.

Knot
Calidris canutus

The waders are a prime example of the way in which the members of a single group may diversify in order to exploit every available feeding niche in a given habitat. Some of their varied feeding techniques are illustrated on page 102, and never is this versatility more vital than in the winter months when millions of waders must leave their arctic breeding grounds for temporary quarters in Africa and Europe.

The Knot is one of the most spectacular migrant waders, often to be seen patrolling the mud-flats in large flocks, moving slowly forward shoulder to shoulder as they feed. At each step the Knot plunges its bill several times into the mud in search of molluscs and crustaceans – leaving the surface a mass of tiny holes.

Breeding in a number of curiously scattered localities in the circumpolar tundra, the bulk of the Knot population migrates to Africa for the winter though a few smaller populations remain around the shores of western Europe. For the immense journeys to and from northern Europe, the birds need "staging posts" where they can rest and build up their reserves of energy for the onward journey. These refuges along the route are of even greater importance in the spring when the birds must rest, moult and replenish their flight feathers, and then fly north to breed. So short is the arctic breeding season that a late arrival has little chance of successfully rearing a healthy brood.

Flight-path interchange

Each year many thousands of waders pass through the British Isles on their way to and from their arctic breeding grounds. For reasons not yet explained, the migrants tend to congregate in the Solway Firth in the autumn and follow the east coast on their journey south. In the spring, the west coast route is favoured – the birds resting on the Dee estuary and in Morecambe Bay before the final stage of the flight north.

Sanderling flies north-west to breed on sandy beaches in southern Greenland

Turnstone heads north-east to breed on rocky shores of northern Scandinavia

1 Solway Firth
2 The Wash
3 Thames estuary
4 South coast
5 Severn estuary
6 Dee estuary
7 Morecambe Bay

Parting of the ways
Inset map shows the preferred routes taken by Sanderling and Turnstone on their annual migrations. Each route links a series of vital "staging posts"

Sanderling
Calidris alba

Turnstone
Arenaria interpres

Knot
Calidris canutus 10in
Success depends on a perfectly timed arrival in the Arctic breeding grounds

The Coast in Summer

Small sandy beaches, protected by rocky headlands, are an attractive feature of much of the coastline of western Europe. Many are so small that they can support only one or two pairs of Ringed Plover, but in remote, undisturbed areas some of these coves support surprisingly large tern colonies.

The situation is markedly different on long, open beaches backed by sand-dunes. Here, shore-nesting birds face a multiplicity of hazards. Few such beaches are free from holidaymakers, whose visits often overlap the birds' breeding season. The lack of headlands exposes the beach to pounding by surf which, particularly in high winds, may produce masses of salt foam. Drifting along the beach, this foam may suffocate, or fatally chill exposed nestlings. The combination of wind and sea keeps the sand surface in constant motion, salt spray may soak the nests, and rough water may deposit piles of seaweed far above the normal high-water mark.

The sterile "soil" of sand and shingle, and the wildly fluctuating weather conditions, limit vegetation to hardy grasses. Plant and associated insect-food is relatively scarce and shore-birds must adapt – either to probing the beach for invertebrates, or, like the terns, to fishing in the shallow coastal waters. Nesting in the slightest depression, shore birds protect their eggs by cryptic colouring, and their young become independent far earlier than most land-birds.

Right: The nest and camouflaged eggs of the Ringed Plover

Oystercatcher
Haematopus ostralegus 16½in
Mollusc shells are no defence against this specialist's bill

Oystercatcher
Haematopus ostralegus

Conspicuous both in colour and in their incessant piping calls, Oystercatchers are a familiar winter sight along the shores of Europe. The majority are immigrants from breeding grounds farther north, and winter sees their greatest concentrations in temperate latitudes.

The Oystercatcher's bill is perfectly adapted for a diet of molluscs – stout and strong and laterally flattened into a chisel near the tip. Chipping through the hard shell of a mussel or cockle, the chisel is used first to sever the muscles holding the shell closed and then, scissor-like, to snip the soft mantle away from the shell. Often, the Oystercatcher will "wash" the mollusc before swallowing it.

This species is curiously vulnerable to foot problems; birds are often seen with a toe or even a whole foot amputated due to weeds or sheep's wool becoming twisted round the leg and restricting circulation.

Herring Gull
Larus argentatus 24in
Predator, scavenger – and cannibal

Herring Gull
Larus argentatus

Barely 50 years ago, the Herring Gull could have been called a "true sea-gull" summer and winter alike, but today it is widespread inland at all seasons, feeding on fish-quays and urban refuse tips with equal success.

The species is omnivorous, a major factor in its expansion, and is a notorious predator on the unguarded eggs and chicks of other birds, particularly members of the auk family. Some pairs even specialize in cannibalizing their own kind.

Territories are small and close-packed and are defended with great ferocity. Serious injury is, however, uncommon as the majority of disputes are settled by ritualized combat which establishes one protagonist's superiority without recourse to physical conflict.

Despite the availability of refuse, the Herring Gull retains its habit of dropping molluscs and crabs on to a hard surface to crack the shells.

Little Tern
Sterna albifrons 10in
*Caught in an ironic
twist of fate*

Living pebbles of the beach

The exposed beach environment offers few defensive nest-sites. Holes and cavities are dangerously unstable and dune vegetation can provide only the most meagre cover. Shore-birds have responded by nesting out in the open, rejecting physical concealment in favour of cryptic colouring. Laid in the barest ground-scrapes, their eggs are patterned with irregular streaks and blotches of colour that break up the tell-tale outline of the egg and allow it to merge unobtrusively with the beach.

1 Lapwing *Vanellus vanellus*
2 Little Tern *Sterna albifrons*
3 Ringed Plover *Charadrius hiaticula*
4 Ringed Plover chick

Little Tern
Sterna albifrons

That cryptic colouring should be counter-productive is a strange quirk of evolution, yet such is the case of the Little Tern. Superbly camouflaged in the barest of ground-scrapes, the clutch of two or three eggs is often crushed underfoot. The normal hazards of exposure, suffered by all shore-nesting birds, take a heavy toll, but the additional losses at the hand, or foot, of man have, over the past few decades, reduced the Little Tern to one of Europe's rarest shore-birds.

Smallest of the European sea-terns, the Little Tern feeds close inshore or in lagoons behind the beach. Often to be seen at close quarters, the bird hovers on flickering wings, bill pointing straight down as it scans the water for food. Plunging on to its prey, the tern may submerge completely for a few seconds before flying off with a sand-eel or shrimp.

Occasionally the Little Tern will nest alone and even its group nesting is better described as "social" than "colonial" as the nests are always well spaced. Most other beach-nesting terns form larger colonies, often over 100, sometimes more than 1,000 pairs strong. Generally these colonies are stable, but the Sandwich Tern, *S.sandvicensis*, is notoriously capricious.

Other terns tend to feed farther out to sea, but they, and even the apparently mild Kittiwake, will harass a Little Tern as it returns, food in bill, to the nest. When this happens, the Little Tern chicks try to scatter to the protection of nearby vegetation, but their extremely short legs prevent them from moving far.

Ringed Plover
Charadrius hiaticula 7¾in
*Supreme exponent of the
"broken wing" trick*

Ringed Plover
Charadrius hiaticula

Ringed Plovers have developed two behavioural adaptations to aid their survival in the exposed habitat of sand and shingle beaches.

The male is bold and aggressive in his defence of the nest, rushing forward at the approach of an intruder (be it bird, man or dog) with his plumage fluffed out to display the bold black markings on the wings and tail. The female is justly re-nowned as the supreme exponent of feigned injury. As an intruder advances, she will stagger from the nest and run away, trailing an apparently broken wing and offering the attacker an irresistibly "easy" prey. As the danger is drawn away from the nest, the chicks crouch or run for cover in response to low calls from the anxious parent.

Outside the breeding season, the Ringed Plover mixes with other shore waders, feeding on small inverte-brates picked from the sand. The Ringed Plover, however, favours drier sand than most waders and is often found higher· up the beach.

133

Cliffs and Offshore Islands

The northern and western coasts of Europe, and the plethora of offshore islands created by wind and sea, are the stronghold of many seabird species. The geology of an area is of great importance as the behaviour of the rock under the forces of erosion will determine the habitats available. The smooth surface of eroded sandstone is useless; its overhangs impossible. Where the rock has been upturned, so that the strata stand vertically, erosion creates knife-edge ridges but few ledges. Such is the case on the island of Skokholm, in Perthshire, a rocky mass completely ignored by the Kittiwakes and Guillemots that crowd on to nearby Skomer.

As a nesting habitat, cliffs are occasionally sheltered, but the majority are wholly at the mercy of the wind and waves that, in northern latitude storms, may crash more than 200 feet up the exposed rock face. However, the ever-present updraughts against the cliff face are a boon to heavily built, unskilled fliers like the auks, and the nesting ledges, perched over a sheer drop of hundreds of feet, are safe from the mammalian predators that plague low-lying colonies. But the cliff-nesters are not immune from predation. Many gulls, notably the Greater Black-backed, Glaucus and Herring Gulls, are experts at snatching poorly guarded eggs and young. This form of predation is serious enough to any species but even more so to the Guillemot whose single egg, once stolen, is very rarely replaced.

Species such as the Cormorant and Shag build bulky nests of seaweed and mud, but the Guillemot has adapted to naked ledges by producing a pear-shaped egg that rolls in a tight circle when dislodged. Most cliff-nesters are colonial, presumably deriving some degree of protection from their vast numbers. The synchronized breeding season that is encouraged by nesting in close proximity, reduces exposure to predators such as the Peregrine, though the latter itself has suffered drastically in recent years from a build-up of chemical pesticides in its natural prey. Colonial nesting also allows a sharing of information on feeding grounds.

Seabird colonies are among the great spectacles of the natural world. The island of St Kilda is home to more than 100,000 Gannets, while some of the northern Little Auk colonies are numbered in millions.

Kittiwake
Rissa tridactyla 16in
*Nests where one wrong
step could be fatal*

Shag
Phalacrocorax aristotelis 30in
*One of the world's most
primitive birds*

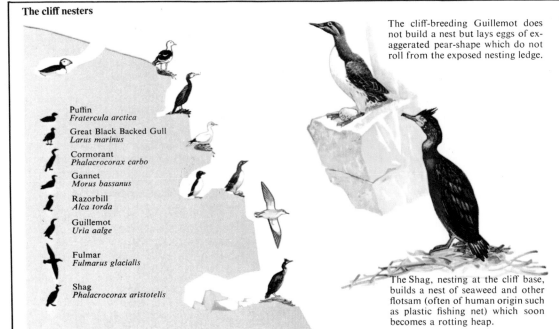

The cliff nesters

Puffin
Fratercula arctica

Great Black Backed Gull
Larus marinus

Cormorant
Phalacrocorax carbo

Gannet
Morus bassanus

Razorbill
Alca torda

Guillemot
Uria aalge

Fulmar
Fulmarus glacialis

Shag
Phalacrocorax aristotelis

The cliff-breeding Guillemot does not build a nest but lays eggs of exaggerated pear-shape which do not roll from the exposed nesting ledge.

The Shag, nesting at the cliff base, builds a nest of seaweed and other flotsam (often of human origin such as plastic fishing net) which soon becomes a rotting heap.

Multi-storey living

However bleak and forbidding to the casual observer, the face of a cliff offers a wide variety of living accommodation.

Structural features such as faults and joints provide ledges; cracks and fissures are created and widened by the incessant action of wind, rain and frost, and below, the pounding of the sea fashions innumerable caves and smaller cavities. All are utilized – indeed, few habitats are able to support such a density of habitation without any apparent ill effect.

Cliff-nesting species tend to produce their young simultaneously, so confining the period of maximum predation to a time when the whole colony is on the alert. The strong territorial instincts of cliff-dwellers also ensure that each bird is constantly alive to the threat to its young.

The diagram, left, illustrates a few of the many species that nest on the cliffs of northern Europe.

Kittiwake
Rissa tridactyla

One of the most graceful and buoyant of gulls in flight, the Kittiwake is probably the most pelagic of all European gulls, dispersing widely overseas outside the breeding season. The young often travel even farther afield than the adult birds. Their colonies are large and characterized by a raucous din and the white splashes surrounding every nest site.

The smallest rock projection, often situated in an impossible position like the overhang of a cave entrance, serves as a base for the nest of seaweed and mud. The adults are equipped with the longest claws of any gull in order to cope with their surroundings and, as one wrong step would be fatal, the adolescent Kittiwakes are among the best-behaved of all young birds. Experimenters have exchanged Kittiwake young for the young of the ground-nesting Black-headed Gull to test the strength of this instinctive behaviour. Within minutes, the Black-headed chicks stepped from the ledge and fell – saved only by the thoughtfully placed safety nets.

Kittiwakes feed mainly on fish and zooplankton, plunging in the manner of terns and sometimes submerging completely.

Shag
Phalacrocorax aristotelis

Unlike most seabirds, the Shag has a long, poorly synchronized breeding season and the single clutch may be laid at any time between March and August. The clutch is unusually large, normally five or six eggs, but the eggs themselves are tiny – a strong indication that the Shag is one of the most primitive species living today.

Shunning exposed cliff-ledge sites, the female builds her nest in the shelter of a cave or rock crevice. Because she is single-brooded, the female is fiercely protective and will warn off any intruder with an impressive threat display, hissing and gobbling with her bright yellow gape wide open and plumage erect.

The Shag is a powerful swimmer, cruising along the surface, frequently dipping its head below water to look for prey, and then pursuing the victim with impressive speed. Its fishing skills are legendary and in many eastern countries the bird, tethered by a tight collar and leash, is used commercially to catch shallow-water fish.

Chough
Pyrrhocorax pyrrhocorax

Contrasting sharply with the healthy population of its Alpine relative, *P.graculus*, the Chough is a dwindling species restricted to rocky coasts of the extreme west of Europe.

Competitive pressures from Rock Doves, feral pigeons and Jackdaws are thought to have contributed to its decline, but equally to blame is the increasing conflict between its highly specialized diet of ants and worms and the savage, salt environment that restricts supplies of these foods in cliff vegetation and coastal fields.

The Chough nests on rock ledges set deep within cliff caves and the single brood of three to five young is raised in an untidy nest of heather and twigs lined with grass.

Deeply slotted wing-tips give the Chough complete mastery of the turbulent air-flow rising against the face of the cliff – a mastery that is superbly displayed in the bird's spectacular tumbling courtship flight.

Puffin
Fratercula arctica 12in
*May carry up to 40
fish at each trip*

Chough
Pyrrhocorax pyrrhocorax 16½in
*Caught in the grip of
a changing environment*

Puffin
Fratercula arctica

While many Puffins nest in clefts in the cliff face, or in cavities in boulder screes, these curious birds show a marked preference for burrow nests situated in the turf-covered soil of ledges and cliff top. The burrows may be dug by the birds themselves, using their strong legs and powerful claws, or may be commandeered from rabbits and Shearwaters. Excavated nests are generally about six feet deep, but those in natural cavities may be much farther from the surface.

Puffins are colonial birds with a strongly developed social structure, often exhibited in social displays. Because of their inquisitive nature and lack of fear Puffins have been exploited by man for food and have played an important role in island economies for centuries. The annual cropping of seabirds, their eggs and young appears nowhere to have exceeded safe limits; strangely, however, the abandonment of this ancient practice does not seem to have arrested the decline in the Puffin population.

Puffins, and their relatives, the Razorbills, *Alca torda*, feed at sea, exploiting the large shoals of small fish that swim near the surface. In turbulent waters, larger fish, particularly sand-eels, are taken. The Puffin's mandibles are armed with backward-facing serrations and the bill opens with the mandibles parallel so that the bird is able to stack up to 40 fish crosswise in the bill before returning to the nest to feed its hungry offspring.

Unlike the Razorbill and Guillemot, the Puffin does not take its young to sea before it is fully grown. Instead, the young bird remains in the burrow until ready to fly and then leaves at night. Rather than being deserted, as is the young Manx Shearwater, it is the young Puffin which deserts its parents. The adult birds will continue to bring food to the burrow after the young has left.

Concrete Cliffs and Gardens

Short of a completely flat and featureless expanse of concrete there can be few habitats more modified by man than the urban sprawl. Two factors, however, ensure that our cities are not completely devoid of birdlife. In every town there are parks and gardens that provide food for a wide variety of birds. Even playing fields, one of the least productive green areas, can support a limited number of gulls during the winter months. Secondly, the remarkable versatility of many species has enabled them to come to terms with man and indeed, to some such as the House Sparrow, the town is a land of endless opportunity.

Tall factory buildings may house families of Black Redstarts; Kestrels and other raptors have bred successfully on the window ledges of high-rise flats, and in coastal towns, Fulmars, Kittiwakes and Herring Gulls have found walls and ledges to be quite acceptable as synthetic cliffs.

Natural food may be in short supply, particularly for the larger birds, but man is careless with his waste and for the majority food is varied and plentiful. Municipal tips provide a rich feeding ground for Rooks, Starlings and gulls, while household scraps help the smaller species. Evergreen trees in parks and gardens are ideal roosting and nesting sites and are far warmer in winter than the leafless deciduous bushes that are the birds' natural home.

Below: Kestrel and young on window-ledge nest

Urban areas of Europe

Blackbird
Turdus merula 10in
Most successful of the urban opportunists

Blue Tit
Parus caeruleus 4½in
Its popularity pays handsomely during the winter months

cans, will serve in the absence of rotten timber, and nest-sites are never a problem. Food, however, may pose difficulties. The clutch size of urban Blue Tits is much smaller (by one to three eggs) than its woodland counterpart, and the success of the young birds is drastically reduced, probably due to a shortage of suitable food.

In winter the situation is much improved due to the widespread practice of feeding birds with energy-rich foods such as fats and peanuts.

Swift
Apus apus

Perfectly adapted for sustained aerobatic flight, the Swift spends most of its time on the wing, twisting and darting in an endless pursuit of flying insects. Its tiny legs seem weak but are in fact well muscled and armed with needle-sharp claws capable of gripping and supporting the bird's weight even on smooth walls.

Such extreme specializations limit the Swift's choice of nest-site as the bird must make its entrance from a rising approach flight. The downward-facing cavities beneath the eaves of buildings are therefore ideal, particularly as there are seldom any nearby perches suitable for competitors such as Starlings.

Quite incapable of feeding on the ground, the Swift is entirely dependent on insects caught in flight. Its mouth is huge and insects are collected into a "food-ball" up to an inch in diameter before being carried back to the nest.

Tawny Owl
Strix aluco

Four birds of prey have adapted more or less successfully to city life; the Kestrel, Lesser Kestrel, Tawny Owl and Black Kite. Of these, the Tawny Owl is remarkable in that it has completely changed its diet in order to accommodate to the new environment.

In the country, over 90 per cent of the Tawny Owl's diet is composed of small mammals; the remainder of birds. In towns, the lack of ground cover excludes most mammals and the proportions are reversed – 90 per cent birds, mainly Starlings and House Sparrows, plus a few mammals and rodents.

The Tawny Owl has amended its normal woodland preferences to include parks and gardens, indeed any open areas with trees substantial enough to provide adequate roosting sites – and dense enough to afford protection from mobbing by flocks of small birds. One of the main threats to its continued success in towns is the work of the tree-surgeon, who, by removing old timber, destroys the cavities in which the owls nest.

The quiet invasion

Spreading slowly from its homeland in Asia, the Collared Dove reached Bulgaria early in the twentieth century. Since then, however, it has colonized Europe at an explosive rate – possibly due to a genetic mutation in birds of the westernmost populations. Reaching Britain in 1955, the westward movement shows no sign of abating: exhausted birds have been found more than 50 miles west of the British Isles and there is no reason why, given favourable winds, the species may not eventually establish itself in the Americas.

The Collared Dove shows great adaptability, nesting in bushes and walls as well as in its preferred pine-forest habitat, and producing as many as five broods each year. It is a grain-eating bird, most commonly found in poultry-breeding areas (where it competes for food) and in towns. It causes little damage, either to farms or gardens, and has generally been welcomed as an attractive addition to the urban bird population.

Collared Dove
Streptopelia decaocto 11in
The peaceful invader of western Europe

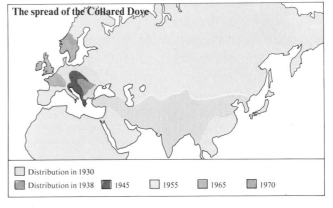

The spread of the Collared Dove

☐ Distribution in 1930				
☐ Distribution in 1938	■ 1945	☐ 1955	☐ 1965	☐ 1970

Swift
Apus apus 7in
The ultimate in flight artistry

Blackbird
Turdus merula

Largely because of its remarkable adaptability, the Blackbird is one of the most common land-birds in Europe. Even in the heart of the city, in tiny gardens and grimy squares, dawn will see chimneys and television aerials dotted with singing males – quite unconcerned at the lack of trees. Females nest in the scantiest vegetation, or on the ledges in and around buildings. The shortage of grass for nesting is no problem to a bird that has quickly learned the versatility of paper and plastics.

Recent studies in major cities have shown that birds exist in far higher densities in the urban environment than in the country. Adult mortality is high but appears to be offset by greater breeding success and more breeding attempts each season. After three weeks of snow in 1968, London Blackbirds were found to weigh 140gm compared with the 80gm body-weight of woodland specimens starving barely 30 miles away. Clearly there is no shortage of food. Garden worms and beetles are plentiful and only in severe weather do the birds rely on domestic scraps.

Blue Tit
Parus caeruleus

Normally an insect-eating resident of the woodland canopy, the Blue Tit had adapted well to urban life, though the Great Tit, *P.major*, is less successful in towns and cities.

For a hole-nesting species, cavities in walls, behind the cladding of buildings, and even in discarded

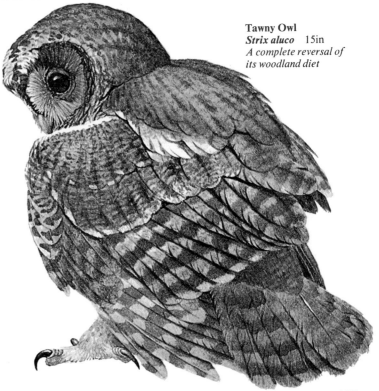

Tawny Owl
Strix aluco 15in
A complete reversal of its woodland diet

Africa
The Ethiopian Realm

Merging imperceptibly with the Palaearctic realm in the rocky wilderness of the northern Sahara, the Ethiopian realm stretches for more than 4,500 miles to meet the cold oceans encircling the southern tip of the continent. Within this vast area, a perfect progression of vegetation zones radiates out from the dense tropical forest of the Congo basin, through wooded and grassy steppes to harsh regions of scrub and semi-desert, varied in the east by snow-capped mountains and great inland waterways. More than 1,500 species make their homes in this rich variety of habitats. In open country the visitor is faced with a bewildering array of plumage colours and behaviour patterns, while the great lakes of the Rift Valley may reward the observer with more than 200 species in a single day. To the wooded and grassy savannas come thousands of millions of winter migrants from the colder climes of Europe and Asia, and many of the 150 visiting species are as abundant as the resident species during the winter months.

Separated from the mainland by the Mozambique Channel, the island continent of Madagascar and the attendant tropical islands of the Malagasy sub-region provided a sheltered theatre of evolution in which many of the world's most curious species lived in peace until the arrival of man early in the sixteenth century.

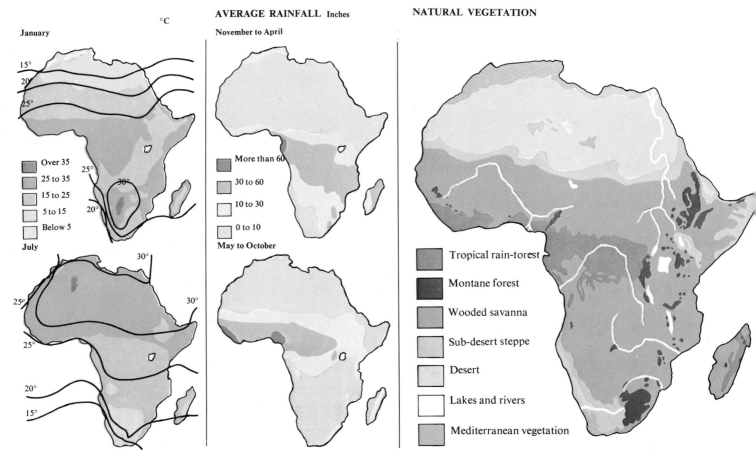

°C

January

15°
20°
25°
25°
30°
20°

Over 35
25 to 35
15 to 25
5 to 15
Below 5

July

30°
25°
25°
30°
20°
15°

AVERAGE RAINFALL Inches

November to April

More than 60
30 to 60
10 to 30
0 to 10

May to October

NATURAL VEGETATION

Tropical rain-forest

Montane forest

Wooded savanna

Sub-desert steppe

Desert

Lakes and rivers

Mediterranean vegetation

BIRDS ILLUSTRATED

1 **White-backed Vulture**
Pseudogyps africanus

2 **Verreaux's Eagle**
Aquila verreauxii

3 **Violet-backed Starling**
Cinnyricinclus leucogaster

4 **Ground Hornbill**
Bucorvus leadbeateri

5 **Pin-tailed Whydah**
Vidua macroura

6 **Greater Flamingo**
Phoenicopterus ruber

7 **Burchell's Gonolek**
Laniarius atrococcineus

8 **Crowned Crane**
Balearica pavonina

9 **African Black Crake**
Limnocorax flavirostra

10 **Wattled Plover**
Vanellus senegallus

11 **Long-tailed Ground Roller**
Uratelornis chimaera

139

Tropical Rain-forest

Gloomy, dank and still, the rain-forests of the Congo basin and the borders of the Gulf of Guinea are rich in birds. But ornithologists must work hard to find them: many species confine themselves to the tree canopy 90 feet or more above ground, and those which live nearer the forest floor are shy and retiring. Conditions for observation are nearly always poor and, screened by trunks and leaves, the habits of many forest birds remain a mystery.

The vegetation that most nearly approaches the widely held conception of "jungle" is not the natural forest but the thick, practically impenetrable tangle of trees, palms and climbing and scrambling lianas that quickly grow where forest has been cleared, farmed and then abandoned. Virgin lowland rain forest, of which little now remains west of Cameroon, consists of tall well-spaced trees with a thick canopy filtering out the light and allowing virtually no understorey to develop. In this world of perpetual twilight a falling leaf attracts the eye, but only the patient and discerning observer will see a bird move. Sounds are important, but skill and experience are needed to distinguish the strange cries of mammals and frogs from the bizarre calls of many of Africa's forest birds.

The tape recorder and mist-net are invaluable aids to the observer: a bird will often be attracted within view by its own voice, while netting safely captures specimens for study.
Right: Lowland tropical forest in West Africa

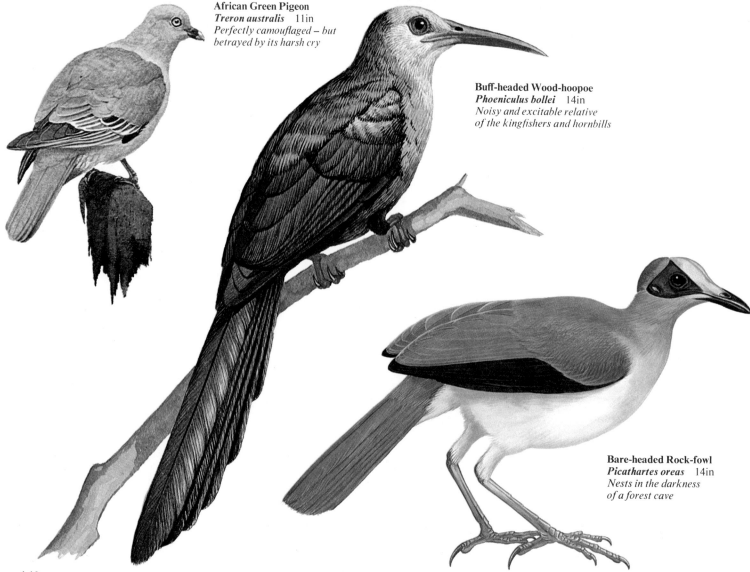

African Green Pigeon
Treron australis 11in
*Perfectly camouflaged – but
betrayed by its harsh cry*

Buff-headed Wood-hoopoe
Phoeniculus bollei 14in
*Noisy and excitable relative
of the kingfishers and hornbills*

Bare-headed Rock-fowl
Picathartes oreas 14in
*Nests in the darkness
of a forest cave*

Tropical forest

Area of forest

Distribution of species

Congo Peacock
Afropavo congensis

Rock-fowl
Picathartes spp.

Congo Peacock
Afropavo congensis 26in
Discovered after a 24-year search

African Green Pigeon
Treron australis

Convergent evolution has produced a remarkable similarity between this heavy-bodied, fruit-eating forest pigeon and the fruit-eating *Poicephalus* parrots. *Treron* pigeons and *Poicephalus* parrots are both green, similar in size and have the same swift, direct flight, moving in small flocks between roosts and fruiting trees. If approached, both species stop feeding and become warily still – their plumage blending invisibly into the rich background of foliage.

Green Pigeons range widely through the forest – sometimes in flocks of hundreds – in search of their favourite fruit, ripe figs. They are solitary nesters, building the loose twig platform characteristic of their family. Unlike the cooing song of most pigeons, their song is an unexpected fast, chuckling purr, punctuated by squeaks and harsh croaks.

Buff-headed Wood-hoopoe
Phoeniculus bollei

Among the noisiest of all forest birds, the Wood-hoopoe forages in chattering flocks among trunks and branches, its slender down-curved bill constantly exploring the bark for grubs, insects and larvae. The birds'

sociable group-feeding is frequently interrupted by ceremonious bowing accompanied by an excited cackling chorus.

The complex social organization even extends to raising the young, the parents being assisted by full-grown young of the previous brood. A member of the kingfisher-roller-hornbill group, the Wood-hoopoe family is confined to Africa: the Buff-headed and Green Wood-hoopoes live in the tropical forest and the smaller, related Scimitar-bills in woodland, savanna and bush.

Bare-headed Rock-fowl
Picathartes oreas

Unlike the highly specialized Oil-birds of the northern Neotropics and the Edible-nest Swiftlets of southern Asia, the Rock-fowl has little need of a sophisticated echo-location system as it seldom flies in darkness. Indeed the Rock-fowl flies very little, preferring to hop along the ground. This secretive bird of the forest caves emerges in the twilight hours, its large eyes searching the forest floor for insects and small vertebrates.

The mud-and-fibre cup nest is cemented high on the cave wall or ceiling and is sometimes anchored in place on a small, deserted wasps' nest. The birds are gregarious, and groups of a dozen or more nests may be found together, each being used year after year by the same family.

Recently, new facts were discovered about the affinities of this bird. Clearly aberrant, it had been placed variously among the crows, starlings and babblers, but studies of egg-white proteins now demonstrate that it *is* probably a babbler.

Congo Peacock
Afropavo congensis

A single feather seen in the head-dress of a Congolese native in 1913; two stuffed specimens lying for years in a Belgian museum and wrongly labelled as the common Indian species – these were the clues that led Dr J. P. Chapin, the Congo's foremost ornithologist, on a 24-year quest after a large, unknown game bird of the forests.

In 1937 his search was rewarded when the first wild specimens of the rare Congo Peacock were observed in the eastern Congo and Ituri forests. Little is known of their biology, but captive birds roost and nest in trees, laying clutches of two to four eggs – a remarkably small clutch for a member of the game-bird family. The erect tuft of crown feathers and the raised tail-covert display are strong indications that the Congo Peacock is descended from an ancestor in common with its larger Asiatic relatives, the Blue Peacock and the Green Peacock.

Red-billed Dwarf Hornbill
Tockus camurus 15in
*Seals his mate in a
tree-hollow fortress*

Fortified nursery
Secure against predators, the
female hornbill spends the
entire incubation period in
the fortified tree-hole nest,
while the male provides food
for the growing family.

Angolan Pitta
Pitta angolensis 7in
*The ventriloquist "Jewel-finch"
whose flight is a sudden burst of
iridescent colour*

Red-billed Dwarf Hornbill
Tockus camurus

Occupying the same niche in the Old
World as the unrelated toucans in the
New, there are 22 known species of
African hornbill and roughly the
same number again in Asia.

Hornbills of the genus *Tockus* are
mostly small gregarious birds with
brown or pied plumage, their far-
carrying piping calls providing the
most characteristic sounds of both
forest and savanna. Their beaks,
vividly coloured and patterned, are
sometimes surmounted by a small
bony casque. Like the toucan's beak,
the hornbill's is an important visual
element in social communication.

Apart from its frequent quavering
call, the Red-billed Dwarf Hornbill
is an inconspicuous bird, keeping
within dense forest and feeding at low
level often in a mixed bird party. Its
food – berries, figs and palm nuts –
is plucked then tipped to the back of
the throat to be swallowed whole.
Live prey is restricted to insects – in
contrast with the larger hornbills,
which often take young birds, lizards
and even young squirrels. Secure
even against predatory bird-eating
snakes, the Hornbill's tree-hole nest
is a fortress – its entrance closed
down to a narrow slit by a rock-hard
mixture of mud and juices. In the
genus *Tockus* both sexes start the
masonry, the female then squeezing
inside to lay her eggs while the male
completes the work of sealing her in.
The Silvery-cheeked Hornbill,
Bycanistes brevis, does all the plastering herself from inside the nest, using
mud pellets passed in by her mate.
During the laying period the female
Hornbill moults completely and is
fed by the male. The five or so eggs
are laid at intervals – the young,
therefore, being graded in age and
size.

Towards the end of the nesting
period the female, her plumage•fully
regrown, chips her way out and the
nest is resealed – leaving a narrow
slit through which the young are fed.
In a remarkable display of instinctive behaviour each of the young in
turn breaks out, and the immature
birds remaining inside – never having
previously seen the operation –
actively help the parents to reseal the
aperture. This process is repeated
until the last of the young is fledged.

Angolan Pitta
Pitta angolensis

Aptly called the "Jewel-thrushes"
this family of 23 brilliantly coloured,
primitive passerine birds is distributed from Africa to the Solomon
Islands, though the forests of Africa
have only the Angolan Pitta and the
Green-breasted Pitta, *P. reichenowi*.
The pittas are shy, thrush-like birds,
moving swiftly over the forest floor
in long easy hops and feeding on a
variety of small invertebrates.

The Angolan Pitta is an alert,
curious bird that normally adopts an
upright posture when examining
anything. When alarmed it drops to
the ground, fluffing out its breast
feathers and crest.

Their swift direct flight through the
forest gloom, and their uncanny
ventriloquist skill, make them difficult to locate, and observations often
consist of little more than a fleeting
glimpse of flashing colour. Strong
evidence suggests that the Angolan
Pitta migrates between Kenya and
southern Tanzania.

Islands in a Forest Sea

Twenty thousand years ago Africa was, on average, 5°C cooler than today. The montane type of forest came to within 1,600 feet of sea-level, making it and its bird-life widespread and continuous. Now that both have retreated to higher altitudes, the montane forests are fragmented and form archipelagos of islands in a sea of lowland forest. In those "islands", isolated as effectively as they would be on an oceanic island, new bird forms have evolved, quite distinct from those in lowland forests. Of 160 species of forest birds in the African mountains, and 290 in the lowlands, only 40 are common to both. The Cameroon highlands, for instance, have no fewer than 16 endemic birds. Eight of these have closely related species in the distant Ruwenzori mountains, and a further 27 species are common to both mountain regions.

Above an altitude of about 5,000 feet, tropical forests have a different character from lowland forests. The approximate upper limit of the timber-line at the Equator is 10,500 feet and above this are unique grasslands, searingly hot by day and bitterly cold by night. Dominated by giant heathers, giant lobelias and treelike *Senecios*, this is the *afro-alpine community*. The bird fauna of these strange moorlands is remarkably similar to that of open country in the lowlands – only a handful of species being truly endemic to the non-forested areas of the mountains.

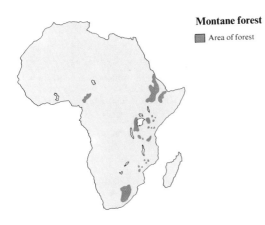

Montane forest

■ Area of forest

Black-billed Turaco
Tauraco schuttii 16in
Consumes fruits that are poisonous to many birds

Eastern Double-collared Sunbird
Nectarinia mediocris 4½in
Lowers its temperature at night to conserve vital energy

Black-billed Turaco
Tauraco schuttii

A squirrel-like movement along tree-top boughs, a deafening communal chorus of ringing "kow-kow-kow" notes, and flashes of crimson wings and brilliant green – these form the characteristic introduction to the turaco. Found only in Africa, these colourful plantain-eaters may be distant relatives of the cuckoos, though the flimsy twig-platform nest and clutch of two white eggs recall pigeons. Many authors think them sufficiently distinctive to comprise a full order.

Lively and gregarious birds of the forest canopy, turacos subsist mainly on fruit and are known to consume some that are disagreeable or even poisonous to other birds. They also take caterpillars and other insects. Small flocks of Black-billed Turacos inhabit montane and lowland forests. They spend much of their time running and hopping along limbs high in trees, only spreading their short round wings in laboured flight when a gap is too wide to be jumped easily.

Eastern Double-collared Sunbird
Nectarinia mediocris

Brilliantly coloured in metallic hues, the sunbirds of the African mountains are superbly adapted to their high-altitude habitat. Intense heat at midday is followed by freezing temperatures at night, and at 11,000 feet in the Kenya Cherangani mountains the Eastern Double-collared Sunbird's temperature may fall by up to 17°C during the night, conserving energy and promoting survival.

N. mediocris is thoroughly montane, seldom venturing below 5,000 feet, and then only when attracted by the flowering of a particularly favoured tree such as the kaffirboom, *Erythrina abyssinica*. At this elevation the sunbird's environment is in harsh contrast to that of its lowland relatives.

Instead of lush forest or rich woodland, the montane Double-collared Sunbirds must survive in a weird landscape of scrub, misty marshes and cold, desolate moorlands, feeding on insects and the nectar of the giant lobelias and red-hot pokers.

The Savanna Woodlands

Between the extremes of rain forest and desert lie a range of habitats loosely called wooded savannas. The South American term "savanna", for grassland, has come to be used for these intermediate biomes of Africa since they are all characterized by a good grass layer, even when extensively wooded.

Such open woodlands, dominated by the fire-resisting trees *Brachystegia* and *Isoberlinia*, occur in a broad zone north and south of the equatorial rain forest, wherever there is sufficient annual rainfall. Farther from the Equator, densely wooded savannas give way to more open country, which towards the Sahara and, in the southwest, the Kalahari, turns to grassland with scattered baobabs and thorny *Acacia* trees. Transitions between these savanna zones are sharp and each holds a distinctive bird fauna. The regions are, however, diversified by watercourses, marshes, granite hills (known as "inselbergs" or "kopjes") and by soils and farming.

The non-forested regions of Africa harbour over twice as many species as the forests – well over a thousand birds. Many native birds migrate within the savannas in keeping with the rains: away from the Equator at the beginning of the wet season (March-May in northern savannas, September-November in southern) and back again at its end. In winter their numbers are greatly augmented by migrants from outside Africa.

Right: Weaver-bird nests in open wooded savanna

Growing fat on other's toil

Killer parasite
All honey-guides are brood parasites, commonly laying their eggs in the nests of barbets and bee-eaters. On hatching the young *Indicator* usually ejects its nest-mates, but may also attack and even kill them, using sharp hooks on the tip of the bill.

Unwitting helper
Attracted by the honey-guide's excited cries the Ratel, *Mellivora capensis*, tears open a bees' nest while the honeyguide waits its turn.

Greater Honey-guide
Indicator indicator

The aptly-named *Indicator indicator*, the Greater Honey-guide, is the most common of the African species – its ringing "vic*tor*" call a familiar sound of the wooded savannas. On finding a bees' nest the Honey-guide darts back and forth in restless flight, uttering an excited, chattering cry to attract the attention of any nearby mammal, commonly the Ratel or Honeybadger. The Honey-guide waits while the nest is broken open and then feeds avidly on bees, larvae and honey – its unique digestive system even coping with the wax of the nest chambers. The two tiny, sharp-billed *Prodotiscus* honey-guides, warbler-like birds of the acacia woodlands, feed on waxy scale-insects, an even more specialized diet.

Some species use their outspread tails to produce a snipe-like drumming "song" in diving flight, and this is particularly well developed in the forest Lyre-tailed Honey-guide, *Melichneutes robustus*.

In addition to digesting wax and taking advantage of unwitting helpers, the remarkable honey-guides are the world's only totally parasitic family.

Pennant-winged Nightjar
Macrodipteryx vexillarius

Standard-winged Nightjar
Macrodipteryx longipennis

Among the more extraordinary manifestations of sexual selection, the breeding males of these closely related nightjars are adorned with greatly elongated flight feathers in the wings. Male Pennant-wings – the largest African nightjars – have the pale seventh, eighth and ninth primaries elongated. The ninth is up to two feet long and in flight the pennant flutters like a white ribbon – an eye-catching sight as the bird darts and turns after its insect prey.

The smaller, nocturnal Standard-winged Nightjars have the ninth primary up to 18 inches long, with broad vanes (the "standards") on the last six inches and the rest of the feather shaft bare. Silhouetted by twilight or moonlight, the shafts are invisible, and the flapping standards look like two small bats closely following every twist and turn of the bird's hunting flight. The Pennant-wing's nuptial display consists of sailing conspicuously above the tree tops, sometimes even by day. Male Standard-wings display by cruising slowly near the ground, the wings held stiffly bowed and vibrating, the standards borne straight up, vibrating with the wings.

Pennant-wings are unusual in nesting during the rains in southern Africa, after which they migrate into the savannas north of the quator. They are thought to bite off the long feathers near the base soon after breeding and to moult the stump after migrating.

After breeding, Standard-winged Nightjars moult the standards, which are replaced by slow-growing feathers. Just before the next breeding season the growth accelerates, transforming them from functional flight feathers into a nuptial adornment.

Marabou
Leptoptilos crumeniferus

Relatives of the Indian adjutants, Marabous are huge African storks which feed largely on carrion but also prey on whatever live animals come their way, from insects to frogs, snakes and rodents. They are by no means confined to waterside habitats and often feed in arid country, jostling with vultures over mammal corpses or on village refuse tips.

Not particularly shy, Marabous nest in the dry season in large trees, often in villages and towns. An inflatable 18-inch-long naked pink throat-pouch is conspicuous during the breeding season. Grotesque on the ground, they are majestic in flight, soaring on thermal up-draughts on wings up to 11 feet in span.

Marabou
Leptoptilus crumeniferus 60in
Soaring scavenger that competes with vultures for carrion

Standard-winged Nightjar
Macrodipteryx longipennis 9in
The impressive nuptial adornments of the male are moulted at the end of the breeding season

Pennant-winged Nightjar
Macrodipteryx vexillarius 12in
The elegant white nuptial display feathers more than double its length

The Open Grasslands

Bateleur
Terathopius ecaudatus 24in
*Perhaps the original Phoenix
of ancient mythology*

Secretary-bird
Sagittarius serpentarius 40in
*Preys on snakes by kicking
and stamping them to death*

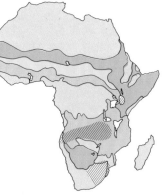

Wooded savanna

Types of savanna

☐ Sudan savanna

☐ Grass savanna

☐ Guinea savanna

Distribution of species

▨ Long-tailed Widow-bird
   Euplectes progne

Bateleur
Terathopius ecaudatus

Thought to be the original Phoenix of mythology, this magnificent fire-backed eagle has a unique flight silhouette that sets it apart from all other eagles. Its flight is graceful and effortless, with a characteristic rocking action. Taking to the wing as soon as the chill of dawn goes, Bateleurs spend the greater part of the day in majestic flight, soaring over savanna and light woodland in their quest for small mammals and birds, reptiles, carrion and even snakes.

Although very different in appearance, the Bateleur may be closely related to the *Circaetus* snake-eagles. Chicks of both species acquire feathers on the crown and back while the undersides are still down-covered. The snake-eagles, which are reared in open, unshaded nests, need these feathers to protect them from the sun. By contrast Bateleurs nest in leafy shade – but the young still bear this evolutionary relict from their *Circaetus*-like ancestors.

Secretary-bird
Sagittarius serpentarius

More the shape of a crane than a hawk, this unique long-legged ground-dwelling bird feeds largely upon snakes – killing them by kicking and stamping. The long, thin shanks have a remarkably powerful forward kick that can inflict painful injury on man and means quick death to small prey. The long legs keep the bird's body clear of striking fangs and enable it to stride through grass in search of prey – for it forages not by soaring like other diurnal predators but by walking hour after hour across savanna and shunning very tall grass and wooded areas.

Secretary-birds take their name from the fanciful resemblance of the crown plumes to quill-pens tucked behind the ear of a clerk. Long eye-lashes enhance the comparison, a rare avian characteristic shared by the ostriches, bustards and ground hornbills. So strange is the terrestrial-hunting habit that ornithologists have long wondered whether the secretary-bird really is a raptor or whether it more properly belongs with the

bustards, as suggested by its hunting technique, egg-protein studies and its strong resemblance to an undoubted bustard relative, the South American Seriema (p 88). The Secretary-bird's breeding biology is, however, very like that of other typical large raptors. Bustard or buzzard, this magnificent bird is one of the most characteristic sights of Africa's grassland habitats.

Helmeted Guinea-fowl
Numida meleagris

Helmeted Guinea-fowl are noisy and gregarious birds, but often inconspicuous when feeding amongst trees and scrub. Towards evening the harsh, abrasive cackles of roosting flocks ring through the trees until silenced by nightfall.

The four species of guinea-fowl comprise a sub-family of game birds mainly confined to Africa, although a population of the Helmeted Guinea-fowl is found north of the Sahara, in Morocco – a country whose bird fauna is much more Palaearctic than Ethiopian. The helmet is bony; its function unknown. In its place some of the forest species, like the Kenya Crested Guinea-fowl, *Guttera pucherani*, have a tuft of crisp curly black feathers, while the Vulturine Guinea-fowl, *Acryllium vulturinum*, of the arid regions of Somalia is without any cranial decoration.

Long-tailed Widow-bird
Euplectes progne

Countless generations of sexual selection have made the Long-tailed Widow-bird one of Africa's most striking weavers. Dowdy and sparrow-like for much of the year, the breeding cocks of the fifteen widow-bird species are resplendent in glossy black plumage boldly relieved by areas of intense yellow and red. In courtship display the Long-tailed Widow-bird bobs and weaves across the nesting ground in a slow, low-level flight, the two-foot-long tail feathers drooping behind.

Often found well above 5,000 feet, the birds inhabit the open wet grasslands and marshes of the highlands of East and South Africa.

Helmeted Guinea-fowl
Numida meleagris 21in
The function of its bony crest is unknown

Long-tailed Widow-bird
Euplectes progne 6in
Resplendent in two-foot-long nuptial display feathers

Red-billed Oxpecker 7in
Buphagus erythrorhynchus
Personal valet to the savanna grazers

Mutual benefits

Wagtails and egrets feed at the feet of cattle, bee-eaters ride goats, and Egyptian plovers supposedly pick at crocodiles' teeth, but no relationship of bird and beast in Africa is as strange as that of the oxpecker.

Probably aberrant starlings, the two species, the Red-billed and the Yellow-billed, *B. africanus*, spend most of their waking hours clinging like woodpeckers to large mammals – antelopes, cattle, giraffes, rhinos and hippos. Moving over the animal's hide, gripping with robust claws and using the stiff tail as an extra support, the oxpecker seeks out the ticks, flies and other parasites that constitute its diet.

Occasionally a small antelope will show signs of irritation, but for the most part mammals tolerate the birds: indeed they should, since they stand to benefit from the association as much as the birds do. Occasionally, however, oxpeckers abuse this symbiotic relationship by pecking at skin wounds and eating pieces of flesh.

At night the birds fly off in small flocks to roost among reeds and trees, but often they simply roost on the host – a technique that saves them having to find a new companion the next morning. Like starlings they nest in tree-holes, lining the nest with animal hairs.

Wooded Savanna

Grey-headed Bush-shrike
Malaconotus blanchoti 10in
*The larger member of
a curiously matched pair*

Red-faced Coly
Colius indicus 13in
*Notorious robber of
orchards and gardens*

Red-faced Coly
Colius indicus

The Coly's fondness for figs, dates and other soft fruits has branded it a pest through farmland and gardens south of the Equator, where its curious habit of running and climbing through the branches with head held low has earned it the unlikely name "mouse-bird". Busy, gregarious birds, the colies have a characteristic fast, direct flight, nearly always accompanied by a clear, loud, whistling call.

The six species of mouse-bird comprise a family and order restricted to Africa and with no known affinities with other groups. All inhabit non-forested regions within the tropics.

Savanna matchmakers

The vividly coloured Grey-headed Bush-shrike *Malaconotus blanchoti* is a shy bird – seldom seen despite its bright colours. Foraging among leafy vegetation with its massive bill, it feeds on insects, mice, lizards and small snakes.

Another striking savanna resident is the Sulphur-bellied Bush-shrike *Chlorophoneus sulfureopectus*, a small, fine-billed bush-shrike which, although much smaller, closely resembles *M. blanchoti* in colouring and has almost exactly the same range. This same remarkable colour-match occurs throughout the wooded savannas wherever the small *Chlorophoneus* and the larger, heavy-billed *Malaconotus* shrikes are found together.

Three closely related species of *Chlorophoneus* inhabit the forest regions – the many-coloured *C. multicolor* lives in the equatorial lowlands and the Black-fronted, *C. nigrifrons*, and Olive, *C. olivaceous*, in the montane forests of eastern and southern Africa. All three are polymorphic.

Among the larger *Malaconotus* bush-shrikes, the montane species are not polymorphic, but in the lowland forest the Fiery-breasted Bush-shrike, *M. cruentus*, and the Angolan Bush-shrike, *M. monteiri*, have crimson, scarlet or yellow plumage – the colour again varying geographically to coincide with the predominant form of local *Chlorophoneus*.

This curious "copycat" situation is as yet not fully understood. Each of the large *Malaconotus* species may be one descendant of a polymorphic ancestor – but this does not explain why *Malaconotus* and *Chlorophoneus* should adopt the same colouring – particularly as their differences in size, bill-form and

food source fit them for different "niches" in the ecology. Perhaps a local population of the smaller *Chlorophoneus* shrikes gains some selective advantage, or protection, in coming to resemble the larger *Malaconotus* in the same area.

The shrikes' colour variants

The map and proportional diagrams below show the predominant colours of the breast and belly plumage of the small bush-shrike *Chlorophoneus multicolor* in different parts of its range. In each area the predominant colour variety of *C. multicolor* closely matches the colouring of the local variety of the larger *Malaconotus* bush-shrike.

1 Red 80%	Yellow 10%	Black 10%	
2 Red 50%	Yellow 50%		
3 Red 66%	Yellow 34%		
4 Yellow 100%			
5 Orange 83%	Red 17%		
6 Yellow 68%	Dark Red 16%	Buff 16%	
7 Dark Red 72%	Yellow 28%		
8 Yellow 66%	Red 29%	Buff 3%	Orange 2%
9 Yellow 56%	Buff 41%	Black & Green 3%	
10 Buff 63%	Orange 37%		

Malaconotus cruentus

Chlorophoneus multicolor

Chlorophoneus multicolor

Malaconotus cruentus

Chlorophoneus multicolor

Malaconotus cruentus

Malaconotus monteiri

Ostrich
Struthio camelus 90in
The world's largest living bird

Red-billed Quelea
Quelea quelea 5in
A devastating pest despite
all attempts at control

Namaqua Dove
Oena capensis 8½in
Nests at all times
of the year

Red-billed Quelea
Quelea quelea

Like feathered locusts, countless millions of these sparrow-like weaver-birds inhabit the savanna grasslands, their swirling flocks a joy to the tourist but an expensive nightmare to the cereal farmer. During the dry season queleas feed on small grass-seeds picked from the ground, turning to larger seeds as the small ones are consumed. In years when the grass-seeds are depleted early, the birds are liable to turn to ripening cereals, particularly millet and guinea corn, devastating crops over huge regions.

International research organizations in a dozen countries have discovered more about the biology of this species than is known about almost any bird in the world – with the exception of the hen – but as yet no effective control measures have been found. Each year millions are killed, but the damage continues.

Ostrich
Struthio camelus

Often weighing more than 300 pounds, the Ostrich is the world's largest living bird, although the recently extinct moas of New Zealand may have weighed three times as much. Today, despite hunting pressures which have reduced or even exterminated local populations, this extraordinary bird is still common enough in many parts of Africa, and in the south its survival is ensured by ostrich-farming based on the valuable plumes and leather.

Much of man's interest in the bird centres upon its remarkable adaptations for life in deserts and arid steppe. In these exposed habitats the bold black and white plumage of the male is conspicuous, and to escape the attentions of large predators it depends upon a turn of speed comparable with a gazelle's. In males the naked thighs and sparsely feathered neck are garishly coloured, varying from flesh-pink in the Sahara to an astonishing bright blue in Somalia.

Females, which far outnumber males, have by contrast an inconspicuous brown-grey plumage, while the vulnerable young are protectively patterned in browns and greys. Succulent plants form the principal diet, but the birds are scavengers and will readily eat berries, seeds, small animals and vegetable refuse.

The Ostrich has a remarkable tolerance of heat, withstanding laboratory air temperatures of 56°C without undue stress. Heat is lost by panting via the well-developed air-sac system, which avoids over-ventilation of the lungs and consequent dangerous water loss. Adaptations of the blood circulatory system permit the body to heat up to a greater extent than in other warm-blooded animals while still keeping the head at a safe temperature.

Namaqua Dove
Oena capensis

The diminutive Namaqua Dove feeds entirely on the ground, on seeds, and is obliged to migrate to drier parts of its range at the beginning of the rains when seeds remaining after the dry season either germinate or become concealed among the flush of growing grasses and herbs.

As with many pigeons, the nesting season is long, and in those latitudes where the species occurs all year, occupied nests may be found at all seasons. The nest itself is a fragile platform of rootlets, leaf-stems and pieces of dry grass built in a low bush or tree-stump. When disturbed, an incubating bird erupts from the nest with a clatter of wingbeats, flying off and deserting the two white eggs.

The Namaqua Dove is one of the few members of its family to show marked sexual dimorphism in plumage colour; the female differs in not having the black throat, chest and face markings characteristic of the male.

The Migrant's Year

Every year more than five thousand million birds leave their breeding grounds in Europe and Asia and fly south to spend the winter months among the lakes, grasslands and forests of Africa.

In autumn the air is full of warblers, chats and wagtails, hawks, waders and myriad waterfowl moving south through Europe to the last "staging posts" along the Mediterranean coast. Beyond these feeding grounds – the Coto Doñana in southwest Spain, the Camargue in southern France, the Danube estuary and others – lies an incredible journey which will take the birds 1,500 miles non-stop across the barren wilderness of the North African deserts.

Nearly one-third of these migrants are destined never to return. Some perish in storms, blown far off course with their reserves of energy burned out. Thousands more fall prey to the predatory hawks lying in wait along the hazardous route and, at the journey's end, millions more die of starvation – too weak to compete for food with other immigrants and the locally resident populations.

Whitethroat
Sylvia communis
The attractive Whitethroat breeds throughout Europe where its rasping, high-pitched call is a common sound in hedgerows, gardens and woodlands. It is one of the most wide-ranging members of the warbler family.

Whitethroat
Sylvia communis

Whitethroat's breeding range

Whitethroat migrates to wintering range

Feeding hours: Europe
Although insectivorous for most of the year, warblers utilize the long daylight hours of late summer to feed up on sugar-rich berries.

June

Whitethroat breeding
Insect diet

July August

Fattening on berries before migration

Crossing to African wintering ground Insect

Eleonora's and Sooty Falcon breeding

September

Eleonora's breeding range

Sooty's breeding range

Whitethroat's winter range

Eleonora's Falcon
Falco eleonorae
Beautiful but deadly, Eleonora's Falcon is the only European bird to breed during the autumn months. Nesting on islands in the Mediterranean and off the coast of North West Africa, it exploits the southward migration of warblers, chats and bee-eaters. The related Sooty Falcon, *F. concolor*, employs the same stratagem – nesting along the Red Sea and preying on migrants crossing from Asia.

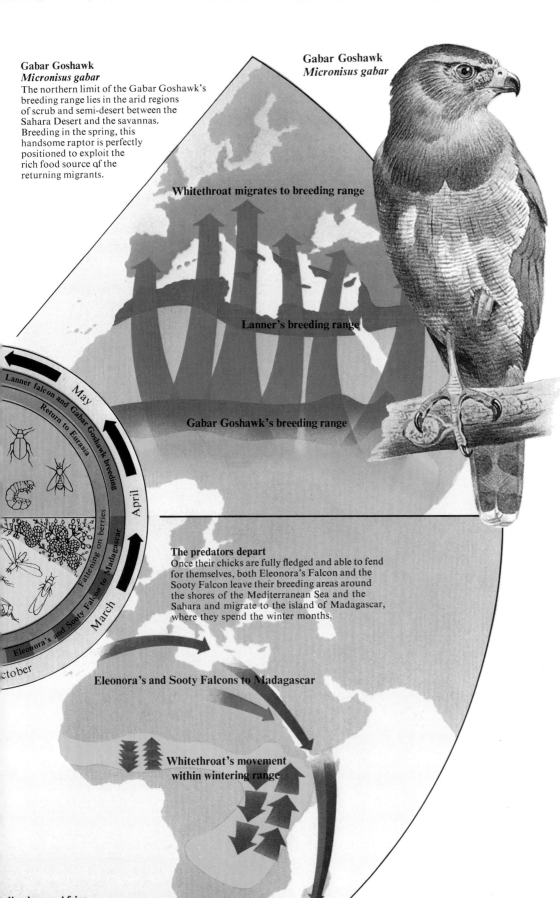

Gabar Goshawk
Micronisus gabar
The northern limit of the Gabar Goshawk's breeding range lies in the arid regions of scrub and semi-desert between the Sahara Desert and the savannas. Breeding in the spring, this handsome raptor is perfectly positioned to exploit the rich food source of the returning migrants.

Gabar Goshawk
Micronisus gabar

Whitethroat migrates to breeding range

Lanner's breeding range

Gabar Goshawk's breeding range

The predators depart
Once their chicks are fully fledged and able to fend for themselves, both Eleonora's Falcon and the Sooty Falcon leave their breeding areas around the shores of the Mediterranean Sea and the Sahara and migrate to the island of Madagascar, where they spend the winter months.

Eleonora's and Sooty Falcons to Madagascar

Whitethroat's movement within wintering range

Lanner falcon and Gabar Goshawk breeding
Return to Eurasia
May
April
Fattening on berries
March
Eleonora's and Sooty Falcon to Madagascar
ctober

eding hours: Africa
the spring, the birds have
ely 12 hours of daylight
their pre-migration feeding
Lantana and *Salvadora* berries.

The migrant's year

Summer
The European Whitethroat, *Sylvia communis*, breeds in May and June throughout Europe as far north as Scandinavia.

In late July the bird abandons its normal insect diet in favour of sugar-rich berries, and in the space of a few weeks its weight is almost doubled by the accumulated store of body fat. As summer ends the migrants move south through Europe to congregate in their millions in the Mediterranean feeding grounds, where they rest for a few days replenishing their energy reserves.

Autumn
The migrants leave Europe along a broad front, travelling singly during the night. Ahead lies a flight of more than 1,500 miles across the barren deserts of northern Africa – a flight which, even in favourable conditions, may take 30 hours. Weak and exhausted birds landing at the few wadis and oases may survive for a few days, but stand little chance of completing their journey.

Those still aloft at dawn over the Mediterranean and northern Africa run the gauntlet of predatory hawks, whose breeding season is timed to exploit the easy prey of migrating birds.

About three weeks after leaving their home range the successful migrants make landfall in the arid semi-desert steppes south of the Sahara.

Winter
The Whitethroat reverts to its normal diet of insects during the winter, moving south through its range as the country dries out in the dry season and then following the equatorial rains north again during the early spring. An important addition to the diet is provided by termites, which reach the winged stage of their life-cycle at this time – just as the Whitethroat begins to feed up in preparation for the return flight to Europe.

Throughout March the birds occupy the extreme northern part of the winter range, near Lake Chad, fattening up on sugar-rich *Lantana* and *Salvadora* berries.

Spring
In April millions of migrant birds take to the air on the first stage of the homeward journey. In the face of seasonal headwinds the long flight across the deserts may take more than 50 hours, and weakened birds fall easy prey to Gabar Goshawks and Lanner Falcons lying in wait along the return route.

After the winter rains the Mediterranean coast of Africa is more hospitable than in the autumn, and the exhausted migrants are able to feed and rest before the final leg of their annual 9,000 mile journey.

Desert and Arid Steppe

Freezing cold by night, searingly hot by day, the extremes of desert climate are problems resolved in birds by various physiological adaptations. Lack of water is an even greater problem and the only birds that can inhabit the Sahara are the few that are specially adapted to overcome it. Larks, sandgrouse and wheatears comprise half the 25 species of Saharan birds and no other genus has more than a single representative in the true desert. Many birds, however, find a living in the arid steppe of the desert margins.

Largest and most inhospitable of the world's deserts, huge areas of the Sahara are sterile sandy wastes, or *ergs*, that receive virtually no rain, although as recently as 5,000 years ago the Sahara was even more extensive and, like the Kalahari today, thinly wooded with scrub that supported a wide variety of animal life.

Although much smaller in area, the other desert regions of Africa – Somalia, the Kalahari and Namibia – have many more bird species and, due to their long history of uninterrupted aridity and isolation from the other Old World deserts, their bird faunas each have many exclusive species. One such restricted species is the rare Herero Chat, *Namibornis herero*, a little-known thrush-flycatcher found in the unique fog-shrouded desert that stretches for nearly 800 miles along the coast of Namibia in South West Africa.
Right: Lanner Falcons nesting in a desert tree, Morocco

Desert

Distribution of species

☐ Lichtenstein's Sandgrouse
Pterocles lichtensteinii

▨ Swallow-tailed Kite
Chelictinia riocourii

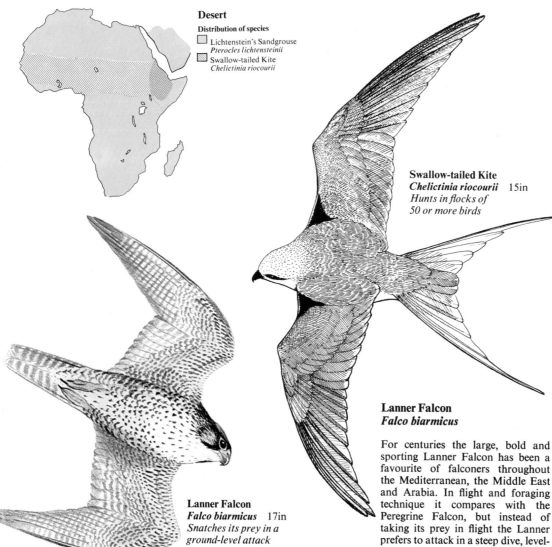

Swallow-tailed Kite
Chelictinia riocourii   15in
*Hunts in flocks of
50 or more birds*

Lanner Falcon
Falco biarmicus   17in
*Snatches its prey in a
ground-level attack*

Lanner Falcon
Falco biarmicus

For centuries the large, bold and sporting Lanner Falcon has been a favourite of falconers throughout the Mediterranean, the Middle East and Arabia. In flight and foraging technique it compares with the Peregrine Falcon, but instead of taking its prey in flight the Lanner prefers to attack in a steep dive, levelling out to snatch its prey from the ground.

No longer very abundant in the Middle East, the Lanner is still common enough throughout the continent of Africa, ranging over farmland, savanna and woodland, arid scrubland and rocky hills, but shunning the forest and most extreme desert regions. It's greatest abundance is reached in the drier savannas from which it displaces the Peregrine by ecological competition – and in townships in the savanna and subdesert zones. Though it normally nests in holes and fissures in cliffs, the Lanner Falcon has adapted to man's presence in the landscape and is now a fairly common sight in towns and cities where it builds its nest on highrise buildings.

Swallow-tailed Kite
Chelictinia riocourii

The African Swallow-tailed Kite is a highly gregarious bird found along the southern borders of the Sahara and in arid parts of eastern Africa. Like a tern, which it strongly resembles in colouring, the Swallow-tail has a light, buoyant and graceful flight. Nesting sociably in thorn trees, sometimes with half-a-dozen twig nests within a few feet of each other, the Swallow-tailed Kite hunts in wheeling flocks of up to 50 birds – catching insects on the wing and taking small lizards in fast, shallow tern-like swoops to ground.

Out of the breeding season these close relatives of the Black-shouldered Kites are widespread – their movements constantly changing with the weather. In western Africa the dustladen Harmattan wind blowing from the desert often carries flocks far to the south of their normal range.

Chestnut-backed Finch-lark
Eremopterix leucotis 4½in
Disruptive plumage conceals it from the desert hunters

Desert
Distribution of species
☐ Chestnut-backed Finch Lark
Eremopterix leucotis
☐ Desert Lark
Ammomanes deserti
☐ Bifasciated Lark
Alaemon alaudipes

Bifasciated Lark
Alaemon alaudipes 7½in
A powerful bill for digging up grubs and larvae

Desert Lark
Ammomanes deserti 5¾in
An undistinguished member of an ancient family

Desert Larks
Eremopterix, *Ammomanes* and *Alaemon* spp.

Walking jerkily to and fro over sun-baked mud or sandy soil looking for seeds, the Chestnut-backed Finch-lark *Eremopterix leucotis* looks more like a finch or weaver-bird than a true lark. If disturbed, the Finch-lark either crouches motionless, its pied and tawny plumage disrupting its outline and concealing it most effectively, or else the whole flock rises high in the air with much twittering to descend abruptly a few hundred yards away where the birds resume feeding immediately.

Representing a family which arose in the great deserts of the Old World, the Desert Lark, *Ammomanes deserti*, and the Bifasciated Lark, *Alaemon alaudipes*, are still found from the western Sahara to Afghanistan, the plain plumage of the Desert Lark contrasting with the strikingly pied livery of the Bifasciated Lark. Though food is scarce and hard-won, both the larks manage to eke out an existence in these searing regions of *hammada* and *erg* – the Desert Larks seeking small seeds, spiders and insects and probing at mammal droppings for undigested seeds, while the larger Bifasciated Lark eats seeds and uses its long powerful curved bill to dig grubs and ant-lion larvae out of the sand.

The desert water-carrier

Lichtenstein's Sandgrouse
Pterocles lichtensteinii

In the late 1890s a reputable naturalist reported that males of this desert bird regularly fly considerable distances to water, there soaking the belly feathers and using them as a sponge to carry water back to the chicks. Although the details were fully documented, the literature of the ensuing 70 years saw the facts ignored and the theory regarded as folklore, finally to be categorically denied in favour of the view that sandgrouse, which drink a lot, must carry water in the crop and then regurgitate it to the young. The unique "sponge" adaptation of the Sandgrouse's plumage sounds so extraordinary that it is perhaps not surprising that scepticism has died hard. But recent studies on Pintailed and Spotted Sandgrouse (*Pterocles alchata* and *P. senegallus*) breeding in Iraq, and Namaqua and Burchell's Sandgrouse (*P. namaqua* and *P. burchelli*) in southern Africa's Kalahari Desert, have confirmed that this is, indeed, how the chicks are watered. With precise timing at dawn or dusk, the adults fly in flocks to watering holes up to 50 miles away. There the males stand in the water, their belly feathers absorbing 15 to 20 times their weight of water. Up to 40 grammes of water can be absorbed in this way and even after the long return flight about half of this remains – enough to water the downy chicks. The male presents his abdomen to the chicks, who drink the water by nibbling and stripping the moist belly feathers.

Water is always a problem for seed-eating birds, but especially so in desert regions. Larks solve the problem by being partly insectivorous and by feeding their nestlings almost entirely on insects which have a high water content.

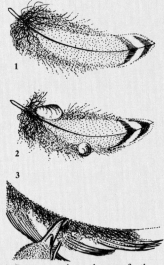

1 Strong, springy breast feather with down-fringed base and edge.
2 Water droplets retained by the helical coils of fuzzy down.
3 The chick drinks by parting the breast feathers and stripping water from the saturated down-layer.

Swamps and Soda Lakes

Spectacular, gaudy, diverse but most of all abundant, the water-fowl are one of Africa's greatest attractions. On a lake such as Naivasha swarm half-a-dozen species of African ducks and geese, their numbers greatly augmented in winter by pintail and other visitors from the Palaearctic. A dozen species of herons and storks frequent the shallows, picking their way between lily-trotters, gallinules and waders. Farther out, cormorants, darters, Pink-backed and White Pelicans ride the open water, and the air-space above is alive with kingfishers and tern. On some of the Rift Valley lakes, and lesser lakes such as Nakuru, Natron and Eyasi, the beautiful Lesser Flamingo congregates in flocks sometimes numbering hundreds of thousands of birds.

Perhaps even richer than these broad and extensive waters are the smaller seasonal lakes and marshes. Vegetation may make their bird-life more difficult to observe, but the reeds, reedmace and *Papyrus* fringing oxbow lakes and marshes harbour not only water-fowl but also scores of songbirds. Open water attracts all manner of land-birds to drink— particularly in the semi-arid regions—and these in turn attract marsh-owls, harriers, falcons and other raptors.

Amongst the countless lakes and marshes of Africa a patient and skilful observer may be rewarded by the sight of over 200 species in a single day.

Right: The Okavango Swamp region, Botswana

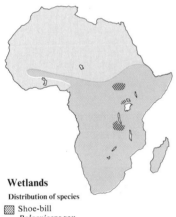

Wetlands

Distribution of species

▨ Shoe-bill
Balaeniceps rex

▢ Hammerhead
Scopus umbretta

Giant Kingfisher
Megaceryle maxima

The kingfisher family is well represented in Africa with 18 species, ranging from pygmies to giants and including several species which are insectivorous and occupy dry-land habitats far from water.

The Giant Kingfisher is the largest of its family and is found throughout most of Africa, usually in small numbers and in very localized areas. It is normally found near streams and rivers but may also nest on the banks of lakes and man-made reservoirs wherever trees grow close to the water's edge. Its characteristic, loud "aark" cry, uttered in flight, and its conspicuous chestnut belly-plumage, make it one of the most easily recognized species. The Giant Kingfisher often takes its prey – usually fresh-water crabs – from a hovering flight, but more commonly dives into the water direct from its perch.

Hammerhead
Scopus umbretta

The small, brown Hammerhead is chiefly remarkable for the huge nest it builds low down in a fork of a waterside tree. Measuring up to six feet in height on the outside and more than four feet from floor to dome inside, the massive structure has a thick waterproof thatch of woven grass and fine twigs. The narrow side entrance and parts of the main chamber are patchily lined with mud and the floor is covered with a layer of dry vegetation.

The Hammerhead, or Hammerkop, gets its name from the thick, permanently erect crest of stiff feathers which gives the bird its characteristic silhouette. Common and widespread throughout Africa, this dusky brown bird is likely to be seen in almost any damp habitat from urban reservoirs to puddles in dry-season river beds, but the most favoured areas are those near slow-moving rivers and streams.

The Hammerhead wades through the shallows in its search for small aquatic invertebrates – often kicking and shuffling its feet in order to dislodge creatures lying in the mud layer at the bottom.

In recent years the Hammerhead has learned to profit from man's activities and, in the early morning, may often be seen patrolling the highway's edge on the look-out for insects and small animals killed by vehicles during the night.

Hammerheads have no close relatives but clearly belong to the same broad group as the herons and storks. Their bizarre appearance and peculiar biology have made them a prominent feature of native folklore and legend.

Giant Kingfisher
Megaceryle maxima   16in
Hovers like a hawk before diving after its prey

Hammerhead
Scopus umbretta   23in
Master-builder of a half-ton nest

Lesser Flamingo
Phoeniconaias minor 40in
*Specialist filter-feeder of
the bitter lakes*

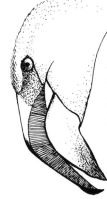

The filter feeders
In the course of a year a million
Lesser Flamingos on a single African
lake may consume over 65,000 tons
of minute blue-green algae – their
sole food source. Water is drawn
into the deeply-keeled bill and
then forced through the filtering
laminae by pressure of the tongue

Lesser Flamingo
Phoeniconaias minor

In the soda lakes of Africa's Rift Valley, the Greater Flamingo, *Phoenicopterus ruber*, and the Lesser Flamingo exist side by side without competition, for their foods are quite different. Greater Flamingos filter small organisms like arthropods, worms and molluscs from the muddy ooze of the lake-bed, but Lesser Flamingos have a more complex filtration apparatus in the bill which enables them to filter microscopic cells of blue-green algae from the clear water above the mud – without ingesting too much alkaline water. Although salt-secreting glands enable them to drink the lake-water, flamingos will drink from freshwater inflows whenever possible.

The saline lakes hold another, hidden danger. A million Lesser Flamingos nest in the middle of the almost dried out Lake Natron. In 1962, when Natron flooded, the birds diverted to the nearby saline, Lake Magadi and thousands of chicks died when their legs became

encrusted with crippling anklets of deposited soda.

A rescue operation was mounted but with limited success. Each year many flamingos must suffer this fate – restricted as they are to warm, shallow, brackish waters.

The Greater Flamingo ranges from South America to the Mediterranean and India. A distinctive species inhabits highland South America from the Equator to Chile, and the Old World sub-species occurs from the Aral Sea in the north to the southernmost parts of Africa. Nowadays their abundance in many areas has been greatly reduced, but the two European populations, in southern France and Spain, have maintained their numbers. The Greater Flamingo reaches its greatest density in the Rann of Kutch, where half a million birds are known to congregate.

The world's other two flamingo species, the Andean Flamingo, *Phoenicoparrus andinus*, and James's Flamingo, *P. jamesi*, are found high in the Bolivian Andes – inhabiting the alkaline lakes of the montane deserts.

Shoe-bill
Balaeniceps rex 60in
*Weighed down by the mass
of its enormous bill*

Shoe-bill
Balaeniceps rex

Surely one of evolution's most bizarre creations, the huge Shoe-bill is found only in dense and extensive *Papyrus* swamps. Although often called the Whale-headed Stork, the Shoe-bill has powder-down like the herons, and in the field resembles a huge heron except that the beak is so heavy that the bird is obliged to rest it on its neck most of the time. The broad, heavy bill is very like that of the South American Boat-billed Heron *Cochlearius cochlearius* – a unique heron of the New World (p44).

Shoe-bills feed mainly on lungfish and catfish which the bird hunts as it wades through the swamp with a curiously exaggerated deliberation. The prey is seized with a lightning thrust of the massive head and is swallowed whole. The nest is a large mound of water-plants hidden in sedges near the water's edge.

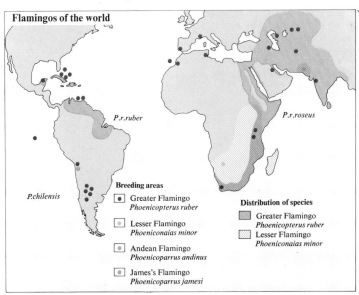

Flamingos of the world

P. r. ruber

P. r. roseus

P. chilensis

Breeding areas

☉ Greater Flamingo
Phoenicopterus ruber

☐ Lesser Flamingo
Phoeniconaias minor

☉ Andean Flamingo
Phoenicoparrus andinus

☐ James's Flamingo
Phoenicoparrus jamesi

Distribution of species

▨ Greater Flamingo
Phoenicopterus ruber

▧ Lesser Flamingo
Phoeniconaias minor

Lakes and Rivers

Rivers and swamps

Distribution of species

☐ Pel's Fishing Owl
Scotopelia peli

☐ African Fish Eagle
Haliaeetus vocifer

⬚ Egyptian Goose
Alopochen aegyptiacus

Pel's Fishing Owl
Scotopelia peli 25in
*Well equipped to deal
with slippery prey*

Egyptian Goose
Alopochen aegyptiacus 24in
*An aggressive water-bird,
domesticated by the
Ancient Egyptians*

African Fish Eagle
Heliaeetus vocifer 30in
*A remarkable free-fall
courtship "flight"*

Egyptian Goose
Alopochen aegyptiacus

This powerful and aggressive water-bird was domesticated by the Ancient Egyptians and, along with the Pintail, figures prominently in the art of that period. The Egyptian Goose is found in Egypt and isolated points on the southern and eastern Mediterranean coasts, throughout the Nile Valley and deep into Africa south of the Equator.

Egyptian Geese feed by grazing on land, but are at home in water – swimming buoyantly and diving when pressed. They are gregarious and, like most water-fowl, flocks consist of small family parties or, near the breeding season, paired birds. Courtship is noisy and protracted, the male spending hours a day displaying before an apparently totally uninterested female.

Nesting takes place in a great variety of situations; on the ground in water-meadows, in tree-holes or on nests deserted by other birds.

Pel's Fishing Owl
Scotopelia peli

Beautifully adapted for snatching fish from the water, Pel's Fishing Owl has long, unfeathered legs and powerful claws and the undersides of the feet are covered with small spines to increase the bird's grip on its slippery prey. This adaptation is shared with the sea-eagles and ospreys.

As the name implies, Pel's Owl feeds principally on fish, which it hunts at night – although quite how the owl detects its prey in the dark and silent river waters remains a mystery.

This large and handsome tawny-plumaged owl is the best known of a trio of rare and poorly studied African species. The other two, confined to the forests of West Africa, are the Rufous Fishing Owl, *S.ussheri*, and Bouvier's Fishing Owl, *S.bouvieri*. All are birds of the forested waterways, but Pel's Fishing Owl also occurs along river courses in the drier, wooded savanna regions.

At night the owl's characteristic hooting call echoes along the watercourses, serving to maintain contact between a hunting pair and to estab-lish ownership of a territory.

Between one and four eggs, pure-white and smoothly rounded like those of all owls, are laid in a hollow tree or in an abandoned nest, but little else is known of the breeding habits of this rare owl.

African Fish Eagle
Haliaeetus vocifer

A wild and far-carrying gull-like "keyow – kow-ow-ow" cry delivered from a vantage point in a waterside tree is one of the most characteristic features of the African Fish Eagle.

Although it is the smallest of the eight species in the sea-eagle genus, this powerful predator is one of the most conspicuous – its snowy head and tail, chestnut shoulders and naked yellow face catching the sun as it swoops in a fast and purposeful glide.

Most of the bird's day is spent perched on a favoured branch, either at rest or scanning the waters for potential prey. Fish are usually taken in a long glide direct from the perch and are adroitly snatched from the surface-waters with one foot. Prey usually weighs about half a kilogramme, but this skilled hunter can take fish up to two kilogrammes and occasionally, rodents and other small mammals. In dry habitats the Fish Eagle will prey on young birds and may also take carrion when live prey is scarce. A pirate by nature, it will chase and harass other fish-eating birds, including other members of its own species, pursuing the victim until it either drops its prey or disgorges the food in its crop.

The courtship flight of the Fish Eagle, like that of many birds of prey, is an impressive sight. Male and female meet high in the air and, with their claws firmly locked together, plummet towards the ground in a tumbling free fall. Parting just above ground level the pair may spiral upward to repeat the performance before finally mating.

The birds' favourite habitats are lakes, wooded rivers, swamps and even coastal mangroves. Individual territories may be small and populations unusually dense for a raptor of this size – indeed, no less than nine pairs were once observed nesting on a 200 hectare island in Lake Victoria.

African River Martin
Pseudochelidon eurystomina

Robust legs, a strong, broad bill and markedly different feeding habits set this peculiar martin apart from the rest of the swallow family.

In 1968 a second species was dramatically discovered over 5,600 miles away in Thailand, where ornithologists netting swallows for migration studies found they had captured a small black swallow with a broad, greenish bill, white rump and central "wires" in the tail. This species is now known as the White-eyed River Martin, *P. sirintarae* – the only other survivor of a presumably once widespread family.

The African species is known only from the lower Ubangi River and adjacent stretches of the River Congo. It nests in large colonies in sandbanks exposed at low water, and when the river-levels rise in April it is obliged to migrate 500 miles downstream to the coast.

Swallow-like in flight, the River Martin is one of nature's supreme flight artists. Very seldom coming to rest, it feeds entirely on the wing – on large, hard-bodied insects.

African River Martin
Pseudochelidon eurystomina 5½in
*Nearly 6,000 miles from
its only known relative*

Relicts of a widespread family

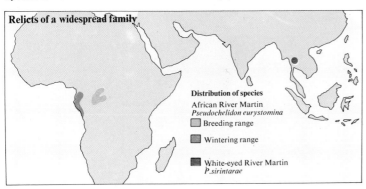

Distribution of species

African River Martin
Pseudochelidon eurystomina
☐ Breeding range

☐ Wintering range

■ White-eyed River Martin
P. sirintarae

Red-throated Bee-eater
Merops bulocki

White-throated Bee-eater
Merops albicollis

Carmine Bee-eater
Merops nubicus

European Bee-eater
Merops apiaster

Bee-eaters – the colourful savanna strike-force

The 17 members of this colourful family feed mainly on bees, ants and wasps and other allied insects – many of which are venomous. Studies of regurgitated pellets containing the indigestible remains of insects show that the stinging workers of the honey-bee comprise a major part of the diet of most bee-eaters. For centuries the honey-bee has been widely cultivated in Africa and this has doubtless encouraged bee-eaters to proliferate.

Carmine Bee-eaters hunting from the back of a Kori Bustard

Several bee-eaters have developed ingenious ways of coping with their dangerous food. The small Red-throated Bee-eater, *Merops bulocki*, hunts bees by "fly-catching" from a perch. With a deft motion the bee's sting is rubbed against the branch until its venom is discharged. The insect is then banged against the perch until it is stunned and is then swallowed whole. Large birds like the Carmine Bee-eater *M. nubicus* sometimes feed on bees in continuous flight. How, or indeed whether, they de-venom them is not known. Bee-eaters have some natural immunity from bee stings, but do occasionally get badly stung.

Carmine Bee-eaters also prey on locusts – particularly when clouds of the insects are disturbed from the grass by large animals or by bush-fires.

The Green Bee-eater, *M. superciliosus*, specializes in taking dragonflies, while the White-throated Bee-eater, *M. albicollis*, eats arthropods and small lizards caught on the ground. *M. albicollis* also feeds commensally with a forest squirrel – adroitly catching strips of skin dropped by the squirrel as it peels the oil-palm fruit to feed on the soft flesh within.

Madagascar: The Island Continent

More than 1,000 miles long, the island of Madagascar forms the main part of the Malagasy Sub-region, with a scattering of oceanic islands making up the remainder. In its vegetation and climate Madagascar is Africa in microcosm. A mountain backbone over 9,000 feet high runs from north to south, separating coastal rain-forests on the eastern seaboard from woodland and open grass savanna in the west, and a wide semi-arid corridor follows nearly 200 miles of the south-western coastline.

Although much of the primeval forest has been cut down to make way for farming – destroying some habitats and drastically reducing others – the island is large and mercifully few animals have been lost from this "island continent". One sad exception is *Aepyornis*, the gigantic flightless "elephant bird" which has become extinct within historic times. Today over 60 species are shared with Africa but, as on all islands, endemism is high and Madagascar boasts no fewer than 125 endemic species. Some have Asiatic rather than African forebears, and several families – notably the woodpeckers and hornbills – are surprisingly absent from the island.

Over 600 miles to the east lie the Mascarene Islands, once the home of a fascinating and unique bird fauna. Alas, since man first landed in 1505, the curious Dodo and 24 other species have been lost for all time but strenuous efforts are now being made to preserve this unique habitat.

The Malagasy Sub-region

Zanzibar

Seychelles Is

Amirantes Is

Aldabra Is

Comoros Is

MOÇAMBIQUE

MASCARENES

Rodriguez

Mauritius

MALAGASY

Reunion

REPUBLIC

☐ East coast rain forest

☐ Plateau forest

☐ Western deciduous forest

☐ Sambirano domain (rain forest)

☐ Semi-arid vegetation

Blue Vanga
Leptopterus madagascarinus 6in
Rare and secretive descendant of African immigrant stock

Scaly Ground Roller
Brachypteracias squamigera 11in
Shy resident of the dense east coast rain-forests

Blue Vanga
Leptopterus madagascariensis

The small Blue Vanga (or Vanga-shrike) is a gregarious resident of the forest canopy and the only colourful member of its 12-strong family. Most of the vangas have black, white, grey or rufous plumage.

Endemic to Madagascar, the vanga-shrikes are rare, and several species are thought to be in danger of extinction.

The Vangidae are probably descended from an African shrike and, in the isolation of their island continent, they have radiated – adapting their bill-forms to a wide range of foods varying from seeds and fruit to large insects.

Scaly Ground Roller
Brachypteracias squamigera

Madagascar makes up for its poor selection of true rollers with five colourful and interesting species of ground rollers.

Little is known of the four species inhabiting the tropical rain-forest of the east coast as they are solitary and unobtrusive birds, but the sandy-coloured Long-tailed Ground Roller, *Uratelornis chimaera*, is a common sight in the arid scrubland of south-western Madagascar.

The four forest ground rollers are beautifully coloured in complementary blue, green, buff and chestnut. They spend much of their time at ground level where the forest floor is free of undergrowth and sparsely covered with herbs and leaf-litter. They forage in the evening shade, feeding on insects and spiders and occasionally taking small reptiles and frogs.

In contrast to the agile African *Coracias* rollers they are stolid birds, moving slowly and taking to the air with a whirr of their short wings only when disturbed. On the ground they resemble thrushes – standing upright when on the look-out and then running for a few paces with head down and tail held high. Their legs are long, as befits ground-dwellers, and even the Short-legged species has longer limbs than *Coracias*.

Although detailed observations are few, the ground rollers are thought to nest in tree-holes and in short tunnels excavated in earth banks. There is also a strong native belief that they hibernate – a notion that deserves respect since at least one other bird, the desert poor-will of America, is known to hibernate.

Dodo
Raphus cucullatus

Its name synonymous with extinction, the Dodo vanished for ever towards the end of the 17th century. Ungainly and inoffensive, these large flightless birds inhabited the island of Mauritius in the Mascarenes – safe and secure until the islands became known to mariners as a source of food and fresh water.

The establishment of permanent settlements, hunting, and the inevitable introduction of cats and dogs, pigs, monkeys and rats, combined to produce intolerable pressures of predation on the defenceless birds. Merchant ships were provisioned in part with Dodos, which were finally exterminated only 85 years after man first settled on Mauritius.

The Dodo's two close relatives are perhaps less well known. The Réunion Solitaire from the neighbouring Réunion Island became extinct about 1750, while the Solitaire of Rodriguez Island, *Pezophaps solitaria*, probably survived until as recently as 1800.

Cuckoo Roller
Leptosomus discolor

While most members of the roller family feed in flight or stoop to the ground to take reptiles or large insects, the Cuckoo Roller of Madagascar feeds high in the forest canopy on caterpillars, stick-insects and, most important of all, chameleons.

Blending its colours to the forest backcloth and seldom leaving the safety of twigs and branches except to cross from one tree to another, the chameleon is an elusive prey. Even on open ground, which it shuns, the chameleon's slow, swaying locomotion makes it difficult to see against the leaf-litter, and the Cuckoo Roller must watch and wait motionless for long periods before a tell-tale movement betrays its victim. Although the bird is common throughout Madagascar, no observer has yet seen exactly how this most specialized and successful predator catches its prey. But successful it is – up to six chameleons a day being fed to the two dove-sized nestlings.

The Cuckoo Roller is about the same size as the European roller and has many features in common with its Palaearctic relatives. Unlike the *Coracias* rollers, however, *Leptosomus* is able to reverse the outer toe, enabling it to perch by gripping the branch with two toes forward and two back.

The tree-hole nest is an untidy affair, without lining. The adult birds make no attempt at sanitation and the nest soon becomes foul and pungent with the smell of ammonia.

Cuckoo Roller
Leptosomus discolor   17in
Preys on the elusive chameleon

Small-billed False Sunbird
Neodrepanis hypoxantha   3¾in
May, by now, be extinct ...

Velvet Asity
Philepitta castanea   6½in
*Builds a hanging nursery
for its eggs and young*

Velvet Asity
Philepitta castanea

Suspended from leafy twigs by a slender woven thread of plant fibres, the hanging nest of the Velvet Asity seems a fragile and delicate structure. In fact such pendent nests are robust. The walls of strongly matted grass and mosses are made inconspicuous by leaves and lichens woven into the outside, while the inside is thickly carpeted with dead leaves – providing a soft, protective bed for the clutch of three glossy white eggs.

Asities inhabit the middle levels of the forest and the undergrowth and thickets of the forest margins. They eat berries and small fruits and, like other forest-dwelling fruit-eaters, are stocky, quiet birds preferring to feed alone, but occasionally joining mixed flocks to forage for insects.

Though different in appearance, the two species of asity are related to the false sunbirds of Madagascar. Anatomical details confirm the relationship, but the only outward similarities are the naked skin wattles round the eye of the male and the yellow plumage of the female.

Small-billed False Sunbird
Neodrepanis hypoxantha

Hovering momentarily before a tropical bloom, the Small-billed False Sunbird of Madagascar's east coast rain-forest feeds by dipping its long slender bill into tubular flowers in its search for nectar, small insects and spiders.

This tiny bird is known only from a few specimens and may, even now, be extinct. The related Wattled False Sunbird, *N. coruscans*, though more widespread, is also rare and seldom observed. The males of both species have attractive plumage but their females are clad in dull olive hues.

The two species look and behave like true sunbirds and were for many years placed in the sunbird family, Nectariniidae. But *Neodrepanis* is not a sunbird – it belongs to a family of primitive songbirds of ancient lineage whose nearest relatives are found in South America and Australasia. Madagascar has very few true sunbirds, and over the course of countless generations *Neodrepanis* has radiated to fill the vacant niche in the forest environment.

Southern Asia
The Oriental Realm

Clearly separated from the Palaearctic
Realm by the formidable barrier of the
Himalayas, the tropical realm of Southern
Asia reaches out in a chain of forested
islands to meet and merge with the islands of
Australasia. Here, where no physical barrier
separates the two great natural regions,
species from north and south meet and
intermingle – creating a unique and
fascinating transitional avifauna.

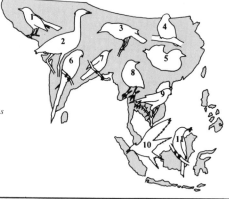

BIRDS ILLUSTRATED

1 **Red-tailed Wheatear**
Oenanthe xanthoprymna

2 **Great Indian Bustard**
Choriotis nigriceps

3 **Violet Whistling Thrush**
Myiophoneus caeruleus

4 **Temmincks Tragopan**
Tragopan temminckii

5 **Mandarin duck**
Aix galericulata

6 **Ring-necked Parakeet**
Psittacula krameri

7 **Common Iora**
Aegithina tiphia

8 **Indian Pitta**
Pitta brachyura

9 **Red-legged falconet**
Microhierax caerulescens

10 **Lesser Crested Tern**
Sterna bengalensis

11 **Red-bearded Bee-eater**
Nyctyornis amicta

AVERAGE TEMPERATURE °C
January

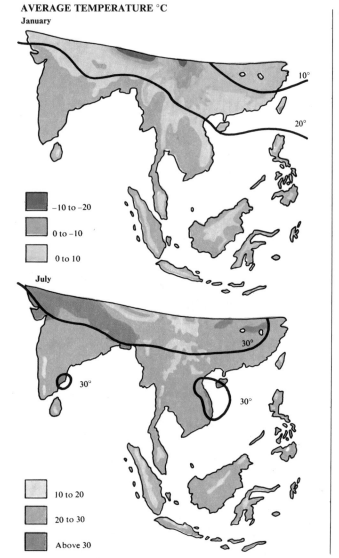

10°

20°

−10 to −20

0 to −10

0 to 10

July

30°

30°

30°

30°

10 to 20

20 to 30

Above 30

AVERAGE RAINFALL Inches
November to April

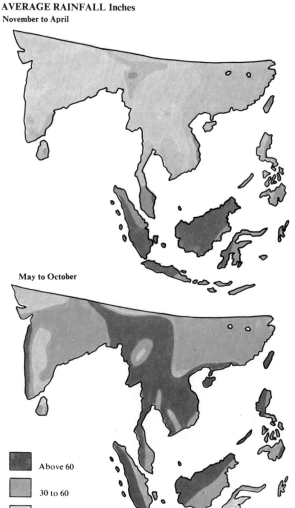

May to October

Above 60

30 to 60

10 to 30

0 to 10

NATURAL VEGETATION

Tropical rain-forest

Savanna vegetation

Steppe vegetation

Rivers and lakes

Temperate rain forest

The Himalayan Foothills

In the bleak and windswept highland plateaux of Tibet and southwestern China, only mosses and lichens can withstand the intense cold and deep snow, though stunted Alpine scrub and grasses will grow in the drier regions. Below 12,500 feet, vegetation is stratified, as the typical forest zones of the Himalayas show. There, wizened conifers, with an understorey of hardy birch and occasional clumps of rhododendron, form the highest Alpine forests. Below these come the dry temperate forests, again predominantly coniferous, but with a leavening of broadleaved species. These are supplanted at about 6,000 feet by a moist temperate zone of mixed forest with a richly varied shrub layer, below which the prevailing forest type varies with the locality, from wet temperate to tropical evergreen forest. Here the canopy is usually dense and decked with mosses, ferns, climbers and epiphytes encouraged by the high humidity and rainfall.

Birds are scarce at the highest altitudes, although Alpine Choughs and Lammergeiers have been seen above 26,000 feet. At the snow-line, Snow Partridges, Snowcocks and several species of pheasant may be seen, and in each descending life-zone, the number of species multiplies rapidly. Altitudinal migration is a feature of the Himalayas; in the spring, birds flock up to occupy the higher zones and move back to the foothills and plains in winter.

Right: A dry waterfall in montane forest at 8,000 ft, East Nepal

The Himalayas

☐ Area of mountain range

Distribution of species

☐ Himalayan Monal
Lophophorus impejanus

⧄ Red-billed Blue Magpie
Cissa erythrorhyncha

Himalayan Monal
Lophophorus impejanus 28in
Decimated by hunters in parts of its mountain range

Spotted Forktail
Enicurus maculatus 11in
A sudden change of direction confuses the pursuer

162

Red-billed Blue Magpie
Cissa erythrorhyncha 27in
Flocks in the company of jays and thrushes

Lammergeier
Gypaetus barbatus 48in
*The bone-eating vulture –
unfairly branded a killer*

Himalayan Monal
Lophophorus impejanus

Bursting from the cover of dense undergrowth with a characteristic wild, ringing cry, the Himalayan Monal is a tempting target to the sportsman, and in many parts of its range this handsome crested pheasant is declining in numbers.

Ranging through the Himalayas from eastern Afghanistan to Bhutan, the Monal inhabits the high forests of rhododendron and deodar between 7,000 and 15,000 feet – favouring steep and precipitous mountain slopes where the forest cover is broken by clearings and ledges rich in grasses and secondary shrub vegetation. The Monal feeds on roots, berries and tubers dug from the ground even when the ground is snow covered.

The call of the polygamous male, a loud ringing cry similar to that of a curlew, is delivered from an exposed rock outcrop commanding a wide view over the hillside. The hen is quiet and dull in comparison with the male – keeping within dense cover for much of the time and building her shallow groundscrape nest in the lee of a boulder or tree.

Spotted Forktail
Enicurus maculatus

Never straying far from the banks of the turbulent mountain streams that provide its food, the Spotted Forktail is found throughout the Himalayas from 2,000 to 12,000 feet above sea level. Living alone, or with a single mate, the Forktail hops daintily over the moss-covered stones of the stream bank in its search for aquatic insects and small molluscs.

At rest, the Spotted Forktail perches on a low branch, gracefully swaying its long tail up and down as it turns to survey its surroundings, but when disturbed it darts swiftly away, flying low over the stream and uttering its sharp alarm cry. If followed, the bird will fly ahead of the intruder in short bursts – finally veering away into the forest to circle back to its starting point when the danger has passed.

During the nesting season, between May and July, the Spotted Forktail lays three or four lightly speckled pale cream eggs in a neatly woven cup of mosses. Lined with leaves and fine rootlets, the nest is carefully hidden in a stream-bank crevice, often hidden by ferns.

Red-billed Blue Magpie
Cissa erythrorhyncha

Noisy birds with a wide variety of harsh, creaking and chattering calls, Red-billed Blue Magpies are also accomplished mimics, copying the calls of many species sharing their forest habitat. Often seen in pairs or in family groups of six or seven, they also form larger flocks and frequently associate with other birds.

Extending from the western Himalayas to Indo-China and Burma, the Blue Magpie inhabits open broadleaf as well as coniferous forest between 3,000 and 6,000 feet above sea level, making small vertical movements according to season. Though mainly arboreal, the Blue Magpie often descends to the ground, hopping about with tail cocked high in its search for insects, grubs and fallen fruit. The species is generally omnivorous and the diet also includes lizards, frogs, small rodents and even the eggs and nestlings of other birds.

The nest is a shallow, flimsy cup of twigs, roots and leaves built up to 20 feet above the ground on wooded hillsides. Five or six cream-coloured, lightly speckled eggs are laid.

Lammergeier
Gypaetus barbatus

With a wing-span of nearly nine feet, the Lammergeier, or "Bearded Vulture", is one of the largest and most spectacular mountain species. Usually seen soaring majestically above mountain peaks and open valleys, the Lammergeier spends much of each day on the wing – scanning the ground below for carrion. Despite its evil reputation there is no authenticated account of this bird ever attacking a living animal, least of all man, and the bones of animals killed in falls or by other predators form the bird's main source of food. Flying up to a great height, the Lammergeier will drop a large bone on to the rocks below, and then descend to feed on the fragments.

In the courtship season, pairs of these magnificent birds perform a dramatic display flight involving sudden dives and mock fights. Turning on to its back, one bird will use its claws to parry the "attack" of the other and the pair will tumble down through the air with talons locked. The huge nest of sticks, bones and animal skins is built high on the face of a mountain precipice.

Monsoon Rain-forest

Extravagantly rich in plant, mammal, bird, reptile and insect life, the tropical rain-forests of southeastern Asia form one of the most complex ecosystems on earth. In this teeming habitat, produced by the monsoon and the rainfall it brings (in some areas exceeding 400 inches), no one species dominates. As many as 2,000 different tree species are found in Malaysia alone, and one square mile of rain-forest can harbour 700 species of beetle. Rich commercial harvests have been reaped from trees, fruits and medicinal herbs originating in these forests, yet thousands of square miles of this invaluable genetic resource have been thoughtlessly destroyed, either for the timber or to make way for agriculture.

A large number of the 1,500 bird species inhabiting southeastern Asia are dependent, directly or indirectly, on the rain-forest, and where this has been destroyed, the decline in bird-life is dramatic. Most rain-forest birds are restricted to the high closed canopy, where brightly coloured hornbills, flowerpeckers, pigeons and parakeets feed among the fruits and nectar-bearing vine flowers. In scattered clearings, for example where a giant tree has fallen under the weight of its strangling vines, orioles, cuckoos, trogons and woodpeckers may be glimpsed, but among the tangled roots in the gloom of the forest floor, even brightly coloured ground-dwelling birds like the pittas, junglefowl and peacock pheasants are seldom observed.

Sultan Tit
Melanochlora sultanea 8in
Colourful and acrobatic member of a widespread family

Common Peafowl
Pavo cristatus 78in
A piercing shriek that warns o approaching danger

Fairy Bluebird
Irena puella 11in
The idle male sings while his mate builds the nest

Tropical rain-forest
☐ Area of rain-forest
Distribution of species
▨ Sultan Tit
Melanochlora sultanea
⬚ Common Peafowl
Pavo cristatus

Red Junglefowl
Gallus gallus 26in
Undisputed ancestor of the world's domestic fowl

Sultan Tit
Melanochlora sultanea

Flitting from branch to branch with a peculiar parachuting action, this boldly coloured member of the "True Tit" sub-family forages through the canopy in small parties, often in the company of other tits. Like most of its relatives, the Sultan Tit is an acrobat – hanging from leaf-fronds and twigs upside-down, sideways and in all manner of positions as it hunts for insects and grubs.

The range of the species extends from the eastern Himalayas through Indo-China to the islands of the Malaysian sub-region, and the bird is always found in wet evergreen and moist tropical deciduous forests – particularly in sub-montane tracts reaching up to 3,000 feet above sea level.

A clutch of seven or eight white eggs, boldly marked with red/brown spots, is laid on a thick pad of moss placed in the safety of a tree hollow, but other details of the Sultan Tit's breeding behaviour and biology are as yet unknown.

Fairy Bluebird
Irena puella

Perhaps one of the most beautiful of all forest birds, the aptly named Fairy Bluebird inhabits dense, humid deciduous and evergreen rain-forests from India eastwards to the Malaysian sub-region. In small parties of six to eight birds, the Fairy Bluebird is constantly on the move – scurrying about the branches or flying from tree to tree, sometimes congregating with hornbills, bulbuls and other fruit-eaters in a particularly fruit-laden tree. Although not truly migratory the Fairy Bluebird is given to constant wandering, particularly in search of favourite fruits like those of the various wild figs.

Unlike many forest birds that nest in the forest margins and clearings, the Fairy Bluebird chooses dense and humid surroundings in which to build a rough shallow nest of twigs and mosses. While the female goes about the task of nest building, her mate

keeps company – encouraging her with loud songs but taking no part in the work. Normally two eggs, olive-grey and irregularly marked, are laid in the nest, high in a tree fork.

Common Peafowl
Pavo cristatus

Raising his six-foot train high over his back in a shimmering fan studded with iridescent "eye" markings, the courting peacock approaches a hen of his choice with mincing steps, hopping from one foot to the other, while the female views the proceedings with affected indifference. During the breeding season, each cock will run a harem of three to five hens, but once the season is over the birds tend to segregate, males in one group, females and immature young in another.

Despite the long train of his breeding plumage, the male is able to move swiftly and silently through the densest undergrowth. The peafowl is endowed with phenomenally keen sight and hearing, and the loud, raucous shriek of its alarm call reverberates through the forest, warning birds and animals alike of approaching danger.

Red Junglefowl
Gallus gallus

Firmly established as the original ancestor of all domestic fowl, this handsome game-bird is known to have been domesticated in the Mohanjodaro civilization more than 2,500 years BC. Today the species shows a remarkable talent for swallowing small fortunes; throughout the ruby mining areas of Burma and elsewhere, rubies and sapphires have been found in the junglefowl's gizzard along with the stones and grit used to aid the comminution of its seed, tuber and fruit food.

Shy and wild, the Red Junglefowl is a fast flier, making for cover at the slightest sign of danger or "chimney-ing" – spiralling vertically upwards to escape through a gap in the forest canopy.

Tropical Rain-forest

Racket-tailed Drongo
Dicrurus paradiseus 27in
A noisy exhibitionist with a flair for mimicry

Shama
Copsychus malabaricus 11in
The forest equivalent of the urban Magpie Robin

Racket-tailed Drongo
Dicrurus paradiseus

The Racket-tailed Drongo is a true exhibitionist; a lively and attractive character who is one of the first up in the morning, calling long before dawn and often still hunting far into dusk. Very noisy and with a large repertoire of loud, metallic calls and melodious whistles, the Drongo is an accomplished mimic, imitating to perfection the calls of a great many species sharing its forest habitat. One of a passerine family of slim arboreal birds, the Drongo is about the size of of a thrush. It is found in several geographical sub-species from India eastwards through the entire Indo-Chinese and Malaysian sub-regions – mainland and archipelagos – in moist deciduous and evergreen forest. Fond of secondary jungle and mixed bamboo forest, it occurs from the lowland plains to about 5,000 feet above sea level.

A good mixer, it is seen singly, in pairs or in groups of five or six, often in the company of woodpeckers, treepies or similar birds. Mixed foraging is noticeable particularly if there is an unexpected food bonus such as a sudden emergence of winged termites from beneath the ground.

The Drongo's flight is noisy and dipping. The long tail feathers produce a humming sound, and, at a distance, the racket ends look just like a pair of angry bumble-bees in pursuit of the bird. Bold and aggressive when nesting, this jaunty little bird attacks recklessly and even puts raptors to flight.

Shama
Copsychus malabaricus

In its general appearance and habits the Shama is instantly recognizable as a close relative of the Magpie Robin, *C.saularis* (p178). Indeed this handsome glossy black bird occupies exactly the same niche in the forest ecology as does the Magpie Robin in open country and towns.

The Shama is one of the most famous song-birds in the Orient. Few species can complete with its range of notes or with the clarity and beauty of its loud melodious song, but its shyness and the inaccessibility of its chosen habitat make it a rare sight, even for the most patient observer. Living in dense tropical forests in hilly country, the Shama favours the narrow ravines and gullies of mountain streams where the continuous forest cover is broken by open glades and stands of bamboo. It feeds mainly at ground level, or among low bushes, scurrying busily about as it searches for insects, worms and fruits.

Nesting between April and June, the Shama builds a shallow cup of rootlets, grasses and bamboo leaves. The nest is placed in a natural tree-trunk cavity or in the base of a dense thicket of bamboo, and provides ample protection for the clutch of four or five dull green, brown-speckled eggs. The Shama has a curious display flight, more pronounced in the breeding season than at other times of the year, in which it strikes the wings together, above the body, as it flies across open glades and clearings.

Crested Swift
Hemiprocne longipennis

The Crested Swift, *Hemiprocne longipennis*, has one of the most fragile of all nests. It is a wispy, shallow half-saucer made of flakes of papery bark and feathers stuck together with the bird's saliva. Attached to one side of a slender, leafless branch high in a tree-top, this tiny nest is barely perceptible from the ground. The bird also makes use of saliva to glue the single egg to the nest to prevent it from coming to grief in a high wind.

Found mainly in India and Malaysia, the Crested Swift inhabits moist deciduous and evergreen forest, hawking after insects high above the canopy. Adroit in flight, the bird drops down occasionally to drink at a stream or pool, dipping at a tangent and barely touching the water surface as it scoops a single droplet, and rises again in a curve.

Scarlet Minivet
Pericrocotus flammeus 9in
*The grey and yellow plumage
of the female and young are
in marked contrast with the
bold colours of the male*

female

Scarlet Minivet
Pericrocotus flammeus 9in
*Camouflages its nest with
lichen, cobwebs and bark*

male

Indian Trogon
Harpactes fasciatus 12in
*An indolent bird, but a
surprisingly agile hunter*

Crested Swift
Hemiprocne longipennis

Cave Swiftlet
Collocalia fuciphaga

Nests of the Asian Swifts
In building their tiny nests, many of
the Asian Swifts make use of their
saliva, a sticky fluid that solidifies
in air to a strong translucent mass.
The Crested Swift makes a small,
shallow cup glued to the side of a
high branch and covered with fragments of lichen so that, from the
ground, the nest is almost invisible.
When brooding, the adult perches on
the branch so that the brood patch
just covers the tiny nest. The Cave,
or Grey-rumped, Swiftlet (p171)
attaches its cup of hardened saliva
high on the wall or roof of a forest
cave, making its nest of saliva alone,
or of saliva reinforced with vegetable
matter, depending on the species.
The Palm Swift, most specialized of
all, glues its diminutive egg to a few
feathers which are themselves stuck
precariously to the underside of a
drooping palm frond.

Palm Swift
Cypsiurus parvus

Indian Trogon
Harpactes fasciatus

An arboreal bird blending in well
with its surroundings, the Indian
Trogon has a rather sluggish per-
sonality, perching bolt upright and
inert for long periods on a tree-
stump or low branch. Now and again
it sets off after winged insects, turning
and twisting with remarkable agility,
before returning either to the same
perch or to one nearby. In addition
to beetles, cicadas, grasshoppers and
other insects the Trogon will occasionally feed on berries and
fallen fruits.

The Trogon has a habit of keeping
its dull-coloured back to the observer
while perching, and the broad tail
looks deceptively like a strip of bark,
enhancing the bird's camouflage in
the dim light of the forest interior.
Often the only indication of its presence, as it carries on hunting well
after sunset, is a flash of white from
the outer tail feathers as the tail is
flicked open and shut in flight.

The Trogon is one of 11 such
forest species found in the Orient.
Slightly bigger than a thrush, the
Indian Trogon is confined to India
and Sri Lanka, in moist deciduous
and wet evergreen forest from plains
level up to about 5,000 feet elevation.
This bird is normally seen alone or in
widely separated pairs.

An unlined tree-hollow, normally
less than 18 feet from the ground,
serves as a nest. Two to four glossy,
ivory-white eggs are laid, but little is
known of the breeding biology or
courtship behaviour.

Scarlet Minivet
Pericrocotus flammeus

The brilliantly coloured Minivet is
distributed in five distinct races
throughout most of the Indian sub-
continent, Bangladesh, Sri Lanka and
Burma, but excluding Pakistan and
the western Himalayas. The slightly
smaller Short-billed Minivet, *P.
brevirostris*, breeds in the Himalayas
and spreads out over the lowland
plains of northern India in winter.

The Scarlet Minivet is exclusively
arboreal, spending the whole of its
life in the dense canopy of tropical
woodland and evergreen forest. Constantly on the move, often in parties
of thirty or more (particularly during
the winter months), the Scarlet
Minivet flits restlessly from branch to
branch – hovering momentarily with
flapping wings in order to "flush out"
insects hidden among the foliage.
Although most of its food is caught
in the canopy, the Scarlet Minivet
will also hunt on the wing, snapping
up stray insects in much the same
manner as a flycatcher.

The birds mate in April through to
July, building a neat cup-nest of
rootlets and fine, fibrous vegetable
matter which is then camouflaged
with lichen, mosses and bark fragments bound together with cobwebs.
Securely fixed to the upper surface of
a horizontal branch up to 40 feet
above the ground, the nest is very
difficult to see, and to complete the
effect, the eggs, two to four in number, are pale green, generously spotted with patches of brown and lavender pigment.

Open Woods and Grasslands

Asia has no equivalent of the long-grass prairies of the Americas. Instead it has the short-grass steppelands of Mongolia, China and Tibet – desolate flat plains with low summer rainfall and harsh, semi-desert conditions in winter. Bustards, larks and pipits are among the few birds typically resident in these windswept plains and even the magnificent Steppe Eagle must, in the virtual absence of trees, forsake the usual nesting habits of its family and make its nest on the bare ground. In winter the steppe seems devoid of life, but in summer many birds of prey find ample food in the abundant small rodents, and in autumn the steppe is alive with flocks of small seed-eating birds.

Much more important to the birds of Asia are the savanna areas with their combinations of grasses, trees and mixed scrub vegetation. Food, in the form of mammals, rodents, insects, fruits and seeds, is plentiful and there is a wide choice of nesting sites for birds of prey, shrikes and other species. Bird-watching in the savanna is much more rewarding than in the closed forest areas, where cover is dense and visibility limited. Unfortunately, the savanna is a declining natural asset, most of it being subjected to severe overgrazing by domestic cattle and to the constant tree-lopping and felling by nomadic and resident native populations. In consequence, many areas of once-verdant savanna have been destroyed.
Right: Dry wooded grassland in northern India

Coucal
Centropus sinensis 19in
Systematically persecutes its weaker neighbours

Savanna and grassland
☐ Area of grassland
Distribution of species
▨ Francolin
Francolinus francolinus
▦ Jungle Babbler
Turdoides striatus

Jungle Babbler
Turdoides striatus 10in
Gregarious habits earn it the sobriquet "Seven Sisters"

Francolin
Francolinus francolinus 13in
A curious blend of the harsh and the musical

Coucal
Centropus sinensis

A large, handsome black cuckoo with chestnut wings and black tail, the Coucal, or Crow-Pheasant, is a terrestrial creature that walks and runs well but is a poor flier, reluctant to take to the air. It is a clumsy bird, but single-minded, stalking pheasant-like through the shrubbery and sometimes flicking open its wings to panic prey that has "frozen" for camouflage. The Coucal works its way methodically along, through bushes and grass fields, or clambers up trees, hopping from branch to branch with great agility and searching every nook and cranny. Few eggs or small birds escape its systematic persecution. The species ranges throughout the Oriental region, exploiting scrub jungle and tall grassland, as well as orchards, village groves and rambling urban gardens. Sedentary, the birds are seen singly or in pairs, and are represented throughout the Oriental realm by a number of geographical races.

The courtship ritual consists of the male strutting grotesquely round and chasing the female in and out of the shrubbery. She pretends to flee, tail down, wings drooping and the chase may continue among low branches and end with the pair mating.

The nest is a large, untidy structure of sticks, twigs, coarse grasses and bamboo leaves, well hidden among tangled vines in a bush or tree.

Jungle Babbler
Turdoides striatus

The Jungle Babbler is best known for its habit of keeping in flocks of six to eight, from which it gets its popular name of "Seven Sisters". The species is gregarious and sociable even during breeding, when two or three flocks, or "sisterhoods", may join up to feed. The birds rummage among fallen leaves for insects, keeping up a continual low chatter.

Occasionally the harmony is disrupted by a row between two individuals. Bill and claws are put to good use, while the rest of the flock looks on. But ranks are closed against intruders: a marauding hawk or cat is attacked and put noisily to rout.

Endemic to India, Jungle Babblers often form the nucleus of the mixed foraging parties made up of birds of the forest. They are as much at home in well-wooded town gardens, village outskirts and cultivated land as in deciduous forest or scrub jungle. Tame and friendly, they make use of back yards and verandas, hopping about fearlessly near human beings.

Domestic chores and chick-rearing are shared on a communal basis. The nest, a loosely constructed affair of grass, twigs and rootlets, is built in a bushy tree in a garden or orchard.

Francolin
Francolinus francolinus

A plump, stub-tailed creature, the Black Partridge or Francolin is a prized game-bird offering excellent sport with the gun. It runs swiftly ahead and rises on whirring wings, flying strongly for no more than 300 yards before touching down. Seldom far from cover, it feeds in the mornings and late afternoons, sauntering about with tail partly cocked.

Found in plains and foothills, the species ranges from Cyprus eastwards through the Near East to India. Favourite habitat is high grass and tamarisk jungle bordering rivers and canals, alternating with millet or sugar-cane cultivation and tea gardens. The bird is found singly, in pairs or in parties of three to five.

The call of the cock-bird is a distinctive blend of the harsh and the musical. It is repeated every few seconds during the morning and evening and far into dusk, and is heard at all hours in overcast, drizzly weather – especially in the breeding season when the calls are taken up by others of its kind.

The nest, a shallow depression scraped in the ground and lined with grass, is sited at the foot of a grass clump or bush and usually contains six to eight brown eggs.

Short-toed Eagle
Circaetus gallicus

The Short-toed Eagle offers a distinctive profile as it circles overhead, quartering the ground like a harrier. Every so often it stops in mid-air, hovering to investigate the ground more closely. With phenomenal eyesight, it spots prey and dives at great speed, flattening out near the ground to pounce on its quarry. It will also saunter about on the ground, picking up the charred remains of small animals caught in a forest fire. Its diet consists of snakes (including poisonous ones), lizards, field rats, disabled birds, locusts and other large insects.

The Short-toed Eagle occurs as a breeding bird or migrant across much of the Palaearctic, Ethiopian and Oriental regions, generally wintering in the south of its range. Preferred territory is open, cultivated plain or grassland, stony deciduous open scrub country and low foothills. The bird is seen singly or in pairs, and in the breeding season pairs circle overhead calling noisily and darting at each other.

The nest is a platform of sticks and twigs with a deep central depression lined with grass. It is usually built near the top of a moderate-sized tree, providing a vantage point in open country. One or two eggs are laid and incubated mainly by the female, though the male helps in feeding the young, initially on small pieces but later on whole prey.

Short-toed Eagle
Circaetus gallicus 26in
May hang in the air for several minutes, scanning the ground for prey

Stone Curlew
Burhinus oedicnemus 16in

Night prowler

The Stone Curlew, *Burhinus oedicnemus*, is a furtive character, only emerging to forage and feed at twilight or in total darkness. If surprised in the open, it slinks quietly away to lie, with outstretched neck, behind some little bush or mound, achieving a miraculous camouflage.

Somewhat larger than a partridge, this is a dark-streaked, sandy-brown bird with a thick head, huge goggle eyes, and yellowish legs with thick knees. It is strictly a terrestrial creature, sluggish and retiring during the daytime, but otherwise running swiftly about with short quick steps, its neck lowered and stretched out in front.

At night the Stone Curlew comes out to forage for insects, worms, slugs, small reptiles and small field-mice. Its distinctive call, a series of sharp, whistling screams, often given in uneven duets or trios, is commonly heard at dusk or dawn in locations where this secretive little bird is hardly ever seen in daylight.

The range is from southern Europe and North Africa across to the Middle East and eastwards as far as India and Indo-China. The species is restricted to dry deciduous and semi-desert habitat – stony, undulating country covered with sparse scrub and dry, shingly river beds. Keeping in pairs, or in parties of six to ten, these birds are often found in groves, orchards and fallow land on the outskirts of towns and villages.

The Stone Curlew's eggs (usually two) are laid in an unlined scrape at the base of a bush or tuft of grass, on stony ground, in a dry shingle bed, or sometimes in a village grove. They are pale buff to olive green in colour, blotched in brown or purple, and, like the incubating bird, extraordinarily well camouflaged in their surroundings. Both male and female share the task of incubating the eggs and the female has a number of very specialized, quiet calls that are used to communicate with the chicks – even before they are hatched. The young are nidifugous at birth; well insulated by thick down and quite capable of running about within a few hours of hatching.

A Multitude of Islands

Tens of thousands of islands, large and small, surround Asia on three sides. The birds of the eastern islands, such as Sakhalin and Japan, belong to the Palaearctic fauna. Those to the southeast, including the Philippines and the 3,000-mile long Indonesian chain, are of the Oriental fauna as far east as the Wallace Line (an imaginary line drawn between Borneo and Celebes, Bali and Lombok), where they merge with the birds of Australasia. In the southwest, the tiny scattered islets of the Indian Ocean have a mixed fauna with Oriental, Ethiopian and Malagasy affinities. These zoogeographic divisions are, however, by no means static. Species are constantly exploring new areas or being carried by the wind from island to island. Typically Oriental species have penetrated eastwards beyond the Wallace Line, but at the eastern end of the Indonesian chain, the birds of the Aru archipelago are almost entirely Australasian.

Most of the larger islands have a prolific avifauna; Borneo for example boasts more than 550 species, almost as many as the Malaysian mainland, while the tiny volcanic and coral islands that abound in the region are home to vast colonies of seabirds. Many of the smaller islands are inhabited by rare and unique birds such as the Frigate Island Magpie Robin, the Cousin Island Brush Warbler and the Mahe Bare-legged Scops Owl and, in the Indian Ocean alone, more than 20 such species are now listed as being in danger of extinction.

The island realm
Distribution of species
▦ Monkey-eating Eagle
  Pithecophaga jefferyi
⬚ Cave Swiftlet
  Collocalia fuciphaga
◻◧ Narcondam Hornbill
  Rhyticeros narcondami
  (Narcondam Island only)

Monkey-eating Eagle
Pithecophaga jefferyi 38in
Only 50 pairs left in the wild

Bornean Bristle-head
Pityriasis gymnocephala 10in
*So little is known that even
its classification is uncertain*

Philippine Monkey-eating Eagle
Pithecophaga jefferyi

Never found outside the Philippines, the spectacular raptor known as the Philippine Monkey-eating Eagle is in grave danger of becoming extinct. The species, once fairly common in the archipelago, is now down to an estimated 50 pairs, chiefly on the islands of Mindanao and Luzon in the eastern Philippines, although there may be a few on some of the other large islands. Reasons for the decline include the clearing of primeval forest and commercial demand for specimens for zoos, museums and private collections.

Now one of the world's rarest eagles, *P. jefferyi* is also one of the largest, measuring up to three and a half feet in length. The short, broad wings, giving great manoeuvrability in the forest habitat, and long, squared tail, produce the flight-silhouette of a gigantic goshawk.

The tousled mane, staring blue eyes and massive, hooked bill give this eagle a particularly fierce look. Its generous diet includes monkeys and squirrels, dogs, pigs and poultry poached from around the villages, and large forest birds like hornbills.

The Monkey-eater's nest is a huge platform of sticks built high up in a lofty tree. This stronghold is occupied year after year and becomes "traditional" if the bird is left undisturbed. It is said that a great pile of debris – bones of prey brought back for the young – accumulates at the foot of a nest tree. One or two white eggs are laid, but normally only a single youngster is fledged.

Bornean Bristle-head
Pityriasis gymnocephala

The Bornean Bristle-head, also known as the Bald-headed Wood Shrike, is a rare arboreal bird of considerable interest – not least because so little is known about it. It is a large, dumpy passerine, superficially resembling a starling or mynah, but of uncertain classification. According to one authority, it is "the most peculiar avian endemic of Borneo".

A resident of lowland forest, the Bristle-head is distributed on the

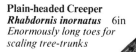

Plain-headed Creeper
Rhabdornis inornatus 6in
*Enormously long toes for
scaling tree-trunks*

Narcondam Hornbill
Rhyticeros narcondami 26in
*The entire world population
confined to one rocky island*

Grey-rumped Swiftlet
Collocalia fuciphaga 4¾in
*Its nest is the basis of one
of the world's great delicacies*

---

island of Borneo up to an altitude of about 12,000 feet, and prefers to keep to the middle canopy. A top-heavy bird, it is slow and ponderous and reluctant to fly. Its food (mainly insects) is taken in clumsy aerial pursuit or from tree-trunks.

In the forest the Bristle-head is located by its curious calls, sometimes uttered in chorus by birds in a party. Little is known about its breeding biology, but it is thought that the nest is a cup-like structure placed in the fork of a tree.

Philippine Creepers
Rhabdornis spp

There are two treecreeper species endemic to the Philippines: the Stripe-headed Creeper, *R.mysticalis*, about the size of a sparrow; and the Plain-headed Creeper, *R.inornatus*, which is similar in coloration, but, as its name suggests, lacks the striping on the crown. The Plain-headed shares at least two islands, Samar and Mindanao, with its striped relative.

The creepers have slender down-curved bills and elongated toes (including the fourth toe or thumb), a development enabling them to scale tree-trunks with ease. They are large, stout, forest-dwelling birds, superficially reminiscent of Spider-hunters, since they have a brush-tipped tongue – an adaptation for nectar eating as in true mellivorous birds; and, besides probing into flowers for their food, creepers also take insects from the crevices of bark as they climb up tree-trunks.

Narcondam Hornbill
Rhyticeros narcondami

The entire world population of Narcondam Hornbills – roughly estimated at about 400 birds – is confined to one solitary rocky island in the Bay of Bengal. Barely two square miles in area, Narcondam is an outlying island of the Andaman group, rising abruptly from the sea to a height of about 1,500 feet.

The Narcondam Hornbill makes its home in the high tropical evergreen forest that carpets the lower slopes of the island down to the sea. The remoteness of the island and a lack of fresh water have deterred settlement, and so the species has no predators. In fact the numbers seem to have doubled in the last 50 years, and probably the increase would be more marked if it were not for the shortage of tree-holes for nesting: many over-mature trees tend to get blown down in the frequent cyclones experienced in the Andaman group.

The Narcondam Hornbill is a noisy bird uttering loud, cackling calls like those of the domestic fowl. Its flight is heavy and slow. Wild figs form the staple diet, although lizards and other animals may be taken whenever animal prey is scarce.

The nest is a natural hollow in a large tree-trunk, usually quite high above the ground. The breeding biology is not documented, but it is thought to follow the general pattern found in other hornbill species. The bird's nearest relatives are 248 miles away in the Mergui Archipelago of southern Burma.

Grey-rumped Swiftlet
Collocalia fuciphaga

There are twenty or so species of so-called Edible-nest Swiftlets – tiny birds whose nests are made of hardened saliva. Some species of swiftlet add straw, feathers and other materials to the nest and these are called "black nests", but white nests, with no foreign matter mixed in, are most sought after for bird's nest soup. This is considered a rare delicacy by the Chinese and tonic properties are claimed for white nests in particular – possibly with some foundation as they are rich in protein (up to 50 per cent) and mineral salts (over 7 per cent).

Most Edible-nest Swiftlets look alike in the field. The Grey-rumped, however, can usually be recognized in good daylight by its pale rump contrasting with the rest of the upper parts. This species ranges over Southeast Asia, chiefly in the Malaysian archipelagos, where offshore islands with sea-caves and grottoes provide roosting and nesting sites.

Often several species use the same grottoes, plastering their tiny nests over the rough rock walls and ceilings. The swiftlets spend the entire daylight hours on the wing, hawking insects. They leave at dawn and return at dusk, covering enormous distances while foraging. In flight, a low, rattle-like call is uttered – an aid to echo-location inside dark caves and a vital aid when the bird flies from daylight into the contrasting dark of the cave – at times crowded with flying birds.

Adaptability Breeds Success

The birds of the Oriental realm have provided students of genetics with ample material for the study of the complex workings of speciation and geographical variation. The species is the basic unit of evolution and is usually constant over a given continuous geographical range. New species may arise when part of the population becomes isolated, for example behind a high mountain range, in a desert region or on an island. The hereditary material of the species is then free to change, and eventually the isolated population may vary so much from the original pattern that it can no longer interbreed with the original stock. It is then defined as a new species. Sub-species, or races, are local populations, usually defined by minor geographical boundaries, which may differ considerably from the original stock, but their differences are usually superficial ones of plumage colour or behaviour and the races are still free to interbreed with other races and with the original "type" species. Only in isolation can the differences become so great as to allow the development of a new, distinct species.

Reproductive isolation is encouraged when a species occupies a new habitat, involving gradual changes in the bird's feeding and nesting habits, for example when a montane species expands and colonizes lowland forest areas or when a woodland species adapts to open grassland. Here natural selection takes over. Any individual not able to cope with the new environment perishes, while those better fitted for the new conditions thrive and go on to produce young. The variations produced by natural selection are never more clearly illustrated than in the populations of small islands. No two islands are identical and even when a single colonizing species occupies a series of new island homes, each island will develop its own unique version of the original, each displaying its own range of plumage variations, feeding habits and nesting techniques. No fewer than 35 different races of the thrush *Turdus poliocephalus* inhabit the islands of Indonesia. Some have adapted to life above the tree-line, others to upland forest; some have made their homes in lowlands while others have radiated to exploit tiny coral atolls. The pigeons and doves, flycatchers, tits and warblers of the Oriental realm also display this remarkable ability to adapt and change and, in the case of the pigeons and doves, have developed into a wide range of beautiful new species.

Emerald Dove 10in
Chalcophaps indica
Successful and widespread throughout evergreen and deciduous forests. Partial to shady, wooded ravines in foothills. Feeds on seeds, berries and termites.

BURMA

INDIA

Nicobar Pigeon
Caloenas nicobarica 16in
An unusual ruff-necked species inhabiting densely forested islands from Malaya to the Solomons. Adapted to a diet of hard seeds, supplemented with fruit and insects.

Green Imperial Pigeon
Ducula aenea 18in
Unlike its predominantly ground-dwelling relatives, the Imperial Green Pigeon is arboreal in habit, plucking fruit direct from the trees. Its unusually short gut allows the passage of hard fruit stones while easily digesting the soft fruit pulp. Widespread from India to the Celebes, the species shows signs of sub-speciation in the restricted islands of its eastern range.

White-bellied Plumed Pigeon
Lophophaps plumifera 8½in
Found throughout the arid, rocky hinterland of northern and central Australia. Feeds almost entirely on seeds but, unlike many desert birds, must drink daily. Also eats grasshoppers, worms and termites. Nests on the ground in the lee of a bush or boulder, but never within cover–apparently preferring ease of escape to nest comfort.

Luzon Bleeding Heart
Gallicolumba luzonica 12in
Sedentary habits and geographical isolation have led to the evolution of five distinct species, each strictly confined to its own island.

Pheasant Pigeon
Otidiphaps nobilis 18in
Four distinct races inhabit New Guinea and neighbouring islands; thought by some to be separate species. A large, shy, terrestial bird capable only of short bursts of flight. Inhabits dense hill forests, feeding on seeds and insects.

Golden Dove
Ptilinopus luteovirens 8in
The Golden Dove, found on Viti Levu in the Fiji Islands, inhabits tall dense forest with little ground vegetation. Like its relatives on neighbouring islands, it is an aberrant product of inbreeding in insolation.

THAILAND
PHILIPPINES
CELEBES
BORNEO
SUMATRA
JAVA
NEW GUINEA

Wonga Pigeon
Leucosarcia melanoleuca 17in
The lack of medium-sized game-birds in Australia has allowed the pigeons to occupy the ground-dwelling, seed-eating niche. The Wonga Pigeon is mainly terrestrial – walking swiftly over the forest floor in search of seeds, fruits and insects.

AUSTRALIA

VANUA LEVU
VITI LEVU
FIJI
SAVAII
SAMOA
UPOLU

Tooth-billed Pigeon
Didunculus strigirostris 13in
A strange aberrant pigeon restricted to the Samoan islands of Savaii and Upolu. Its massive hooked bill has serrated edges. Feeds in small flocks, on berries and plantains, in montane forest.

173

Swamp-forest and Marshland

Throughout the world, wetlands are of paramount importance to birds, but as the human population expands, so too does the demand for land and new water resources. Marshes and lakes, rivers and tidal mudflats, even mangrove swamps are reclaimed for man's use. Rivers are diverted or dammed, and countless miles of river and stream polluted by the poisonous effluent of industry and agriculture. Asia, no less than Europe or America, has suffered losses of wildlife in consequence of these actions and unfortunately her controls on pollution, like her conservation efforts, are, though rapidly developing, still in their infancy.

When the lakes of northern and central Asia freeze in winter, millions of birds migrate to the south to feeding grounds in the Indian peninsula. Here they face persecution by commercial netting and shooting and habitat disturbance through intensive fish-netting and reed-cutting. Cranes, egrets, herons and pelicans are also liable to be shot as unwelcome predators on commercial fisheries. Fortunately India, Pakistan, Bangladesh and several other countries have created wetland reserves for winter visitors and, with help from the international conservation agencies, some very rare species, such as the White-winged Wood Duck and the Marbled Teal, have been successfully reintroduced into reserves in Assam and Pakistan.

Right: A typical "jheel", or shallow lake, in Bharatpur, India

Wetlands

Distribution of species

White-breasted Kingfisher
Halcyon smyrnensis

Masked Finfoot
Heliopais personata

Mandarin Duck
Aix galericulata

Masked Finfoot
Heliopais personata 22in
*Frequents secluded pools
in dense swamp forest*

Masked Finfoot
Heliopais personata

One of a small family of water-birds found in the tropical zones of South America, Africa and Asia, the Masked Finfoot is a shy, secretive individual roughly the size of the domestic duck. Olive-brown and white, it has a velvety black mask and a conspicuous orange-yellow bill, and, on the water, could easily be mistaken for a large grebe.

The Masked Finfoot ranges eastwards from Bangladesh and eastern Assam to Malaysia, keeping to secluded pools and streams in dense, swampy forest. It rides high on the water, swimming like a coot with rhythmic jerks of the head at each stroke. When alarmed it submerges, with only the head and neck showing above the water. The Finfoot takes off like a coot, too, pattering along the surface for a few yards before becoming airborne; flight is fairly strong, but low. On land the body is carried erect, and, when danger threatens, the bird will run at great speed, taking cover in the nearest thicket.

This is a species seen only singly or in pairs, often perched on a low branch overhanging water. A distinctive feature is the curious, high-pitched bubbling call – rather like the sound of air being blown through a tube into water.

Its diet consists of molluscs, crustaceans, aquatic insects, small fish and vegetable matter, and the bird makes its home in a partly submerged tree in dense jungle swamp. The nest is a circular pad of twigs placed on a horizontal branch. Five or six eggs are laid and both sexes incubate, but little else is known about its biology.

Striated Weaver
Ploceus manyar

The Striated Weaver is a streaked, brown, sparrow-like bird about six inches long, with a yellow line over the eye and another behind the ear. It is found beside rivers and canals and in reed-beds throughout India, Sri Lanka, Burma and Java, and in Tenasserim south to Moulmein.

Generally the Striated Weaver breeds only on stretches of water choked with reed-beds or on watercourses where the banks are lined with reeds and rushes or bordered with thickets of high grass. The species thrives in this environment, with numerous birds nesting in the reeds and feeding in flocks on grass seeds or insects found in grass.

Individual colonies, however, are small – half a dozen nests, each suspended from 40 or 50 ends of grasses or rushes, which are bent over by the birds and incorporated in the nests. The nest itself is of woven vegetation, with a short, tubular entrance leading to a chamber where the eggs (usually two) are laid.

Weaver colonies are founded by the males, who busy themselves with nest-building before the hen-birds arrive. As soon as the first clutch is laid, the cock moves on to build a second nest for another prospective hen. If circumstances are favourable he may even make similar provision for a third female.

This regime explains why males are so conspicuous in the weaver colonies, and also accounts for the number of unfinished "cock-nests" found in weaver territory: these are second or third homes abandoned by the male birds as the reproductive initiative begins to wane.

Brahminy Kite
Haliastur indus

Essentially a water-loving hawk, the Brahminy Kite relies largely on the wetlands for its diet of fish, crabs, frogs, snails, small reptiles and insects. Also, with other species, the Brahminy hawks winged termites emerging from rain-sodden ground: the insects are seized in the talons and transferred to the bill in mid-air.

This handsome, chestnut-coloured raptor ranges over the entire Oriental region and parts of Australasia. On the coast it is found in ports, fishing villages, tidal creeks and mangrove swamps, and inland habitats include rivers, lakes, irrigation reservoirs and rice fields. It is given to seasonal wandering, especially during the monsoon season.

The nest, a loose structure of twigs and sticks lined with rags and wool, is placed high in a tree near water.

White-breasted Kingfisher
Halcyon smyrnensis

Though only medium-sized, the White-breasted Kingfisher is a keen hunter, preying on insects, crabs, frogs, small reptiles and rodents, fledgling birds and fish. When suitable prey appears, the bird swoops to the ground like a shrike, carries its victim back to the perch and batters it against the perch before bolting it down.

Mainly a plains-dweller, the White-breasted Kingfisher is also seen in the hills. The species ranges from Asia Minor eastwards to Hainan and southwards to the Philippines. Usually it is found near water, but it also exploits seemingly inappropriate habitat like dry, deciduous forest.

Between four and seven white eggs are laid in a nest chamber at the end of a tunnel driven into an earth bank or the side of a well.

Mandarin Duck
Aix galericulata

The Mandarin Duck holds an important place in Japanese folklore as a symbol of conjugal fidelity, and in paintings and embroidery the ornate cock-bird is nearly always accompanied by his faithful, somewhat plain spouse.

With its exquisite colouring, the Mandarin Duck is a feature of almost every zoo, and is, therefore, better known than many commoner species. In the wild, however, these birds face the destruction of their habitat by modern forestry management. The Mandarin breeds from Amur south through Korea, eastern China and the Japanese islands to Taiwan, generally wintering in the south of the range. Its habitat is the secluded forest pond or stream. The nest, a pad of grass thickly lined with down, is usually placed in a tree-hollow.

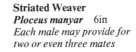

Striated Weaver
Ploceus manyar 6in
Each male may provide for two or even three mates

Brahminy Kite
Haliastur indus 19in
Monsoon floods increase the fish-hawk's feeding range

White-breasted Kingfisher
Halcyon smyrnensis 11in
Batters its prey against the perch before feeding

Mandarin Duck
Aix galericulata 17in
Forest management is eroding much of the Mandarin's habitat

Lakes, Rivers and Marshes

Pheasant-tailed Jacana
Hydrophasianus chirurgus

Larger and more aggressive than the male, the polyandrous female Pheasant-tailed Jacana will do battle with her rivals for the attentions of a cockbird. Laying a clutch of four eggs on a floating pad of grass and weeds, the female immediately deserts her mate to go in search of fresh conquests, and a single male may raise up to three broods in a season with no help at all from the wayward hen.

Jacanas, also known as "lilytrotters", are rail-like water-birds with long bare legs and enormously lengthened toes that, by spreading the birds' weight, enable them to step gracefully across floating vegetation. Feeding on plant matter, aquatic insects and molluscs, the Jacana frequents ponds and lakes even in populated areas and seems completely unafraid of man.

The Pheasant-tailed Jacana's long elegant tail-plumes are a part of its breeding plumage, but outside the breeding season, shorn of its nuptial finery, the bird is a plain brown, nondescript creature, distinguished only when its brilliant white, black-tipped wings flash open in flight.

Common throughout the lowlands of the whole Oriental realm – eastwards to Taiwan and southwards to the Philippines – the Pheasant-tailed Jacana is occasionally found up to 10,000 feet above sea level.

Sarus Crane
Grus antigone

The pair-bond forged by the Sarus Crane is lifelong and the legendary marital devotion of the species has earned it a popularity amounting to near sanctity. Protected by this popular sentiment, the birds are trusting and unafraid of man, and they stalk about, quite unconcerned, though always alert, within a few feet of cultivators at work in the fields.

Standing about five feet high, the Sarus is one of the world's largest cranes. It is found throughout the wetlands of northern India and deep into the Indo-Chinese region, wherever there are open, well-watered plains and marshes rich in fish, frogs, insects and crustaceans which, with plant-foods, make up the crane's diet.

The courtship dance, like that of most cranes, is a spectacular and beautiful display. The birds bow and curtsy, flicking open their great wings and throwing back their heads to utter loud trumpeting calls. So strong is the pair-bond that seldom is a solitary bird seen. They travel either in pairs, with their young, or in small flocks made up of two or three family groups. The nest is a huge pile of reeds and rushes on raised ground within the marsh, and the eggs and young are tended by both parents – the hen taking the major share of the 28-day incubation while the male stands guard.

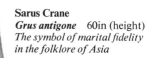

Sarus Crane
Grus antigone   60in (height)
*The symbol of marital fidelity
in the folklore of Asia*

Pheasant-tailed Jacana
Hydrophasianus chirurgus   20in
*The elegant male is deserted
by his faithless mate*

176

Spoonbill
Platalea leucorodia   34in
*Feverish activity is punctuated
by bouts of total lethargy*

Black-winged Stilt
Himantopus himantopus   10in
*Exceptionally long legs reduce
the need to compete for food*

Black-winged Stilt
Himantopus himantopus

The exceptionally long legs of this pied black and white marsh-bird enable it to forage for food in much deeper water than most of its marshland associates, thus reducing the degree of competition in the habitat. With its head submerged, the Stilt probes the bottom with its slender, pointed bill in search of molluscs, worms and insects, or picks the seeds from sedges and other marsh plants.

Closely related to the more familiar Avocet, *Recurvirostra avosetta*, the Black-winged Stilt is represented in the Oriental region by at least two geographical races. The northern breeding populations are true long-distance migrants, but elsewhere the birds move only locally – following favourable feeding conditions in times of flood and drought.

The nest may be built in a depression in the ground, on a river sand-bank, or on a raised platform of pebbles in shallow water. The four eggs are incubated for about 26 days by both parents and intruders near the nest are warned off by noisy, wheeling alarm displays.

This gregarious species is normally found in parties numbering between 20 and 100 individuals, the feeble, flapping flight, shrill piping calls and distinctive flight silhouette making them easy to identify, even at a considerable distance.

Spoonbill
Platalea leucorodia

The feeding habits of the Spoonbill are almost as curious as its broad spatulate bill. Wading into shallow water, either in the morning or evening, the Spoonbill sweeps its bill from side to side in a scything motion, raking up fish, crustaceans, molluscs and plant material from the bottom ooze. If food is abundant, the birds will jostle each other greedily, feeding almost at a run, but these bursts of hectic activity are punctuated by periods of complete inaction when the birds stand inert and listless with no apparent interest in food.

This gregarious species is common throughout much of Europe, North Africa and Asia; migratory in some parts of the range, sedentary in others. The Spoonbill's flight is clumsy and ponderous – slow, deliberate wingbeats carrying the bird through the air with neck outstretched and legs trailing behind. About the size of a domestic duck, the Spoonbill has patches of naked yellow skin on the face and neck, the colour of which intensifies during the breeding season when the bird also acquires a long, white nuchal crest.

Three or four eggs are laid in a platform nest of twigs built in a tree or among reeds, and the Spoonbill may often be found in mixed breeding colonies of ibises and egrets.

The cranes of Asia – a family in danger

In the past, persecution by man has played a major part in the decline of many of the world's cranes. The Siberian White Crane has been killed in large numbers – it is regarded as a delicacy in some areas; and the eggs of the prolific breeding Black-necked Crane have for many years been collected for food. However, it is the destruction of breeding habitats that has reduced many of these handsome marshland birds to their present plight. The cranes typically require large areas in which to breed successfully; they cannot tolerate crowding and any reduction in the size of their territory, through the reclamation of marshland for agricultural use, leads automatically to a reduction in the population. For some there is hope. A sanctuary is being prepared near Hokkaido for the Japanese Crane, and another is projected in Irkutsk for the protection of the Siberian White Crane.

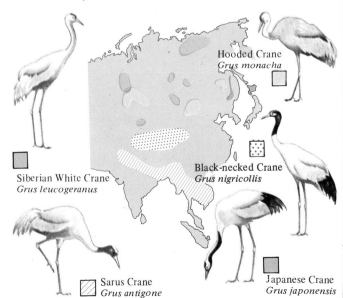

Hooded Crane
Grus monacha

Siberian White Crane
Grus leucogeranus

Black-necked Crane
Grus nigricollis

Sarus Crane
Grus antigone

Japanese Crane
Grus japonensis

177

Garden, Field and City Park

Since time immemorial the birds of Asia have lived in close proximity to man. Some, like the Junglefowl and Peafowl, have long been domesticated, while many others have been kept as household pets or, as with the falcons, for sport. Countless cities and villages have Black Kites nesting on rooftops, and these agile hunters join with the familiar crows, scavenging in the streets. Brahminy Kites and a wide variety of gulls and terns feed in the harbours and estuaries, following ships to plunge on to scraps of refuse thrown overboard and thronging the markets and fish quays.

City parks, mosques and temple gardens are alive with colourful birds, and noisy flocks of parakeets and mynahs wheel over the traffic-filled streets. Cattle Egrets, jacanas, herons and kingfishers frequent towns and villages, feeding unmolested at ponds and cattle-wallows. In the tree-lined streets of major cities one may see more than 100 species in the space of a few days. The molestation of small birds has no place in the traditions of Asia, but in some countries the trade in captured wild birds is a major industry. In Bangkok alone, hundreds of thousands of birds change hands every year and for each one that survives, hundreds die in capture or in transport. Despite such waste, however, it is impossible to travel through Asia without being impressed by the richness of its avian life in town and country alike.

Right: Rice-fields and cultivated land in the Celebes

Red-rumped Swallow
Hirundo daurica 7½in
Its beautifully made nest may become a death-trap

Magpie Robin
Copsychus saularis 8in
Fierce in defence of his garden territory

Red-rumped Swallow
Hirundo daurica

Descending on their winter quarters in enormous droves, Red-rumped Swallows sun themselves during the early morning on telegraph wires, taking off as the day warms to wheel about the sky as they hawk after flying insects.

Breeding at altitudes up to 10,000 feet, the Red-rumped Swallow is common from southern Europe and North Africa eastwards through the Middle East to Mongolia and southwards to Sri Lanka. Highly gregarious in the winter months, they spend the rest of the year in scattered pairs or small family groups.

The birds build a retort-shaped nest of mud-pellets stuck together with saliva. The short horizontal entrance chamber leads to a bulbous egg chamber lined with grass and soft down; the whole structure is cemented to the eave of a building or to a bridge or culvert. Both birds roost in the nest when incubating and many deaths have been recorded due to the freshly cemented entrance passage constricting during the night, trapping the birds so that they starve to death.

Magpie Robin
Copsychus saularis

Just eight inches high, the Magpie Robin becomes quite ludicrously pugnacious in the breeding season, defending its territory with great vigour. Puffed up like a ball, the cock struts and postures before his rivals, or bears down on them like a shrike stooping on prey.

The Magpie Robin is a trim black and white bird with a jauntily cocked tail. Widely distributed throughout the Orient, it is found in dry, deciduous forest and open secondary jungle. Characteristically it is seen near human habitation – in orchards, village groves, city parks and rambling gardens. This delightful bird keeps singly or in pairs, perching on walls and roof-tops. It descends to the ground now and then, progressing in sprightly hops to forage for insects and worms.

Home is a rough pad or cup made of grass, rootlets and hair. This untidy nest, containing three to six eggs, is placed in a tree-hollow, drainpipe or a hole in a building.

Paradise Flycatcher
Terpsiphone paradisi

In contrast with his delicate appearance the Paradise Flycatcher male has a disappointing vocal range. Apart from harsh, nasal call-notes, he has only a rather indifferent warbling song. In courtship display he sings with wings fluttering, tail raised and spread, before taking off to fly around in circles, with long tail streamers arching gracefully behind.

This slim, dainty flycatcher frequents gardens, orchards and other well-timbered localities close to human habitation. It is also found in deciduous forest and bamboo-clad watercourses in plains and foothills up to about 6,560 feet.

The range is from East Africa to Afghanistan and eastwards to South China and Korea. Keeping singly or in pairs, these birds participate in the mixed hunting parties of insectivorous forest birds.

Black Kite
Milvus migrans

The Black Kite is an efficient municipal scavenger, regularly visiting garbage dumps, slaughter-houses, meat and fish markets and other locations where there are easy pickings to be had. The preferred diet is of carcases of small animals, rarely live prey, but urban sites are more likely to yield offal and garbage. Also, these predators often poach from poultry holdings, especially when there are nestlings on hand.

With its forked tail – a striking feature in flight – the Black Kite is a familiar sight in seaports, towns and cities throughout Southeast Asia. In built-up areas it is seen perched on roof-tops or telegraph poles or circling overhead scanning the ground for tit-bits. Suddenly it swoops, as if from nowhere, to carry off a dead rat or bit of offal, twisting and turning adroitly in flight to dodge the clutter of overhead cables and the bustling traffic of a busy Oriental thoroughfare.

The Black Kite's range covers the south of Europe, North Africa and most of the Orient, as well as New Guinea and Australia. There is considerable local migration.

These birds share communal roosts in selected trees or groves, congregating noisily at dusk. The nest is a large, untidy platform of sticks, wire, rags, tow and other rubbish, placed high in the fork of a tree. Two to four eggs are laid, varying a great deal in colour, and heavily marked with streaks and blotches.

Paradise Flycatcher
Terpsiphone paradisi 8in
Compensates for its poor song with graceful display flights

Black Kite
Milvus migrans 24in
Impudent raider in the midst of the urban sprawl

Tailor Bird
Orthotomus sutorius 5in

Master tailor

The Tailor Bird, *Orthotomus sutorius*, immortalized in Rudyard Kipling's *Jungle Book*, is an amazingly resilient character who thrives in tiny back yards and town squares, in dense housing developments and shopping precincts right in the heart of bustling towns and cities. Despite heavy losses brought about by cats, rodents and, at times, children, this bird holds its own, remaining fearless and confident in the most congested conditions.

The Tailor Bird keeps in pairs and is usually delightfully tame, boldly taking over the verandas of occupied bungalows and hopping about among the pot plants, often within a few feet of the inhabitants.

The nest, a cup made of soft vegetable down and other matter, is contained in a funnel of living leaves painstakingly stitched together by the bird, using its fine, pointed bill as a needle and cotton wool shreds as yarn. The nest, which is close to the ground, is often built in the leaves of a large-leaved pot plant. Three to four eggs are laid and the female does most of the incubating.

Choosing the site
The site chosen for the nest is generally within a few feet of the ground. Often a single pendent leaf, large enough to contain the nest when folded and sewn, is used, but a cluster of three or four living leaves may be stitched together.

Preparing the purse
Having obtained several strands of vegetable cotton, fine grass or wool, the bird punctures the leaf margin with its bill and uses bill and feet to manipulate the thread through the hole. The fibrous material tangles to form a knot – preventing the leaf from reopening when tension is released.

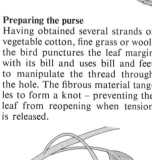

Building the nest
Once the margins of the purse are firmly sewn, with an entrance gap at the top or side, the female makes a neat conical nest inside, using soft vegetable down, fine grass, wool scraps and some feathers to form a warm, safe cocoon for her eggs.

Australia and New Zealand
The Australasian Realm

The islands of the Australasian realm were separated from each other, and from mainland Asia, many millions of years before the advent of modern birds, but the bird-life of Australia and the associated islands is nevertheless thought to be of Oriental ancestry, derived from a steady traffic of migrant birds along the chain of islands linking the two realms. The earliest arrivals have undergone extensive differentiation in the isolation of their adopted home and account for the very high proportion of endemic species; later arrivals show much closer affinities with the birds of the Oriental and Palaearctic realms.

From the vast arid plains of central Australia, the vegetation zones radiate outwards through increasingly benign grasslands to the lush and humid forests of the southeast and southwest and the tropical rain-forests of the north coast. Australia's smaller neighbours, however, have a richness and diversity of habitat unequalled by the mainland continent. The mild, temperate regime of New Zealand supports more than 250 species, while the dense forests and high mountain tracts of tropical New Guinea harbour more than 650 species – as many as are found in the whole of Australia.

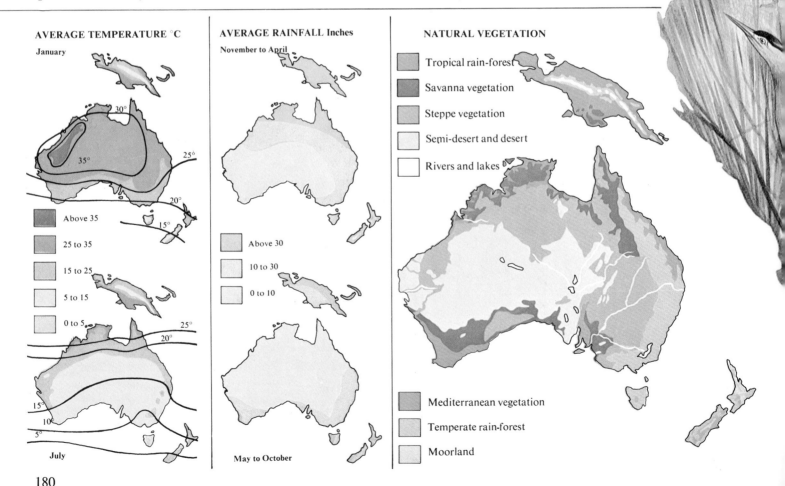

AVERAGE TEMPERATURE °C

January

- Above 35
- 25 to 35
- 15 to 25
- 5 to 15
- 0 to 5

July

AVERAGE RAINFALL Inches

November to April

- Above 30
- 10 to 30
- 0 to 10

May to October

NATURAL VEGETATION

- Tropical rain-forest
- Savanna vegetation
- Steppe vegetation
- Semi-desert and desert
- Rivers and lakes
- Mediterranean vegetation
- Temperate rain-forest
- Moorland

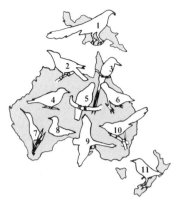

BIRDS ILLUSTRATED

1 Pheasant Coucal
Centropus phasianus

2 Blue-faced Honeyeater
Entomyzon cyanotis

3 Long-tailed Kingfisher
Tanysiptera sylvia

4 Flock Pigeon
Histriophaps histrionica

5 Galah
Kakatoe roseicapilla

6 Satin Bowerbird
Ptilonorhynchus violaceus

7 Little Bittern
Ixobrychus minutus

8 Banded Plover
Zonifer tricolor

9 Black Swan
Cygnus atratus

10 Eastern Whipbird
Psophodes olivaceus

11 Wrybill
Anarhynchus frontalis

The Northern Rain-forests

The east coast and mountains of Australia, the mid-western coastal reaches of Tasmania, and isolated pockets scattered across northern Australia are clothed in dense, luxuriant tropical rain-forests commonly called "big scrubs". They are characterized by a completely continuous canopy and are often formed of several storeys, including a rich ground layer of ferns and perennial herbs.

Three distinct forest types are recognized. True tropical rain-forest, one of Australia's most important bird habitats, has a rich flora with little tendency to domination by any one species, except in swamp areas where palms may predominate. Many of the trees are buttressed and festooned with lianas, mosses and orchids, providing a wealth of food for fruit- and seed-eating birds. Temperate rain-forest differs in having fewer tree species, often with a tendency for one species to dominate, and in having fewer lianas. The third form, also known as monsoon forest, is a depauperate rain-forest, generally having only a low tree layer which is intermingled with eucalypts and has a very dense shrub layer. Pockets of monsoon forest extend into the sclerophyll forests and fringe many of the northern rivers. It has few endemic species, but harbours both rain-forest and woodland birds.

Though many bird species range throughout the tropical forests, some have very restricted local ranges.

Right: Tropical rain-forest in northern Queensland

Rain-forest
☐ Area of forest
Distribution of species
☐ Cassowary
Casuarius casuarius
▨ Topknot Pigeon
Lopholaimus antarcticus
▤ Regent Bowerbird
Sericulus chrysocephalus

Cassowary
Casuarius casuarius 60in
Protective helmet or sexual adornment?

Cassowary
Casuarius casuarius

Distributed throughout much of northeastern Queensland, the Aru Islands, Ceram and New Guinea, this large, heavily built ground-dwelling bird is one of the most shy and wary of all forest birds. Ever alert to danger, the Cassowary keeps to the most densely overgrown areas of tropical rain-forest, remaining hidden for most of the day and emerging during the early morning and late evening to forage for fruit, seeds and berries. The huge bony crest adorning its forehead is not fully understood; like many such ornaments it may have a significance in species recognition and breeding behaviour, but may also function simply as a protective shield as the bird forces a passage through dense vegetation. Unlike many forest birds, the Cassowary is an accomplished swimmer and fish form a part of its natural diet.

Between July and September the birds mate; each pair building a large untidy platform of sticks and leaves, usually in dense cover at the base of a tree. The three to five eggs, pale green in colour, have a very characteristic coarse, granular shell.

Topknot Pigeon
Lopholaimus antarcticus

The nomadic life-style of the Topknot Pigeon has enabled it, unlike some of its less fortunate relatives, to survive the pressures created by man's domination of the environment. Though extensively shot for food in the past, the species is now protected by law and its once-depleted numbers have recovered.

For much of the year the Topknot travels from one forested region to the next, following the ripening of various fruits. Its habit of migrating in large flocks has earned it the additional common name of Flock Pigeon and, in particularly rich feeding grounds, the earth below the pigeons' roosts may be thickly strewn with the excreted seeds of wild figs, bangalow fruits and the seeds of the cabbage-tree palm. The birds generally roost until late in the morning, in high trees on the hillsides, coming down into the valleys and ravines to feed and then returning to their roosts.

In October and November the birds pair off and prepare to mate. Little is known of their courtship behaviour but, typical of their family, the nest is a strong platform of stout twigs placed high above the ground – often in the slender branches at the very top of a casuarina tree.

Regent Bowerbird
Sericulus chrysocephalus

The Regent Bowerbird is an "avenue builder" – one of a group of bowerbirds whose courtship ritual centres around a carefully constructed and often highly decorated stage. At the start of the breeding season the male clears a space on the forest floor and carefully lays down a low platform of twigs some 12 by 14 inches in size. Upright twigs about ten inches long are planted in this ground layer to form two walls with a clear space or "avenue" between them. The bird then collects a variety of small objects – snail shells, leaves, berries and even scraps of paper – generally of a yellow or green colour, with which to adorn

Topknot Pigeon
Lopholaimus antarcticus 17in
*Millions were shot for
their rich, dark meat*

Regent Bowerbird
Sericulus chrysocephalus 11in
*Its courtship bower is
furnished, painted and decorated*

Yellow Figbird 11in
Sphecotheres flaviventris
*Noisy and gregarious birds of
the mixed northern forests*

Fernwren
Oreoscopus gutturalis 5½in
*Tosses debris aside as
it searches for food*

his bower. (The Satin Bowerbird, *Ptilonorhynchus violaceus*, is blue-black in colour and adorns its bower with blue objects.) The avenue may also be "painted" with a mixture of saliva and vegetable pulp applied with a wad of macerated plant material. The male then jumps around his bower, excitedly picking up and moving the decorative items until a female is enticed into entering the walled avenue. Copulation takes place within the avenue and the female leaves to nest alone. The bower and display are for mating only; the female builds her saucer-like nest of twigs among dense vines up to 40 feet above the ground and incubates her two eggs alone. The breeding behaviour of the bowerbirds is one of the outstanding features of the bird-life of Australasia and is discussed further on pp198-199.

These attractive forest birds inhabit the dense east-coast rainforests from southern Queensland to the Hawkesbury River in New South Wales. Having paired during the breeding season (October to January) the birds tend to form small flocks in the autumn and winter – constantly moving about as they feed on the fruits and berries of vines and shrubs.

Yellow Figbird
Sphecotheres flaviventris

In pairs or small sociable groups, Yellow Figbirds inhabit the mixed woodlands and rain-forests of Northern Territory and northeastern Queensland. Their feeding parties are noisy and active and, in areas where fruit is plentiful, the birds may form mixed parties, flocking together with orioles and other fruit-eating

species. Though fruit and berries form the bulk of the figbird's diet, individuals have been observed to occasionally catch large flying insects on the wing.

The Yellow Figbird's sociable nature extends to its nesting habits, and the shallow, unlined saucer of twigs and vine tendrils may often be placed high in a tree shared by Drongos and Helmeted Friarbirds. So loose is the nest construction that the three pale green eggs are often clearly visible from below. In the southern coastal forests the Yellow Figbird is replaced by the closely related Southern Figbird, *S.vieilloti*, while far to the north the genus is represented on Timor by the Green Figbird, *S.viridis*, and on the islands of the Banda Sea by the White-breasted species, *S.hypoleucus*.

Fernwren
Oreoscopus gutturalis

So vigorous is the Fernwren's search for insects and larvae that it often tosses debris into the air as it works away at the rotten bark of a fallen tree or tugs at a dense pad of mosses and ferns. The bird itself is normally quiet, apart from a low and plaintive call, and the sound of its busy scratching is often the first clue to its whereabouts.

The Fernwren inhabits the tropical montane forests of the northeast, generally staying within its own small territory in a sheltered, damp locality. Its neat dome-shaped nest is made from fresh green mosses and black fern stems, placed on the ground among concealing vegetation or partly hidden in a hole in an earth bank.

Coastal Sclerophyll Forest

Sclerophyll, a term meaning hard-leafed, is applied in Australia to the eucalypt forests of the east and southwest in areas receiving more than 30 inches of rainfall a year. Wet sclerophyll consists of very tall, straight-trunked eucalypts and angophoras with an understorey of dense shrubs, ferns and small trees. It could almost be termed eucalypt rain-forest, but the canopy is not as dense as rain-forest and vines are virtually absent.

There are three layers of birds: those of the tree-tops – often 200 feet above ground – like small honeyeaters; those of the undergrowth foliage, including thornbills, fantails and robins; and ground birds foraging in the damp litter, such as lyrebirds (particularly in dense gullies), scrub birds and whipbirds.

Dry sclerophyll is much more open, and the eucalypts spread laterally as they grow, with the trunk branching from a low level. The understorey is less dense, too, with the ground covered with small plants and dry litter. Typical birds are whistlers, robins, honeyeaters, thornbills, Quail-thrush and Painted Quail.

Within the sclerophyll forests some micro-habitats support specialized birds, for example the Rock Warbler of the Hawkesbury Sandstone around Sydney, and the very localized Helmeted Honeyeater near Melbourne.

Right: Typical mixed sclerophyll forest; New South Wales

Sclerophyll forest
▨ Area of forest
Distribution of species
▨ Golden Whistler
Pachycephala pectoralis
▢ Lyrebird
Menura superba

Sulphur-crested Cockatoo
Cacatua galerita 19in
A beautiful wild bird too often doomed to a life in captivity

Sulphur-crested Cockatoo
Cacatua galerita

Flocks of Sulphur-crested Cockatoos inhabit both wet and dry sclerophyll forests as well as areas of drier, more open woodland. Where clearing has taken place they may be observed feeding at ground level on seeds, nuts, berries and insects, with sentries posted around the feeding group to warn of approaching predators. Each flock has an habitual roost, usually a dense, old tree hidden deep in the forest. It has been suggested that the pure-white phase of the Grey Goshawk, *Accipiter novaehollandiae*, enjoys its great success as a hunter because of its superficial similarity to the Cockatoo. However, the Cockatoos themselves are not deceived; if a Goshawk appears, the whole flock will rise in a white cloud to the top of a prominent tree, perching there with crests raised and wings spread as they shatter the forest silence with their ear-splitting shrieks of alarm.

At the beginning of the breeding season (in the dry winter season in the north and in spring and early summer in the east), the flocks split up into pairs. A deep hollow, usually in the trunk of an old eucalypt tree, is chosen as the nest-site, and two white eggs are laid on a bed of decaying wood-dust in the base of the hollow. Both parents share the 30-day incubation period.

Many young cockatoos are taken from the nest and sold as cage-birds, doomed to a life of misery in small, totally unsuitable cages. Their loud screeches, occasioned by boredom, often result in the birds changing hands at frequent intervals and many are thoughtlessly released to perish in the unfamiliar outside environment.

Island variations

The Golden Whistler, *Pachycephala pectoralis*, proliferates in many forms in the islands northeast of Australia. On the mainland, however, it is rather more conservative. The males of the two Australian forms are very similar, only the females differing – one with yellow underparts, the other grey. One form inhabits the mangroves of the northern coasts, the other the forests and woodlands of the south and east. The latter is predominantly a bird of sclerophyll forests where its pleasant whistling song is a characteristic sound.

The male assists in building the flimsy nest and incubating the two or three eggs. These are variable in colour, ranging from white to buff with darker spots.

The chicks tend to leave the nest before they are fully fledged, and may be seen perched some considerable distance away, still downy and showing bare patches on neck and abdomen. They are bright rufous in colour, but the head and body feathers moult within a few weeks and are replaced by grey plumage.

Tasmania

Louisiade Archipelago

Tanimbar Islands

Geographical variations
The Golden Whistler is known in more than 70 racial variations widely distributed over mainland Australia and the northern islands. Birds of the warmer northern regions tend to be smaller and more brightly coloured than their southern relatives – a reflection of the processes of natural selection at work in different habitats. Bill form, too, varies considerably from one area to another and never more so than between the races inhabiting the isolated off-shore islands around the Australian coast. Three such races, from widely separated localities, are illustrated above.

Golden Whistler 7in
Pachycephala pectoralis

Superb Lyrebird
Menura novachollandiae

In the wild the Superb Lyrebird is very difficult to observe, for this shy and secretive bird inhabits densely vegetated gullies in the most inaccessible temperate rain-forest and wet sclerophyll forest.

The outer tail feathers of the male are lyre-shaped, with a notched appearance due to alternate bands of light and dark colours. The remaining tail feathers are delicate filaments, dark grey or blackish on the upper surface and silver on the underside. When the bird is walking normally only the dark upper sides of the tail feathers are visible, but during display they are thrown forwards over the head and made to quiver so that the silver underside forms a shimmering veil.

The male prepares a number of dancing mounds, each in a small clearing. Soil and leaves are raked into a heap and flattened to form a platform. Sometimes the clearing is scraped clear of debris altogether and occasionally a fallen log is used as a display ground. The male visits each of his mounds in turn, although there is usually a favourite. When a receptive female visits, the male's singing and dancing become frenzied and, at the climax, she is enclosed in the veil and mating takes place.

The female builds the domed nest from sticks and moss, placing it on a tree-stump, on a ledge or among dense vines, and lining the chamber with feathers plucked from her flanks. Only one egg is laid, greyish-brown in colour with darker streaks. Nest hygiene is rather unusual: the female carries all droppings from the nest and deposits them in a stream.

Superb Lyrebird
Menura novachollandiae 38in
Mating takes place beneath the shimmering veil of the male's tail plumes

Pink Robin
Petroica rodinogaster 5in
Its nest is beautifully decorated with cobwebs and pieces of lichen

Pink Robin
Petroica rodinogaster

The Australian Robins, which cover most of the territory apart from the tropical north, are members of the flycatcher family. They are totally unrelated to the European Robin, *Erithacus rubecula*, and only the five species with red or pink breasts even remotely resemble it. The Pink Robin's closest relatives are the Spotted Flycatcher of Europe (p107) and the Paradise Flycatcher of Asia (p178).

The Pink Robin is an unobtrusive bird, sitting quietly on a low branch, occasionally flicking its wings and uttering a low metallic "tick-tick". Its food consists of a wide variety of insects taken either in flight or on the ground. The female is very different from the striking male and has a dark brown back, pale undersides and buff bars on the wings. The nest is a superb piece of construction. Placed in a lichen-encrusted fork near the ground, the delicately woven cup is decorated with fragments of bark and lichen held in place by strands of cobweb. The birds breed between September and December and both adults share the 14-day task of incubating their three pale-green spotted eggs. Once hatched, the young birds are fed constantly by their parents, food being provided at intervals of between five and 20 minutes.

The Pink Robin favours the wet sclerophyll forests of the southeast and Tasmania, spending the hotter months at high altitudes but moving down to lower altitudes, and into the drier forests, in winter. Some individuals are nomadic and a few have been recorded as travelling as far as southeastern Queensland.

Sandy Heath and Scrub

Heaths are restricted, treeless plains of densely packed shrubs, sedges and grasses growing in sandy soil often poor in minerals. Many of these "sandplains" are, in spring, covered by a wealth of wild flowers, ranging from ground orchids to dwarf eucalypts, banksias and dryandras rich in nectar. In other seasons however, the terrain is drab and featureless, and offers little variety of food to birds.

Hidden for much of the time among dense shrubby vegetation, the heathland birds are often difficult to observe and many have not been studied in detail. Best known are the scrub birds, probably the most primitive of all passerines. These are so localized in habit, and thus so vulnerable, that they are close to being extinct. Also vulnerable are the Western Whipbird and the Ground Parrot. Species such as the Field Wren and the Tawny-crowned Honeyeater are common.

Because heaths are so easy to clear, they are disappearing. Fortunately, due to public interest in the threatened species, some national parks have been retained.

An extension of heath habitat, where larger trees grow among the vegetation, is known as "tree heath". This is rich in honeyeaters, particularly the Little Wattle Bird and New Holland Honeyeater; it also provides cover for the elegant Brush Bronzewing pigeon.

Right: Typical dense ground vegetation in heathland

Heath

■ Area of heath

Distribution of species

▨ Ground Parrot
Pezoporus wallicus

▢ Brush Bronzewing
Phaps elegans

Brush Bronzewing
Phaps elegans 11in
Iridescent wing feathers are a feature of one of Australia's two major pigeon groups

Brush Bronzewing
Phaps elegans

Heavily built and powerfully winged, the Brush Bronzewing is one of the fastest of all Australian birds, and the Peregrine Falcon, *Falco peregrinus*, is probably the only predator which can overtake it in level flight.

It takes its name from iridescent feathers in the wing, a characteristic that identifies one of the two groups of pigeons that occupy Australia. The first of these groups eats fruit and is more or less confined to rain-forest, wet sclerophyll and mangrove; the second feeds on seeds and is found in areas of lower rainfall. Most of the pigeons in the group to which the Brush Bronzewing belongs, have adapted to arid and desert conditions, but the Bronzewing lives in heath and coastal brush country in the wetter southwest and southeast.

The bronze speculae on the wings are best seen during courtship displays. The male bows with the wings slightly opened and tilted so that the sun glances from the iridescent feathers towards the female. The display is accompanied by typical cooing. The nest of twigs, usually containing two white eggs, is placed on the ground or on a tree-stump surrounded by new growth.

Rufous Bristlebird
Dasyornis broadbenti

Though plumaged in dull colours, the Bristlebird has a lacquered appearance (an unusual feature shared by some other members of the endemic Australian warbler family *Maluridae*) that is possibly an adaptation for shedding water in rain-soaked, dense undergrowth. Unfortunately the number of bristlebirds has fallen in recent years until only relict populations now exist.

The Rufous Bristlebird inhabits the heaths of the southeast and the extreme southwest. In the latter area it is one of the rarest of birds, having been sighted only a few times this century. Even where it is comparatively common it is difficult to see because it is a ground bird, flying only with extreme reluctance, and lives in a tangled habitat.

The bird's name derives from two or three bristles at the base of the bill – possibly a mechanism to protect the eyes in dense heath.

Breeding tends to be late in the year, and December is the optimum month. Coarse grasses form the outer casing of the dome-shaped nest, built by the female, and the lining is of soft, fine grasses and moss.

New Holland Honeyeater
Phylidonyris novaehollandiae

Honeyeaters consititute Australia's most successful bird family, with 69 species, most of which are endemic. A remarkable feature of the honeyeaters is the variety in the length of bill and in the size of the birds themselves – from the four-inch Grey Honeyeater, *Lacustroica whitei*, to the Yellow Wattle-bird, *Anthochaera curunculata* of Tasmania, measuring 18 inches.

The New Holland Honeyeater is about seven inches long and has a curved bill suitable for probing the deep nectaries of its favourite blossoms, banksia and dryandra. It often flies up above the heaths to take passing insects, turning over and dropping straight down – a flight pattern repeated in courtship.

The breeding season is long, from later autumn to late spring. The cup-shaped nest, usually built in a low bush, is made of grass, rootlets and bark and holds two or three eggs, pinkish-buff in colour with red and grey spots. Incubation is shared by both parents. When one of the adults arrives with food, the insect in its beak is given to the nearest chick and then each chick is rapidly fed a drop of regurgitated nectar.

Ground Parrot
Pezoporus wallicus

Like many of the ground birds of the heaths, the Ground Parrot is difficult to observe. Although it flies well, under normal circumstances during the day it does not do so, but prefers to run and walk among the dense ground vegetation. If startled, it takes to the wing like a quail, and its zig-zag flight, long tail and pale wing bar are distinctive. In the evening it becomes active and may be seen flying.

Once heath becomes overgrown, seeds are more difficult to reach and the parrots, whose requirements are particular, find it difficult to feed. Thus, they probably require fairly regular natural slow burning of parts of the environment to maintain optimum conditions. Destruction of habitat has already taken its toll of their numbers and the Gound Parrots may soon be in need of protection.

Two or three white eggs are laid in a grass-lined depression under a tussock of grass or a leafy bush. The young are able to run before fledging and, if disturbed, they scurry away into the surrounding vegetation.

Rufous Bristlebird
Dasyornis broadbenti 9½in
*Tough bristles at the base
of the bill may protect the
eyes in coarse vegetation*

New Holland Honeyeater 7 in
Phylidonyris novaehollandiae
*Nectar-feeding member of
Australia's most successful
bird family*

Ground Parrot
Pezoporus wallicus 12in
*Threatened by the loss
of its heathland habitat*

Signposts to a lost landscape

In 1842 a small and fleet-footed ground bird was discovered in the dense scrub-forest of southwestern Australia. At first known as the Western Scrub-bird, the species was later renamed the Noisy Scrub-bird, *Atrichornis clamosus*, a name chosen to reflect the bird's most notable feature – a remarkably powerful and varied voice. Extremely shy by nature, few in numbers and inhabiting a densely vegetated environment, this species remained clouded in mystery for many years. Only 20 specimens were collected by the turn of the century and when, in 1961, a second small population was discovered, the bird was immediately placed under rigid protection.

In 1865 a second species was dis-covered, more than 2,500 miles away in the east-coast forests of New South Wales. Like its western relative, this bird was shy, terrestrial in habit and possessed of a loud and varied voice; its more pronounced reddish colouring giving rise to the name Rufous Scrub-bird, *A.rufescens*. Close study revealed that both species lined their nests with a curious paste of wood-pulp that dried to the consistency of cardboard, a feature found in no other Australian bird.

There can be no doubt that the two species represent the remnants of a once widespread family, isolated at the close of the ice ages when arid conditions replaced the scrub woodland of central Australia.

Rufous Scrub-bird
Atrichornis rufescens

Noisy Scrub-bird
Atrichornis clamosus

Scrub-birds
Atrichornis spp

▨ Former range

▉ Present range

Noisy Scrub-bird
Atrichornis clamosus 8in

Savanna Woodland

Strictly savanna implies grassland, but in Australia the term is used to describe scattered trees with a rich understorey of grasses and shrubs. In savanna woodland the trees are fairly close and are mainly eucalypts. Savanna woodland is usually found in areas receiving approximately 20 to 30 inches of rainfall annually, but in the tropics it is also found on wetter ground, and, in drier country, along water-courses.

Tropical savanna woodland is an important habitat in northern Australia and species like the White-winged Sittella, Black-tailed Treecreeper, Long-tailed Finch and Blue-winged Kookaburra are typical. Many birds in this area are species in the making – for example, the Red-collared Lorikeet, Black-ringed Finch, Northern Brown Goshawk, Yellow Weebill and Northern Shrike-tit.

The sub-tropical woodland of eastern Australia is in two basic forms, one predominantly eucalypt with typical birds such as the Barking Owl and Kookaburra, and the other a mixture of low scrub vegetation and acacia, known as brigalow. The latter has no endemic bird species, but is a most important habitat as it provides an insect-rich winter ground for southeastern migratory birds, notably small honeyeaters and fantails. With higher rainfall brigalow scrub may become very dense, even to the point where it can support some rain-forest birds.

Right: Savanna woodland from the Grant Range, W.A.

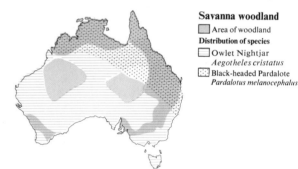

Savanna woodland
- Area of woodland

Distribution of species
- Owlet Nightjar
  Aegotheles cristatus
- Black-headed Pardalote
  Pardalotus melanocephalus

Tawny Frogmouth
Podargus strigoides 19in
Its distinctive varieties may prove to be separate species

Tawny Frogmouth
Podargus strigoides

Although it is common, the Tawny Frogmouth has only been studied superficially, probably because of its nocturnal habits, and the three or four distinctive forms so far recorded may eventually prove to be separate species. In the northwest are two small forms, one red, the other pale grey. In the rain-forests of south-eastern Queensland is a darker form, the Plumed Frogmouth, already regarded by some as a different species.

Frogmouths are lethargic by day, relying instinctively on their "broken branch" appearance to escape detection. If disturbed on its roosting perch, the bird will freeze with its head upright and keep one almost closed eye towards the intruder.

At night the Tawny Frogmouth is an efficient, kookaburra-like hunter, diving down on to any insect, gecko or small mammal moving on the ground. The powerful, cavernous bill is used to mangle the prey for swallowing. The nest is a scanty platform of twigs, holding the bird's two lustrous white eggs.

Black-headed Pardalote
Pardalotus melanocephalus

Pardalotes are aberrant flower-peckers occurring only in Australia. They are very small, colourful birds that feed predominantly on the scale insects that infest eucalypt trees. Very much birds of the eucalypt canopy, they abound in savanna woodland. The Spotted Pardalote, *P. punctatus*, is the most colourful and tends to occur in denser woodland than the other species, sometimes extending into sclerophyll forests.

The Black-headed Pardalote digs a burrow in a loamy bank for its nest. Male and female share the work, entering the burrow with grass and slivers of bark bristling from the bill, like moustaches. Four white eggs are laid and both sexes incubate.

Orange-winged Sittella
Neositta chrysoptera

The five or six forms of Australian sittella are in an interesting phase of development, having almost reached species status. No two forms occupy the same area, but where two

Black-headed Pardalote
Pardalotus melanocephalus 3¼in
*Male and female share the building
of a well-lined burrow nest*

Orange-winged Sittella
Neositta chrysoptera 4¼in
*This agile bird can hop along
the underside of a branch*

meet intergradation occurs. Southern forms have an orange patch on each wing, visible in flight; northern forms have white patches. In general, they are birds of all forms of woodland, usually moving in small, noisy flocks of up to a dozen birds.

Possibly the most fascinating aspect of their feeding behaviour is the way they can hop upside down along the underside of a limb looking for insects. Foraging flocks follow a circular or elliptical route, returning to re-examine in sequence trees searched an hour before.

These birds are among the many species in Australia that practice sociable breeding. Members of a flock combine to build the nest, although one bird, possibly the productive female, does most of the work. The cup-shaped nest is superbly camouflaged, placed in a vertical fork and decorated with small strips of bark.

Usually three bluish-white speckled eggs are laid. One female does most of the incubation, although the task is shared and the sitting bird is fed by the others. Once the chicks hatch, one bird does most of the feeding, but here again the others help.

Owlet Nightjar
Aegotheles cristatus

The Owlet Nightjar occupies a taxonomic position about half way between the frogmouths and night-jars, but its nesting behaviour is rather like that of the small owlets. It roosts during the day in hollow eucalypt branches, often sunning itself at the entrance to the hollow.

At night it is very active chasing insects. The angle of the eyes is such that it can probably see above its head without looking directly upwards. When a suitable insect passes, the Nightjar darts up like a flycatcher taking its victim in flight. Like many passerine flycatchers, its broad gape is surrounded by bristles.

Two phases exist, the more common being grey and a characteristic bird of savanna woodland; the red phase often roosting among rocks in arid zones.

The breeding season extends from July to December. Three or four white eggs are laid on a leafy pad at the bottom of a hollow branch and as soon as one brood has fledged, another clutch may be laid in the same hollow.

Kookaburra
Dacelo gigas 18in

Woodland Kingfisher

The voice of the Kookaburra, *Dacelo gigas*, euphemistically described as laughter, features among the background noises of many jungle films; a ludicrous invention of the film-maker as this curious bird is found only in Australia and is far more typical of woodland than tropical forest.

Much of this large kingfisher's popularity in Australia derives from its often reported, but seldom observed, snake-killing propensities. One ornithologist, after examining all available published photographs of Kookaburras holding snakes, found that they invariably involved tame birds with clipped wings. He felt that the stories accompanying these pictures were, therefore, discredited. However, to add some objectivity to his scepticism, he kept watch at a nest and within the first hour the Kookaburra fed its chicks with two still writhing dugites (highly venomous snakes), one measuring about 15 inches and the other 25 inches.

Kookaburra relatives
The kingfishers of Australia have evolved a number of different bill-forms, partly, though not exclusively, related to their feeding habits. The Kookaburra, found in savanna woodlands, and the Forest Kingfisher, *Halcyon macleayi*, have broad, strong bills and feed on a variety of insects, crustaceans and small vertebrates. The Little Kingfisher, *Alcyone pusilla*, has the slender stiletto bill more suitable to its fishing habit. It is generally thought that terrestrial feeders are the more primitive forms and that the fishing habit is a late behavioural exploitation of a "pre-adapted" bill.

Little Kingfisher
Alcyone pusilla 5in

Forest Kingfisher
Halcyon macleayi 9in

Owlet Nightjar
Aegotheles cristatus 17in
*A curious species mid-way between
the frogmouths and nightjars*

Brigalow Scrub and Grassland

Tropical savanna woodland merges imperceptibly into grassy forest, the two habitats differing only in the density of the trees. Generally they may be regarded as a single entity. As far as birds are concerned they form a large wooded grassland stretching across the north of Australia, rich in species and in endemic forms. Although eucalypts are the dominant trees, many other species, some deciduous, are important to the birds' ecology. Most obvious is the Baobab, an important nest site for raptors of all kinds, and babblers; however, most important is *Bauhinea*, a small and abundant tree rich in both insects and nectar. A pair of White-winged Trillers near Derby, Western Australia, was observed to feed its chicks solely from insects caught in one of these favoured nest-trees. Honeyeaters are particularly prevalent and many species such as the Banded and Rufous-throated Honeyeaters are endemic. Many other birds such as chats, trillers and wood swallows regularly take nectar from bauhineas.

Although spectacular flocks of finches are characteristic of savanna grasslands, some species, notably the Gouldian and Masked finches, also inhabit tropical savanna woodland.

Seed-eating birds such as doves, quail and parrots are numerous, sometimes congregating in flocks of millions near water-holes during the dry seasons. At such times, birds of prey also congregate and a patient observer may compare the hunting techniques of as many as five species of falcon.

Golden-backed Honeyeater
Melithreptus laetior 6in
Mutual preening and "licking" remove sticky nectar from the birds' plumage

The migrant cuckoos

One of the most interesting examples of seasonal migration in the Australasian realm is provided by the two closely related cuckoos, the Golden Bronze Cuckoo, *Chalcites lucidus plagosus*, and the Shining Bronze Cuckoo, *C.l.lucidus*.

The Golden Bronze Cuckoo inhabits eastern and southeastern Australia, the island of Tasmania and the southwestern region of Australia. Distinguished from its close relative by the strong bronze colouring of its nape and neck, it frequents forests and woodlands where it is a popular species with foresters and farmers because of its predation on harmful caterpillars. It makes no nest and like many cuckoos, lays its eggs in the nests of other birds.

The Shining Bronze Cuckoo of New Zealand is similar in habit, feeding on a wide variety of insects and caterpillars, and laying its eggs in the nests of small insect-eating birds. This species is also found sparsely distributed in the eastern coastal forests of the Australian mainland where it probably occurs only as a passing migrant.

Bronze Cuckoo
Chalcites lucidus 6in

Arriving from the north in mid-August, the Bronze Cuckoos reach their breeding grounds in October and "nest" immediately. The southern hemisphere summer is spent in the breeding range, and the birds depart north again in late March to winter in the islands north of Australia. The races utilize the prevailing winds on their annual migrations but there is no intermingling; each race adheres strictly to its own particular wintering zone.

Migration of the Bronze Cuckoo

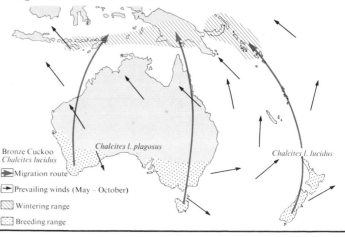

Bronze Cuckoo
Chalcites lucidus
▶ Migration route
➡ Prevailing winds (May – October)
▨ Wintering range
⬚ Breeding range

Chalcites l. plagosus

Chalcites l. lucidus

Golden-backed Honeyeater
Melithreptus laetior

The Golden-backed Honeyeater is one of a group of similar honeyeaters characterized by a black head, white nape and fleshy wattle over the eye. Members of the group share many behavioural traits, but, as some cover the same range, they probably differ in their ecological requirements. Where the ranges of the Golden-backed Honeyeater and the White-throated Honeyeater, *M.albogularis*, overlap, the birds occupy different habitats, the former preferring open woodland and the latter riverine forest.

One of Australia's many sociable birds, the Golden-backed Honeyeater moves in small flocks of up to seven or eight birds. It has a most unusual communal activity which at first sight appears to be mutual preening but is more like mutual licking. One bird sits upright on a branch while its fellows go over it with beaks slightly open and brush-tipped tongues darting in and out among the feathers – possibly removing nectar or pollen which has saturated the plumage. However, the Striped Honeyeater, *Plectorhyncha lanceolata*, a species which relies little on nectar, behaves similarly.

Barking Owl
Ninox connivens

The Barking Owl's bark is less of a conversation-stopper than its scream, which, horrifically reminiscent of a woman crying out in terror, was for many years attributed to the much larger Powerful Owl. The normal call, a low "wook-wook", is uttered by both sexes.

In size midway between the common Boobook, *N.boobook*, and the giant Powerful Owl, *N.strenua*, the Barking Owl preys on birds (parti-

Barking Owl
Ninox connivens 14in
*Finally exposed as the elusive
"screaming woman" bird*

White-winged Triller
Lalage sueurii 7in
*Northern populations carry a
tell-tale clue to their winter feeding
habits*

cularly frogmouths), beetles and quite large mammals, including opossums and rats. Like the Boobook it is particularly active shortly after dark, but also takes prey in daylight. It is not confined to woodland, but also occurs in forests, particularly along river courses.

Breeding occurs between August and October. The nest site is a large, open tree-hollow lined with chips scraped from the surrounding wood Two or three white eggs are laid at intervals of two to three days. Incubation commences with the laying of the first egg and takes 37 days for each egg. After about four weeks the female ceases to roost with the young.

White-winged Triller
Lalage sueurii

In the south, the White-winged Triller is a strict migrant, arriving to breed in September or October and leaving in March. In the north, however, it is sedentary. Possibly triller migration is of the leapfrog variety, in which the southern birds migrate to the north of the sedentary population.

In April the trillers moult and the pied male assumes drab female-like colours, although he retains the wing, rump and tail feathers of the former plumage. Between June and August, the male dons a completely new set of black and white feathers. The female moults only once a year.

Trillers usually feed on insects, but

in winter in northern Australia they also feed on nectar, and the forehead is often daubed with orange or yellow patches of pollen, confusing the unwary bird-watcher.

In the north, breeding extends from August to April, but the migratory population in the south breeds between late September and February, with a peak in November and December. The nest, a small cup placed in a horizontal fork, is made of grass and cobwebs.

Red-backed Kingfisher
Halcyon pyrrhopygia

Throughout the summer the Red-backed Kingfisher inhabits dry savanna woodland, particularly where there are earthen banks, but in winter it often moves into wetter areas and even into cleared areas of rain-forest. Its food consists of lizards, skinks, grasshoppers, spiders and centipedes. Its loud mournful cry carries for hundreds of yards and is one of the most characteristic calls of the inland regions.

The nest is a tunnel drilled into an earth bank or termite mound. Angled upwards with two grooves on the floor made by the birds' feet, the tunnel ends in a nesting chamber hidden below the level of the main passage so that it is not visible from outside. Both birds dig the nest, diving bill first at the bank while uttering a chuckle peculiar to the kingfishers of the genus *Halcyon*.

Red-backed Kingfisher
Halcyon pyrrhopygia 9in
*A cunningly angled nest-tunnel
protects the young from prowling
hunters*

Dry Savanna Grassland

Savanna grassland is basically a continuous grassy plain with scattered trees or shrubs. In many parts of Australia agricultural techniques have changed other habitats into an approximation of savanna grassland and some of the species inhabiting natural grasslands have invaded these newly created niches. Galahs, Cockatiels, Stubble Quail and Black-shouldered Kites now occur in enormous numbers and are still spreading. Pipits, Bushlarks and Crested Pigeons, as well as larks and wrens, are now much more numerous than they were a century ago. In the natural grasslands the highest populations of birds are found near watercourses lined with eucalypts. Even during long periods of drought the trees provide a focus for multitudes of parrots, doves and finches that feed on seeding grasses. Perhaps the most spectacular sights are the large flocks of finches flying in dense packs to and from the feeding grounds. Chestnut-breasted and Yellow-rumped Finches in particular occur in millions on occasions. Many of the grassland birds are influenced by seasonal conditions, breeding in enormous numbers where the climate is favourable and dying in millions when droughts occur. Their biology is such that they can tolerate violent population fluctuations.

The Flock Pigeon, once common in the grasslands, appeared to be in danger after a number of bad breeding seasons but has recently staged a revival.

Right: Eucalypt grassland, west of the Great Divide

Savanna grassland

Area of grassland
Distribution of species
Cockatiel
Nymphicus hollandicus
Budgerigar
Melopsittacus undulatus

Cockatiel
Nymphicus hollandicus 12½in
Constantly on the move in search of new feeding grounds

Budgerigar
Melopsittacus undulatus 7½in
Huge flocks settle like blossom on water-side trees

Cockatiel
Nymphicus hollandicus

By far the smallest member of the cockatoo family, the Cockatiel averages between 12 and 13 inches long, though most of this is tail – long and graduated with pointed central feathers. Also known as the Quarrion, Crested Parrot or Cockatoo Parrot, this species is distinguished by its long crest and its pleasant chattering calls.

Cockatiels are found throughout the interior of Australia and as far west as the coast. Most types of open country are utilized, but the birds seldom move very far from water and hence are found in great numbers near creeks and waterholes. Apart from a few escaped cage-birds the species has not been recorded in Tasmania.

In the wild they are usually seen in groups, often in very large flocks, constantly on the move in search of food. The seeds of grasses and herbaceous plants form the basis of the bird's diet, but the seeds of acacia trees, grain, fruit and berries are all taken in varying amounts. The flight is swift and direct with strong, regular wing-beats and the birds usually utter a long, warbling call in flight.

Often several Cockatiels nest together, forming a loosely knit colony based on an old tree that provides hollow branches and trunk cavities in which the birds may nest. Each pair will usually lay between four and seven eggs, which are incubated for about 22 days by both adults. The young birds are fed by the parents for about five weeks in the nest, and for several weeks after they have become fully fledged.

Budgerigar
Melopsittacus undulatus

Although domesticated budgerigars are probably the most popular of cage-birds, in parts of Australia it is an offence to keep wild budgerigars in captivity. The budgerigar has the freedom of the skies, and, after plentiful rain, huge flocks of these little birds gather near water in the arid interior, completely covering the trees like blossom,

Soon the flocks split into pairs, busily inspecting the tree-trunks for suitable hollows. The ideal is a little cavity with a floor of wood dust and a knot-hole aperture just big enough to permit entrance. Suitably accommodated, the pairs spend much time in mutual preening. When the eggs are laid, the female incubates and is fed on the nest by her mate.

About a month after the chicks are hatched the family party rejoins the flock, ready to depart in search of fresh supplies of water. In the parched terrain of the interior the need for water is paramount and wild birds will even alight on a human's cupped hands to drink. If the flocks find water, they survive; if not, the birds die in their thousands.

Another great threat are the birds of prey. Falcons and goshawks wait for budgerigar flocks to settle and then dash forward, plucking victims from the panicking horde. Often several species of falcon circle overhead with the less predatory kites waiting at lower levels for birds struck but not carried off.

Even so, such is the resilience of the species and the rapidity with which they exploit good conditions that budgerigar numbers remain constant in the wild.

Wedgetailed Eagle
Aquila audax

The stories told about the Wedge-tailed Eagle are truly incredible. Most of them are, in fact, folk yarns woven round the doings of the Golden Eagle, but even this heavier bird could hardly carry off a bullock! The average wing-span of the Wedgetail is about six feet eight inches, and the weight ranges from six to ten pounds. But the carrying power of this eagle is phenomenal; on one occasion a small wallaby weighing fourteen pounds was lifted and carried some distance.

The Wedgetail builds its stick nest in a tree, often very high and with a commanding view. One or two eggs are laid but usually only one chick survives. The young Wedgetail retains its brown and gold plumage for between four and seven years, contrasting with the black of the adult bird.

Crested Pigeon
Ocyphaps lophotes

With iridescent feathers and prominent crest, the Crested Pigeon is one of the most eye-catching residents of the savanna. Strangely, this is a bird which seems to be proliferating as rapidly as other species are disappearing – probably due to the creation of artificial savanna grassland in the form of grain fields.

The Crested Pigeon has remarkable flying ability. On take-off it gives a few flaps then glides at tremendous speed. When it seems only will-power is keeping it aloft, a few more flaps send it forward again and in this fashion the bird can easily outpace the Little Falcon, *Falco longipennis*.

Like other bronze-winged pigeons, the Crested has a spectacular display in which the iridescent wing feathers play a prominent part.

Emu
Dromaius novaehollandiae

The Emu, largest bird native to Australia, is inferior in size only to the Ostrich among the world's birds. It is common in many habitats but is probably most numerous in savanna grassland. But, since it has been heavily persecuted in some parts of Australia, it is seldom seen near human settlements. Even so, the Emu is extremely curious and can be attracted towards the observer with a waving handkerchief. Often people sitting quietly in the bush have been surprised to see a group of emus walk up and circle a few yards from them, uttering their eerie, bubbling grunts.

Males are smaller than females and the roles of the sexes are largely reversed. Females initiate courtship behaviour, signalled by loud booming and inflated necks. The task of incubating the clutch of six to 12 eggs falls to the male, who also bears the responsibility for looking after, and feeding, the young.

Singing Bushlark
Mirafra javanica

The Singing Bushlark is like a small skylark. Across the north of Australia breeding takes place during and immediately after the summer rainy season. At the onset of rain, the bushlarks take territories and the males spend much of their time in the air above, pouring out their beautiful, rather metallic song. These ground-dwelling birds show a remarkable variation in plumage colour. Those living in areas of red soil have a reddish plumage; those on black soils are dark, and so on throughout the range.

The nest, built on open ground or under a grass tussock, is a neat cup often with a flimsy hood or an entrance to one side.

Wedgetailed Eagle
Aquila audax 40in
Impressive enough without the wild claims of folklore

Crested Pigeon
Ocyphaps lophotes 12½in
One of the few to benefit as man changes the land

Singing Bushlark
Mirafra javanica 6in
Plumage colour varies to blend with the local soil

Emu 72in (height)
Dromaius novaehollandiae
Second only to the Ostrich in size

Mallee Scrub

Mallee vegetation consists of a number of species of dwarf eucalypt, all having many stems growing from an underground bole or woody tuber. Some species, known as Marlocks, have the "lignotuber" reduced. In general, mallees rarely exceed 15 to 20 feet in height. They grow quite densely and have a ground layer of shrubs, or, in drier areas, grasses such as spinifex. A number of birds are endemic to the mallee associations, including the Mallee Emu-wren, Mallee Fowl, Black-winged Currawong and Mallee Honeyeater. In areas where the mallees are associated with a dense undergrowth of shrubs, a tree heath is formed and provides a habitat for such secretive species as the Southern Scrub-robin, Western Whipbird, Fieldwren and Shy Heathwren.

Much of the mallee in wetter areas has been cleared and some birds are now quite rare – the Western Whipbird being just one species that has suffered from the destruction of its habitat. On the other hand, man's interference has indirectly benefited one species, the Yellow-tailed Pardalote, which digs its nesting tunnel in the mounds of earth thrown up along roadside ditches. However, even dry mallee scrub is being cleared and, though conservationists were able to save one such area in the Little Desert of Victoria; rash clearance of scrublands may have far-reaching consequences – not only for the endemic wildlife of the mallee, but also for the millions of migrant nectar feeders that are supported during the spring.

Purple-crowned Lorikeet
Glossopsitta porphyrocephala   6in
Brush-tongued denizen of the flowering eucalypt woodlands

Mallee and mulga

☐ Area of mulga

▨ Area of mallee

Distribution of species

▦ Bourke's Parrot
Neophema bourkii

▤ Mallee Fowl
Leipoa ocellata

Mallee Fowl
Leipoa ocellata   22in
"A remarkable feat of thermal engineering . . ."

Mallee Fowl
Leipoa ocellata

This large ground-dwelling bird is one of Australia's most remarkable species and its nesting habits provide a superb example of the way in which a bird may utilize natural heat-producing processes to incubate its eggs. The Mallee Fowl belongs to a small group of mound-nesting birds called the megapodes, but unlike its forest-dwelling relatives, this species has adapted to arid habitats and, living out in the open, it has also developed cryptic colouring.

A heavy bird, the Mallee Fowl seldom takes to the air, although it does flap clumsily into trees and bushes to roost. During the day it forages for a variety of foods including fruits, insects and plants.

The breeding season lasts from September to April and begins with the birds building up a huge mound, four feet high and up to 14 in diameter, consisting of vegetation covered with loose earth. Sealed under the earth, the vegetable matter rots, producing considerable heat. At intervals of about six days the hen deposits 15 to 24 large white eggs in a hole made in the top of the mound. The male then assumes the main responsibility for the remainder of the incubation period. Testing the temperature of the mound with the sensitive mouth-lining and tongue, he makes constant adjustments – piling on more earth or removing earth and "compost" to expose the egg chamber to the air. The temperature is maintained to within one degree of 92°F and, as the total incubation period lasts for some eight months, this represents a remarkable feat of thermal engineering, unequalled by any other species.

On hatching, the chicks dig their way out of the mound unaided. They are able to fly within a week and receive virtually no help or protection from their parents from the moment they emerge from the mound. As with all ground-nesting birds, losses through predation are high and up to 50 per cent of the eggs laid fail to produce young.

Purple-crowned Lorikeet
Glossopsitta porphyrocephala

The Purple-crowned Lorikeet ranges across southern Australia and is the only member of its family to occur in the southwest. It is a nomadic bird, following the flowering of eucalyptus trees, which, in any one area, have mutually exclusive blooming periods, thus ensuring an almost constant supply of food.

The mallee usually flowers in summer and as the trees are closely packed and heavy with blossom, a rich environment is created for nectar-feeding species. The lorikeets clamber over the trees, robbing the blooms of their nectar with long, brush-tipped tongues. In the feeding process, the plumage becomes matted with nectar and requires constant attention, often including mutual preening by pairs of birds.

The Purple-crowned Lorikeet nests late in the year, timing the arrival of young to coincide with the local availability of blossom. A small patch of bush, well-endowed with suitable hollows, may harbour several pairs, each of which will produce four to six eggs. Incubation, and care and feeding of the young, is shared by both parents.

194

Mulga Scrub

A number of species of acacias, or wattles, principally of the type *A.aneura*, are collectively known as mulgas and form a large and important area of arid low-layered woodland. The mulga habitat consists of low acacia trees with a discontinuous shrub layer and a more or less continuous ground cover of grasses. Many species of birds are endemic to the mulga, including the Cinnamon, Chestnut-breasted and Western Quail-thrushes, Grey Honeyeater, Bourke's Parrot, Slate-backed Thornbill and Banded Whiteface. A large number of birds spend much of their time in the mulga but irrupt into other habitats in dry seasons – a habit common to the White-browed and Masked Woodswallows, Crimson Chats, Pied and Black Honeyeaters.

After rain, the mulga country is an area of great beauty with carpets of white, pink and yellow flowers and flocks of breeding birds. In times of drought it looks like desert but the speed with which it blossoms after rain is truly incredible. Many of the sedentary endemic birds of the mulga, such as the Quail-thrushes and Spotted Nightjar, are equally remarkable in their ability to withstand the harsh extremes of climate, particularly those encountered on stony ridges. One of the most recent bird discoveries in Australia, Hall's Babbler, is resident over about 90,000 square miles of mulga, and yet remained undiscovered until 1964 – lost to view in the vast expanse of this virtually unpopulated area.

Princess Parrot
Polytelis alexandrae

The Princess Parrot makes its home in mulga country, where there is a dense understorey of spinifex or porcupine grass, and also in open spinifex country broken by watercourses lined with eucalypts.

Following the intermittent rains, and the brief burst of seeding and plant growth that attends them, the Princess Parrot is a nomad, ranging widely over the arid interior. Small colonies of birds flock together and nest in close proximity, often as many as a dozen nests being built in a single stream-side tree. While the female incubates her clutch of four to six eggs, the male flies in search of food, carrying seeds back to the nest for the hen.

Bourke's Parrot
Neophema bourkii

Bourke's Parrot is one of the tamest of species in the wild, content to continue feeding within a few yards of an observer. However, the observer himself must be attentive, for the parrot's soft colouring and quiet habits protect it well from the eyes of friendly observers and hunting predators alike. When alarmed, the bird utters a shrill disyllabic note far removed from its normal soft warbling.

Like most arid-land parrots, Bourke's Parrot is nomadic, generally following the rains, but stable colonies may form near permanent watercourses. The female lays her clutch of three to six eggs in a hollow low down in a mulga tree and, during the incubation period, is fed by her mate on the nest or on a nearby branch.

White-browed Wood-swallow
Artamus superciliosus

Most common in mulga country, the White-browed Wood-swallow is also nomadic, moving into open forest areas in the summer months when the mulga environment is harsh. During the winter, the mulga is alive with these attractive little birds. Huge flocks fly so high that they can scarcely be seen and their presence is betrayed only by their clear, cheerful call-notes. Wheeling to the ground, the birds settle in their hundreds on the scattered trees.

Cinnamon Quail-thrush
Cinclosoma cinnamomeum

Members of the ground babbler family, the quail-thrushes have adapted to exploit the uncompromising micro-habitat of stony hillsides – a niche generally shunned by other birds. The Spotted Quail-thrush, *C.punctatum*, occupies this habitat in forest areas, the Chestnut, *C.castanatum*, in dry eucalypt country and the Cinnamon in the desolate mulga regions. Though it may seem that nothing could eke out a living in these barren hills, the Cinnamon Quail-thrush thrives here, drinking only in the brief period after rains and normally taking its water requirements from grasshoppers, caterpillars and moths. When the insects die off in times of drought, this remarkable bird turns to seeds as its main food source.

On a thin bed of dry leaves placed in a natural hollow, the female lays a small clutch of pale buff eggs. Once hatched, the young leave the nest to forage alone.

Bourke's Parrot
Neophema bourkii 7in
The attentive male collects food for the brooding female

Princess Parrot
Polytelis alexandrae 16in
Ranges in small flocks through the arid interior

White-browed Wood-swallow
Artamus superciliosus 8½in
One of Australia's few truly aerial species

Cinnamon Quail-thrush
Cinclosoma cinnamomeum 9in
Adapts its life-style to the most severe conditions

Desert Grassland

Vast areas of the interior of Australia are covered with grasses, often referred to as hummock grassland, adapted to withstand long periods of drought and to exploit brief, erratic showers and storms. The sandy deserts are structurally in the form of vast parallel sand ridges, usually less than a mile apart. The dunes are clothed with hummock grasses; canegrass on the tops of the ridges and spinifex on the slopes. Between the dunes grow saltbush, blue-bush and similar plants. An interesting example of how birds have exploited this harsh environment is illustrated by the grasswrens; two very similar species being easily identified by the way in which they exploit the dunes. The Thick-billed Grasswren lives on the saltbush plains between the sand ridges, while the Dusky Grasswren, with a rather more slender bill, is confined to the spinifex on the slopes. In a confined area the extremely rare Eyrean Grasswren inhabits the canegrass on the crests of the ridges. Spinifex is not confined to the sandy deserts, but clothes even rugged ironstone ranges. A number of birds are adapted to life in the spinifex and have extensive ranges in the desert, for example, the Rufous-crowned Emuwren, Striated Grasswren and Spinifexbird. The Night Parrot is a fascinating bird, never common but now extremely rare – possibly even extinct. However, the grasslands are vast and more than one species, thought to be extinct, has later been rediscovered.
Right: Porcupine grass and low scrub in red sand desert

Striated Grasswren
Amytornis striatus 7in
Most widespread member of ah elusive desert family

Night Parrot 9in
Geopsittacus occidentalis
Recent reports have allayed fears of its extinction

Rufous-crowned Emuwren
Stipiturus ruficeps 5in
A far cry from its namesake

Striated Grasswren
Amytornis striatus

The various grasswrens inhabit some of the most inhospitable parts of Australia. Their shyness and inaccessibility is illustrated by the fact that the Grey Grasswren, *A.barbatus*, was not described until 1968; the Eyrean Grasswren, *A.goyderi*, has been seen only on two occasions; the Black Grasswren, *A.housei*, was considered a lost species until it was rediscovered recently, and the White-throated Grasswren, *A.woodwardii*, is one of only two or three Australian species whose nests have yet to be discovered.

The Striated Grasswren is one of the most widely distributed, although in parts of its range it seems to be disappearing. It is invariably found in association with spinifex or porcupine grass. It is inconspicuous, given away only by its barely audible squeak and musical bubbling song. The domed nest is built in the crown of a spinifex clump of grass lined with plant down. Three eggs are laid. Breeding depends on rainfall and may occur at any time of the year when conditions are right.

Night Parrot
Geopsittacus occidentalis

Among Australian bird-watchers, the Night Parrot, last collected in 1912, has generated its own legend. There are many reports that it has been found, although these usually turn out to refer to Bourke's Parrot.

However, two recent reports of substance suggest that it is premature to declare the Night Parrot extinct. Certainly it is hard to imagine the species dying out, for its range covers millions of acres of the least traversed territory in Australia.

In the desert spinifex there are countless unknown waterholes where the Night Parrots could drink. Possibly their ecology is such that they need water only on the hottest days. The fact that the bird is nocturnal indicates the degree of adaptation to an arid environment. During the heat of summer days it probably rests deep in the spinifex.

Not surprisingly, little is known about the Night Parrot. A terrestrial bird, it can fly well, but usually runs when disturbed.

Rufous-crowned Emuwren
Stipiturus ruficeps

The emuwrens are the lightest Australian birds but with long tails, they measure more than other small species like the Weebill, *Smicrornis* sp, and the Mistletoe Bird, *Dicaeum hirundinaceum*. The unique tail feathers are held in a cocked position. The filamentous structure, rather like that of emu feathers, accounts for the name, although no two birds could be less alike than the emu and the emuwren.

There is some disagreement as to whether there are one, two or three species of emuwren. All three forms are different and occupy different habitats. The Rufous-crowned Emuwren inhabits desert spinifex, particularly stony ridges and sandhills and is one of the most elusive of birds. The nest is a domeshaped structure placed in a spinifex clump. Usually only two eggs are laid. Nesting occurs at any time of the year following rain.

Gibber Desert

Gibbers are rounded stones. In some areas they lie in millions forming huge stony deserts. No habitat on earth can look more desolate yet it supports numbers of birds including one endemic species, the Gibber Chat. Other birds found on the gibber plains have a wider distribution, but have a definite preference for stony ground wherever they occur. Probably the most famous of the gibber deserts is Sturt's Stony Desert, now a National Park, which proved a stumbling block to several early transcontinental expeditions, but the gibbers extend from central Western Australia across northern South Australia into western Queensland and northeastern New South Wales.

Although gibber deserts look so desolate they support a surprising population of insects and lizards. During summer temperatures are extreme and every patch of shade is exploited; exertion is kept to a minimum. In winter the temperature may drop below freezing point at night. When rain comes, the gibber deserts blossom – grasses and flowers grow almost overnight and the birds breed, even if it is the coldest time of the year. Passing flocks of birds such as Crimson Chats or songlarks may stop and feed while the good conditions last. They move on, but the Gibber Chats, Australian Dotterels, Pipits and Australian Pratincoles remain, relying for survival on their exceedingly complex adaptations for limiting the loss of water.

Desert grass and Gibber desert
Area of grass
Area of desert
Distribution of species
Night Parrot
Geopsittacus occidentalis
Gibber Chat
Ashbyia lovensis

Australian Dotterel
Peltohyas australis

Also known as the Inland Dotterel and the Desert Plover, the Australian Dotterel has the perfect colouring for a bird of the arid regions. Mottled dark grey-brown and gold above with white and orange-brown markings and a characteristic black Y-shaped bar across the breast, its colour and pattern blend perfectly with the bare earth and rock of its habitat.

In pairs, or in small flocks of a few dozen individuals, the Australian Dotterel ranges over the arid and semi-arid regions of inland Australia. The birds frequent open plains and the margins of lakes and streams and, like many desert species, are nomadic – constantly moving in search of new feeding grounds in a harsh and relatively unproductive environment. Their main sources of food are seeds and insects – both extremely sensitive to the vagaries of climate and both equally liable to sudden shortages.

The Australian Dotterel's call is a sharp metallic "quick", a distinctive sound that carries well in open country. When at rest, or feeding quietly, the bird has a low soft "kroot" call, probably used to maintain contact within the feeding group.

From April to October the birds breed, laying their eggs in shallow ground depressions with no lining material. Whenever the parent bird leaves the nest, the eggs are carefully covered with a layer of soil or dust that effectively screens the clutch from the eyes of predators and protects the eggs from overheating in the direct glare of the sun.

Gibber Chat
Ashbyia lovensis

The small family of Australian chats, consisting of five species, contains some of the most fascinating and colourful of birds. The Gibber Chat is the most unusual of all, living on the Gibber plains of central Australia. There is some evidence to suggest that at least a few Gibber Chats spend all their lives within a small area, regardless of the severity of the seasons. Some do move about within their arid range, but not so much as the Orange, *Epthianura aurifrons*, and Crimson Chats, *E. tricolor*, both of which are nomadic.

Food consists of insects and seeds gathered while running on the ground. Chats have brush-tipped tongues and some species, notably the Crimson, take nectar, so presumably the Gibber Chat feeds from flowers on the rare occasions when they are available.

On hot days the Gibber Chat shelters in whatever shade is available, even in lizard holes, and is most reluctant to move if disturbed. If it is forced to fly it does so in a lark-like manner, fluttering high then diving back to earth. When running it pauses, pipit fashion, to bob the tail up and down.

Breeding may occur at any time if conditions are suitable. In good seasons more eggs are laid than in poor years. The nest, made of dried grasses and leaves, is placed on the ground, usually in a small depression. Any disturbance by a potential predator provokes a "broken-wing" display.

Australian Dotterel
Peltohyas australis 8in
When the parent is absent, a covering of earth protects the eggs from predators

Gibber Chat
Ashbyia lovensis 5in
Ekes out an existence in Australia's harshest desert

Stage-makers, Gardeners and Avenue-builders

Though many species, including whydahs, ruffs, grouse and lyrebirds, use cleared patches of ground, or arenas, as the focal point of their courtship rituals, only the remarkable bowerbirds of Australia and New Guinea are known to decorate their courting grounds. Promiscuous breeding appears to be a natural corollary of arena and bower behaviour. The male is sexually active throughout the prolonged breeding season and is kept in a state of readiness by his constant attention to the maintenance and decoration of his bower. Similarly, the bower acts as a beacon to receptive females, ensuring that during her brief receptive period, each female will be able to find a willing mate.

The bowers themselves illustrate one aspect of natural selection; the more ornate bowerbirds build relatively simple display structures while less colourful species, like the Gardener and Yellow-breasted Bowerbirds, build extremely elaborate bowers. This ornate courtship ground is also the focal point of each male's territory, and in autumn and winter much of the male's bower activity is probably a symbolic display of territorial defence.

The drive to construct a bower is inherent in the male but juveniles must learn the techniques from adult birds. Early in the year, young males frequent the sites of the mature birds, shifting leaves and twigs about in the owner's absence as they mimic his building activities.

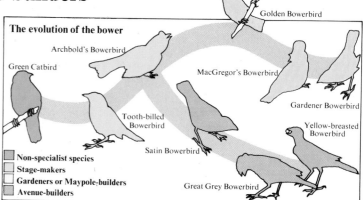

The evolution of the bower

Golden Bowerbird

Archbold's Bowerbird

Green Catbird

MacGregor's Bowerbird

Gardener Bowerbird

Tooth-billed Bowerbird

Yellow-breasted Bowerbird

Satin Bowerbird

Great Grey Bowerbird

■ Non-specialist species
□ Stage-makers
□ Gardeners or Maypole-builders
■ Avenue-builders

Archbold's Bowerbird
Archboldia papuensis 14½in

Green Catbird 14in
Ailuroedus crassirostris

Tooth-billed Bowerbird
Scenopoeetes dentirostris 10½in

Arenas and stages

The two catbirds of the genus *Ailuroedus* build no recognizable display arena and are typically passerine in their nesting habits. The first of the "stage-maker" species, the Tooth-billed Bowerbird, *Scenopoeetes dentirostris*, is thought to be closely related to the catbirds. Like them it has serrated bill-margins but utilizes this adaptation to cut fresh leaves with which to decorate a cleared area of the forest floor. The male displays in his court with a wide variety of loud calls, often copying the calls of his neighbours and developing variations on a basic song. Once a female

has been attracted, and copulation has taken place, the pair separate; the female nests alone in the manner of the more advanced bowerbirds and in marked contrast to the catbirds, who remain together.

Archbold's Bowerbird, *Archboldia papuensis*, is an advanced stage-maker, decorating his five-foot mat of ferns and grasses with shells and beetle wings and festooning nearby branches with ferns and mosses. The male's behaviour is probably very like that of *Scenopoetes*, but the song display is always performed from a perch above the stage. *Archboldia* represents the final development of

the stage – beyond which the bowers become far more complex.

Maypoles and gardens

The Golden Bowerbird, *Prionodura newtoni*, builds a massive bower consisting of heaps of sticks banked, pyramid-fashion, against two adjacent saplings – a prime factor in the bird's choice of site being the presence of a third horizontal branch that serves as a display perch. The bower of this species may be regarded as the first stage in evolution of the complex maypoles of the *Amblyornis* species.

A less complex bower is built by MacGregor's Bowerbird, *A.mac-*

gregoriae, but the bird compensates by means of its beautiful golden-orange crest. Its bower is a simple four-foot tower of twigs placed around a sapling in the centre of a shallow depression. By contrast, the dowdy Gardener Bowerbird, *A. inornatus*, constructs a house. It banks long sticks against a central sapling to form a roof and clears an open space, or garden, at the front in which to display its collection of stones, shells and other ornaments.

The avenue builders

Bowerbirds of the genera *Chlamydera* and *Ptilonorhynchus* show an entirely

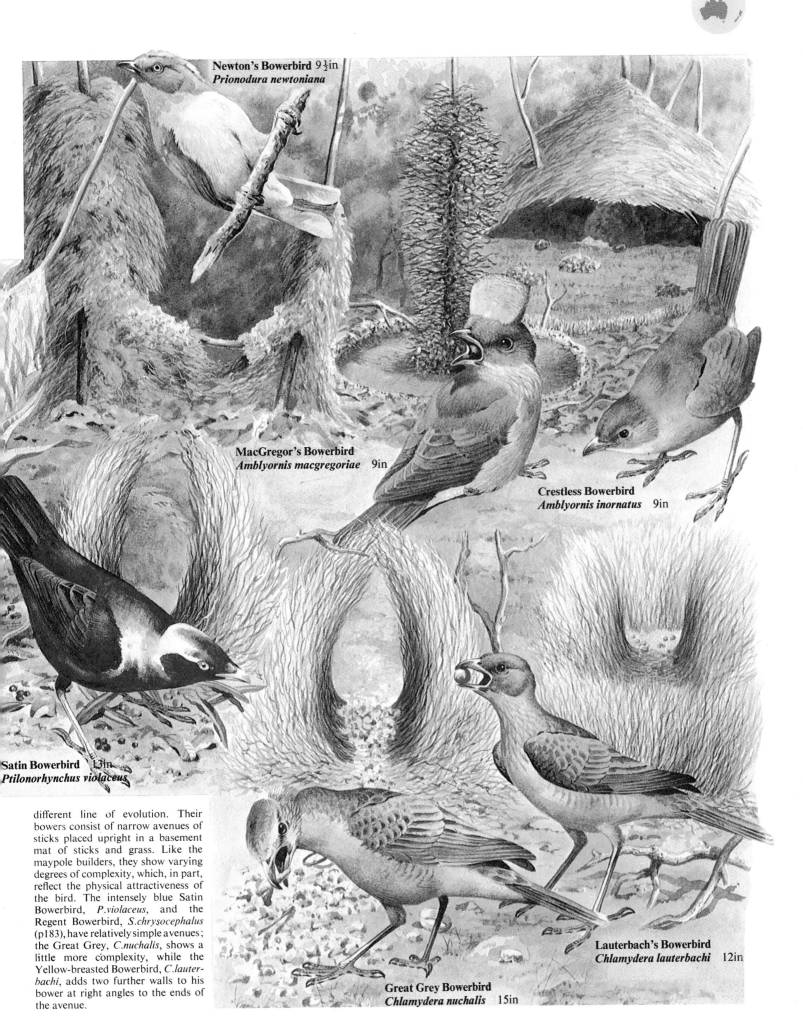

Newton's Bowerbird 9½in
Prionodura newtoniana

MacGregor's Bowerbird
Amblyornis macgregoriae 9in

Crestless Bowerbird
Amblyornis inornatus 9in

Satin Bowerbird 13in
Ptilonorhynchus violaceus

different line of evolution. Their bowers consist of narrow avenues of sticks placed upright in a basement mat of sticks and grass. Like the maypole builders, they show varying degrees of complexity, which, in part, reflect the physical attractiveness of the bird. The intensely blue Satin Bowerbird, *P.violaceus*, and the Regent Bowerbird, *S.chrysocephalus* (p183), have relatively simple avenues; the Great Grey, *C.nuchalis*, shows a little more complexity, while the Yellow-breasted Bowerbird, *C.lauterbachi*, adds two further walls to his bower at right angles to the ends of the avenue.

Lauterbach's Bowerbird
Chlamydera lauterbachi 12in

Great Grey Bowerbird
Chlamydera nuchalis 15in

Marshes and Flood-lakes

Australia is a dry land with deserts inferior in size only to the Sahara, but in the northern and eastern arc from Broome in the northwest to Adelaide in South Australia, for two or three hundred miles from the coast, the country is relatively well watered, and springs, lakes and rivers are abundant. Many are ephemeral, some are salt. All support wildlife, birds in particular. Most of the remainder of the mainland, except the southwest, receives irregular rainfall, or regular rainfall for only a short time each year. Surface water seldom lasts long and is quickly exploited by birds adapted to move vast distances in search of the brief, rich explosions of life that follow rain.

Some of the "wetlands" shown prominently on maps of Australia are dry for most of the time, and many inland rivers, such as the Diamentina and Cooper's Creek, dry up completely for years on end during drought periods. However, many of the rivers flowing into the Darling flow from catchments in the hinterland of the Gulf of Carpentaria to feed fresh-water lakes, such as Dynevor Lake, in arid country. Dynevor supports several large colonies of Black Swans, each numbering hundreds of nesting pairs with an extended breeding period. Silver Gulls and Caspian Terns also nest on islands in the lake while nearby Bullawarra, a small tree-lined oasis on the Buloo river system, supports hundreds of nesting ibis, spoonbills, herons and cormorants.

Right: Magpie Geese and Plumed Egrets; Northern Territory

Wetlands

Major lakes and rivers

Distribution of species

Magpie Goose
Anseranas semipalmata

Black Swan
Cygnus atratus

Spotted Crake
Porzana fluminea

Black Swan
Cygnus atratus

A native of Australia, the Black Swan is smaller than its close relative, the Mute Swan, *C.olor*, but still has an average wing-span of more than six feet. Because of its sombre aspect, black but for the white trailing edges of its wings, it was once thought by countryfolk to be in league with the devil and undoubtedly many Black Swans were killed on the strength of this fear. This may be why the species never became established in the wild in Europe and America. Introduced to these continents in the eighteenth century, it has never become established in the wild.

In Australia distribution is predominantly southern, although vagrants have been recorded throughout the territory wherever conditions are right. The Black Swan's preference is for large, permanent expanses of water, brackish or fresh, but it is also seen on temporarily flooded areas and coastal rivers.

Once thought to be sedentary, the species is now known to be highly mobile. There is no set pattern of migration, but adverse conditions such as drought force the birds into travelling vast distances. There is also some "moult migration". Like other water-fowl, Black Swans lose all their flight feathers at once and, flightless for about a month, they seek safety on large, open waters.

Like the migrations, breeding depends on weather conditions and the availability of suitable habitat. In unfavourable areas, birds respond to any rainfall and nest at almost any

Black Swan
Cygnus atratus 58in
Once persecuted as a "familiar" of the devil

Spotted Crake
Porzana fluminea 8in
This opportunist breeder will exploit briefly flooded claypans

time. If the rains fail, they desert the nests and sometimes do not lay at all (or the young are lost). The nest is a heap of vegetation as much as three feet in diameter and about a foot high. The average clutch size is five to six eggs and both parents incubate.

Spotted Crake
Porzana fluminea

Crakes, which live mainly among reeds, are difficult to see and the average bird-watcher comes across them only by accident, though some species, like the White-browed Crake, *Poliolimnas cinereus*, are noisy and draw attention to themselves. The Spotted Crake is less shy than most and is sometimes seen walking on floating vegetation or in shallow water within easy reach of protective reeds, its long toes well adapted to coping with both tangled reeds and floating weed. It swims well and looks like a diminutive moorhen.

Its food consists mainly of insects and aquatic animals, with some vegetable matter. The bird is reluctant to fly when alarmed, and only does so as a last resort, yet it will fly long distances at night. Spotted Crakes may be found on isolated, newly filled claypans as soon as the grasses are long enough to hide them; they breed quickly and leave with their offspring before the water dries up.

The nest is usually well hidden in reeds, but may be found in the open, built on a partly submerged samphire bush. The sitting bird pulls nearby grasses over the cup-shaped nest to give added protection. Four to six

eggs are laid, dark olive in colour with darker spots. The small, dark chicks leave the nest as soon as they are dry and are immediately able to swim.

Magpie Goose
Anseranas semipalmata

The Magpie Goose is one of those fascinating birds which causes endless controversy and speculation. Is it swan, goose or duck? Or does it deserve its own separate status? It does not fit precisely into any other group of water-fowl: its feet are only partly webbed; it can fly throughout the moult period; it perches and roosts in trees; it has a large knob on the forehead, and it has abnormally long legs.

The Magpie Goose is a bird of the marshes and swamps, feeding in shallow water while wading or by up-ending in deep water; it also grazes to some extent. Large numbers occur across the north, but in the south-east the species has almost entirely disappeared. Due to a tendency in the dry season to congregate in any location where water is available, flocks sometimes cause damage to irrigated crops such as rice and sorghum. Many small waterholes used by Magpie Geese in the dry season are being destroyed by the increasing herds of introduced water-buffalo.

With the onset of the wet season, sprouting grasses in the water trigger breeding behaviour. Grasses are flattened to make a foundation for the nest, a heap of swamp plants, in which a clutch of six to ten white eggs is laid.

Brolga
Grus rubicunda 46in

Magpie Goose
Anseranas semipalmata 34in
Swan, goose or duck?

The dancing cranes

The graceful dances of the Brolga, *Grus rubicunda*, although not so different from those of other cranes, have captured the imagination of its admirers. The agility and elegance of the ritual have inspired stories and corroborees among the Aboriginals, and bird-watchers come from far and wide to areas such as the Townsville Common, where the Brolgas congregate, in the hope of seeing them in action.

Superficially like the more widely spread Sarus Crane (p176), the Brolga was thought to be merely a race of that bird until both were found breeding recently in northern Australia. The most obvious difference between the two species is the more extensive red area on the head of the Sarus.

Brolgas frequent marshes on the margins of fresh and brackish water, even in arid areas; their preference is for damp and irrigated pastures. They gather in large flocks, particularly on marshes where their favourite food, the subterranean tuber of bulburu sedge, is abundant.

Before becoming airborne, the Brolga runs into the wind for some distance. The sight of a take-off run often triggers nearby birds into following suit, and a whole flock may find itself airborne on the whim of one bird. Certain predators trigger flight; the White-breasted Sea Eagle, *Haliaeetus leucogaster*, is the most feared, yet the larger Wedge-tailed Eagle, *Aquila audax*, is ignored.

The nest, a large platform of grass and sticks, is placed on the ground, usually in some marshy location, although it may be a long way from water; even a flattened spinifex bush may be used.

Courtship dance of the Brolga Crane

A recurring theme in many traditional Aboriginal dances

The Urban Landscape

In ecological terms the urban environment, seen through the eyes of a bird, may vary from near-desert to the equal of some of the richest scrub or wooded savanna. Particularly in those areas where plots are large, with abundant shrubs and trees, ample near-natural nesting sites and feeding areas are available. Newer, unvegetated plots, and completely controlled areas, such as parks and swimming-pool areas, may often be less attractive to birds. Add to these urban opportunities the abundant and varied nesting sites afforded by the overhanging eaves of buildings, and the artificial nesting boxes placed in gardens; add also the foodstuffs put out by benevolent housewives (particularly in winter, when flocking species like the Pied Currawong descend on the towns in hoards) and a very rich habitat emerges.

Clearly the hazards in the urban environment are also greater than in the wild. Nest disturbance is a common feature and the toll of adults and young alike may be very high. Domestic livestock such as dogs and cats are a constant threat to nesting birds, as are man's less welcome commensals – rats. Natural predators, particularly birds of prey, are generally less common in towns than in the wild, the bulk of the urban bird population usually being made up of the more adaptable, smaller seed- and insect-eaters. Water-birds are also common colonists of man-made waterways and are a familiar sight in parks and ornamental gardens.

Superb Blue Wren
Malurus cyaneus 5in
The male returns to a non-descript brown at the close of the mating season

Magpie Lark
Grallina cyanoleuca 11in
So aggressive it will fiercely attack its own reflection

Superb Blue Wren
Malurus cyaneus

Classified either as Australian Wrens or as Old World Warblers, the blue wrens are a widespread family many of which are far more brilliantly coloured than the Superb Blue Wren.

Most of the family, however, are shy by nature and quickly retreat in the face of advancing civilization, but the Superb Blue Wren is tolerant of man and is common in gardens of the southeastern towns and cities wherever shrubs are plentiful.

M.cyaneus is usually seen in pairs or in groups of six or seven, each group usually having one brightly coloured male; other males may be in eclipse plumage.

The dome-shaped nest is built in dense shrubbery or tussock grass. Two spotted, pale pink eggs are laid and incubated by one of the hens. The sitting female may leave the nest to receive food from the others and is immediately recognizable by her bent tail.

Magpie Lark
Grallina cyanoleuca

One of Australia's most common birds, the adaptable Magpie Lark is found in all habitats except rainforest and true desert. Even in arid country it may be seen alongside watercourses and near boreholes. It is a common resident in towns and cities, where it feeds, like a wagtail, on lawns and ornamental gardens. Pugnacious by nature, the Magpie Lark will often attack its own reflection in a window or car hub-cap, thinking that an intruder has encroached on its territory.

Its unusual nest of mud strengthened with grass stems is attached to a horizontal branch. The breeding season varies with locality; in the north it is dependent on the rains and nesting usually occurs between January and May. In inland areas the birds will nest whenever mud is available, while the southern populations generally nest in spring and summer. Once the three or four young are fledged, the family splits up. The juveniles form flocks and feed in pastoral country, but the adult birds tend to remain in their home territory.

Willy Wagtail
Rhipidura leucophrys

The Willy Wagtail is a ubiquitous resident of parks and gardens and one of Australia's most popular birds. Completely fearless, it will attack cats, dogs, snakes and lizards and will even alight on the back of an eagle if its nest or territory are threatened.

Each adult pair is sedentary and maintains a territory throughout the year, often raising as many as four broods. The juveniles are driven from the home territory as soon as they are fledged and join the migrating flocks that spend the autumn and winter months in the brigalow scrublands.

Spiders, a favourite food, are taken in a direct flight through the web. To remove the clinging strands, the bird then wipes its head across a branch giving a significant clue to the origin of its nest type – a neatly woven cup of grass and cobwebs. The head-wiping action is identical to the nest-making movements.

Pied Currawong
Strepera graculina

The Pied Currawong is a bird of many names; two are derived directly from its cries, "curra-wa, curra-wong" giving the most commonly used name, while the protracted "chilla-wong" cry is rendered as the name Chillawong. The bird's natural habitat of forest and scrubland, ranging from lowland to mountain, has also given rise to alternative names, among them the Mountain Magpie and Scrub Magpie.

The birds spend much of their time in pairs but, outside the breeding season, and particularly in the colder months of the year, may congregate into huge flocks, descending on the towns and cities of eastern Australia in search of extra food. They are omnivorous feeders, taking seeds, fruit and insects and preying on the eggs and nestlings of many other species. Though attractive and at times impressive in hill country, the Pied Currawong is branded a pest in areas of fruit growing and poultry farming where the flocks may do extensive damage.

Crimson Rosella
Platycercus elegans

In the vulnerable period of the nesting season, the brilliantly coloured Crimson Rosella avoids the attentions of many native predators by nesting in the protection of tree-holes. A natural cavity is chosen and enlarged where necessary, but the nest is unlined and the clutch of between five and eight eggs is laid on the bed of wood dust at the bottom of the cavity. The young are further protected by cryptic colouring and the predominant dark green of the juvenile plumage blends with the surroundings in the dim light of the bird's forest habitat.

Ranging over much of south-eastern Australia, the Crimson Rosella inhabits dense forest, scrubland and open woodland. It feeds mainly at ground level, picking the seeds of grasses and other plants from the forest litter; it also takes fruit and berries from bushes. Like many fruit- and seed-eating species the bird may become a pest in fruit-growing areas but its depradations are partly balanced by its useful predation on damaging scale insects.

An interesting relationship may exist between the Crimson Rosella and the Tasmanian Rosella *P.caledonicus*. The adult plumage of *P.caledonicus* is very like the immature plumage of the Crimson Rosella and its has been suggested that the island form may originally have been *P.elegans* but that the adult plumage colour has been lost in the course of evolution.

Yellow-tailed Thornbill
Acanthiza chrysorrhoa

When flushed from the cover of its woodland habitat the Yellow-tailed Thornbill, or Tomtit, flies only a short distance before coming to ground to carry on feeding on insects, grubs and larvae picked from the ground vegetation and leaf litter of the forest floor.

Its nest is one of the most curious of all Australia's woodland birds. Built into the dense foliage in the crown of a tree, or in the bushy extremity of a drooping bough, the nest has a double-chambered construction. The main structure, of dry grasses, stems and fibres, matted together with cobweb, is dome-shaped and has a narrow side entrance. This chamber is warmly lined with hair, wool and feathers and is the main nesting chamber for the female and her clutch of three or four speckled, off-white eggs. The nest is surmounted by a second cup-like structure which may be a roosting perch for the male but may equally well be of no functional significance.

Pied Currawong
Strepera graculina   18in
A bird of many names

Crimson Rosella
Platycercus elegans   13in
*A safe retreat in
a hollow tree*

Willy Wagtail
Rhipidura leucophrys   8½in
*The juveniles are ruthlessly
evicted as soon as they are fledged*

Yellow-tailed Thornbill
Acanthiza chrysorrhoa   4in
*Its curious nest has an
unexplained upper storey*

New Guinea

New Guinea is separated from Queensland only by the 100-mile-wide Torres Strait, but this narrow water barrier has effectively prevented some of the most fabulous birds known to man from entering and establishing themselves in the mainland forests of Australia. An island in name, but considered by many to be a minor continent in its own right, New Guinea is clothed in some of the most magnificent tropical rain-forests in the southern hemisphere. The knife-edged ridge, reaching 15,000 feet in places, that forms the spine of the island, is largely tree clad and covered at higher levels with Alpine tundra vegetation, varied by many unique relict plants. The mountain ridges are extremely steep and deeply dissected by hidden valleys, many of which have rarely – if ever – been trodden by man. The shoulders of the ridges are densely covered with montane rain-forests, dominated by the *Nothofagus* beech at high altitudes, and by oak below, merging imperceptibly into the steaming splendour of the lowland rain-forest of the coastal belt beyond which the coastline itself is hidden by tangled mangrove swamps. Creepers and epiphytic plants, including many ferns and bromeliads, are abundant, as are some very curious relict plant species such as the *Araucaria* and *Drimys*. High temperature and humidity encourages vast insect populations which, with the lush fruits, provide a veritable cornucopia for feeding birds.

Right: Rain-forest canopy in tropical New Guinea

Papuan Hawk Owl
Uroglaux dimorpha   11in
*Rare nocturnal hunter
of the New Guinea forests*

Black-mantled Goshawk
Accipiter melanochlamys   14in
A specialist in ambush tactics

Papuan Hawk Owl
Uroglaux dimorpha

Considering how difficult daylight bird-watching is in parts of New Guinea, it is not surprising that the problems of making observations by night, particularly of forest species, are almost insurmountable. It is for this reason that night birds offer a new and unexplored field of study.

The main groups of night birds inhabiting New Guinea are nightjars, owlet-nightjars, frogmouths and owls. All the Australian owls (except the Powerful Owl) occur also in New Guinea. In addition, there are two endemic owls as well as the little Papuan Scops Owl that occurs only on Biak Island.

The Papuan Hawk Owl is rare, an intriguing bird quite unlike other owls. The small head and long tail lend it a hawk-like aspect, and the unusual combination of horizontally barred back and vertically streaked front give it the specific name of *dimorpha*. It feeds on insects and rodents, but nothing is known of its breeding behaviour.

Black-mantled Goshawk
Accipiter melanochlamys

At one time goshawks and sparrow-hawks were placed in separate genera. Now they are merged into one large genus, *Accipiter*. There is a basic similarity between them: most have piercing yellow eyes and long, powerful yellow legs with black talons; the wings are rounded and the tail is long, allowing the bird to explode from a perch in a short, furious dash in pursuit of a fleeing victim.

In general, the hunting method is ambush and the whole nature of the bird is geared to this. A typical example, the Black-mantled Goshawk, flies to a concealed perch near a waterhole or feeding place. At its approach, birds scatter and go into hiding, through some of the more pugnacious species harass the hawk for a while. The predator then waits, often perching on one leg, until the panic abates and the birds continue feeding. Soon they forget the hawk is there. Then it dashes among them and, singling one out, follows it until it can reach out a long leg and snatch the victim in flight.

New Guinea could be described as the home of the Accipiter, for eight species occur here. Among these are some remarkable birds: Burger's Goshawk, *A.buergersi*, is a large, rather primitive form with massive legs; the Variable Goshawk, *A.novaehollandiae*, has colour phases ranging from pure white to dark grey with an apricot breast, and the Black-mantled appears closely allied to the Variable.

In most countries Accipiter species do not actively compete with each other. They are nicely graduated in size so that each plunders a different larder; even males and females of the same species, different in size, have varying requirements.

Victoria Crowned Pigeon
Goura victoria

New Guinea, with 44 species, has more than its fair share of the world's 300 species of pigeon. With its vast areas of forest graded by altitude and divided by mountain ranges, the environment is ideal for these colourful fruit-eating birds.

Many pigeons are well hidden among the foliage and fruits where they feed, but, as a ground feeder, the Crowned Pigeon is conspicuous. When disturbed, it flies heavily up to perch on a horizontal branch – a habit well known to hunters in the heyday of the plume trade.

Food consists of fallen fruits gathered while walking in small parties of five to ten birds. The habits of the three species are much the same, but as they occupy different geographical ranges there is no competition. The Common Crowned Pigeon, *G.cristata*, inhabits lowland forest in western Papua; Sheepmaker's Crowned Pigeon, *G.scheepmakeri*, occurs in southern New Guinea, and the Victoria Crowned Pigeon is found in northern New Guinea.

The nest is a large, flat structure of sticks, leaves and stems on a horizontal forked branch at heights up to 50 feet. Only one egg is laid.

Threatened survivor

The curious Kagu, *Rhynochetos jubatus*, of New Caledonia is the sole member of its family. A primitive heron-like bird, it was initially thought to be related to the herons, but current theories place it in the same group as the finfoots and sunbitterns of South America though the relationship remains obscure.

Once widespread throughout the forests of New Caledonia, several factors have led to the Kagu's decline. Pigs, dogs, cats and rats introduced by settlers (Melanesians initially, followed by white settlers in the mid-nineteenth century) have preyed on the Kagu and also competed fiercely and successfully for the available food. Lumbering, mining and forest clearance have forced the birds to retreat ever farther into the inaccessible montane areas, while a long history of hunting, mainly for the bird's attractive plumes, has added its toll. The Kagu is now fully protected by law, but whether or not the weakened population will survive, only time will tell.

The Kagu is largely nocturnal in habit and spends the greater part of its time on the ground, alternately running swiftly forward and then pausing motionless as it forages for worms, grubs and insects. Its short, rounded wings are apparently rather ineffectual and the bird very seldom takes to the air. The wings are, however, used extensively in various displays but, surprisingly, this fascinating bird has not yet been fully investigated and little is known of its breeding habits or behaviour. Some authorities are even doubtful of its nocturnal habit, though the bird is certainly at its most vociferous in the hours of darkness, shattering the quiet with its harsh calls.

New Caledonia

Kagu
Rhynochetos jubatus   23in

Victoria Crowned Pigeon
Goura victoria   33in
Once persecuted for its magnificent plumes

New Guinea
Distribution of species

◻ Blue Crowned Pigeon
Goura cristata

◼ Sheepmaker's Crowned Pigeon
G.scheepmakeri

◼ Victoria Crowned Pigeon
G. victoria

Paradise Island

Spectacular even in the extravagant company of New Guinea's other birds, the birds of paradise represent one of nature's most stunning examples of functional beauty, for the elaborate plumage of the males and the displays that show them off are a crucial part of courtship. The polygamous behaviour of many birds of paradise often leads to birds mating outside their own species and producing hybrid offspring. To prevent hybridization within their family, birds of paradise show a bewildering variety of form, colour and behaviour. An iridescent black is the commonest plumage shade, but few other generalizations are possible. Three-foot long tails, iridescent feather fans, plume-tufted flanks and long "wires" hanging from the neck are all instances of the need to be recognizably different. The form of the display also preserves distinctions between the species; some birds display from trees, others use an arena on the forest floor, some perform complex and energetic routines, while others employ more subdued tactics to woo their mates.

For human observers, however, pride of place among the birds of New Guinea must belong to the seven magnificent *Paradisaea* species. Since their discovery more than 450 years ago, their plumes have commanded high prices, but, while their numbers could absorb the pressures of primitive hunting, the advent of modern firearms has introduced a new and more serious threat to their continued safety.

King of Saxony Bird of Paradise
Pteridophora alberti   8in
*One of five species hunted to
the verge of extinction for their
magnificent feathers*

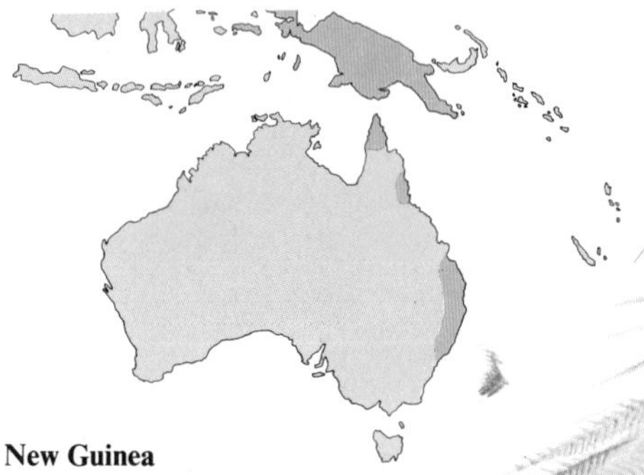

New Guinea
Distribution of Birds of Paradise

Greater Bird of Paradise
Paradisaea apoda   18in
*An amusing misnomer born
out of ignorance*

Magnificent Riflebird
Ptiloris magnificus 13in
*A sombre aspect until caught
by the rays of the sun*

King of Saxony Bird of Paradise
Pteridophora alberti

Although the export trade in plumes was banned in 1924, illicit hunting continues and, combined with the pressures created by the destruction of forest habitat, has brought five members of the family Paradisaeidae to the point of threatened extinction. The range of "Kiss-saa-baa", the native name derived from the bird's loud sibilant call, extends from the Snow Mountains to the Central Highlands of New Guinea. The three races, distinguished by variations in the females' underparts, inhabit the middle and upper cloud forest between 4,800 and 7,800 feet.

Each male chooses a display perch, normally a dead branch above, or a pliant young branch below, the main canopy, and situated at least 400 yards from the nearest rival male. Bouncing his perch up and down, the male opens and closes the cape on his back while bringing the two 15-inch head plumes forward in an elegant bow towards the approaching female.

Greater Bird of Paradise
Paradisaea apoda

For many Europeans this species made a bizarre and misleading introduction to the birds of paradise. Prepared by native traders, the original specimens arrived without wings or legs (hence the specific name *apoda*) prompting a belief that the birds never landed but were kept permanently aloft by their plumes.

The Greater Bird of Paradise inhabits lowland forest on the Aru Islands and southern New Guinea, interbreeding with the Raggiana Bird of Paradise where their ranges overlap.

The elegant plumes characteristic of *Paradisaea* males are long, lacy specialized feathers growing from the sides of the upper breast and protruding between body and wing to hang down over the back and tail. The two central feathers are elongated into "wires" that vary in form from species to species. The plumes of the Greater Bird of Paradise may be 20 inches and the wires 30 inches long – both far exceeding the bird's body length.

During display, perhaps 20 males will gather in one tree, hopping on their perches and posturing momentarily with wings open, backs bent and plumes erect. When a female arrives, the males freeze in the display posture while she selects a mate. Beyond the fact that two streaked, brown-buff eggs are laid, nothing is known of their breeding and nesting.

Magnificent Riflebird
Ptiloris magnificus

The loud cry of the Magnificent Riflebird is usually the first clue to its presence high in the canopy. Climbing with great agility it clings to trunks and branches, probing under the bark for spiders and insects, or among the foliage for fruit. In shadow, the male appears black but direct sunlight sends bursts of brilliant turquoise and purple from the iridescent patches on the crown, throat and tail.

The male selects a favourite perch from which to make his solitary display. The wings, which rustle harshly in flight, are fully extended and the head stretched upwards to show off the colourful throat gorget. The black plumes on the flanks, inconspicuous at other times, are spread wide. The male is polygamous and may mate with several females, each one of which will build her own nest without help from the male. The cup-shaped nest of rootlets and leaves is often decorated with fragments of snakeskin, paper, bark and dried leaves. Two eggs are usually laid, cream in colour and longitudinally streaked with grey and brown.

Princess Stephania Bird of Paradise
Astrapia stephaniae

The Princess Stephania Bird of Paradise inhabits the dense forests of the eastern highlands between 5,000 and 9,000 feet, subsisting on fruit gathered in the upper reaches of the canopy. Like many other species it has suffered greatly from hunting pressures and may be in danger of extinction. The 24-inch tail plumes are much sought after by tribesmen of the highlands, whose head-dresses are among the most ornate in the world.

Although their plumage rustles audibly in flight, the *Astrapias* are quiet birds adding little to the general cacophony of the forest. Their display is also subdued and static, performed high on a branch in the canopy. The tail hangs in a long inverted vee as the wings are raised and the head craned forward. One pale brown egg is laid in a cup-shaped nest of leaves and creepers placed high above the forest floor.

The Ribbon-tailed Bird of Paradise, *A.mayeri*, is restricted to one small forest zone between 8,000 and 10,000 feet and, where the two birds coincide, hybridization is common.

Princess Stephania Bird of Paradise
Astrapia stephaniae 32in
*Quiet and subdued by comparison
with many of its relatives*

New Zealand : 1

The two major land masses and their adjacent islands that constitute New Zealand stretch approximately northeast-southwest and span some 12 degrees of latitude. Compressed into this (in global terms) small area is a tremendous variety of landforms and associated environments suitable for birds. From tip to tip the climate may be described as equable and mild, though this description must apply only to lowland regions. Both the North and South Islands have mountain ranges and those of the South Island carry glaciers in the upland valleys and permanent snowfields on the summits. The South Island mountains form a long ridge running parallel to the west coast and, with the prevailing westerly wind systems, receive a far higher annual rainfall than the eastern parts of the island.

Astonishingly, even the nearby mainland mass of Australia has had little effect on the plant and animal population of New Zealand. There could be no clearer indication of the extent of New Zealand's isolation as, in terms of habitat alone, the islands would appear to have all the opportunities necessary to support a well-diversified fauna. Additionally, the obvious success of many introduced European species of animals and birds, and the more recent colonists from Australia, indicates that suitable niches are abundantly available.

Right: Mount Cook National Park, South Island, New Zealand

New Zealand

Distribution of species

- ● Kakapo
  Strigops habroptilus
- ☐ Kea
  Nestor notabilis
- ▢ Rifleman
  Acanthisitta chloris

Kakapo

Strigops habroptilus 25in
A species in decline, even before the arrival of man

Kakapo
Strigops habroptilus

It is easy to attribute the decline of disappearing species to the impact of man on the landscape, and often the criticism is justified; the rats, cats and dogs released by man have damaged many environments and, in New Zealand, weasels and deer have also placed pressures of competition on native fauna. Some species, however, were in decline even before man's arrival on the scene and it is likely that the range of the Kakapo has been shrinking for several hundred years. It disappeared from the Chatham Islands about 150 years ago and the last sighting on the North Island was in 1927. By surrendering the use of its wings in a mild and predator-free environment the Kakapo was bound to suffer an acceleration of its decline on man's arrival. The only known population remaining inhabits the Cleddau watershed in Fjordland on the South Island.

The primary habitat requirements of this curious ground-dwelling parrot are beech forest with nearby grassland or sub-Alpine scrub and snow meadow. During the day, the birds shelter among overhanging vegetation or rock, moving out to feed at night on blades of tussock grass, ferns, mosses and berries. In the past they used well-worn paths to their feeding grounds – scampering down the hillsides with great agility or alternately hopping and gliding.

Fernbird
Bowdleria punctata

The diminutive Fernbird, charac-terized by the peculiar ragged appear-ance of its tail feathers, inhabits swamp and marshy areas throughout New Zealand from sea level up to 3,000 feet. Although widespread, it is nevertheless very localized and while forest clearance has temporarily boosted its range in some localities, as scrub vegetation and ferns have replaced the forest growth, the reclamation of marginal land for agriculture and housing has destroyed much of its natural habitat.

The Fernbird is represented by a number of sub-species both on the mainland and on outlying islands. The Snares Island sub-species departs from the shy habits of its relatives and spends much of its time in the open – often feeding in penguin col-onies and in open forest.

Both male and female take part in building a neatly woven cup-nest of dry grass and rushes, placing it deep among sedges and rushes where it is well protected from the elements. The nest is so thickly lined with feathers that the clutch of two or three white eggs may be barely visible. The young hatch after $12\frac{1}{2}$ days' incubation and are fed on moths, grubs and cater-pillars until fully fledged.

Kea
Nestor notabilis

Among the many cases of conflict between man's pastoral interests and native wildlife, the Kea's story is, alas, but one of many. Based on isolated instances and circumstantial evidence, the Kea was branded an inveterate sheep-killer and, for many years, was the victim of a widespread and determined eradication campaign. Keas certainly feed on carrion and, like the majority of scavenging

Kea
Nestor notabilis 18in
An undeserved reputation brought this mountain parrot to the brink of extinction

Fernbird
Bowdleria punctata 7in
Forced to retreat as the marshlands are reclaimed

New Zealand Pigeon
Hemiphaga novaeseelandiae 20in
Adaptable feeding habits have aided its recovery

species, will often hasten the end of a sick or injured animal, but it is scarcely credible that the bird could kill a healthy mature sheep.

The Kea is a large olive green parrot restricted to the mountainous areas of the South Island though it will move down into forested montane valleys, and even out on to open river flats, in order to feed. In appearance it is very like the closely related forest-dwelling Kaka, *N.meridionalis*. Both have similar colouring with scarlet underwing patches, but the Kaka is distinguished by its scarlet abdomen. The Kea's prime habitat is the Alpine grassland and sub-Alpine scrub found at high altitude, and it is the only parrot in the world to be found at the snow-line.

The birds breed between July and January with a peak of activity in October. Two to four white eggs are laid in a hole at ground level, beneath a pile of fallen rocks, or inside a hollow log.

New Zealand Pigeon
Hemiphaga novaeseelandiae

This large and beautifully plumaged forest-dwelling pigeon is a member of the fruit-pigeon sub-family. Native fruits, flowers and young leaves form the bulk of its diet but it has also developed a taste for several introduced species, including clover, holly and rowan. In the past, shooting and forest clearance have caused serious diminution of its numbers, but protective measures, and its acceptance of exotic food-species, have allowed the bird to recover over much of its range, though the Chatham Island subspecies appears to be in danger of extinction.

On the mainland, the New Zealand Pigeon nests high in a tree, but the island sub-species more commonly nest near the ground. Thin twigs are used to construct a shallow cup for the single white egg, and, though both parents share the incubation, the female appears to shoulder the main responsibility. The chick remains at the nest for six to seven weeks and a second brood may be undertaken once the fledgling has become independent.

Rifleman
Acanthisitta chloris

One of the four families endemic to the isolated islands of New Zealand contains four oddly proportioned birds known collectively as the New Zealand Wrens. The Stephen Island species, *Xenicus lyalli*, is now extinct – the total population having been wiped out by the lighthouse-keeper's cat within months of the bird's discovery in 1894. The Bush Wren, *X.longipes*, is a rare and little-known insectivorous species feeding mainly among the outer leaves of trees, and the Rock Wren, *X.gilviventris*, lives on fruit and insects in the sub-Alpine scrub of the mountains, feeding at ground level and building its bulky nest in a rock cavity.

The Rifleman is more common than its relatives. Running about tree-trunks and branches, it hunts for spiders and insects, rapidly flicking open its wings to flush its prey from the bark or from hanging fronds of moss. Its large nest is placed behind a peeling slab of bark or in a hollow branch and the four or five young of the first brood sometimes assist the parents in raising a second brood.

Rifleman
Acanthisitta chloris 3in
The most common of New Zealand's rare diminutive wrens

New Zealand : 2

In recent geological ages gigantism has been a marked feature of New Zealand's avifauna – the huge moas of the family Dinorthidae reaching a maximum size of 12 feet in height. But the catalogue of New Zealand's curious residents does not end with the extinct species. The present-day Acanthisittidae, the bushwrens, are primitive passerine birds; the Kiwis are relics of a bygone age; genera like *Callaeas*, the wattlebirds, are endemic to the islands and are very difficult to classify, while the Kea and Kakapo are parrots unique to the islands of New Zealand.

The North Island has an element of tropical lushness enhanced by active volcanic vents, hot springs and bubbling mud pools. The fringing forests are mainly of *Nothofagus* beech with a wide variety of tree-ferns, epiphytes and podocarps (New Zealand yews). The northwest is extensively clothed in heathland varied with scattered marshes. The South Island, cooler in climate and divided by a mountainous spine, offers many contrasts. Much of the southwest is barely explored and largely inaccessible without air support. The mountains themselves are deeply dissected by rushing torrents that feed upland marshes – the favoured haunt of the Takahe. The eastern parts of the island, in part covered by mixed temperate woodland, have been cleared of much of their native cover of woodland and tussock grassland in order to make way for sheep rearing.

Tui
Prosthemadera novaeseelandiae

The three species of honeyeater that inhabit New Zealand are probably the descendants of vagrants carried to the islands, by winds, in the distant past.

Of the three, the Tui is the most spectacular in behaviour and appearance. It is an active and vigorous bird with remarkable aerobatic abilities and a talent for mimicry. One of New Zealand's most accomplished songsters, it has an extensive repertoire of calls and songs including a "whisper" song in which, apparently for its own amusement, it quietly recreates the songs of other forest residents. Another of its songs rises far above the limit of human hearing.

The Tui's food consists mainly of nectar, collected from flowers with the brush-like tip of the tongue, and of fruits, berries and insects. Its nest is a bulky, cup-shaped structure of sticks and twigs lined with grasses and moss. The female incubates the clutch of two to four eggs for about 14 days, relieving the monotony with frequent snatches of song.

Takahe
Notornis mantelli

If the story of the Stephen Island Wren (p209) is a conservationist's nightmare, that of the Takahe must be a dream. The Wren became extinct almost before it was known to science; the Takahe was thought to be extinct long before the first live specimens were found. Sub-fossil bones were described as *Notornis* early in the nineteenth century; later four live specimens were discovered (between 1849 and 1898), but when no further specimens were found, the bird was declared extinct. In 1948 it was rediscovered on the shores of Lake Orbell and the present population in the tussock grassland of the Musgrave and Kepler Ranges is jealously guarded.

A large, flightless swamphen, or gallinule, the Takahe was once widespread on both the North and South Islands. Probably environmental changes brought about by climatic fluctuations were the basic cause of its decline, but the predations of the early Maori settlers took a heavy toll.

Tui
Prosthemadera novaeseelandiae 12½in
Mimics its neighbours in a curious "whisper song"

Kokako
Callaeas cinerea 15in
Surviving relative of New Zealand's most remarkable bird

Takahe
Notornis mantelli 25in
"*Extinct*" . . . *until rediscovered on
the shores of a mountain lake*

Survivor from a bygone age

The Brown Kiwi, *A.australis*, is the most common and widespread of the three species and is the lone survivor on the North Island. It inhabits forest areas and despite its adaptability, it has withdrawn from areas of clearance. Its three sub-species have been successfully introduced to offshore islands where they are safe from predators.

The Little Spotted Kiwi, *A.oweni*, also successfully established on offshore islands, is confined to western districts of the South Island, but inhabited the North Island as recently as 1875. It is easily identified by its small size and its "spots" – due to banding and mottling of the feathers. The Great Spotted Kiwi, *A.haasti*, has not been so greatly affected by settlement as the others and may even be expanding its range through the forests of the South Island.

Breeding takes place between July and February and, though little is known of the nesting habits of the spotted species, statistics for the Brown Kiwi are impressive. The egg weighs about one pound – representing almost 25 per cent of the adult's body weight – and is incubated for 75 to 80 days by the male, who may sit for periods of a week without leaving the burrow. Once the egg is hatched, the female may re-lay, leaving her mate to incubate while she cares for the nestling.

New Zealand's primeval isolation, wide variety of habitats and dearth of native mammals allowed many bird species the freedom to occupy niches more usually filled by mammals. Free from predators, many birds relinquished the power of flight and attained huge proportions. The most prodigious were the twenty or so species of moa, ranging from the size of a turkey to giants standing 12 feet tall. Like many isolated creatures, the moas were vulnerable to any drastic change and, in the company of 20 other species, they became extinct some 700 years ago. Curiously, the three species of Kiwi, *Apteryx spp*, have survived, even though they are flightless, probably of the same stock as the moas, and presumably just as vulnerable. Despite their solid bone structure and vestigial wings, there is a good deal of evidence to suggest that the Kiwi probably could fly, many millions of years ago.

During the day, the Kiwi rests in a well-protected labrynthine burrow excavated beneath tree roots. Emerging to feed at night, it compensates to some extent for its poor eyesight by using sensitive tactile bristles about the base of the bill. Waddling through the undergrowth, it uses these bristles, and the nostrils – uniquely positioned at the tip of the bill – to search for worms and insects in the forest-floor leaf-litter.

Kokako
Callaeas cinerea

The three birds that make up the endemic family of New Zealand wattle-birds share few obvious characteristics beyond the wattle of coloured flesh at the base of the bill and the dense feathering between the eye and the bill. As a group, they have not fared well since the arrival of man; one is presumed to be extinct while the others have drastically reduced ranges.

The blue wattled Kokako still exists on the North Island, but the South Island form, distinguished by its predominantly orange wattles, is confined to a few isolated areas. Its song is a resonant medley of two rich organ-like notes followed by three whistling "pips" and can be heard for miles. To many observers it is New Zealand's finest song-bird. The Kokako is a reluctant flier. To gather the fruits, flowers and leaves on which it feeds, it glides from tree to tree. Alighting, it hops up the trunk, gathering food on the way and, on reaching a vantage point, it glides down to the trunk of the next tree to start over again.

Breeding takes place between November and March, but the pairs re-main together throughout the year. The nest is a stick and twig structure placed in the fork of a large tree or amid dense foliage in the canopy.

The Saddleback, *Philesturnus carunculatus*, is identified by its chestnut saddle and orange wattles. Both the North and South Island forms now only exist on a few offshore islands. Pairs of Saddlebacks remain together as they move through the forest in search of food. Every bark crevice is examined for insects, and loose or dead bark is torn away with the powerful bill. The Saddleback normally shuns the main forest canopy, preferring to feed among the shrubs and bushes of secondary growth.

The Huia, *Heteralocha acutirostris*, now presumed extinct, has been described as "one of the world's most remarkable birds". A quite extraordinary differentiation had occurred in the bill form and function of the male and female. The male's bill was stout and powerful, strongly curved and almost as long as its head, while the female was equipped with a slender scimitar bill, suggesting that the pair worked in concert – the male tearing a breach in a decaying log so that the female could insert her bill and extract the larvae of boring insects.

Brown Kiwi
Apteryx australis 20 in

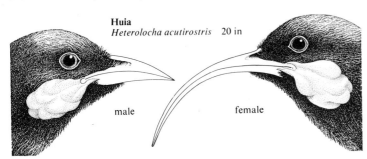

Huia
Heterolocha acutirostris 20 in

male

female

A curious relict

The illustration, left, shows the position and form of the Kiwi's vestigial wing, normally this defunct limb is completely hidden by the bird's loose, shaggy plumage. The egg, drawn here to scale, is (in proportion to body size) the largest of any living bird and may represent roughly one-quarter of the adult bird's body weight.

Coasts and Fringing Islands

Inevitably the interface between two physical environments as different as land and sea must provide both a wide variety of physical features and a richness of exploitable food reserves. The sheer length of the Australian coastline provides further variety; the northern coasts washed by warm, tropical waters; the southern coast swept by cold waters upwelling from the Antarctic Ocean, laden with planktonic life that forms the basis for a complex food-web supporting millions of fish, aquatic mammals and oceanic birds.

The land masses of the southern hemisphere are much smaller than those north of the Equator but a great many shore-birds and sea-birds breed in the Palaearctic and travel south in the autumn to winter in the more benign conditions of the Australasian realm. Not all the coasts are suitable for the winter migrants, but even the less inviting, such as the mangrove coasts, can support a few specialist visitors, including the *Gerygone* warblers, various honeyeaters and the Mangrove Kingfisher. At the other extreme, sandy shores and muddy estuaries teem with food and provide a rich and easily exploited wintering ground for waders, ducks and gulls.

In the breeding season, the diversity of the coast – from sand-dunes to cliffs – is fully utilized. The auks, familiar to northern eyes, are absent; gulls are poorly represented, but their place is taken by a wide variety of albatrosses, petrels, prions and shearwaters.

female

Red-headed Honeyeater
Myzomela erythrocephala 5in
An unexpected glow of colour

male

Red-capped Dotterel
Charadrius ruficapillus 6in
Considered by many to be identical to the Kentish Plover

Common Diving Petrel
Pelecanoides urinatrix 8in
Bursts from the water into flight without pause

Red-headed Honeyeater
Myzomela erythrocephala

One of the smallest of all Australian birds, the Red-headed Honeyeater is one of about 20 species that are virtually confined to mangrove swamps. Only the male is brilliantly coloured and the scarlet feathers of the head and rump glow like embers against the dim light of the swamp habitat. Equally at home in riverine or tropical ocean mangroves, the bird finds an abundant supply of nectar and insects on which to feed, in addition to extensive dense cover that provides protection against predators. The only real threat to the Honeyeater comes from the Black Butcher-bird, *Cracticus quoyi*, a cunning and voracious nest-robber.

Red-headed Honeyeaters are found in small parties, very localized and rarely moving far from their home territory unless tempted briefly away by nearby flowering trees. Even then, at the first sign of danger these shy birds dart back into the gloom of the mangroves.

The small cup-shaped nest is swung like a hammock between two twigs and in it the hen lays two speckled white eggs, sharing the incubation with her attentive mate.

Red-capped Dotterel
Charadrius ruficapillus

The Red-capped Dotterel, thought by many to be conspecific with the Kentish Plover of Europe, is a common resident of sand and pebble beaches, estuaries and mangrove swamps and even inland salt lakes. Unlike most Australian waders it does not migrate, but there is some nomadic movement within the home range and Red-capped Dotterels have been found inhabiting flooded claypans, even in arid desert areas.

Breeding extends from September to March over most of the continent but winter breeding is also common in the north. A small scrape in the ground, often beneath a rock or piece of driftwood, serves as a nest for the two beautifully camouflaged eggs. The chicks, too, are cryptically patterned and "freeze" with eyes closed at the first sign of danger while both the parents will make distraction displays.

Common Diving Petrel
Pelecanoides urinatrix

In appearance the Common Diving Petrel closely resembles the unrelated Little Auk, *Plautus alle*, of northern Europe and, like the auk, has an extensible throat-pouch used for holding food caught while hunting under water.

The Diving Petrel is a powerful swimmer, diving into the sea at a shallow angle and using its short wings as paddles while swimming. In taking to the air, the petrel bursts from the water and takes flight immediately, without pausing on the surface. Gathering in small flocks, these active birds feed well out to sea, often in the company of other petrels and shearwaters, diving and swimming among shoals of krill and plankton.

The Common Diving Petrel nests on islands in the southern oceans, making its nest in a burrow dug among tussock grass. In Australian waters, the greatest concentration is among the islands of the Bass Strait.

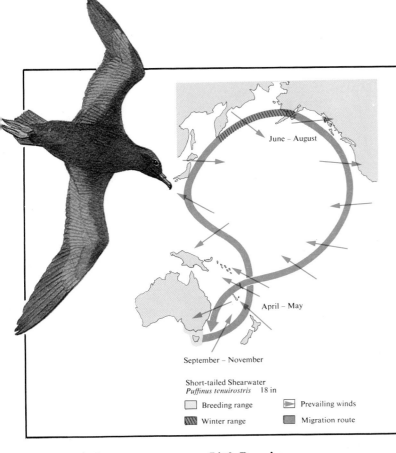

The 20,000-mile commuter

Many of the world's seabirds are long-range migrants but few, apart from the Arctic Tern, *Sterna paradisea*, can match the annual 20,000-mile round trip of the Short-tailed Shearwater, or Tasmanian Mutton Bird, *Puffinus tenuirostris*. Leaving their nesting territories late in April, these medium sized, dark grey seabirds fly out to sea and then swing back on to a course that takes them northwards to Japan, sometimes covering this 5,500-mile stage in a month. Pushing farther to the north, the birds spend June, July and August in the Pacific Arctic before "riding" the trade winds and westerlies on the return leg of their remarkable figure-eight journey.

Mutton Birds breed on the shores of Tasmania, southeastern Australia and on many islands in the south Pacific, and even conservative estimates put their total numbers in tens of millions. Late in September, the birds return to the breeding grounds and the quiet of evening is shattered by the noisy cries of their courtship displays. Kicking and

digging with their powerful webbed feet, the birds burrow between three and nine feet into the soft earth to prepare a nest chamber, often sharing their burrow with one of several species of snake.

As with most shearwaters, the Mutton Bird shuns the day, preferring to remain underground apart from feeding excursions in search of fish and shoals of krill. Early in November the densely crowded colony is deserted. For up to 18 days the birds remain at sea, during which time the eggs develop within the females. Immediately on their return, the females retire to the burrows to lay their single large white eggs, leaving again almost at once to feed at sea. The male incubates the egg for the first two weeks after which the two adults take turns, each sitting for 10 to 15 days at a stretch, for the duration of the 55-day incubation period.

Blind, and thickly covered with down, the chick receives little parental care beyond the regurgitated meals of fish and krill delivered during the first 3 months.

Short-tailed Shearwater
Puffinus tenuirostris 18 in
☐ Breeding range   ▶ Prevailing winds
▨ Winter range   ▨ Migration route

June – August

April – May

September – November

Cape Barren Goose
Cereopsis novaehollandiae

Like many Australian birds, the Cape Barren Goose poses problems for those concerned with classification. It is not clear from what stock the species evolved, nor to what extent its gooselike form is simply an adaptation to its mode of living. A similar form once inhabited New Zealand, but beyond that evidence the evolutionary record remains silent. Based on the appearance of the downy young, present theories suggest that it may be related to the shelducks and that the species may be a primitive link with the geese.

The Cape Barren Goose breeds on small offshore islands, notably those in the Bass Strait. Male and female are similar in appearance and make the small hollow, nasal sounds but the male is distinguished by a high-pitched trumpeting call. Breeding takes place in winter in western regions and between May and December in the east. Both sexes join in building the shallow nest of grass, lined with down, which is placed on the ground either in the open or among low bushes. The clutch of between four and seven eggs is incubated by the female alone for up to 40 days while the drake remains in close attendance. The eggs are unusual in having a limy coating.

Feeding entirely on grass, the Cape Barren Goose often visits the mainland to feed alongside sheep. In the past this has lead to extensive shooting as local belief held that sheep would not graze in areas fouled by geese. The species now enjoys protection and, despite an earlier alarming decline, numbers are rapidly increasing again.

Little Penguin
Eudyptula minor

Although a number of penguin species are found around the southern shores of Australia, most are nomads that have travelled from the huge island breeding colonies far to the south. Only the Little Penguin breeds in Australia and, unlike its relatives, this species lives in very small colonies.

By day, the Little Penguin feeds well out to sea, swimming buoyantly and diving after fish, the feeding group communicating with each other by means of high-pitched yapping barks. After sunset, the birds return to the shore, again heralding their arrival by an excited chorus of barks.

Living in warmer waters than most penguins, the Little Penguin has less need for insulation and consequently has shorter feathers and a less extensively developed blubber layer beneath the skin. By day it remains at sea, avoiding the higher temperatures on land as much as possible. Only during the breeding season does the Little Penguin spend any appreciable part of the day on land, and even then the bird remains in the shade of its nest-burrow.

The Little Penguin prepares for the annual moult by feeding heavily and increasing its body weight. It then rests for four or five days, in the burrow, before the first new feathers begin to appear. On the fifth and sixth days the old feathers start to fall, beginning with those on the face, flippers and lower back. Replacement of the plumage takes about 14 days, during which time the scruffy and dejected-looking bird spends the majority of its time preening.

Cape Barren Goose
Cereopsis novaehollandiae 33in
Thought to be a primitive relative of the true geese

Little Penguin
Eudyptula minor 16in
The only penguin to breed in Australian waters

Birds of the Great Oceans

The interconnected ocean system, covering more than 70 per cent of the earth's surface, provides a potentially global habitat for sea-birds; and yet very few species actually range over all the world's oceans. Differences in water temperature and salinity separate the oceans into distinct regions with markedly different properties, among which food supply is but one major factor. The clearest distinction is between the polar and tropical waters; the cold Arctic and Antarctic waters, and the cold upwellings along the western coasts of Africa and South America, are far richer in food than the meagerly supplied warm waters of the tropics.

The sea-birds' freedom of movement has removed many of the pressures that normally result in speciation and, of a total of more than 8,600 bird species, only 285 are sea-birds. The almost uninterrupted band of tropical waters circling the globe allows the tropical species to roam far and wide. In contrast, the polarization of cold water masses at high latitudes has encouraged separate evolution. Penguins have never colonized the northern hemisphere, but convergent evolution has ensured that the "penguin role" is filled – by the members of the auk family.

A few species, like the Gannet, do occur in both hemispheres, but the most wide-ranging birds of all are those that, like the Arctic Tern, winter in the southern polar regions and breed in the high Arctic tundra.

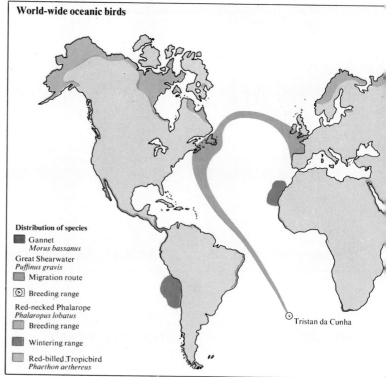

World-wide oceanic birds

Distribution of species

Gannet
Morus bassanus

Great Shearwater
Puffinus gravis
Migration route

Breeding range

Red-necked Phalarope
Phalaropus lobatus
Breeding range

Wintering range

Red-billed Tropicbird
Phaethon aethereus

Tristan da Cunha

Red-necked Phalarope
Phalaropus lobatus 7in
A complete reversal of the usual courtship roles

Red-necked Phalarope
Phalaropus lobatus

Unlike most waders the phalaropes spend most of their time at sea and use the land only during the breeding season. Physically they are well adapted to their aquatic life style: the toes are fringed with flattened scales to give added swimming power, and the dense plumage of the underparts greatly increases the birds' buoyancy. This latter adaptation does, however, create its own hazard. The phalarope rides very high in the water and, in high winds, the birds are very prone to being blown on to a lee shore.

A model of diffidence beside his larger, more colourful and domineering mate, the male phalarope leaves the female to take the initiative during courtship. He, in turn, is left to shoulder the main responsibility for incubating the eggs and caring for the young. This reversal of the usual roles is common to all phalaropes; the female displays in flight, chooses the nesting site and defends it against competing females.

The Red-necked Phalarope breeds throughout the Arctic region. In the calm waters of the breeding grounds the crustaceans and larvae that provide the bulk of its diet are often too deep to be accessible by up-ending and so the feeding bird spins like a top, creating its own turbulence that brings the food nearer the surface of the water.

Courtship feeding

Despite its world-wide distribution, the strictly colonial behaviour of the Roseate Tern, *Sterna dougallii*, limits its breeding to a few well-defined localities within each part of its total range. Roseate Terns usually nest in mixed tern colonies on safe off-shore islands. Within these colonies they tend to nest among vegetation, leaving sand and shingle sites to their shorter-legged relatives. Like other terns, their breeding habits are erratic and breeding itself is sporadic; colonies will unaccountably make a wholesale shift to a new site in the middle of the season.

Breeding is preceded by complex aerial courtship displays, including the phenomenon of "courtship feeding". The male tern displays by flying around with a fish held in its bill, offering the token to any unmated female. Females accept food from a number of males initially but eventually confine themselves to feeding with one chosen mate, both at sea and in the colony. This behaviour is generally supposed to initiate and cement the pair bond before the more binding elements of the relationship, like the nest and family, are established. However, this extra food is probably important during the stressful period of laying. Even after they are firmly paired some male terns renew this feeding if the female loses the first clutch and is going to re-lay. This supports the view that the feeding is more than just courtship behaviour, and, in the mid-season food shortages that often hit tropical areas, it may be crucial in stimulating the female to lay again. Furthermore, in fish-carrying species, the capacity of the male in bringing food to the female is related to the number of young reared so ensuring that the "fittest" adults breed together.

Roseate Tern
Sterna dougallii 15in

Gannet
Morus bassanus

Aided by acute binocular vision, the brilliant white Gannet plummets down on its fish prey from up to 100 feet above the ocean. Shock-absorbing cellular structures beneath the skin, externally closed nostrils and a strengthened skeleton all give the bird added protection from the terrific impact of a dive that takes it deep into the shoal – probably to enable it to turn and attack fish silhouetted against the surface.

The Gannet usually bobs buoyantly to the surface after three to ten seconds, its prey already consumed. Although many dives are probably unsuccessful it is thought that "bill-washing" actions often seen immediately after the bird bobs to the surface, indicate a successful strike.

The dazzling white plumage serves a dual function; the bird is difficult to see against a bright sky, and the repeated flash of a diving bird attracts more Gannets – the combined attack of hundreds of birds sending the shoals of fish into a chaotic and vulnerable panic. Young Gannets are fed by the parents on regurgitated food for ten to 12 weeks and then suddenly leave the colony.

Red-billed Tropicbird
Phaethon aethereus

Known to seafarers as the "bosun-bird" because of its shrill, piping cry, the Tropicbird roams far across the warm Atlantic and western Pacific Oceans and Persian Gulf. Solitary for much of the year, it ranges with swift, graceful wingbeats then hovers briefly before plunging with half-folded wings to take fish and squid just below the surface.

A faint pink tinge to its plumage, for long a mystery, is now known to be caused by an orange-red oil used to waterproof the feathers. Of the three tropicbird species, the Red-billed is the largest, ousting its smaller relatives whenever competition arises for nesting sites on cliff ledges and sandy cays. No nest is built, the single egg being laid on a rock ledge or shallow ground-scrape and incubated for 28 days by both male and female.

Great Shearwater
Puffinus gravis

Leaving their breeding grounds a week or two ahead of their chicks, adult Great Shearwaters embark on a wind-assisted migration northwards from their remote breeding grounds in the South Atlantic. Their journey, which may take more than nine months, follows the course of the prevailing winds and describes a circle over the North Atlantic. The mammoth journey starts from three tiny, predator-free islands in the Tristan Da Cunha group – the main breeding locality of this spectacular migrant.

During the highly synchronized breeding season, the four-million-strong colony on Nightingale Island uses every available nesting space, and the central plateau of the 400-acre island is honeycombed with their burrows. Like most pelagic sea-birds, the Great Shearwater is awkward on land. Legs set far back on the body make walking difficult, and the bird's take-off and landing are both laborious and clumsy.

Gannet
Morus bassanus 36in
Its powerful hunting dives send shoals of fish into a vulnerable panic

Red-billed Tropicbird
Phaethon aethereus 30in
The "bosun-bird", a familiar sight to early seafarers

Great Shearwater
Puffinus gravis 18in
This long-range migrant spends nine months of each year travelling over the Atlantic Ocean

The Island-dwellers

When islands first emerge from the sea, only nesting sea-birds and turtles can find a use for these barren hulks of rock and coral. Land-based birds arriving at this stage must either depart or perish; only after vegetation is well established can these species have any chance of surviving. Purely insectivorous species must wait even longer before the island can provide a life-supporting food supply. Those few birds that do settle tend, in contrast to mainland species, to become more versatile and adaptable than their mainland counterparts, and exploit as many feeding niches as possible. With time to adapt to these conditions the pioneers offer formidable competition for later arrivals, most of which are unable to adapt and relinquish the island to its first tenants.

However, the tables are easily turned on resident species, and both internal and external disturbances have profound effects on the few species that inhabit islands. Over a quarter of all island species have become extinct through over-specialization, and the fortunes of the remainder turn on the delicate ecological balance of their habitat; the smaller the island the finer the thread on which survival depends. On the smallest islands, extinction may follow natural fluctuations in population, and the arrival of man, with his introduction of rival bird species and predators, does nothing to improve the survival prospects of island birds.

Right: Blue-footed Boobies nesting on the Galapagos Islands

Galapagos Hawk
Buteo galapagoensis 20in
Its indiscriminate predation led to massive reprisals

Galapagos Hawk
Buteo galapagoensis

Several island groups have a resident hawk species, usually of the *Buteo* genus, which is peculiar to their area. The Galapagos Hawk probably evolved from the migratory Red-backed Hawk, *B.polyosoma*, of the Americas, and is among the rarest of these island hawks. It has all the appearance of a typical buzzard: blackish-brown plumage; strongly hooked beak and powerful legs and feet. However, in most other respects comparison with mainland species is impossible. Like many isolated creatures, it shows an innocent confidence in the world at large, which, even after repeated betrayal, remains apparently unshaken. The first settlers to arrive on the islands clubbed thousands of birds to death to protect their poultry from predation. The effects of this persecution were exacerbated by the birds' haphazard opportunist feeding habits. Had they hunted in an orthodox fashion, within defined territories, only those birds on inhabited islands would have been killed. As it was, an abundant and static food source attracted birds from the whole group of islands.

Despite their past experience, the 130 pairs remaining are as tame as ever, and will still approach a man to feed from his hand. These survivors are now confined to only nine of the hot, dry islands. To make life more difficult in these barren conditions, the hawks must face competition from escaped cats and dogs and as a result a number of uninhabited islands with a suitable food supply remain largely unexploited.

Even though each bird hunts over a large area, food is deceptively scarce and only the varied diet typical of island birds, readily adjusted to the prevailing food supply, makes survival possible. The basic diet of native rats, doves, lizards, finches, mockingbirds and giant centipedes is supplemented with marine iguanas, shearwaters, migrant shore-birds, sealion placenta and carrion. Galapagos Hawks may be seen stooping after small birds, in the manner of Peregrines; snatching large insects from the air like nightjars, or wheeling round carrion like vultures. Individual birds have marked food preferences and the partners in a pair will often concentrate on different prey. The female, as befits her greater size, deals with large iguanas and the carcases of goats unable to survive on the meagre local resources. The more agile male takes small birds both in the air and on the ground.

Providing for the young places an extra burden on the hard-pressed pair, forcing them to wait for the fructifying but infrequent tropical rains before nesting. In some territories, two or three males will mate with a single female. Each specializes in a different type of prey, so supplying a full and varied diet for the female and her young. The onus to provide food for the young falls largely on the male, for the female guards the young constantly and rarely leaves the nest unattended. The bulky twig nest is usually sited on a rock or in a tree with a commanding view over the harsh volcanic landscape. Although clutches of three eggs have been recorded, usually only one chick is reared, and it seems probable that, even after it is fully grown, the bird remains with its parents for some time.

Nene
Branta sandvicensis 25in
A captive breeding programme saved the species from extinction

Flightless Cormorant
Nannopterum harrisi 36in
Weight proved to be more valuable than flight

Nene (Hawaiian Goose)
Branta sandvicensis

Guns, escaped mongooses and dogs, and man's compulsive clearance of natural habitat had, by the mid-twentieth century brought Hawaii's largest native bird to the brink of extinction. In 1949 and 1950 three pairs were captured and taken to the Wildfowl Trust in England, where a selective breeding programme was established. So productive was this programme that in 1960 the first captive-bred birds were successfully reintroduced to their original island.

Probably evolved from the migratory North American Canada Goose, *Branta canadensis*, the Nene has adapted well to its volcanic island habitat. The partly webbed feet have thickened soles affording protection from the sharp volcanic rocks; the legs are set well forward for walking (thus losing the waddling gait of most geese), and the heavy bill is ideally suited to grazing the rough island vegetation. Although now well established, the Nene will only be secure in the wild if alien predators on Hawaii are controlled.

Flightless Cormorant
Nannopterum harrisi

This Cormorant is, apart from the penguins, the only flightless sea-bird living today. The entire world population of some 700 to 800 pairs is confined to 200 miles of coastline in the Galapagos Islands. Arriving early in the island group's history, the Cormorant's ancestors thrived in its rich, cold, coastal waters. Since there were no land predators and their food (bottom-feeding octopi, eels and reef fish) was close to shore, flight, for escape and transport, was not important. Weight, however, is a valuable diving aid, and over countless generations, the bird has become so dense that it now swims with its back awash.

Unlike the penguins, the Flightless Cormorant does not use its wings for swimming. Its breast-bone has lost the ridge, or keel, to which the flight muscles are normally anchored, and it relies instead on powerful legs for swimming and for landing on the rough lava shores. Curiously, this bird still hangs its wings out to dry after each fishing expedition.

The Hawaiian Honeycreepers

The Iiwi is one of the three Honeycreeper species still fairly common on Hawaii and is readily identified as a specialist nectar feeder by its slender decurved bill.

More successful than its two neighbours, the Iiwi has a longer and stronger bill and is able to feed on the nectar of deep tubular flowers, many of which are inaccessible to the other two species. All three are known to supplement their diet with a wide variety of insects.

The Iiwi is very aggressive in the defence of its nest and may, occasionally, drive rivals away from a favourite feeding area. Groups, however, do forage amicably and volubly in the same tree during the flowering season. Their harsh, strident calls are most noticeable in the breeding season, and particularly during courtship. Little is known of the Iiwi's nesting behaviour, but nestlings have been recorded between February and July.

Iiwi
Vestiaria coccinea 5½in

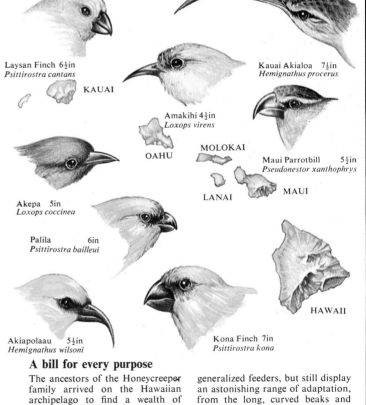

Laysan Finch 6½in
Psittirostra cantans

KAUAI

Kauai Akialoa 7½in
Hemignathus procerus

Amakihi 4½in
Loxops virens

Akepa 5in
Loxops coccinea

OAHU

MOLOKAI

LANAI

Maui Parrotbill 5½in
Pseudonestor xanthophrys

MAUI

Palila 6in
Psittirostra bailleui

HAWAII

Akiapolaau 5½in
Hemignathus wilsoni

Kona Finch 7in
Psittirostra kona

A bill for every purpose

The ancestors of the Honeycreeper family arrived on the Hawaiian archipelago to find a wealth of different vegetation zones. In this isolated and largely unexploited habitat, the honeycreepers managed an unrivalled degree of divergence, evolving to fill niches usually taken by other groups of birds. However, such opportunism had its penalties; of the 22 honeycreeper species, eight made fateful commitments to their chosen way of life and over-specialization led to their extinction. The 14 surviving species are more generalized feeders, but still display an astonishing range of adaptation, from the long, curved beaks and brush-tipped tongues of the nectar-sippers, through the straight, slender beaks of the insectivorous species, to the stout, crunching bills of the seed-eaters.

On Hawaii, the Akiapolaau, *Hemignathus wilsoni*, a rare, perhaps extinct, species apes the woodpecker by using its stout lower mandible to hammer and lever off bark. Its long decurved upper mandible then probes for exposed insects.

World-wide Birds

The formation and separation of the earth's continents many millions of years ago confined many species of birds to their own land-masses. With the passage of time, these birds consolidated their positions in the local ecology and, in many cases, evolved specialized adaptations to suit their particular circumstances. The oceans that divide the land areas, and the birds' own specializations, prevented many species from greatly extending their ranges once they became established. Truly world-wide species are uncommon, but convergent evolution has produced beguiling similarities in birds of quite different species. The tree-creepers of Australia, South America and the Palaearctic, all distinct species despite their common ancestors, have evolved convergently to develop common characteristics of behaviour and appearance – where a bird does not exist to fill an available niche, evolution will generally ensure that a species will adapt to fill that niche.

Man has greatly influenced the range of many species, rarely without some adverse effect on the local fauna and flora. The success of artificial introductions depends on the new arrival finding an unexploited gap in the new habitat, and the more crowded the habitat the greater the problems of survival. Predators and water-birds, the most successful and widespread land-based birds, have always shown this crucial versatility.

Swallow
Hirundo rustica 7½in
Late chicks may be deserted by their migrating parents

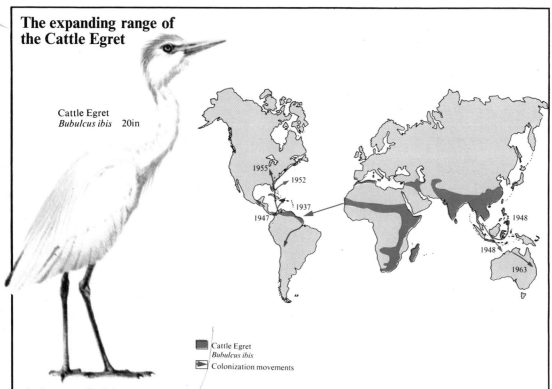

The expanding range of the Cattle Egret

Cattle Egret
Bubulcus ibis 20in

1955
1952
1937
1947
1948
1948
1963

Cattle Egret
Bubulcus ibis
Colonization movements

In the space of a little more than 60 years, the Cattle Egret has achieved an astonishing expansion of its range outside its native areas in Africa and Asia. Crossing the Atlantic in the early part of this century, this egret successfully colonized Guyana – filling the niches in South America that had been created by extensive forest clearance. In a newly created grassland habitat the Cattle Egret faced little competition for the large insects and small amphibians that form the bulk of its diet. One of the major factors in the Cattle Egret's success has been its adaptability. In the absence of large native herbivores the bird has taken to feeding in the company of domestic livestock – pouncing on insects and other prey as they are flushed from the grass by the grazing beasts. It has also adopted the habit of feeding at roadside verges and even on urban lawns, and will roost readily in both country and urban surroundings.

During the breeding season, the male egret develops long buff plumes on the crown, breast and back, while the legs flush a deeper, more alluring pink. Courtship is hectic, with a great deal of bustling activity and crooning. Once paired the birds nest communally with other herons, building untidy platform nests of stout sticks on which to lay their eggs. In the northern part of the range, the usual clutch is of six eggs, but clutches in the tropics are smaller. In open country the nests are constructed in thickets or in low trees where they are shielded from wind and rain. In tropical areas, rain is vital in the weeks following hatching; without it the chicks would soon become dehydrated.

Swallow
Hirundo rustica

The Swallow is one of the most aerial of all birds, its rolling, twisting aerobatic flight enabling it to pursue and catch individual insects in addition to its scooping runs through dense insect clouds. In order to obtain food throughout the year, this exclusively insectivorous bird must migrate from its northern range each winter.

Irrigation systems and reservoirs, both of which harbour millions of breeding insects, partly explain the bird's success in Europe, but during their migration journeys the Swallows have no such man-made aids and, for birds that feed on the wing, the 1,000 mile two-day flight across the Sahara is a severe test. Unlike many migrants that pause to feed *en route*, the Swallows feed as they go and, in order to see their flying prey, are forced to fly during the day in the full glare of the sun. Exhaustion overtakes many thousands of birds each year, and only their prolific breeding balances a mortality rate as high as three out of every five adults and four of every five young.

The very high mortality rate has been indirectly helped by man's ever-increasing urbanization; the roofs and eaves of buildings afford excellent sites for the Swallow's neatly made mud cup-nest – well out of range of most predators and well protected from the elements. Two or three clutches, each of between four and six eggs, are laid each season. Most of the young are successfully fledged, but late chicks are in danger of being deserted as the migration instinct may override the adults' parental instincts.

Barn Owl
Tyto alba

The Barn Owl, often hunting on nights too dark even for its acute night vision, depends heavily on hearing to locate the small ground animals on which it feeds. Its ears are asymmetrically positioned on either side of the heart-shaped facial disc, which itself may act as a sound-reflector. This lop-sided setting causes a slight timelag in sound reception so that the owl is able to obtain an immediate bearing on the sound source. To prevent the prey being disturbed and their muted sounds being drowned, the owl's long, wide wings have soft fringed feathers. This creates a smooth airflow which is the secret of their uniquely silent flight.

Coloured a nondescript buff and brown, and roosting in dark places, this nocturnal hunter is rarely seen in the day, except for occasional hunting forays in the breeding season. Food indeed determines breeding; two clutches, averaging between four and eight eggs, will be laid in a reasonably plentiful year.

At present the Barn Owl and its numerous sub-species are widespread throughout most of the world, living in every type of open country from arid desert scrub to water-meadow. In many parts of its range, however, the Barn Owl has suffered from the effects of agricultural programmes. Reduction of forested areas has greatly reduced the bird's hunting range and crop-spraying activities have introduced a number of lethal, persistent pesticides into its food.

Barn Owl
Tyto alba 13½in
Directional hearing is the nocturnal hunter's weapon

Osprey
Pandion haliaetus

Despite a superficial resemblance to some other eagles, the Osprey is unique – the sole member of the family Pandionidae. Almost exclusively a fish eater, it has become perfectly adapted to catching and carrying its slippery and elusive prey. Its massive talons are all of equal length and the outer one (like that of the owl) is reversible, enabling the bird to obtain a secure grip.

Cruising over the surface of a lake or river, between 40 and 100 feet high, the Osprey scans the surface waters for fish. Its prey sighted, the bird hovers momentarily and then plunges with wings half folded – entering the water feet first in a cloud of spray to clamp its talons, two each side, around the fish. So powerful is the Osprey's dive that the bird is almost submerged, often only the wing tips showing above water. The Osprey, though handsome in flight and when perched on the nest, is a strangely ungainly bird in the water. In its attempts to take off clutching its prey, it thrashes itself clear of the water with flailing wings, vigorously shaking the water from its plumage as soon as it is airborne. Once the bird is in flight, the prey is adjusted in the grip into a head-forward position to reduce drag – an important consideration as the 3½ lb Osprey normally takes prey 1 to 2 lb in weight. When fish are scarce the Osprey may take frogs and, very rarely, small birds.

The young, usually reared from a clutch of two to four eggs, are fed at the nest two or three times each day for up to ten weeks, after which they leave the nest to hunt for themselves.

Osprey
Pandion haliaetus 22in
Powerful talons and spiny soles secure a firm grip on the most slippery prey

Antarctica

Of the forty-three species that breed in the barren windswept lands of the Antarctic, all but five are sea-birds. Larger and better insulated than most land species, they are better able to withstand the extreme cold of the southern regions and the dangerous flights across some of the world's stormiest oceans. In contrast to the empty lands, the southern oceans teem with food – fish, squid and plankton – and provide an abundant supply of food for more than half the year. Most Antarctic species breed on the rocky islands scattered through the northern fringe of the region, where tussock grass and other tundra vegetation provides a degree of cover and shelter from the elements. Nineteen species range farther south to breed on the ice-fringed shores within the pack-ice zone, and only ten species, all sea-birds, penetrate to the mainland of Antarctica itself.

The 19 species that breed in the pack-ice zone include eight petrels and five penguins – all oceanic birds that forage far out to sea in search of food and return to breed in huge shore-based colonies. Antarctica's gulls terns, cormorants and skuas feed in the shallower coastal waters and breed in smaller colonies on headlands where food is locally abundant in the spring. The solitary land-bird of the Antarctic proper is the pigeon-like Sheathbill – a ubiquitous scavenger of the shore-line and breeding colonies.

Right: Adelie Penguin colony, Avian Island, Antarctic Peninsula

Wilson's Petrel
Oceanites oceanicus 7in
Appears to walk on water as it picks food morsels from the surface

Giant Petrel
Macronectes giganteus

Largest by far of the fulmar petrels, these solid, heavily built birds sweep the southern oceans like over-weight albatrosses on wings spanning six feet or more. Two sub-species have recently been recognized; a northern form having generally darker plumage, and a more variable southern form.

Curiously ugly at close quarters, with small pale eyes and a heavily fluted bill, the Giant Petrel breeds in solitary pairs or small colonies from the sub-Antarctic islands south to the continental mainland. The northern populations breed in September and October while egg-laying occurs about one month later in the south. The eggs are incubated for eight to nine weeks and, once hatched, the chicks must be carefully guarded for a further three weeks to protect them from the skuas that habitually lurk on the fringes of the breeding colonies to prey on unguarded eggs and young.

The chicks remain at the nest for up to 16 weeks, wrapped in dense down and protected by fat deposits. Though physically weak, they defend themselves effectively by vomiting streams of sticky red oily fluid – a defence mechanism common to many members of the fulmar family. The parents return to the nest periodically, carrying fish, squid and blubber gleaned from carcasses found at sea. They also scavenge in the penguin colonies, taking eggs and young and attacking weak and injured birds.

Immature birds often roam as far north as South Africa and South America before returning, several years later, to breed near their birth-place.

Wilson's Petrel
Oceanites oceanicus

They are thrush-sized birds with unusually large parasol wings that enable them to perform the most remarkable low-speed manoeuvres without stalling. They hunt in large, straggling flocks, rising, swirling and then settling on the surface of the water like leaves in a gale, sometimes hanging motionless, facing into the wind and treading the water as they inspect the surface for morsels of food. Occasionally the birds will dive after planktonic organisms – bobbing buoyantly to the surface within two or three seconds.

The diminutive Wilson's Petrel is not only the smallest member of the petrel family but is also probably the most numerous of all oceanic birds. Because of its distribution, over the least-populated areas of the world's surface, accurate estimates are difficult, but its total population is thought to be hundreds of millions.

The birds nest throughout the Antarctic and sub-Antarctic region, inhabiting almost every one of the thousands of small islands that dot the circumpolar oceans and extending south to well within the Antarctic Circle. They nest in crevices among bare rocks and on boulder-strewn scree slopes, or in burrows driven into the soil of the more northerly islands. At the end of the summer both adults and juveniles leave the Antarctic waters and spend the months between April and October far out to sea.

Giant Petrel
Macronectes giganteus 35in
Largest member of the "tube-nosed" fulmar family

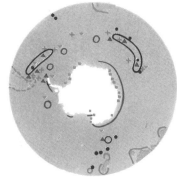

Distribution of species

- ----- Magellanic Penguin
  Spheniscus magellanicus
- + Macaroni Penguin
  Eudyptes chrysolophus
- ── Southern Blue Penguin
  Eudyptula minor minor
- ── Jackass Penguin
  Spheniscus demersus
- ▼ Chinstrap Penguin
  Pygoscelis antarctica
- ■ Emperor Penguin
  Aptenodytes forsteri
- ▲ Gentoo Penguin
  Pygoscelis papua
- ── Adelie Penguin
  Pygoscelis adeliae
- ── King Penguin
  Aptenodytes patagonica
- ● Rockhopper Penguin
  Eudyptes crestata

Antarctic Penguins

Although penguins are popularly associated with the Antarctic regions, only three species (Emperor, Adelie and Chinstrap) nest entirely within this frozen habitat of ice and snow. Seven species are distributed throughout the sub-Antarctic islands and spend much of each year in Antarctic waters, but more than half the known species are restricted to temperate latitudes and three species are found only within the tropics. Despite this range of habitat, however, the penguins share a number of remarkable features that immediately set them apart from all other birds. Gone are the light-weight body structure and the broad wings and fan-shaped tail of the flying bird. In their place the penguin has evolved a heavy, compact, streamlined body, well protected from cold by a layer of subcutaneous blubber and completely covered with short, dense feathers that are underlain by a layer of warm down. This padded sheath protects the bird from heat loss and from the tremendous poundings encountered when landing on a rocky shore or leaping for the edge of an ice-floe.

Emperor Penguin
Aptenodytes forsteri 48in
Incubation means a gruelling two-month ordeal for the male

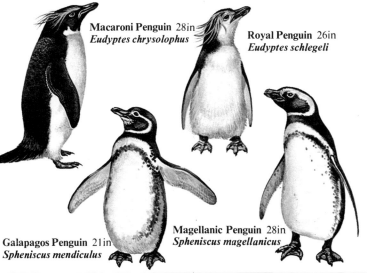

Macaroni Penguin 28in
Eudyptes chrysolophus

Royal Penguin 26in
Eudyptes schlegeli

Galapagos Penguin 21in
Spheniscus mendiculus

Magellanic Penguin 28in
Spheniscus magellanicus

Emperor Penguin
Aptenodytes forsteri

As soon as the sea-ice re-forms at the onset of winter, the Emperor Penguins return to their breeding grounds on the Antarctic continent and on the sea-ice and rocky islands off the continental coast.

Each female lays a single, large white egg which is immediately passed into the care of the male, who, throughout the eight-week incubation period, carries the egg on the upper surface of his feet, covered by the warm, protective mass of his abdomen. The female spends the whole winter at sea and returns in time for the hatching, unerringly finding her mate even in a colony of many thousands. She then takes over the brooding while the male, a weakened and emaciated shadow of his former 65 lb self, heads out to sea to feed.

Both parents carry food to the young, taking turn to hunt at sea. The whole breeding cycle takes nearly six months and ensures that when the young are ready to go to sea in mid-summer, they do so when the food supply of the southern oceans is most abundant.

Adelie Penguin
Pygoscelis adeliae

After spending the winter months far out to sea where temperatures are higher than on land, the Adelie Penguins return to their Antarctic breeding grounds in September and October.

The breeding cycle is attended by complex ritual. The male presents, to his chosen mate, a pebble – the basic building material of the crude nest – and only if this token is accepted may the remaining courtship rituals follow. Two eggs are usually laid in a shallow saucer of stones and throughout the incubation period the birds remain on land, gradually becoming dirtier and more emaciated. Once the chicks are hatched, the parents may leave the colony in turn to feed at sea and later, when the chicks are more advanced, they may be left in "crèches" guarded by a few adults.

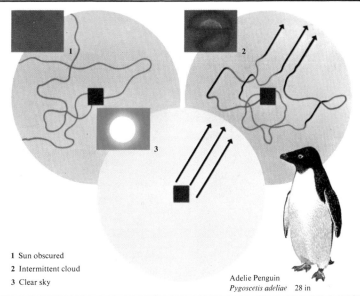

1 Sun obscured
2 Intermittent cloud
3 Clear sky

Adelie Penguin
Pygoscelis adeliae 28 in

Navigational skills

Year after year, millions of Adelie Penguins find their way unerringly back to their traditional breeding grounds after a winter spent at sea. Sometimes, at the end of their journey, the birds must walk up to 200 miles across sea-ice but even when the ground is covered with snow the birds are able to locate the nesting sites used in previous years.

Birds taken from their home range were released on a featureless plain many hundreds of miles away. Under a cloudy sky, their movements were completely erratic, but, with the sun in full view, the birds headed in a direction that would, under normal circumstances, have carried a lost bird straight back to its home colony.

The studies proved that the penguin's navigation is based on the sun, and that an inbuilt "clock" enables the bird to compensate for the sun's movement.

The Sub-Antarctic Islands

North of the Antarctic Convergence, where the cold waters of the Antarctic oceans meet those of the southern Atlantic and Pacific, sea temperatures are milder and island climates more benign. The sub-Antarctic islands are clothed in grasses, shrubs and even trees and provide a wide variety of habitats for both land- and sea-birds. Not all the available habitats are utilized as the islands are often not readily accessible to land-birds, but on the Falkland Islands, favourably situated off the coast of South America, two-thirds of the resident breeding species are land-birds, while the sub-Antarctic islands in the Australian sector have acquired many land-birds, including parrots, starlings and blackbirds, from temperate Australia.

On the vast majority of these islands, however, sea-birds predominate, often breeding in huge colonies either on beaches and cliffs, or in burrows excavated in the soft soil. Penguins are an important element in the avifauna of the circumpolar islands. Although these birds are often associated with the frigid wastes of Antarctica, most of the species are temperate birds, inhabiting the southern shores of Australia, South Africa and South America. Gulls, skuas, terns and cormorants abound along the coasts and throughout the year the oceans themselves are alive with birds, the magnificent albatrosses ranging for thousands of miles as they endlessly cruise along on the Southern Hemisphere wind systems.

Grey-headed Albatross
Diomedea chrysostoma 23in
Would-be attackers are met with a jet of sticky red fluid

Blue-eyed Shag
Phalacrocorax atriceps 29in
Its sodden plumage must be thoroughly dried after each hunting session

Blue-eyed Shag
Phalacrocorax atriceps

Two species of shag, or cormorant, both closely akin to South American populations, have penetrated the colder parts of the southern oceans. The Kerguelen Cormorant, *P.albiventer*, is widespread on the sub-Antarctic islands and crosses the Antarctic Convergence at Iles Kerguelen. The Antarctic, or Blue-eyed Shag, breeds on cliffs and islands in the Scotia Arc and the Antarctic Peninsula.

Both species nest in small colonies, usually on a cliff or headland, and usually close to an area of rich, disturbed water where food is plentiful. In the far south, colonies are common near reefs and shoal water where the ice is seldom thick in winter and breaks up quickly at the onset of the spring thaw. Cormorants dive for their food and often remain submerged for a minute or more in a prolonged chase after a fish, or while searching the sea-bed for molluscs and worms. They remain in the water for up to half an hour at any one time, but then emerge to stand on a prominent rock with wings outstretched in order to dry their sodden plumage.

The shag's untidy nest is made of seaweed, feathers and even bones built up into a mound and cemented with the bird's own droppings. In the far south, two to three eggs form the usual clutch – farther north, three to four is more normal. The young are ready for independent life in February or March, by which time they have acquired the basic hunting skills, and are able to feed up during the summer months before facing their first Antarctic winter.

Grey-headed Albatross
Diomedea chrysostoma

Typical of the smaller albatrosses, or "mollymawks" (a name given to the birds by seamen), the Grey-headed Albatross has a wing-span of about six feet and weighs between four and nine lb. The large, though slender, bill has extremely sharp edges and a powerful hooked tip ideally suited to grasping and tearing slippery prey. Like its many relatives, the Grey-headed Albatross feeds mainly on squid, fish and large surface-dwelling crustaceans caught in the surface waters in long, far-ranging hunting flights.

Grey-headed Albatrosses range as far south as the outer limit of the pack-ice and north into temperate latitudes, frequently keeping company with other, related species. They breed in colonies on the isolated islands of the sub-Antarctic zone, their nests often packed quite close together on the flat tops of the islands or on narrow, grass-covered ledges part way up the cliffs. The nest is a neat cylinder of trampled tussock grasses and mud topped with a shallow hollow in which the single egg is laid. The breeding cycle is a protracted affair and, after ten weeks' incubation, the chick is fed on the nest for up to 30 weeks – throughout the summer, autumn and early winter. Once the chick has attained a reasonable size, both parents leave to hunt for food, leaving the chick to fend for itself. Like most other petrels, its defence is to vomit a stream of oily fluid at any attacker and the sticky fluid is enough to mat the feathers of a raiding skua and cause inconvenience or even death, when the bird next attempts to fly.

Great Skua
Catharacta skua

This predatory brown gull with clawed toes and a powerfully hooked bill, is found on nearly every island and coast in the Antarctic and sub-Antarctic zone. It nests either alone or in small colonies, each nest surrounded by a small but fiercely defended territory. Two richly speckled eggs are laid but usually only a single chick is raised. Outside the breeding season, skuas leave the breeding range and wander widely, living out in the open oceans and travelling into the warmer latitudes of the Equator. In the breeding season they frequent colonies of penguins, petrels and skuas, preying on unguarded eggs, chicks and even weak or injured adults.

Yellow-billed Sheathbill
Chionis alba

The two species of this pigeon-like scavenger are restricted to the shores of Antarctica and the sub-Antarctic islands. The two are separated geographically; *C.alba*, to the western sector, the Black-billed, *C.minor*, to the east. The Sheathbill is the only land-bird to breed in the Antarctic, and although able to fly strongly, this ugly bird spends most of its time running and hopping over the beaches on its tough, un-webbed feet. The birds nest in rock crevices and abandoned petrel burrows, building an untidy nest of shells and pebbles.

They are voracious scavengers – interrupting feeding penguins to rob the chick of its meal of regurgitated krill and often stealing eggs and killing weak or injured birds.

Great Wandering Albatross
Diomedea exulans 40in
The world's largest flying bird

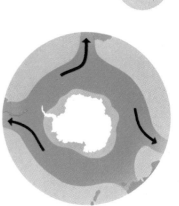

The albatross latitudes
A broad belt of westerly winds encircles the southern hemisphere and, riding these winds, the albatrosses cover enormous distances between their breeding grounds and distant winter quarters.

Great Skua
Catharacta skua 21in
A constant threat to the eggs and young of breeding penguins

Sheathbill
Chionis alba 15in
Antarctica's only resident land-bird

Great Wandering Albatross
Diomedea exulans

Largest of all the world's flying sea-birds, the Great Wanderer measures up to ten feet from wing-tip to wing-tip and may weigh up to 24lb. Breeding mainly on the flat-topped sub-Antarctic islands, the species ranges far and wide across the southern oceans avoiding only the pack-ice zone to the south. Birds banded in South Georgia have been recorded at Gough Island (in the Tristan da Cunha group), off the mouth of the River Plate, and in New South Wales where they tend to congregate in the winter. Great Wanderers from Iles Kerguelen have been recovered off Western Australia and Cape Horn and there is growing evidence that both young and mature birds have regular wintering areas far from their breeding localities.

These magnificent birds feed far out at sea, swooping low over the wave-tops and then settling with wings folded, like huge marine geese, to dabble for squid and other large surface-dwelling creatures. In very calm conditions the Great Wanderer may have difficulty becoming air-borne again, but the normal conditions of the southern oceans almost invariably give the bird full scope to exercise its renowned aerial skills.

The Great Wanderer breeds in colonies on the tops and hillsides of islands where prevailing winds are always available to aid take-off. The courtship "dance", an elaborate and beautiful ritual, culminates in copulation and the single egg is laid in a large, untidy nest similar to that of the Grey-headed Albatross (p222). The egg is incubated for 80 days and the chick must be brooded for a further month or more.

Classification

For early man a crude classification of plants and animals was probably one of the first and most important functions of primitive language; obvious advantages would accrue from an ability to classify species into groups that were dangerous, harmless, poisonous or safe to eat. The grouping of species according to distinct and recognizable features constituted the first steps in taxonomy.

Any system that uses economical generalizations provides a convenient and efficient means of assembling and communicating information, but for animal taxonomists, the arrangement of systematic groups into a hierarchy has the added advantage of providing a "blueprint" in which the various levels of the hierarchy reflect different degrees of evolutionary divergence. The blueprint can help to indicate the probable course of evolution and the relationships that may exist between different groups. Unfortunately, a hierarchical framework cannot adequately reflect the immense complexity of evolutionary history, and examples of convergent evolution (the development of superficial similarities between unrelated species) constantly bedevil the taxonomist.

Though the exact number and sequence of categories may vary between authorities, the basic divisions are universally agreed. Within the animal kingdom, birds belong to the Phylum CHORDATA, within which they form the Class AVES. The Class is divided into 28 ORDERS, further subdivided into Families, Genera and Species. Each bird is known by a "bi-nomial" label consisting of its generic and specific names. The Carrion Crow bears the name *Corvus coròne*, but where more than one race, or sub-species, occurs, a "trinomial" system may be used. Thus, the common, all-black race of the Carrion Crow is more correctly described *Corvus corone corone (C.c.corone)*, while the part-black, part-grey phase, known as the Hooded Crow, is *Corvus corone cornix*.

Key to symbols

HABITAT	Symbols indicate the preferred habitat, or habitats, of the family. For large and varied families, additional labels qualify the symbols shown	fresh water · pelagic · cliff	shore · boreal forest	temperate forest · tropical forest	scrub · desert	marsh · grassland	
NESTING	Most common nest-type shown for each family though individual members of large families may show considerable variation	enclosed · ground-hole	hanging · tree-hole	ground-scrape · open cup	platform	communal	
FEEDING HABIT	The predator classification includes all birds feeding on live prey, e.g. insectivores (insects), piscivores (fish) and carnivores (flesh)	P predator S scavenger	V vegetarian O omnivore	day	night	crepuscular	
FOOD SOURCE	A general indication only, many species having individual preferences. Crustacean symbol = aquatic invertebrates; worm symbol = terrestrial invertebrates	eggs and birds · mammals	fish · reptiles	insects · crustaceans · worms	seeds · grass	fruit and berries	
SOCIAL	Symbols indicate the main type of social organization, or "family life" and the sharing of responsibilities in raising the young	SOCIAL ORGANIZATION solitary · faithful pair · gregarious		PARENTAL CARE male · female · both parents			

ORDER
STRUTHIONIFORMES

Ostrich
Struthio camelus

Struthionidae
Ostrich family
1 species

CHARACTERISTICS The largest living bird, ostriches can be up to 96in tall and weigh up to 350lb. They are flightless, and wing and tail plumes are decorative only. They have a long neck, long strong legs and two toes (3rd, 4th). Neck and thigh muscles are well developed, and unfeathered. Plumage is black and white in males, brown and white in females. Eyesight and hearing are both keen. HABITAT Semi-desert, thorn scrub, plains. DISTRIBUTION S and E Africa, Sahara, S Syria.

Species illustrated
Ostrich 149

BEHAVIOUR Ostriches are non-migratory and rove in flocks of 10-50, often with herds of herbivorous animals, in search of food. FEEDING They eat succulents, insects, small vertebrates. BREEDING In display the male squats and waves his wings; the neck and thighs blush red. Usually silent, the male has a hollow booming call in the breeding season. Some 3-5 females per male lay 15-50 eggs in a communal nest scooped in the ground; the eggs are cream-coloured with pitted surfaces. Males incubate by night, females by day. CARE OF YOUNG The young leave the nest within 24 hours. BIRD & MAN Eggs are used by Kalahari Bushmen as food and to carry water; plumes were once fashionable in Europe. The Arabian sub-species is now presumably extinct.

HABITAT	NESTING	FEEDING	FOOD SOURCE	SOCIAL
		O		

ORDER
RHEIFORMES

Greater Rhea
Rhea americana

Rheidae
Rhea family
2 species

CHARACTERISTICS The heaviest New World bird, rheas can weigh up to 55lb. Height is up to 60in. Neck and legs are long, and there are three toes (2nd, 3rd, 4th). The bill is wide and flat. Rheas are flightless and have short wings. Plumage is loose, greyish in colour, darker on the neck; there are no tail plumes. The sexes are similar, the male being slightly larger. HABITAT Grasslands and open brush country. DISTRIBUTION S Peru, E and Central Brazil, Agentina.

Species illustrated
Greater Rhea 87

BEHAVIOUR Rheas are mainly gregarious (old males may be solitary). Living in non-migratory flocks of 20-50, often in company with Bush Deer or domestic cattle, they are rapid runners and swim well. FEEDING They eat vegetable matter, insects, small vertebrates, molluscs. BREEDING The male displays to 3-8 females, running and spreading his wings and uttering a roaring call. He scratches a hollow in the ground and lines it with grass. There the females lay up to 30 or more eggs, which are incubated by the male for 35-40 days. CARE OF THE YOUNG The young leave the nest early and communicate by whistling calls. Full size is reached in five months, sexual maturity in two years. BIRD & MAN The feathers are used as dusters in South America.

HABITAT	NESTING	FEEDING	FOOD SOURCE	SOCIAL
		O		

ORDER
CASUARIIFORMES

Cassowary
Casuarius casuarius

Casuariidae
Cassowary family
3 species

CHARACTERISTICS These large ratites, or flightless birds, are up to 63in tall. Neck and legs are long, and there are three toes (2nd, 3rd, 4th), the second having a long, sharp claw. The bristly plumage, black in colour, is absent from the head, which bears a bony casque; the wings are greatly reduced. Coloured wattles hang from the neck (except in *C.bennetti*). The sexes are similar, the female being larger. HABITAT Tropical forest. DISTRIBUTION New Guinea, NE Australia and nearby islands.

Species illustrated
Cassowary 182

BEHAVIOUR Occurring singly or in pairs, occasionally in groups of up to six, cassowaries are rapid runners and good swimmers. Shy, and partly nocturnal, they are common but seldom seen, and known to be extremely aggressive, even killing humans, leaping to strike with the claws of both feet. FEEDING They eat all kinds of vegetation (mainly fruit and berries) and insects and spiders. BREEDING They are monogamous, and the female lays 3-8 light-green eggs in a shallow scrape filled with sticks and leaves. The male incubates for 49-52 days. CARE OF YOUNG The nidifugous young, striped above, are defended by the male and fed by both parents. BIRD & MAN The legs are eaten in New Guinea; the feathers serve as head-dresses.

HABITAT	NESTING	FEEDING	FOOD SOURCE	SOCIAL
		V P		

Emu
Dromaius novaehollandiae

Dromaiidae
Emu family
1 species

CHARACTERISTICS This large ratite is 72in high and weighs more than 100lb. It has a long neck and long strong legs, with three toes (2nd, 3rd 4th); the claws are short and strong. The Emu's wings are very short. It has coarse, hairlike plumage, dark above, lighter below. The skin of the head and throat is blue. The sexes are similar. HABITAT Savanna parklands, scrub, open plains. DISTRIBUTION Widespread in Australia, extinct in Tasmania.

Species illustrated
Emu 193

BEHAVIOUR Gregarious, rapid runners and capable swimmers, emus become prevalent in settled areas during times of drought. FEEDING Their food is mainly vegetable, especially fruit; some insects also are eaten. BREEDING The female develops a nuptial plumage of black feathers on the neck, and the blue skin darkens. The nest is a trampled platform of vegetation on the ground under a tree. Some 9-20 eggs are laid and are incubated by the male for 58-61 days. CARE OF YOUNG The nidifugous young may stay up to 18 months with the male. BIRD & MAN Contrary to the predictions of the nineteenth-century naturalist Gould, the Emu has flourished, reaching pest proportions in some areas, notably W Australia in recent years.

HABITAT	NESTING	FEEDING	FOOD SOURCE	SOCIAL
		V		

Classification

ORDER APTERYGIFORMES

Apterygidae
Kiwi family
3 species

Brown Kiwi
Apteryx australis

CHARACTERISTICS These medium ratites, 19-33in long, weigh up to 75lb. They have no tail, the wings are vestigial and hair-like feathers disguise the shape of the body. The legs are short and stout with four toes. They have a long, flexible, decurved bill with bristly hairs at the base and nostrils at the tip. Their eyes are small and their sight is weak. The sexes are similar, the female being larger. HABITAT Humid forest and semi-cleared areas. DISTRIBUTION New Zealand.

Species illustrated
Brown Kiwi 211

BEHAVIOUR Kiwis are nocturnal, somewhat gregarious and notable for their extraordinary appearance – a pear-shaped mass of hairy feathers. Their voice is similarly individual, consisting of two notes, "Ki-Wi", which sound reedy in the male and hoarse in the female. FEEDING The senses of hearing, touch and smell serve as the principal detectors of food – usually worms, insects and fallen berries. BREEDING The nest is a hole in the ground, often dug among tree roots. The female lays 1-2 elongated eggs (weighing approx. 1 lb) which are incubated by the male for 75-80 days. CARE OF YOUNG The young are not fed for the first six days, then they find their own food. BIRD & MAN As the protected national bird of New Zealand, they are in little danger of extinction.

HABITAT	NESTING	FEEDING	FOOD SOURCE	SOCIAL

ORDER GAVIIFORMES

Gaviidae
Diver family
4 species

Black-throated Diver
Gavia arctica

CHARACTERISTICS These foot-propelled diving birds, 26-38in long, have a strong pointed bill, small pointed wings and a short tail. The toes (1st, 2nd, 3rd) are webbed. Body plumage is dense and black and white in colour. The head, neck and back are striped, spotted or barred in bold patterns. The sexes are alike. HABITAT Lakes and ponds, also the sea in winter. DISTRIBUTION N Eurasia, northern N America. Most of the divers are migratory.

Species illustrated
Arctic Loon 36

BEHAVIOUR Divers are usually found singly or in pairs, but may form loose flocks at sea in winter. They swim and dive well and can remain submerged for more than 40sec. Flight is strong though the larger species need a long take-off run. FEEDING Food is mainly fish, with some crustaceans and marine molluscs. BREEDING Divers go ashore only to nest and are awkward on land. Nests are built on small lake islands or by the shore and vary from a slight depression in the ground to a large heap of vegetation. Usually two olive-brown eggs are laid, and incubated by both parents for 28-30 days. CARE OF YOUNG The downy young, fed by both parents, fledge in 45-60 days. BIRD & MAN Great Northern Divers are hunted in Greenland for their neck skins, to make carpets.

HABITAT	NESTING	FEEDING	FOOD SOURCE	SOCIAL

ORDER PODICIPEDIFORMES

Podicipedidae
Grebe family
20 species

Great-crested Grebe
Podiceps cristatus

CHARACTERISTICS Grebes are aquatic diving birds, 9-20in long. Their wings are short and they have almost no tail. The neck is long and the bill sharply pointed (except *Podilymbus*). The toes are lobed. Plumage is a satiny grey or black above, and white, mottled or rufous below. There are lateral tufts on the head. The sexes are alike. HABITAT Fresh-water lakes with plenty of vegetation. Sea coasts in winter. DISTRIBUTION World-wide, except extreme north and south and some islands.

Species illustrated
Pied-billed Grebe 63
Great Crested Grebe 126
Slavonian Grebe 131

BEHAVIOUR Flying little except on migration, grebes are highly adapted to an aquatic life. Usually they are solitary or slightly gregarious. Migration is carried out at night on the wing; by day they swim along the sea-shore, feeding en route. FEEDING They eat aquatic invertebrates, some vegetable matter, and fish in the larger species. BREEDING The courtship display is elaborate and, according to species, includes head shaking, weed presentation and the pair rushing across the water side by side. The nest is built, tethered or floating, in water from sodden aquatic plants. There are 2-9 white, blue or green eggs, elliptical in shape. Incubation is by both sexes for 20-30 days. CARE OF YOUNG The streaked or spotted young are cared for by both parents.

HABITAT	NESTING	FEEDING	FOOD SOURCE	SOCIAL

ORDER SPHENISCIFORMES

Spheniscidae
Penguin family
17 species

Emperor Penguin
Aptenodytes forsteri

CHARACTERISTICS Penguins are flightless birds, 16-48in tall, with paddle-like, non-folding wings. The tail is very short. The legs are short and set well back on the body; the three front toes are webbed. Dense plumage covers the whole body, with no bare patches; colouring is black and white, and some species have a yellow neck. The sexes are similar. HABITAT Sea coasts. DISTRIBUTION Antarctic, New Zealand, south coasts of all southern continents, Galapagos.

Species illustrated
Penguins: Little 213, Emperor 221, Adelie 221, Magellanic 221, Macaroni 221, Royal 221, Galapagos 221

BEHAVIOUR Penguins are gregarious and highly adapted to their marine life and to intense cold. They are awkward on land but versatile in the water, where they can swim submerged, using their wings as flippers, and also leap forward out of the water like porpoises. FEEDING They eat mainly fish, squid and crustaceans. BREEDING Display in some species includes stone presentation. Some species nest in burrows, others in the open. The female lays 2-3 eggs, incubated by both parents. CARE OF YOUNG Crèches form of up to 200 half-grown chicks among those species that nest in the open. Although they are left unguarded by the adults for most of the time, the chicks are nevertheless fed by their own parents, by regurgitation.

HABITAT	NESTING	FEEDING	FOOD SOURCE	SOCIAL
pelagic		P		

ORDER
PROCELLARIIFORMES

Diomedeidae
Albatross family
14 species

Wandering Albatross
Diomedea exulans

CHARACTERISTICS Albatrosses are large, stout-bodied, oceanic birds, 28-53in long. Their wings are long and narrow, their tail short. They carry their webbed feet open in flight. Plumage is brown, black and white or all white. They have a stout hooked bill covered with horny plates. The sexes are similar (except in the Wandering Albatross). HABITAT Oceanic. DISTRIBUTION Southern oceans from 30°S to Antarctica. North in Pacific to Bering Sea. Most species are migratory, covering vast distances.

Species illustrated
Grey-headed Albatross 222
Great Wandering Albatross 223

BEHAVIOUR Albatrosses are often gregarious and form colonies on remote islands, favouring the windward side to make taking off easier. Their long, narrow wings make them superb gliders. FEEDING They alight on the water to feed, mainly on squid and also fish and other marine organisms. Individuals follow ships, often for days, to scavenge. BREEDING Courtship displays are elaborate. In the nest, consisting of a scrape or mound, a single white egg is laid. CARE OF YOUNG In some species the fledging period approaches a year, and so breeding occurs every two years. The nidicolous young are fed by both parents by regurgitation. They defend themselves by vomiting stomach oil at attackers. BIRD & MAN Albatrosses can be an aircraft hazard.

HABITAT	NESTING	FEEDING	FOOD SOURCE	SOCIAL
	mound	P_S ☀		

Procellariidae
Shearwater family
56 species

Fulmar
Fulmarus glacialis

CHARACTERISTICS These oceanic birds, 11-36in long, have long pointed wings and a short tail. The legs are short to medium, the feet webbed. Plumage consists of combinations of white, black, brown and grey. Some species show two colour-phases. In some the bill is short and heavy, in others it is long and slender, hooked and covered with horny plates. Shearwaters have a characteristically musty smell. HABITAT Oceanic. DISTRIBUTION World-wide. Most species are migratory.

Species illustrated
Fulmar 73
Short-tailed Shearwater 213
Great Shearwater 215
Giant Petrel 220

BEHAVIOUR Like the albatrosses, this family is more at home at sea, using the land largely for breeding. FEEDING They feed from the surface, either in flight or after landing. Food is mainly plankton, fish and squid. Some birds may be taken, also offal, refuse and oil. BREEDING Large colonies form in season, and complex vocal displays take place. Nests are made in burrows or crevices; the larger species may prefer to nest on open ground. The female lays 1-2 white eggs, incubated by both parents; there is much noise at shift-changing. CARE OF YOUNG The nidicolous young are fed by both parents and fledge in 3-5 months. They defend themselves by discharging oil from the mouth. BIRD & MAN Mutton Birds are harvested as food by Bass Strait islanders.

HABITAT	NESTING	FEEDING	FOOD SOURCE	SOCIAL
		S P ☀		

Hydrobatidae
Storm petrel family
18 species

Storm Petrel
Hydrobates pelagicus

CHARACTERISTICS Smallest of the web-footed sea-birds, storm petrels are 5½-10in long. They have a frail appearance, with longish thin legs, long wings and a medium to long tail that is square or forked in shape. The neck is short, the bill slender and hooked. Plumage is brown, black or grey; many species have a white rump or underparts. The bill and legs are black, the webs yellow in some species. The sexes are similar. HABITAT Oceanic. DISTRIBUTION World-wide. Population numbers very high.

Species illustrated
Wilson's Petrel 220

BEHAVIOUR These birds seem almost too delicate for an oceanic life; their legs are so weak that they cannot support themselves on land without assistance from their wings; their flight is erratic and bat-like. They are nocturnal, presumably to avoid predation by larger sea-birds. FEEDING Food is mainly plankton, crustaceans and oily scraps from ships. BREEDING They breed colonially in a burrow or crevice. A single egg is incubated by both parents, each for several days at a time, for 5½-7 weeks. CARE OF YOUNG The downy young are fed by regurgitation until they are larger than the parents; they are then deserted. When feathers have replaced down, the young make their way to the sea. BIRD & MAN They are also known as Mother Carey's Chickens.

HABITAT	NESTING	FEEDING	FOOD SOURCE	SOCIAL
		S P ☾	plankton	

Pelecanoididae
Diving petrel family
5 species

Common Diving Petrel
Pelecanoides urinatrix

CHARACTERISTICS These small birds, 6½-10in long, have a squat body, short wings and neck, and a stumpy tail. Their legs are short and their toes are webbed. The bill is short and hooked with upward-opening nasal tubes. Plumage is black above, white below. The sexes are similar. HABITAT Oceanic, nesting on cliffs or islands. DISTRIBUTION Diving petrels are found in southern oceans from the coast of S America east to New Zealand, between latitudes 35°S and 55°S.

Species illustrated
Common Diving Petrel 212

BEHAVIOUR These aptly named birds are spectacularly skilful in the water, diving straight into the sea for food or to escape from enemies. Their wings can be used for under-water propulsion and they are able to re-emerge directly into flight. FEEDING Food comprises fish, crustaceans and other animal matter. BREEDING They breed nocturnally, probably to avoid predation since they are slow and clumsy on land. Nests are made in burrows in soft soil, up to 50in long, the same pair using a burrow for several seasons. A single white egg is incubated by both parents for about five weeks. CARE OF YOUNG Chicks lack any natal down and are brooded continuously for the first 8-10 days; they are then visited nightly by one or both parents.

HABITAT	NESTING	FEEDING	FOOD SOURCE	SOCIAL
		P ☀		

Classification

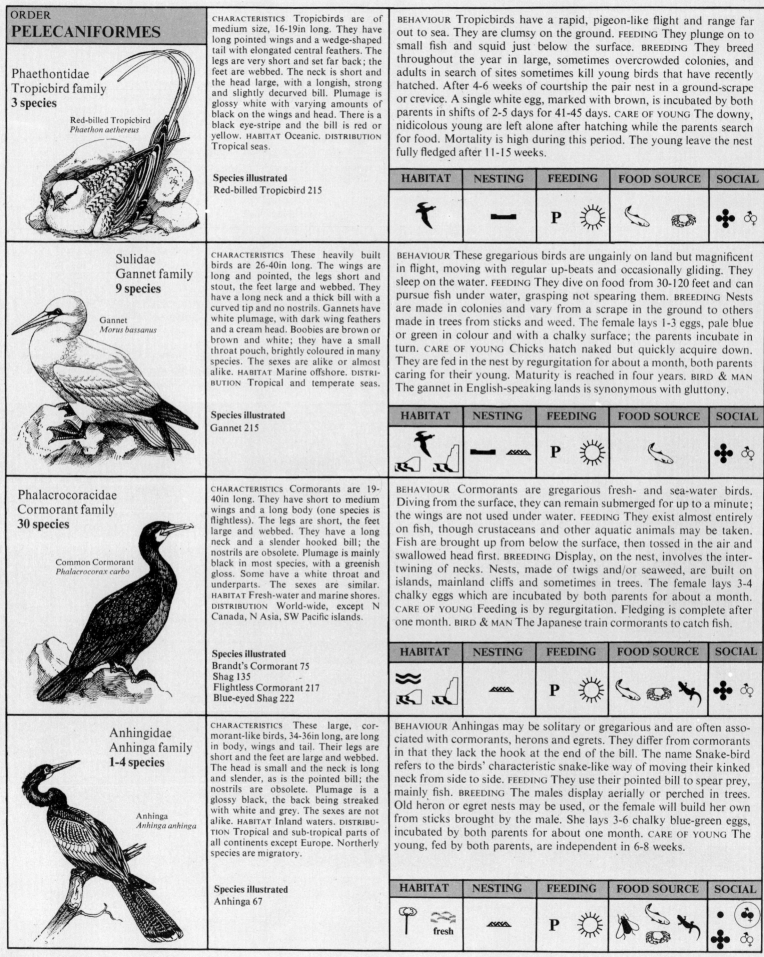

ORDER PELECANIFORMES

Phaethontidae
Tropicbird family
3 species

Red-billed Tropicbird
Phaethon aethereus

CHARACTERISTICS Tropicbirds are of medium size, 16-19in long. They have long pointed wings and a wedge-shaped tail with elongated central feathers. The legs are very short and set far back; the feet are webbed. The neck is short and the head large, with a longish, strong and slightly decurved bill. Plumage is glossy white with varying amounts of black on the wings and head. There is a black eye-stripe and the bill is red or yellow. HABITAT Oceanic. DISTRIBUTION Tropical seas.

Species illustrated
Red-billed Tropicbird 215

BEHAVIOUR Tropicbirds have a rapid, pigeon-like flight and range far out to sea. They are clumsy on the ground. FEEDING They plunge on to small fish and squid just below the surface. BREEDING They breed throughout the year in large, sometimes overcrowded colonies, and adults in search of sites sometimes kill young birds that have recently hatched. After 4-6 weeks of courtship the pair nest in a ground-scrape or crevice. A single white egg, marked with brown, is incubated by both parents in shifts of 2-5 days for 41-45 days. CARE OF YOUNG The downy, nidicolous young are left alone after hatching while the parents search for food. Mortality is high during this period. The young leave the nest fully fledged after 11-15 weeks.

HABITAT	NESTING	FEEDING	FOOD SOURCE	SOCIAL

Sulidae
Gannet family
9 species

Gannet
Morus bassanus

CHARACTERISTICS These heavily built birds are 26-40in long. The wings are long and pointed, the legs short and stout, the feet large and webbed. They have a long neck and a thick bill with a curved tip and no nostrils. Gannets have white plumage, with dark wing feathers and a cream head. Boobies are brown or brown and white; they have a small throat pouch, brightly coloured in many species. The sexes are alike or almost alike. HABITAT Marine offshore. DISTRIBUTION Tropical and temperate seas.

Species illustrated
Gannet 215

BEHAVIOUR These gregarious birds are ungainly on land but magnificent in flight, moving with regular up-beats and occasionally gliding. They sleep on the water. FEEDING They dive on food from 30-120 feet and can pursue fish under water, grasping not spearing them. BREEDING Nests are made in colonies and vary from a scrape in the ground to others made in trees from sticks and weed. The female lays 1-3 eggs, pale blue or green in colour and with a chalky surface; the parents incubate in turn. CARE OF YOUNG Chicks hatch naked but quickly acquire down. They are fed in the nest by regurgitation for about a month, both parents caring for their young. Maturity is reached in four years. BIRD & MAN The gannet in English-speaking lands is synonymous with gluttony.

HABITAT	NESTING	FEEDING	FOOD SOURCE	SOCIAL

Phalacrocoracidae
Cormorant family
30 species

Common Cormorant
Phalacrocorax carbo

CHARACTERISTICS Cormorants are 19-40in long. They have short to medium wings and a long body (one species is flightless). The legs are short, the feet large and webbed. They have a long neck and a slender hooked bill; the nostrils are obsolete. Plumage is mainly black in most species, with a greenish gloss. Some have a white throat and underparts. The sexes are similar. HABITAT Fresh-water and marine shores. DISTRIBUTION World-wide, except N Canada, N Asia, SW Pacific islands.

Species illustrated
Brandt's Cormorant 75
Shag 135
Flightless Cormorant 217
Blue-eyed Shag 222

BEHAVIOUR Cormorants are gregarious fresh- and sea-water birds. Diving from the surface, they can remain submerged for up to a minute; the wings are not used under water. FEEDING They exist almost entirely on fish, though crustaceans and other aquatic animals may be taken. Fish are brought up from below the surface, then tossed in the air and swallowed head first. BREEDING Display, on the nest, involves the intertwining of necks. Nests, made of twigs and/or seaweed, are built on islands, mainland cliffs and sometimes in trees. The female lays 3-4 chalky eggs which are incubated by both parents for about a month. CARE OF YOUNG Feeding is by regurgitation. Fledging is complete after one month. BIRD & MAN The Japanese train cormorants to catch fish.

HABITAT	NESTING	FEEDING	FOOD SOURCE	SOCIAL

Anhingidae
Anhinga family
1-4 species

Anhinga
Anhinga anhinga

CHARACTERISTICS These large, cormorant-like birds, 34-36in long, are long in body, wings and tail. Their legs are short and the feet are large and webbed. The head is small and the neck is long and slender, as is the pointed bill; the nostrils are obsolete. Plumage is a glossy black, the back being streaked with white and grey. The sexes are not alike. HABITAT Inland waters. DISTRIBUTION Tropical and sub-tropical parts of all continents except Europe. Northerly species are migratory.

Species illustrated
Anhinga 67

BEHAVIOUR Anhingas may be solitary or gregarious and are often associated with cormorants, herons and egrets. They differ from cormorants in that they lack the hook at the end of the bill. The name Snake-bird refers to the birds' characteristic snake-like way of moving their kinked neck from side to side. FEEDING They use their pointed bill to spear prey, mainly fish. BREEDING The males display aerially or perched in trees. Old heron or egret nests may be used, or the female will build her own from sticks brought by the male. She lays 3-6 chalky blue-green eggs, incubated by both parents for about one month. CARE OF YOUNG The young, fed by both parents, are independent in 6-8 weeks.

HABITAT	NESTING	FEEDING	FOOD SOURCE	SOCIAL

fresh

Pelecanidae
Pelican family
6 species

White Pelican
Pelecanus onocrotalus

CHARACTERISTICS Pelicans are 50-72in long. They have a large body, short, stout legs and webbed feet. The wings are large, the tail short. Their bill is long, straight and flat, the lower mandible having a large distensible pouch. Plumage is white, brown or grey; the face and bill are brightly coloured in some species. The sexes are alike. HABITAT Inland waters and estuaries. DISTRIBUTION America south to Galapagos, Africa, dispersed in SE Europe, S Asia, E Indies, Australia.

Species illustrated
Brown Pelican 67

BEHAVIOUR Pelicans are highly social birds and flock in large numbers. They move heavily on land but are fine fliers and gliders. FEEDING They live by fishing, often communally, sometimes driving fish to shallower water with heavy wing-beats. The fish are scooped up in the beak pouch as in a net. Adults can eat more than 20lb a day. BREEDING There are relatively simple rituals for pre-mating and at incubation change-over. Nesting is carried out in colonies. The female lays 1-4 white eggs which hatch after about 30 days. CARE OF YOUNG The young, hatching naked, acquire a dark brown down after three days. Fed at first by regurgitation, they feather in eight weeks and can then begin to fish. The young peck at a red spot on the adult's bill to initiate feeding.

HABITAT	NESTING	FEEDING	FOOD SOURCE	SOCIAL
≈ 🪶	⌃⌃	P ☀	🐟	✿ ⚥

Fregatidae
Frigatebird family
5 species

Magnificent Frigatebird
Fregata magnificens

CHARACTERISTICS Frigatebirds are 31-41in long and have the largest wing area, in proportion to body weight, of any bird; their span is up to 96in. They have short legs, a forked tail and a hooked bill. Plumage is black, the male bearing a scarlet throat sac that inflates in display. The female is larger, white breasted, and has no throat sac. HABITAT Coastal waters. DISTRIBUTION Frigatebirds are found in tropical and subtropical zones throughout the world. Also known as the "bo'sun bird".

Species illustrated
Magnificent Frigatebird 99

BEHAVIOUR Frigatebirds live gregariously in areas remote from man. FEEDING Although they are fishers, they never alight on water because they can quickly become waterlogged if they do. Instead they snatch fish from the water while on the wing and pluck flying fish out of the air. Frigatebirds often chase their own and other species, forcing them to disgorge food which they then take. BREEDING The display of the male is spectacular: the throat sac expands to a crimson balloon as big as a man's head. Nests 10-15 feet in diameter are built in trees or, sometimes, on the ground. A single white egg is incubated by both sexes for about 40 days. CARE OF YOUNG The naked young are closely brooded and fledge in 4-5 months, but remain dependent on their parents for up to a year.

HABITAT	NESTING	FEEDING	FOOD SOURCE	SOCIAL
🪶	⌃⌃	P ☀	🐟 🦀	✿ ⚥

ORDER
CICONIIFORMES

Ardeidae
Heron family
64 species

Grey Heron
Ardea cinerea

CHARACTERISTICS These birds vary in height from 11-56in. They have large wings and a short tail. The legs and toes are long, as is the neck, which is bent in an S-shape. The beak is long and pointed (except in the Boat-billed Heron). Plumage is loose and may be all white, brown, grey, blue or patterned in speckles or streaks. The sexes are alike. HABITAT Tree-lined shores and marshes, fresh or salt. DISTRIBUTION World-wide except northern N America and some Pacific islands.

Species illustrated
Great Blue Heron 64, Great White Heron 68, Boat-billed Heron 94
Bittern 125
Cattle Egret 218

BEHAVIOUR Herons are solitary or gregarious according to species, but some may become gregarious of necessity in the breeding season. Many species are crepuscular, some are nocturnal. FEEDING They feed in shallows, standing or walking slowly in search, primarily, of fish, they also eat other aquatic animals, small mammals, reptiles, young birds and insects. BREEDING Nesting is usually colonial, the nest itself being made of sticks and sited in a tree or, less often, on the ground. Courtship display can be elaborate, less so in the more secretive species. The female lays 3-6 eggs, white, blue or buff in colour, which are incubated by both parents. CARE OF YOUNG Chicks are fed by regurgitation and are ready to leave the nest after two months.

HABITAT	NESTING	FEEDING	FOOD SOURCE	SOCIAL
🪶 〰	⌃⌃	P ☀ ☽	🐛 🪰 🦎 🐟 🦀 🐇	✿ ⚥

Balaenicipitidae
Shoe-billed Stork family
1 species

Shoebill
Balaeniceps rex

CHARACTERISTICS These large, stork-like birds are about 46in tall and have a wing span of up to 102in. Their legs are long, their neck longish. The bill is very large, broad and flattened and has a hooked tip. Plumage is grey, darker above, with blackish-grey flight feathers. The sexes are similar. HABITAT Marshes and swamps. DISTRIBUTION The Shoe-billed Stork is found in Africa from N Uganda and E Zaire north as far as the valley of the White Nile in the southern Sudan.

Species illustrated
Shoe-billed Stork 155

BEHAVIOUR These large, slow-flying, inelegant birds are inclined to be solitary and largely nocturnal, and are not easily approached for observation in the papyrus swamps which they usually inhabit. FEEDING They feed while wading, mainly on fish, also frogs, snakes, molluscs, cructaceans and carrion. Their enormous bill may also be employed to dig up lungfish (*Protopterus*), which have been found in their stomachs. BREEDING The nest consists of a platform of rushes built on the ground and lined with finer rushes and grass. There are two eggs, white with a tinge of blue. CARE OF YOUNG The young are downy and nidicolous. Parental care is unknown. BIRD & MAN The birds are recognizable in wall paintings from tombs in Ancient Egypt.

HABITAT	NESTING	FEEDING	FOOD SOURCE	SOCIAL
〰	⌃⌃	P ☀ ☽	🐟 🦀 🦎	•

Classification

Scopidae Hammerhead family
1 species

Hammerhead
Scopus umbretta

CHARACTERISTICS Hammerheads are heavy-looking, stork-like birds, 20in tall, with relatively short legs. The bill is straight, long and laterally compressed. They have a backward-pointing crest which is conspicuous on the ground though not in the air. Plumage is dull brown with faint markings of grey and lighter brown; there is a slight purplish sheen on the upper parts and flight feathers. **HABITAT** Marshes, rivers and lakes. **DISTRIBUTION** Africa south from 12°N.

Species illustrated
Hammerhead 154

BEHAVIOUR Hammerheads are usually found singly or in pairs. **FEEDING** They feed in shallow water mainly on fish, amphibians, large insects and crustaceans. **BREEDING** An enormous roofed stick nest, up to 72in high, is built by both partners in a tree and lined with mud. The male decorates the exterior with brightly coloured objects, often stolen from man, and with dead animal bodies. The female lays 3-6 eggs which, apparently incubated by both birds, hatch at such wide intervals that the first chick may be leaving the nest when the last is hatching. **CARE OF YOUNG** The young are fed by both parents. **BIRD & MAN** The Hammerheads' bizarre style of nest decoration has earned them a reputation for witchcraft and bad luck.

HABITAT	NESTING	FEEDING	FOOD SOURCE	SOCIAL
		P		

Ciconiidae Stork family
17 species

White Stork
Ciconia ciconia

CHARACTERISTICS These large, long-legged birds, 30-60in tall, have long, broad wings, a long neck and a long bill which is either straight, recurved or decurved. The toes are webbed at their extreme base. Plumage is either black and white or all black, the black being generally glossed with purple, blue or green. The sexes are alike. **HABITAT** Lakes, marshes, fields, plains. **DISTRIBUTION** Eurasia to 60°N, Africa, E Indies, Philippines, Australia, S USA, C and S America.

Species illustrated
American Wood Stork 67
Marabou Stork 145

BEHAVIOUR Most storks are gregarious and probably also diurnal. They are strong fliers, the majority flying with the neck extended and the legs trailing behind. **FEEDING** They feed chiefly on animals, especially insects, molluscs, amphibians and fish; one group, the Marabou and Adjutant Storks, are also carrion feeders. **BREEDING** Various courtship displays include elaborate dancing movements and bill clattering. Many nest in trees, some on buildings (notably the White Stork) and on cliffs, often in colonies. In the stick platform-nest 3-6 white eggs are laid which are incubated by both parents. **CARE OF YOUNG** The nidicolous young, naked at first but later downy, are cared for by both parents. Family includes the Wood Ibises of America and Africa.

HABITAT	NESTING	FEEDING	FOOD SOURCE	SOCIAL
		P_s		

Threskiornithidae Ibis family
28 species

Sacred Ibis
Threskiornis aethiopicus

CHARACTERISTICS Medium to large in size, 19-42in tall, these birds have long wings and a short tail. The toes are webbed at the base. Neck and bill are long, the latter decurved in Ibises, broad and spatulate in Spoonbills. Plumage is white, grey-brown or black with a greenish gloss (except for one pink and one scarlet species). The sexes are nearly alike. **HABITAT** Marsh and water in some species, dry areas in others. **DISTRIBUTION** Eurasia, Africa, Australia, S USA, C and S America.

Species illustrated
White Ibis 67, Scarlet Ibis 94
Roseate Spoonbill 67
Eurasian Spoonbill 177

BEHAVIOUR Most species are more or less gregarious. They fly strongly with the neck extended, sometimes gliding. **FEEDING** They eat insects, crustaceans, fish, amphibians, reptiles and some vegetable matter. Spoonbills sift food from the water by holding their bill vertically and moving it from side to side. **BREEDING** A nest of sticks or rushes is built either on the ground, on a cliff or in a tree. There are 2-5 eggs, white, blue or buff in colour, some with spots. **CARE OF YOUNG** Incubation and feeding are carried out by both parents. **BIRD & MAN** The Sacred Ibis was to the ancient Egyptians a symbol of the god Thoth, and thousands of mummified birds have been discovered. Sadly they are now extinct in the land where they were so revered.

HABITAT	NESTING	FEEDING	FOOD SOURCE	SOCIAL
		P		

Phoenicopteridae Flamingo family
4 species

Greater Flamingo
Phoenicopterus ruber

CHARACTERISTICS Flamingos are large water birds, up to 48in tall. They have very long legs and a long neck. The wings are large, the tail short, the face bare. Their bill is unique, being decurved from the middle with a trough-like lower jaw and a lid-like upper jaw. Plumage is pale to deep pink; the wing tips are black. The sexes are alike. **HABITAT** Large, shallow, brackish or salt-water lakes and lagoons. **DISTRIBUTION** S Europe, SW Asia, India, Africa Mexico, W Indies, S America.

Species illustrated
Lesser Flamingo 155

BEHAVIOUR The shape and size of the flamingo's bill are adapted for the pumping and filtering mechanism on which it depends for feeding. The bill is held upside-down in the water and the tongue works like a piston to force water in and out over specialized filtering structures. **FEEDING** The smaller species feed mainly on microscopic plankton (algae, diatoms), the larger mainly on molluscs, crustaceans, insects, annelids, protozoa, algae, diatoms and seeds. **BREEDING** They breed in colonies, often in enormous numbers, usually on bare mud, in shallow water or on lake islands. The nest is a low, truncated cone of mud. The female lays one chalky white egg which is incubated by both partners for 28 days. **CARE OF YOUNG** The nidifugous young are fed by both parents.

HABITAT	NESTING	FEEDING	FOOD SOURCE	SOCIAL
salt water	mud cone	P	aquatic invertebrates plankton	

ORDER
ANSERIFORMES

Southern Screamer
Chauna torquata

**Anhimidae
Screamer family
3 species**

CHARACTERISTICS Screamers are stoutly built and of medium size, 28-36in tall. The wings are long and broad, with two spurs on each carpal edge. The tail is short, the legs sturdy and of medium length with long, stout toes that are webbed at the base. Their bill is short and pheasant-like and a short neck is surmounted by a small head. Plumage is grey or black above, white or grey below and barred. HABITAT Marsh and wet grasslands. DISTRIBUTION S America, except Andean chain and Patagonia.

Species illustrated
Southern Screamer 86

BEHAVIOUR Largely terrestrial, screamers are gregarious at times, flocking in their thousands. They frequent areas of shallow water, wading slowly in search of food. Their bulk makes taking off awkward, but once in the air they can soar to great heights. Screamers are aptly named, the two-note call of a single bird being audible at a mile, and a "concert" of a whole flock, usually delivered at night, can be almost deafening. FEEDING Their diet is mainly vegetarian. BREEDING In season there is much calling and wheeling about in the air, presumably as part of a display. A shallow, cup-shaped nest of rushes and grasses is built among cover on marshy ground. The 4-6 eggs are incubated by both partners. CARE OF YOUNG The nidifugous young are cared for by both parents.

HABITAT	NESTING	FEEDING	FOOD SOURCE	SOCIAL

**Anatidae
Duck family
147 species**

Mallard
Anas platyrhynchos

CHARACTERISTICS These essentially aquatic birds range from 11-60in long. The legs are medium to short, the toes fully webbed, the hind toe being small and elevated. Wings are moderately long and pointed, tails usually short and pointed. They have a medium to long neck and bills are typically lamellate, broad and flat with a rounded tip. Plumage is dense and in varied colours, often elaborately patterned. HABITAT Rivers, lakes, sea coasts, marshes. DISTRIBUTION World-wide.

Species illustrated
Ducks: Canvasback 63, Torrent 93, Black-headed 95, Eider 128, Mandarin 175
Geese: Canada 65, Egyptian 156, Magpie 201, Cape Barren 213, Hawaiian 217
Swans: Mute 126, Black 200
Shelduck 128, Merganser 131

BEHAVIOUR This closely related, monophyletic family shows a remarkable anatomical uniformity, and hybridization frequently occurs. Habits are varied; many species are gregarious, most fly well, a few are flightless. *All* are flightless for some weeks after the breeding season, when flight feathers moult simultaneously. All swim well and many dive (the Torrent Duck lives and feeds in rapids). FEEDING Their diet ranges from entirely vegetarian to entirely animal. BREEDING Most species nest on the ground, some in holes or trees. The nest is usually lined with the female's breast-down. There are 2-16 eggs, white, buff or greenish in colour, and these are incubated by one or both parents. CARE OF YOUNG Either parent, or both, care for the nidifugous young.

HABITAT	NESTING	FEEDING	FOOD SOURCE	SOCIAL

ORDER
FALCONIFORMES

King Vulture
Sarcoramphus papa

**Cathartidae
American Vulture family
6 species**

CHARACTERISTICS New World Vultures are medium to very large, 25-44in long, with a bulky body and broad wings. The tail is medium to long, the legs short to medium with an obsolete hind toe; the claws are weak. They have a thick hooked bill and the head and neck are bare. Plumage is brown or black, with a light area under the wings; head and neck may be red, black or yellow. HABITAT Forest, plains, desert, mountains. DISTRIBUTION S Canada, N America, W Indies, S America.

Species illustrated
Turkey Vulture 50
California Condor 53

BEHAVIOUR The Andean Condor is one of the largest living birds, weighing up to 26lb and having a wing span of up to 125in. All species soar and glide well, often at great heights. Their voices consist merely of hisses and grunts. FEEDING They have a large olfactory chamber and some species use their sense of smell to locate food. Diet is mainly carrion, and some small animals, fruits and vegetables are also taken. BREEDING Nesting takes place on cliffs, in caves and sometimes in trees. Condors usually lay one egg, the smaller vultures two; these are white or grey-green, plain or blotched, and are incubated by both parents for 32-58 days. CARE OF YOUNG The nidicolous young, at first fed by regurgitation, remain in the nest for up to 12 weeks.

HABITAT	NESTING	FEEDING	FOOD SOURCE	SOCIAL

**Accipitridae
Hawk family
217 species**

Golden Eagle
Aquila chrysaetos

CHARACTERISTICS Varying from 8-45in long, these birds have large rounded wings, strong medium-sized legs and claws, the latter being hooked. The neck is short, as is the hooked bill. Plumage is brown or grey and barred or streaked. In most species the sexes are nearly alike, with the female larger. HABITAT Open country, woods, forests, swamps, cliffs, marshes, deserts, seashores. DISTRIBUTION This family is found world-wide, except in the Arctic, the Antarctic and most oceanic islands.

Species illustrated
Eagles: 69, 85, 97, 110, 117, 123, 146, 156, 169, 170, 193 Kites: 69, 152, 175, 179 Buzzards (Am.=hawks): 42, 55, 102, 216 Sparrowhawks: 39, 106, 204
Lammergeier 163
Harriers (Am.=hawks): 63, 88, 125

BEHAVIOUR Habits vary greatly in this family. Some are gregarious, more are solitary. All are fine fliers and many soar. FEEDING Apart from the carrion-feeding vultures, they generally hunt live prey. Many take their food on the wing; the African Fish Eagle plunges feet-first into water, often submerging completely. Food includes mammals, birds, amphibians, reptiles, insects, eggs and offal. BREEDING Nests are varied, usually being made of sticks in trees, less often on cliffs or on the ground. The eggs are white in most species and either unmarked or marked with brown, red and grey. The larger species lay 1-2 eggs, the smaller 3-5. CARE OF YOUNG The downy, nidicolous young are generally fed by the female on food which the male brings.

HABITAT	NESTING	FEEDING	FOOD SOURCE	SOCIAL
all land habitats				

Classification

Pandionidae
Osprey family
1 species

Osprey
Pandion haliaetus

CHARACTERISTICS Ospreys are large birds, about 24in long, and have long pointed wings. The bill is short and hooked. Claws are large, the outer toe being reversible, and there are spines on the soles of their feet. Plumage is brownish-black above, white below. A black line runs through the eye to the back of the neck. The sexes are alike. HABITAT Near water, either the sea or inland. DISTRIBUTION Europe, Asia, N Africa, E Indies, Australia, N America to Gulf Coast, C America, Bahamas.

Species illustrated
Osprey 219

BEHAVIOUR Ospreys are invariably associated with water, either inland or sea. FEEDING They are fishers and take their prey with the claws, hovering and then diving, the feet flung forward an instant before entering the water; often they submerge completely. The fish is carried to the nest or perch to be eaten. Their diet is almost exclusively fish, although small mammals and birds, including domestic fowl, are occasionally taken. BREEDING This occurs communally where ospreys are common. Usually three eggs, white or fawn with brown markings, are laid in a nest of sticks high in a tree, or on rocks or on the ground. Incubation is by the female. CARE OF YOUNG The downy, nidicolous young are fed by the female and fledge in 8-10 weeks.

HABITAT	NESTING	FEEDING	FOOD SOURCE	SOCIAL
≈ ≋	∿∿	P ☀	🐟	⊛ ♂♀

Falconidae
Falcon family
61 species

Peregrine Falcon
Falco peregrinus

CHARACTERISTICS Falcons are of small to medium size, 6-25in long. Their wings are long and pointed, the tail medium to long as are the legs, which end in long toes with strong hooked claws. The neck is short, also the bill, which in most species features a hooked upper mandible with a tooth. Plumage is brown or grey and often barred or streaked. The sexes are usually alike, the female being larger. HABITAT Varied. DISTRIBUTION World-wide, except Antarctic and most oceanic islands.

Species illustrated
Falcons: 56, 73, 150, 152
Hobby 119, Merlin 123
Crested Caracara 87

BEHAVIOUR Most species of true falcon are solitary. Flight is direct and swift with less soaring than in other birds of prey. FEEDING Their live prey is usually taken in the feet after aerial pursuit, or in an air-to-ground dive. Diet consists of vertebrate and invertebrate animals in most species, though some (such as caracaras) depend on carrion. BREEDING Some build nests (*Polyborus* and *Milvago*), others (*Falco* and related genera) utilize abandoned nests. There are 2-6 white eggs, often so heavily spotted with brown that the ground colour is obscured. Incubation is by the female or, less often, by both sexes. CARE OF YOUNG Generally the downy, nidicolous young are cared for by the female, food being delivered by the male.

HABITAT	NESTING	FEEDING	FOOD SOURCE	SOCIAL
all land habitats	∿∿	P$_S$ ☀	🐦 🦎 🐰	• ♂♀

Sagittariidae
Secretary Bird family
1 species

Secretary Bird
Sagittarius serpentarius

CHARACTERISTICS These large birds of prey, 50-60in tall, have long wings and long slender legs with short, powerful, partly webbed toes and long claws. The 12-feathered tail features an elongated central pair. The neck is fairly long and the bill is short with a hooked tip. Plumage is pale grey on the body, with black thighs, tail and flight feathers. There is a conspicuous grey crest. The sexes are alike, the female larger. HABITAT Grassy plains, DISTRIBUTION Africa south of Sahara.

Species illustrated
Secretary Bird 146

BEHAVIOUR These terrestrial birds hunt by running and walking with long strides. They fly well but infrequently. FEEDING Their food includes reptiles, mammals, insects and young birds, all taken on the ground. Large snakes are killed by a powerful stamp of the foot, or by being dropped from a height. BREEDING Courtship display is carried out in the air. The pair build a bulky nest of sticks at the top of a tree or bush. The female lays 2-3 eggs and incubates them alone for six weeks. CARE OF YOUNG The downy young receive mainly regurgitated insects for about six weeks, then go on to more solid food. Gradually the parents begin abandoning the young for increasing periods and at ten weeks they are ready to leave the nest.

HABITAT	NESTING	FEEDING	FOOD SOURCE	SOCIAL
⋀⋀⋀	∿∿	P ☀	🐦 🦎 🐰	⊛ ♂♀

ORDER
TINAMIFORMES

Tinamidae
Tinamou family
45-50 species

Crested Tinamou
Eudromia elegans

CHARACTERISTICS Tinamous have a squat, compact body and are 8-21in long. Their wings are short and rounded and the tail is also short and often hidden by dense rump feathers. The legs are short and bear three front toes; the hallux is absent or elevated. The neck is of medium length, the bill weak, elongated, pointed and slightly decurved. Plumage is tawny, brown or grey and patterned in streaks, spots or bars. The sexes are similar. HABITAT Varied. DISTRIBUTION S Mexico to S Argentina.

Species illustrated
Great Tinamou 82

BEHAVIOUR Tinamous are rather poor fliers and prefer a terrestrial life, protecting themselves from predators by crouching motionless and using their patterned plumage as camouflage. Some are gregarious, many are solitary, shy and crepuscular. FEEDING They eat mainly fruit, seeds and some insects. BREEDING The males often mate with several females, while the females lay eggs in several nests; these are made in a ground indentation and lined with vegetation. The eggs, 1-12 in number, are glossy and either green, blue, yellow or purplish-brown, and they are incubated by the male. Some species cover their eggs with leaves or feathers. CARE OF YOUNG The young hatch in 19-20 days and leave the nest in the next two days, guarded by the male.

HABITAT	NESTING	FEEDING	FOOD SOURCE	SOCIAL
all land habitats	—	V$_P$ ☀	🌿 🥚 🦟	⊕ ♂

ORDER
GALLIFORMES

Megapodidae
Megapode family
12 species

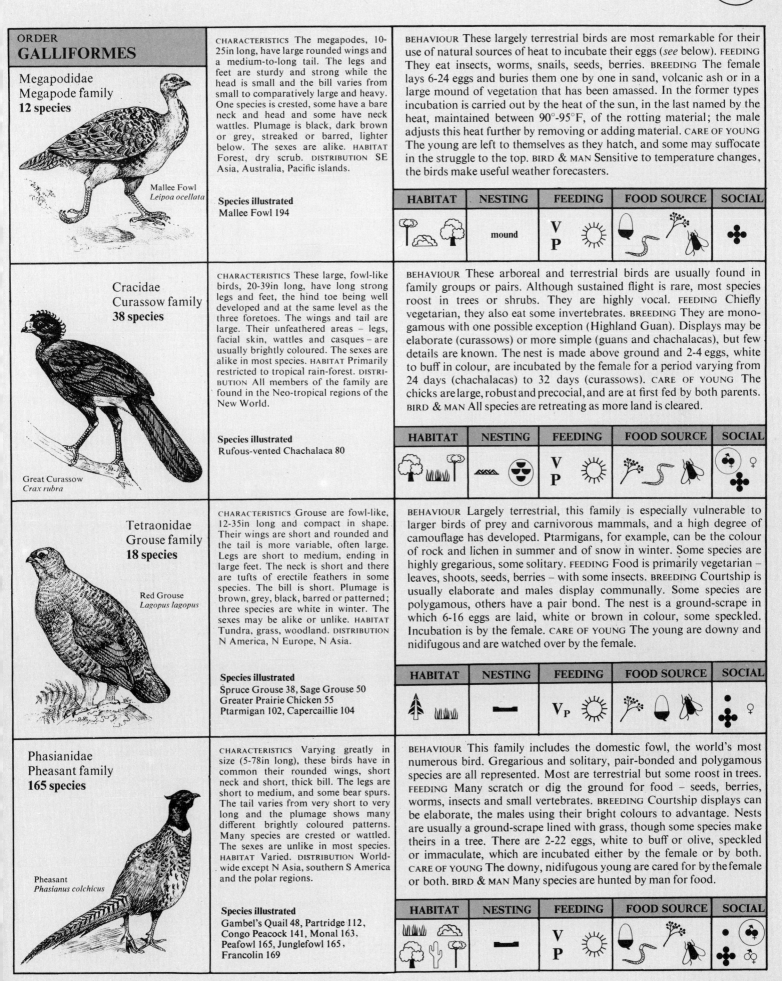

Mallee Fowl
Leipoa ocellata

CHARACTERISTICS The megapodes, 10-25in long, have large rounded wings and a medium-to-long tail. The legs and feet are sturdy and strong while the head is small and the bill varies from small to comparatively large and heavy. One species is crested, some have a bare neck and head and some have neck wattles. Plumage is black, dark brown or grey, streaked or barred, lighter below. The sexes are alike. HABITAT Forest, dry scrub. DISTRIBUTION SE Asia, Australia, Pacific islands.

Species illustrated
Mallee Fowl 194

BEHAVIOUR These largely terrestrial birds are most remarkable for their use of natural sources of heat to incubate their eggs (*see* below). FEEDING They eat insects, worms, snails, seeds, berries. BREEDING The female lays 6-24 eggs and buries them one by one in sand, volcanic ash or in a large mound of vegetation that has been amassed. In the former types incubation is carried out by the heat of the sun, in the last named by the heat, maintained between 90°-95°F, of the rotting material; the male adjusts this heat further by removing or adding material. CARE OF YOUNG The young are left to themselves as they hatch, and some may suffocate in the struggle to the top. BIRD & MAN Sensitive to temperature changes, the birds make useful weather forecasters.

HABITAT	NESTING	FEEDING	FOOD SOURCE	SOCIAL
	mound	V P		

Cracidae
Curassow family
38 species

Great Curassow
Crax rubra

CHARACTERISTICS These large, fowl-like birds, 20-39in long, have long strong legs and feet, the hind toe being well developed and at the same level as the three foretoes. The wings and tail are large. Their unfeathered areas – legs, facial skin, wattles and casques – are usually brightly coloured. The sexes are alike in most species. HABITAT Primarily restricted to tropical rain-forest. DISTRIBUTION All members of the family are found in the Neo-tropical regions of the New World.

Species illustrated
Rufous-vented Chachalaca 80

BEHAVIOUR These arboreal and terrestrial birds are usually found in family groups or pairs. Although sustained flight is rare, most species roost in trees or shrubs. They are highly vocal. FEEDING Chiefly vegetarian, they also eat some invertebrates. BREEDING They are monogamous with one possible exception (Highland Guan). Displays may be elaborate (curassows) or more simple (guans and chachalacas), but few details are known. The nest is made above ground and 2-4 eggs, white to buff in colour, are incubated by the female for a period varying from 24 days (chachalacas) to 32 days (curassows). CARE OF YOUNG The chicks are large, robust and precocial, and are at first fed by both parents. BIRD & MAN All species are retreating as more land is cleared.

HABITAT	NESTING	FEEDING	FOOD SOURCE	SOCIAL
		V P		

Tetraonidae
Grouse family
18 species

Red Grouse
Lagopus lagopus

CHARACTERISTICS Grouse are fowl-like, 12-35in long and compact in shape. Their wings are short and rounded and the tail is more variable, often large. Legs are short to medium, ending in large feet. The neck is short and there are tufts of erectile feathers in some species. The bill is short. Plumage is brown, grey, black, barred or patterned; three species are white in winter. The sexes may be alike or unlike. HABITAT Tundra, grass, woodland. DISTRIBUTION N America, N Europe, N Asia.

Species illustrated
Spruce Grouse 38, Sage Grouse 50
Greater Prairie Chicken 55
Ptarmigan 102, Capercaillie 104

BEHAVIOUR Largely terrestrial, this family is especially vulnerable to larger birds of prey and carnivorous mammals, and a high degree of camouflage has developed. Ptarmigans, for example, can be the colour of rock and lichen in summer and of snow in winter. Some species are highly gregarious, some solitary. FEEDING Food is primarily vegetarian – leaves, shoots, seeds, berries – with some insects. BREEDING Courtship is usually elaborate and males display communally. Some species are polygamous, others have a pair bond. The nest is a ground-scrape in which 6-16 eggs are laid, white or brown in colour, some speckled. Incubation is by the female. CARE OF YOUNG The young are downy and nidifugous and are watched over by the female.

HABITAT	NESTING	FEEDING	FOOD SOURCE	SOCIAL
		V P		

Phasianidae
Pheasant family
165 species

Pheasant
Phasianus colchicus

CHARACTERISTICS Varying greatly in size (5-78in long), these birds have in common their rounded wings, short neck and short, thick bill. The legs are short to medium, and some bear spurs. The tail varies from very short to very long and the plumage shows many different brightly coloured patterns. Many species are crested or wattled. The sexes are unlike in most species. HABITAT Varied. DISTRIBUTION Worldwide except N Asia, southern S America and the polar regions.

Species illustrated
Gambel's Quail 48, Partridge 112,
Congo Peacock 141, Monal 163,
Peafowl 165, Junglefowl 165,
Francolin 169

BEHAVIOUR This family includes the domestic fowl, the world's most numerous bird. Gregarious and solitary, pair-bonded and polygamous species are all represented. Most are terrestrial but some roost in trees. FEEDING Many scratch or dig the ground for food – seeds, berries, worms, insects and small vertebrates. BREEDING Courtship displays can be elaborate, the males using their bright colours to advantage. Nests are usually a ground-scrape lined with grass, though some species make theirs in a tree. There are 2-22 eggs, white to buff or olive, speckled or immaculate, which are incubated either by the female or by both. CARE OF YOUNG The downy, nidifugous young are cared for by the female or both. BIRD & MAN Many species are hunted by man for food.

HABITAT	NESTING	FEEDING	FOOD SOURCE	SOCIAL
		V P		

Classification

Numididae Guineafowl family
7 species

Helmeted Guineafowl
Numida meleagris

CHARACTERISTICS Guineafowl are 17-29in long and have a stocky body with a medium tail and wings, the latter rounded. Their legs are strong and the hind toe is located above the level of the three front toes. The head and neck are bare though there may be a casque, crest or wattles. The bill is short and stout, the tail medium. Plumage is black, spotted and striped with white. Sexes alike. **HABITAT** Forest, brush, grassland. **DISTRIBUTION** Africa south of Sahara, Madagascar.

Species illustrated
Helmeted Guineafowl 147

BEHAVIOUR Although capable of strong flight guineafowl are mainly terrestrial, and many species choose to run rather than fly when threatened; nevertheless, they usually roost in trees. Most species are gregarious. **FEEDING** They eat all kinds of vegetable matter, also insects, molluscs and frogs. **BREEDING** The nest is a ground-scrape, sparsely lined. There are 7-20 eggs, white to light brown in colour, which are incubated by the female. **CARE OF YOUNG** Both parents care for the downy, nidifugous young. **BIRD & MAN** Guineafowl were domesticated in ancient times by the Romans as table birds and they are still hunted as game today. Some authorities classify guineafowl as a sub-family within the Phasianidae.

HABITAT	NESTING	FEEDING	FOOD SOURCE	SOCIAL

Meleagrididae Turkey family
2 species

Turkey
Meleagris gallopavo

CHARACTERISTICS Turkeys are fat and heavy, 33-43in long. The wings and tail are broad and rounded, the legs medium to long and spurred with large feet. The neck is long and bare, coloured blue and red and wattled. The bill is short. Plumage is dark brown to greenish-black with buff and white on wings and tail and black tips to the tail feathers. The sexes are similar. **HABITAT** Wooded country. **DISTRIBUTION** Dispersed throughout much of the USA and eastern Mexico.

Species illustrated
Turkey 43

BEHAVIOUR Although terrestrial, turkeys can fly strongly for short distances. They are gregarious. **FEEDING** Their diet is largely vegetarian, with some insects, worms and other animals. **BREEDING** In display the male fans his wings and tail, making a characteristic gobbling sound. A male will mount many females, each then building her own nest, a ground hollow, and herself incubating the 8-18 buff eggs. **CARE OF YOUNG** The downy, nidifugous young are her charge alone; they are able to fly at two weeks. **BIRD & MAN** Turkeys were farmed by the Aztecs and were introduced to Europe by about 1540. At one time dangerously depleted in the USA, they were protected and special farms were set up.

HABITAT	NESTING	FEEDING	FOOD SOURCE	SOCIAL

ORDER GRUIFORMES

Rallidae Rail family
132 species

Moorhen
Gallinula chloropus

CHARACTERISTICS Rails are small to medium birds, 5½-20in long, with short wings and a very short tail. The body is often laterally compressed. Legs are longish, the tibiae partly bare, with long toes that in the coot (*Fulica*) are lobed. The bill is strong and varies from long and curved to short and stout. Plumage is grey, black, brown, blue or green, often streaked above and barred below. The sexes are usually alike. **HABITAT** Mainly marsh and lake. **DISTRIBUTION** World-wide except polar regions.

Species illustrated
Sora Rail 64, Clapper Rail 70, Horned Coot 95, Spotted Crake 201, Takahe 210

BEHAVIOUR Many species of rail are solitary and secretive, and often nocturnal or crepuscular. A large number are aquatic, and though some others are terrestrial, nearly all swim well. Some are weak fliers, but generally long distances can be achieved; a few island species are flightless. Flight feathers are moulted simultaneously. Rails walk with a characteristic bobbing of the head and a flirting tail. **FEEDING** Food varies greatly, including many kinds of animal and vegetable matter. **BREEDING** A flat or domed nest of vegetation is built either in water, on the ground or low in a bush. The female lays 2-16 eggs, white, buff or olive in colour and speckled, which are incubated by both parents. **CARE OF YOUNG** The downy, nidifugous young are tended by both parents.

HABITAT	NESTING	FEEDING	FOOD SOURCE	SOCIAL

Heliornithidae Finfoot family
3 species

Sungrebe
Heliornis fulica

CHARACTERISTICS These medium-sized birds, 12-24in long, have short wings and a long broad tail. Their legs are short and stout with long, broadly lobed toes. The bill is longish, strong and tapered. A small thin head rests on a long neck. Plumage is blackish or brown above, pale buff below; the head and neck carry distinct white stripes. The sexes are nearly alike. **HABITAT** Streams, lakes, marshes. **DISTRIBUTION** C and S Africa, Asia from NE India to Sumatra, C and northern S America.

Species illustrated
Masked Finfoot 174

BEHAVIOUR These largely aquatic birds are very shy and are found in family parties, in pairs or singly. They are strong fliers, but only for short distances, and when disturbed on land they react by running. They swim with a coot-like bobbing of the head; it is not universally agreed whether they dive or not. **FEEDING** Food comprises insects, molluscs, crustaceans, amphibians, small fish, leaves and seeds. **BREEDING** A bulky nest of sticks, twigs, leaves and grass is built in a bush or low in a tree. There are 2-7 spherical eggs, cream or pale green with darker blotches, incubated by both parents. **CARE OF YOUNG** The role of the parents in looking after the downy, nidifugous young is at present not known. Habits and structure show affinities with grebes, darters, ducks and rails.

HABITAT	NESTING	FEEDING	FOOD SOURCE	SOCIAL

Rhynochetidae
Kagu family
1 species

Kagu
Rhynochetos jubatus

CHARACTERISTICS These medium-sized birds, about 22in long, have broad and rounded wings; the tail is also broad but longish. Their legs are long and red, the hind toe elevated. A crested head is set on a short neck. The bill is red and fairly long and flattened, sharp and slightly decurved. Plumage is grey-brown on back and tail, with a whitish head, crest, chest and belly. The sexes are nearly alike. HABITAT Forests. DISTRIBUTION Restricted to the island of New Caledonia.

Species illustrated
Kagu 205

BEHAVIOUR The shy, solitary Kagu is active towards dusk and after dark, when its piercing guttural, rattling calls are heard. Terrestrial, it is apparently flightless and escapes by running with spread wings. FEEDING Food consists of insects, worms, molluscs and frogs. BREEDING In courtship the birds face each other with spread wings to reveal normally hidden stripes and also whirl round holding a wing-tip in the bill. A single buff egg, speckled with brown, is laid in a cup-shaped nest made on the ground of sticks and leaves. The parents share the 36 days of incubation. CARE OF YOUNG Both tend the downy chick for one month, by which time it can feed itself. BIRD & MAN This is a threatened species, prey to rats, pigs and dogs, all introduced by man.

HABITAT	NESTING	FEEDING		FOOD SOURCE			SOCIAL	
		P						

Eurypygidae
Sunbittern family
1 species

Sunbittern
Eurypyga helias

CHARACTERISTICS. Wading birds of medium size, 18in long, Sunbitterns have broad wings and a long broad tail. Legs and toes are long. The head is large and the bill and neck are long. Plumage is a barred and mottled black, brown, grey and white. Spread wings are boldly patterned with black, brown, yellow, olive and white. There are two white bands on the side of the black head. The sexes are alike. HABITAT Tropical forests. DISTRIBUTION Sunbitterns are found in C America and the Amazon system.

BEHAVIOUR Solitary and terrestrial, the Sunbittern is found wading at the water's edge where it searches for food. These birds fly gracefully, and the voice is a long whistle and a plaintive-sounding piping. When alarmed, the bill is rattled. FEEDING They eat insects, crustaceans and small fish. BREEDING Display includes a spectacular spreading of the wings, revealing a richly coloured upper surface which combines with the raised tail to form a complete semi-circle. A nest of leaves, twigs, moss and mud is built in a tree by both birds. There are 2-3 oval-shaped buff eggs, blotched with brown, and these are incubated for about four weeks by both parents. CARE OF YOUNG Feeding is shared until, after about three weeks, the young can fly to the ground.

HABITAT	NESTING	FEEDING		FOOD SOURCE			SOCIAL	
		P						

Mesoenatidae
Mesite family
3 species

Bensch's Rail
Monias benschi

CHARACTERISTICS Thrush-sized terrestrial birds, 10-11in long, the mesites have rounded wings and tail, the former short, the latter long. Medium-sized legs may be slender or stout. The head is small and the neck medium. The bill is medium, slender and straight in *Mesitornis*, long and sickled in the monias. Plumage is brown or grey and olive, the throat and breast pale, spotted or barred. The sexes are alike except the monias. HABITAT Forest and brush. DISTRIBUTION Madagascar.

BEHAVIOUR The mesites are entirely terrestrial and apparently incapable of flight. They are usually found in pairs, except the monias which live in flocks of 30 or more. FEEDING They eat fruit, seeds and insects. BREEDING They are thought to be polyandrous, as males greatly outnumber females. A nest of sticks and leaves is made up to six feet above ground in a tree or bush (always accessible without flying). There are 1-3 eggs, white, greenish-white or greyish-buff, incubated by either or both parents. CARE OF YOUNG It is generally believed that the downy, nidifugous young are tended by the male. BIRD & MAN A difficult family to place, the sum of their characters suggests that they are possibly closest to the Sunbittern and the hemipodes.

HABITAT	NESTING	FEEDING		FOOD SOURCE			SOCIAL	
		V P						♂

Turnicidae
Hemipode-quail family
15 species

Andalusian Hemipode
Turnix sylvatica

CHARACTERISTICS The hemipodes are small, 4½-7½in long, and stout bodied. Their wings are short and rounded, the tail very short. Short strong legs bear three toes (2nd, 3rd, 4th). A small head is set on a short neck; the bill is short and varies from stout to slender. Plumage is brown, black and grey, patterned above and plain below. HABITAT Brush, grassland. DISTRIBUTION S Spain and Portugal, Africa, India, SE Asia, Philippines, Solomons, New Guinea, Australia.

BEHAVIOUR Superficially resembling the true quail, though with only three toes, the hemipodes are secretive and terrestrial. They rarely fly, usually only when startled. Most species are solitary or live in pairs, though some keep together in groups of 15-30. FEEDING They scratch the ground for seeds, young shoots and insects. BREEDING In courtship the female takes the dominant role, uttering a booming call and attacking other females. A nest of grass is made on the ground, and 2-4 eggs are laid, white, grey or olive, and spotted with brown; these are then abandoned for the male to incubate. The incubation period, 12-13 days, is one of the shortest among birds. CARE OF YOUNG The male also broods and feeds the downy, nidifugous young.

HABITAT	NESTING	FEEDING		FOOD SOURCE		SOCIAL	
		V P					♂

Classification

Pedionomidae
Collared-hemipode family
1 species

Plains Wanderer
Pedionomus torquatus

CHARACTERISTICS These small birds, 6-7in long, have a compact body with short wings and a very short tail. The legs are fairly long and there are four toes. The neck, head and bill are of medium size, the latter pointed. Plumage is buff, brown and black, patterned above with pale underparts and a white collar spotted with black. The female is larger and more boldly patterned and has a brown collar below the white one. HABITAT Open plains. DISTRIBUTION SE Australia.

BEHAVIOUR The Plains-wanderer rarely flies, though there is evidence that it may do so at night. Usually it walks upright, on tiptoe. FEEDING Food consists of seeds, vegetable matter and insects. BREEDING The female is dominant in courtship (and terrestrial behaviour). The nest is a ground-hollow, protected by tufts of grass. There are four eggs, yellowish- or greenish-white and spotted with olive and grey; these are incubated by the male. CARE OF YOUNG The male also cares for the young, which are presumed to be nidifugous. BIRD & MAN The Plains-wanderer population has been considerably reduced by foxes and dogs, introduced by man, and by the generally changing character of its habitat brought about by highly mechanized agriculture.

HABITAT	NESTING	FEEDING	FOOD SOURCE	SOCIAL
		P V		♂

Gruidae
Crane family
14 species

Whooping Crane
Grus americana

CHARACTERISTICS The cranes, 31-60in tall, have large wings (the secondaries modified for display) and a short tail. The legs and toes are long, the hind toe elevated. The neck and bill are long, the latter straight. The head may be plumed or have bare red areas. Plumage is brown, grey or white. The sexes are alike. HABITAT Open country of various kinds, particularly wet land areas. DISTRIBUTION N America south to Mexico, and W Indies, Europe, Asia, Africa, Madagascar, Australia.

Species illustrated
Whooping Crane 65
Demoiselle Crane 110
Sarus Crane 176, Brolga Crane 201

BEHAVIOUR Cranes are gregarious birds, except during the breeding season. They spend much of their time on the ground but are good fliers, moving through the air with the neck extended, often soaring. Their particularly resonant voice is caused by an elongated trachea which is coiled in the sternum. FEEDING They eat a great variety of animal and vegetable matter. BREEDING Display includes elaborate dancing rituals in which two or more birds participate. The nest, made of vegetation either on the ground or in water, varies in size. There are 2-3 eggs, white, blue, brown or buff, and spotted, which are incubated by both parents. CARE OF YOUNG Both parents also tend the downy, nidifugous young.

HABITAT	NESTING	FEEDING	FOOD SOURCE	SOCIAL
		O	varied	⚥

Aramidae
Limpkin family
1 species

Limpkin
Aramus guarauna

CHARACTERISTICS Limpkins are large birds, 23-28in long, with broad and rounded wings and a broad tail. The legs and toes are long, the claws sharp. The neck and bill are long, the latter slightly decurved and laterally compressed. Plumage is dark brown with white streaks on the head, neck, breast and back. The sexes are alike. HABITAT Wooded or open swamps (drier country in W Indies). DISTRIBUTION Parts of the Americas – Florida, S Georgia, Antilles, S Mexico, C America to C Argentina.

Species illustrated
Limpkin 68

BEHAVIOUR Solitary or slightly gregarious, Limpkins are largely terrestrial. When they fly, they do so like the cranes, with neck and legs outstretched. They swim efficiently, and have a variety of calls which are usually described as screams, wails and yells. FEEDING They feed to a very great extent on water snails (*Pomacea*), supplementing this basic diet with a few insects and seeds. Feeding is often crepuscular or nocturnal. BREEDING A flat nest of reeds and sticks is built in a bush or tree or on the ground near water. The female lays 4-8 buff eggs, spotted with brown, which are incubated by both parents. CARE OF YOUNG Both parents tend the downy, nidifugous young. BIRD & MAN Limpkins have disappeared from areas denuded of snails through marsh drainage.

HABITAT	NESTING	FEEDING	FOOD SOURCE	SOCIAL
fresh water		V P		⚥

Psophiidae
Trumpeter family
3 species

Common Trumpeter
Psophia crepitans

CHARACTERISTICS Trumpeters, 17-21in long, are heavily built, "hump-backed" and have very broad wings. The tail is short with elongated coverts, and the legs are long. They have a long neck and a short stout bill. Plumage is mainly black with a green, mauve or bronze iridescence; elongated secondaries and tertials are white, brown or grey. The sexes are alike. HABITAT Tropical rain-forest. DISTRIBUTION Parts of S America – the Amazon basin, Guianas, and southern Venezuela.

BEHAVIOUR Trumpeters are gregarious and largely terrestrial; they are weak fliers and do so only when threatened, or to roost in trees. They bathe often, and afterwards lie with their wings spread to dry. FEEDING Their diet consists of fruit, berries and other vegetable matter, also insects. BREEDING An elaborate courtship display, with dancing, strutting and leaping, is performed in a forest clearing. The nest is made either in a tree-hole, in the crown of a palm or on the ground. There are 6-10 white or green eggs, incubated by the female. CARE OF YOUNG The downy young that hatch from ground-nests are nidifugous; it is not known how long tree-hatched birds take to leave the nest. BIRD & MAN The birds are often kept as pets by Indians.

HABITAT	NESTING	FEEDING	FOOD SOURCE	SOCIAL
		V P		♀

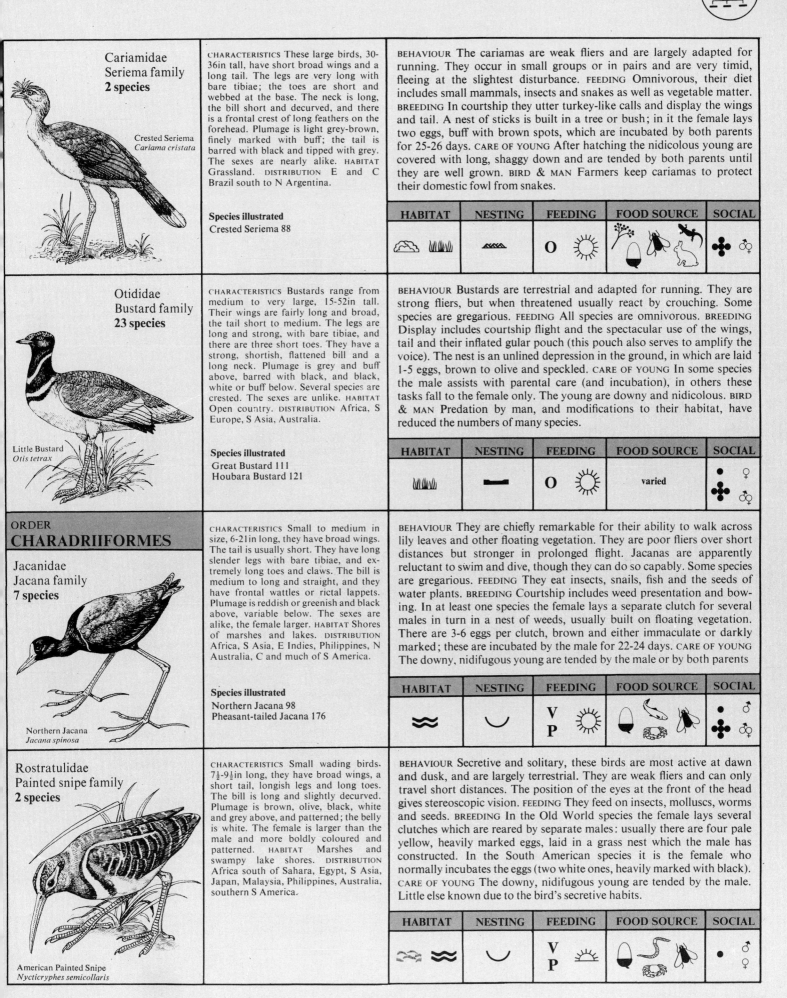

Cariamidae
Seriema family
2 species

Crested Seriema
Cariama cristata

CHARACTERISTICS These large birds, 30-36in tall, have short broad wings and a long tail. The legs are very long with bare tibiae; the toes are short and webbed at the base. The neck is long, the bill short and decurved, and there is a frontal crest of long feathers on the forehead. Plumage is light grey-brown, finely marked with buff; the tail is barred with black and tipped with grey. The sexes are nearly alike. HABITAT Grassland. DISTRIBUTION E and C Brazil south to N Argentina.

Species illustrated
Crested Seriema 88

BEHAVIOUR The cariamas are weak fliers and are largely adapted for running. They occur in small groups or in pairs and are very timid, fleeing at the slightest disturbance. FEEDING Omnivorous, their diet includes small mammals, insects and snakes as well as vegetable matter. BREEDING In courtship they utter turkey-like calls and display the wings and tail. A nest of sticks is built in a tree or bush; in it the female lays two eggs, buff with brown spots, which are incubated by both parents for 25-26 days. CARE OF YOUNG After hatching the nidicolous young are covered with long, shaggy down and are tended by both parents until they are well grown. BIRD & MAN Farmers keep cariamas to protect their domestic fowl from snakes.

HABITAT	NESTING	FEEDING	FOOD SOURCE	SOCIAL

Otididae
Bustard family
23 species

Little Bustard
Otis tetrax

CHARACTERISTICS Bustards range from medium to very large, 15-52in tall. Their wings are fairly long and broad, the tail short to medium. The legs are long and strong, with bare tibiae, and there are three short toes. They have a strong, shortish, flattened bill and a long neck. Plumage is grey and buff above, barred with black, and black, white or buff below. Several species are crested. The sexes are unlike. HABITAT Open country. DISTRIBUTION Africa, S Europe, S Asia, Australia.

Species illustrated
Great Bustard 111
Houbara Bustard 121

BEHAVIOUR Bustards are terrestrial and adapted for running. They are strong fliers, but when threatened usually react by crouching. Some species are gregarious. FEEDING All species are omnivorous. BREEDING Display includes courtship flight and the spectacular use of the wings, tail and their inflated gular pouch (this pouch also serves to amplify the voice). The nest is an unlined depression in the ground, in which are laid 1-5 eggs, brown to olive and speckled. CARE OF YOUNG In some species the male assists with parental care (and incubation), in others these tasks fall to the female only. The young are downy and nidicolous. BIRD & MAN Predation by man, and modifications to their habitat, have reduced the numbers of many species.

HABITAT	NESTING	FEEDING	FOOD SOURCE	SOCIAL
		O	varied	

ORDER
CHARADRIIFORMES

Jacanidae
Jacana family
7 species

Northern Jacana
Jacana spinosa

CHARACTERISTICS Small to medium in size, 6-21in long, they have broad wings. The tail is usually short. They have long slender legs with bare tibiae, and extremely long toes and claws. The bill is medium to long and straight, and they have frontal wattles or rictal lappets. Plumage is reddish or greenish and black above, variable below. The sexes are alike, the female larger. HABITAT Shores of marshes and lakes. DISTRIBUTION Africa, S Asia, E Indies, Philippines, N Australia, C and much of S America.

Species illustrated
Northern Jacana 98
Pheasant-tailed Jacana 176

BEHAVIOUR They are chiefly remarkable for their ability to walk across lily leaves and other floating vegetation. They are poor fliers over short distances but stronger in prolonged flight. Jacanas are apparently reluctant to swim and dive, though they can do so capably. Some species are gregarious. FEEDING They eat insects, snails, fish and the seeds of water plants. BREEDING Courtship includes weed presentation and bowing. In at least one species the female lays a separate clutch for several males in turn in a nest of weeds, usually built on floating vegetation. There are 3-6 eggs per clutch, brown and either immaculate or darkly marked; these are incubated by the male for 22-24 days. CARE OF YOUNG The downy, nidifugous young are tended by the male or by both parents

HABITAT	NESTING	FEEDING	FOOD SOURCE	SOCIAL
		V P		

Rostratulidae
Painted snipe family
2 species

American Painted Snipe
Nycticryphes semicollaris

CHARACTERISTICS Small wading birds. 7½-9½in long, they have broad wings, a short tail, longish legs and long toes. The bill is long and slightly decurved. Plumage is brown, olive, black, white and grey above, and patterned; the belly is white. The female is larger than the male and more boldly coloured and patterned. HABITAT Marshes and swampy lake shores. DISTRIBUTION Africa south of Sahara, Egypt, S Asia, Japan, Malaysia, Philippines, Australia, southern S America.

BEHAVIOUR Secretive and solitary, these birds are most active at dawn and dusk, and are largely terrestrial. They are weak fliers and can only travel short distances. The position of the eyes at the front of the head gives stereoscopic vision. FEEDING They feed on insects, molluscs, worms and seeds. BREEDING In the Old World species the female lays several clutches which are reared by separate males: usually there are four pale yellow, heavily marked eggs, laid in a grass nest which the male has constructed. In the South American species it is the female who normally incubates the eggs (two white ones, heavily marked with black). CARE OF YOUNG The downy, nidifugous young are tended by the male. Little else known due to the bird's secretive habits.

HABITAT	NESTING	FEEDING	FOOD SOURCE	SOCIAL
		V P		

Classification

Haematopodidae
Oystercatcher family
6 species

Oystercatcher
Haematopus ostralegus

CHARACTERISTICS These medium-sized waders, 15-20in long, have plump bodies and long pointed wings. The tail is short and the legs long and stout; there are three toes, slightly webbed. The neck is short and the bill long, stout and laterally compressed. Plumage is blackish or dark brown with a black head. The sexes are alike. HABITAT Sea coasts and margins of inland waters. DISTRIBUTION Temperate and tropical coasts from Iceland and Aleutians to Cape Horn and Tasmania. Inland in parts of Eurasia.

Species illustrated
Oystercatcher 132

BEHAVIOUR Outside the breeding season oystercatchers are gregarious and gather in enormous flocks, sometimes numbering thousands. On the ground they usually walk, though they can run swiftly. FEEDING Food is mainly molluscs, with worms, crustaceans and a few insects. BREEDING An elaborate "piping ceremony" involving birds of both sexes is believed to assist identification of the sexes and the formation of pairs. The nest is a ground-scrape decorated with stones, shells and bones. There are 2-4 yellowish eggs, marked with brown and black, which are incubated by both sexes for 26-27 days. CARE OF YOUNG The downy, nidifugous young are tended by both parents and fledge in five weeks. Breeding does not begin until the fourth year.

HABITAT	NESTING	FEEDING	FOOD SOURCE	SOCIAL

Ibidorynchidae
Ibisbill family
1 species

Ibisbill
Ibidorhyncha struthersii

CHARACTERISTICS Ibisbills, 16in long, have square wings and long legs with three toes, slightly lobed and webbed between the middle and outer. The neck and bill are long, the latter strongly decurved from the middle point. Plumage is greyish-brown with a black face and chin, breast band and top of head. The bill and legs are red. The sexes are alike. HABITAT Mountain lakes and streams. DISTRIBUTION Southern C Asia, with some migration in winter to foot-hills of Himalayas.

BEHAVIOUR Ibisbills usually live in pairs or parties of 3-8 in tranquil areas near mountain streams. Flight is swift and gull-like, the voice loud and melodious. FEEDING They feed by wading with the head and neck submerged, or dipped in alluvial grass, on crustaceans, insects and molluscs. BREEDING This begins in early March, when the nest is made among pebbles on the shore; it may be unlined or lined with a floor of tamped-down small pebbles. Eggs, usually four in number, are greyish-green with patches of sepia. Incubation is shared by both parents, the sitting bird being virtually invisible when motionless on the sunken nest. CARE OF YOUNG The chicks are downy and nidifugous, and are probably cared for by both parents.

HABITAT	NESTING	FEEDING	FOOD SOURCE	SOCIAL

Recurvirostridae
Avocet family
6 species

Avocet
Recurvirostra avosetta

CHARACTERISTICS These slender waders, 11½-19in long, have long pointed wings and a short tail. Their legs are long, the toes slightly webbed. The neck is longish and the bill long, slender and either straight or recurved. Plumage is black or brownish and white above, white below. HABITAT Marshes, lakes, rivers and estuaries. DISTRIBUTION Africa, Madagascar, C and S Europe and Asia, Malaysia, Philippines, Australasia, Hawaii, S USA, W Indies, C and S America, Galapagos.

Species illustrated
Black-winged Stilt 177

BEHAVIOUR These gregarious waders are good fliers: the northern species are migratory in winter. FEEDING They mostly feed in shallow water on molluscs, crustaceans, insects and, less often, on fish, reptiles, amphibians and vegetable matter. A characteristic feeding method of avocets is a sideways sweeping movement of the bill, skimming the surface of the water. BREEDING Nesting is colonial, the nest itself either a platform of vegetation or a ground-scrape. In some species a bowing ceremony precedes copulation. Usually there are four eggs, light brown to olive and patterned with darker colours; these are incubated by both parents. CARE OF YOUNG The young are nidifugous and are tended by both parents.

HABITAT	NESTING	FEEDING	FOOD SOURCE	SOCIAL
		V P		

Dromadidae
Crab-plover family
1 species

Crab Plover
Dromas ardeola

CHARACTERISTICS Crab Plovers are medium-sized waders, 15in long, with long pointed wings and a short tail. The legs are long, the neck rather short, and the bill strong and laterally compressed. Plumage is mainly white with black and blackish-brown flight feathers, scapulars and central feathers on back. The female is smaller. HABITAT Sea coasts, estuaries, the shores of islands. DISTRIBUTION Shores of Indian Ocean, from Natal and Madagascar to southern Red Sea and Burma.

BEHAVIOUR Noisy and highly gregarious, Crab Plovers are to be seen in great numbers on beaches, running in short rushes and flying about strongly. Uncommon on African shores between November and February, they are common during the same months on Arabian and Indian shores, which would indicate some migratory habits. FEEDING Their food consists of crabs, which they crack open with their heavy bill, and other crustaceans, molluscs and worms. BREEDING They nest in a burrow excavated in the sand up to 90in long, in the chamber of which a single egg, 2¼ × 1¾in (very large for that size of bird) is laid, white and unmarked. The period of incubation is unrecorded. CARE OF YOUNG The downy, nidicolous young are tended by both parents.

HABITAT	NESTING	FEEDING	FOOD SOURCE	SOCIAL

Burhinidae
Thick-knee family
9 species

Stone Curlew
Burhinus oedicnemus

CHARACTERISTICS Medium to large, 14-20½in long, the thick-knees have longish, broad and pointed wings and a medium tail. Their legs are long, ending in three slightly webbed toes. The head and eyes are large and the bill is short to medium, stout and straight. Plumage is mainly brown, grey or buff, barred and streaked. The sexes are alike. HABITAT Open stony and sandy ground. DISTRIBUTION Temperate and tropical Europe, Africa, Asia, Australia, C and S America, Hispaniola (W Indies).

Species illustrated
Stone Curlew 169

BEHAVIOUR These crepuscular and nocturnal birds are gregarious in some species. They rarely fly; when they do they are silent and stay close to the ground FEEDING Food includes insects, worms, crustaceans, molluscs, amphibians, small mammals and the nestlings of other birds. BREEDING Display by the male precedes the laying of (usually) two eggs, white to buff and blotched with brown, in an unlined ground-hollow, sometimes decorated with pebbles, shells, etc. *B.vermiculatus* nests unscathed in the breeding grounds of crocodiles. Incubation, for 25-27 days, is by the female, assisted by the male. CARE OF YOUNG The young are downy and cared for by both parents. Family shows similarities to bustards but more closely related to plovers.

HABITAT	NESTING	FEEDING	FOOD SOURCE	SOCIAL

Glareolidae
Pratincole family
16 species

Pratincole
Glareola pratincola

CHARACTERISTICS These small to medium birds are 6-10in long. Pratincoles have long pointed wings, a forked tail, medium legs with four toes, and a short bill. Coursers have short, broad wings and tail, long legs with three toes, and a long tapered bill. In both the middle toe is elongated. Plumage is buff, grey, brown, olive, boldly marked with black, white, brown. The sexes are similar but may differ in size. HABITAT Stony or sandy ground. DISTRIBUTION S Europe, Africa east to SE Asia and Australia.

Species illustrated
Pratincole 121

BEHAVIOUR Most species are gregarious. The pratincoles are strong fliers and resemble starling-sized swallows as they dive through the air. Coursers are terrestrial and, as the name suggests, swift runners. FEEDING Pratincoles dive and take locusts and other insects in the air. Coursers feed on insects, molluscs, reptiles, seeds and, possibly, fish; several species feed while wading. BREEDING Some species breed colonially. There are 2-4 eggs, buff and boldly marked with black and brown; they are laid on the ground, often in a hollow, and are sometimes protected from the sun by a parent's outstretched wing. Incubation may be mainly, or entirely, by the female. CARE OF YOUNG The young are downy, basically nidifugous, and are probably cared for by both parents.

HABITAT	NESTING	FEEDING	FOOD SOURCE	SOCIAL

Charadriidae
Plover family
56 species

Grey Plover
Pluvialis squatarola

CHARACTERISTICS These small to medium waders, 6-15½in long, have sturdy bodies and long wings. The tail is medium to short. The legs are short to long and the toes are medium, the hallux vestigial or lacking. Neck, head and bill are of medium size, the latter being straight in most species. Plumage is a combination of brown, olive, grey, black and white. Some species have a crest, face wattles or a carpal spur. The sexes are alike or nearly so. HABITAT Open country. DISTRIBUTION World-wide.

Species illustrated
Golden Plover 36, Killdeer 58, Sociable Plover 111, Ringed Plover 133, Australian Dotterel 197, Red-capped Dotterel 212

BEHAVIOUR These swift-running terrestrial birds form a largely gregarious family. They are strong, direct fliers, and many species are active by night. FEEDING They feed on insects, molluscs, worms, crustaceans, seeds and other vegetable matter. BREEDING The nest, a ground-hollow, is either unlined or scantly lined with vegetation. There are 2-5 eggs (usually four), buff or grey and heavily marked with black or brown. Incubation is by both parents (the male only in *Eudromias*). CARE OF YOUNG The downy, nidifugous young are tended by both parents (male only in *Eudromias*). Many species distract predators from their young by feigning injury. *Thinornis novaeseelandiae* is reduced to an estimated 70 pairs living on a small island in New Zealand.

HABITAT	NESTING	FEEDING	FOOD SOURCE	SOCIAL

Scolopacidae
Sandpiper family
85-89 species

Common Snipe
Gallinago gallinago

CHARACTERISTICS Small to medium in size, 5-24in long, these birds have long wings and a short to medium tail. The legs are short to long, the toes long. The neck is medium to long and the bill is usually long, straight, and decurved or recurved. Plumage is buff, grey or brown above, and white, buff, brown or black below. Many species are elaborately barred, streaked or spotted. The sexes are mostly alike. HABITAT Open country, usually near water. DISTRIBUTION World-wide. Most species are migratory.

Species illustrated
Dunlin 103, Woodcock 109, Ruff 125, Sandpiper 127, Redshank 129, Knot 131, Red-necked Phalarope 214

BEHAVIOUR Usually living near water, these birds are often found outside the breeding season in large flocks by the seashore; two species of phalarope live on open tropical oceans. FEEDING Food is mostly animal, in particular small invertebrates which are taken from the surface of the ground, mud or water, or by probing in mud or sand. BREEDING Many species perform an elaborate display either on the ground or in flight. The nest is usually on the ground, though a few use old nests built by other birds in trees or burrows. There are 2-4 eggs, buff, olive or brown, incubated by both, by the female alone or mainly by the male. CARE OF YOUNG The downy, nidifugous young are tended by both parents, by the male or by the female.

HABITAT	NESTING	FEEDING	FOOD SOURCE	SOCIAL

Classification

Thinocoridae
Seedsnipe family
4 species

Gay's Seedsnipe
Attagis gayi

CHARACTERISTICS The seedsnipes are smallish, plump and 6¾-11in long. The wings are long and pointed, the tail short to medium. They have short legs and small feet. Neck and bill are short, the latter pointed and finch-like. Plumage is brown with pale feather edgings above, buff or white with dark markings below. The sexes are unlike. **HABITAT** Open country. **DISTRIBUTION** Western S America along Andes and coastal area south from Ecuador.

Species illustrated
Least Seedsnipe 86

BEHAVIOUR They are terrestrial birds, two species resembling finches, two resembling partridges. They run rapidly and either crouch or creep away when disturbed. Flight is snipe-like, rapid and zig-zag. Their neutral coloration makes them almost invisible against the ground. **FEEDING** Food is mainly seeds, with leaves and other vegetable matter, and some insects. **BREEDING** The nest is a ground-hollow lined with varying amounts of plant material. There are 3-4 eggs, cream, brown, olive, spotted and blotched. Details of the sitting bird and the length of the incubation period have yet to be recorded. **CARE OF YOUNG** Although it is known that the young are downy and nidifugous, there is no record relating to parental care.

HABITAT	NESTING	FEEDING	FOOD SOURCE	SOCIAL

Chionididae
Sheathbill family
2 species

Yellow-billed Sheathbill
Chionis alba

CHARACTERISTICS Plump and of medium size, 14-17in long, the sheathbills have longish wings and a short rounded tail. Their legs are short, the toes slightly webbed. The bill is short and stout, the base of the maxilla covered with a horny sheath. The neck is short and the face partly bare, carunculated at the base of the bill. Plumage is all white, the bill yellow or black and yellow. The sexes are alike, the male larger. **HABITAT** Sea coast. **DISTRIBUTION** Antarctic and sub-Antarctic coastal regions.

Species illustrated
Yellow-billed Sheathbill 223

BEHAVIOUR Although sheathbills are not notably gregarious, they do breed in large numbers in colonies shared with penguins. They rarely fly, preferring to walk, run or hop. Swimming is also rare; nevertheless, they can swim well. **FEEDING** Food includes offal and refuse, carrion, insects, molluscs, crustaceans, algae, lichens and eggs and nestlings of other birds. **BREEDING** A bulky nest of feathers, shells and assorted refuse is built in a natural hole, a petrel burrow or some similar site. Pairs remain faithful and occupy the same site annually. There are 2-4 white eggs, blotched with brown, which are incubated by both parents for 29 days. **CARE OF YOUNG** The downy, nidifugous young are tended by both parents. Often only one chick reaches maturity.

HABITAT	NESTING	FEEDING	FOOD SOURCE	SOCIAL

Sterocorariidae
Skua family
4 species

Great Skua
Catharacta skua

CHARACTERISTICS These stout-bodied birds, 17-24in long, have long pointed wings and a medium wedge-shaped tail. The legs are short, ending in webbed feet and hooked claws. The neck is longish, the bill medium and strong with a hooked tip. Plumage, which varies according to light and dark phases, is brown or blackish above, lighter to white below, plain or barred with brown. The sexes are alike. **HABITAT** Oceanic. **DISTRIBUTION** High latitudes in N and S Hemispheres. Migratory.

Species illustrated
Parasitic Jaeger 37
Great Skua 223

BEHAVIOUR They are strong fliers capable of spectacular aerobatics. Except in the breeding season they may remain away from land for indefinite periods: at sea they are solitary but near land tend to be gregarious. They are aggressively predatory, often living in or near bird colonies and forcing other species to disgorge food in flight. **FEEDING** Their food includes small mammals, eggs (including their own), and birds, insects, fish, crustaceans, molluscs, carrion, offal and some vegetable matter. **BREEDING** They breed colonially, nesting in a ground-depression, lined or unlined, in which 2-4 eggs, light greenish to dark brown, are incubated by both parents, who fiercely defend the nest. **CARE OF YOUNG** Both parents care for the semi-nidifugous young.

HABITAT	NESTING	FEEDING	FOOD SOURCE	SOCIAL

Laridae
Gull family
82-85 species

Common Gull
Larus canus

CHARACTERISTICS Stout-bodied, 8-30in long, the gulls have long pointed wings and a medium to long tail, square or forked. The legs are short to medium, the feet webbed. The bill is slender to stout, pointed to hooked. Plumage is grey, white and black in differing combinations; many species are mainly white. The bill and feet are often brightly coloured. Terns are crested. The sexes are alike. **HABITAT** Sea coasts, rivers, lakes, marshes. **DISTRIBUTION** World-wide. Most species are migratory.

Species illustrated
Gulls: 65, 73, 129, 132, (*Larus*)
Kittiwake 135
Terns: 71, 133, 214

BEHAVIOUR Best known of the sea-birds, gulls are strong fliers, often soaring and gliding. They swim freely, but only a few species dive. All are gregarious. **FEEDING** Food comprises fish, molluscs, crustaceans, insects, carrion and vegetable matter. **BREEDING** They often breed in large colonies. The nest is built of grass, seaweed, etc., on a cliff or in a tree, on a tussock of grass in a marsh, or is an unlined ground-scrape usually made in the open on sand or shingle. *Larosterna* nests in burrows. There are 1-4 eggs, ranging from almost white to dark buff; these may be incubated by both parents, by the female alone or largely by the female, who is fed by the male. **CARE OF YOUNG** The downy, semi-nidicolous young are cared for by both parents.

HABITAT	NESTING	FEEDING	FOOD SOURCE	SOCIAL

Rynchopidae
Skimmer family
3 species

Black Skimmer
Rynchops nigra

CHARACTERISTICS Skimmers, 14½-23in long, have very long pointed wings and a short forked tail. Their legs are short, their feet small and webbed. They have a long, pointed and very compressed bill; the lower mandible is much longer. Plumage is dark brown or black above, whitish below. The sexes are alike, the female smaller. HABITAT Shores of seas, lakes, rivers. DISTRIBUTION Africa south of Sahara, India, Burma, coasts of USA to C America, Amazon system and coasts to south. Partly migratory.

Species illustrated
Black Skimmer 71

BEHAVIOUR Skimmers are gregarious, and inclined to be crepuscular and nocturnal. Unique among birds is the vertical pupil of the eye which, presumably, gives protection from glare reflected off the water. When not feeding they rest in numbers on a sand-bank, their heads all pointing in the same direction. FEEDING They take their name from their habit of feeding while flying along the surface of still water, the lower mandible immersed, scooping up fish and plankton. Crustaceans are also taken. BREEDING They nest in a scrape in the sand: there the female lays 2-5 eggs, buff to greenish and heavily blotched with brown, which she incubates possibly with the assistance of the male. CARE OF YOUNG Both parents tend the downy, nidicolous young.

HABITAT	NESTING	FEEDING	FOOD SOURCE	SOCIAL

Alcidae
Auk family
22 species

Puffin
Fratercula arctica

CHARACTERISTICS Small to medium, 6½-30in long, these stout-bodied birds have short wings, tail and legs; the feet are webbed. The neck is short and the bill varies from short and strong to long and slender. Plumage is black, brown or grey above, white below in most species. Some are crested and some are brightly coloured in bill and feet. HABITAT Sea coasts. DISTRIBUTION Members of the Auk, Murre and Puffin family are found in the Arctic, the N Pacific and the N Atlantic.

Species illustrated
Guillemot 73, Razorbill 73, Murrelet 75, Tufted Puffin 75, Auklet 75, Common Puffin 135

BEHAVIOUR Auks come to land only to breed, spending most of their year on the high seas, though some, e.g. the Black Guillemot, stay close to the shore. They are all good swimmers and divers but seldom fly far (the Great Auk, extinct since 1844, was flightless). FEEDING They eat mainly fish, molluscs and crustaceans, which are usually pursued under water. BREEDING Most species nest colonially. Since there is little or no nesting material available, the eggs are laid either on bare ground, on ledges, in crevices or burrows. A clutch consists of 1-2 eggs, white, buff, light green, immaculate to heavily marked, incubated by both parents. CARE OF YOUNG The downy, nidicolous young are tended by both parents.

HABITAT	NESTING	FEEDING	FOOD SOURCE	SOCIAL

ORDER
PTEROCLIDIFORMES

Pteroclidae
Sandgrouse family
16 species

Pallas's Sandgrouse
Syrrhaptes paradoxus

CHARACTERISTICS Small to medium birds, 9-16in long, sandgrouse are stout-bodied and have long pointed wings. Their tail is medium to long and pointed. The legs are short with stout toes. A small head rests on a shortish neck; the bill is short and stout. Plumage is thick and patterned, with buff, rufous or grey above; the underparts are usually boldly marked with white, black, brown, yellow. The sexes are unlike. HABITAT Open steppes, semi-desert. DISTRIBUTION Africa, SW Europe, SW to S Asia.

Species illustrated
Pallas's Sandgrouse 121
Lichtenstein's Sandgrouse 153

BEHAVIOUR All species are terrestrial and highly gregarious, congregating near water at dawn or dusk. Water can be carried back to nestlings in the crop, and, though long doubted, it has been proved that some species carry water back by soaking their breast feathers and transporting it thus. FEEDING Their diet is berries, seeds, buds, leaves and insects. BREEDING They nest in a ground-scrape, furnished with little or no lining, or on the bare ground. There are 2-3 eggs, white, buff or green, marked with brown; these are incubated by both parents for 20-24 days. CARE OF YOUNG The downy, nidifugous young are cared for by both parents. Some species of sandgrouse are known to rear several broods in one season.

HABITAT	NESTING	FEEDING	FOOD SOURCE	SOCIAL

ORDER
COLUMBIFORMES

Columbidae
Pigeon family
289 species

Wood Pigeon
Columba palumbus

CHARACTERISTICS These small to medium birds, 6-33in long, have a compact body, short to medium wings and a medium to long tail, either square or pointed. The legs are short to medium, the bill is medium and slender to stout. Plumage is dense and soft and highly variable in colour and pattern. Some species are crested. The sexes are usually alike. HABITAT Varied, including open country and dense forest. DISTRIBUTION World-wide except in extreme latitudes and some oceanic islands.

Species illustrated
Pigeons: Green 140, Topknot 182, Bronzewing 186, Crested 193, Victoria Crowned 205, New Zealand 209,
Doves: Mourning 50, Collared 13 Namaqua 149, Ruddy Quail-dove

BEHAVIOUR Most species are more or less gregarious in this highly varied family that includes game-like terrestrial and arboreal forms. FEEDING Their food is predominantly vegetable – seeds, buds, fruit, etc.; a few species take insects, worms and snails. BREEDING Courtship display may be aerial or terrestrial. Most species build flimsy nests of sticks in trees or on ledges, while a few breed on the ground in tree-holes or burrows. Some nesting is colonial. Usually there are 1-2 white or buff eggs, incubated by both parents. CARE OF YOUNG The naked, nidicolous young are at first fed on "pigeon's milk", produced in the crop of the parents, later on regurgitated solids. BIRD & MAN The last Passenger Pigeon, once widespread in the USA, died in captivity in 1914.

HABITAT	NESTING	FEEDING	FOOD SOURCE	SOCIAL

Classification

ORDER
PSITTACIFORMES

Psittacidae
Parrot family
315-339 species

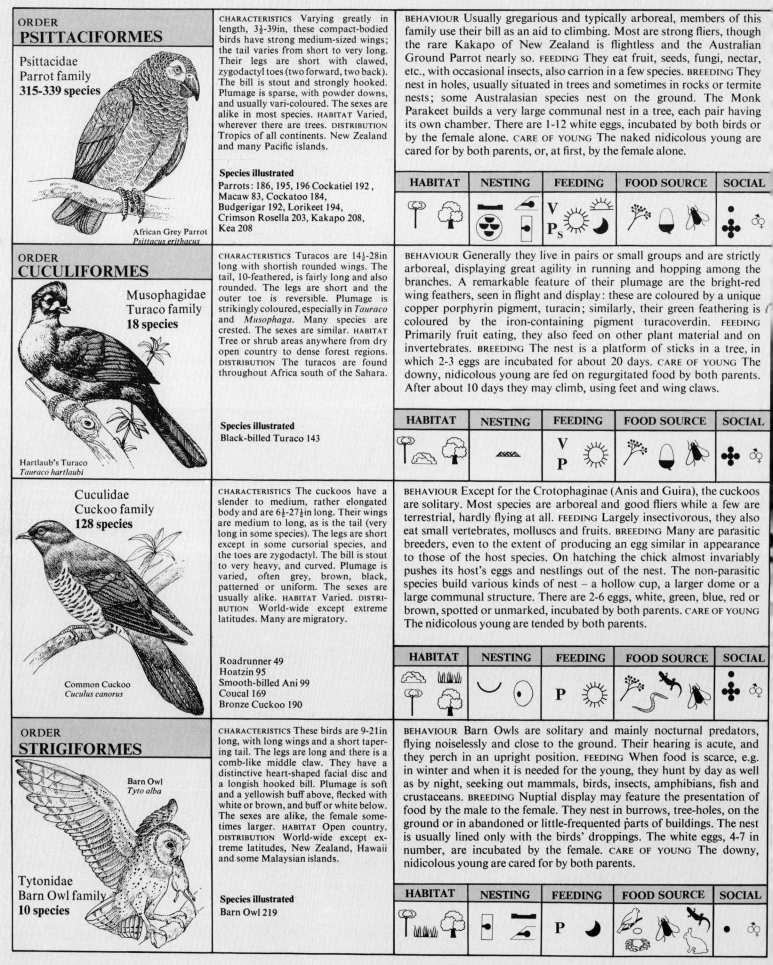

African Grey Parrot
Psittacus erithacus

CHARACTERISTICS Varying greatly in length, 3½-39in, these compact-bodied birds have strong medium-sized wings; the tail varies from short to very long. Their legs are short with clawed, zygodactyl toes (two forward, two back). The bill is stout and strongly hooked. Plumage is sparse, with powder downs, and usually vari-coloured. The sexes are alike in most species. HABITAT Varied, wherever there are trees. DISTRIBUTION Tropics of all continents. New Zealand and many Pacific islands.

Species illustrated
Parrots: 186, 195, 196 Cockatiel 192 , Macaw 83, Cockatoo 184, Budgerigar 192, Lorikeet 194, Crimson Rosella 203, Kakapo 208, Kea 208

BEHAVIOUR Usually gregarious and typically arboreal, members of this family use their bill as an aid to climbing. Most are strong fliers, though the rare Kakapo of New Zealand is flightless and the Australian Ground Parrot nearly so. FEEDING They eat fruit, seeds, fungi, nectar, etc., with occasional insects, also carrion in a few species. BREEDING They nest in holes, usually situated in trees and sometimes in rocks or termite nests; some Australasian species nest on the ground. The Monk Parakeet builds a very large communal nest in a tree, each pair having its own chamber. There are 1-12 white eggs, incubated by both birds or by the female alone. CARE OF YOUNG The naked nidicolous young are cared for by both parents, or, at first, by the female alone.

HABITAT	NESTING	FEEDING	FOOD SOURCE	SOCIAL

ORDER
CUCULIFORMES

Musophagidae
Turaco family
18 species

Hartlaub's Turaco
Tauraco hartlaubi

CHARACTERISTICS Turacos are 14½-28in long with shortish rounded wings. The tail, 10-feathered, is fairly long and also rounded. The legs are short and the outer toe is reversible. Plumage is strikingly coloured, especially in *Tauraco* and *Musophaga*. Many species are crested. The sexes are similar. HABITAT Tree or shrub areas anywhere from dry open country to dense forest regions. DISTRIBUTION The turacos are found throughout Africa south of the Sahara.

Species illustrated
Black-billed Turaco 143

BEHAVIOUR Generally they live in pairs or small groups and are strictly arboreal, displaying great agility in running and hopping among the branches. A remarkable feature of their plumage are the bright-red wing feathers, seen in flight and display: these are coloured by a unique copper porphyrin pigment, turacin; similarly, their green feathering is coloured by the iron-containing pigment turacoverdin. FEEDING Primarily fruit eating, they also feed on other plant material and on invertebrates. BREEDING The nest is a platform of sticks in a tree, in which 2-3 eggs are incubated for about 20 days. CARE OF YOUNG The downy, nidicolous young are fed on regurgitated food by both parents. After about 10 days they may climb, using feet and wing claws.

HABITAT	NESTING	FEEDING	FOOD SOURCE	SOCIAL

Cuculidae
Cuckoo family
128 species

Common Cuckoo
Cuculus canorus

CHARACTERISTICS The cuckoos have a slender to medium, rather elongated body and are 6½-27½in long. Their wings are medium to long, as is the tail (very long in some species). The legs are short except in some cursorial species, and the toes are zygodactyl. The bill is stout to very heavy, and curved. Plumage is varied, often grey, brown, black, patterned or uniform. The sexes are usually alike. HABITAT Varied. DISTRIBUTION World-wide except extreme latitudes. Many are migratory.

Roadrunner 49
Hoatzin 95
Smooth-billed Ani 99
Coucal 169
Bronze Cuckoo 190

BEHAVIOUR Except for the Crotophaginae (Anis and Guira), the cuckoos are solitary. Most species are arboreal and good fliers while a few are terrestrial, hardly flying at all. FEEDING Largely insectivorous, they also eat small vertebrates, molluscs and fruits. BREEDING Many are parasitic breeders, even to the extent of producing an egg similar in appearance to those of the host species. On hatching the chick almost invariably pushes its host's eggs and nestlings out of the nest. The non-parasitic species build various kinds of nest – a hollow cup, a larger dome or a large communal structure. There are 2-6 eggs, white, green, blue, red or brown, spotted or unmarked, incubated by both parents. CARE OF YOUNG The nidicolous young are tended by both parents.

HABITAT	NESTING	FEEDING	FOOD SOURCE	SOCIAL

ORDER
STRIGIFORMES

Barn Owl
Tyto alba

Tytonidae
Barn Owl family
10 species

CHARACTERISTICS These birds are 9-21in long, with long wings and a short tapering tail. The legs are long and there is a comb-like middle claw. They have a distinctive heart-shaped facial disc and a longish hooked bill. Plumage is soft and a yellowish buff above, flecked with white or brown, and buff or white below. The sexes are alike, the female sometimes larger. HABITAT Open country. DISTRIBUTION World-wide except extreme latitudes, New Zealand, Hawaii and some Malaysian islands.

Species illustrated
Barn Owl 219

BEHAVIOUR Barn Owls are solitary and mainly nocturnal predators, flying noiselessly and close to the ground. Their hearing is acute, and they perch in an upright position. FEEDING When food is scarce, e.g. in winter and when it is needed for the young, they hunt by day as well as by night, seeking out mammals, birds, insects, amphibians, fish and crustaceans. BREEDING Nuptial display may feature the presentation of food by the male to the female. They nest in burrows, tree-holes, on the ground or in abandoned or little-frequented parts of buildings. The nest is usually lined only with the birds' droppings. The white eggs, 4-7 in number, are incubated by the female. CARE OF YOUNG The downy, nidicolous young are cared for by both parents.

HABITAT	NESTING	FEEDING	FOOD SOURCE	SOCIAL

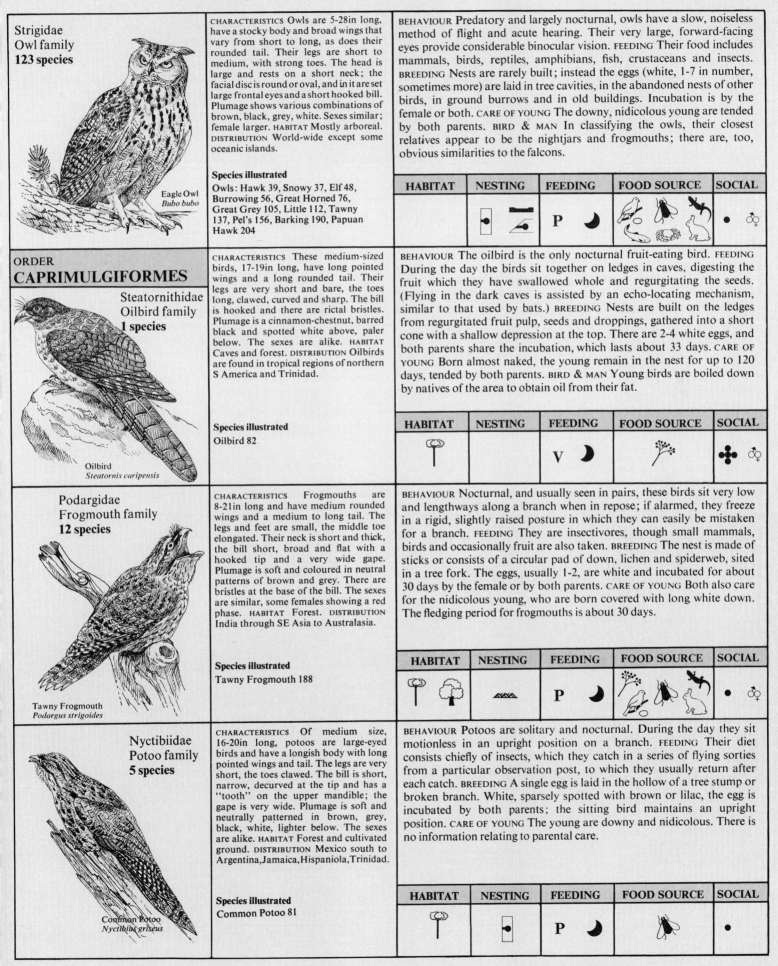

Strigidae Owl family
123 species

Eagle Owl
Bubo bubo

CHARACTERISTICS Owls are 5-28in long, have a stocky body and broad wings that vary from short to long, as does their rounded tail. Their legs are short to medium, with strong toes. The head is large and rests on a short neck; the facial disc is round or oval, and in it are set large frontal eyes and a short hooked bill. Plumage shows various combinations of brown, black, grey, white. Sexes similar; female larger. **HABITAT** Mostly arboreal. **DISTRIBUTION** World-wide except some oceanic islands.

Species illustrated
Owls: Hawk 39, Snowy 37, Elf 48, Burrowing 56, Great Horned 76, Great Grey 105, Little 112, Tawny 137, Pel's 156, Barking 190, Papuan Hawk 204

BEHAVIOUR Predatory and largely nocturnal, owls have a slow, noiseless method of flight and acute hearing. Their very large, forward-facing eyes provide considerable binocular vision. **FEEDING** Their food includes mammals, birds, reptiles, amphibians, fish, crustaceans and insects. **BREEDING** Nests are rarely built; instead the eggs (white, 1-7 in number, sometimes more) are laid in tree cavities, in the abandoned nests of other birds, in ground burrows and in old buildings. Incubation is by the female or both. **CARE OF YOUNG** The downy, nidicolous young are tended by both parents. **BIRD & MAN** In classifying the owls, their closest relatives appear to be the nightjars and frogmouths; there are, too, obvious similarities to the falcons.

HABITAT	NESTING	FEEDING	FOOD SOURCE	SOCIAL

ORDER
CAPRIMULGIFORMES

Steatornithidae Oilbird family
1 species

Oilbird
Steatornis caripensis

CHARACTERISTICS These medium-sized birds, 17-19in long, have long pointed wings and a long rounded tail. Their legs are very short and bare, the toes long, clawed, curved and sharp. The bill is hooked and there are rictal bristles. Plumage is a cinnamon-chestnut, barred black and spotted white above, paler below. The sexes are alike. **HABITAT** Caves and forest. **DISTRIBUTION** Oilbirds are found in tropical regions of northern S America and Trinidad.

Species illustrated
Oilbird 82

BEHAVIOUR The oilbird is the only nocturnal fruit-eating bird. **FEEDING** During the day the birds sit together on ledges in caves, digesting the fruit which they have swallowed whole and regurgitating the seeds. (Flying in the dark caves is assisted by an echo-locating mechanism, similar to that used by bats.) **BREEDING** Nests are built on the ledges from regurgitated fruit pulp, seeds and droppings, gathered into a short cone with a shallow depression at the top. There are 2-4 white eggs, and both parents share the incubation, which lasts about 33 days. **CARE OF YOUNG** Born almost naked, the young remain in the nest for up to 120 days, tended by both parents. **BIRD & MAN** Young birds are boiled down by natives of the area to obtain oil from their fat.

HABITAT	NESTING	FEEDING	FOOD SOURCE	SOCIAL

Podargidae Frogmouth family
12 species

Tawny Frogmouth
Podargus strigoides

CHARACTERISTICS Frogmouths are 8-21in long and have medium rounded wings and a medium to long tail. The legs and feet are small, the middle toe elongated. Their neck is short and thick, the bill short, broad and flat with a hooked tip and a very wide gape. Plumage is soft and coloured in neutral patterns of brown and grey. There are bristles at the base of the bill. The sexes are similar, some females showing a red phase. **HABITAT** Forest. **DISTRIBUTION** India through SE Asia to Australasia.

Species illustrated
Tawny Frogmouth 188

BEHAVIOUR Nocturnal, and usually seen in pairs, these birds sit very low and lengthways along a branch when in repose; if alarmed, they freeze in a rigid, slightly raised posture in which they can easily be mistaken for a branch. **FEEDING** They are insectivores, though small mammals, birds and occasionally fruit are also taken. **BREEDING** The nest is made of sticks or consists of a circular pad of down, lichen and spiderweb, sited in a tree fork. The eggs, usually 1-2, are white and incubated for about 30 days by the female or by both parents. **CARE OF YOUNG** Both also care for the nidicolous young, who are born covered with long white down. The fledging period for frogmouths is about 30 days.

HABITAT	NESTING	FEEDING	FOOD SOURCE	SOCIAL

Nyctibiidae Potoo family
5 species

Common Potoo
Nyctibius griseus

CHARACTERISTICS Of medium size, 16-20in long, potoos are large-eyed birds and have a longish body with long pointed wings and tail. The legs are very short, the toes clawed. The bill is short, narrow, decurved at the tip and has a "tooth" on the upper mandible; the gape is very wide. Plumage is soft and neutrally patterned in brown, grey, black, white, lighter below. The sexes are alike. **HABITAT** Forest and cultivated ground. **DISTRIBUTION** Mexico south to Argentina, Jamaica, Hispaniola, Trinidad.

Species illustrated
Common Potoo 81

BEHAVIOUR Potoos are solitary and nocturnal. During the day they sit motionless in an upright position on a branch. **FEEDING** Their diet consists chiefly of insects, which they catch in a series of flying sorties from a particular observation post, to which they usually return after each catch. **BREEDING** A single egg is laid in the hollow of a tree stump or broken branch. White, sparsely spotted with brown or lilac, the egg is incubated by both parents; the sitting bird maintains an upright position. **CARE OF YOUNG** The young are downy and nidicolous. There is no information relating to parental care.

HABITAT	NESTING	FEEDING	FOOD SOURCE	SOCIAL

Classification

Aegothelidae
Owlet-frogmouth family
8 species

Australian Owlet-nightjar
Aegotheles cristatus

CHARACTERISTICS Small and plump-bodied, 7½-12½in long, they have long wings and tail, the latter wedge-shaped. The legs and feet are slender and weak, with long toes and claws. The neck is short, as is the bill which is flat, hooked and has a wide gape. Plumage is soft, mottled and spotted in combinations of grey, buff, black and browns. There are long erectile bristles on the forehead. The sexes are alike or nearly so. HABITAT Open and wooded country. DISTRIBUTION Australia, New Guinea, Moluccas.

Species illustrated
Owlet-nightjar 189

BEHAVIOUR The owlet-frogmouths are solitary and nocturnal. During the day these arboreal birds rest in tree-hollows, sitting upright in an owl-like posture. Flight is silent, direct and limited to short distances. FEEDING They are insectivorous, taking their food in the air and from the ground, mostly the latter. In general their feeding habits are halfway between those of the frogmouths and the true nightjars. BREEDING Nesting is in a hollow tree, sometimes in a hole in a bank; the nest may be lined with leaves or animal fur, or left unlined. There are 3-5 white eggs, immaculate or marked. Details of the sitting bird are not known. CARE OF YOUNG The young are downy and nidicolous; information about parental care is not known.

HABITAT	NESTING	FEEDING	FOOD SOURCE	SOCIAL

Caprimulgidae
Nightjar family
67 species

Common Nighthawk
Chordeiles minor

CHARACTERISTICS These birds are 7½-11½in long and have medium to long wings and tail. Their legs are short, the toes and claws small. A large head, tufted in some species, is set on a short neck; the bill is small but with a very wide gape. Plumage is soft and black, white, grey, buff, rufous, and cryptically patterned. The sexes usually differ. HABITAT Varied, from arid regions to forest. DISTRIBUTION World-wide except extreme latitudes, New Zealand and some oceanic islands.

Species illustrated
Poorwill 47
European Nightjar 119
Pennant-winged Nightjar 145
Standard-winged Nightjar 145

BEHAVIOUR Usually solitary and nocturnal or crepuscular, the nightjars rest motionless during the day on a branch or on the ground, made almost invisible by their coloration. FEEDING They are largely insectivorous. Insects are hawked from a vantage point, and taken on the wing in the bird's capacious mouth. BREEDING Most species lay their eggs directly on the ground, a few in trees or on flat roofs. Usually there are 1-2 eggs, white to pinkish, blotched with black, brown or violet. Incubation is by both parents. CARE OF YOUNG The downy, nidicolous young are tended by both parents. BIRD & MAN One species, the Poorwill, *Phalaenoptilus nuttalli*, is known to the American Indians as the "sleeper" because of its annual hibernation.

HABITAT	NESTING	FEEDING	FOOD SOURCE	SOCIAL

ORDER
APODIFORMES

Apodidae
Swift family
76 species

Common Swift
Apus apus

CHARACTERISTICS Small, 3½-9in long, these compact-bodied birds have long pointed wings; the tail varies from short and square to long and forked. The legs and feet are very small, as is the bill which is decurved at the tip and has a wide gape. Plumage is from bluish-black to grey-brown with white throat, collar, rump or belly. The sexes are alike. HABITAT Varied. DISTRIBUTION World-wide except extreme latitudes and some oceanic islands. Many species are migratory.

Species illustrated
White-throated Swift 52
European Swift 137
Edible-nest Swiftlet 171

BEHAVIOUR The family name Apodidae means, literally, legless. It derives from the birds' extremely small legs and feet and their almost entirely aerial way of life. At rest they cling to an upright surface. Most species are gregarious. FEEDING They are entirely insectivorous and all food is taken on the wing. BREEDING Sometimes breeding colonially, the nest is constructed of a salivary secretion, with or without fragments of twigs and other plant material, on a cliff, in a cave or tree hollow, under a protecting branch or palm leaf, or in an abandoned burrow. There are 1-6 white eggs, incubated by both parents. CARE OF YOUNG The young hatch naked, are nidicolous and are cared for by both parents.

HABITAT	NESTING	FEEDING	FOOD SOURCE	SOCIAL

Hemiprocnidae
Crested-swift family
3 species

Crested Swift
Hemiprocne longipennis

CHARACTERISTICS These small birds, 6¼-13in long, have a longish slender body, long pointed wings and a long forked tail. The legs are very short, the toes long, the 1st not reversible. The bill is flat and broad with a wide gape. They have large eyes. Plumage is soft, grey or brown, and some species have a green or blue gloss on the back and/or breast. All have an erectile crest. The sexes differ. HABITAT Open and wooded areas. DISTRIBUTION India to SE Asia, New Guinea, Philippines, Solomons.

Species illustrated
Crested Swift 166

BEHAVIOUR Conspicuously aerial (though they also perch in trees), they tend to be gregarious and are most active at the beginning and end of the day. FEEDING They are adept at hawking insects, their only food, on the wing. They drink by means of a low pass over the water. BREEDING The nest is of a salivary secretion that hardens when exposed to the air; feathers are combined with the mixture and the nest is attached to a twig high in a tree; in size it appears far too small for the bird, being about 1in wide and ½in deep. A single pale blue-grey egg is incubated by both parents. The Whiskered Treeswift usually sits on the supporting twig rather than the fragile nest. CARE OF YOUNG The downy, nidicolous chick is tended by both parents.

HABITAT	NESTING	FEEDING	FOOD SOURCE	SOCIAL

Trochilidae Hummingbird family
319-331 species

Magnificent Hummingbird
Eugenes fulgens

CHARACTERISTICS The smallest birds, 2¼-8½in long, they have long narrow wings and a tail that varies from very short to very long. The legs are short, the feet small and weak. The neck is very short, the bill slender, straight or decurved and shortish to very long. Plumage is greatly varied, with green, brown and black predominant. Some species are crested. The sexes mostly differ. **HABITAT** Mainly tropical forest and scrub. **DISTRIBUTION** S and C America, some species farther north.

Species illustrated
Andean Hillstar 92

BEHAVIOUR These tiny birds are remarkable for their agility in the air, their wings moving at high speed (up to 80 beats per second in some). By contrast, they are virtually incapable of walking and use their feet only to perch. They are mainly solitary and aggressive. Bathing is frequent. **FEEDING** Their high metabolic rate makes a high rate of feeding essential. Insects, arachnids and nectar are taken, usually as the bird hovers above vegetation; some insects may be taken in the air. **BREEDING** Some species are said to be polygamous. The nest is a deep cup of spider-web, moss and down built mostly by the female, who also incubates the eggs (two, white). **CARE OF YOUNG** The young, born naked and blind, are usually tended by the female, in some species by both parents.

HABITAT	NESTING	FEEDING	FOOD SOURCE	SOCIAL
		V P		

ORDER COLIIFORMES

Coliidae Mousebird family
6 species

Mousebird
Colius indicus

CHARACTERISTICS These birds are 11½-14in long, their stiff narrow tail more than two-thirds the total length. They have short wings and small slender legs with four toes directed forward, the outer two reversible. Neck and bill are short, the latter stout and slightly decurved and set in a small head. Plumage is soft, grey or brown, the neck blue, the throat black or chestnut, lighter below. The sexes are alike. **HABITAT** Wooded areas and brushland. **DISTRIBUTION** Africa south of Sahara.

Species illustrated
Red-faced Coly 148

BEHAVIOUR Highly gregarious, often flying in flocks of 5-30, they roost huddled together and practise mutual preening and dust bathing. In trees they clamber about using the bill as well as the feet, rather like parrots. **FEEDING** Their diet consists mainly of fruit. **BREEDING** In at least one species nuptial display is by the female. The pair build a hollow cup of sticks and bark in a tree, lining it with wool, cotton or leaves. There are 2-4 eggs, white, immaculate or streaked with brown, incubated by both parents. **CARE OF YOUNG** The young are downy and nidicolous. Long before leaving the nest permanently they make preliminary sorties, clambering about the tree and returning to be brooded at night.

HABITAT	NESTING	FEEDING	FOOD SOURCE	SOCIAL
		V		

ORDER TROGONIFORMES

Trogonidae Trogon family
34 species

Mexican Trogon
Trogon mexicanus

CHARACTERISTICS Stocky birds, 9-13in long, they have short wings and a long, broad, square tail. Legs and feet are small, the 1st and 2nd toes reversed. The neck and bill are short, the latter broad, bristled at the base and serrated in some species; the nostrils are also bristled. Plumage is soft and varied with red, green, blue, brown, black, white and yellow in often sharply defined areas. The sexes mostly differ. **HABITAT** Forests. **DISTRIBUTION** Tropics of America, Africa, Asia.

Species illustrated
Quetzal 96
Indian Trogon 167

BEHAVIOUR Trogons are solitary and arboreal and sit erect for long periods. Their feathers seem to be loosely fixed in their delicate, oily skins. Many species are said to be weak fliers. **FEEDING** Food is mainly fruit and insects, the former predominating with the American species, the latter with the African and Asian. Snails, reptiles and frogs have also been recorded; despite the birds' alleged weakness in the air, some insects may be taken on the wing. **BREEDING** Aerial display often precedes mating. Nesting is in a tree-hollow, sometimes in a termite nest. There are 2-4 eggs, white, buff or bluish, incubated by both parents for about 18 days. **CARE OF YOUNG** The young hatch naked and are fed by regurgitation by both parents.

HABITAT	NESTING	FEEDING	FOOD SOURCE	SOCIAL
		V P		

ORDER CORACIIFORMES

Kingfisher
Alcedo atthis

Alcedinidae Kingfisher family
87 species

CHARACTERISTICS Kingfishers, 4-18in long, have compact bodies and short wings. The tail varies from stumpy to very long. The legs are short with three or four syndactyl toes. A large head rests on a short neck; the bill is straight, thick and heavy. Plumage is brown, green, blue, purple, black, white. Many are collared, some crested. The sexes may be alike or unlike. **HABITAT** Forest or open wooded areas. **DISTRIBUTION** World-wide except extreme latitudes and some oceanic islands.

Species illustrated
Giant Kingfisher 154
White-breasted Kingfisher 175
Kookaburra 189
Red-backed Kingfisher 191

BEHAVIOUR Inclined to be solitary, they fly strongly but for short periods only. Some species hover. Most emit sharp calls or harsh rattles. **FEEDING** Food is taken by swooping from a perch, either into water to seize fish or amphibians or to the ground to take insects, reptiles or small mammals; birds, crustaceans and worms have also been recorded. **BREEDING** Nesting is in a hole either in a tree, burrow or termite nest. There are 2-7 white eggs, incubated by both parents. **CARE OF YOUNG** The young hatch naked (except *Dacelo* which are downy) and are tended by both parents. The growing feathers remain in their sheaths until just before the young are ready to fly. **BIRD & MAN** The hysterical laughter of Kookaburras alarmed the first pioneers in Australia.

HABITAT	NESTING	FEEDING	FOOD SOURCE	SOCIAL
		P		

Classification

Todidae — Tody family — 5 species

CHARACTERISTICS Small and plump-bodied, 3½-5in long, these birds have short wings, a medium tail and slender legs and feet, the toes long and syndactyl. A large head rests on a short neck; the bill is long, straight and pointed. Plumage is green above, white or pastel shades below with under-tail coverts and a yellow abdomen. The throat is red and there is a white cheek stripe. The bill is reddish, the feet orange. HABITAT Varied, from tropical forests to grasslands. DISTRIBUTION Greater Antilles.

Species illustrated
Puerto Rican Tody 99

Puerto Rican Tody
Todus mexicanus

BEHAVIOUR Usually seen in pairs, these small birds are fairly weak fliers and move through the air with a characteristic whirring rattle of the wings. They are highly territorial and perch in shrubs and trees. FEEDING They dart from their perch to take flying insects; they also eat small lizards, sometimes striking their prey against a limb before eating it. BREEDING The pair share the work of digging a burrow up to 25in long in a bank, ending in a chamber. There the female lays her eggs (usually four, white in colour). The parents also share the incubation. CARE OF YOUNG The nidicolous young are tended by both parents. The juvenile birds do not acquire the characteristic red throat until the first moult.

HABITAT	NESTING	FEEDING	FOOD SOURCE	SOCIAL
		P		

Momotidae — Motmot family — 8 species

CHARACTERISTICS Small to largish birds, 6½-20in long, motmots have short rounded wings and a long tail (except *Hylomanes*) that takes up more than half the birds' total length and is racquet-tipped in many species. Their legs are short, their toes syndactyl. The longish bill is broad, decurved and usually serrated. Plumage is green, blue, brown. The crown, face or throat are black, blue or brown. HABITAT Forests. DISTRIBUTION Found throughout the American tropical region.

Species illustrated
Blue-diademed Motmot 96

Blue-diademed Motmot
Momotus momota

BEHAVIOUR Usually solitary. Individuals perch for long periods on a branch, twitching their tails in pendulum fashion. FEEDING They dart suddenly from their perch to seize an insect, spider, worm, snail or lizard which they then carry back to the perch, usually beating it against a branch before eating it. Some insects are taken in the air; they also feed on fruit. BREEDING Nesting takes place either in a burrow dug by the pair or, in limestone areas, in caves or natural niches. The chamber may be as much as 15 feet from the entrance, though most are much less. There are 3-4 white eggs, incubated on the bare floor by both parents. CARE OF YOUNG The young hatch blind and naked and are fed and brooded by both parents.

HABITAT	NESTING	FEEDING	FOOD SOURCE	SOCIAL
		P_V		

Meropidae — Bee-eater family — 24 species

CHARACTERISTICS These small to medium birds, 6-14in long, have a longish compact body and long wings and tail, the former pointed. The legs are slender, as are the syndactyl toes. The bill is long, slender, laterally compressed and decurved. Plumage is a variety of bright colours, green and red predominating. The sexes are alike or nearly so. HABITAT Forests to open country areas. DISTRIBUTION Temperate and tropical parts of Europe, Africa, Asia, Australia. Most species are migratory.

Species illustrated
Red-throated Bee-eater 157

European Bee-eater
Merops apiaster

BEHAVIOUR Most species are gregarious, sometimes massing in huge flocks, and mainly arboreal. FEEDING Most hawk their food—bees and other insects—in the air, either continuously over a period or in repeated sallies from a perch. At least one species, *M.superciliosus*, de-venoms the bees it captures by rubbing their sting-end against a branch (they can apparently distinguish between the stinging worker and the non-stinging drone). This species is also believed to take fish from the surface waters. Some species also feed on tiny lizards. BREEDING Many nest colonially. Both parents dig a tunnel in a bank up to 40in deep and leading to an unlined chamber. There are 2-5 white eggs, incubated by both. CARE OF YOUNG Both parents tend the naked, nidicolous young.

HABITAT	NESTING	FEEDING	FOOD SOURCE	SOCIAL
		P		

Leptosomatidae — Cuckoo-roller family — 1 species

CHARACTERISTICS Stoutly built, 16-18in long, they have long pointed wings and a long square tail. The legs are short with long toes. A large head rests on a short neck; the bill is stout and slightly hooked. Plumage varies according to sex: in the male it is dark grey above with dark iridescent green and copper wings and tail, lighter grey below; the female is duller and browner than the male above, spotted with black below. HABITAT Forests and brush. DISTRIBUTION Madagascar, Comoro Islands.

Species illustrated
Cuckoo-roller 159

Cuckoo-roller
Leptosomus discolor

BEHAVIOUR These conspicuous and largely arboreal birds are often seen wheeling about in the air in small groups. FEEDING Their food is taken from trees and beaten against a branch before it is swallowed. Diet includes insects of all kinds, in particular locusts and caterpillars, and chameleons and other lizards. BREEDING The nuptial display is carried out in the air. The female lays 3-5 white eggs, usually in an unlined tree-hole, occasionally in a ground-hole in a bank. Only the female incubates, fed by the male, for a period of about 20 days. CARE OF YOUNG The young remain in the nest for about 30 days until they fledge, taking on a downy plumage similar to that of the female parent.

HABITAT	NESTING	FEEDING	FOOD SOURCE	SOCIAL
		P		

Coraciidae
Roller family
17 species

European Roller
Coracias garrulus

CHARACTERISTICS Rollers are 9½-18in long with long wings and tail, the latter square, emarginate or forked. The legs are short. A fairly large head rests on a short neck; the bill is broad, strong, of medium length, slightly decurved and hooked. Plumage is a variety of bright colours in most species. The sexes are alike or nearly so. **HABITAT** Varied. **DISTRIBUTION** Europe and Asia except extreme north, Africa, E Indies, Philippines, N and E Australia east to Solomons. Some species are migratory.

Species illustrated
European Roller 117
Long-tailed Ground-roller 139
Scaly Ground-roller 158

BEHAVIOUR Rollers take their name from their acrobatic display flights. Except in migration they are usually solitary, perching at a vantage point from which they swoop on ground prey. Ground Rollers are mainly terrestrial, inhabiting dense forest or brush. **FEEDING** They mostly eat small animals, especially insects. Small birds are sometimes taken, fruit more rarely. **BREEDING** The rolling and tumbling aerial display precedes nesting in a hole in a tree or bank, or among rocks, sometimes in an abandoned magpie nest. The nests have little or no lining. There are 3-6 white eggs, incubated by both or possibly by the female only. **CARE OF YOUNG** The young hatch naked and are cared for in the nest by both parents.

HABITAT		NESTING		FEEDING		FOOD SOURCE		SOCIAL	
				P	☀	🪰	🦎	•	♂♀

Upupidae
Hoopoe family
1 species

European Hoopoe
Upupa epops

CHARACTERISTICS Hoopoes are 10-12in long, with broad rounded wings and a medium square tail. The 3rd and 4th toes are fused at the base; the claws are short. They have a long, slender, decurved bill. Plumage is cinnamon to chestnut, conspicuously marked with black and white bands. There is an erectile crest, tipped with black. The sexes are similar. **HABITAT** Semi-open country. **DISTRIBUTION** C and S Europe, Africa except central areas, C and S Asia to Japan. Some species migratory.

Species illustrated
Hoopoe 118

BEHAVIOUR Usually living singly or in pairs, and in small groups during migration, they are slow, erratic fliers and prefer environments that give them trees for roosting as well as plenty of open ground in which to search for food. **FEEDING** Mainly they feed on the ground, walking or running with a characteristic bobbing of the head. They eat mostly insects as well as other invertebrates and small vertebrates. **BREEDING** Nesting is in a hole either in a tree, bank, wall or termite nest. Usually 5-8 eggs are laid, long and greenish-white, which are incubated by the female for about 18 days; she is fed by the male. **CARE OF YOUNG** The young are downy and fed in the nest by both parents. They fledge after 20-27 days.

HABITAT		NESTING		FEEDING		FOOD SOURCE			SOCIAL	
				P	☀	🪰	🪱	🦎	•	♂♀

Phoeniculidae
Wood-hoopoe family
6 species

Green Wood-hoopoe
Phoeniculus purpureus

CHARACTERISTICS These birds, 8½-15in long, have short rounded wings and a long graduated tail. Their legs are short with long toes, the 3rd and 4th fused at the base; their claws are long and curved. The bill is long and slender and varies from almost straight to sickled. Plumage is blackish with a metallic gloss of blue, green or purple; some have white spots near the end of the tail. The sexes are similar, the female smaller in some species. **HABITAT** Forests, wooded areas. **DISTRIBUTION** C and S Africa.

Species illustrated
Buff-headed Wood-hoopoe 140

BEHAVIOUR Usually solitary or found in small groups, they are infrequent fliers and do so briefly and in a laboured manner. The family has a strong musty smell, unpleasant to humans. **FEEDING** They mainly eat invertebrates, taking food from among the branches of trees where they climb with great skill, sometimes hanging upside down and using the tail as a prop. Berries and seeds are also taken. **BREEDING** Little is known of their breeding habits in the wild. They do not build a nest, the female laying her eggs in a tree cavity. There are 3-5 pale greenish-blue eggs which are incubated by the female. **CARE OF YOUNG** Both parents care for the downy, nidicolous young.

HABITAT		NESTING	FEEDING		FOOD SOURCE		SOCIAL	
			P$_v$	☀	🌿	🪰	•	♂♀

Bucerotidae
Hornbill family
45 species

Great Indian Hornbill
Buceros bicornis

CHARACTERISTICS Hornbills are medium to very large, 15-63in long, with a slender to stout body, strong wings and a long broad tail. The legs are short, the toes syndactyl. The neck is long, the bill massive and decurved, surmounted in most by a horny casque. Plumage is wiry in combinations of black, white, brown. The bill is usually black, white, red or yellow. The sexes may be alike or unlike. **HABITAT** Forests, open woods. **DISTRIBUTION** Africa south of Sahara, tropical Asia, Philippines, Malaysia.

Species illustrated
Red-billed Dwarf Hornbill 142
Narcondam Hornbill 171

BEHAVIOUR They are arboreal and usually found in pairs or small flocks. The wings of the larger species can be loud in flight. **FEEDING** Ground Hornbills are virtually omnivorous; Tree Hornbills eat chiefly fruit and insects. **BREEDING** While Ground Hornbills nest unimprisoned in rock or tree-holes, in other species the female walls herself up in a tree-hole with clay or dung, leaving only a narrow aperture through which the male passes food. She lays 1-6 white eggs, incubating them for 30-50 days, during which period she moults. **CARE OF YOUNG** The young hatch naked and are tended by the female, who feeds them on food passed in by the male. In some species the female leaves the hole before the young are fully fledged; they then replaster the aperture.

HABITAT		NESTING	FEEDING		FOOD SOURCE			SOCIAL	
			O	☀	🌿🐦	🪰	🐰	•	♂♀

247

Classification

ORDER PICIFORMES

Galbulidae Jacamar family
15 species

Rufous-tailed Jacamar
Galbula ruficauda

CHARACTERISTICS Jacamars are small to medium, 5-12in long, with short wings and a long tail. Their legs are short, the toes usually zygodactyl. A large head rests on a short neck; the bill is long, slender and almost straight. Plumage is soft, black or iridescent green above, black or tawny below. The throat is usually white or buff. The sexes are dissimilar. **HABITAT** Tropical forests. **DISTRIBUTION** S Mexico to S Brazil, the main concentration being in the Amazon area.

Species illustrated
Rufous-tailed Jacamar 83

BEHAVIOUR Lively and usually solitary, jacamars communicate with squeaking and whistling calls. **FEEDING** They appear to be entirely insectivorous, in particular taking butterflies on the wing after spotting them from a vantage point in a tree; the prey is then beaten against a branch until the wings fall off, and the body is swallowed. **BREEDING** The nest is a burrow excavated by both sexes in a bank or in a termite nest. At the end the tunnel opens into an unlined chamber where 3-4 almost spherical white eggs are laid; incubation is by both parents. **CARE OF YOUNG** The newly hatched young are covered with long white down and have well-developed heel pads. They are tended by both parents in the nest.

HABITAT	NESTING	FEEDING	FOOD SOURCE	SOCIAL

Bucconidae Puffbird family
32 species

White-whiskered Puffbird
Malacoptila panamensis

CHARACTERISTICS These solidly built birds, 5½-12½in long, have short rounded wings and a medium to long square tail. The legs are short, with zygodactyl toes. A short neck supports a large head; the bill is strong, broad and straight or decurved with a hooked tip. Plumage is soft and thick and predominantly black, white and brown with yellow and reddish browns, often spotted and streaked. The sexes are alike or nearly so. **HABITAT** Tropical forest. **DISTRIBUTION** S Mexico to Brazil and Paraguay.

Species illustrated
White-fronted Nunbird 85

BEHAVIOUR Closely related to jacamars, these primarily arboreal birds are inclined to be solitary, sitting motionless on a branch for long periods. **FEEDING** They suddenly dart from their perch to take insects either from the air or on the ground. The prey is beaten against a branch before it is swallowed. **BREEDING** Nesting is on the ground. Both sexes excavate a hole up to 60in long either in an earth bank, level ground or a termite nest; the entrance is sometimes concealed with vegetation. There are 2-3 glossy white eggs, incubated by both parents. **CARE OF YOUNG** The young hatch naked and blind. In the illustrated species the brooding is by the male, the feeding mainly by the female: this is the reverse of the usual pattern among birds.

HABITAT	NESTING	FEEDING	FOOD SOURCE	SOCIAL

Capitonidae Barbet family
76 species

Black-collared Barbet
Lybius torquatus

CHARACTERISTICS Small to medium, 3¼-12½in long, barbets are stout-bodied and have short to medium wings and tail. The legs are short with large zygodactyl feet. They have a large head and bill, the latter heavy and slightly decurved. Plumage is a great variety of bright colours, spotted in some, tufted over the nostrils in many, and many have rictal and chin bristles. The sexes are mostly alike. **HABITAT** Forests. **DISTRIBUTION** Africa to Asia, Indonesia, Philippines, Central and South America.

BEHAVIOUR Primarily arboreal, barbets frequent the tops of trees, and some species are able to climb tree trunks. Usually they are seen alone or in pairs: they are weak fliers and do so for limited periods only. **FEEDING** Most are mainly vegetarian and their diet includes fruit, berries and seeds. Many also take insects, a few being chiefly insectivorous. **BREEDING** The bill is used to excavate holes in trees or banks and occasionally to burrow into termite nests. A few species nest colonially. The female lays 2-4 white eggs which are incubated by both parents. **CARE OF YOUNG** The young hatch naked and are tended in the nest by both parents for a relatively long period.

HABITAT	NESTING	FEEDING	FOOD SOURCE	SOCIAL

Indicatoridae Honeyguide family
12 species

Greater Honeyguide
Indicator indicator

CHARACTERISTICS Small and compact-bodied, 4¼-8in long, honeyguides have long wings and tail, the former pointed. Their legs are short with zygodactyl toes and long hooked claws. The neck is short, as is the bill which varies from stout and blunt to slender and pointed. Plumage features browns and grey above, lighter below; some species are streaked or spotted and some have yellow patches. **HABITAT** Forests and brushland. **DISTRIBUTION** Africa south of Sahara, Himalayas, Borneo, Sumatra.

Species illustrated
Greater Honeyguide 144

BEHAVIOUR Largely solitary and arboreal, honeyguides are rapid fliers and their vernacular name refers to the habit of several African species of leading animals, including man, to the nests of wild bees. As well as leading, they also attract potential honey-eaters by display. **FEEDING** After the hive has been plundered, the bird takes food for itself. Their diet includes honey and beeswax, bees and their larvae and other insects. **BREEDING** All species so far investigated are parasitic breeders, using the holes of tree- or burrow-nesting birds (*P.insignis* uses the open nest of a passerine). There is one white egg, incubated by the host bird. **CARE OF YOUNG** The young hatch naked and are tended in the host nest. Both mandibles are hooked in some nestlings.

HABITAT	NESTING	FEEDING	FOOD SOURCE	SOCIAL

Ramphastidae
Toucan family
37 species

Keel-billed Toucan
Ramphastos sulfuratus

CHARACTERISTICS Medium to largish, 12-24in long, toucans have short rounded wings and a long tail. Their feet are strong, clawed and zygodactyl. They have a hugely enlarged, brightly coloured bill and a long "fringed" tongue. Plumage is loose with black, white and various bright colours, usually in bold combinations. The sexes are alike in most species. HABITAT Forests. DISTRIBUTION Toucans are found throughout the Neotropical regions.

Species illustrated
Keel-billed Toucan 85

BEHAVIOUR Toucans are fairly gregarious, arboreal birds. The smaller species fly swiftly and directly; the larger, heavier species tend also to flap and glide. They are fond of bathing, mutual preening, mock fencing and grappling with their huge bills. Their voice is limited to croaks, rattles and shrill cries. FEEDING They eat fruit and berries, insects, spiders and, in the larger species, eggs and nestlings and also fish. BREEDING There are 2-4 glossy white eggs, laid in an unlined tree cavity that may be natural or made by other birds. Both parents share the incubation. CARE OF YOUNG The young hatch naked and blind and equipped with heel pads. They are tended by both parents.

HABITAT	NESTING	FEEDING	FOOD SOURCE	SOCIAL

Greater Spotted Woodpecker
Dendrocopos major

Picidae
Woodpecker family
210 species

CHARACTERISTICS These birds, $3\frac{1}{2}$-$23\frac{1}{2}$in long, have medium wings and tail, the latter rounded or wedge-shaped. The feet are zygodactyl or three-toed. The neck is long, slender and strong (short in *Jynx*). They have a large head and a straight, strong chisel-like bill. Plumage is black, white, brown, green, red, yellow. The sexes mostly differ. HABITAT Forests, wooded areas. DISTRIBUTION World-wide except extreme latitudes, Madagascar, Papua, Australia and most oceanic islands. Some species migratory.

Species illustrated
Woodpeckers: 42, 44, 45, 49, 108
Yellow-bellied Sapsucker 41
Olivaceous Piculet 80
Andean Flicker 93

BEHAVIOUR Arboreal and largely solitary, woodpeckers are well known for their habit of boring holes in trees to reach insects. They have a long flexible tongue that is smooth, brush-like or barbed. They cling upright to tree trunks using their stiff tail as a bracing third leg (except *Jynx* which usually perches). It is likely that the drumming sound of bill on wood serves in some species as a territorial and/or courtship signal. FEEDING In addition to insects, sap is also said to be taken, as well as fruit and nuts. *Jynx* takes insects from the surface. BREEDING The nest is an unlined hole in a tree or an earth bank. There are 2-12 glossy white eggs, incubated by both parents. CARE OF YOUNG Most species are born naked, some downy; all are tended by both parents.

HABITAT	NESTING	FEEDING	FOOD SOURCE	SOCIAL

ORDER
PASSERIFORMES

Eurylaimidae
Broadbill family
14 species

Lesser Green Broadbill
Calyptomena viridis

CHARACTERISTICS Broadbills are dumpy, 5-11in long, with short to long wings and tail, the latter square-shaped. Their legs are short, the feet strong and syndactyl with long hooked claws. A broad flat head rests on a short neck. Plumage is commonly bright green or blue; other bright colours occur, also black, white, brown. The sexes are alike in most species. HABITAT Dense forests, undergrowth and more open wooded areas. DISTRIBUTION Africa, India east to Borneo and Philippines.

BEHAVIOUR Solitary or gregarious, broadbills habitually sit silent and motionless for long periods on tree branches. Some species are crepuscular. FEEDING They mostly eat insects which they either hawk from the air or take from branches or the ground. Small frogs, lizards and fruit are also taken. BREEDING The nest is a pendant sac of grass and twigs, decorated with moss and having a porched entrance in the side. Usually the nest is built over water, and streamers of material hang down for 30-40in or more. The female lays 3-5 white or pinkish eggs which are incubated by both parents. CARE OF YOUNG Both also care for the naked, nidicolous young.

HABITAT	NESTING	FEEDING	FOOD SOURCE	SOCIAL

Dendrocolaptidae
Woodcreeper family
47 species

Spot-crowned Woodcreeper
Lepidocolaptes affinis

CHARACTERISTICS Woodcreepers are $5\frac{3}{4}$-$14\frac{1}{2}$in long, and have medium rounded wings and a long tail with strong rigid feather shafts. The legs are short, the feet and claws strong. The bill varies from short and straight to long and compressed. Plumage is a variety of browns streaked, barred or spotted with black, white, buff. Most species have rufous wings and tail. The sexes are alike or nearly so. HABITAT Forests and brush. DISTRIBUTION Mexico, C and S America.

Species illustrated
Streak-headed Woodcreeper 80

BEHAVIOUR Arboreal and solitary, though sometimes associating with other species, woodcreepers are strong fliers but do so for short periods only. Unlike woodpeckers they do not tap wood though their stiff tail is used as a prop to support the body upright on the trunk while they probe the bark with their bill. FEEDING This probing method is used to locate insects and spiders. The bird works its way methodically up a tree then flies to the base of another to start again. Some species also feed on the ground. BREEDING There are 2-3 white to greenish eggs, laid in a tree cavity that is either natural or made by other birds and lined with bark and leaves. Incubation is shared by both parents. CARE OF YOUNG Both tend the blind, downy, nidicolous young.

HABITAT	NESTING	FEEDING	FOOD SOURCE	SOCIAL

Classification

Furnariidae
Ovenbird family
212 species

Rufous Ovenbird
Furnarius rufus

CHARACTERISTICS Small to medium birds, 4¾-11in long, their wings vary from short and rounded to long and pointed, the tail from short to long. The legs are short to medium and slender. They have a small head and a slender bill, short to long and either straight, decurved or recurved. Plumage consists of browns above, marked in some with darker colour, and lighter below. HABITAT Mountains, forests, seashores, rivers, semi-desert. DISTRIBUTION Mexico, C and S America.

Species illustrated
Rufous-fronted Thornbird 81
Rufous Ovenbird 88

BEHAVIOUR This is probably the most diverse of all the bird families, and only the broadest generalizations are possible. Most are active but unobtrusive and many seem to move about in pairs. Different species may be solitary or gregarious, arboreal or terrestrial, strong or weak fliers. FEEDING The range includes insectivores, vegetarians, scavengers in sewage effluent and offshore kelp feeders. BREEDING Nesting habits are similarly diverse. Up to nine eggs, usually 2-5, all white or nearly so, are laid in a ground- or tree-hole or in a domed mud structure built in a tree, a building or on a post; alternatively the nest may be a domed grass or stick structure in a bush or on the ground. CARE OF YOUNG The downy, nidicolous young are tended by both parents.

HABITAT	NESTING	FEEDING	FOOD SOURCE	SOCIAL

Formicariidae
Antbird family
221 species

Rufous-capped Ant-thrush
Formicarius colma

CHARACTERISTICS Smallish, 3¾-14½in long, these rather plump birds have short rounded wings and a short to long tail. Their legs are short in the arboreal species, long in the terrestrial. The bill is of medium length and slightly to strongly hooked. Plumage consists of combinations of browns, black, white, grey; some are streaked, spotted or barred. The female is usually browner than the male. HABITAT Forests, brushland. DISTRIBUTION S Mexico south to C Argentina.

Species illustrated
Bicoloured Antbird 85

BEHAVIOUR Arboreal or terrestrial, but always settling in areas that afford good cover, these birds tend to be secretive and are usually solitary or live in pairs. They are weak fliers and do so for brief periods only. FEEDING They are largely insectivorous; some also eat fruit and berries and some are said to take young birds. A number accompany marching ant columns, taking insects flushed by them. BREEDING Nests take many forms including a woven open cup, semi-pendant or set in a tree-fork or bush, a cup on the ground or a lined tree-hole. Usually there are two eggs, white or buff, speckled or streaked, incubated by both parents. CARE OF YOUNG The young are naked or downy and are cared for in the nest by both parents.

HABITAT	NESTING	FEEDING	FOOD SOURCE	SOCIAL

Conopophagidae
Antpipit family
10 species

Black-bellied Gnat-eater
Conopophaga melanogaster

CHARACTERISTICS These small birds, 4-5½in long, have plump bodies, short rounded wings and a very short tail. The legs are slender, from short to fairly long, with long toes. A large head is set on a short neck; the bill is broadish and flattened. Plumage is made up of varieties of brown, rufous, black, olive above, lighter below. Some species have a contrasting patch on the throat and/or crown. The sexes are similar. HABITAT Forests. DISTRIBUTION Northern S America to about 30°S.

BEHAVIOUR The exact number of species is uncertain but all superficially resemble the juvenile Robin, *Erithacus rubecula*. Timid, secretive and solitary, they are also weak fliers. FEEDING They spend much of their time scratching among fallen leaves for the insects which form their diet. BREEDING The nest is an open cup of leaves, twigs, moss and grass constructed either low in a bush or on the ground. Usually there are two eggs, buff with streaks and spots of brown or pink. Incubation is apparently shared by the parents who (at least in *C.melanops*) use the tactic of feigning injury as a means of distracting intruders. CARE OF YOUNG Information is lacking both on the young and on parental care.

HABITAT	NESTING	FEEDING	FOOD SOURCE	SOCIAL

Rhinocryptidae
Tapaculo families
26 species

Unicoloured Tapaculo
Scytalopus unicolor

CHARACTERISTICS Small, 4½-10in long, they have plump bodies and short rounded wings; the tail varies from short to long and is often raised. The legs are fairly long with large strong feet and claws. They have a short neck and a pointed bill, slender to stout. Plumage is brown, grey or black, some rufous and/or barred below. The sexes are alike or nearly so. HABITAT Forests, grassland, semi-arid brush DISTRIBUTION Americas south from Costa Rica except Brazil and Amazon system.

Species illustrated
Unicoloured Tapaculo 92

BEHAVIOUR Almost entirely terrestrial, they fly very rarely but are rapid runners, usually moving with the tail held erect. One of the most distinctive anatomical features of the family is the operculum or lid-like structure that covers the nostrils. Their rather monotonous calls seem to have ventriloquial properties that make them difficult to locate. FEEDING They creep secretively about, scratching the ground for their diet of insects and seeds. BREEDING They nest mainly in holes either in a bank, a hollow stump, in crannies of rotting trees or between the bark and the trunk. There are 2-4 white eggs, probably incubated by both parents. CARE OF YOUNG The young are downy and nidicolous and are tended by both parents.

HABITAT	NESTING	FEEDING	FOOD SOURCE	SOCIAL

Cotingidae
Cotinga family
90 species

Cock-of-the-rock
Rupicola rupicola

CHARACTERISTICS Cotingas are 3½-18in long with short to long wings and tail, the latter forked in one species. The legs are short, the feet large. The bill is fairly broad and slightly hooked. Plumage is brightly coloured in some males, otherwise browns, greys, black and white predominate in both sexes. Some have an elaborate crest, some a bare throat pouch. The sexes may be alike or unlike. HABITAT Forests. DISTRIBUTION S USA, C America, West Indies, S America south to about 30°S.

BEHAVIOUR An enormously varied family, usually solitary and arboreal, these forest birds frequent the tops of trees. Their calls include a penetrating bell-like note, whistles, grunts and croaks. They are fairly strong fliers. FEEDING They eat insects and fruit. BREEDING The display of the Umbrella-bird involves spreading the crest to cover the entire head. Nests include a tree-hole, a platform of vegetation, an enclosed structure of vegetation with a side entrance, and a mud cup plastered to a rock wall. The White-winged Becard prefers to build next to a wasps' nest. There are 1-6 eggs, variously coloured, which are incubated by the female. CARE OF YOUNG The young hatch naked or downy and are probably tended in the nest by both parents.

HABITAT	NESTING	FEEDING	FOOD SOURCE	SOCIAL
		V P		

Pipridae
Manakin family
59 species

Long-tailed Manakin
Chiroxiphia linearis

CHARACTERISTICS These small, stout-bodied birds, 3½-6½in long, have short wings and a very short tail, some with elongated feathers. The legs are short, the 3rd toe fused at the base with the 2nd or 4th. Their neck is very short, their bill short and broad and slightly hooked. Plumage in the male is usually black with various brightly coloured areas; the female is typically olive green. HABITAT Tropical forests. DISTRIBUTION Manakins are found from S Mexico south to Paraguay.

Species illustrated
Golden-collared Manakin 85

BEHAVIOUR Manakins, usually solitary, are occasionally found in small flocks. Flight is rapid and direct. FEEDING Their diet consists of fruit and some insects. BREEDING The most outstanding feature is the display in some species of groups of males at a "lek", a cleared area around a single sapling which forms the principal display perch. The female chooses a male and copulation occurs at the lek. The female then leaves to carry out all the nesting duties alone. Other species have an aerial display and the Yellow-thighed Manakin *P.mentalis* performs an elaborate display of acrobatic tumbling on a branch. The nest is a woven hammock, often constructed over water. There are two spotted eggs. CARE OF YOUNG The downy, nidicolous chicks are tended by the female.

HABITAT	NESTING	FEEDING	FOOD SOURCE	SOCIAL
		V P		♀

Tyrannidae
Tyrant-flycatcher family
365 species

Eastern Kingbird
Tyrannus tyrannus

CHARACTERISTICS These birds, 3-16in long, show great variations. Their wings range from short and rounded to long and pointed, the tail from very short to very long. Legs and feet are small except in the terrestrial species. The bill is usually short, broad and flattened. Plumage varies, but protective shades of brown, grey, black are common, with a few areas of bright colour. The sexes are mostly alike. HABITAT Forests to open country. DISTRIBUTION N and S America.

Species illustrated
Scissor-tailed Flycatcher 59
Cattle Tyrant 89

BEHAVIOUR This enormous family is exceeded in numbers only by the finches and Old World Warblers. Usually arboreal, flight is weak but agile and used by many to hawk insects by sorties from a perch. They are highly territorial, fearlessly attacking large birds that approach the nest. Their voice is limited and weak. FEEDING Their food includes insects, fruit, small mammals, reptiles, amphibians and fish. BREEDING Courtship display is aerial in many species. The various nest-forms include an open cup in a tree or on the ground, a tree- or ground-hole, a pendant enclosed structure and a conical nest built in reeds. There are 2-6 white, cream or buff eggs, usually incubated by the female, sometimes by both. CARE OF YOUNG Both tend the downy or naked, nidicolous young.

HABITAT	NESTING	FEEDING	FOOD SOURCE	SOCIAL
		O		

Oxyruncidae
Sharpbill family
1 species

Sharpbill
Oxyruncus cristatus

CHARACTERISTICS Small, about 6½in long, they have longish rounded wings and a medium square tail. The legs are short, the toes fairly long, strong and sharp-clawed. The bill is long, straight, pointed. Plumage is olive green above, whitish yellow below, spotted with brown. There is a bright orange crest, the face is white with a dark scale-pattern. The sexes are similar. HABITAT Tropical forests. DISTRIBUTION Discontinuous in Costa Rica, Panama, Guyana, Paraguay, S Brazil.

BEHAVIOUR Little is known about this aberrant bird. Structurally it is similar to the tyrant-flycatchers but it may be as closely related to the todies. For the present it appears to merit family status. It flies strongly and perches in tree-tops. FEEDING Fruit appears to be the sole diet, as indicated by the stomach contents of some individuals, though the bird has been observed only rarely. BREEDING/CARE OF YOUNG No nest has been described and there is no record of the Sharpbill's habits in display or breeding, nor about the eggs it lays nor about parental care.

HABITAT	NESTING	FEEDING	FOOD SOURCE	SOCIAL
		V		

Classification

Phytotomidae
Plant-cutter family
3 species

Plantcutter
Phytotoma rutila

CHARACTERISTICS They have a stocky body, are about 6½in long and have short pointed wings and a longish tail. The legs are short, the feet large. The bill is short, thick, pointed, serrated. Plumage in the male is plumbeous washed with olive, the crown and underparts rufous or bright red, the wings and tail black. The female is mainly grey above, buff below. HABITAT Open brushland, fields, gardens. DISTRIBUTION W Peru (isolated), Chile, Bolivia, Argentina to about 40°S.

BEHAVIOUR Superficially they resemble finches, in particular the grosbeaks. They fly rather weakly, are sometimes solitary and sometimes seen in small flocks. The voice is described as rasping, squeaking, croaking. FEEDING Their name derives from their habit of clipping off vegetation with their serrated bill; they eat fruit, leaves, shoots, buds and seeds. Much of what they cut off is wasted. BREEDING A cup-shaped nest of twigs and fibres is built in a tree or bush, usually near the ground. There are 2-4 bluish-green eggs, incubated by the female alone. CARE OF YOUNG The nidicolous young are cared for by both parents. BIRD & MAN Plantcutters are unpopular with farmers because of the large amount of crops they destroy.

HABITAT	NESTING	FEEDING	FOOD SOURCE	SOCIAL

Pittidae
Pitta family
23 species

Steere's Pitta
Pitta Steerii

CHARACTERISTICS Small to medium, 6-11in long, these stout-bodied birds have short wings and tail, long legs and large feet. The neck is short, the bill strong and slightly curved. Plumage is a variety of bright colours, each usually occupying a sharply defined area. Some species have crest or ear tufts. The sexes may be alike or unlike. HABITAT Forests and brushland. DISTRIBUTION Pittas are found in C and S Africa, India and SE Asia, E Indies, N Australia.

Species illustrated
Angolan Pitta 142

BEHAVIOUR Largely solitary and usually terrestrial (although they are strong fliers), pittas are by nature retiring and are more easily heard than seen. Their calls are melodious trills and whistles. They roost in trees. FEEDING They usually feed among leaves on the ground, hopping rapidly along in search of insects and other invertebrates; fruit and some small vertebrates are also taken. BREEDING The nest is a large domed construction of twigs, leaves and roots built with a side entrance either on the ground, on a stump or low in the branches of a tree. There are 2-7 eggs, white or buff and marked with darker colour, which are incubated by both parents. CARE OF YOUNG The nidicolous young hatch naked and are fed in the nest by both parents.

HABITAT	NESTING	FEEDING	FOOD SOURCE	SOCIAL

Xenicidae
New Zealand Wren family
4 species

New Zealand Bush Wren
Xenicus longipes

CHARACTERISTICS These very small, plump-bodied birds are 3-4in long with short rounded wings and a very short tail. Their legs and toes are long and slender, the outer and middle toes united at the base; they have long sharp claws. The neck is very short, the bill straight, slender and pointed. Plumage is brown or greenish-yellow above, whitish below; there is some black on the primaries. The sexes are unlike. HABITAT Forests and scrub. DISTRIBUTION New Zealand.

Species illustrated
Rifleman 209

BEHAVIOUR Largely solitary and arboreal, sometimes seen in small groups, they fly poorly and spend much time hopping over the branches of trees and, less often, running on the ground. *Acanthisitta* are also known as Riflemen, the name deriving from the "zing" of their call. FEEDING Their food consists of insects, grubs and spiders, for which they probe tree barks with their pointed bill. BREEDING *Xenicus* build a domed nest of vegetation, approached by a woven tunnel, on the ground; *Acanthisitta* line a natural tree-hole with vegetation, and also build an entrance tunnel. There are 2-5 eggs, white and immaculate, which are incubated by both parents. CARE OF YOUNG Both parents also tend the naked, nidicolous young.

HABITAT	NESTING	FEEDING	FOOD SOURCE	SOCIAL

Philepittidae
Asity family
4 species

Velvet Asity
Philepitta castanea

CHARACTERISTICS These small birds, 4-6½in long, have medium rounded wings and a shortish tail. The legs and feet are large, the claws long. Their bill varies from medium and slightly decurved to long, sharp and sickled. Plumage consists of various combinations of blue, green and yellow, or is largely black with touches of those colours. The orbital skin is bare in the male. The sexes are unlike. HABITAT Forests. DISTRIBUTION Madagascar.

Species illustrated
Velvet Asity 159
Small-billed Sunbird 159

BEHAVIOUR The four species are divided between two greatly divergent genera and are regarded as the remnants of a very ancient family. They are largely arboreal and solitary, though sometimes they keep company with flocks of other species. Flight is strong but not sustained and they tend to be rather inactive. FEEDING Food includes fruit, buds, nectar, insects, spiders. BREEDING Behaviour is recorded only for the Velvet Asity, *P.castanea*. They build a pendant nest of fibres, leaves and moss, each having a roofed side entrance. Three white, immaculate, elongated eggs were found in the nest examined. CARE OF YOUNG Nothing is known of incubation or parental care, or of the young themselves.

HABITAT	NESTING	FEEDING	FOOD SOURCE	SOCIAL

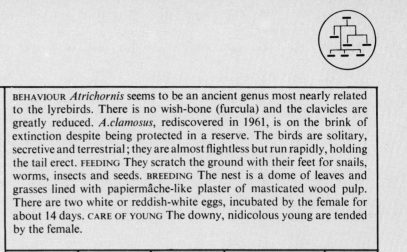

Atrichornithidae
Scrub-bird family
2 species

Noisy Scrub-bird
Atrichornis clamosus

CHARACTERISTICS Small, 6½-12in long, with a plump body and very short wings, scrub-birds have a long broad tail and sturdy legs with large feet. The neck is short, the bill strong and pointed. Plumage is rufous and a variety of browns, vermiculated above, lighter below. The sexes are unlike. **HABITAT** Dense scrub. **DISTRIBUTION** Specific regions of Australia: *A.clamosus* is found only in SW Australia, while *A.rufescens* is confined to New South Wales.

Species illustrated
Noisy Scrub-bird 187

BEHAVIOUR *Atrichornis* seems to be an ancient genus most nearly related to the lyrebirds. There is no wish-bone (furcula) and the clavicles are greatly reduced. *A.clamosus*, rediscovered in 1961, is on the brink of extinction despite being protected in a reserve. The birds are solitary, secretive and terrestrial; they are almost flightless but run rapidly, holding the tail erect. **FEEDING** They scratch the ground with their feet for snails, worms, insects and seeds. **BREEDING** The nest is a dome of leaves and grasses lined with papiermâche-like plaster of masticated wood pulp. There are two white or reddish-white eggs, incubated by the female for about 14 days. **CARE OF YOUNG** The downy, nidicolous young are tended by the female.

HABITAT	NESTING	FEEDING	FOOD SOURCE	SOCIAL
		V P		♀

Menuridae
Lyrebird family
2 species

Superb Lyrebird
Menura novaehollandiae

CHARACTERISTICS Ranging in length from 30-40in, lyrebirds have short wings and a long tail that is very elaborate in the male. Their legs and feet are large and strong with long claws. The neck is long, the bill stout, straight and pointed. Plumage consists of combinations of browns and grey, darker above. There is bluish skin around the eyes. The sexes are unlike. **HABITAT** Forests, scrub. **DISTRIBUTION** Lyrebirds are found in SE Australia and have also been introduced into Tasmania.

Species illustrated
Superb Lyrebird 185

BEHAVIOUR Solitary and terrestrial, though they roost in trees, lyrebirds are rapid runners and jumpers; they fly rarely, gliding down from trees. The tail of the male Superb Lyrebird is both substantial and fantastic, consisting of 12 filamentary feathers, two wire-like plumes and two wider feathers marked with silvery-mauve and golden-brown. **FEEDING** Food is insects, spiders, worms and molluscs. **BREEDING** The male has an elaborate ritual display, and there is some evidence of polygamy. The female alone undertakes all nesting duties: she builds a domed stick-nest either on the ground, on a stump or high in a tree. Incubation of the single purplish-brown egg is for about 42 days. **CARE OF YOUNG** The nidicolous chick hatches almost naked and stays in the nest for six weeks.

HABITAT	NESTING	FEEDING	FOOD SOURCE	SOCIAL
		P		♀

Alaudidae
Lark family
75 species

Skylark
Alauda arvensis

CHARACTERISTICS Larks, 4¾-9in long, have longish wings, usually pointed, and a short to medium tail. Their legs are short to longish and in most species the hind claw is long and sharp. The neck is short, the bill varying from short and stout to fairly long and curved. Plumage is variously brown, grey, buff, black, white. Some have a crest or ear tufts. The sexes are mostly alike. **HABITAT** Open country. **DISTRIBUTION** World-wide except extreme latitudes, New Zealand, oceanic islands.

Species illustrated
Larks: Skylark 113, Shore 131, Desert 153, Bifasciated 153, Chestnut-backed Finch 153, Singing Bushlark 193

BEHAVIOUR Many of the larks are treasured by man for their songs which are often elaborate and may be uttered as the bird soars in flight. Most species in this wide-ranging family are gregarious and are to be found in areas ranging from Arctic tundra to desert scrub – though not in forested regions. **FEEDING** Larks are ground-feeders, taking insects, molluscs, seeds and buds. **BREEDING** They nest on the ground in a scrape, lined or unlined, in a grass cup in a hollow or in a domed structure made of grass. *Ammomanes* and *Eremopterix* protect their sand-scrapes with a low wall of pebbles on the windward side. There are 2–6 eggs, usually speckled, which are incubated largely by the female. **CARE OF YOUNG** The young hatch with a thick down and are tended by both parents.

HABITAT	NESTING	FEEDING	FOOD SOURCE	SOCIAL
		V P		♂♀

Hirundinidae
Swallow family
75 species

Swallow
Hirundo rustica

CHARACTERISTICS Swallows are small and slender-bodied, 3¾-9in long, with very long pointed wings. The tail varies from long and forked to medium and square. Legs and feet are small and the neck and bill are short, the latter also flat and having a wide gape. Plumage is black or a dark colour above, white or pale below; some are streaked below. The sexes are alike in most species. **HABITAT** Greatly varied. **DISTRIBUTION** World-wide except extreme latitudes and some oceanic islands. Many species migratory.

Species illustrated
Swallows: Cliff 53, Red-rumped 178, European 218
Martins: Purple 76, African River 157

BEHAVIOUR Swallows and martins are quick and extremely agile in the air, though on the ground they can only shuffle. They perch on twigs, reeds, wires, and cling to their nests or surrounds. Gregarious at all times, some species form enormous flocks before the autumn migration. **FEEDING.** They are insectivorous. **BREEDING** Some species excavate ground burrows, some use natural holes in trees or rocks, and some make mud nests, either cup-shaped or enclosed and having an entrance tunnel, on ledges, in trees or often in roofs or the eaves of buildings. There are 3–7 eggs, white, some with speckling, which are incubated by both parents. **CARE OF YOUNG** Some species may rear as many as three broods in a season; the older offspring help to rear the later chicks.

HABITAT	NESTING	FEEDING	FOOD SOURCE	SOCIAL
		P		♂♀

Classification

Campephagidae Cuckoo-shrike family
72 species

Black Cuckoo-shrike
Campephaga phoenicea

CHARACTERISTICS These small to medium birds, 5-12½in long, have a longish, rather stout body, medium to long wings and a long graduated tail, forked in some. Their legs are short, their feet varying from weak to strong. They have a medium bill, rather heavy and hooked. Plumage is soft and coloured in combinations of greys, with black and white in shrikes and additional red, yellow and orange in minivets. HABITAT Forests, cultivated land. DISTRIBUTION Pantropical except Americas.

Species illustrated
Scarlet Minivet 167
White-winged Triller 191

BEHAVIOUR Varying from sparrow- to pigeon-size, the cuckoo-shrikes are, with the exception of the Ground Cuckoo-shrike of Australia, primarily arboreal and strong fliers. They are often gregarious and most have a noisy harsh voice. FEEDING Their diet consists of insects and berries. BREEDING Courtship display in many species involves calling while alternately raising their unopened wings. The nest is a shallow cup of twigs and vegetation, usually lined and sometimes camouflaged with spider-web and pieces of bark; usually it is built on a horizontal branch. There are 2-4 eggs, white, green or blue, mostly marked, which are incubated by both parents. CARE OF YOUNG Both parents also care for the nidicolous young.

HABITAT	NESTING	FEEDING	FOOD SOURCE	SOCIAL
		P		

Pycnonotidae Bulbul family
109 species

Red-vented Bulbul
Pycnonotus cafer

CHARACTERISTICS These smallish birds, 5½-11¼in long, have short to medium wings and a medium to long tail. Their legs are short, as is the neck, while the bill varies from short to medium and is slender and slightly curved. Plumage consists of browns, greys and yellow in most species with patches of red, yellow or white in some. One species is black. Many are crested. The sexes are mostly alike. HABITAT Forests, brush, gardens. DISTRIBUTION Africa, Madagascar, India to SE Asia. Northern species migratory.

BEHAVIOUR Although they are rather feeble fliers, most bulbuls are agile and lively. Many are gregarious but some are extremely secretive, keeping to dense forest areas, while others frequent parks and gardens. Most are noisy chatterers and some mimic other birds. FEEDING Berries, fruit, buds and insects in differing proportions form their diet; they cause a great deal of destruction in orchards and gardens. BREEDING The nest is an open cup of vegetation, usually built fairly low in a bush or tree, sometimes in a hanging flower-basket on a veranda or similar site, occasionally very high in a tree. There are 2-4 pink, white or cream eggs, incubated by both parents. CARE OF YOUNG The nidicolous young, who possibly hatch naked, are tended by both parents.

HABITAT	NESTING	FEEDING	FOOD SOURCE	SOCIAL
		V P		

Irenidae Leaf-bird family
14 species

Fairy Bluebird
Irena puella

CHARACTERISTICS Small, 4¾-9½in long, with medium wings and tail, they have short thick legs and small feet. Their bill is medium and slender to stout, slightly curved and notched in some. Plumage is long and soft, bright green and black with areas of yellow, olive and black. Some species have longer neck feathers. The sexes are unlike. HABITAT Forests, undergrowth, gardens. DISTRIBUTION India, SE Asia, S China, Philippines, Malaysia, Borneo.

Species illustrated
Fairy Bluebird 165

BEHAVIOUR Three distinct genera, *Irena* and *Aegithina* (the ioras) and *Chloropsis* (leafbirds) are retained here as one family; sometimes they are grouped under the Oriolidae (orioles) or Pycnonotidae (bulbuls) or separated under another family, e.g. Chloropseidae. They are lively arboreal birds, rapid fliers and have whistling and chattering voices. Most species are gregarious though inclined to be retiring and timid. FEEDING Insects supplement a diet of fruit, berries, nectar, seeds and buds. BREEDING Nests are cup- or saucer-shaped and built either in scrub or in a tree (sometimes at a great height). There are 2-4 eggs, grey, cream or pink, marked with brown, incubated by both or by the female alone. CARE OF YOUNG The nidicolous young are tended by both parents.

HABITAT	NESTING	FEEDING	FOOD SOURCE	SOCIAL
		V P		

Laniidae Shrike family
74 species

Great Grey Shrike
Lanius excubitor

CHARACTERISTICS Shrikes are 6-14½in long. They have medium wings and a long narrow tail. The legs and feet are strong with sharp claws. The head is large and the bill strong, hooked and toothed in some. Plumage usually consists of contrasting dark and light patterns; African species are often brightly coloured or black. The sexes may be alike or unlike. HABITAT Open or semi-open country. DISTRIBUTION Africa, Europe, Asia to New Guinea, N America to S Mexico.

Species illustrated
Great Grey Shrike 119
Red-backed Shrike 119
Grey-headed Bush-shrike 148
Bornean Bristlehead 170

BEHAVIOUR Shrikes are typically solitary, aggressive and strong fliers; they are also known for their habit of impaling their prey on a thorn. FEEDING They watch from a perch for insects, small reptiles, birds and mammals. The wood-shrikes *Prionops* and *Eurocephalus* tend to be more gregarious and feed only on insects. BREEDING Nesting is colonial in some species, the nest consisting of a cup of grass, leaves and roots in which more than one female lay a total of 2-6 eggs. Other species build a bulky nest in a bush or tree and 2-8 spotted eggs are laid; these are incubated largely by the female, or in *Prionops* by several associated adults. CARE OF YOUNG The downy, nidicolous young are tended by both parents or by associated adults.

HABITAT	NESTING	FEEDING	FOOD SOURCE	SOCIAL
		P		

Vangidae
Vanga-shrike family
13 species

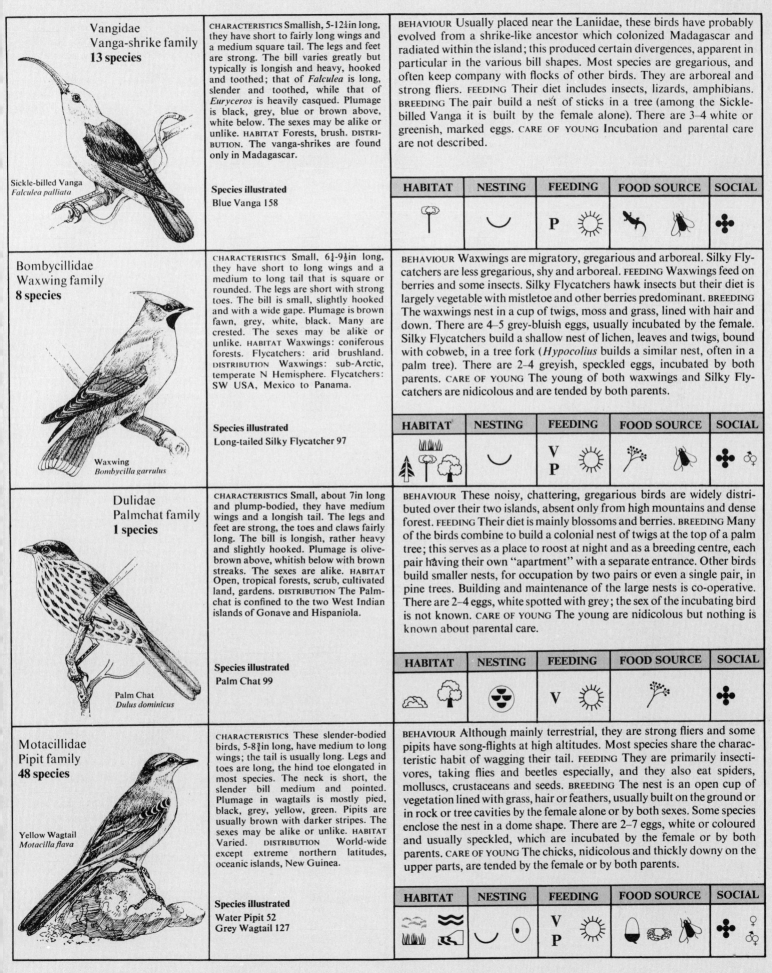

Sickle-billed Vanga
Falculea palliata

CHARACTERISTICS Smallish, 5-12¼in long, they have short to fairly long wings and a medium square tail. The legs and feet are strong. The bill varies greatly but typically is longish and heavy, hooked and toothed; that of *Falculea* is long, slender and toothed, while that of *Euryceros* is heavily casqued. Plumage is black, grey, blue or brown above, white below. The sexes may be alike or unlike. HABITAT Forests, brush. DISTRIBUTION. The vanga-shrikes are found only in Madagascar.

Species illustrated
Blue Vanga 158

BEHAVIOUR Usually placed near the Laniidae, these birds have probably evolved from a shrike-like ancestor which colonized Madagascar and radiated within the island; this produced certain divergences, apparent in particular in the various bill shapes. Most species are gregarious, and often keep company with flocks of other birds. They are arboreal and strong fliers. FEEDING Their diet includes insects, lizards, amphibians. BREEDING The pair build a nest of sticks in a tree (among the Sickle-billed Vanga it is built by the female alone). There are 3–4 white or greenish, marked eggs. CARE OF YOUNG Incubation and parental care are not described.

HABITAT	NESTING	FEEDING	FOOD SOURCE	SOCIAL

Bombycillidae
Waxwing family
8 species

Waxwing
Bombycilla garrulus

CHARACTERISTICS Small, 6¼-9½in long, they have short to long wings and a medium to long tail that is square or rounded. The legs are short with strong toes. The bill is small, slightly hooked and with a wide gape. Plumage is brown fawn, grey, white, black. Many are crested. The sexes may be alike or unlike. HABITAT Waxwings: coniferous forests. Flycatchers: arid brushland. DISTRIBUTION Waxwings: sub-Arctic, temperate N Hemisphere. Flycatchers: SW USA, Mexico to Panama.

Species illustrated
Long-tailed Silky Flycatcher 97

BEHAVIOUR Waxwings are migratory, gregarious and arboreal. Silky Flycatchers are less gregarious, shy and arboreal. FEEDING Waxwings feed on berries and some insects. Silky Flycatchers hawk insects but their diet is largely vegetable with mistletoe and other berries predominant. BREEDING The waxwings nest in a cup of twigs, moss and grass, lined with hair and down. There are 4–5 grey-bluish eggs, usually incubated by the female. Silky Flycatchers build a shallow nest of lichen, leaves and twigs, bound with cobweb, in a tree fork (*Hypocolius* builds a similar nest, often in a palm tree). There are 2–4 greyish, speckled eggs, incubated by both parents. CARE OF YOUNG The young of both waxwings and Silky Flycatchers are nidicolous and are tended by both parents.

HABITAT	NESTING	FEEDING	FOOD SOURCE	SOCIAL

Dulidae
Palmchat family
1 species

Palm Chat
Dulus dominicus

CHARACTERISTICS Small, about 7in long and plump-bodied, they have medium wings and a longish tail. The legs and feet are strong, the toes and claws fairly long. The bill is longish, rather heavy and slightly hooked. Plumage is olive-brown above, whitish below with brown streaks. The sexes are alike. HABITAT Open, tropical forests, scrub, cultivated land, gardens. DISTRIBUTION The Palmchat is confined to the two West Indian islands of Gonave and Hispaniola.

Species illustrated
Palm Chat 99

BEHAVIOUR These noisy, chattering, gregarious birds are widely distributed over their two islands, absent only from high mountains and dense forest. FEEDING Their diet is mainly blossoms and berries. BREEDING Many of the birds combine to build a colonial nest of twigs at the top of a palm tree; this serves as a place to roost at night and as a breeding centre, each pair having their own "apartment" with a separate entrance. Other birds build smaller nests, for occupation by two pairs or even a single pair, in pine trees. Building and maintenance of the large nests is co-operative. There are 2–4 eggs, white spotted with grey; the sex of the incubating bird is not known. CARE OF YOUNG The young are nidicolous but nothing is known about parental care.

HABITAT	NESTING	FEEDING	FOOD SOURCE	SOCIAL

Motacillidae
Pipit family
48 species

Yellow Wagtail
Motacilla flava

CHARACTERISTICS These slender-bodied birds, 5-8¾in long, have medium to long wings; the tail is usually long. Legs and toes are long, the hind toe elongated in most species. The neck is short, the slender bill medium and pointed. Plumage in wagtails is mostly pied, black, grey, yellow, green. Pipits are usually brown with darker stripes. The sexes may be alike or unlike. HABITAT Varied. DISTRIBUTION World-wide except extreme northern latitudes, oceanic islands, New Guinea.

Species illustrated
Water Pipit 52
Grey Wagtail 127

BEHAVIOUR Although mainly terrestrial, they are strong fliers and some pipits have song-flights at high altitudes. Most species share the characteristic habit of wagging their tail. FEEDING They are primarily insectivores, taking flies and beetles especially, and they also eat spiders, molluscs, crustaceans and seeds. BREEDING The nest is an open cup of vegetation lined with grass, hair or feathers, usually built on the ground or in rock or tree cavities by the female alone or by both sexes. Some species enclose the nest in a dome shape. There are 2–7 eggs, white or coloured and usually speckled, which are incubated by the female or by both parents. CARE OF YOUNG The chicks, nidicolous and thickly downy on the upper parts, are tended by the female or by both parents.

HABITAT	NESTING	FEEDING	FOOD SOURCE	SOCIAL

Cinclidae Dipper family
5 species

Dipper
Cinclus cinclus

CHARACTERISTICS These solidly built birds, 5½-7½in long, have short pointed wings and, a short tail. The legs and toes are long and strong with short claws. The bill is straight, slender, laterally compressed and slightly hooked. Plumage is dense with a downy underlay, chestnut and brownish-black above and on the belly. The sexes are alike. HABITAT Swift-flowing mountain and hill streams. DISTRIBUTION Europe, C Asia to China and Japan, Americas from Canada to Argentina.

Species illustrated
Dipper 123

BEHAVIOUR Exclusively aquatic, dippers use their wings under water as flippers; they can also walk on the bottom. Flight is direct with rapid wing beats. They are active birds and have a characteristic bobbing of the body. FEEDING They feed on insects and their larvae, worms, molluscs, crustaceans, fish and some vegetable matter which they take from the swift streams they mostly frequent. BREEDING The nest is large and domed and has a side entrance; it is built of moss and grass, lined with leaves and sited in natural cavities in rocks or banks or under a bridge or some other protected location, possibly even on a rock or log in mid-stream. There are 4–5 white, unmarked eggs, incubated by the female. CARE OF YOUNG The downy, nidicolous young are tended by both parents.

HABITAT	NESTING	FEEDING	FOOD SOURCE	SOCIAL

Troglodytidae Wren family
63 species

Common Wren
Troglodytes troglodytes

CHARACTERISTICS Small and plump-bodied, 3¾-8½in long, wrens have short rounded wings and a short to long tail. The legs and feet are strong, the neck is short, the bill slender, medium to long and curved. Plumage is a variety of browns with white, grey or black, barred, streaked or spotted in most species. The sexes are alike or nearly so. HABITAT Varied. DISTRIBUTION Europe and Asia except extreme north in both and extreme S Asia, N America except extreme north, S America, NW Africa.

Species illustrated
Cactus Wren 49
Long-billed Marsh Wren 70

BEHAVIOUR Active, restless birds, usually solitary except for some tropical species which congregate outside the breeding season. Habitat varies but they are typically birds of low, dense vegetation. The tail is characteristically carried erect. Flight is generally weak; song highly developed and elaborate in most species. FEEDING The diet consists mainly of insects. BREEDING Some species are polygamous. The nest is built in a hole in a tree, bank, wall, or among rocks or sometimes as a separate structure in a tree or in grass. Usually both sexes work on the construction. Two to ten eggs are laid, white with brown or lilac speckles, sometimes unmarked. The males of many species build unlined "false nests". CARE OF YOUNG Mainly by the female.

HABITAT	NESTING	FEEDING	FOOD SOURCE	SOCIAL

Mimidae Mockingbird family
30 species

Northern Mockingbird
Mimus polyglottos

CHARACTERISTICS These birds, 8-12in long with short wings and a long tail, superficially resemble thrushes. Their legs are longish, the middle and outer toes adherent at the base. The bill is strong, medium to long and almost straight to decurved. Plumage is mainly drab greys and browns, lighter below, spotted in many species; but iris yellow, orange or red is often present. The sexes are alike or nearly so. HABITAT Varied. DISTRIBUTION Americas from S Canada to SC Argentina, W Indies, Galapagos.

Species illustrated
Sage Thrasher 51
Mockingbird 77

BEHAVIOUR These birds' powers of mimicry are probably more limited than may be generally believed, possibly because their reputation is falsely based on their great repertoire of notes and calls which by coincidence resemble those of other birds. They are arboreal or terrestrial and live either alone or in pairs. Most species make only short flights and some can run rapidly. FEEDING Their diet consists of insects, fruit and seeds. BREEDING The nest takes the form of a bulky open cup and is constructed either in a bush or on the ground. There are 2–5 eggs, buff, blue or green, and speckled, which are incubated by both parents or by the female alone. CARE OF YOUNG The nidicolous young, naked or slightly downy, are cared for by both parents.

HABITAT	NESTING	FEEDING	FOOD SOURCE	SOCIAL

Prunellidae Dunnock family
12 species

Dunnock
Prunella modularis

CHARACTERISTICS These birds, 5-7in long, have a stout body and wings that vary from short and rounded to medium and pointed. The tail is short to medium, the legs and feet strong. They have a medium, slender, pointed bill. Plumage consists of drab browns and greys, lighter below; in many the chin is a contrasting colour. The sexes are alike or almost so. HABITAT Scrub and rocky places, often at high altitudes. DISTRIBUTION N Africa, Europe, Asia. Most species are migratory.

BEHAVIOUR Apparently sharing characteristics in common with thrushes, buntings, flycatchers and Old World warblers, most species are inclined to be solitary and secretive. They walk or hop on the ground with a characteristic flicking of the tail. FEEDING They feed mainly on the ground, taking mostly insects, other vertebrates and berries in summer, and mostly seeds in winter. BREEDING The nest is an open cup of plant materials and feathers, constructed in a bush, on the ground or in a crevice among rocks. Usually there are 3–4 eggs, bluish or bright blue; these are incubated either by the female alone or by both parents in turn. CARE OF YOUNG The nidicolous, downy young are cared for by both parents.

HABITAT	NESTING	FEEDING	FOOD SOURCE	SOCIAL

Muscicapidae Thrush family
1,153 species

Mistle Thrush
Turdus viscivorus

CHARACTERISTICS Small to medium birds, 3½-20in long, their wings vary from short to long, their tail from very short to very long, fan-shaped or forked. The legs are short to long, slender to stout. The bill is small to long, slender or stout, straight or curved. Plumage in most consists of drab browns and greys; some flycatchers are brightly coloured. A few species are crested. The sexes may be alike or unlike. HABITAT Greatly varied. DISTRIBUTION World-wide except extreme latitudes.

Species illustrated
Thrushes, Warblers, Chats, etc. 41, 46, 47, 58, 77, 106, 108, 116, 119, 121, 123, 125, 137, 140, 150, 163, 166, 169, 178, 179, 181, 183, 185, 186, 195, 196, 197, 202, 203, 208

BEHAVIOUR Included here in this very large family are the thrushes (Turdinae), babblers (Timalinae), Old World warblers (Sylviinae), Old World flycatchers (Muscicapinae), rail-babblers (Cinclosomatinae), parrotbills (Paradoxornithinae), gnatcatchers (Polioptilinae), Australian wrens (Malurinae) and thickheads (Pachycephalinae). Only the most general remarks are possible. The birds may be gregarious or solitary, arboreal or terrestrial, their flight strong or weak. FEEDING They eat insects and other invertebrates, including spiders and molluscs, and vegetable matter. BREEDING There are 2–12 eggs, incubated by the female or both in a cup- or dome-shaped nest built in a tree, bush or natural cavity. CARE OF YOUNG Both parents tend the naked or downy, nidicolous young.

HABITAT	NESTING	FEEDING	FOOD SOURCE	SOCIAL

Paridae Titmouse family
65 species

Great Tit
Parus major

CHARACTERISTICS Small, 3-8in long, with a rather sturdy body, they have short to medium rounded wings and a tail that varies from very short to long and graduated. The legs are short, as is the bill which may be stout or slender. Plumage features combinations of black, white, grey, yellow, blue, green, orange, either sharply defined or blended. HABITAT Varied. DISTRIBUTION Africa, Eurasia except extreme north, New Guinea, Polynesia, Australia, N America to Guatemala.

Species illustrated
Chestnut-backed Chickadee 41
Black-crested Titmouse 46
Blue Tit 137
Sultan Tit 165

BEHAVIOUR Active, fairly gregarious and arboreal, the family are generally weak fliers. Although some northern species migrate, others remain throughout the winter, some living off food stored during the autumn behind the bark of trees. FEEDING They are largely insectivorous, and seeds and nuts are also taken. BREEDING The nest is usually built of moss or some soft material and sited in a tree or a ground- or rock-hole; others are pendant or covered, made in a bush or tree. There are 4–14 white or pinkish eggs, immaculate or marked, incubated in most species by the female alone. CARE OF YOUNG The nidicolous young hatch naked or downy and are tended by both parents. BIRD & MAN The sturdy nests of the Penduline Tits are used as purses in parts of Africa.

HABITAT	NESTING	FEEDING	FOOD SOURCE	SOCIAL

Sittidae Nuthatch family
29 species

Nuthatch
Sitta europaea

CHARACTERISTICS Small, 3¾-7½in long, they have long wings and a short to medium tail. The tarsi are short, the toes long. The bill is slender, straight and pointed or slightly hooked and notched. Plumage is a slate grey, blue or black above, streaked or plain, lighter below. Most *Sitta* have an eye stripe, others a broad white or buff band across the spread wing. HABITAT Woodlands, rocky areas. DISTRIBUTION Eurasia, N America, Japan, Malaysia, Philippines, New Guinea, Australia.

Species illustrated
Plain-headed Woodcreeper 171
Orange-winged Sitella 188

BEHAVIOUR Included here are the treerunners, wallcreepers and the Philippine creepers. Most inhabit trees, which they climb obliquely, almost hanging from the upper foot, and are able to descend head-first. Some are gregarious, some solitary. Flight is undulating. FEEDING They eat insects, spiders, nuts and seeds; the latter are pushed into cracks to secure them and then hammered open with the bill. BREEDING Nesting is in a natural cavity in a tree or rock which is lined and plastered. The Australasian species build an open cup of spider-web, hair, cocoons and bark high in a tree, in which 3–4 eggs are incubated by both parents. The Eurasian species produce 4–12 eggs, incubated largely by the female. CARE OF YOUNG In all species both parents care for the nidicolous young.

HABITAT	NESTING	FEEDING	FOOD SOURCE	SOCIAL

Certhiidae Creeper family
6 species

Treecreeper
Certhia familiaris

CHARACTERISTICS Small, about 5in long, with short wings and tail, the latter stiff and pointed, treecreepers have large feet and long curved claws. The bill is long, slender and decurved. Plumage is brownish and streaked above, white below. The sexes are alike. HABITAT Trees and, to a lesser extent, rocky areas. DISTRIBUTION Treecreepers are found dispersed throughout Eurasia, N America and N Africa.

Species illustrated
Treecreeper 107

BEHAVIOUR Creepers have much in common with the nuthatches and were at one time included in the Sittidae. One difference is in the way they use their stiff tail as a prop when climbing, another the fact that they rarely climb downwards. Usually they ascend with short jerky movements, then fly to the base of the next tree to start again. FEEDING Their food is almost entirely insects; seeds are sometimes taken. BREEDING The nest is a cup of twigs, grasses and moss lined with feathers and bark and sited in a natural crevice, either behind ivy or similar, or behind loose bark. The eggs, 5–7, white and marked with red spots and blotches, are incubated by the female alone or assisted by the male. CARE OF YOUNG Both parents tend the downy, nidicolous young.

HABITAT	NESTING	FEEDING	FOOD SOURCE	SOCIAL

Classification

Climacteridae
Australian Treecreeper family
6 species

Brown Treecreeper
Climacteris picumnus

CHARACTERISTICS Small birds, about 6in long, their wings are long, their tail short and rounded. The legs and toes are long, the claws long and curved, especially the hallux. The bill is long, slender and decurved. Plumage is greyish-brown to rufous and black above, lighter below and streaked; the wings bear a whitish to rufous bar, and there is also an eye stripe. **HABITAT** A variety of trees from wet eucalyptus forests to semi-arid country. **DISTRIBUTION** Australia and New Guinea.

BEHAVIOUR Inclined to be sedentary and arboreal, these birds appear to represent an ancient colonization and are possibly related to the honey-eaters (Meliphagidae), though superficially they resemble the Australian warblers, *Acanthizinae*. Similarities between their feeding habits and those of the Northern Hemisphere treecreepers (Certhiidae) may be due to convergence. **FEEDING** The Australian treecreepers are insectivorous, feeding sometimes from the ground but usually from tree trunks, which they ascend spirally. **BREEDING** A nest of grass, down, fur and bark is built in a tree-hollow or fallen log. There are 2–3 eggs, white or flesh-coloured, marked with brown, incubated by the female, sometimes assisted by the male. **CARE OF YOUNG** Both tend the downy, nidicolous young.

HABITAT	NESTING	FEEDING	FOOD SOURCE	SOCIAL
	P_V			

Dicaeidae
Flowerpecker family
51 species

Orange-bellied Flowerpecker
Dicaeum trigonostigma

CHARACTERISTICS These small birds, 3-7½in long, have shortish wings and tail, the latter stumpy. The legs and neck are short, the bill varying from thin and serrate to stout and unserrate. Plumage in many males is dark and glossy above, lighter below and with bright red or yellow on breast, head or rump; some are streaked below. Other males and all females are dull-coloured. **HABITAT** Forests. **DISTRIBUTION** Tropical Asia through Indonesia to New Guinea and Australia.

Species illustrated
Black-headed Pardalote 188

BEHAVIOUR Usually found in pairs or loose groups, they are primarily arboreal. **FEEDING** They are energetic and noisy when searching for food, and typically feed on berries, nectar, insects and spiders. In some species a close association has developed with their main food, the mistletoe, and it is they who are responsible for much of its spread. Berries may be swallowed whole or the seed separated from the flesh. In those species that feed on nectar the tongue divides into two semi-tubular tips. **BREEDING** The nest consists of a cup or hanging pouch built in a tree or bush or (in *Pardalotus*) in a tree- or ground-hole. There are 1–4 eggs, white, some spotted, incubated by the female or both. **CARE OF YOUNG** Both parents care for the nidicolous young.

HABITAT	NESTING	FEEDING	FOOD SOURCE	SOCIAL
		$\begin{matrix}V\\P\end{matrix}$		

Nectariniidae
Sunbird family
104 species

Malachite Sunbird
Nectarinia famosa

CHARACTERISTICS Small to Medium, 3¾-10in long, they have short rounded wings and a tail that varies from short and square to long and pointed. The legs and feet are short and strong. The bill is long, curved and finely serrate. Plumage in many features a great variety of bright colours. **HABITAT** Tropical forests, scrub, gardens. **DISTRIBUTION** Africa south of Sahara, Madagascar, Middle East, India, SE Asia to C China, E Indies, New Guinea, NE Australia.

Species illustrated
Eastern Double-collared Sunbird 143

BEHAVIOUR Usually seen in small flocks in a variety of habitats, sometimes at high altitudes, they are nomadic and very active, mainly arboreal and strong fliers. **FEEDING** They roam widely in search of their foods – nectar, fruits, insects and spiders. They mostly feed from a perch, occasionally in flight. **BREEDING** The nest consists typically of a pouch with a side entrance, porched in some instances; this is suspended from a twig, a clump of grass or projecting roots or is sewn on to the underside of a large leaf. There are 2–3 eggs, speckled or blotched, which are incubated by the female for about 15 days; on rare occasions she is assisted by the male. **CARE OF YOUNG** The nidicolous young, downy above, are tended by the female or by both parents.

HABITAT	NESTING	FEEDING	FOOD SOURCE	SOCIAL
		$\begin{matrix}V\\P\end{matrix}$		

Zosteropidae
White-eye family
80 species

Indian White-eye
Zosterops palpebrosa

CHARACTERISTICS These small birds, 4-5½in long, have short pointed wings with only nine primaries. The tail is medium and square, the legs rather short. The neck is short, the bill slender, straight or decurved. The tongue is bifid and protractile. Plumage is greenish or yellowish, often with a ring of white feathers around each eye. The sexes are alike. **HABITAT** White-eyes favour wooded areas of all kinds. **DISTRIBUTION** They are widely dispersed from Africa to Asia and Australasia.

BEHAVIOUR Most species are placed in the genus *Zosterops*, but there is some confusion caused by a great deal of convergence and by the multiple invasions of islands by neighbouring species. They are active, restless birds, arboreal and often seen in company with flocks of other species. Most have a rather melodious song in addition to a range of twittering sounds. **FEEDING** They eat insects, fruit and nectar – piercing the fruit with the bill and extracting the juice with the tongue. **BREEDING** The nests of all species are very similar, consisting of a semi-pendant cup of plant material in a forked twig. There are 2–4 white, pale blue or green eggs, incubated by both parents for about 10 days (one of the shortest periods for birds). **CARE OF YOUNG** Both tend the nidicolous young.

HABITAT	NESTING	FEEDING	FOOD SOURCE	SOCIAL
		$\begin{matrix}V\\P\end{matrix}$		

Meliphagidae
Honey-eater family
160 species

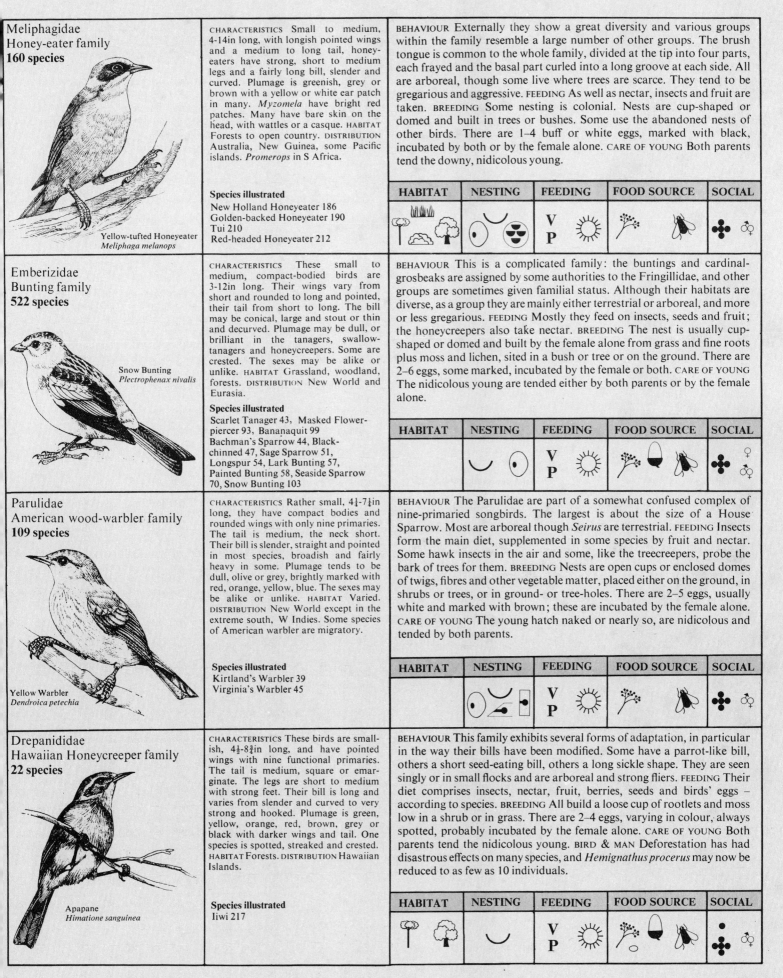

Yellow-tufted Honeyeater
Meliphaga melanops

CHARACTERISTICS Small to medium, 4-14in long, with longish pointed wings and a medium to long tail, honey-eaters have strong, short to medium legs and a fairly long bill, slender and curved. Plumage is greenish, grey or brown with a yellow or white ear patch in many. *Myzomela* have bright red patches. Many have bare skin on the head, with wattles or a casque. HABITAT Forests to open country. DISTRIBUTION Australia, New Guinea, some Pacific islands. *Promerops* in S Africa.

Species illustrated
New Holland Honeyeater 186
Golden-backed Honeyeater 190
Tui 210
Red-headed Honeyeater 212

BEHAVIOUR Externally they show a great diversity and various groups within the family resemble a large number of other groups. The brush tongue is common to the whole family, divided at the tip into four parts, each frayed and the basal part curled into a long groove at each side. All are arboreal, though some live where trees are scarce. They tend to be gregarious and aggressive. FEEDING As well as nectar, insects and fruit are taken. BREEDING Some nesting is colonial. Nests are cup-shaped or domed and built in trees or bushes. Some use the abandoned nests of other birds. There are 1–4 buff or white eggs, marked with black, incubated by both or by the female alone. CARE OF YOUNG Both parents tend the downy, nidicolous young.

HABITAT	NESTING	FEEDING	FOOD SOURCE	SOCIAL

Emberizidae
Bunting family
522 species

Snow Bunting
Plectrophenax nivalis

CHARACTERISTICS These small to medium, compact-bodied birds are 3-12in long. Their wings vary from short and rounded to long and pointed, their tail from short to long. The bill may be conical, large and stout or thin and decurved. Plumage may be dull, or brilliant in the tanagers, swallow-tanagers and honeycreepers. Some are crested. The sexes may be alike or unlike. HABITAT Grassland, woodland, forests. DISTRIBUTION New World and Eurasia.

Species illustrated
Scarlet Tanager 43, Masked Flower-piercer 93, Bananaquit 99
Bachman's Sparrow 44, Black-chinned 47, Sage Sparrow 51, Longspur 54, Lark Bunting 57, Painted Bunting 58, Seaside Sparrow 70, Snow Bunting 103

BEHAVIOUR This is a complicated family: the buntings and cardinal-grosbeaks are assigned by some authorities to the Fringillidae, and other groups are sometimes given familial status. Although their habitats are diverse, as a group they are mainly either terrestrial or arboreal, and more or less gregarious. FEEDING Mostly they feed on insects, seeds and fruit; the honeycreepers also take nectar. BREEDING The nest is usually cup-shaped or domed and built by the female alone from grass and fine roots plus moss and lichen, sited in a bush or tree or on the ground. There are 2–6 eggs, some marked, incubated by the female or both. CARE OF YOUNG The nidicolous young are tended either by both parents or by the female alone.

HABITAT	NESTING	FEEDING	FOOD SOURCE	SOCIAL

Parulidae
American wood-warbler family
109 species

Yellow Warbler
Dendroica petechia

CHARACTERISTICS Rather small, 4¼-7¼in long, they have compact bodies and rounded wings with only nine primaries. The tail is medium, the neck short. Their bill is slender, straight and pointed in most species, broadish and fairly heavy in some. Plumage tends to be dull, olive or grey, brightly marked with red, orange, yellow, blue. The sexes may be alike or unlike. HABITAT Varied. DISTRIBUTION New World except in the extreme south, W Indies. Some species of American warbler are migratory.

Species illustrated
Kirtland's Warbler 39
Virginia's Warbler 45

BEHAVIOUR The Parulidae are part of a somewhat confused complex of nine-primaried songbirds. The largest is about the size of a House Sparrow. Most are arboreal though *Seirus* are terrestrial. FEEDING Insects form the main diet, supplemented in some species by fruit and nectar. Some hawk insects in the air and some, like the treecreepers, probe the bark of trees for them. BREEDING Nests are open cups or enclosed domes of twigs, fibres and other vegetable matter, placed either on the ground, in shrubs or trees, or in ground- or tree-holes. There are 2–5 eggs, usually white and marked with brown; these are incubated by the female alone. CARE OF YOUNG The young hatch naked or nearly so, are nidicolous and tended by both parents.

HABITAT	NESTING	FEEDING	FOOD SOURCE	SOCIAL

Drepanididae
Hawaiian Honeycreeper family
22 species

Apapane
Himatione sanguinea

CHARACTERISTICS These birds are small-ish, 4¼-8¾in long, and have pointed wings with nine functional primaries. The tail is medium, square or emarginate. The legs are short to medium with strong feet. Their bill is long and varies from slender and curved to very strong and hooked. Plumage is green, yellow, orange, red, brown, grey or black with darker wings and tail. One species is spotted, streaked and crested. HABITAT Forests. DISTRIBUTION Hawaiian Islands.

Species illustrated
Iiwi 217

BEHAVIOUR This family exhibits several forms of adaptation, in particular in the way their bills have been modified. Some have a parrot-like bill, others a short seed-eating bill, others a long sickle shape. They are seen singly or in small flocks and are arboreal and strong fliers. FEEDING Their diet comprises insects, nectar, fruit, berries, seeds and birds' eggs – according to species. BREEDING All build a loose cup of rootlets and moss low in a shrub or in grass. There are 2–4 eggs, varying in colour, always spotted, probably incubated by the female alone. CARE OF YOUNG Both parents tend the nidicolous young. BIRD & MAN Deforestation has had disastrous effects on many species, and *Hemignathus procerus* may now be reduced to as few as 10 individuals.

HABITAT	NESTING	FEEDING	FOOD SOURCE	SOCIAL

Classification

Vireonidae
Vireo family
42 species

Red-eyed Vireo
Vireo olivaceous

CHARACTERISTICS Small, 4-7½in long, they have short to long wings, the 10th primary short to vestigial, and a medium tail. The legs are short, as is the neck. The bill is medium to fairly long and thick and slightly to conspicuously hooked. Plumage is usually greenish or greyish above, whitish or yellowish below. The sexes are alike or almost so. HABITAT Forests or brush. DISTRIBUTION Americas except extreme north and south beyond 30°S, W Indies. The northern species are migratory.

Species illustrated
Yellow-throated Vireo 43

BEHAVIOUR Inclined to be solitary, they live in trees and shrubs, where they have been described as moving about "rather deliberately", sometimes hanging upside-down to look under leaves. Their calls and songs are loud and repetitive. FEEDING They feed mostly in the trees on insects and fruit; ground feeding is rare. BREEDING A cup-shaped nest is built in a horizontal fork of a bush or tree. Contrary to the usual pattern among birds, vireos are reported as being fairly tame on the nest. The female alone, or both parents, incubate 2–5 white or pinkish slightly speckled eggs for about 12–16 days. CARE OF YOUNG At hatching the young are naked or slightly downy above; they are cared for in the nest by both parents.

HABITAT	NESTING	FEEDING	FOOD SOURCE	SOCIAL

Icteridae
Troupial family
87 species

Wagler's Oropendola
Zarhynchus wagleri

CHARACTERISTICS Varying in size from 6¾-21½in long, their wings are long and pointed in most, short in some, with nine primaries. The tail is short to long, broad in many. The legs and feet are very strong. The bill is conical and varies from short and heavy to longish and slender. Plumage is black alone or with brightly coloured areas. Some have a neck ruff, some are crested. The sexes are mostly unlike. HABITAT Tropical forests to open wooded areas. DISTRIBUTION Americas, W Indies.

Species illustrated
Meadowlark 55, Cowbird 56, Bobolink 59, Yellow-headed Blackbird 62, Red-winged Blackbird 62, Montezuma Oropendola 97

BEHAVIOUR This is a varied family. They may be solitary or gregarious, arboreal or terrestrial, and some species walk when on the ground. FEEDING Their food is insects, crustaceans, amphibians, fish, small mammals and birds, fruit, seeds and nectar. BREEDING Nesting may be isolated or colonial. Some species are polygamous. Nests include a pensile or semi-pensile structure, a cup built in trees or on the ground or in reeds above water. Some nest in holes or rock crevices or are parasitic (the Cowbirds). There are 2–7 eggs, variously coloured, usually with strong markings, incubated by the female. CARE OF YOUNG Both parents tend the downy or naked, nidicolous young.

HABITAT	NESTING	FEEDING	FOOD SOURCE	SOCIAL

Fringillidae
Finch family
122 species

Chaffinch
Fringilla coelebs

CHARACTERISTICS Small birds, 4¼-8½in long, their wings vary from short and rounded to long and pointed; all except *Urocychramus* have nine functional primaries. The tail is 12-feathered and short to long, the legs medium. The bill ranges from slender and pointed to massive and pyramidal. Plumage features combinations of yellow, blue, green, black, white, brown, red, gold. HABITAT Varied, from wooded to arid regions. DISTRIBUTION World-wide except Australasia.

Species illustrated
White-winged Crossbill 38, Cassin's Finch 41, Rosy Finch 53, Variable Seedeater 89, Brambling 105, Hawfinch 108

BEHAVIOUR Only the Fringillinae (chaffinches) and the Carduelinae (goldfinches, crossbills, etc.) are included here. Though primarily arboreal, some finches are terrestrial. Most are gregarious and social and have a well-developed flight song. FEEDING They eat mainly seeds, buds and to a lesser extent insects. BREEDING Typically the nest is a lined cup built by the female from twigs, grass, roots, plus possibly moss and lichens. There are 3–7 eggs, bluish, green or pale brown, more or less spotted or streaked with brown or red; these are incubated by the female alone. CARE OF YOUNG The young are nidicolous and are cared for by both parents.

HABITAT	NESTING	FEEDING	FOOD SOURCE	SOCIAL

Estrildidae
Waxbill family
108 species

Zebra Finch
Poephila guttata

CHARACTERISTICS Small, about 4in long, their wings are short, the outer primary reduced. The tail is short to long, the legs and toes short to fairly long. A shortish bill varies from medium to massive and from straight to curved or hooked. Plumage is usually a variety of bright colours, though browns, greys and black predominate in some. The sexes may be alike or unlike. HABITAT Tropical forest to semi-desert. DISTRIBUTION Africa, Middle East to India, Ceylon, SE Asia and Australasia.

BEHAVIOUR This is a family of largely gregarious birds. FEEDING Most are seed-eaters, some also take insects, nectar and buds. BREEDING Display in the male includes leaping, swaying and grass-presentation. Both sexes build the nest, an untidy structure in which 2–6 white or coloured eggs are incubated by both parents for about 21 days. CARE OF YOUNG The young usually have conspicuous white or black and white swellings or nodules around the gape, and a conspicuously spotted palate. Both parents care for the young in the nest. Sexual maturity may be reached in a few months. BIRD & MAN The family includes a number of well-known cagebirds such as the Zebra Finch, Cordon Bleu, Java Sparrow and the Fire Finch.

HABITAT	NESTING	FEEDING	FOOD SOURCE	SOCIAL

Ploceidae
Weaverbird family
156 species

House Sparrow
Passer domesticus

CHARACTERISTICS Small to largish, 3-25½in long, their wings vary from short and rounded to long and pointed; there are ten primaries, the outer rudimentary. The tail is very short to very long. The legs are short in most. The bill ranges from short and thick to thin and pointed. Plumage includes browns and greys, yellow, red, black, blue, green, often in bold patterns, many conspicuously barred or spotted. The sexes are alike or unlike. **HABITAT** Woods, scrub, arid bush. **DISTRIBUTION** Eurasia, Africa.

Species illustrated
Snow Finch 123
Long-tailed Whydah 147
Red-billed Quelea 149
Striated Weaver 174

BEHAVIOUR Arboreal or terrestrial, many species are gregarious. **FEEDING** Their diet includes seeds and insects. **BREEDING** A number of species nest colonially, some are monogamous and others are polygamous. Nests are diverse and found in a variety of situations, ranging from a mere lined pad of grass to bulky domed nests lined with feathers and elaborate suspended nests intricately woven from vegetable fibres, some of which have entrance tunnels. One species is parasitic on the grass warblers *Cisticola* and *Prinia*. There are 2–8 eggs, white, green or blue, some speckled, which are incubated by the female or by both. **CARE OF YOUNG** The nidicolous young are usually tended by both parents.

HABITAT	NESTING	FEEDING	FOOD SOURCE	SOCIAL
		V_P		

Sturnidae
Starling family
103 species

Starling
Sturnus vulgaris

CHARACTERISTICS Medium to largish, 7-17in long, their wings range from short and rounded to long and pointed. The tail is short to long, the legs and feet strong. The bill is strong, straight and slender in most, heavy and hooked in some. Plumage is usually dark with a pronounced iridescence in many. Some have lappets, wattles or bristles. **HABITAT** Varied. **DISTRIBUTION** Africa, Eurasia except extreme north, Malaysia, New Guinea, NE Australia, Pacific islands. Some are migratory.

Species illustrated
Rosy Pastor (Starling) 111
Red-billed Oxpecker 147

BEHAVIOUR Most starlings are gregarious. All, whether arboreal or terrestrial, fly strongly, and many species mass in great aerial formations. **FEEDING** Their food includes insects, fruit, grain, offal, eggs, crustaceans and lizards. **BREEDING** Most nest in tree-hollows, some build an enclosed structure, a few dig a ground-burrow and many nest in eaves and on the ledges of buildings. The white or blue eggs (usually 3–4) are incubated by the female or both parents. **CARE OF YOUNG** Both care for the downy, nidicolous young. **BIRD & MAN** Many starlings live in close proximity to man, and are either valued for their work in disposing of insect pests or else detested for the damage they cause to crops.

HABITAT	NESTING	FEEDING	FOOD SOURCE	SOCIAL
		O		

Oriolidae
Oriole family
28 species

Golden Oriole
Oriolus oriolus

CHARACTERISTICS Orioles are medium-sized, robust birds, 7-12in long, with long wings and a medium to long, 12-feathered tail. Their legs are short and strong. They have a strong pointed bill, slightly hooked. Plumage is yellow, green, brown, red, black, with black or dark wings and tail and much black on the head. The sexes are unlike in most. **HABITAT** Forests, parkland. **DISTRIBUTION** Africa, Eurasia except in the north, E Indies, Philippines, N and E Australia. Some species are migratory.

Species illustrated
Yellow Figbird 182

BEHAVIOUR All species are arboreal and most are tropical. They are usually solitary and wary and have a rapid, undulating flight. Many of the island species have evolved characteristics typical of isolated groups, e.g. loss of colour in *O.crassirostris* and *O.bouroensis*, and greatly shortened wings in the former. **FEEDING** Their diet is insects and fruit; the European Golden Oriole, which lives in the Mediterranean area, takes figs in particular. **BREEDING** Most nest in a semi-pendant woven cup, often of lichen, sited high in a tree. *Sphecotheres* build a much more flimsy saucer-shaped nest. There are 2–5 white or pinkish eggs (greenish in *Sphecotheres*), incubated by both parents, mainly the female. **CARE OF YOUNG** Both care for the downy, nidicolous young.

HABITAT	NESTING	FEEDING	FOOD SOURCE	SOCIAL
		P_V		

Dicruridae
Drongo family
20 species

Racket-tailed Drongo
Dicrurus paradiseus

CHARACTERISTICS Medium to largish, 7-25in long, they have long wings and a ten- or 12-feathered tail that is medium and square to very long and either forked, curled or racket-tipped. The legs and feet are short and stout. The bill is stout, slightly hooked and notched. Plumage is black and iridescent or grey. The sexes are alike, the male larger. **HABITAT** Forests, clearings, gardens. **DISTRIBUTION** Africa south of Sahara, Madagascar, India, SE Asia, Philippines, New Guinea, Australia, Solomons.

Species illustrated
Racket-tailed Drongo 166

BEHAVIOUR Solitary, arboreal and good fliers, drongos are highly aggressive towards large birds such as crows and hawks; a consequence of this appears to be that some smaller birds build their nests close to those of drongos, for protection. They have a variety of calls and mimic other birds. **FEEDING** They eat insects, small frogs and lizards, also nectar. **BREEDING** Nests are saucer- or cup-shaped, made of twigs, roots, stems, bound with cobweb and set in a horizontal fork near the outside of a tree at least 15 feet from the ground. There are 2–4 white or coloured eggs, incubated by the female alone, who is sometimes assisted by the male. **CARE OF YOUNG** Both parents care for the downy, nidicolous young.

HABITAT	NESTING	FEEDING	FOOD SOURCE	SOCIAL
		$\begin{array}{c}V\\P\end{array}$		

Classification

Callaeidae Wattlebird family
3 species

Kokako
Callaeas cinerea

CHARACTERISTICS Medium, stout-bodied, 10–21in long, with medium wings (the first primary very long), they have a long square tail, arched in profile. The legs and feet are large and strong. The bill is stout to fairly slender and decurved. Fleshy orange or blue wattles hang from the corners of the mouth. Plumage is blue-grey or black with a chestnut saddle. The sexes are alike in plumage, unlike in size and shape of wattle. HABITAT Forests. DISTRIBUTION New Zealand.

Species illustrated
Kokako 210

BEHAVIOUR Like so many New Zealand birds, the wattlebirds are virtually flightless. Usually found in pairs or small groups, they travel in long hops across the ground or over tree branches in search of food. They have a variety of calls including whistling, fluting, mewing and some harsh notes. FEEDING They eat insects, fruit, leaves and nectar. Food is sometimes held in the claw, as parrots do. BREEDING The nest is of sticks lined with feathers and grass, placed in a tree-hole or fork. There are 2–3 eggs, grey or brown, spotted and blotched, which are incubated by both parents for 20–21 days. CARE OF YOUNG Both parents care for the downy, nidicolous young, the male sometimes passing the food to the female who gives it to the chicks.

HABITAT	NESTING	FEEDING	FOOD SOURCE	SOCIAL

Grallinidae Mudnest-builder family
4 species

Magpie Lark
Grallina cyanoleuca

CHARACTERISTICS Medium and solidly built, 7½–19½in long, their wings vary from short and rounded to long and pointed. The tail is short to very long, the legs medium to fairly long and strong. The bill ranges from short and stout to long and curved. Plumage is black and white or dark blue and grey. HABITAT They are chiefly found near water in forests, marshes, parkland. DISTRIBUTION Australia and NW New Guinea. Some mud-nest builders are migratory.

Species illustrated
Magpie Lark 202

BEHAVIOUR The various species are strikingly different and have little in common except their bowl-shaped mud nests, and until recently they were classified apart. Gregarious at times, they are fairly weak fliers; in trees they jump from branch to branch. FEEDING Mostly they feed on the ground, taking insects (including water insects), seeds, fruit and molluscs. BREEDING Nesting is communal: the mud bowl is lined with grass and feathers and placed high on a branch. There are 3–8 white or reddish eggs, incubated by both parents. CARE OF YOUNG Both parents also tend the downy, nidicolous young.

HABITAT	NESTING	FEEDING	FOOD SOURCE	SOCIAL

Artamidae Wood-swallow family
10 species

White-browed Wood-swallow
Artamus superciliosus

CHARACTERISTICS Small and plump-bodied, 5¾–8in long, they have long pointed wings and a medium tail. The legs are very short and strong; the feet are also strong. The bill is stout, slightly curved, longish, pointed, and has a wide gape. Plumage consists of browns, greys and black, with white markings in some. The sexes are alike or almost so. HABITAT Near water in open country or clearings. DISTRIBUTION Australia east to Fiji, India, SE Asia, SE China, E Indies, Philippines.

Species illustrated
White-browed Wood-swallow 195

BEHAVIOUR Graceful fliers, they are the only passerines, apart from the raven, that can glide for long periods. They are highly gregarious, and often rest clustered together in numbers. They are aggressive and will fearlessly attack larger birds. FEEDING They are primarily insectivorous, capturing insects rather as swallows do; they also forage from a perch like flycatchers, and sometimes feed on the ground, taking seeds as well as insects. BREEDING Nesting is at times colonial. A shallow cup of grass, fibres, feathers, etc., is built in a tree, occasionally in a bush. One species nests in a tree cavity. There are 2–4 whitish or greenish speckled eggs which are incubated by both parents. CARE OF YOUNG Both also tend the downy, nidicolous young.

HABITAT	NESTING	FEEDING	FOOD SOURCE	SOCIAL

Cracticidae Bellmagpie family
10 species

Grey Butcherbird
Cracticus torquatus

CHARACTERISTICS Largish and solidly built, 10–15in long, their wings vary from rather short to long and pointed. The tail is fairly large. Legs are medium to long and strong. The bill, very large and stout, hooked in most species, is set in a large head. Plumage is pied black and white, grey and white, or plain black. Some show brown phases. The sexes may be alike or unlike. HABITAT Open woodland, scrub, gardens. DISTRIBUTION Australia, Tasmania, New Guinea and neighbouring islands.

Species illustrated
Pied Currawong 203

BEHAVIOUR These birds are strongly territorial and aggressive, usually gregarious and arboreal though sometimes feeding on the ground. They have clear, loud, mellow calls and are reputed to be the best of the Australian songsters. FEEDING They eat insects, small animals including birds, eggs and fruit. Butcherbirds are so named for their habit of impaling food on thorns, either to store or to tear it apart. BREEDING The nest is a large open cup of twigs lined with grass and other material, high in a tree. There are 3–5 eggs, varying in colour but usually spotted. The female incubates, assisted rarely by the male. CARE OF YOUNG Both parents tend the downy, nidicolous young, helped perhaps by the previous brood, who remain with their parents for more than a year.

HABITAT	NESTING	FEEDING	FOOD SOURCE	SOCIAL

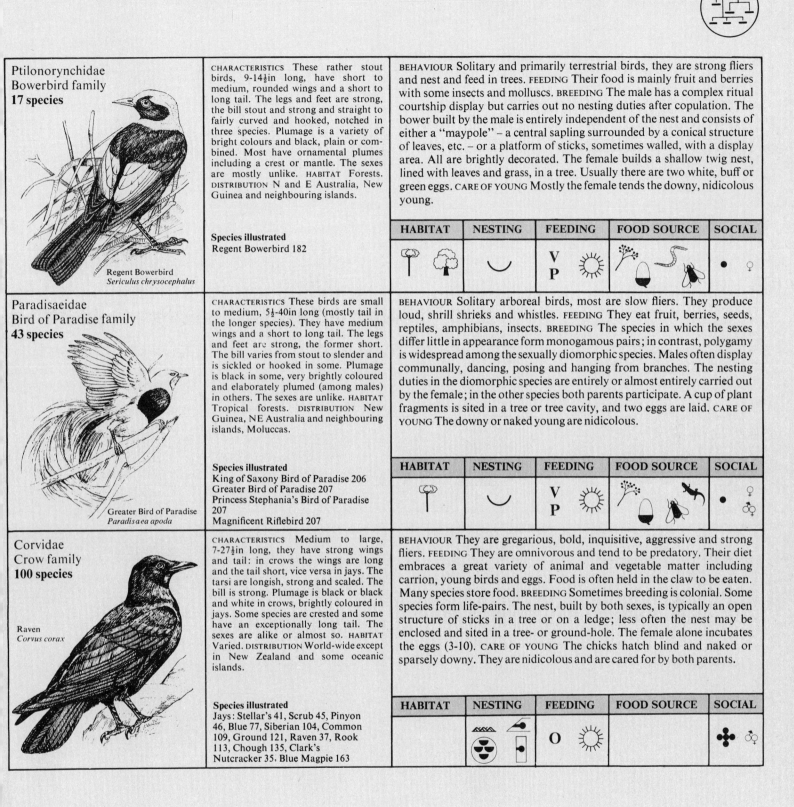

Ptilonorynchidae
Bowerbird family
17 species

Regent Bowerbird
Sericulus chrysocephalus

CHARACTERISTICS These rather stout birds, 9-14½in long, have short to medium, rounded wings and a short to long tail. The legs and feet are strong, the bill stout and strong and straight to fairly curved and hooked, notched in three species. Plumage is a variety of bright colours and black, plain or combined. Most have ornamental plumes including a crest or mantle. The sexes are mostly unlike. HABITAT Forests. DISTRIBUTION N and E Australia, New Guinea and neighbouring islands.

Species illustrated
Regent Bowerbird 182

BEHAVIOUR Solitary and primarily terrestrial birds, they are strong fliers and nest and feed in trees. FEEDING Their food is mainly fruit and berries with some insects and molluscs. BREEDING The male has a complex ritual courtship display but carries out no nesting duties after copulation. The bower built by the male is entirely independent of the nest and consists of either a "maypole" – a central sapling surrounded by a conical structure of leaves, etc. – or a platform of sticks, sometimes walled, with a display area. All are brightly decorated. The female builds a shallow twig nest, lined with leaves and grass, in a tree. Usually there are two white, buff or green eggs. CARE OF YOUNG Mostly the female tends the downy, nidicolous young.

HABITAT	NESTING	FEEDING	FOOD SOURCE	SOCIAL

Paradisaeidae
Bird of Paradise family
43 species

Greater Bird of Paradise
Paradisaea apoda

CHARACTERISTICS These birds are small to medium, 5½-40in long (mostly tail in the longer species). They have medium wings and a short to long tail. The legs and feet are strong, the former short. The bill varies from stout to slender and is sickled or hooked in some. Plumage is black in some, very brightly coloured and elaborately plumed (among males) in others. The sexes are unlike. HABITAT Tropical forests. DISTRIBUTION New Guinea, NE Australia and neighbouring islands, Moluccas.

Species illustrated
King of Saxony Bird of Paradise 206
Greater Bird of Paradise 207
Princess Stephania's Bird of Paradise 207
Magnificent Riflebird 207

BEHAVIOUR Solitary arboreal birds, most are slow fliers. They produce loud, shrill shrieks and whistles. FEEDING They eat fruit, berries, seeds, reptiles, amphibians, insects. BREEDING The species in which the sexes differ little in appearance form monogamous pairs; in contrast, polygamy is widespread among the sexually diomorphic species. Males often display communally, dancing, posing and hanging from branches. The nesting duties in the diomorphic species are entirely or almost entirely carried out by the female; in the other species both parents participate. A cup of plant fragments is sited in a tree or tree cavity, and two eggs are laid. CARE OF YOUNG The downy or naked young are nidicolous.

HABITAT	NESTING	FEEDING	FOOD SOURCE	SOCIAL

Corvidae
Crow family
100 species

Raven
Corvus corax

CHARACTERISTICS Medium to large, 7-27½in long, they have strong wings and tail: in crows the wings are long and the tail short, vice versa in jays. The tarsi are longish, strong and scaled. The bill is strong. Plumage is black or black and white in crows, brightly coloured in jays. Some species are crested and some have an exceptionally long tail. The sexes are alike or almost so. HABITAT Varied. DISTRIBUTION World-wide except in New Zealand and some oceanic islands.

Species illustrated
Jays: Stellar's 41, Scrub 45, Pinyon 46, Blue 77, Siberian 104, Common 109, Ground 121, Raven 37, Rook 113, Chough 135, Clark's Nutcracker 35, Blue Magpie 163

BEHAVIOUR They are gregarious, bold, inquisitive, aggressive and strong fliers. FEEDING They are omnivorous and tend to be predatory. Their diet embraces a great variety of animal and vegetable matter including carrion, young birds and eggs. Food is often held in the claw to be eaten. Many species store food. BREEDING Sometimes breeding is colonial. Some species form life-pairs. The nest, built by both sexes, is typically an open structure of sticks in a tree or on a ledge; less often the nest may be enclosed and sited in a tree- or ground-hole. The female alone incubates the eggs (3-10). CARE OF YOUNG The chicks hatch blind and naked or sparsely downy. They are nidicolous and are cared for by both parents.

HABITAT	NESTING	FEEDING	FOOD SOURCE	SOCIAL

Scientific and Common Names

Scientific name	Britain	North America	Australia
Where a bird species occurs over a wide geographical range it may be known by a variety of common names. The table below illustrates some of the more common variations that exist in three major English-speaking continents. Many species also bear a large number of very localized common names.			
Gavia arctica	Black-throated Diver	Arctic or Pacific Loon	
Podiceps auritus	Slavonian Grebe	Horned Grebe	
Puffinus tenuirostris		Slender-billed Shearwater	Short-tailed Shearwater
Phalacrocorax carbo	Cormorant	European Cormorant	Black Cormorant
Nycticorax nycticorax	Night Heron	Black-crowned Night Heron	Black-crowned Night Heron
Branta bernicla	Brent Goose	Brant or American Brant	
Mergus merganser	Goosander	American Merganser	
Buteo lagopus	Rough-legged Buzzard	Rough-legged Hawk	
Haliaetus albicilla	White-tailed Eagle	Grey Sea Eagle	
Circus cyaneus	Hen Harrier	Marsh Hawk	
Falco columbarius	Merlin	Pigeon Hawk	
Lagopus mutus	Ptarmigan	Rock Ptarmigan	
Perdix perdix	Partridge	Hungarian Partridge	Grey Partridge
Charadrius alexandrinus	Kentish Plover	Snowy Plover	Red-capped Dotterel
Pluvialis dominica	Lesser Golden Plover	American Golden Plover	Eastern Golden Plover
Pluvialis squatarola	Grey Plover	Black-bellied Plover	Grey Plover
Arenaria interpres	Turnstone	Ruddy Turnstone	Ruddy Turnstone
Calidris alpina	Dunlin	Red-backed Sandpiper	Dunlin
Phalaropus lobatus	Red-necked Phalarope	Northern Phalarope	Red-necked Phalarope
Stercorarius parasiticus	Arctic Skua	Parasitic Jaeger	Arctic Skua
Larus canus	Common Gull	Short-billed or Mew Gull	
Sterna sandvicensis	Sandwich Tern	Cabot's Tern	
Sterna albifrons	Little Tern	Least Tern	Little Tern
Rissa tridactyla	Kittiwake	Black-legged Kittiwake	
Plautus alle	Little Auk	Dovekie	
Alca torda	Razorbill	Razor-billed Auk	
Uria aalge	Guillemot	Common Murre	
Uria lomvia	Brunnich's Guillemot	Thick-billed Murre	
Eremophila alpestris	Shore Lark	Horned Lark	
Hirundo rustica	Swallow	Barn Swallow	Barn Swallow
Lanius excubitor	Great Grey Shrike	Northern Shrike	
Troglodytes troglodytes	Wren	Winter Wren	
Certhia familiaris	Tree Creeper	Brown Creeper	
Calcarius lapponicus	Lapland Bunting	Lapland Longspur	
Loxia curvirostra	Crossbill	Red Crossbill	
Loxia leucoptera	Two-barred Crossbill	White-winged Crossbill	

Although less common than variations in the naming of individual birds, the common names of whole families may vary from one area to another. Several such differences occur between the nomenclature of Britain and North America.

Paridae	Tits or Titmice	Titmice or Chickadees	
Gaviidae	Divers	Loons	
Stercorariidae	Skuas	Jaegers	

Conversely, settlers in a new area often gave the same common name to a bird or bird family bearing a superficial resemblance to familiar birds of the "home" country – though in many cases the birds were later found to be unrelated.

Common name			
Sparrows	Ploceidae	Emberizidae	
Flycatchers	Muscicapidae	Tyrannidae	
Warblers	Muscicapidae	Parulidae	
Blackbirds	Muscicapidae	Icteridae	
Treecreepers	Certhiidae	Certhiidae	Climacteridae
Robin	Erithacus rubecula	Turdus migratorius	Petroica spp.
Sparrowhawk	Accipiter nisus	Falco sparverius	
Dipper	Cinclus cinclus	Cinclus mexicanus	
Catbird		Dumetella carolinensis and Pipilo fuscus	Ailuroedus spp.
Spotted Crake	Porzana porzana		Porzana fluminea
Great White Heron	Egretta alba	Ardea herodias occidentalis	

Glossary

Apterium: pl Apteria; an area of skin from which no feathers grow, except down feathers (cf. pteryla).

Arboreal: of life-style; inhabiting trees, often the canopy.

Carnivorous: Meat-eating.

Caruncle: An unfeathered flap or appendage of fleshy texture, often brightly coloured and possibly significant in display or species recognition.

Casque: An enlargement on the upper surface of the bill in front of the head (hornbills) or on top of the head as in cassowaries.

Cryptic: of coloration; providing concealment or disguise either by colour or pattern.

Cursorial: adapted to running but not necessarily flightless, e.g. Roadrunner.

Crepuscular: of twilight; those birds which are most active during the hours of dawn and dusk.

Decurved: Curved downwards.

Diurnal: Active during the day.

Gular pouch: a "throat sac" often very distensible, for capturing prey (Pelican), brightly coloured for display (Frigate-bird), or for sound production (Prairie Chicken).

Hallux: The first toe, usually "opposed" (pointing backwards). In birds it is often reduced or absent.

Herbivorous: Plant-eating.

Insectivorous: Insect-eating.

Lammellate: (adj. of lamella, a plate or layer); in thin plates or layers.

Lappet: a wattle, particularly at the corners of the mouth ("Rictal lappet").

Lore: (pl. lores); the area between the base of the upper mandible and the eye.

Mandible: without qualification – the lower part of the jaw. Often used for both parts of the jaw qualified by "upper" or "lower".

Maxilla: the upper jaw or upper mandible.

Monophyletic: A group of species derived from a common evolutionary ancestry.

Nidicolous: Young birds which remain in the nest after hatching – often blind and naked but not necessarily so. The chicks are dependent on the parents for food.

Nidifugous: Young birds which leave the nest immediately, or soon, after hatching. They are down covered, have strong legs, their eyes are fully open and they are often independent of parents.

Olfactory: Pertaining to the sense of smell.

Omnivorous: Eating both flesh and plant foods.

Pelagic: of birds; those which spend the greater part of their lives at sea out of sight of the land.

Piscivorous: Fish-eating.

Plumbeous: lead coloured.

Precocial: of chicks (cf. nidifugous); capable of locomotion immediately, or soon, after hatching. Semi-precocial young have eyes open, are down covered, but are not immediately able to walk.

Ratite: A bird with a keel-less sternum. A feature characteristic of flightless, running birds, formerly grouped together as "Ratitae", e.g. Ostrich, Cassowary, Emu, Kiwi, Rhea, Moa, Elephant-bird.

Syndactyl: having toes three (III) and four (IV) coalescent (fused) for part of their length.

Taxonomy: The science of classification.

Vestigial: (adj. of vestige); a physical feature that, during the course of evolution, has become greatly reduced or even functionless, e.g. Kiwi wing.

Wattle: a caruncle (q.v.) or fleshy appendage, chiefly of the face and neck, often with a sexual significance (display or threat).

Zygodactyl: having two toes directed forward and two back.

Index

Index

Index

Index

Index

Index

Acknowledgements

GENERAL ACKNOWLEDGEMENTS

A great many individuals and institutions have given invaluable help and advice during the preparation of *The World Atlas of Birds*. The publishers wish to extend their thanks to them all, and in particular to the following:

Ian MacPhail, for his help in planning the Atlas; Dr Philip Ashmole of Edinburgh University; The Director, Michael Walters and Staff of the British Museum (Natural History); The Members and Staff of The British Trust for Ornithology, Tring; The Director and Staff of the Edward Grey Institute of Field Ornithology, Oxford; Dennis Elphick, Dr Pat Hall, The Director, Curator of Zoology and Staff of the Leicester Museum; The Director, Keeper of Vertebrate Zoology and Staff of the Liverpool and City Museums; The Chief Librarian and Staff of the National Research Library of Science and Invention, London; The Director, Chief Librarian and Staff of the Royal Society for the Protection of Birds; The Chief Librarian and Staff of the Westminster Library, London; The Hon. Director, Dr Janet Kear, Mike Garside and Staff of the Wildfowl Trust, Slimbridge; The Director, Dr Gwynne Vevers, Chief Librarian and Staff of the Zoological Society of London; The Director, Curator of Zoology and Staff of the Maidstone Museum and Art Gallery

ARTISTS

Illustrations on pages 1-33: Sidney Woods, Brian Delf, Advent Graphics, Michael Woods, John Davis, Maurice Pledger/Linden Artists; Terry Pastor and George Underwood/Andrew Archer Associates; Terry Collins **Bird portraits (colour) on pages 36-223:** Robert Morton, Ken Lilly, John Barber, Bryon Harvey, Jill Platt, Peter Hayman, Chloë Talbot Kelly, Anthony Morris, Charles Raymond, John Rignall/Linden Artists; Don Cordery **Line illustrations on pages 36-223:** Peter Hayman, Sean Milne, Richard Orr/Linden Artists **Location maps and diagrams on pages 36-223:** Advent Graphics, John Davis **Line illustrations on pages 224-263:** Harry Titcombe (224), Richard Orr/Linden Artists **Section title pages, 34-35, 78-79, 100-101, 138-139, 160-161, 180-181:** Maurice Pledger/Linden Artists (bird artwork), Derek Hogg (maps) **Special topic spreads on pages 60-61:** Robert Morton; **90-91** Robert Morton and John Davis; **114-115** John Davis; **150-151** Robert Morton and Bryon Harvey; **172-173** Ken Lilly and Bryon Harvey; **198-199** Robert Morton

PHOTOGRAPHERS

1 Jane Burton/Bruce Coleman; **2-3** Jane Burton/Bruce Coleman; **4-5** David and Katie Urry/Bruce Coleman; **6-7** David and Katie Urry/Bruce Coleman; **8-9** David and Katie Urry/Bruce Coleman; **12** Svante Lundgren; **14-15** David and Katie Urry; **14-15** (Barn Owls) Eric Hosking; **16** Eric Hosking; **18** George Nystrand/Frank Lane; **24-25** J.A.F. Fozzard of Clare College, Cambridge (for Dr J.R.G. Bradfield of Trinity College, Cambridge); **36** Norman Lightfoot; **38** Norman Lightfoot; **40** Leonard Lee Rue/Bruce Coleman; **48** P. Morris/Ardea; **50** James Tallor/NHPA; **52** James Tallor/NHPA; **54** Tom Willcock/Ardea; **58** P. Morris/Ardea; **62** J. Drajewicz/Canada Wide; **66** S. Dalton/NHPA; **72** Fred Breummer; **74** Fred Breummer; **76** Picturepoint; **82** © Royal Society/Royal Geographical Society; **86** Fransisco Erize/Bruce Coleman; **94** James Simon/Bruce Coleman; **102** Arthur Christiansen; **104** Lennart Norström; **106** L.E. Perkins/NSP; **110** Novosti; **112** D.N. Dalton/NHPA; **116** Lennart Norström; **118** M. Savonius/NHPA; **120** Lennart Norström; **122** J.J.M. Flegg; **124** Lennart Norström; **128** Heather Angel; **130** W.S. Paton; **132** K.J.V. Carlson; **136** A.C. Parker; **140** Picturepoint; **144** Arthur Christiansen; **152** C.A. Walker/NSP; **154** Anthony Bannister/NHPA; **162** K.H. Hyatt/NSP; **168** C.H. Fry; **174** M.D. England/Ardea; **178** A. Eddy/NSP; **182** Hans and Judy Beste/Ardea; **184** Hans and Judy Beste/Ardea; **186** Graeme Chapman; **188** C. Frith/NSP; **192** Graeme Chapman; **196** Graeme Chapman; **200** Hans and Judy Beste/Ardea; **204** M.E. Bacchus/NSP; **208** W.J. Knight/NSP; **216** Heather Angel; **220** Martyn Bramwell

SOURCES OF REFERENCE

A vast number of books, journals and scientific papers have been referred to during the preparation of *The World Atlas of Birds*. The publishers wish to thank the authors and publishers, and in particular the following:

General References Abercrombie, M., Hickman, D.J. & Johnson, M.L. (1951) *A Dictionary of Biology* Penguin. Alexander, W.B. (1954) *Birds of the Ocean* Putnam. Amos, W.H. (1967) *The Life of the Pond* McGraw-Hill. Austin, O.L., Singer, A. (1962) *Birds of the World* Paul Hamlyn. Brooks, M. (1966) *The Life of the Mountains* McGraw-Hill. Craighead, J.J. & Craighead, F.C. (1969) *Hawks, Owls & Wildlife* Dover Publications Inc. Fisher, J., Lockley, R.M. (1954) *Sea-birds* Collins. Fisher, J., Simon, N. & Vincent, J. (1969) *The Red Book* Collins. Gilliard, E.T. (1958) *Living Birds of the World* Doubleday & Co. Gooders, J. (Ed.) (1969) *Birds of the World* I.P.C. Partwork Ltd. Guggisberg, C.A.W. (1970) *Man & Wildlife* Evans Bros. Ltd. I.U,C.N. (1966) *Red Data Book* (*Aves.*) Lack, D. (1956) *Swifts in a Tower*. Leopold, A.S. (1969) *The Desert* Time-Life. McCormick (1966) *The Life of the Forest* McGraw-Hill. Mellanby, K. (1967) *Pesticides and Pollution* Collins. Murton, R.K. (1971) *Man and Birds* Collins. Murton, R.K. and Wright, E.N. (1968) *The Problems of Birds as Pests* Academic Press. Mohr, C.E., Poulson, T.L. (1966) *The Life of the Cave* McGraw-Hill. Niering, W.A. (1966) *The Life of the Marsh* McGraw-Hill. Peters, J.L. *et al* (1931) *Check-list of Birds of the World* Harvard University Press. Reader's Digest Association (1970) *The Living World of Animals*. Thomson, A. Landsborough (Ed.) (1964) *A New Dictionary of Birds* Nelson. Urry, D. & Urry, K. (1970) *Flying Bird* Vernon & Yates Ltd. Usinger, R.L. (1967) *The Life of Rivers and Streams* McGraw-Hill. Van Tyne, J. & Berger, A.J. (1971) *Fundamentals of Ornithology* Dover Publications Inc. Walker, E.P. (1968) *Mammals of the World* The John Hopkins Press. Welty, J.C. (1964) *The Life of Birds* Constable & Co. Wood, G.L. (Ed.) (1972) *The Guinness Book of Animal Facts and Feats* Guinness Superlatives Ltd. **Species and Groups** Brown, L., Amadon, D. (1965) *Eagles, Hawks and Falcons of the World* Country Life. Chapman, F.M. (1968) *Warblers of North America* Dover Publications Inc. Gilliard, E.T. (1969) *Birds of Paradise and Bower Birds* Weidenfeld & Nicolson. Goodwin, D. (1967) *The Pigeons and Doves of the World* British Museum (Natural History). Greenewalt, C.H. (1960) *Hummingbirds* Doubleday. Howard, H.E. (1907-14) *The British Warblers* London. Marshall, A.J. (1954) *Bowerbirds* Clarendon Press. Murton, R.K. (1965) *The Woodpigeon* Collins. Newton, I. (1972) *Finches* Collins. Scott, P. (1957) *A coloured key to the Wildfowl of the World* Wildfowl Trust. Scott, P. (1972) *The Swans* Michael Joseph. Wayre, P. (1970) *A Guide to the Pheasants of the World* Country Life. **Introduction** Armstrong, E.A. (1965) *Bird Display and Behaviour* Dover Publications Inc. Berger, A.J. (1961) *Bird Study* Dover Publications Inc. Dorst, J. (1962) *Bird Migration* Heinemann. Greenway, J.C. (1967) *Extinct and Vanishing Birds of the World* Dover Publications Inc. Lack, D. (1954) *The Natural Regulation of Animal Numbers* Oxford University Press. Lack, D. (1968) *Ecological Adaptations to Breeding in Birds* Methuen. Lack, D. (1971) *Ecological Isolation in Birds* Blackwell Scientific Publications Ltd. Marshall, A.J. (Ed.) (1960) *Biology and Comparative Physiology of Birds* Academic Press. Moreau, R.E. (1972) *Palaearctic/African Bird Migration Systems* Academic Press. Saunders, J.T., Manton, S.M. (1931) *A manual of Practical Vertebrate Morphology* Oxford University Press. Simkiss, K. (1963) *Bird Flight* Hutchinson. Simon, N., Geroudet, P. (1970) *Last Survivors* P.S.C. Swinton, W.E. (1958) *Fossil Birds* British Museum (Natural History). Yapp, W.B. (1970) *The Life and Organisation of Birds* (Edward Arnold). **Nearctic Realm** Bent, A.C. (1919) *Life Histories of North American Birds* Smithsonian Institution. Bond, J. (1960) *Birds of the West Indies* Collins. Chapman, F.M. (1966) *Handbook of Birds of Eastern North America* Dover Publications, Inc. Farb, P. (1968) *The Land and Wildlife of North America* Time-Life. Gabrielson, I.N., Jewett, S.G. (1970) *Birds of the Pacific Northwest* Dover Publications Inc. National Geographical Society (1964) *Song and Garden Birds of North America*. National Geographical Society (1964) *Water, Prey and Game Birds of North America*. Palmer, R.S. (1962) *Handbook of North American Birds* Yale University Press. Peterson, R.T. (1941) *A Field Guide to Western Birds* Houghton Mifflin. Ridgeway, R. Friedmann, H. (1901-50) *Birds of North and Middle America* US National Museum Bulletin, Sanderson, I.T. (1957) *The Continent We Life On – North America* Hamish Hamilton. Shelford, V.E. (1963) *The Ecology of North America* University of Illinois Press. **Neotropical Realm** Bates, M. (1969) *The Land and Wildlife of South America* Time-Life. De Schauensee, R.M. (1970) *A Guide to the Birds of South America* Oliver & Boyd. Dorst, J. (1967) *South America and Central America* Hamish Hamilton. Goodall, J.D., Johnson, A.W., Philippi, B. *2nd Supplement to the Birds of Chile*. Haverschmidt, F. (1968) *The Birds of Surinam* Oliver & Boyd. Johnson, A.W. (1965-67) *The Birds of Chile* Buenos Aires. Skutch, A.F. (1954-69) *Life Histories of Central American Birds* Cooper Ornith. Soc. Skutch, A.F. (1972) *Studies of Tropical American Birds* Nuttall Ornith. Club. **Palaearctic Realm** Bannerman, D.A., Lodge, G.E. (1953-63) *Birds of the British Isles* Oliver & Boyd. Bruun, B. (1970) *The Hamlyn Guide to Birds of Britain and Europe* Hamlyn. Campbell, B., Ferguson-Lees, J. (1972) *A Field Guide to Birds Nests* Constable. Coward, T.A., Barnes, J.A.G. (Ed.) (1969) *The Birds of the British Isles and their Eggs* Warne. Dement'ev, T.N., Gladkov, H.A. *et al* (Eng. Trans. 1966) *Birds of the Soviet Union* Israel Program for Scientific Translation. Donaldson, J.G.S., Barber, D.F. (1969) *Farming in Britain Today* Allen Lane – Penguin Press. Etchecopar, R.D., Hue, F. (1967) *The Birds of North Africa* Oliver & Boyd. Etchecopar, R.D., Hue, F. (1970) *Les Oiseaux du Parche et du Moyenorient* N. Boubec GIE. Fitter, R.S. (Ed.) (1969) *Book of British Birds* Drive Publications/Reader's Digest/A.A. Heinzel, H., Fitter, R., Parslow, J. (1972) *The Birds of Britain and Europe* Collins. Peterson, R.T., Mountfort, G., Hollom, P.A.D. (1954) *A Field Guide to the Birds of Britain and Europe* Collins. Ruttledge, F.R. (1966) *Ireland's Birds* H.F. & G. Witherby. Simms, E. (1971) *Woodland Birds* Collins. Vaucher, C.A. (1967) *Andalousie Sauvage* Libraire Marguerat-Lausanne. Vaurie, C. (1959) *The Birds of the Palaearctic Fauna* H.F. & G. Witherby. Voous, K.H. (1960) *Atlas of European Birds* Thomas Nelson. Witherby, H.F. *et al* (1938-41) *The Handbook of British Birds* H.F. & G. Witherby. Yapp, W.B. (1951) *Birds and Wood* Oxford University Press. **Ethiopian Realm** Benson, C.W. (1971) *Birds of Zambia* Collins. Hall, B.P., Moreau, R.E. (1970) *An Atlas of Speciation in African Passerine Birds* British Museum (N.H.). Mackworth-Praed, C.W., Grant, C.H.B. (1952) *Handbook of African Birds* Longmans. Moreau, R.E. (1966) *The Bird Faunas of Africa and its Islands* Academic Press. Prozesky, O.P.M. (1970) *A field guide to the Birds of Southern Africa* Collins. Williams, J.G. (1963) *A Field Guide to the Birds of East & Central Africa* Collins. **Oriental Realm** Ali, S., Ripley, S.D. (1968) *Handbook of Birds of India and Pakistan* Oxford University Press. Baker, E.C.S. (1932-35) *The Nidification of Birds of the Indian Empire*. Baker, E.C.S. (1922-30) *Fauna of British India: Birds* Taylor & Francis. Henry, G.M. (1955) *Guide to the Birds of Ceylon* Oxford University Press. Pfeffer, P. (1968) *Asia, a Natural History* Hamish Hamilton. Ripley, S.D. (1965) *The Land and Wildlife of Tropical Asia* Time-Life. Smythies, B.E. (1960) *Birds of Borneo* Oliver & Boyd. Smythies, B.E. (1953) *Birds of Burma* Oliver & Boyd. Whistler, H. (1928) *Popular Handbook of Indian Birds* Oliver & Boyd. **Australasian Realm** Cayley, N.W. (1931) *What Bird is That?* Angus & Robertson. Falla, R.A., Sibson, R.B. & Turbott, E.G. (1966) *A Field Guide to the Birds of New Zealand* Collins. Frith, H.J. (Ed.) (1969) *Birds in the Australian High Country* A.H. & A.W. Reed. Gilliard, E.T., Rand, A.L. (1967) *Handbook of the Birds of New Guinea* Weidenfeld and Nicolson. Keast, A. (1966) *Australia and the Pacific Islands* Hamish Hamilton. MacDonald, J.D. (1973) *Birds of Australia* H.F. & G. Witherby. Slater, P.S. (1971) *A Field Guide to Australian Birds* Oliver & Boyd. **Classification** Sibley, C.G. (1970) *Comparative Study of Egg-white Proteins of Passerine Birds* Peabody Museum of Natural History (Yale University) Bull. 32. Sibley, C.G., Ahlquist, J.E. (1972) *Comparative Study of Egg-white Protein of Non-passerine Birds*. Peabody Museum of Natural History (Yale University) Bull. 39. Wetmore, A. (1951) *A revised classification for the Birds of the World* Smithsonian Mis. Coll. 117 (4), 1-22. **Journals** *Alauda*, Société d'Etudes Ornithologiques. *Annual Report*, The Wildfowl Trust. *Ardea*, Nederlandse Ornithologische Unie. *Auk*, American Ornithologists Union. *Birds*, Royal Society for the Protection of Birds. *Bird Study*, British Trust for Ornithology. *British Birds*, Macmillan Journals Ltd. *Bol. Soc. Venezolana Cien. Nat.* Bulletin of the American Museum of Natural History. Bulletin of the United States National Museum. *The Condor*, Cooper Ornithological Society. *Emu*, Royal Australasian Ornithologists Union. *Field Studies in Natural History*, American Museum of Natural History. *Ibis*, British Ornithologists Union. *Journ für Ornithologie*, Deutsche Ornithologische Gesellschaft. *Limosa*, Nederlandse Ornithologische Unie. *Living Bird*. *L'Oiseau et la Revue Francaise d'ornithologie*, Société Ornithologique de France et de l'Union Francaise. *National Geographic Magazine*, National Geographic Society. *Nature*, MacMillan Journals Ltd. *New Scientist*, New Science Publications. *Newsletter*, Cornell Laboratory of Ornithology. *Ornithological Monographs*, American Ornithologists Union. *Postilla*, Peabody Museum, Yale University. Proceedings of the International Ornithological Congress. Proceedings of the United States National Museum. *Scientific American*, W.H. Freeman & Co. *Travaux de L'Institut Francais d'Etudes Andines*. *Wilson's Bulletin*, Wilson's Ornithological Club. *Zoologica*, New York Zoological Society.